PERSONNEL MANAGEMENT

THE IRWIN SERIES IN MANAGEMENT

CONSULTING EDITOR   JOHN F. MEE   *Indiana University*

AMMER *Materials Management* rev. ed.

BRENNAN *Wage Administration: Plans, Practices, and Principles* rev. ed.

BROOM *Production Management* rev. ed.

CHAMPION & BRIDGES *Critical Incidents in Management* rev. ed.

EELLS & WALTON *Conceptual Foundations of Business* rev. ed.

FARMER & RICHMAN *Comparative Management and Economic Progress*

GREENE *Production Control: Systems and Decisions*

HANEY *Communication and Organizational Behavior: Text and Cases* rev. ed.

HOUSTON *Manager Development: Principles and Perspectives*

JONES *Executive Decision Making* rev. ed.

JUCIUS *Personnel Management* 6th ed.

JUCIUS & SCHLENDER *Elements of Managerial Action* rev. ed.

LING *The Management of Personnel Relations: History and Origins*

MCDONOUGH & GARRETT *Management Systems: Working Concepts and Practices*

MEGGINSON *Personnel: A Behavioral Approach to Administration*

MOORE *Manufacturing Management* 5th ed.

MOORE & KIBBEY *Manufacturing: Materials and Processes*

MORRIS *The Analysis of Management Decisions* rev. ed.

NADLER *Work Design*

NIEBEL *Motion and Time Study* 4th ed.

PATTON, LITTLEFIELD, & SELF *Job Evaluation: Text and Cases* 3d ed.

PRINCE *Information Systems for Management Planning and Control*

REED *Plant Layout: Factors, Principles, and Techniques*

RICHARDS & GREENLAW *Management Decision Making*

ROSCOE *Organization for Production: An Introduction to Industrial Management* 4th ed.

ROSCOE *Project Economy*

SCOTT *Organization Theory: A Behavioral Analysis for Management*

SEIMER *Cases in Industrial Management*

SIEGEL *Industrial Psychology* rev. ed.

SIMONDS & GRIMALDI *Safety Management: Accident Cost and Control* rev. ed.

SPRIEGEL & MYERS (eds.) *The Writings of the Gilbreths*

TERRY *Principles of Management* 5th ed.

THAYER *Communication and Communication Systems: In Organization Management and Interpersonal Relations*

TIMMS *The Production Function in Business: Fundamentals and Analysis for Management* rev. ed.

VORIS *Production Control: Text and Cases* 3d ed.

WEBBER *Culture and Management: Text and Readings in Comparative Management*

PERSONNEL

MANAGEMENT

BY MICHAEL J. JUCIUS, Ph.D.

Professor, College of Business and Public Administration

University of Arizona

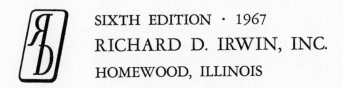

SIXTH EDITION · 1967

RICHARD D. IRWIN, INC.

HOMEWOOD, ILLINOIS

SIXTH EDITION

First printing, March, 1967
Second printing, November, 1967
Third printing, July, 1968
Fourth Printing, June, 1969

Library of Congress Catalog Card No. 66–29193

PRINTED IN THE UNITED STATES OF AMERICA

To C. U. J.

E. G. J.

PREFACE

The basic aim of the earlier editions of *Personnel Management* was to supply the college student with a realistic survey of principles and practices in this area. It was hoped that others, too, in various positions in, or related to, business might find it useful.

But the college student, with his needs and in his situation, was uppermost in mind. His exposure to personnel management could be made most meaningful, therefore, through preparatory readings by means of which his interaction in the classroom with his peers and instructor would make for a stimulating experience.

This concept, so favorably received in earlier editions, has continued to guide the current revision. Into the overview of personnel practices and principles has been inserted a variety of new developments such as systems, civil rights, behavioral contributions, and managerial aids. Moreover, various users of the text have suggested changes in style, presentation, and emphasis which have been adopted with gratitude. And a number of additions and revisions have been made in the questions and case problems.

The organization of the chapters is based primarily upon the broad functions which management must perform in order to build and cooperate with an effective and satisfied group of people. At the outset attention is directed to the scope of personnel management, major factors of personnel management, and the organization of personnel activities and staff. Here are stressed the managerial functions, structures, and guiding principles which are universally significant in personnel relationships and interactions.

Attention is then turned to the major tasks of procuring, developing, maintaining, and utilizing the working members. Specifically, such detailed topics are taken up as specifying job and manpower requirements; screening, interviewing, and testing people; developing employees and executives; establishing compensation and service programs; dealing with collective bargaining, grievances, and disciplinary cases; and carrying on research evaluation programs.

In assigning these materials, various instructors may desire to follow somewhat differing sequences than those in this outline. There is no reason why those so inclined should not do so. For example, some might prefer to take up the materials on grievances earlier than presented in the text. Or the materials on job evaluation and classification might be taken up after job specifications. Such preferences are a matter of personal choice and are easily possible with the subject matter of this text.

To name the many fellow-workers, business executives, associates, and students whose aid and assistance are incorporated in this text is impossible. But to all, I am grateful beyond words but not beyond continual remembrance and indebtedness.

MICHAEL J. JUCIUS

Tucson, Arizona
January, 1967

TABLE OF CONTENTS

TABLE OF CASES

CHAPTER **1**

THE FIELD OF PERSONNEL MANAGEMENT

The Challenge of Human Relations

From many sides, we are constantly being reminded of the importance of the human factor in business. News channels give prominence to various incidents in labor-management relations. Politicians, governmental agencies, educators, and various community groups express their interest in the aims and problems of employees. Business and labor leaders voice their deep concern with human matters. And ever-widening research in the behavioral sciences is casting new light on interpersonal relations in the working environment.

But perhaps more impressive than the foregoing to most individuals are their own personal experiences. From childhood to old age, a large segment of their lives is encompassed by business affairs. Their standards of living and earning power are dependent upon their jobs and economic condition. Much of what and how they think is determined by job factors. Their aspirations and fears, as well as those of their families, are bound up in the business environment.

Thus, in numerous ways, all employees, from top administrators to manual and from professional to unskilled, are made aware of their interdependence in business affairs. All types consequently are concerned with the challenge to improve human relations in business.

The Human Factor in Business

In undertaking the study of personnel management, it is well to make clear what is meant by the terms "labor" and "personnel." Both terms are used interchangeably here. Others sometimes restrict "labor" to operative workers; and some use "personnel" as a more euphonious term. But here, it is proposed to use each in the broadest sense as the

1

human factor in the business enterprise. Thus, everyone from the president of the enterprise to the salesman, mechanic, or clerk is "labor" or "personnel." To be sure, operative levels of employees have received much attention in personnel management, but interest here is also directed to professional, scientific, technical, staff, and managerial groups of labor. Thus a vice president may be concerned with subordinate levels of labor, but he nonetheless is encompassed in the term "labor."

A number of terms have been used to designate various aspects of the subject of people in business. "Industrial relations," for example, has been used to refer to multilateral relations between employees, employers, and government. To others, it means the relations between employees and management within the confines of a given enterprise. "Labor relations," in the language of one use, may refer to collective bargaining and, in that of another, to grievance handling. And still others have tagged some of these subjects with such terms as "human engineering," "labor management," "human relations," "personnel services," "personnel administration," and "manpower management."

Because of the absence of standard definitions, the reader must make certain that he is aware of the meanings of particular terms in any given case. When any of these terms are used here in subsequent discussions, their meaning will be noted. Here, the general concept of the human factor in business is taken up under the name of personnel management.

In order to indicate the scope and meaning of personnel management, this chapter is devoted to the following aspects of this term:

1. Definition and description of the field of personnel management
2. Groups of managers concerned with personnel management
3. Basic guides in personnel management
4. Qualifications and training of personnel executives

Definition of Personnel Management

No definition can be expected to describe fully any concept or subject. It can, however, serve as a springboard for fruitful analysis and amplification. With these thoughts in mind, personnel management is defined here as follows:

The field of management which has to do with planning, organizing, directing, and controlling the functions of procuring, developing, maintaining, and utilizing a labor force, such that the—

1. Objectives for which the company is established are attained economically and effectively.
2. Objectives of all levels of personnel are served to the highest possible degree.
3. Objectives of the community are duly considered and served.

1. *Managerial Phases.* This broad statement emphasizes, to begin with, that personnel management is a responsibility of management. This does not preclude others from participating in consideration of matters important to them. It does mean, however, that management must assume constructive leadership in personnel work, or else the advantages of the principle of specialization of effort cannot be fully gained. Such managerial specialization encompasses four broad functions: planning, organizing, directing, and controlling.

The planning functions pertain to the steps taken in developing a personnel program and in specifying what operative personnel functions are to be performed, and how. Such plans are often unwritten, but it is usually preferable to set down such programs in printed form. More is said on this subject in Chapter 4.

After plans have been developed, organizing is next in order. This step calls for procuring the staff necessary to carry out the plan, designing appropriate systems for executing plans, and establishing lines of authority and communication between the various parties working with or receiving benefit from the personnel plans. Which aspects of plans will be handled by the personnel department and which by the line executives must be determined in this managerial phase. In Chapter 5, various schemes of organizing personnel work will be discussed.

Directing refers to the function of running the organization units responsible for carrying out specific plans. Thus, it is particularly relevant to the work of leadership either at the operative or at the upper levels. Here, active direction must be given to such tasks as motivating and supervising people. Specific examples of direction will be noted throughout various parts of the text.

By means of control, management evaluates results in comparison with desired objectives. Controls guide the personnel ship along the lines laid out in the program. When the ship docks (at the end of the program year, let us say), controls are exercised to determine how effectively desired personnel objectives were attained. Thus, through direct observation and direct supervision, as well as reports, records, and audits, management assures itself that its organization is carrying out planned personnel programs. Reference to managerial controls will be made throughout many of the subsequent chapters.

2. *Operative Phases of Personnel Work.* In the second place, the foregoing definition places emphasis upon four broad and fundamental phases of personnel work. These arise out of the fact that a working force must be procured, developed, maintained, and utilized. These are termed here the operative phases of personnel management and will be examined more fully in later chapters.

Each involves, of course, many detailed duties and tasks. Procurement calls for performance of such functions as locating sources of supply, interviewing applicants, giving tests, and inducting selected applicants. Development calls for training and education, morale building, good communications, promotion and transfer plans, suggestions systems, and similar plans. Maintenance encompasses activities which serve to support the skills and favorable attitudes of employees, such as adequate wages and working conditions, supervision, grievance machinery, recreational and social programs, and housing plans. Of course, all of the foregoing impinge upon the utilization of labor, which is concerned with the working effectiveness of the employee.

To perform these tasks, management must employ a variety of tools, devices, forms, records, and procedures. As a consequence, these sometimes seem to be the substance of personnel work. They are a means to an end, however, and should be viewed as such. To allow forms to become the keystone of a personnel program is to convert personnel management into a clerkship. Appropriate references to these tools will be made in subsequent chapters.

3. *Objectives.* The description of personnel management, in the third place, stresses the point that personnel work is intended to attain a number of important objectives. High place must at once be given here to success in producing a service or commodity which earns a reasonable profit. This is patently dependent upon the effectiveness with which the various members of the business team work together. Personnel management must seek, therefore, to make employees effective contributors to the success of the enterprise. Unless a particular enterprise is successful, it can neither continue to exist nor have use for labor or management.

The foregoing definition recognizes clearly and unequivocally that the performance of personnel duties must also keep in view the objectives of people. Nonfinancial as well as financial needs of people must be fairly and sincerely considered in the plans of management. If not, others will be more than eager, in ways which may run counter to those considered good by the employer, to help people attain desired goals.

And finally, the definition recognizes the obligations personnel management has to the communities in which the company operates. The plural is used because a company must

    a) Be a good neighbor in its local neighborhood.
    b) Live according to the best interests of its regional and national location.
    c) In some cases, give due consideration to its international obligations.

Briefly, this means that a company should act to enhance the development of community life and to avoid doing harm to living conditions.

In summary, this analysis of personnel management may seem somewhat idealistic. After all, few companies are performing all the personnel functions cited here, and all companies do not take the views toward labor proposed here. Nevertheless, the practices and viewpoints of companies which have had the best results from their personnel activities tie in closely with the foregoing suggestions.

Responsibility for Personnel Management

The responsibility for performing the functions by which desired objectives are to be attained has in the foregoing been placed upon management. But how is this obligation divided among various levels of managers, and between line and staff executives? Answers to this question will be proposed in greater detail in Chapter 5, but a few comments are in order here.

The primary responsibility for personnel management must be assumed by the top management of a company. To the president, subject to the approval of the board of directors, must be assigned the task of setting the tone of human relations. He must establish the broad objectives, plans, and policies of personnel management. He must assign to various subordinate executives the specific duties they are to carry out. He must coordinate their personnel efforts. He must check to see that personnel plans are executed. And he must evaluate the effectiveness with which desired objectives have been attained so that (1) future personnel plans can be improved and (2) responsible executives can be appropriately rewarded or penalized.

Of course, the chief executive cannot—except in the smallest companies—perform the functions of personnel management throughout all levels of the organization. He must rely upon the executives at each level to carry out personnel duties appropriate to their respective organization units. These are the ones who actually put personnel practices into effect. How well they manage personnel depends upon their skills, the guidance they get from above, and the help they may get from a personnel department, if there is one.

The personnel department provides a third segment of personnel management. During the last thirty years or so, it has attained a formal stature in most companies having more than one hundred employees. It is generally established for the purpose of serving others by helping to hire employees, train them, operate recreational and safety programs, and carry on negotiations with labor unions. But its services must be approved by those it serves or by some higher authority. Since it does so much personnel work, it is often assumed to be personnel management. While the contributions of this department may be great, assigning to it the paramount role is questionable; the other two areas are the major vehicles carrying the load of human relations.

These three groups of people are the ones through whom personnel management in business is carried out. No one should be ignored nor any one given exclusive jurisdiction; so all are the concern of this text.

Basic Guides in Personnel Management

The field of personnel management cannot be adequately described, however, by defining its functions, listing its objectives, and denoting its responsible leaders. Stopping here establishes the form of personnel management. But to what degree should various objectives be sought? How balance the interests of various groups? To what extent should the several functions be performed? What ideals and ethics should guide management?

Answers to these questions add substance to form; they determine what personnel management really is in any given company. Guides to such answers depend upon the philosophy and principles adopted by a company.

1. *A Philosophy of Personnel Management.* The most basic guide to personnel action in any company derives from its philosophy toward people. The mere fact that a business philosophy is not written down does not mean that none exists. Informally or subconsciously, if not openly, a philosophy exists in every company.

Broadly speaking, a personnel philosophy may take either of two directions. First, labor may be viewed as a factor which tends more or less passively or actively to resist managerial leadership. People must therefore be molded and controlled by management to achieve company objectives. Second, labor may be viewed as a factor with inherently constructive potentials. Management's task, then, is to provide an environment in which this force will willingly exert itself to the fullest.

Until recent years, the first of these philosophies has generally prevailed in business. In such instances, management has adopted the pattern of close control and supervision of people. Of course, there have been exceptions; some have actively encouraged the initiative of people. And there are signs of change. On the one hand, confidence has been shaken in the efficacy of getting the best results through a tough role toward employees. On the other hand, varied research seems to add support to a small but increasing number of practitioners that the constructive forces in people are realized when a positive attitude underlies management's programs.

2. *Principles of Personnel Management.* The broad terms of a philosophy must be interpreted in detail to be practically useful. Hence, it is desirable to establish bench marks that guide particular personnel programs and practices along lines that take account of the attitudes and behavioral patterns of the human factor. Such bench marks are not immutable and inflexible laws. As conditions alter, as time and experience reveal, as new purposes are established, and as executives change, it will be found that principles should be modified or amended.

Without implying that the list is complete or should be adopted in all cases, the following discussion is illustrative of the lines along which a set of principles could be built.

a) Establish fair levels of wages, hours, and working conditions. Although unassailable standards of fairness are not available, and although everybody would not agree as to the exact meaning of fairness, nevertheless the basic watchword of personnel management is fairness. Anything less, sooner or later, will undermine a personnel program and the confidence of employees in management.

b) Add to fairness the appearance of fairness. Be fair, but also appear to be fair. For example, it may be company policy to pay at or above community rates. This, it would seem, lends itself to fairness. But the appearance of fairness can readily be spoiled if the basis for gathering data on community rates seems biased or is not explained.

It is not argued here that appearance of fairness takes precedence over being fair (although some seem to follow the inversion of the rule). Were an inverted policy adopted, the ultimate and certain discovery of unfairness would make irreparable the breach between labor and management. The maxim as stated here recognizes the simple truth that all of us are influenced by how things are presented to us, as well as by what is presented.

c) Supply employees with relevant information. Communication on matters of mutual interest is imperative. On the one hand, there is little reason for believing that important information can be kept from employees. As a permanent policy, it cannot be done. Attempts to do this merely antagonize employees. Sooner or later, the hidden information turns up, often in a form which tends to weaken the cofidence of employees in their company.

On the other hand, it is unwise to withhold information on the ground that employees cannot understand and therefore are likely to misinterpret, for example, a revenue and expense statement. Whether they can or not is irrelevant (for that matter, no one except the accountant who drew it really understands it), because that is not at issue. To employees, the availability of such a statement (and particularly one drawn in a form designed for their benefit) is assurance that the company has nothing to hide.

d) Make employees feel worthwhile and related. "Men do not live by bread alone" is a saying that applies to personnel. Of course, all of us are anxious to get our pay envelopes; these are morale boosters, particularly when they are bulging. But feeling significant is also important during the intervals between paydays. Personal feelings of accomplishment, pride in one's craft or profession, and a harmonious kinship with fellow workers are day-to-day needs if technical productivity is to be of the highest order.

It is important to emphasize that feelings of worthwhileness and relatedness are tied in not only with individual needs and perceptions but also with how well individuals identify with their associates. This means that group reactions, group customs, and group norms are of great importance.

e) Rewards should be earned, not given. Gift giving is not the province of business, is not wanted by mature employees, and is rarely appreciated. Yet, one often hears that employees were given a 10-cent-an-hour raise, were given a vacation with pay, or were given a paid-up insurance policy. Such gifts invariably induce no extra efforts. Indeed, employees soon assume that the gifts must be continued as a deserved reward.

If these rewards are earned, they should not be termed gifts. The relationship between effort and reward should be clearly stated as earnings. Then the worker is not put in the position of having to be grateful. It is unwise to subject a person to the feeling of subservience when the situation reflects accomplishment and satisfaction with a job well done.

f) Build programs with due consideration for how employees react to them. Managerial action should not be based on the idea that "here is how I would react were I in their position." Rather, it is necessary to be sensitive to how employees feel. And this sensitivity should relate to group as well as individual feelings.

This matter of sensitivity cannot be overemphasized. Indeed, the recent widespread interest in the organizational behavior of people is basically a realization that the economic and technical success of a business is largely influenced by personal feelings and attitudes. Incorporating these forces in personnel relations is good not only for employees but also for business.

g) Do not underestimate the intelligence or strength of people. It is courting trouble to assume that employees (organized or not) are neither strong nor generally intelligent. Sometimes, management so assumes because people are slow to action. Once aroused, however, employees have shown that they know not only what they want but also how to get it, both in the national area and in the individual company.

An interesting point can be made here regarding the charge that employees are not wise enough to participate in decisions affecting their interests. But the point is irrelevant. Employees exert an influence upon every decision management reaches. When employees have no direct voice in bargaining, for example, they may malinger, seek employment elsewhere, or have recourse to the ballot box. In short, they act indirectly when not invited to do so directly. Hence the real issue is how and by what means employees should be brought into the decision-making processes.

h) "Sell" the personnel program. It must be sold. Education, indoctrination, yes, even good propaganda are justifiable. This follows because employees will learn by themselves or from others, if management does not teach them. In which case, will management like what they learn?

Time must be taken and effort exerted through understandable language to sell management's beliefs. On the one hand, it should be clear that policies or programs that have taken executives perhaps months to develop cannot be assimilated in the time it takes to read a notice on the bulletin board or in the company magazine.

On the other hand, the selling should be done in terms that can be clearly understood. Whether oral or printed, words and expressions should be used which convey desired meanings with clarity.

In the last analysis, the real significance of one's principles will be found in whether or not they are a part of daily routines and executive acts. All the talk in the world is ineffective unless it is backed with action. In short, the "good" life must be lived by management in order that labor can be sure that what is said is really meant.

Personnel Executives

Some comments are now in order regarding the qualifications, breadth of knowledge, and education expected of those whose jobs entail personnel management. Obviously, what is said here must be somewhat general. Conditions are certainly not the same in all kinds and sizes of businesses. And the kind and degree of personnel responsibilities within the same company will not be the same for top, middle, first-line, and staff executives. Hence a standard specification for everyone is out of the question. Nevertheless, there are points which have some application to all.

1. *Qualifications.* As to qualifications, one frequently hears from those seeking to prepare themselves for personnel work that they made the choice because they "like to work with people." This is highly commendable but should scarcely be the deciding factor. After all, one must like to work with people in almost all fields of professional and technical endeavor. Moreover, the words "working with people" are too indefinite—they may mean such things as helping others out of trouble (of which there are many kinds, and not all are of interest to the business enterprise); simply liking to work side by side with others (no more than ordinary gregariousness); and telling people what they should or should not do (often a mere desire for power).

Success in personnel management depends upon skill and ability in three areas: managerial, technical, and behavioral. By its very emphasis in the title, it should be patent that managerial talents are involved. In the case of top, middle, bottom, and staff managers, a premium is placed on ability to plan, organize, direct, and control the work of others. The emphasis is upon managing the work of others, not upon doing the work oneself. Therefore, any executive concerned with personnel activities must be proficient in leading others and in coordinating his organizational unit with the procedures and organizational areas of other executives.

A manager must, by definition, manage somebody regarding something. He must therefore possess competence in the technical field being managed. In the personnel area, he must be skilled in the tools, techniques, and practices of procuring, developing, maintaining, and utilizing a labor force. If the executive in question happens to be the personnel manager, the depth of his technical skill should be much more detailed and comprehensive than that of line executives. The latter should concern themselves with policy determination and programming technical matters the higher they are in the organization, and with application of technical matters the lower they are.

And since managers must manage somebody, they must possess skill in working personally with subordinates. The way a leader reacts to or behaves toward his subordinates determines in part how effective he will be in executing his managerial and technical functions. The top executive, for example, may be autocratic or democratic in his relationships with subordinate executives. The personnel manager may be patronizing, cooperative, officious, or contemptuous toward those he serves. And the supervisor may be "work-centered" or "person-centered" in dealing with his employees. The behavioral pattern—friendly, stern, standoffish, pleasant, gruff, or understanding, to cite but a few examples—has a significant effect upon the reactions an executive will get from his team and associates.

2. Breadth of Knowledge. Another useful view of executives concerned with personnel may be taken by (*a*) viewing the fields of knowledge that can contribute to their work and (*b*) discussing the extent of specialization in the various fields.

a) *Fields of Knowledge.* The following listing illustrates the major fields of knowledge which have a contribution to make in the personnel area:

1. Philosophy, which seeks for the underlying explanations of human nature and conduct
2. Ethics, which is concerned with moral and value judgments
3. Logic, which is concerned with rules and principles of reasoning
4. Mathematics, which treats of exact relations between quantities, magnitudes, and systems
5. Psychology, which deals with the phenomena of individual consciousness and behavior
6. Sociology, which deals with the forms and functions of human groups
7. Anthropology, which is concerned with physical and environmental relations to man's social and cultural patterns
8. Medicine, which in all its branches is concerned with the well-being of man
9. History, which seeks to record and explain the past events of man
10. Economics, whose interests are in optimizing choices among competing uses of limited resources
11. Management, which is concerned with skillful leadership of organized groups
12. Politics, which in the best sense is concerned with how men are governed and govern themselves

b) *Extent of Specialization.* For how many of the foregoing fields should an executive be responsible? Some interesting trends may be noted. Going back only a little more than a century or two, a man was not considered educated unless he was a master of many fields. In our own country, such men as Washington, Jefferson, and Franklin were not only governmental figures of renown, but were also proficient in military, agricultural, business, philosophical, and cultural affairs. And in other countries, too, business leaders could claim the same cosmopolitan skill and knowledge.

Then, gradually, came the era of specialization. The outpouring of knowledge in each field seemed to require the full attention and time of anyone who pretended to be an expert. The philosopher had time only for philosophy, the doctor only for medicine, the psychologist only for psychology, the manager only for business, etc. To each, his vocation monopolized his time to such an extent that elsewhere he could claim perhaps at best only amateur standing.

But in recent years, there has been a swing back. And of particular interest in the study of labor problems in business is the development of the behavioral sciences. This trend has taken hold in the last dozen years or so. It proceeds on the lines that to specialized effort must be added collaboration. The psychologist, the sociologist, the economist, the mathematician, etc., must join forces to solve human problems.

Such joining of forces involves a number of things. It is desirable, for example, to improve communication between fields, to compare theories of human behavior, to study approaches and skills used by each other, to note similarities and differences of findings about human beings, to discuss systems of measurement and empirical research, and to seek generalizations about human behavior.

This trend undoubtedly will accelerate. Man in the business environment cannot be effectively studied like the elephant which was examined by the blind men. Each in his specialized "view" was partly right and partly wrong. And difficult though it is, the studies of specialists must be brought together. Fortunately, the developments in mathematics, decision making, electronic computers, interdisciplinary research, and mixing of professional groups and societies are providing major breakthroughs. In this text, it is deemed axiomatic that the interrelations of man and management are best approached through combined viewpoints.

3. *Education.* It is undoubtedly true that as of the present, most executives engaged in personnel work, as a phase of either a line position or a full-time staff position, gained managerial and technical competence on the job and through self-education. This school of experience has until recently been the only one available. It is exacting and thorough. But it is also somewhat haphazard, costly, and time-consuming. Indeed, by the time one receives his "diploma," he is also ready to receive his pension.

It is not surprising, therefore, that graduates of this school themselves advocate formal education whenever possible. And more and more companies prefer such training. As a consequence, formal offerings at the collegiate level have in the past two or three decades been increasing steadily.

Formal education need not, nor should it, stop with a college degree. For example, special short courses in many of the foregoing areas are also made available to executives by such groups as the American Management Association and the Society for the Advancement of Management, and by a variety of executive development programs conducted by private companies, consulting organizations, trade associations, and universities.

Thus, through appropriate combinations of formal education and working experience, competence in personnel work will be better achieved. Indeed, this may well raise personnel management to a professional status. Such a level cannot be attained so long as personnel work is viewed as a routine set of procedures. But professional status—to which many in personnel management aspire—can be gained. This is not beyond the realm of possibility because, more and more, personnel work calls for (*a*) technical study and training beyond the borders of mere trade knowledge, (*b*) large responsibilities toward those served, and (*c*) a high level of ethics in dealing with labor, management, and the community. When appropriate standards in these areas are promulgated and accepted generally, the field of personnel management will deserve inclusion in the family of professions.

Outline of Subsequent Chapters

It is the task of subsequent chapters to fill out the outline of personnel management sketched in this chapter. The next four chapters provide subject material that is pertinent to all aspects of personnel management. Perspective, human relations, programming, and organization cut across all areas and specific tasks of personnel work.

The next group of chapters (Chapters 6–13) is largely concerned with the procurement function. Some of the chapters take up materials (in particular, interviewing, transfers and promotions, and merit evaluation) that are also important to topics taken up in later chapters, such as those on training and labor-management relations.

The remainder of the text is divided into sections dealing with programs of training, compensation, labor relations, service plans, and research. Chapters 14–17 are concerned with training and education for various levels of an organization. Chapters 18–21 deal with compensation principles, practices, and problems. Chapters 22–24 are devoted to a variety of programs relating to the maintenance of staffs of people. Chapters 25–27 treat important aspects of labor relations. And the final chapter is devoted to some pertinent comments on research and information as important contributions to the planning and control of personnel functions.

QUESTIONS

1. Check the definition of personnel management given in this text against personnel practices in the companies in your community or in companies with which you are acquainted. Explain any differences you may note.
2. How would you proceed to prove the contention that personnel management is a specialized phase of management?
3. Illustrate concretely examples of planning, organizing, directing, and controlling of personnel functions.
4. Does industry have social responsibilities? If so, what are they? Have such obligations changed much in the past fifty years?
5. Who, in the final analysis, is the personnel manager in an industrial or business enterprise? Upon what grounds do you justify your answer?
6. Why is a philosophy important in personnel management? What different directions may such a philosophy take? How do principles of personnel management differ from a philosophy?
7. How far would you go in supplying employees with company information? Would your answer be the same during a strike as during a period of relative peace?
8. Why must personnel management seek to make employees feel that they are worthwhile and significant members of the company team? Cannot employees see this for themselves?
9. What qualifications should be possessed by a personnel executive? With what areas of knowledge should he be acquainted? How much weight would you give to the quality of "liking to work with people"?
10. Why is training so essential to the development of those interested in entering the field of personnel management? What is the alternative to formal training? What is the major shortcoming of the alternative?

CHAPTER 2

A PERSPECTIVE OF PERSONNEL MANAGEMENT

Importance and Scope of Perspective

Personnel management must deal with the present and be concerned with the future. It must build programs that solve problems in the framework of today and tomorrow. But if it is to perform its tasks as effectively as possible, it must also be aware of the past. Forces and factors and experiences in the past have their impact upon the present and future.

Study in this text of personnel matters can proceed on firmer grounds, therefore, by directing attention at the outset (1) to a review of pertinent historical trends and (2) to an estimate of the present status and future prospects in this field.

HISTORICAL CHANGES

Many impressive changes have taken place in the status and position of employees in the United States, particularly since the Civil War. Of course, comparisons with earlier periods and with conditions in foreign countries would be even more startling. For present purposes, however, a brief description and study of important changes during the period specified will suffice.

The forces that have been and are at work in the field of employee and management relations are closely intertwined. Hence, within the limited scope of these pages, any attempt to unravel the threads of cause and effect must perforce be arbitrary and no more than suggestive. In the following discussion a study of historical changes is based (with the knowledge that the classifications are not mutually exclusive) upon the following general classes or types of changes:

1. Technological conditions of business
2. Cultural and social background
3. The role of government
4. Trends in organized labor
5. Management attitudes

Technological Changes

Technological changes have had a profound effect upon the working population. At one time, production and distribution were confined within narrow geographical areas and business units of family size. The Industrial Revolution changed all this. Thousands of workers have been brought into modern factories, offices, and distributive units. Work was once performed manually with the aid of simple tools. Now, all types of business operations are increasingly being carried on by complex, integrated, power-driven, and electronically controlled equipment. The age of automation is upon us.

The figures in Table 2–1 disclose dramatically the tempo of techno-

TABLE 2–1

ESTIMATED RELATIVE SUPPLY OF "WORK ENERGY" FROM MINERAL
FUELS AND WATER POWER, WORK ANIMALS, AND HUMAN
WORKERS, 1850–1960, IN PERCENTAGES*

Year	Mineral Fuels and Water Power	Work Animals	Human Workers
1850	5.8	78.8	15.4
1860	6.5	79.2	14.3
1870	11.5	73.1	15.4
1880	17.2	68.6	14.2
1890	27.5	60.5	12.0
1900	37.8	51.7	10.5
1910	56.9	34.7	8.4
1920	73.5	20.8	5.7
1930	83.7	11.7	4.6
1940	90.0	6.4	3.6
1950	94.0	3.0	3.0
1960	96.3	1.3	2.4

* SOURCE: J. Frederic Dewhurst and Associates, *America's Needs and Resources* (New York: Twentieth Century Fund, 1947), p. 787.

logical change. It is shown here that the contribution of human energy to the total supply of work energy is estimated to have decreased from 15.4 to 2.4 percent from 1850 to 1960. The estimate for mineral energy shows an increase of from 5.8 to 96.3 percent for the same period. In other words, within this relatively short span of time the physical work of manufacturing has been largely turned over to the machine.

As might be expected, such technological changes have left their impact upon employees. Instead of large numbers of craftsmen, the working population has until recent years been made up largely of machine tenders, desk workers, and service employees. Instead of jobs in which employees had opportunities for personal expression, the average job, in and of itself, has been repetitive and restrictive. Instead of experiencing the satisfactions of making a complete product, the workers too often have been little more than cogs in a machine. Moreover, the workers no longer own the tools of a trade and hence have lost a strong link of pride in work. Of course, there have been some offsetting social gains of mass production. Nevertheless, the worker has lost something in the working situation which has to be gained elsewhere (as some believe, in the structure of the unions) if his working days are to be more than an uninspiring round of drudgery.

But more recent technological trends presage new and improved opportunities. In particular, automation, electronic data processing, and computerization have desirable implications. To be sure, this trend has negative, short-run problems of unemployment and retraining that must be solved.

On the positive side, however, this trend calls for higher levels of skills not only in manufacturing but also in such areas as marketing, commercial enterprises, communications, and transportation.

The call for higher levels of skills increases in urgency. Since 1950, about 85 percent of the increase in total employment in the United States has been in the white-collar occupations (professional, technical, managerial, clerical, and sales). Looking ahead to 1975, it is estimated that industrial jobs will show no increase, whereas the demand for professional and technical workers will be up about 40 percent, for engineers and scientists about 150 percent, for clerical workers about 33 percent, and for service workers about 40 percent. In some industries, such as aerospace, white-collar workers now exceed production workers. Hence, as technology advances, the highest qualities of people in increasing quantities are required. Work consequently has a challenging, not a dismal, prospect for much of humanity.

Cultural and Social Background

In dealing with people, it is essential to know the influence of cultural and social forces. This follows because group customs and norms vitally affect the actions of employees. In these respects, some significant changes have taken place in the United States since the Civil War. Although many forces have been at work, attention will be restricted to study of trends in education, immigration, rural and urban population, age groups, and some sociological patterns of business.

1. *Educational Background.* In regard to education, a much larger percentage of the population is now exposed to formal training. In the age group from 5 to 20 years, for example, the proportion of the population which attended school was under 60 percent in 1910, but over 90 percent in 1963. In the age group of 18 to 64 years (that of the labor force) the median level of education is now 12 years of school—the equivalent of a high school education; yet, just prior to World War II, the average was nine years. Obviously, as the base of education broadens, management must plan to deal with employees on a higher plane of logical interactions and involvement.

2. *Factors of Immigration.* Changes in the population makeup, too, are striking. For example, the relation between the native-born population and that caused by immigration has changed drastically. Immigration provided a major source of the population increase from 1880 to 1910. Since 1910, however, the wave of immigration has fallen off rapidly. Indeed, during the decade starting with 1930, emigration exceeded immigration. Since the late thirties, however, immigration has slightly exceeded emigration.

Such changes in the working population are of vital consequence to the student of personnel management. Native-born workers now have largely replaced the immigrants. Their framework of reference and comparison makes them unwilling to accept the word of the boss as final and unequivocal. Employees want to know what is going on and often want to have a voice in affairs affecting their interest. Indeed, employees place themselves on an equal plane in their relationships with management.

3. *Rural and Urban Population.* Another trend of population change of interest here is that relating to changes in the rural and urban population. These changes are impressive. From 1850 to the 1960's the percentage of the population living in rural areas has decreased from about 85 percent to about 30. On the other hand, the urban areas have been growing. A striking example of this may be seen in the fact that there were no cities of a million in 1850; but in 1963, one third of the population lived in areas defined as metropolitan centers.

As greater numbers of workers congregate in large cities, they become less independent than they once were. They are affected more directly by the business cycles and less by the cycles of agricultural plenty and scarcity. Less and less can they fall back upon their own resources when depression hits. Their views consequently revolve with increasing intensity around the need of attaining economic security. Perhaps for this reason, the contention is heard frequently that business must accept certain social responsibilities, which is another way of saying that business must be prepared to support employees during bad as well as good times.

4. *Age Groups.* The dispersion of workers according to age groups also has interesting implications. As seen in Figure 2–1, a large

FIGURE 2–1

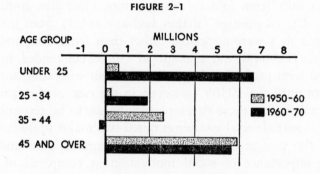

SOURCE: United States Department of Labor, *Manpower—Challenge of the 1960's* (Washington, D.C.: U.S. Government Printing Office, 1960), p. 6.

increase in young workers and older workers has occurred during the 1960's, whereas a decrease occurred in the 35–44 age bracket. Briefly, this implies having to provide programs of training for younger workers, programs to hold experienced middle-aged workers, and programs effectively to utilize older workers.

5. *Sociological Patterns.* A most significant trend is that pertaining to the sociological status of people in the community and in their place of work. At one time, employees enjoyed relative stability regarding their place in the community and in business.

Most workers had a sense of security deriving from this relative stability. From the job a worker held, he was accorded a definite station in the eyes of his fellow workers and his neighbors. This scale of prestige values was informal, yet was recognized and respected by all concerned. A worker knew that if his current job was low in the scale of values, there was a ladder of jobs of greater prestige which he might climb through the years.

But for a number of reasons, this rigid structure has largely disappeared. Technological mass production, concentration of financing in a few large cities, and improvements in communication brought telling changes in social relations and modes of living. Jobs, companies, and whole areas change so rapidly that social patterns are in a constant state of flux. As a consequence, the insecurity and tensions in the community tend to carry over to the work place.

Within the business enterprise, also, there were social changes of significance. For one thing, social groups were created that never existed before. The mere fact that numbers of people were brought together under the single roof of a factory, store, or office added a new framework of social relationships to the older combinations. And status tended to shift from jobs to other factors. Operative employees, for example, derived prestige (if they had any at all) from the company with which they were associated rather than from the particular jobs they held. Technical and managerial employees tended to be more concerned with professional attachments than with company loyalties. It was not until the 1930's, however, in the case of the famous Hawthorne studies, that these developments began to be recognized.

These internal social groupings raised two major problems: (a) the clash of the worker class against the managerial class and (b) the growing importance of social motivation as compared to economic interests. Employees in an affluent society often are as concerned with the approval of their peers as with economic matters or technological progress.

The impact of sociological patterns upon employee-management relations cannot be overestimated. How an employee feels about his job and his company is greatly influenced by how his neighbors rate and respect them. The status accorded him has a strong effect upon his sense of satisfaction and stability. And the role he plays—often to the consternation of management—is less technical and more attitudinal and group-inspired.

The Role of Government

Momentous changes have also taken place in the relation of government to labor and business. This may be seen by reviewing trends in governmental attitudes toward labor and management, and its own role in the business community.

1. *Earlier Governmental Attitudes.* From an earlier attitude of general disinterest and passiveness in labor-management matters, government has in some cases taken giant steps in the direction of positive intervention. And from a role in which it tended invariably to side with capital, government has turned more and more in the direction of becoming a protagonist and guardian of the interests of employees.

Perhaps the increasing proportion of votes that are coming from the side of labor has much to do with this change.

About the time of the Civil War and for some time afterward, employees possessed few powerful friends in governmental circles. The concept of interstate commerce had not been extended to cover manufacturing, so that the legislative branch of the federal government was in no position to interest itself in the problems of the workingman. The state assemblies were preoccupied with such matters as expansion and state versus federal rights, and therefore had little time to become concerned with labor matters. Moreover, the nation was as yet largely an agricultural, pioneering, and maritime country, so that labor problems arising in industry and commerce were considered to be relatively unimportant and so were easily passed over.

Then, too, the executive branch of the federal government had not yet attained any real measure of political strength. It was without the power to have helped workers, even had it been disposed to do so. And the judicial branch based its views on the preeminence of property rights, so that it invariably sided with capital interests whenever labor issues were placed before it. Indeed, court injunctions were a favored and easily obtained weapon of employers to combat picketing and boycotts, to stop strikes, and to limit union activities.

2. *Changing Conditions.* But a number of forces acted to change the role of government. Workers grew in numbers, so that their voting power became influential. Moreover, several costly strikes at the turn of the century focused attention upon the injury being done to the public welfare as well as to the parties involved. In addition, the public was aroused about sweatshops and poor working conditions as exposed by private reformers and organized labor. And federal concern with monopolies led to a reexamination of the concept of interstate trade.

As a result, at the turn of the century, some protective legislation primarily at the state level could be found pertaining to child labor and industrial safety. About a decade later, state after state began to provide for workmen's compensation in the event of industrial accidents. At about this time, too, the federal government passed significant labor laws covering accidents to railroad employees, the eight-hour day on the railroads, and the issuance of labor injunctions in the federal courts. Most labor legislation (with the exception of that relating to industrial compensation) traveled a rough road, especially through the courts; hence, very little was actually accomplished until after World War I.

Beginning with a liberalization of the powers of the government in the field of public utilities, the movement to side with labor spread to other business areas in the thirties. Particularly significant were federal legislation and executive action on such subjects as collective bargaining, minimum and overtime wages, and social security.

In recent years the federal government has moved in the direction of establishing, by suggestion and legislation, guide lines that business should follow in respect to labor matters. It has proposed, for example, that wage increases sought through collective bargaining be restricted to noninflationary wage-price considerations. It has made available plans for upgrading the skills and knowledge of various unemployed and underprivileged groups. And it has enacted provisions for equalizing employment opportunities irrespective of race, color, sex, or creed.

Such legislation has been predicated upon changed concepts of interstate commerce and industry's social responsibilities. On the one hand, the federal Congress proceeded upon the assumption (with which the courts largely concurred) that manufacturing and labor matters came within the province of interstate commerce. As such, they were consequently subject to federal regulation. On the other hand, there was a growing feeling that the economic security of employees was more or less a responsibility of industry. This view found favor not because industry was necessarily at fault for economic crises, but because it was considered best able to assume the burden the crises brought on.

Thus the federal government in all its branches—legislative, judicial, and executive—and many of the state assemblies have moved in the direction of strengthening the position of employees. Some are disturbed by this trend. They see the government taking on the role of a participant—and a partial one at times—rather than an umpire in the solution of labor problems. They would prefer that employees and management themselves resolve their difficulties.

Some contend that such trends in favor of employees are leading to the welfare state form of government. They see capitalism, democracy, and the profit system being swept aside. They see business being removed from the realm of private enterprise to that of planned regulation. If government does throw its weight in this direction, patently management prerogatives and employee relations as we now think of them will be drastically recast.

Trends in Organized Labor

No perspective of people in business would be complete without a view of the changing role of organized labor. Unions have existed for a long time, but their growth has been most influential since the thirties. A few unions, such as those of the typographers, stonecutters, and hat finishers, were in existence about the time of the Civil War, but the membership was relatively small. Perhaps the first real strength of unions was displayed in the growth of the Knights of Labor, which reached a peak membership of about 700,000 in the 1880's. For various reasons, however, it went into a decline from which it never recovered. Nevertheless, this group left its imprint upon subsequent union activities.

Believing that the Knights of Labor were wrong in participating in political activities, others in the labor movement took steps to form the American Federation of Labor. The growth of this federation of local and autonomous unions has been slow but steady. Its membership grew as follows:[1]

1881	45,000	1920	3,970,000
1890	220,000	1930	2,950,000
1900	550,000	1940	4,250,000
1910	1,580,000	1950	8,000,000

In 1935, dissatisfaction with the principles and policies of the American Federation of Labor led to the formation of the Congress of Industrial Organizations (originally called the Committee of Industrial Organization). The CIO was intended to unionize workers on a vertical or industry basis as compared with the craft or horizontal basis of the AFL. Its membership in the 1950's reached over six million. In December, 1955, the two unions decided to merge into a united AFL–CIO. Their combined membership is now estimated to be over 15 million. Independent unions such as the Teamsters Union and the United Mine Workers account for another three million members. Total membership, as shown in Figure 2–2, has grown to around 18 million. Thus, out of a working force of close to 75 million, almost one out of every four is a union member.

In the course of the foregoing changes, there has come a significant readjustment in employee-employer relations. The era of unquestioning acceptance of the decisions of the employer is on the wane. So, too, is the era of subservient employees. In their place looms a scene in which the working population is more articulate, highly organized, and politically potent. Employees not only have strong views regarding what they want but also have shown that they know how to achieve their objectives. This does not mean that an era of warefare is at hand. On the contrary, it might well be argued that equality of strength is a prerequisite to mutual understanding of each other's problems. Indeed,

---

[1] R. A. Lester, *Economics of Labor* (New York: Macmillan Co., 1941), p. 550; and estimates of the United States Department of Labor.

labor-management relations that have developed in such industries as clothing, printing, and the steel industry on such matters as joint job evaluation, for example, are highly encouraging that cooperation is not a dreamer's ideal.

FIGURE 2–2. Membership of National and International Unions, 1935–65 (Exclusive of Canadian Members)*

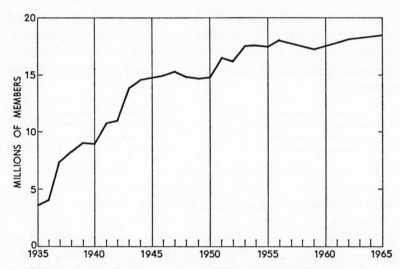

Midpoints of membership estimates made in a range for the years 1948–52 were used.
* Includes a relatively small number of trade union members in areas outside the continental United States other than Canada. In 1954 and 1956, approximately 100,000 union members fell in this category; comparable data for earlier years are not available.
SOURCE: Bureau of Labor Statistics.

Management Attitudes

Another perspective of this field may be taken by examining the attitudes employers have taken toward employees. There is much overlapping in conceptual trends, so that it cannot be said either that one concept was held until such and such a date or that all are agreed upon a particular point of view at present.

Until the turn of the present century, labor was most widely viewed as a factor of production. As such, it was to be handled like any other technical or economic resource of production. The main considerations were costs and returns. Perhaps something could be said for this concept if the emotional and social characteristics of people could be segregated from and did not influence the working situation. Such, however, is obviously impossible. Hence, this attitude has proved untenable, although occasionally some employers may be seen casting longing glances in that direction.

The first departures from the factor-of-production concept took place around 1900. Some employers became concerned with employees as human beings. Believing that they knew what was best for employees, they installed recreational, pension, and insurance programs at their own expense. Such employer-initiated programs have been termed paternalism.

With the passage of time, paternalism encountered serious opposition. On the one hand, employees began to resist being treated like children. They wanted a voice in programs which affected their interests. As a consequence, some paternalists, grieved that employees did not appreciate their well-meaning efforts, decided to concern themselves only with running their businesses. They decided to let each employee take care of himself according to his own standards of what was good for him. Unfortunately for those who held such views, once the gates of social and welfare programs were opened, the pressures of competition, union demands, and governmental legislation forced a continuation of these programs; but now, they were jointly sponsored or administered.

On the other hand, some employers saw the good that could flow if the limitations of paternalism were removed. The logic was to treat employees as mature individuals, welcome their participation in various programs, and thereby bring forth their most effective cooperation.

In turn, the economic success of a business would be enhanced if various human needs were served, but in joint collaboration with employees. This concept accepts a social responsibility by business and also listens to labor's voice in determining the human needs to be served.

In recent years the human aspect has been expanded to stress sociological factors. There is growing recognition of the fact that an employee must be dealt with not only in terms of individual characteristics but also in terms of his group perceptions, reactions, and needs. This approach assumes that productivity and loyalty are conditioned as much by what an employee thinks others feel about his status and role as by what he himself would like to do or say.

Another concept which has pushed itself into the foreground is derived from the political power of labor, of significant strength since the 1930's. The AFL–CIO Committee on Political Education gives indication that in addition to other political methods, the movement of labor in politics, both directly and indirectly, is likely to accelerate rather than slow down. And this applies to local and state levels as well as the federal level.

Political action in national and local politics finds its counterpart within the business enterprise. Certainly, the term "industrial democ-

racy," which is often heard, refers to more direct participation in industrial affairs that affect the interests of labor. This goes beyond the
normal role and mode of operation of the union. It implies a movement
in the direction of a partnership in which many, if not all, of the major
decisions in a business will be a matter of direct concern to labor as well
as management. This has been formalized under the designation "codetermination" in Germany, where labor has by law been given a significant place on the boards of directors of specified types of business
concerns. Although the movement has not gained much headway here,
it nonetheless represents a concept of labor which cannot be discounted.

In summary, management may approach its dealings with employees from any one of several viewpoints: the economic or factor-of-
production point of view, various shades of the human and social
condition, and various degrees of the political and partnership stand-
point. All have some bearing upon the matter of how to get along with
labor in the best interests of all. It does seem that those who are giving
greater weight to the human, social, and democratic aspects are more
likely to be successful in their labor-management solutions. At least,
this appears to be true for the foreseeable future.

PRESENT STATUS AND FUTURE PROSPECTS

To conclude this discussion of perspectives, it is desirable (1) to
draw an over-all picture of personnel problems, (2) to examine management's role in their solution, (3) to note possible approaches to the
solution of these problems, (4) to note obstacles to solutions, and (5)
to comment on future prospects.

General Nature of Problems

Management must allocate some of its time, skill, and resources to
personnel because of various problems that call for solution. At this
juncture, therefore, it is desirable to note the range of problems that
arise in connection with employees. These include the following categories:

1. *Measurement of Quantities.* How much, for example, is a fair wage, a
   fair day's pay, or a fair pension payment? Or what is the right number of
   hours to be worked, the right length of a vacation, or the right number of
   holidays with pay?
2. *Dimensions of the Human Factor.* To what extent should consideration
   be given to the technical, economic, psychological, sociological, political,
   and ethical aspects of the human factor in business?
3. *External Relationships.* In what ways and in regard to what topics

should management work with governmental agencies, labor groups, community agencies, and educational institutions in the matter of personnel problems?

4. *Internal relationships.* Through what systems and structures should management and employees work out solutions to common problems?

Management's Role

It is pertinent to look at the question of what relation management has to problems listed in the foregoing classification. Certainly, management cannot, nor should it, claim exclusive jurisdiction over the various problems that must be solved. Either directly or indirectly, however, it is involved in all of them. But the same can also be said of other groups. How and to what degree each should participate in their solution is debatable. As may be deduced from the earlier discussion of trends, the roles of the several groups have been in a constant state of flux. And there is no reason to conclude that it will be otherwise in the future.

There are areas, however, within which the prerogatives of management are sharper than in others. Its rights of decision are more clearly defined over internal business operations. At least, it is invariably held responsible for what happens within the internal framework. Others—such as union and governmental agencies—have inserted themselves into the internal picture in varying degrees and ways, usually in the form of controls, agreements, and limitations over unrestricted freedom of managerial choice of action. Beyond this, at least in the United States, there is little if any outright sharing of decision making by management with organized labor or government.

Approaches to Personnel Problems

A number of approaches may be used by management in tackling the problems with which it is confronted. These may be classified into three large groups according to (1) the extent to which problems are anticipated, (2) the nature of facts brought to bear upon labor-management problems, and (3) the kinds of knowledge required in dealing with these problems.

1. *Cure and Prevention.* Looking first at the extent to which problems are anticipated, personnel management can tackle problems after or before they develop. For example, after an employee expresses resentment or belligerence, after a work stoppage occurs, or after a supervisor is faced with noncooperation, steps are taken to correct the situation. Unfortunately, personnel management has been characterized largely by the use of curative methods.

There is a distinct trend toward the use of preventive measures.

Management is attempting more frequently to anticipate possible sources of trouble or irritation by establishing constructive personnel programs. Job evaluation, attitude surveys, and merit-rating plans, to be discussed later in this book, are cases in point.

There are also those who are cognizant of the need of positive measures to maintain the equilibrium when relations between labor and management are said to be good. For example, recent studies of companies that have experienced long years of relatively satisfactory relations may provide personnel management with better suggestions than can the studies which stem from cases in which trouble has occurred. The analogy to this is the matter of studying healthy individuals as well as those who are ill.

2. *Factual Basis of Personnel Problems.* Another way of looking at the approach to personnel problems which management employs is to note the basis used to solve problems. Such solutions may be founded upon one's own experiences, upon the experiences of others, or upon scientific analysis of problems.

Under the first-mentioned plan, the personnel executive reaches decisions in terms of his own experience, which are therefore subject to the wisdom a limited personal experience can provide. When a problem is encountered, a decision is reached on a cut-and-try, hit-or-miss, or rule-of-thumb basis; if the decision does not work, it is a case of trying something else. It is very simple and quick in execution but highly unpredictable in results. Nevertheless, it is undoubtedly the most widely used plan in personnel as well as other fields of management. Yet, decisions based on such methods are difficult to explain to the satisfaction of labor.

Next, the executive may add the experience of others to his own before reaching a decision. By means of attendance at conventions, discussions with various experts, visits to the plants of others, and study of business literature, the executive broadens the horizons of his limited experience. When a problem arises, the executive attempts to find in his files or his memory a plan or solution which someone else has used with success in similar circumstances. This scheme is relatively simple, not too expensive to use, and hence rather frequently applied. But finding plans of other that will fit one's own problems is often equivalent to looking for the proverbial needle in a haystack. And when one tries to explain why the plan of a given company was selected, one may find a counterproposal that the plan of some other company should be chosen.

Finally, some executives attempt to solve their problems by scientific methods. Under this method, solutions are sought by gathering, analyzing, classifying, and interpreting pertinent data. Starting with a careful statement of the problem, the scientific system includes such major steps as establishing a working hypothesis, collecting data, reaching a tentative solution, checking the solution, and then applying the solution. Obviously, such an approach to problems of labor is time-consuming, often costly, and invariably calls for close attention to details. Hence, this approach, though the best in theory, is the hardest to apply and thus the least frequently used. Yet, it represents the line along which attempts must increasingly be made, since it is the only one that has a logical basis for continued success. And it is the only one in which both employees and management can join forces without fear that a solution prejudicial to the other is being sought.

3. *Knowledge Requirements.* What areas of knowledge are pertinent to the solution of personnel problems? Specific areas were noted in the preceding chapter in the section devoted to the education of executives concerned with personal matters. It will suffice here to comment upon the basic aspects of man for which knowledge is indispensable. The business executive must learn as much as possible about three aspects of man: what he does, why he does what he does, and by what means he seeks to attain his goals.

What does man do? He thinks, he feels, he acts. So such fields of knowledge as logic, psychology, medicine, etc., are helpful in learning how labor, for example, thinks, feels, and acts in regard to various subjects of interest.

Why does he do what he does? He has certain values, needs, goals, and interests. So ethics, for example, seeks to throw light on grades of values in human life. Sociology is interested in group needs and satisfactions. And history has given us clues on how various goals have shaped human events.

What means does he use to accomplish his goals? Man has striven to attain desired ends through either individual or group effort. So psychology, sociology, and political science are contributors to our knowledge of such efforts. And economics and management have contributed to the wisdom and organizing skills needed for such decisions.

The foregoing listing does not imply that enough is now known in all areas to provide quick and simple solutions. The listing merely recites basic subject matter which cannot safely be left unstudied.

Obstacles to Problem Solving

It is well to recognize also that the problems that confront personnel management are by no means simple. It is not child's play to tussle with such issues as fair wages, the way in which employees should exercise their voice in matters of interest to them, reactions to political activities, and how far one has a right to go into matters pertaining to private lives and community affairs.

Complex though these problems are, their solutions are made even more difficult by the following obstructions:

1. Precise methods of measuring labor's interests or contributions are lacking.
2. The human factor is hard to interpret, and its probable future actions are difficult to forecast.
3. The common human shortcomings of ignorance, selfishness, and prejudice interfere with the application of logical methods.

If these obstructions could be removed, a long stride would be taken in reducing labor problems. For example, how much room for argument could there be if a measuring device were available that could determine precisely what an employee in a given case was worth? Imagine how quickly wage disputes could be settled with a thermometer of wage rates. But such a device is nonexistent, and it is improbable that one will be developed in the foreseeable future. Of course, methods of giving approximate answers are available, but they all leave something to be desired. Is it any wonder, therefore, that disputants over wage matters so often have recourse to tests of power in order to reach decisions in their quarrels? And is it any wonder, then, that employee-management problems, handled thus, have a habit of recurring?

The human factor also is a source of perplexing problems. On the one hand, it acts in ways that are often difficult to understand, let alone forecast. On the other hand, even the fairest of men is not above some selfishness or ignorance—sometimes reasonably so and sometimes not. Although it may be argued that the human race is improving in these matters, we still have a long way to go in learning how to live together peacefully and equitably.

These difficulties are cited as a warning to the student to be realistic about personnel matters. It would be much better if logic could always be used. Unfortunately, the perversity of nature and man must be considered. When trial-and-error methods must sometimes be used, this should not give rise to cynicism; rather, it is only realistic to recognize the complete nature of things as they are. Under such conditions, measurable improvement rather than artificial perfection should be the test of results achieved.

Future Prospects

From the foregoing, it is clear that labor in business has traveled many roads and has involved many groups. Changes in relationships have been numerous and continuous. It is not unreasonable, therefore, to expect that present patterns will be reconstructed with the passage of time. What are the future prospects?

What the future may bring is of course conjectural. But several possibilities are worth mentioning. In the first place, it is almost certain that employees will exert more influence on decisions which affect their interests. Whether this influence will emphasize voluntary cooperation with management, intervention through union representatives, legislative controls, or some combination of these is uncertain. But in view of past trends and current developments, there is reason to expect the voice of employees to become louder rather than more subdued.

In the second place, it is almost certain that the government will take an increasing role in labor-management affairs. One the one hand, it will be forced to do so by the growing voting power of labor. Anyone who aspires to political office will be careful to avoid being tagged as an enemy of labor. Conversely, he will seek to aid in the enactment of laws which are favorable to labor. On the other hand, government as an agency of all the people must seek ways and means of balancing the interests and protecting the rights of all who are involved in and affected by labor relations.

Thirdly, technological change can be expected to be more striking than it has been in the past and its impact upon personnel relations more electrifying. Such trends as automation are bound to intensify problems in this area. Merely to list the following is enough to illustrate the problems that must be solved as automation gains momentum: how to provide for employees displaced by machines, how to share in the productive powers of mechanization, how to develop the needed engineers and technicians, and how to design supervisory and organizational techniques to meet these new challenges.

Technological changes will also affect the factor of mobility of workers. This will involve changes in jobs, employers, occupations, industry, and geographic area, as well as movements in and out of the labor force itself. The increasing rate at which technology and business have been changing will, on the one hand, see increased movements of labor in the dimensions just mentioned. And on the other hand, such changes will call for (1) greater flexibility on the part of people, (2) more attention by management to personnel problems of a more dynamic society, and (3) better solutions to the needs of those displaced or adversely affected.

In the fourth place, it is certain that new insights will be provided toward the end that employees and management may work together more harmoniously and effectively. Certainly, agreement is general that labor cannot be viewed simply as a technical or economic factor of production. Contributions from the behavioral sciences are particularly encouraging.

Varied research has pointed up the fruitful possibilities of improvement that lie in the areas of industrial sociology, group dynamics, and interpersonal relations. Perhaps most gratifying is the realization that human problems in business should be approached from an interdisciplinary rather than a specialized point of view.

And lastly, one can expect business to take a broader view of its responsibilities than it has in the past. Once, it was rather universally accepted that business should be judged solely by the profit test. Management was appraised according to how well it protected the interests of the financial investor. Gradually, other tests have been added. It is therefore neither radical nor impractical to state that the future will see even more weight given to success in serving personal and psychological needs, community and social responsibilities, and appropriate roles in political, religious, and educational affairs.

QUESTIONS

1. What are the differences to employees of the short-run and long-run effects of technological unemployment?
2. How has the cultural and social background of labor in the United States changed since the Civil War? What effect have such changes upon the problems of employee-employer relations?
3. If the status of a person depends upon some factors apart from what has usually been considered the normal working conditions and situation, what right has business to interest itself in such matters? Cite some of these factors in your answer.
4. Do you view the greater role of government in employee-employer relations with favor or disfavor? Cite examples of trends that please or displease you.
5. The concept that business should accept responsibility for labor's economic security is based upon what grounds? Do you expect this concept to receive greater or less acceptance in the future? Why?
6. What obstacles stand in the way of perfect solutions to personnel problems? What room for optimism is there if perfect solutions can never be expected?
7. Since logic cannot always be brought to bear upon personnel problems, what are the alternatives? What safeguards or warnings would you suggest in connection with the alternatives?
8. About what basic aspects of man must the business executive learn as much

as possible? In which of these areas have the frontiers of knowledge been pushed the farthest? About which do we know the least?

9. Trace the attitudes management has taken toward employees over the past fifty years. To what extent, if at all, do you favor a trend toward a more eclectic approach?

10. What do you expect will be the status of personnel management a quarter of a century hence? You may find it of interest to write out your forecast and save it, to be checked at that future date.

CHAPTER 3

HUMAN RELATIONS IN PERSONNEL MANAGEMENT

The Human Factor

Personnel management seeks, as already noted, to help build an effective and satisfied working force. Both line and staff executives, in their personnel responsibilities, must therefore give due consideration to the technical skills required of people for the jobs to be done. This is the factor-of-production aspect of people.

But to stop here would be far from adequate. Man possesses other attributes. He brings to the work place, whether management likes it or not, various feelings, desires, perceptions, motives, values, and drives. Thus, man—at operative, professional, and managerial levels—may be concerned about security, relations with fellow workers, status and roles, and personal and family needs. When a man is unsettled about such matters, his technical effectiveness will be impeded and his cooperation difficult to obtain. On the other hand, an individual whose various sides are harmoniously attuned will be more effective in the working situation. He must therefore be dealt with as a human being as well as a technical factor.

Dealing with the Human Factor

The human capacities and needs thus cannot escape the concern of personnel management. They manifest themselves through group as well as individual reactions. And they are subjective and changeable, varying with business events, managerial decisions, and time. Hence, management is dealing with a qualitative and dynamic subject.

Is management's work here esoteric, mystical, and dependent upon some nebulous, occult touch? Much that is bandied about concerning human relations seems to imply an affirmative answer. Since scientific contributions are as yet negligible in this area, credibility is lent to the assumption that the human factor must be dealt with in some vague fashion.

But such loose treatment is to skate on the edge of trouble. It will make management suspect, as it has in the past, in the case of such practices as wage incentives, merit rating, and testing. And once discredited, human relations practices can regain their proper role only with great difficulty. Hence, it behooves management to move in this area with extreme care.

And move it must, because in everything it does, management meets the impact of the human factor. Throughout this book, therefore, specific allusions to human relations will frequently be made at pertinent points. But to reduce unnecessary duplication, it is proposed in this chapter to note how the human factor is related to the following:

1. The functions of personnel management
2. Motivation
3. Interpersonal relations
4. Executive behavior

Human Relations and Personnel Functions

Some of the mystery associated with human relations can be dissipated by (1) defining the basic factors of human relations and (2) describing how these factors pertain to the functions of building an effective and satisfied working force.

1. *Basic Factors of Human Relations.* The members of an organization not only perform their respective tasks but also affect each other's actions. Each member can be viewed partly as an isolated performer. He must carry out the responsibilities assigned to him. Each member, however, affects and in turn is affected by others. He relates to and is related to others.

The relationships may be technical or human. On the one hand, a research supervisor, for example, may instruct a subordinate on the engineering limits within which a particular project is to be confined. This, as far as it goes, may be construed as a relationship involving technical subject matter. On the other hand, the supervisor may weigh how his own attitudes and behavior in giving technical instructions will affect the feelings of the subordinate, and therefore his ultimate research performance. This illustrates a human side of the supervisor-subordinate relationship.

Human relations thus has reference to how the behavior of people is affected by their interaction in such matters as feelings, perceptions, motivation, attitudes, and value systems. In other words, people are psychological, sociological, political, and ethical creatures as well as economic and technical factors of production. They interact in terms of these human dimensions concurrently with the economic and technical dimensions. And the impact of these human aspects upon productivity may well be as important as that of the technical factors. Hence, how management deals with the factors of human relations is of utmost significance.

2. *Management of Human Relations.* If management is to concern itself successfully with human relations, a planned course of action is needed. Various comments along these lines will be made throughout the text. For the present, it is sufficient to note how the functions of procuring, developing, maintaining, and utilizing a working force can contribute to better human relations.

a) *The Procurement Function.* Human relations can be no better than the kind of people who are hired. Hence, it is desirable to place emphasis upon human relations right from the start when specifying job needs, in attracting and screening candidates, and in inducting and placing people.

Turning attention to the first of these, jobs must be viewed not solely in technical terms (which are discussed in a later chapter). They must also be analyzed to ascertain such facts as the following:

1. Personal contacts that are involved
2. Percentage of time spent with various classes of people
3. Status and role implications
4. Perceptions of job values and norms
5. Union, governmental, and community contacts

Such inquiries help to describe the kind of a person it takes to meet specific human situations of a particular job. In the case of a research chemist, for example, to what degree should he be an introvert to satisfy the professional demands and to what degree an extrovert to keep him in balance with the types of people with whom he will be associated? How balance the respect he must have for the professional opinions of others with the confidence and judgment to push hard for his own ideas? Answers here may be qualitative, but that is better than evading a consideration of such crucial matters.

Having established criteria, the next step is to screen prospects. Good interviewing and testing, for example, have much to offer in checking personal qualities. Much useful information can be gathered regarding personality patterns, emotional stability, social awareness, interests, and the like.

The induction and placement phase also has a place in improving human relations. Useful here are practices which serve to adjust the new employee as a person to his new surroundings, to relieve tension, and to provide a friendly managerial atmosphere.

b) *Development of Human Relations Potential.* Having hired employees with good human relations characteristics, the next step is to develop them as fully as possible. The following questions, for example, illustrate the areas which might require attention:

1. What should be done on the job, or after working hours, to raise the understanding of people regarding political, community, and economic problems and affairs?
2. How should human relations factors be fed into the training of executives?
3. What help or information of a psychological nature, for example, should be made available to employees and executives?
4. How relate ethical and social norms into the working situation?

The fact that fully satisfactory answers to such questions as these will likely never be found is not a valid excuse to defer all action. Some progress is much better than none.

c) *Maintenance of Desirable Human Relations.* Essentially, maintenance of desirable human relations involves three stages: removal of undesirable situations, improvement of desired situations, and cultivation of assisting situations.

Good human relations cannot be maintained so long as situations are allowed to exist which bring about dissatisfaction among employees and management. Grievances represent a common form of employee disatisfaction with management. Disciplinary action is indicative of management's dissatisfaction with employees. In either case, as discussed more fully in later chapters, appropriate procedures and policies should be established to minimize the sources of dissatisfaction.

Improvement of desired situations has to do largely with motivational practices and morale building. As noted in the next section, motivation is concerned with stimulating employees to take desired courses of action. It must take into account the personal factors which determine the enthusiasm with which employees apply their technical skills. Closely allied to this is morale building. Here, concern is with the attitude of mind—the spirit—which governs willingness to cooperate in the projects of management.

Cultivation of assisting situations has reference to a wide range of plans which affect human relations. For example, recreational and social programs can provide an opportunity to exercise and indulge in a wide variety of human relations skills, desires, and energies. Or employee service plans of a legal, medical, and counseling nature help to reduce tensions and solve disturbing personal problems. And bringing employees into the decision-making process on matters of mutual interest can gain group acceptance and cohesion.

d) *Utilization of Human Relations.* The payoff of human relations comes on the job. Procurement, development, and maintenance are intended to have an effect upon job performance. But the job itself raises a variety of human implications. The work place, to begin with, has an effect on and is affected by feelings, attitudes, status, and social significance. Useful information on these, obtained by attitude surveys on likes and dislikes, such as that depicted in Figure 3–1, is helpful in determining the degree to which management and employees see eye to eye.

Personal associations on the job are particularly significant in their effect upon human relations. First and foremost is the supervisor. He must be alert to the reactions and needs of his subordinates; he must know how and to what extent he can deal with these reactions and needs; and he must know how to relate human relations forces to company objectives. Second, in this age of modern technology, staff experts must render their services without undue straining of the feelings of those who may have to accept technical or specialized services. In this regard, such outside agencies as unions must be brought into the working situation in a graceful and cooperative manner; otherwise, employees become resentful of management's actions. And third, management must not interfere with justifiable informal contacts between employees which are helpful in maintaining their status, roles, and feelings.

Human Relations and Motivation

Perhaps the most unique aspect of the human factor is that relating to motivation. Man, undoubtedly more than any other living creature, is captain of his destiny. He can vary his efforts over a wide range; how he applies his technical skills depends upon how he is motivated— partly a financial matter but also a human relations matter. To examine the latter phase, attention is here directed to basic aspects, classes, steps, and rules of motivating.

1. *Basic Aspects of Motivation.* Motivation, simply defined, is the act of stimulating someone or oneself to take a desired course of action. If it were as simple as that, there would be little, if any, excuse to fail as a motivator.

To begin with, there are buttons beyond number which might be

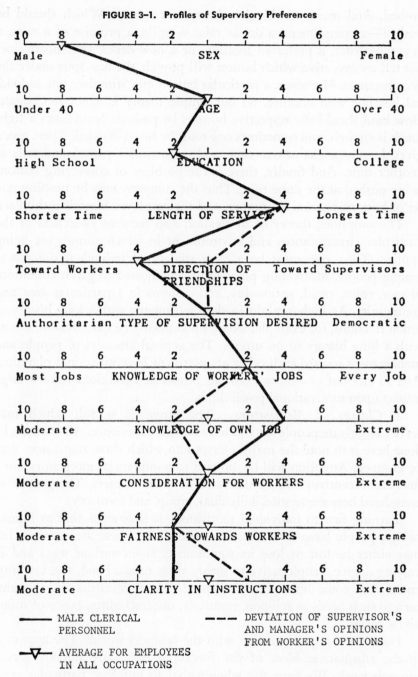

FIGURE 3–1. Profiles of Supervisory Preferences

SOURCE: Howard M. Vollmer and Jack A. Kinney, "Informal Requirements for Supervisory Positions," *Personnel*, Vol. XXXIII, No. 7, p. 433.

pushed. And many would give the same response. Which should be pushed—a compliment, a dollar raise, a smile, a promise of a raise, a new typewriter, a preferred location, or a new desk? The theory does not tell an executive which button will provide the best spur under the circumstances. Moreover, a particular button may stimulate one individual but fail with another. So our simple theory is again inadequate. How hard should the respective buttons be pushed? Sometimes a light touch is enough, and sometimes one must be heavy-handed. Then, too, a given button works at one time with a particular person and fails at another time. And finally, there is the problem of conflicting buttons being pushed at the same time. Thus the company may be pushing one set of buttons, the union another, and the employee himself a third set.

The simplified theory of motivation also requires awareness of the particular circumstances and environment in which stimuli are being applied. Thus, one must be a close student of individual differences among people. Motivating plans must be adjusted to given conditions of race, color, creed, nationality, and customs in a particular area and community. And what might work in a company with a long history of union relations, for example, would undoubtedly be questionable in one with a long history of no unions. The general attitudes of people and management toward each other are pertinent in motivational planning. And to cite but one more example, economic conditions have a large impact upon motivational possibilities.

2. *Classes of Motivators.* The range of stimuli which may serve to motivate people is as wide as human experience. All that can be done here is to note the major classes into which these motivators may be grouped. Attention will be directed to nonfinancial motivators, since financial incentives will be discussed in later chapters. The groupings considered here are termed individual, group, and company.

Turning first to individual motivators, it is obvious that as human beings, people have certain basic needs. Unless these are satisfied, life may either be lost or lose its significance. So in various ways and in varying degree, people strive to satisfy these needs. Food, sex, clothing, and shelter come immediately to mind. But as immediately, thoughts turn to such needs as religion, creativity, understanding, peace of mind, and security.

Have these any connection with the business world? The answer is in the affirmative. Most of the foregoing needs are directly served through work. We earn the wherewithal to purchase particular commodities and services which will satisfy our material needs. Moreover, the work itself may satisfy such personal needs as craftsmanship, artistic feelings, creation, and feelings of significance and accomplishment.

No less potent as motivators are the stimuli which arise out of social interactions. Without doubt, we are very powerfully affected by what others think of us and our actions. Even the areas of basic wants—food, sex, shelter, and religion—are invariably influenced by what will gain group approval or be attached with group disapproval. Why do we live in particular communities, wear certain kinds of clothing, trade our cars before they wear out, and prefer certain occupations? The answer in many instances is adherence to the group opinion of our families, neighbors, or working associates.

As life becomes more "civilized," the power of group motivators grows. Management should seek to utilize group pressures and when possible improve their quality and standards. For example, as shown in Figure 3–2, production is higher in cases in which employees have a feeling of group solidarity.

Attention is warranted to the specific relation of nonfinancial motivators to the business situation. It may sometimes seem that what people want out of life cannot be gained in the business environment. A

FIGURE 3–2. Group Solidarity and Productivity

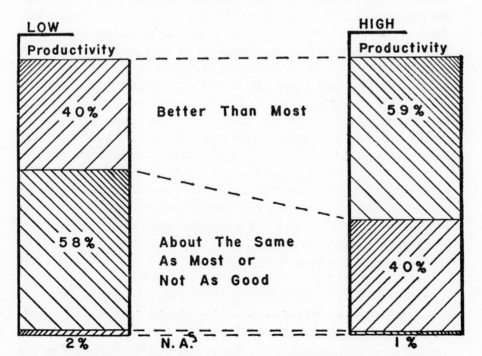

SOURCE: Rensis Likert, *Motivation: The Core of Management*, Personnel Series, No. 155 (New York: American Management Association), p. 13.

little thought shows, however, that business is not necessarily inimical to human needs. To begin with, man must ordinarily earn his bread by the sweat of his brow. If he does not work for a business enterprise, he nonetheless will have to work somewhere.

Viewed in this light, management should be able to show that business provides people with one of the best opportunities to gain what they want. In few types of enterprise is the relation between working and leisure hours so favorable. This relationship should be stressed by management in its communications to labor.

In addition, if man must work, should he not seek the environment in which work will in itself be most satisfying? This does not imply that work, like play, will be pleasurable in all ways. But it does imply that work has potentialities for deep satisfaction. Through the centuries, the philosophers have argued that work—yes, hard work—brings the fullest returns of contentment. And the thought is echoed by the doer as well as the thinker.

Here again, management should bring out this salient thought. In the first place, business has innumerable jobs which can challenge the skill, imagination, and ambitions of anyone. Just to go through a modern factory, office, or store is to be struck by the complex tasks that are everywhere. But some may retort that for every challenging job, there are thousands of boring, dull positions. True, but here again, business can show how it is attempting to turn such work over to machines. Moreover, employees themselves can help to develop new ways of working better and can learn to operate the new machines.

3. *Steps of Motivation.* It is now appropriate to see how management may actually proceed to motivate employees. This activity divides itself into two parts: (a) what is to be done, and (b) how and why what is done is done. The former are steps in motivation, and the latter are rules governing the steps. Both are performed simultaneously, of course. But for purposes of discussion, it is preferable to take them up separately. This section is devoted, therefore, to steps and the next to rules of motivation. The major steps include the following:

a) Sizing up situations requiring motivation
b) Preparing a set of motivating tools
c) Selecting and applying the appropriate motivator
d) Following up the results of the application

a) *The Size-up.*   The first stage of motivation is to ascertain motivational needs. Which employees need motivation? All, of course, but of varying kinds and degrees. Thus, one person will bestir himself to get champagne and caviar; another wants only beer and pretzels. One worries about a college education for his children; another is more than satisfied if his children learn how to read and write. Or one takes pride in the quality of his work, while another is simply interested in quantity. Stress in the size-up stage must therefore be laid upon individual differences.

Size-up requires reference to groups as well as individuals. At times, individuals are group-influenced. For example, office workers tend to act and feel somewhat differently than shop workers; craftsmen take a different view of their work than unskilled labor; and some of the views of supervisors are different from those of their subordinates. Hence an executive must determine what group-inspired differences exist in individuals as well as what egocentric drives motivate them. Sometimes, there is a conflict, as in the case of a person who likes his job but goes out on strike because of loyalty to the group. Then, executives must be careful to avoid irritating employees who already are torn by frustrating tensions.

b) Preparing a Set of Motivating Tools. Having determined the motivational needs of a particular person or group, an executive must then be ready to select and apply specific tools of motivation. But this means that he must have available a list from which choices may be made. Such a list should be compiled in advance and added to as information on motivational devices is obtained from one source or another. An executive, from his own experience, from the experiences of others, and with the help of the personnel division, can distill a list of what devices seem to work, with what types of people, and under what conditions.

c) Selecting and Applying Motivational Plans. The critical stage in motivation is, of course, application. This involves selection of the appropriate plan, the method of application, and the timing and location of applications.

The choice of a plan depends on answers to a number of pertinent questions. Who is involved? What has worked or not worked in the past? Are there any precedents or other employees involved? What does the selected motivational device require in terms of executive time, skill, and resources?

Having decided, for example, that an employee is to be complimented on his craftsmanship, thought must be given to application. One must think through the words he will use, the tone of his voice, and his own gestures when paying the compliment. He should rehearse his contemplated act, for he is an actor. In this connection, role playing has proved effective as advance preparation.

And finally, consideration should be given to where and when motivation is to be applied. Using the compliment as an example, some employees like to be told in public of their good deeds; others prefer to avoid the spotlight. Timing, too, is important. How soon after a good deed has been done should an employee be told of management's appreciation? Too late may be worse than useless. So it is imperative that the time factor be watched in the application of a motivational plan.

d) The Follow-up. The final stage of motivation is the follow-up. The primary purpose of feedback is to determine if an individual has been motivated. If he has not, some other device must be applied. This is necessary because the desired objective—whether higher output, lower costs, greater loyalty, or whatnot—has not been attained. A secondary purpose of follow-up is to evaluate motivational devices for future reference. It provides information regarding how devices should be classified as to their possible future use.

4. *Rules of Motivating.* In the performance of the steps of motivation, management should be guided by some fundamental rules or bench marks. These are not laws; we do not as yet know enough about motivation to be that certain. But past experience has taught some useful lessons which provide a basis for building one's own list of guides.

a) Self-Interest and Motivation. Without doubt, motivation is largely built on selfishness. This may seem to be an undesirable foundation. To the extent that selfishness tends toward greediness, undesirability is not denied. But selfishness may be intelligent. This is so when a person realizes that his own purposes are best served when he helps others, too, to attain their goals. For example, an employee may be ambitious to climb the executive ladder. He can try to accomplish this by climbing over others and letting the devil take the hindmost. Or he can try to climb by helping others become more effective team members. Both methods are selfish, but one is intelligent.

b) Attainability. It may seem too obvious to say so, but motivation must establish attainable goals. What we hold out for a particular person must be attainable by him. This does not mean easily or at once. Such a goal as a better job or a supervisory position may take years to attain. But it must be within reach.

But in all cases, goals should be attainable only through deserved effort. How much have we lost in good labor-management relations because work standards, for example, have been poorly established! A standard is set which employees beat. So management cuts the rate. The workers beat it again. So management cuts the rate again. Soon labor is so suspicious that it mistrusts every effort of management to stimulate production.

c) Proportioning Rewards. Good motivation is dependent also upon proper proportioning of rewards between people and for the same person at different times. A uniform plan of compensation for salesmen, for example, loses its punch after a while. That is why various types of contests with different rewards should be set from time to time. At one time a contest may be based on sales of new products; at another, on percentage of increase; at another, on the number of new customers; and at still another, on service calls made. And the rewards may vary— once, a trip to an exclusive resort for the salesman and his wife; another time, some desired product such as a new car or a mink coat for his wife; at still another, a college scholarship for the children of the winners.

d) The Human Element. It is well to refer again to the idea that the actions of people are caused by their feelings as well as by their thinking. One needs to work with employees for only a short time to learn how quickly their actions can turn into undesirable channels if their feelings are hurt, their egos or personalities insulted, or their pet ideas slighted. An executive may have been absolutely right in his facts, logic, and decisions. But by giving a wrong impression, or by rubbing a person's fur the wrong way, the executive's actions do not bring off the desired results.

e) Individual-Group Relationships. Finally, motivation must be based upon group- as well as individual-centered stimuli. For a long time, management acted as though employees were solely and simply ego-centered creatures. If action was desired, attention had only to be paid to the individual drives and needs of people. To an extent, this is true. Each of us is to a large degree an island unto himself.

But more recently, research has disclosed the terrific impact groups have upon individuals. As a consequence, management in its motivational efforts must determine what the group thinks about particular goals and appeals before putting them into a plan of action. For example, can a wage incentive plan succeed if the group is against such a plan? Can desired productivity standards be attained if the group considers them unfair?

Interpersonal Aspects of Human Relations

The matter of group behavior is worthy of further comment. Attention is directed (1) to manifestations of group behavior and (2) to explanations of them.

1. *Manifestations of Group Behavior.* To the beginner on the management team, employees may seem to be rugged individuals. Before long, however, the new supervisor notes that employees do things for reasons other than personal likes or dislikes. He notes, for example, that a particular worker whom he considered to be good and loyal is going along with a group slowdown even though it means either a loss of high incentive earnings or a low merit rating. Such group-inspired reactions are even more apparent during strikes, when otherwise conservative and reserved employees resort to violent and physical demonstrations.

On the other hand, good teamwork may be due to group-influenced behavior. Rush orders are pushed through in record time, overtime hours are worked without complaint, and undesirable jobs are performed with enthusiasm. The orders and instructions of executives are accepted willingly and, indeed, at times are anticipated and acted upon before orders are issued.

Group relations are not restricted to business matters. Both on the job and off, groups may participate in various social activities. During work, gregarious needs will be served by conversation, gossiping, and rumor-mongering while working, during coffee breaks, and at the lunch hour. Group pressures of retaliation against nonconformists or positive assistance of "good" members may be noted. After work, members of work groups tend to associate in recreational, social, and athletic programs. All of these nonbusiness interactions serve to strengthen the group in its common efforts to cooperate or not during working hours on company business.

2. *Explanations of Group-Influenced Behavior.* What are the causes of such behavior? Are they hereditary in origin or environmental? Both undoubtedly are causal. Trying to separate the two is perhaps impossible and certainly beyond the purposes of this text. A few comments on both are, however, in order.

The drive of self-preservation, for example, is certainly significant in group reactions. Whether it is an acquired or inherited instinct, people have found that in groups their chances for survival are increased. Such survival need not be viewed solely as a matter of life or death; it can have reference to any goals individuals consider valuable. Thus, employees may act in unison if they feel their security (job, pay, or prestige, for example) is threatened. Many of our fears certainly seem to diminish when we have a group with which to face them.

One is perhaps on safer ground in arguing that group-influenced behavior arises out of environmental and social causes. The cultural patterns of a people, for example, have much to do with how employees react in a business situation. In some countries an employee stands with hat in hand when he talks to his supervisor. He does this because all employees do so and would consider it shocking if he were to act otherwise. But in other countries the worker considers himself an equal of his supervisor. To act in a menial manner would be to invite insults from his fellow workers.

Other environmental factors are religious and political in nature. In some countries, religious feasts seem to occur every other day, and no worker would dare work on these days. His fellows would look with great disfavor upon him if he thought so little of his religious transgressions. Political views and forces also influence the behavior of employees. In some instances, political movements separate labor into one party, and management and capital into another. And the political disagreements are carried from the outside right into the working environment.

Executive Behavior and Human Relations

In dealing with individuals and groups, an executive affects people not only by the functions he performs but also by how he acts, his demeanor, and his appearance. Subordinates are often as much impressed by appearances and behaviorisms as by what executives are communicating. Hence, it is important for management to concern itself with how its behavior and its attitudes influence human relations.

1. *Behavior Patterns.* It is not surprising to hear such comments from employees as the following: "Keep away from the boss today; he just passed me without seeing me." "The boss smiled this morning; I wonder who is going to get the ax today?" "The boss is wearing his brown suit today; don't ask him for any favors."

These statements are evidence of the observational powers of people. The lesson has been learned that such overt manifestations as preoccupation, a smile, or the type of clothes worn are indicative of the way an executive is likely to act on a given day. The way an executive talks, the subjects about which one wants to talk, how one looks and dresses, and bodily mannerisms also provide clues to his mood. Or the way in which an executive dresses up his office often notifies people what his relations with others are likely to be. By reading such signs, people learn when to avoid the boss and when he can be favorably approached.

Executive Attitudes. Of great significance in affecting individual and group reactions is the set of attitudes an executive holds toward how his organization should be operated. Differences may be found in attitudes toward (*a*) group control, (*b*) factors of success, and (*c*) latitude of action.

a) *Type of Group Action.* How an executive directs his organization can fall into a variety of categories. For a long time in this country —and it is still true in many other countries—the theory of the autocrat prevailed. The executive was king, and his wishes were expected to be obeyed loyally, completely, and without question. There were no human relations problems. The "problems" kept to themselves or were discharged. As long as everyone thought that management had the right to act autocratically, the system operated with relative efficiency and satisfaction.

All autocratic executives have not been heartless. Many have felt a strong responsibility for providing for the personal needs and welfare of their employees. So it was not uncommon to find managers who provided various recreational, health, and benefit services. It was not unlike a good parent who takes care of his children; hence the term "paternalism" has been applied to this type of management behavior.

But children grow up and want to do things and decide things for themselves. As a consequence, the autocrat and the paternalist in business, by force or by choice, have tended to move toward participative action. Participation may take a voluntary form by means of suggestion systems, grievance plans, and joint conferences. The final plans and decisions remain in the hands of management. Yet, this type of change makes the human factor react in ways other than just as a technical factor; it has taken on a more significant role in the business world.

A more advanced stage of human relations is attained when management shares decision-making powers with employees—in other words, when democratic processes prevail. This stage has been reached already in the subjects covered by collective bargaining. Labor and management work out the basis upon which wages, hours, and working conditions will be established in return for the skills and effort of the working force.

There is no doubt that each of these types of leadership will be found to exist in the United States today. Indeed, each executive uses some of these forms himself; he is seldom if ever always a pure autocrat, paternalist, collaborator, or democrat. Sometimes, it pays to be decisive; sometimes, it is better to be a complete humanitarian, sometimes a consultant, and sometimes an equal partner. He should adjust so that the human being with whom he must cooperate will react most favorably for the total good. And he is wisest when he consciously calculates which vehicle of leadership is best to use under various conditions.

b) *Factors of Success.* Executives differ, too, regarding the factors they consider important in measuring success and progress. Since almost everyone is interested in getting ahead—or at least likes to think he is so motivated—it is important to know how one's superior measures success. The executive should therefore be aware of the various measures which seem to be most effective from a human relations point of view.

FIGURE 3–3. Supervisory Effectiveness

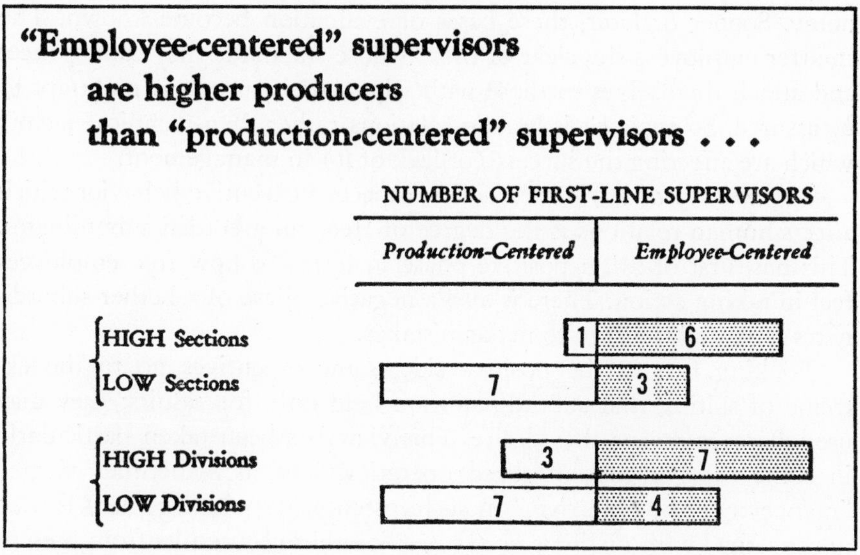

"Employee-centered" supervisors are higher producers than "production-centered" supervisors . . .

NUMBER OF FIRST-LINE SUPERVISORS

	Production-Centered	Employee-Centered
HIGH Sections	1	6
LOW Sections	7	3
HIGH Divisions	3	7
LOW Divisions	7	4

SOURCE: Rensis Likert, *Motivation: The Core of Management*, Personnel Series, No. 155 (New York: American Management Association), p. 6.

Of particular relevance in this connection is the attention which has been recently directed to the "work-centered" versus the "person-centered" boss, as shown in Figure 3–3. Studies of these types seem to indicate that more work is accomplished under the latter type of supervisor than the former. Thus the work-oriented executive deals with his subordinates in terms of meeting schedules, getting out production, keeping down costs and spoilage, and being careful with machines and tools. The person-oriented executive, on the other hand, shows concern for the problems his subordinates have and with the difficulties they encounter on the job. And his success is higher than the other's.

Other examples may be cited of executive attitudes toward success factors. Some executives rate a subordinate high if he keeps his desk in neat order. Another is impressed by on-time performance. Some like a particular style of report writing and dislike others. Some rate terseness as a sign of ability, and others consider it as a sign of emptiness. Some are impressed by quantity and others by quality. Is it any wonder that subordinates are on the alert as to how a particular superior evaluates things?

These likes and dislikes also run along lines of personal qualities. An executive may show partiality toward fraternity brothers, those of a given nationality or religion, members of a particular club, those from a particular part of a town or a social stratum, those who dress well or have polished manners, or those of a particular coloration or physiognomy. Sooner or later, these bases of evaluation become known. The smarter employees shy clear of those whose standards they cannot meet and attach themselves to those with whom their success is more apt to be assured. So again, it is human relations rather than technical factors which are affecting the success (or lack of it) in management.

c) Latitude of Action. Another aspect of executive behavior which affects human relations is the degree of freedom accorded subordinates. This has, first of all, a positive phase in terms of how free employees feel in taking action. There is also a negative phase of whether subordinates have any freedom to make mistakes.

Looking first at the positive side, some executives go to the extreme of stating that subordinates are held only for results; they may use whatever means they desire. This view has been taken particularly in some cases of decentralized operations and is sometimes termed "management by objective." In such instances, top management is then unconcerned with methods or excuses; it either gets results from present managers or hires new ones. This may give subordinates freedom of action, which is usually desired by most people; however, it also provides for swifter penalties but, by the same token, greater rewards.

Looking now at the negative side of latitude of action, there are differing opinions on the mistakes subordinates may make. Some executives look with such contempt upon errors that subordinates refrain from taking action. They are almost immobilized for fear of penalties. They avoid mistakes by slowing down action until they can consult with their superiors on what should be done. Their mistake record is clear, and the danger of chastisement is reduced, but so is production.

On the other hand, some executives believe subordinates should be freed of this fear, that they have a right to make mistakes. And this finds foundation in the theory of learning which states that we learn more from our mistakes than from our successes. Of course, the proponents of this idea do not contend that success will be in proportion to mistakes. Rather, the idea is that removal of fear opens vast powers of constructive action which hitherto have been walled up by fear of executive displeasure. Moreover, review of mistakes is a good way to clear the road for better future planning and action.

QUESTIONS

1. With what phases of the man factor of production is human relations concerned? Do you expect this concern to increase or decrease in the coming years? Why, or why not?
2. In what ways can procurement, development, maintenance, and utilization of an effective working force be designed to take into account the human relations factor?
3. To what extent, if any, would you recommend that supervisors associate with their subordinates in order to gain a more personal contact in the matter of human relations? What are the dangers of close association, and can they practically be overcome?
4. What is the theory of motivation? If it is simple to state, why is it so difficult to put into effect?
5. What steps should be taken and what principles followed when motivating?
6. Why are group forces seemingly of equal if not greater importance in affecting individual behavior? What are the sources or explanations for such group forces?
7. To what extent do you think religious and political forces exert influence within the business unit? Do legal restrictions rule out these factors in business operations?
8. What is your opinion of the importance of executive behavior in influencing individual actions? Should subordinates allow such personal factors to affect their attitudes and performance? Why?
9. Whch type of executive attitude toward his organization do you think is most effective and desirable? How do you take into account the influence of time and situation upon the attitude an executive might assume?
10. In what ways may executives differ regarding factors they consider important in measuring success and progress? How would you rate these factors in terms of their usefulness and fairness?

CHAPTER 4

PERSONNEL PROGRAMMING

Scope and Importance

The field of personnel management in a given company may be like a patchwork or like a map of well-defined dimensions. In the former case, there will be contradictions between policies, gaps in and duplications of functions, and poorly budgeted operations. In the latter case the various phases of personnel work will have been integrated into a well-designed system. The difference between the two lies in managerial planning—the degree of predetermining the means by which desired objectives are to be sought in a forthcoming period.

By establishing a planned program, management recognizes that all parts of personnel work are interacting and complementary. Good selection procedures, for example, reduce excessive training and abet good training. Again, such work as collective bargaining is not left to chance but is based upon careful research regarding wages, hours, and working conditions. And auditing of personnel work is not an afterthought but is planned for at the same time as the activities the auditing procedure is intended to check.

Establishing a program requires the integration of several factors. Assuming that a basic foundation of philosophy and principles (as outlined in Chapter 1) has been devised, attention must be directed to the following aspects of programming:

1. Objectives to be sought through the program
2. Functions to be performed in seeking desired objectives
3. Assignment of responsibility for performance of functions
4. Policies guiding those responsible for programs
5. Budgetary aspects of programs
6. Research needs of programming

OBJECTIVES

The Importance of Objectives

Perhaps the most fundamental factor in a personnel program, next to a basic philosophy, is that of objectives. It is impossible, on the one hand, to establish effective personnel plans until one has definite ideas of what results one hopes to accomplish. For example, a morale-building program cannot be designed just to raise morale; it must be based upon some estimate of the degree by which it is hoped to increase morale. Or a pension plan, to be successful, must serve specific needs of employee as well as company goals.

On the other hand, it is difficult to prescribe remedies for (i.e., a plan to correct) personnel shortcomings if one does not know what the specific results should have been. If a hiring procedure is to be improved, for example, it is necessary to know how far it has fallen short of producing desired results. Only then can one decide whether the procedure should be completely replaced or merely changed in some parts. Moreover, when objectives are established only after troubles are encountered with particular programs, employees suspect that executives are making a case to suit themselves.

Classes of Personnel Objectives

To develop a concept of personnel objectives, it is necessary to study the objectives of the company of which the personnel are a part. In general, the aims of most companies encompass the following:

1. Produce and distribute an acceptable product or service
2. Continuously yield satisfactory profits to investors and satisfactory wages, salaries, and other personal values to employees at all levels
3. Meet community and social obligations
4. Attain the foregoing objectives economically and effectively

1. *Service Objectives.* At the outset, it is imperative to recognize the fundamental importance of the objective of service. Business is an institution by means of which society seeks to satisfy the desires of its members for goods and services. To those who help attain the service objectives, various personal rewards are forthcoming, such as profits, wages, and other personal satisfactions. It is therefore incumbent both on management in its personnel work and on employees in their willingness to cooperate to recognize the significance of the service objective.

The design of a personnel program thus starts with a clear picture of the service objectives a company seeks to attain. Personnel functions and personnel cooperation must be directed toward efficient output of good and services.

2. *Personal Objectives.* Of course, the objectives of service, efficiency, and profits do not take precedence over the personal goals employees seek, nor vice versa. Obviously, the goals of employees also must be attainable, or trouble will ensue. Hence, personnel management must give due consideration to the desires of employees. But what are the personal goals which must be satisfied?

It is not difficult to list the kinds of goals that are generally in the minds of employees, but the question of how much of each kind is desired is another matter. Specific answers have to be hammered out on the anvil of actual experience, but wants of employees may be classified as follows:

a) Fair wages, hours, and working conditions
b) Participation and involvement in decisions
c) Economic security
d) Opportunity for advancement and self-improvement
e) Worthwhile accomplishment and individual significance
f) Positive group feeling

a) *Fair Wages and Working Conditions.* The keystone of any personnel program is an acceptable wage structure. Unless employees are reasonably satisfied that their wages are fair, it is invariably futile to expect much good from other parts of a personnel program, such as recreational plans, company periodicals, suggestion systems, training plans, and insurance plans. Hence, it is imperative (1) to establish as fair a wage policy as possible and (2) to seek to convince the employees of the intrinsic fairness of the plan. Even the best of wage plans will not meet expectations if employees, for one reason or another, will not accept it or do not understand it and therefore are suspicious of it.

In the matter of hours of work, there is less probability of trouble as long as rules governing working periods, rest periods, holidays, vacations, and shift rotations are definitely stated, are uniformly applied, and conform to general community practice. Unfortunately, these matters have often been considered only after grievances have stemmed from them.

Working conditions also merit attention in a personnel program. Physical aspects of working conditions, such as heating, lighting, safety devices, and clean work places, can usually be established without too much difficulty. However, supervision—the human aspect of working conditions—is more difficult to manage and often has caused trouble. And what constitutes correct work loads and reasonable rights of employees in job assignments can cause deep-seated grievances unless carefully worked out.

b) Participation. Participation and involvement in decisions which affect their interests are increasingly desired by all levels of employees. Fair wages, for example, seem fairer when employees have something to say about their establishment. Even on such matters as deciding on the installation of new processes or equipment, ultimate efficiency depends upon the manner in which employees are involved in the decision-making process. Although this seems to run counter to the prerogatives of management, what good are such prerogatives if they are nullified by the noncooperation of labor? If an end is desirable, the fitting question is what means are most effective in their attainment.

c) Economic Security. Another group of personal objectives in which employees are interested is that of economic security. Such events as accidents, seasonal or cyclical depressions, or technological changes hold a constant threat to an employee's earning power. To be sure, federal and state legislation has been enacted that serves to alleviate some of these losses. And unions have obtained concessions along the lines of supplementary unemployment benefits and are working toward the guaranteed annual wage. But a long road must be traveled before substantial relief is obtained.

d) Opportunity for Employees. Less tangible than the foregoing, and for that reason perhaps less frequently considered, is the desire of employees for the opportunity for self-improvement and advancement. There is a subtle distinction here that must be grasped. Obviously, all employees do not want advancement and promotions; to many, the responsibilities of new jobs are too great, and the feeling of self-assurance in their present positions is too satisfying to give up. But there are very few employees who do not like to think that if they wanted to get ahead, the opportunity for such development would be open to them. So long as the open-door policy is maintained, employees do not develop into less efficient workers by reason of the repressive feeling caused by having lost a rightful privilege.

e) Individual Feeling of Significance. Perhaps modern business has been most negligent in the matter of making employees feel that their individual accomplishments are significant and worthwhile. This is due in part to the conviction that a good wage is all that is needed to express management's satisfaction with its employees. This is not enough. Nor are mere words, such as unsupported compliments. Management must seek the ideas of employees, thus assuring them that their brains as well as their brawn can make useful contributions. And when respect is evidenced for the various human qualities of people, the individual will return a more cooperative response.

f) Group Feeling of Significance. There is growing recognition, too, that personnel management must consider the feelings of significance that are generated by interpersonal relations within groups. If a group feels, for example, that a job or company is inferior, that the status of various positions is of a low order, or that cooperation with management is undesirable, individuals will feel likewise. Hence, it is wise for management to build its personnel programs with a view to favorable development of group perceptions, feelings, and values.

3. *Community and Social Objectives.* Many forces have been at work for many years to bring about the realization that what happens within the walls and during the working hours of a business organization has an effect upon the community and, in turn, upon the efficiency of the company. For example, failure to provide safe working conditions, taking advantage of child labor, or sweatshop wage rates have in their time adversely affected the community. Eventually, there has been a reaction against all business as well as the offending companies. Legislation on these matters is a case in point.

It is not implied that all business has been callously unaware of such losses. Nevertheless, the failure of enough employers to take constructive action has led to the enactment of various restrictive laws by the states as well as by the federal government. In recent years the passage of compensatory and welfare legislation concerning such matters as unemployment insurance, old-age pensions, and medical care is additional evidence of what happens when business itself has not (and, some argue, for good reason) accepted such social obligations itself.

4. *Economy and Effectiveness.* All the foregoing objectives must invariably be attained economically and effectively. This follows for the simple reason that a company's resources are not unlimited. If its resources, and that includes manpower, are not utilized effectively, a company will eventually lose out in the competitive race. The importance of economy and effectiveness must be understood by employees, too, since their personal goals can best be attained only by successfully operated companies.

In summary, the various objectives the employer and employees seek must be incorporated in a well-designed personnel program. This relation between objectives and the program is aptly summarized in Figure 4–1, developed by Professor John F. Mee.

FIGURE 4–1. Relation of Objectives, Personnel Program, and Leadership

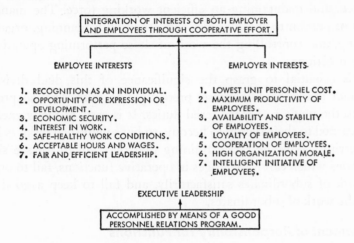

SOURCE: John F. Mee, *Management Organization for a Sound Personnel Relations Program*, Bulletin 2 (Bloomington: Bureau of Business Research, School of Business, Indiana University), p. 2.

FUNCTIONS

Nature of Functions

Having established the objectives of personnel management, the next important question to be settled is that of how desired goals are to be attained. The answer, basically, is through the performance of functions (activities).

The kind and quality of functions chosen in any given case are affected by the company's objectives. For example, a company that recognizes the psychological needs of employees will have to undertake a variety of activities that would be unnecessary if these objectives were not considered. Or in a company that is conscious of the secondary objectives of economy and effectiveness of its personnel programs, control and audit functions will be installed which others would ignore. And a company that proposes, for example, to set wages upon community levels must undertake surveys which are of no interest to those that follow a traditional or hit-or-miss system of setting wage differentials.

Although details of actual practice vary considerably, the general outline of personnel functions is much the same among progressive companies. These functions fall into two major classes: operative and managerial. Since they have been described in the first chapter and will be taken up in detail in succeeding chapters, only a brief comment on each is needed now. The operative functions of personnel management include the activities specifically concerned with procuring, developing, utilizing, and maintaining an efficient working force. The managerial functions pertain to the activities concerned with planning, organizing, directing, and controlling the work of those performing operative personnel functions.

It is essential to grasp the significance of this dual division of personnel functions. Otherwise, preoccupation with detailed problems leads to the neglect of managerial duties. It is easy, as many executives have learned to their regret, to become so busy with such tasks as hiring, transferring, counseling, and training that they fail to foresee shifting conditions which call for changes in operative functions, fail to organize the work of subordinates satisfactorily, and fail to keep a good check upon the work of subordinates.

Assignment of Responsibility for Functions

The personnel program must not only spell out needed functions but must also establish them into organized responsibility patterns. This requires the design of (1) procedural or systems structures and (2) organization structures.

1. *Procedural Responsibility.* Procedural or systems responsibility refers to the manner in which functions are arranged in complementary and sequential relationships for the accomplishment of desired objectives. References to such procedures will be made throughout the text, so only a few comments are in order here.

A personnel procedure is the basic tool for getting work done, i.e., accomplishing objectives. The broad function of hiring, for example, to be effective, must consist of an orderly sequence of a number of detailed functions. Each subfunction must feed into the next, so that good candidates are retained and poor ones rejected. Such details as application forms, interviews, tests, and references should be arranged so that evaluation of candidates can proceed effectively in arriving at correct decisions. Or on a larger scale, various broad personnel procedures—training, motivation, counseling, wage administration, collective bargaining—should be orderly not only within themselves but also in relation to each other and to the major functions of the business, such as production, sales, finance, research, and engineering.

The management of personnel systems has taken on an increasing importance as companies have grown in size. Information data and flows have increased to such an extent that decision making in personnel matters would be obstructed without carefully designed and integrated procedures. The economical and full use of computers, data-processing equipment, and communication devices is impossible unless their incorporation into personnel systems is carefully planned to the smallest detail. The demands of coordinating the personnel activities of a large and often geographically decentralized organization have underlined indelibly the need of refined systems in a personnel program.

2. *Organizational Responsibility.* Organizational responsibility refers to the manner in which functions and procedures are grouped under particular executives and to the relationships between these executives. This aspect is the concern of the next chapter, so only a few comments are in order now.

The organization structure must specify three areas of responsibility for the preparation, execution, and control of personnel functions. First, the personnel duties and responsibilities of each member of the management team must be specified. Second, the role of staff personnel units must be established, designating over what functions they have authority and which of their services are subject to approval by line executives. And third, the relationship between line and staff executives needs to be clearly indicated as to their specific areas of authority, responsibility, and conditions of cooperation and consultation.

PERSONNEL POLICIES

The performance of personnel functions specified in a personnel program is significantly conditioned by personnel policies. A useful overview of policies may be gained by noting their nature and purposes, how they may be established, and how they may be controlled.

Nature and Purposes

Policies are basic rules established to govern functions so that they are performed in line with desired objectives.[1] A few comments will serve to clarify this definition. First, while policies are guides to action, they are not the action. Functions and procedures constitute the action. For example, a selection policy might state: "Hire only high-school graduates or the equivalent." The hiring would be done through the selection process; the policy restricts those going through the process. Second, while policies guide action toward objectives, they are not the objectives. Thus, in the selection policy just cited, policies help achieve effectiveness in hiring by removing some candidates from the selection

---

[1] To some, the term "policies" has reference to the basic principles or philosophy upon which an organization is built or operated. While such principles or philosophy are basic to policy making, it is preferred here to follow the more restricted connotation of "policy."

process who presumably are undesirable. And third, while personnel policies are a tool of management, they cannot think for or replace management. Management must design appropriate policies and see that they are properly applied.

Policies serve two major purposes. On the one hand, they restrain executives from performing undesirable functions or from mishandling specified functions. As an example of the former, a policy which states that unauthorized collections among employees shall not be permitted on company premises upon penalty of discharge serves to prevent such activities from being performed. Or as an example of the latter, a policy which states that candidates for employment shall be selected only from those who possess a grammar school education or its equivalent serves to screen out those who would, in the opinion of the company in question, fail to succeed if employed.

On the other hand, policies are positive in nature by providing standard decisions when action has to be taken. Hence, they make it unnecessary for subordinates to ask their superiors how a given problem or case should be handled. Consider, as an example, the policy that all employees will be evaluated every four months to determine which ones deserve raises. This policy is restrictive, to be sure, in that the subject of raises is to be taken up only at specified time periods; but it states definitely when each employee can expect to have his record reviewed, which certainly is not true in the absence of such a policy. As a consequence of this policy, when an executive is asked about raises, he is in a position to give a prompt answer.

Coverage

In general terms, policies should cover situations which tend to repeat themselves. A useful classification can be derived by grouping policies according to the organizational areas to which they pertain and the kinds of functions they are intended to guide. Study of all of these is beyond the scope of this book. From time to time in subsequent chapters, however, the subject of policies will be discussed in connection with various subjects. Some insight can be gained at this juncture from the following listing and the brief examples in each:

1. Organizational grouping of policies:
    a) General company policies which must be followed by all units of a company; e.g., it may be a company policy to subsidize educational programs of study carried on by any executive or employee in various schools.
    b) External policies which guide an organization in relation to outside groups and agencies; e.g., it may be the policy to approve the partici-

pation of executives in part-time assistance to community, charity, and welfare agencies.

  c) Internal policies which guide the internal relations between organization units; they may be vertical or horizontal.
   (1) A vertical policy is intended to guide a lower level in an organization; e.g., the sales manager may rule that all district managers are to evaluate salesmen every quarter.
   (2) A horizontal policy is intended to guide relationships between departments on the same level; e.g., a policy may be set to the effect that the personnel department must consult with and get approval of departments it serves before establishing, let us say, training procedures.
  d) Centralized policies which have pertinence for companies with several locations and have reference to the degree of autonomy local units will have in setting policies and procedures which fit their respective conditions.

2. Functional grouping of policies:
  a) Policies which guide managerial functions of personnel planning, organizing, directing, and controlling; e.g., it may be the policy that every manager must submit a plan of action for personnel activities in his unit by December 1 for the next operating year.
  b) Policies which guide technical functions of procuring, developing, maintaining, and utilizing labor; e.g., it may be the policy that any employee who has a grievance has the unqualified right to go to his superior or the personnel division, as he may choose.

Responsibility for Establishing Policies

Many personnel policies undoubtedly have, like Topsy, just grown. In such instances, everyone seems to know, without being told and without knowing where it originated, that a certain type of decision will be made in certain situations. Such policies are informal, and their establishment is beyond analysis. But useful comments can be made about formal methods of establishing policies.

Most personnel policies are best established at the higher levels of management with the advice and assistance of staff personnel. To see the desirability of this, take the matter of severity of penalties. Every executive must at one time or another take disciplinary action. It would be unwise, however, to allow each executive to set his own policies on penalties. The result would be inconsistent and nonuniform penalties. Hence, such policies should be set at a high level to cover all parts of the organization in which discipline is a recurring problem.

Middle and supervisory levels will be more concerned with transmission and application of policies. Middle management will be responsible for communicating the policy formulations to operating levels. Such communications would involve interpreting policies, clarifying areas of uncertainty and misunderstanding, and training lower levels in policy application. And the first-line supervision and, in some instances, the personnel department would be responsible for applying personnel policies in their respective areas of duties.

There is an important question of the form in which policies should be communicated. As already noted, many are informal or stated in oral form. It is not uncommon, for example, to hear an executive say: "Our policy is to pay wages equal to or above the community rate." But nowhere is this written down, and the amount of the premium seems to vary with the passage of time and business conditions. Written policies are an obvious improvement. They require more time to prepare and issue. They have advantages of permanence and ease of transmission, can be used as training manuals, and can be quickly arranged for auditing and evaluation. Hence, many companies find it desirable to prepare carefully worded printed statements of their policies.

Policy Control

Personnel policies will be most effective if they are established in accordance with good standards and are carefully reviewed from time to time. A set of standards is very useful in checking to see if a proposed personnel policy will be a good policy. Without seeking the answers, note how the following questions immediately give clues regarding such a policy as "Hire only high-school graduates or the equivalent."

1. Is the policy based upon a careful analysis of the objectives and ideals of the company?
2. Is it definite, unambiguous, complete, and accurately stated?
3. Is it reasonably stable and not subject to change because of temporary changes in existing conditions?
4. Does it have sufficient flexibility to handle normal variations in conditions?
5. Is it related to policies of other sections of the company so that a proper balance of complementary policies is established?
6. Is it known and understood by all who must work with it or are affected by it?

Periodic review of personnel policies is also needed to determine which should be changed or dropped and where additional policies are needed. A variety of appraisal methods is available, as follows:

1. All policies should be subject to some, if not extended, evaluation annually.
2. Some policies should come up for review at specific times, such as when collective bargaining agreements must be renegotiated.

3. Policies of each department or division may be reviewed when budgetary requests are made.
4. Spot or overall appraisal of policies may be made by outside consultants. This could be done after trouble develops; but preferably, it should be a constructive preventive measure.
5. Policies may be subject to review when the desirability is indicated by employee suggestions, employee grievances, or unsatisfactory reports on employee performance or behavior.
6. Policies should be subject to review whenever a company plans a major expansion or contraction, a change to a new location, or a change of methods.

BUDGETARY ASPECTS OF PROGRAMS

The budget is a particularly useful device in personnel programming. It shows, in financial terms for a coming period of time, the amounts which may be spent for various personnel activities. It is, therefore, a quantitatively expressed plan of action. During the period covered by the budget, it is useful in guiding the actions of those performing personnel functions. But in addition, at the end of the budget period, it can be used as a basis of comparison with actual expenditures. Hence a personnel budget assists management in performing not only its functions of planning and organizing but also that of controlling.

The possible contributions of budgeting to programming may be seen by describing the steps of budgetary preparation and usage. To begin with, establishing budgets involves a forecast of the specific goals which are to be sought and the tasks which must be undertaken in a forthcoming period. Such questions as the following must be answered:

1. How many people are to be hired, trained, counseled, transferred, and pensioned?
2. What types of recreational, social, and athletic activities shall be scheduled, and how often?
3. How many grievance or collective bargaining sessions are likely to be held?
4. How many workers are likely to have accidents, become sick or disabled, or require hospitalization?
5. How much of a staff—administrative, technical, and clerical—will be needed to carry out personnel functions?
6. What equipment, space, and other resources will be needed to carry out personnel functions?

Obviously, answers to these questions depend in part on the basic attitude of a company toward human relations. For example, a company which believes, as some do, that it is desirable to provide facilities for religious contemplation on company premises will entail expenditures that would not be incurred by those that feel otherwise.[2] Thus the budget aids in giving concrete expression to basic personnel philosophy and principles.

In setting forth estimates of personnel expenditures, it is invariably necessary, in the second place, to communicate extensively between organization levels. Thus, it is usually customary to ask lower levels of an organization to submit their estimates of what personnel duties must be performed by them and how much money will be required for these purposes. These are reviewed as they ascend the organization structure. The top management then combines all estimates, checks to see if they conform with total business prospects, and then returns the budgets in amended or original form. At times, it may be desirable to go up and down the channels more than once before all parties are satisfied. In any event, this up-and-down process of communication provides an excellent means of educating all levels on personnel matters and of integrating the various elements of an organization into a more effective team as regards personnel goals.

In the third place, working up a budget can serve to minimize gaps, imbalance, or duplications in programming. This can be illustrated in Tables 4–1 and 4–2. By reviewing the subdivisions in Table 4–1, management can be sure that all phases of personnel have been covered. Dividing the budget according to organizational divisions, as evidently has been done in this case, is a particularly useful plan. And by comparing elements of expense in various budgets, duplication of effort can be uncovered. Thus, in Table 4–2, Department #1 has a budgeted amount for training and safety salaries. If these have been approved, it is only because they are valid supplements to the amounts requested for training and safety work in the budget of the staff personnel division.

Finally, such budgets can be useful in comparing what happened with original expectations. Thus, at the end of the budget period, actual expenditures can be entered in a column adjacent to budgeted amounts. Differences can then be entered either as absolute or as percentage values. Reasons and explanations for deviations can then be sought. Search for causes of variations can serve two purposes: (1) to determine who deserves censure or praise and (2) to adjust future plans to take advantage of past successes and avoid past mistakes.

Through the use of budgets, comparisons may also be made with other companies or with industry-wide data. In the past decade, more

---

[2] As an example, see the illustration in Figure 4–2.

FIGURE 4–2.   A Company Chapel

'THINE TO WORK AS WELL AS PRAY'

— Whittier

TALL pines guard the approaches to an attractive chapel within the mill area of a steel company in eastern Texas.

To this interdenominational sanctuary, built and staffed by the company and dedicated just three years ago this month, come as many as 50 employees in one day.

Although some seek the personal counsel of the company's chaplain, many others fulfill the primary purpose of this house of worship, as inscribed on its cornerstone: ". . . For prayer and meditation, where all men find light for darkness, assurance for confusion, and faith for doubt and despair."

The eyes of those who enter soon come to rest upon the unusual stained glass window above the altar. As Robert Harmon, the artist, describes it:

"There is the large Hand of God, the Creator. From His hand flow all things of creation, fish, water, animals, birds, stars and plant life — all these being apparent throughout the window.

"At the top of this abstract Tree of Life is the figure of man silhouetted against the sun, because man is the crowning glory of God's creation."

From little reflections of man's belief in God, such as these, sprang the inspiration for this Chapel in the Pines: two employees saying grace one day in the plant cafeteria . . . a knot of men on the Sunday shift holding a brief service during noon hour.

Amid the tensions, pressures and complexities of modern living, the chapel stands serene; the sound of organ music, flowing forth through an amplifying system to every part of the mill during shift changes, seeming to say:

Take comfort,
Have faith,
Find peace.

SOURCE: *Steelways*, November, 1958, published by American Iron and Steel Institute.

TABLE 4–1

THE STANDARD MANUFACTURING CO. OPERATING BUDGET
Personnel Division, 1966

Administrative expenses:

Administrative salaries	$30,000
Clerical salaries	12,000
Office supplies	1,000
Traveling expenses	4,000
Telephone and telegraph	800
Total	**$ 47,800**

Employment division:

Advertising	$ 3,000
Manager's salary	9,500
Interviewers' salaries	15,000
Technical salaries	10,000
Clerical salaries	12,000
Office supplies	4,000
Traveling expenses	6,000
Telephone and telegraph	2,500
Total	**62,000**

Training division:

Manager's salary	$ 8,500
Trainers' salaries	14,000
Technical salaries	9,500
Clerical salaries	6,000
Training supplies	4,500
Traveling expense	2,100
Telephone and telegraph	600
Total	**45,200**
Medical division*	32,700
Safety division*	21,800
Employee relations division*	61,800
Benefits and service division*	78,300
Personnel research division*	19,500
Grand total	**$369,100**

* Breakdown of detail not shown.

TABLE 4–2

THE STANDARD MANUFACTURING CO. LABOR BUDGET
Department #1

Supervisory salaries	$ 17,000
Clerical salaries	16,000
Training costs	4,200
Safety engineer	4,400

Drill press operators:

Grade 1	$49,300
Grade 2	31,500
Grade 3	12,250
Total	**93,050**

Bench hands:

Grade 1	$21,000
Grade 2	4,900
Total	**25,900**
Truckers	6,000
Grand total	**$166,550**

and more information has been forthcoming on such relationships as personnel expenditures per employee and the number of personnel staff members per one hundred employees on the payroll. It would be most helpful to a company if its records were kept so that it could make comparisons with others similar to it, as shown in Table 4–3.

TABLE 4–3

PERSONNEL COSTS
Average Functional Cost per Employee per Year

1. Administration...$ 7.38
2. Planning policy and organization............................. 3.88
3. Staffing: job analysis, selection, recruitment, induction.......... 9.06
4. Training... 5.13
5. Promotion and transfer....................................... 2.47
6. Personnel rating... 2.04
7. Labor relations.. 6.08
8. Employee services, including communications.................... 9.14
9. Medical, health, and safety................................... 11.68
10. Wage and salary administration............................... 4.82
11. Records and reports.. 5.66
12. Audit and review.. 1.51
13. Research.. 1.46
14. Overhead and miscellaneous.................................. 6.57
       All functions...$76.88

SOURCE: A. C. Thornton, *Practical Personnel Budgeting*, Personnel Series, No. 173 (New York: American Management Association), p. 55.

RESEARCH NEEDS OF PROGRAMMING

It should be apparent by this time that much information will be required in programming personnel work. How well this job of collecting information is done will determine how successfully responsible executives can reach decisions on personnel objectives, functions, policies, and principles. Reliance in such matters is often placed upon personal experience or the experience of others. Yet, it is contended here that much more emphasis will have to be placed upon logical, scientific research for needed information.

A number of research tools are already available for these purposes and will be touched upon in later chapters. It is worth noting here, however, a few examples of information gathering through research. Such techniques as job analysis and man specifications, merit rating and job evaluation analysis, procedural analysis, turnover and absenteeism studies, morale and attitude surveys, wage and salary surveys, and policy audits and evaluations can provide indispensable information basic to program development. Such investigations need not be perfect analyses of these subjects. Of course, the more thorough, the better. But for all practical purposes, much data can be gathered with a minimum of fanfare and expenditure. There is needed only the sincere desire to seek facts for decisions in the place of personal hunches and limited experience.

The purpose of this chapter has been to call attention to certain basic factors to which consideration must be given early in the study or development of any personnel program. Decisions must be reached on such matters as objectives, functions, assignment of responsibilities, policies, and principles in building an effective personnel plan. Some believe that such matters may be resolved by cut-and-try methods. But there is no shortcut solution to the complex problems of human relations. The only hope in the long run for fair and equitable solutions is along the path of facts and information. Hence the subject of research has been given special emphasis in this chapter on programming. Research is without doubt the key to effective planning of personnel activities.

QUESTIONS

1. What are the purposes of a personnel program? Are the purposes solely for the interests of the company?
2. Can you illustrate the argument that a personnel program serves to tie together various personnel activities?
3. Make a list of personnel objectives. Which do you think are the most difficult to attain?
4. How would you prove in a given case that the investment in a personnel program was justified?
5. How would you classify the wants of employees? Can you cite specific illustrations in support of your classification? To what extent are these wants selfish?
6. Do you believe it is feasible for a company to include in its personnel program all the activities listed in this chapter? Which ones do you believe are performed less frequently and which more frequently?
7. What are the purposes of personnel policies? Do employees have a voice in their determination?
8. What is the relation between personnel policies and employee booklets of rules and regulations?
9. What contributions can budgets make to personnel programming? Is it possible to put a dollar sign on personnel work and human relations?
10. What is the relationship between programming, budgets, and research? Can these relationships be expressed quantitatively, or must they be stated in general, qualitative terms?

CHAPTER 5

ORGANIZATION OF PERSONNEL MANAGEMENT

Scope of Organization

The attainment of various objectives of personnel management requires the coordinated effort of many people. If objectives, efforts, and people are to be integrated effectively in an ongoing, dynamic fashion, an appropriate operational organization must be designed and maintained. Such an organization must include (1) the sequence in which various functions are to be performed and (2) the authority-responsibility relationships of the people who perform the functions. The former is commonly referred to as systems or procedures, and the latter as organization structure. These comprise the major divisions of this chapter.

SYSTEMS OF PERSONNEL MANAGEMENT

It has been noted that personnel management must procure, develop, maintain, and utilize people. Even the briefest consideration of any of these four functions is sufficient to disclose that each consists of more than one step. Procurement, for example, invariably involves a number of subfunctions. How these subfunctions are arranged in orderly sequences determines the system of procurement used in a particular case. It is important, therefore, that systems be carefully established if each of the basic four functions is to attain desired goals. To understand the role of systems in personnel management, the discussion here is concerned with (1) the nature of systems and (2) systems in personnel management.

Nature of Systems

A system, as already noted, is a sequential arrangement of functions leading to the attainment of desired objectives. Such an arrangement consists of the following parts:

1. The objectives of the system
2. The functions and subfunctions to be performed
3. The information flows needed to operate and control functions
4. The resources (technical and human) to operate and manage the various parts
5. The sequential relationships between the foregoing

FIGURE 5–1.   A Hiring System

STEPS

STEP # 1	STEP # 2	STEP # 3	STEP # 4	STEP # 5	OBJECTIVE
Applicant fills out application blanks.	Interviewer talks to applicant.	Candidate takes psychological tests.	Supervisor talks to candidate.	Personnel and payroll records are completed.	Vacancy filled by successful candidate.

INFORMATION FLOWS

Various Information on Application Blanks	Interviewer's Evaluations	Test Scores	Supervisor's Evaluation.	Final Decision	

The relationships in a system can be seen more clearly by reference to the simple hiring system illustrated in Figure 5–1. The objective of filling a vacancy is the only justification for the existence of the system. The five steps that deal directly with candidates must be performed with that end in mind. Each step derives information to advance subsequent steps and is dependent upon previous flows of information. For example, the interviewer in the personnel department derives information useful (1) to himself in deciding whether or not to reject a given candidate and (2) to others who follow him in the procedure. But the interviewer could not do his work so effectively if he had not been supplied with information from the application blank, job specifications, and man specifications. And of course, the interviewer is a human resource indispensable to the execution of his particular function in the system.

Hiring can be used to illustrate decision-making aspects of systems in personnel work. As noted, hiring invariably involves rejections as well as selections. Each stage of the hiring process provides a basis for deciding whether or not a given candidate is to be retained as a candidate. The decision presumably is based upon the information generated by the various stages of the process. Quantity and quality of information are therefore critical to decision making. As a consequence, systems design in personnel requires that attention be directed to the collection and channeling of information to and through the various stages of every personnel procedure.

Building a system consists of two steps: (1) The various components must be ascertained, (2) the components must be fitted together. The first step is accomplished in one of three ways: seeing what has been done in the past by one's own company, seeing what is being done by other companies, or determining needs by research and logical analysis. This is not the place to delve into these methods and their relative merits. But it may be noted that in complex enterprises, systems study is being accorded well-deserved scientific analysis.

The second step of fitting components together deserves more space than is available here. A few comments are, however, called for. An orderly sequence implies two dimensions of order: time and place. If, for example, five functions must be performed to hire a person, which should come first, which second, etc.? Sometimes an answer is obvious; it would be unwise to interview a candidate without having a filled-out application blank. But at times, answers are not so obvious. Is it better to give psychological tests and then interview, or interview and then give tests? The interviewer would be in a better position to interview if test scores were available. But by interviewing first, fewer tests would need to be given. So cost, as well as information needs, is a significant factor in sequencing functions.

Since orderliness implies space relationships, this dimension must also be considered. Much of the hiring process or system takes place in the physical location of the employment office of the personnel department. Yet, in a well-designed selection procedure the executive under whom an employee is to work must have a voice. Shall the candidate go to the executive, or shall the executive go to the candidate? Again, such factors as cost, safety, and convenience will have to be weighed. The space factor also becomes important when needed data are stored in some central location. Then the system flow must accommodate itself to the physical storage of records.

Systems in Personnel Management

Inasmuch as discussion of systems is best related to particular tasks of personnel management, various references to this subject are made throughout the text. It is appropriate here, however, to note the growing awareness to a systems approach to personnel management as business enterprises become more complex. As long as business units were relatively small and stable in their operations, it was feasible to let systems just grow and, in a sense, take care of themselves.

But as a company grows and is subject to various changes in operations, the traditional approach to systems building leads to informational strangulation and excessive costs. Growth generates tremendous amounts of personnel information that can be handled only by expensive technical and human resources. But the use of well-designed electronic data-processing equipment makes possible the efficient and rapid flow of information to both line and staff departments. Moreover, a well-designed system of such equipment can be flexible enough to handle various new informational needs that develop after the original installation.

Another phase of system design that merits attention is how the personnel management system ties in with the total company and divisional systems. Personnel management cannot be considered as something that is off somewhere by itself in a personnel department. It must be fitted into an ongoing, developing, changing operation incorporated throughout all units of a company. Thus a supervisory training program for project leaders in the engineering division is not a self-contained, isolated undertaking. It must be related to such matters as overall company long-range planning, current production plans, budgetary requirements, promotional plans, and appraisal plans covering the ambitions of particular staff members. So this training plan, like all subsystems, must be blended into other subsystems and into the total company operating system. Such an approach makes for a total system design for personnel management.

ORGANIZATION STRUCTURE

If personnel procedures and systems could be made self-coordinating, our general survey of organizations could have ended with the preceding section. But the people who are an essential part of working procedures must be made accountable to and given direction by superiors. This is accomplished by an organization structure. The present section is concerned with the place of personnel management in various schemes and patterns of organization structure. The discussion is taken up under the following headings:

1. Formal types of organization structure
2. Informal types of organization structure
3. Relations between executives
4. Factors of structural design

Formal Structures

A formal structure is one which has been expressly established in an enterprise to spell out who has authority and responsibility over whom and for what. There are three major types of formal structures: the line, the functional, and the line and staff.

1. *Line Form of Structure.* The line form is simplicity itself, as shown in Figure 5–2. Each executive is given complete charge of the

FIGURE 5–2. The Line Form of Organization Structure

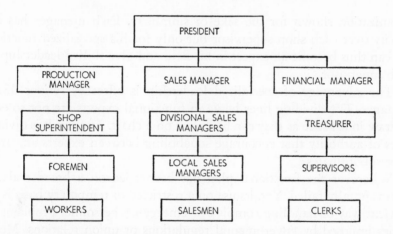

work assigned to him, subject only to the superior to whom he reports. And each executive must perform for himself, subject only to whatever advice or help he can get from his superior, all personnel duties which are helpful in the performance of his primary task, such as producing, selling, or financing.

There are good and bad sides to this form. The line form is simple, it permits quick decision making, and responsibility for personnel matters is easy to determine. But it is asking much of an executive to be a good personnel manager and a good technical manager at the same time.

The advantages of the line form tend to outweigh the disadvantages when (*a*) a company is relatively small, (*b*) the executives at all levels and in all parts of the company are well seasoned, and (*c*) the problems of the company are neither complex nor changing rapidly. Obviously, its sphere of usefulness is limited.

2. *Functional Form of Structure.* The pure functional form of structure is, like the pure line form, of limited use, but it has some desirable features. It is illustrated in Figure 5–3, with only part of an

FIGURE 5–3. The Functional Form of Organization Structure

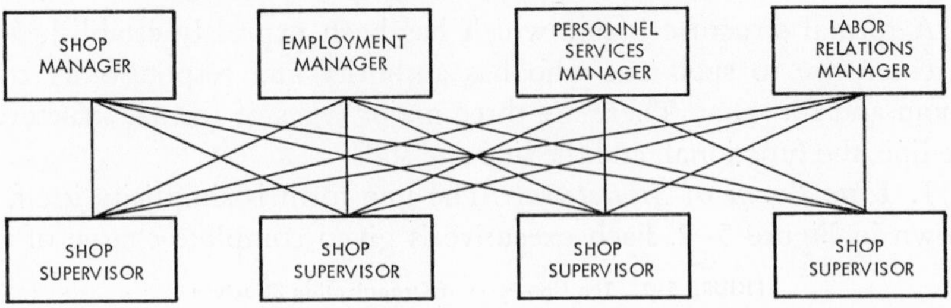

organization shown for the sake of simplicity. Each manager has authority over each shop supervisor but only for his specialized function. He can thus become an expert in his field and give skilled leadership to each supervisor.

The advantage of specialized leadership is offset by serious disadvantages. The dividing lines between functional experts are not so easy to draw in practice as they can be drawn on a chart. The result is divided lines of authority that encourage squabbling between experts and frustrate subordinates.

Wherever the functional plan has been tried on a broad scale, it has eventually failed. Yet, its use on a restricted or temporary basis is an efficient way of handling complex or emergency personnel problems or duties imposed by governmental regulations or union relations. Moreover, in the case of automated processes, it has sometimes been found necessary to place authority for such processes in the hands of functional experts. And finally, the functional form deserves mention because it serves to clarify the operation of the line and staff form, which is, in one sense, a cross of the line form and of the functional form.

3. *Line and Staff Form of Structure.* The most widely used form in personnel work is the line and staff, a simple diagram of which is shown in Figure 5–4. The most striking feature of the line and staff form is that in it each person reports to one and only one supervisor, yet receives specialized service and help from various experts. To illustrate, let us examine the hiring procedure, which is operated by the employment section of the personnel division, as shown in Figure 5–4. This unit screens applicants for jobs and then directs those selected as desirable employees to the supervisors for their acceptance or rejection. Since the employment unit cannot compel supervisors to follow its recommendations, the line of authority between the foreman and the superintendent remains undivided and the allegiance of the former to the latter is not placed in question.

FIGURE 5–4.   The Line and Staff Form of Organization Structure

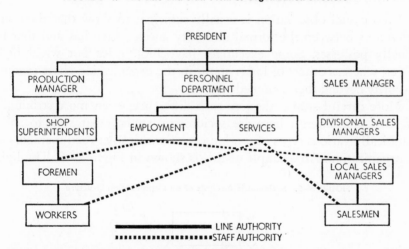

The advantages of the line and staff form are readily apparent. Experts are available for service, but their services need not be accepted by the line. Obviously, it would ordinarily be unwise to refuse to avail oneself of such services, since the staff frees line executives so that they may concentrate upon their primary responsibilities.

The major disadvantage of the line and staff form is that staff specialists sometimes attempt to force their suggestions and services upon others. In such a situation, subordinate executives do not know whether to obey their immediate superiors or the staff. This leads to the divided-line weakness of the functional form, which can be avoided if staff experts are expressly warned from above against exceeding their assigned scope of activity.

Under emergency conditions, it may be desirable to give staff units direct authority. Some companies found it desirable during the war years, for example, to turn disciplinary authority to the personnel department because it was impossible to train large numbers of supervisors in the proper handling of this task. These allocations were intended to be temporary, for it was hoped to return such duties to the supervisors as soon as they could effectively handle disciplinary responsibilities.

Except in small-sized enterprises, in which the line form of organization seems best suited, the line and staff form has evolved as the best all-around type of structure. Of course, this form would seldom be as simple as that shown in Figure 5–4. Ordinarily, there are numerous staff personnel—public relations experts, lawyers, accountants, office help, etc.—scattered throughout an organization.

Informal Executive Authority

Even casual observation is usually sufficient to show that there are differences between the formal authority an executive has and that he actually possesses. Some executives have high titles but wield little power, whereas others of lower status in the organization chart exercise authority beyond their assigned station.

More careful studies disclose such differences even more strikingly. Of particular interest here are sociometric studies that seek to show graphically various types of working relationships between members of an organization. An example of this is shown in Figure 5–5. The light

FIGURE 5–5.   Sociometric Analysis of an Organization Structure

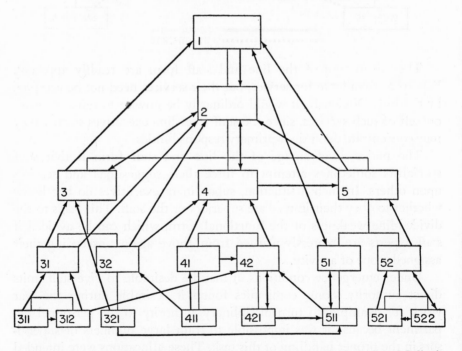

Source: The Ohio Leadership Studies, Personnel Research Board, Ohio State University. From C. L. Shartle, "Leadership and Executive Performance," *Personnel*, Vol. XXV, No. 5, p. 6.

lines depict the formal lines of relationship between levels of the organization structure. The heavy lines show the relationships based upon a study of the question with whom most time is spent in getting work done. It is clear from the heavy lines running to the positions marked 4, 42, and 511 that because of their respective levels in the structure, their significance is greater than that of the other positions.[1]

Such informal relations develop for a number of reasons. First, it may be time-consuming to go through channels; a friendly visit to the personnel department may get a transfer arranged, for example, quickly and quietly. Second, an accounting supervisor may have little confidence in or respect for the accounting manager, so he short-circuits him when he decides to seek a raise. Third, it may give a person a greater feeling of prestige if he makes a contact with executives other than his own supervisor. Fourth, some executives attract followers because of personal qualities of sympathetic understanding and wisdom. And finally, and perhaps foremost, informal relations develop because the formal structures fail to provide for the full needs of the organization and the people. Thus a structure which is based on the technical procedures soon will be interlaced with channels which provide for the emotional, psychological, and sociological needs of people.

As yet, not too much is known about informal structures. Their existence is well known; the "grapevine" is a case in point. But how to react to them is another matter. Perhaps the best advice is to try to determine how the formal structures are failing and then rebuild them so that the need of the informal is minimized. Certainly, a company that provides good channels of communication will have a minimum of unfounded rumors floating around.

Informal Employee Authority

Whenever people organize, the careful observer will soon note that unofficial groups form among employees. Each group will have a structure of leaders and be led as rigidly as any put down formally on paper. The appointment of the leaders in such groups comes about in a number of ways. Some become recognized because they are born leaders of men; they are naturally accepted because of an aptitude for performing leadership functions. Others are accorded leadership status because of some institutional factor—for example, seniority, type of work, position in a line, pay received, age, or special technical skills.

---

[1] It is to be noted that such sociometric measurements may be superimposing procedural analysis upon structural elements, in which case they may be depicting procedural relationships as well as structural importance.

These informal structures also are composed of a hierarchy of positions of prestige. There is not just one leader, but usually several of varying importance or of specialized areas of significance. Thus the group may look to a particular employee on matters pertaining to wages, to another for advice on how to deal with recalcitrants, and to still another when a spokesman is needed to talk to the supervisor. In a way, each member of the group is assigned some place that determines his status. Thus it is that one observes an employee being "put in his place" by a second employee, who feels that the first has not as yet earned the right to be heard. And the other employees will support the second, or reject him, depending upon the status of leadership which the first has not, or has, attained.

These hierarchies carry duties as well as privileges. The informal leaders are, on the one hand, expected to play the role attached to their assigned specialties. The old-timer is expected to counsel those in need of advice. The spokesman is expected to present to supervisors the thoughts which need to be conveyed in that direction. And the organizer of social gatherings is looked up to as the arbiter in these matters.

On the other hand, varying types and degrees of rights and privileges—status—are accorded informal leaders. Such status not only is recognized within the working areas but also is often extended into the community. Consequently, the employee himself and, at times, his wife and family are accorded respect that is not the lot of the average employee. In addition to this social status, it will also be found that the natural leaders are considered to be immune from performing menial tasks or are permitted various liberties which others are not.

While these hierarchies are informal, they nonetheless are well fixed in the minds of employees. The newcomer in a group, for example, is soon made aware of the need for respecting the informal group standards, or he is placed outside the pale; and failure to be accepted by a group is a penalty few wish to pay. Indeed, it is felt by some that the pressures of the informal social system are much more important than the so-called "logical" factors of individual motivation.

RELATION OF LINE AND STAFF EXECUTIVES

It is now pertinent to inquire into the particular roles of line executives and of staff executives in personnel matters. This may perhaps best be done by examining who has authority over and who is responsible for personnel work. It is impossible here to establish boundaries of authority and responsibility in every case. All that can be done is to note (1) the application of these terms to line and staff executives (taken up in this section) and (2) some factors which tend to change the boundaries of authority and responsibility in different cases (taken up in the next section).

Authority in Organization Structure

Authority, in its broadest sense, means the right to command the performance of others. It implies the right to give orders to others and to expect obedience from those to whom the orders are given.

But what is the source of authority, and how far does authority extend? In a formal sense, any executive obtains authority by delegation from a superior. Thus a personnel director may be empowered by the vice president (1) to organize and operate a personnel department and (2) to render personnel services to various other groups in the organization. The first part of this delegation gives him authority over the staff and the workings of his organization unit. The second part of the delegation indicates that his direct line of authority stops at the borders of his own department. Beyond these limits, his authority is advisory, which, in the final analysis, means that he has no authority.

In an informal sense, the authority derived by delegation may be strengthened and the borders of authority may be extended by earning the right to lead. In the case of line executives, this means incorporating some degree of participation and consultation in dealing with subordinates. In the case of staff executives, such as the personnel director, this means serving the interests of others with proficiency and sensitivity.

Responsibility in Organization Structure

If an executive has authority, he also has responsibilities. By responsibility is meant the obligation (1) to do an assigned task and (2) to look to someone for the assignment. Obligation implies a willingness to accept, for whatever rewards one may see in the situation, the burden of a given task and the risks which attend in the event of failure. Usually, more than one person or organization unit incurs obligations in a personnel procedure. For example, in selecting a salesclerk, the employment section suggests hiring a given candidate, but the departmental sales manager approves or disapproves the recommendation. Then, who is responsible if the salesclerk eventually proves unsatisfactory?

An answer to this question could be provided if the areas of responsibility had been defined before the hiring took place. In that event, assignment would have been made for each step of hiring. Such assignments could have specified the procedural responsibilities of both the staff and the line units. It would have been a relatively simple matter to determine which one failed to eliminate the salesclerk in the screening process.

Relations of Authority to Responsibility

Having discussed the terms "authority" and "responsibility" separately, it is now appropriate to comment upon (1) the need for clear assignments of authority and responsibility, (2) the need for coequality of authority and responsibility, and (3) the importance of lines of communication.

1. *Assignments of Authority and Responsibility.* From what has already been said, it should be apparent that each phase of personnel work should be clearly assigned to a given individual or organization unit. Take training as an example. Planning of program development, teaching methods, and training aids may well be assigned to a training section in the personnel division. Actual training may be assigned to each supervisor, who will use these services and aids. Here, there is a clear division of authority and responsibility for particular phases of training. Such an analysis of training also serves to emphasize the need of line and staff cooperation. Delineation of obligations for all other personnel functions should be made in the same manner.

2. *Equality of Authority and Responsibility.* One frequently encounters the statement that authority and responsibility should be coequal. This contention holds true, however, only when the person on a given job is capable of accepting responsibility and of handling authority. Any executive is justified in being reluctant to place authority over people in untried hands because of the losses occasioned by misused authority. It is usually less likely that responsibility will be mishandled. However, as a person proves himself, authority is gradually increased; eventually, it is made coequal with responsibility for personnel matters.

3. *Importance of Lines of Communication.* Authority and responsibility for a given job are also related by the lines of communication which are established between upper and lower levels of an organization. To begin with, such a line invariably runs downward from a superior to his subordinates. This is used to transmit orders, information, and advice.

Downward lines of communication also carry specialized services of various kinds. To illustrate, a sales manager may authorize a sales supervisor to add salesmen to his unit, but the personnel department may be authorized to screen candidates for the sales supervisor, thus freeing him for other duties.

The lines of responsibility, on the other hand, run upward. The main obligation is, and always should be—except in emergency cases, as noted earlier—to one's immediate superior because this insures single and undivided accountability. Lines of information may be established, however, to various staff experts. For example, if a sales supervisor sends a report to his superior regarding the number of people who left his unit and regarding their reasons for leaving, he may also send a copy of this report to the personnel department. In this way, the results will be examined not only by the line executive but also by staff experts. This does not mean that the sales supervisor reports to two executives. The line of single accountability remains inviolate, but the added line of communication offers a means of gaining expert advice on how poor results can be reduced and good results continued.

INTEGRATION OF PERSONNEL FUNCTIONS AND UNITS

From what has been said thus far, it is apparent that a number of executives and departments are involved in personnel management. It could be easy to get into conflicts of authority or evasions of responsibility. One way to avoid such conflicts and evasions is to adopt an integrated approach to authority over and responsibility for personnel functions, as suggested in Figure 5–6.

This diagram illustrates an application of the check list principle. It lists the functions, factors, objectives, and departments in any way related to personnel. Then, it is up to the user of the check list to see what each department is doing or not doing about the functions and factors of personnel. From such a review, gaps or duplications in personnel matters will be revealed, and appropriate remedial action can be taken.

The use of the diagram can be quickly illustrated. Each series of squares represents a major division of the company. Then, for each division, it would be necessary to determine:

1. What objectives, policies, and functions must be established for
2. Planning, organizing, directing, and controlling the
3. Procuring, developing, maintaining, and utilizing of the
4. Physical, mental, psychological, sociological, and ethical aspects of a labor force, with due regard for
5. Situational conditions, limiting factors, and basic philosophy.

FIGURE 5–6. An Integrated Personnel Plan

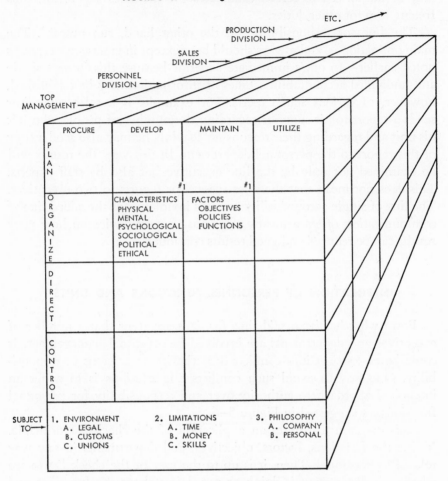

This check list may be used to relate top management, the person-nel division, production, sales, finance, engineering, etc., as they are concerned with personnel matters. Thus, it serves to integrate the work of personnel at all levels and throughout all divisions.

FACTORS IN SPECIFIC STRUCTURAL DESIGNS

It is now appropriate to note the formal place given to personnel in the organization in actual practice. Practice varies, depending upon a number of factors, the more important of which are the following:

1. The degree to which top management considers personnel subjects impor-tant
2. Interaction of people and organizations

3. The size of the company and the location of its units
4. Influence of such outside factors as legislation and labor unions
5. Types of labor or company problems calling for solution

Of course, these are more or less interrelated; but for the sake of simplicity, the foregoing will be used as an outline of exposition.

Attitude of Management

The opinion of top management of the importance of personnel is undoubtedly the most compelling factor in determining its place in the organization structure. In some companies, there is no personnel department worthy of the name, nor are line executives expected to spend much time on personnel duties. Opposed to the foregoing are other companies that have elaborate and highly placed personnel divisions as well as personnel-minded line executives.

In instances in which top management takes a comprehensive and understanding view of the subject, a personnel division approximately along the lines of that shown in Figure 5–7 would be the result. It should be noted that this chart is a composite developed from actual practice, and not just a theoretical conception.

Interaction of Personnel and Structure

Although only in the threshold stage, the introductory work of the behavioral sciences gives evidence of the need of adjusting structure to personnel as well as accommodating personnel to structure. Thus, on the one hand, different types of organization structure have varying influences on employee attitudes, reactions, and needs. And on the other hand, employees can influence for good or bad the structure employed in a given company. Because of such interaction, the design of structure must be one of reciprocal accommodation with personnel, and not a unilateral decision.

To see this in its practical aspect, a subordinate in a line and staff organization must relate to (and is, in turn, affected by) not only his immediate superior but also such staff units as the personnel department. If the subordinate feels adversely controlled by an autocratic line superior and more at ease with the permissive role of the staff department, he can readily tend to undermine the former. Particularly is this probable as rights of employees gain more legal and union support, which tends to reduce the autocratic powers of management. But the reverse is possible, in that structures may be weak in dealing with personnel. At times and with particular kinds of employees, strong executive action may be called for.

FIGURE 5–7. Composite Personnel Relations Functional Chart

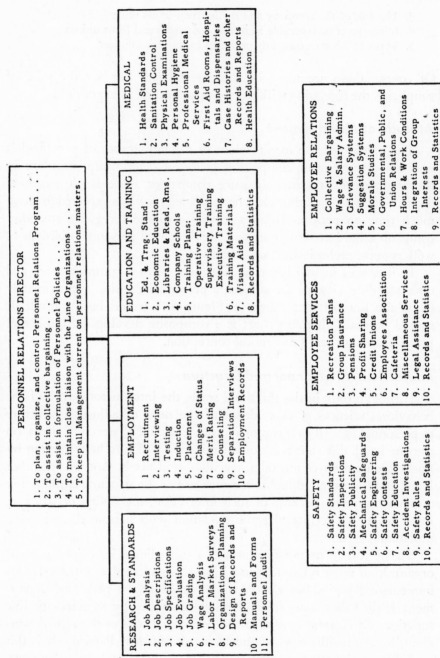

PERSONNEL RELATIONS DIRECTOR

1. To plan, organize, and control Personnel Relations Program . . .
2. To assist in collective bargaining . . .
3. To assist in formulation of Personnel Policies . . .
4. To maintain close liaison with the Line Organizations . . .
5. To keep all Management current on personnel relations matters.

RESEARCH & STANDARDS

1. Job Analysis
2. Job Descriptions
3. Job Specifications
4. Job Evaluation
5. Job Grading
6. Wage Analysis
7. Labor Market Surveys
8. Organizational Planning
9. Design of Records and Reports
10. Manuals and Forms
11. Personnel Audit

EMPLOYMENT

1. Recruitment
2. Interviewing
3. Testing
4. Induction
5. Placement
6. Changes of Status
7. Merit Rating
8. Counseling
9. Separation Interviews
10. Employment Records

EDUCATION AND TRAINING

1. Ed. & Trng. Stand.
2. Economic Education
3. Libraries & Read. Rms.
4. Company Schools
5. Training Plans:
   Operative Training
   Supervisory Training
   Executive Training
6. Training Materials
7. Visual Aids
8. Records and Statistics

MEDICAL

1. Health Standards
2. Sanitation Control
3. Physical Examinations
4. Personal Hygiene
5. Professional Medical Services
6. First Aid Rooms, Hospitals and Dispensaries
7. Case Histories and other Records and Reports
8. Health Education

SAFETY

1. Safety Standards
2. Safety Inspections
3. Safety Publicity
4. Mechanical Safeguards
5. Safety Engineering
6. Safety Contests
7. Safety Education
8. Accident Investigations
9. Safety Rules
10. Records and Statistics

EMPLOYEE SERVICES

1. Recreation Plans
2. Group Insurance
3. Pensions
4. Profit Sharing
5. Credit Unions
6. Employees Association
7. Cafeteria
8. Miscellaneous Services
9. Legal Assistance
10. Records and Statistics

EMPLOYEE RELATIONS

1. Collective Bargaining
2. Wage & Salary Admin.
3. Grievance Systems
4. Suggestion Systems
5. Morale Studies
6. Governmental, Public, and Union Relations
7. Hours & Work Conditions
8. Integration of Group Interests
9. Records and Statistics

SOURCE: Edgar G. Williams, *Indiana Personnel Executives—Their Programs and Practices*, booklet of the Indiana State Chamber of Commerce, Indianapolis (1952), p. 5.

This restrictive impact of organization structure has been particularly evident in large enterprises. As a consequence, developments in decentralization and the splitting-off of product units as self-contained organizations have been favored by some. These seem to raise employee efficiency and satisfaction. Personnel as well as other problems can be handled more effectively in relation to the particular situational conditions of the decentralized units. And the personnel have a greater feeling of association with such units than with the total organization of which they are a part.

Physical Factors

As suggested earlier, size of company, location of offices and plants, and the importance of labor problems affect the specific place such a division would be given in a particular organization. For example, a medium-sized company with one plant and no unusual labor problems might get along very well with the setup shown in Figure 5–8. As

FIGURE 5–8. Personnel Functions in a Small Company

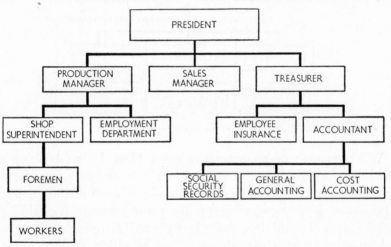

illustrated there, an employment section has been installed in the production division to serve its needs, whereas employment functions apparently are performed by the sales manager himself. (A larger company might establish a setup such as that shown in Figure 5–7.) In the case of personnel matters affecting all employees, central units have been established in the accounting department to handle social security records and in the treasurer's department to handle pension and insurance programs. Most of the relations with employees are handled directly by line supervisors and foremen.

But as an organization grows, the volume of personnel work increases to a point where it becomes a burden on all line executives. It is therefore as desirable for the sales manager, let us say, to divest himself of some personnel duties as it was in earlier decades for the production manager. As a consequence, as illustrated in Figure 5–4 (p. 75), the employment section "hires" for all line executives. Thus, in larger companies (employees running into the thousands), a centralized personnel department performs many service and advisory duties, thereby freeing line executives to concentrate on (*a*) important decisions in personnel matters and (*b*) face-to-face human relations.

FIGURE 5–9. **Decentralization of Personnel Functions**

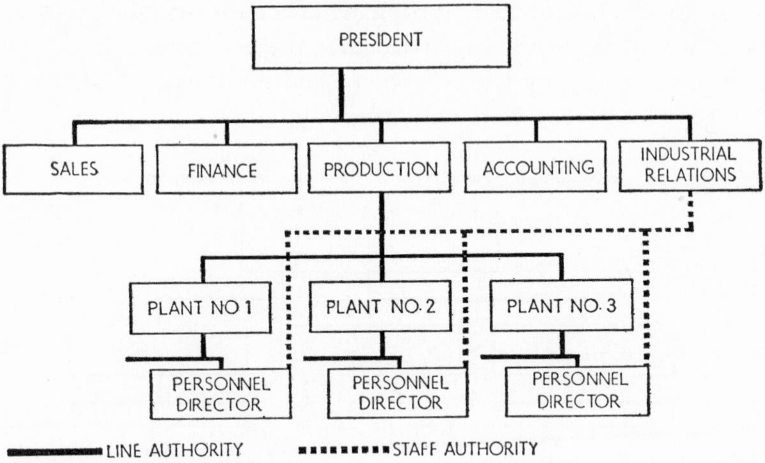

When growth of an enterprise takes place by establishing additional locations, the question arises as to where and by whom personnel functions should be performed. One answer is illustrated in Figure 5–9. A personnel department, subject to the plant manager, is established at each location. In addition, there is a central personnel unit to which each may turn for expert advice and from which uniform plans and policies are derived. By this arrangement, local autonomy, with its advantages, is secured; yet, uniform practices are assured for the company. In some instances the foregoing arrangement is changed by making the local personnel units responsible to the central personnel unit instead of to the respective plant managers. This relationship is used because of the more specialized direction which is given to the local personnel units. This advantage is attained only at the cost of lowered cooperation between the local personnel units and the plants they serve.

Effect of Legislation and Unions upon Structure

Such factors as legislation and labor unions have also influenced the design of organization structures. For example, the installation of such units as safety and unemployment compensation can be ascribed almost entirely to legislative regulations or requirements. Also, the right of employees to organize and bargain collectively has resulted in the addition of organization relationships, as illustrated in Figure 5–10.

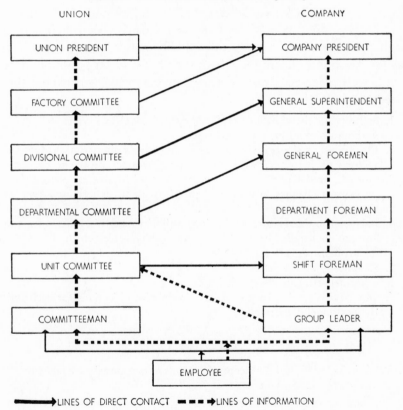

FIGURE 5–10. Structure of Collective Bargaining

Problems Faced

In the last analysis, the type of personnel functions performed depends largely upon the problems to be solved. This explains why personnel management usually developed first in the production divisions of most companies. Here, labor problems among large aggregations of workers were encountered.

But as other areas of problems developed, personnel units were established to deal with them. For example, it is not uncommon to find personnel units concerned primarily with such groups as research and development personnel, engineering staffs, women workers, and night-shift employees.

TESTS OF GOOD STRUCTURE

The foregoing discussion of the theory and practice of organization structure has been undertaken with a view to providing the student with a background of material essential to, and an understanding of the place of personnel management in, an enterprise. In conclusion, it is worth pointing some remarks toward the matter of tests by which it may be possible to determine whether or not a given personnel department is well organized. In general, a good personnel department should possess the following characteristics:

1. Stability, or the ability to replace key personnel executives or employees with a minimum loss of effectiveness
2. Flexibility, or the capacity to handle effectively short-run changes in the volume of personnel work or in the personnel problems encountered
3. Growth, or the feature of being prepared with advance plans to handle permanent changes in personnel problems or in underlying labor conditions
4. Balance, or the feature of having authority and resources adequate in amount to handle the functions and problems for which the personnel department is made responsible
5. Simplicity, or the feature of keeping personnel lines of relationship to other departments clear and simple
6. Objectivity, or the feature of having definite objectives for each unit in the personnel department

QUESTIONS

1. What is included in the concept of systems of personnel management? Why is this concept important?
2. How are personnel systems designed?
3. Why is a limited use of the functional form of organization structure desirable during periods of emergency? Illustrate this in connection with conditions that exist during wartime or when much labor legislation is being enacted.
4. Essentially how much authority does a staff executive, such as the personnel manager, have in a pure line and staff structure? Where and how does he ever build any influence over personnel matters?

5. Of two executives on the same plane organizationally, it was found that during a given period of time, one was contacted by subordinates and other executives on an average of thirty times a day; the other, five. What are the possible explanations?

6. If employees appoint informal leaders among themselves, why does not business seek out these leaders and put them on the management team?

7. Why not suppress informal organizations among employees and require all relationships to conform to the formal chart of the organization structure? Explain.

8. Can you cite any examples of how employees use the informal structure among themselves? If you cannot from your own experience, ask some old-timer about this subject, but do not use the term "informal structure" when talking to him.

9. Upon what factors does the place accorded the personnel department in a company organization structure usually depend? Illustrate by concrete examples.

10. What is meant by centralization of personnel functions? Distinguish between authority and performance as factors of centralization. May one be centralized and the other decentralized at the same time?

CHAPTER **6**

JOB AND MANPOWER REQUIREMENTS

The Hiring Function

The broad background and managerial functions of personnel were the subject matter of the preceding chapters. It is now pertinent to turn attention to the operative functions of personnel management. These, as will be recalled, are procuring, developing, maintaining, and utilizing a labor force. Each of these involves detailed activity, specific methodology, and careful application of principles. As a consequence, it will be necessary to devote the next several chapters to a discussion of procurement; the other functions will be studied in subsequent chapters.

Personnel procurement may be defined as the task of hiring people to fill current or future job vacancies. If hiring practices are to be most effective, answers must be sought to a number of important questions, among which are the following:

1. What are the requirements of the jobs to be filled?
2. What kinds of and how much manpower must be procured?
3. From what sources may the required manpower be procured?
4. What procedures should be used to screen candidates for employment?
5. What is the use of such tools as interviewing and testing in the selection procedure?
6. What is the place of transfers and promotions in the procurement function?

The present chapter is devoted to the first two of these questions; the other questions are considered in the next several chapters. The first section of this chapter takes up a number of pertinent job definitions. Then, attention is turned (1) to specifying job and man requirements and (2) to estimating quantitative requirements.

Definitions

Unfortunately, a standard set of definitions for terms used in connection with jobs does not exist. For present purposes, definitions have been selected because they have currency among technicians, although they do not conform with the loose usage of the layman. Hence, when various job terms are encountered elsewhere, their meanings must be ascertained in the particular case. In this section, definitions are given for the concepts of jobs, specifications, and job studies.

1. *Job Terms.* A number of terms are used in connection with the work people perform. By a *job* is meant an assignment of work calling for a set of duties, responsibilities, and conditions that are different from those of other work assignments. The foregoing elements determine work limits and not the location of a particular task. For example, two salesclerks who are performing similar duties and who require similar training, experience, and personal characteristics would, according to the foregoing definition, be said to hold the same kind of job. Yet, these two clerks may be working in widely separated parts of the store. On the other hand, two other sales clerks who do not have the same range of duties would be said to be working on different jobs, even though they happened to be located side by side.

The term *job* may be clarified by comparing it with "position" and "occupation." The term *position* is sometimes used as a synonym for "job," although in better practice a distinction is made between the two. Thus, when several persons are doing similar work, each one is said to have the same job, but all have different positions. The latter term refers to the number of people at work, not to the nature of their work assignments. The term *stations* is similar in meaning to that of "positions." There invariably are more positions or stations in a company than jobs.

The term *occupation* refers to a group of jobs with common characteristics. Although selling, for example, may be divisible into a number of jobs, depending on the complexity of the selling work, a group of closely related selling jobs may be considered as an occupation. *Job families* is another term used to cover the idea of groupings of similar jobs.

Within a particular job, two or more *grades* may also be recognized. For example, a wide range of work may be performed in the case of a single-spindle drill press operation. Some of the work might involve intricate drilling, and other batches might be more or less simple. Hence, it would be desirable to distinguish between operators on this machine according to whether they were, let us say, Class I, Class II, or Class III operators, meaning that they were highly skilled, semiskilled, and learners, respectively.

2. *Specifications.* *Specifications* are statements which describe something about the jobs of a company. They may describe the job itself

(strictly speaking, a *job specification*). They may describe the kind of a person who should fill a given job (strictly speaking, a *man specification*). Or they may describe both job and man characteristics (strictly speaking, a *job and man specification*). In practice, the term is used to

FIGURE 6–1. Performance Standards—Stenographer-Typist and File Clerk

	Hours	Minutes	%
1. Total Hours Paid For: (Daily)	8	480	100
Total Hours Allowance: (Daily)	1	60	12.5
Total Net Productive Hours: (Daily)	7	420	87.5

LINES

2. 30 Lines Per Letter: Dictated and Transcribed
30 Lines Per Letter: Straight Copy

LETTERS

3. Production (Net Production Time). - In Seven (7) Hours, or 420 Minutes:
Dictated and Transcribed Letters (30 lines each) = 10-1/2 letters, or Straight Copy Work
(30 lines each) = 21 letters

TIME STUDY ANALYSIS

4. Fifteen (15) Minutes Average Dictation Time for 30-Line Letter
Twenty-Five (25) Minutes Average Transcription Time for 30-Line Letter
Twenty (20) Minutes Average Copy Time for 30-Line Letter

AVERAGE DAILY TIME

5. Net Production Time: Seven (7) Hours, or 420 Minutes:
Minutes Per Dictated Letter (40) = 10-1/2 - 30-Line Letters In Seven (7) Hours
Minutes Per Copied Letter (20) = 21 - 30-Line Letters in Seven (7) Hours

Note: *Typing time to transcribe a full page or equivalent from voicewriting
machine cylinders or records is figured at 20 minutes per letter. The
average cylinder contains approximately 120 lines of typing. The
number of cylinders completed per day should total 7 or more.
In general, stenographers spend 65% of productive time on dictation
and transcription and 35% on typing from copy or manuscript, resulting
in a combined total production of 13 full pages per day.*

FILING

6. (a) Fifty (50) Units of Mail Per Hour using a numerical file system is the average and
includes General File upkeep.
(b) One hundred fifty (150) Units of Mail Per Hour, filing alphabetically, is the average
and includes General File upkeep.

These production standards are based on the results of numerous surveys of stenographic work
and represent actual production of stenographers having average ability.

CODE ARRANGEMENT:

Have steno or typist place initials on copy.
Use "T" for transcribing from longhand material or typed copy.
Use "D" for dictated letters.
Use "V" for voicewriting machine.
Make notation on working paper describing material typed if not practical to make
copy such as contracts, complicated statements, and legal documents.
Show typing time on each letter or typed material.

include varying amounts of both job and man information, yet it may be entitled a job specification.

These specifications do not disclose how much detail must be included in a specification. About all that can be said in this connection is that detail should be sufficient for the purposes of a particular company. In some cases, it might be sufficient to specify that a stenographer, for example, takes dictation, transcribes shorthand notes, types, and keeps various files. In other cases, it might be very desirable to specify in some detail, as is illustrated in Figure 6–1, how much work is expected from a stenographer on various duties. And in many cases, it might be wise to translate job requirements into statements of human characteristics such as finger dexterity, physical strength, hand-eye coordination, and emotional poise needed on the job.

3. *Job Studies.* A number of terms which are used in connection with the derivation of job and man specifications, or which may be confused therewith, merit definition at this juncture. *Job analysis* refers to the process of studying the operations, duties, and organizational aspects of jobs in order to derive specifications or, as they are called by some, *job descriptions.* Another term of interest is *job classification,* which refers to a system of relating jobs with similar or family characteristics into a logical grouping of classes. The term *job evaluation,* which subject is studied in a later chapter, has reference to monetary measurement of jobs. And *man evaluation,* also studied later, has reference to processes by which the relative value of employees is measured.

It is well to note here that although interest in these tools at present is in relation to hiring, they are also of use in connection with other personnel tasks. For example, training, counseling, safety work, job evaluation, promotion plans, and personnel research are scarcely possible without a good plan of job analysis, specifications, and classifications. These are discussed in later chapters.

SPECIFICATION OF REQUIREMENTS

Since employees are hired to carry out specific tasks, it would seem axiomatic that knowledge of work assignments is a basic prerequisite for performing the procurement function. Such knowledge is often kept only in the minds of line executives. But best practice, certainly in companies of any size, calls for the preparation of job specifications. And when hiring is done by a personnel department, such specifications are indispensable.

The task of developing such information may be conveniently discussed under the following headings:

1. Job specification information
2. Man specification information
3. Responsibility for collecting information
4. Methods of gathering information
5. Writing up specifications

Job Specification Information

The first step in a well-rounded program of job specifications is to prepare a list of all jobs in the company and where they are located. Information on job titles may be derived by checking payroll records, organization chart titles, supervisors, and employees. The *Dictionary of Occupational Titles,* a publication of the federal government, may be used as a basis of industry-wide comparison.

In general, the information sought usually includes the following:

1. Job titles, including trade nicknames
2. Number of employees on the job and their organizational location
3. Names of immediate supervisors
4. Materials, tools, and equipment used or worked with
5. Work or instructions received from whom and to whom delivered
6. Salary or wage levels and hours of work
7. Conditions of work
8. Complete listing of duties, separated according to daily, weekly, monthly, and casual, and estimated according to time spent on each
9. Educational and experience requirements
10. Skills, aptitudes, and abilities required
11. Promotional and transfer lines from and to the job
12. Miscellaneous information and comments

Figure 6–2 illustrates how such information was gathered by means of a questionnaire in the retail field.

Man Specification Information

A job specification, in and of itself, does not describe what kind of person is needed to fill a job. Hence, for hiring purposes, job information must be converted into required man characteristics. A man specification is called for which describes needed physical, mental, emotional, social, and behavioral requirements.

1. *Physical Specifications.* An easy approach to the task of writing man specifications is to list the physical qualifications which are called for on given jobs. This has reference to the obvious fact that various kinds and degrees of physical capacities are required on different

FIGURE 6–2

QUESTIONNAIRE FOR JOB ANALYSIS

Your Name   *Jane White*   Date   *2-9-54*

Title or Designation of Your Job   *Inspector-wrapper*

Regular or Extra   *Regular*

Your Department   *Coat and Gown Room*

To Whom Do You Report Directly (Name and Title):   *Miss Nancy Brown*

floor supervisor.

The purpose of this questionnaire is to ask each person here to write down exactly what his or her job is and also to write down the duties and the responsibilities of that job. This information will be of great assistance in carrying out the store's employment, training, and promotion program.

In the space below, please write a brief description of your work under the eight main headings indicated. To do this successfully, reflect for a few minutes on your activities, making a few notes of the things you do daily, periodically, and occasionally; any supervision of others which you may do; your contacts with other individuals and departments; any business contacts outside the Company, and whether personally, by telephone, or by correspondence; finally a notation of the equipment and material you use. Endeavor to put the essential things first and in order of their performance, then the lesser items.

Next, write four or five sentences covering that portion of your work falling under each of the headings. Do any revising necessary to make the statements more concise. Whenever possible, begin each statement with word denoting action. For example: "open mail, type forms," etc. (Omit "I"). Finally, copy this below in legible print or longhand (on typewriter if convenient).

Use additional paper if necessary and attach securely.

1. Description of Work

A—DAILY DUTIES: Describe in detail the work you perform regularly each day. In case of selling, include the lines of merchandise sold and the price range. Where there are several steps involved in your job, show each separately and in order of performance.

Source: M. J. Jucius, H. H. Maynard, and C. L. Shartle, *Job Analysis for Retail Stores* (Columbus, Ohio: Bureau of Business Research, Ohio State University, 1945), pp. 15–17.

FIGURE 6–2 (Continued)

1. Check and put away supplies received from supply department.

2. Straighten and clean wrapping desk including washing paste jar, filling tape machine with water and tape.

3. Complete wrapping of after-four merchandise.

4. Receive sales check and merchandise from salesperson to be wrapped for takewith or delivery giving precedence to takewiths.

5. Open tube carriers for authorized saleschecks and check same against merchandise, noting quantity, price and condition of merchandise.

6. If salescheck is unauthorized, notify section manager. If there is change to be returned to customer, count and call sales-person.

7. Select correct size box, line with tissue, fold merchandise and prepare box for takewith or delivery, according to routines learned in training period.

8. Paste customer's address docket on packages and pin triplicate of sales-check on packages to be delivered in town or out of town and make record of shipments.

9. Bag layaways, fold sales check and place in slot of layaway tag and place on hook of the hanger.

10. Keep stubs for stock record purposes.

11. Answer phone calls for section managers and salespeople.

12. Check supplies and make requisition for needed items.

13. Count dockets of merchandise wrapped the previous day.

14. Make out desk report if there is more than one person in the desk.

B—PERIODICAL DUTIES: Describe in detail the work you perform regularly at stated periods, as, for instance, each week, each month, etc. If none, so state.

None.

C—OCCASIONAL DUTIES: Describe those duties you are called upon to perform at irregular intervals, that is, duties which are special or fill-in work.

None.

2. Job Knowledge Requirements

A—STORE PROCEDURE AND METHODS:

1. Handling of sales transactions and authorizations according to store procedure.

2. Handling of wrapping according to store procedure.

3. Handling of inspector-wrapper reports according to store procedure.

4. Handling of delivery record of coat department.

5. Type and quantity of supplies needed.

FIGURE 6-2 *(Continued)*

B—MERCHANDISE:

1. Check mechandise for defects.

3. What Equipment Do You Use?

Inspector stamp, tape machine, paste bottle, scissors.

4. What Materials Do You Work with or Sell?

Wrapping paper, tissue paper, boxes, tape, twine and miscellaneous forms.

5. If You Supervise the Work of Others, State How Many and What Their Jobs Are (for example: Two file clerks).

None.

6. What Persons in Other Jobs Do You Contact Regularly in Your Work?

A—WITHIN THE COMPANY

Section manager	Assistant buyer
Salesperson	Floor supervisor
Buyer	Head supervisor

B—OUTSIDE OF THE COMPANY

Answer customers' phone calls to salespeople and questions of customers at desk.

7. To What Job Would You Normally Expect to Be Promoted?

Stock record clerk, Credit Department clerk, Adjustment office clerk, Shopping Service, Salesperson.

8. From What Job Were You Transferred to Your Present Job?

Hired for job—no previous retail experience.

jobs. Thus a stock chaser has to do a lot of walking, whereas a drill press operator does almost all of his work sitting or standing. And an assembler of parts in the tail section of an airplane should be small in stature, whereas a warehouseman should possess a large and strong physique. A specification of physical demands for the position of a tool designer is illustrated in Figure 6–3.

2. *Mental Specifications.* In regard to mental specifications, this has reference to the various mental processes called for on particular jobs, such as an ability to solve problems, to think, or to concentrate. A general approach to mental processes has been to specify for a given job the required schooling or experience. In this way a given educational level, let us say four years of high school in the case of a stenographer, may be used as an indirect measure of the level of mental processes required on a particular job. The intelligent quotient (IQ) of the psychologist is also a generally accepted measure in this area.

FIGURE 6–3*

PHYSICAL DEMANDS FORM

Job Title __TOOL DESIGNER_____   Occupational Code __O-48.41__

PHYSICAL ACTIVITIES		WORKING CONDITIONS	
1 __X__ Walking	16 __O__ Throwing	51 __X__ Inside	66 __O__ Mechanical hazards
2 __O__ Jumping	17 __O__ Pushing	52 __O__ Outside	67 __O__ Moving objects
3 __O__ Running	18 __O__ Pulling	53 __O__ Hot	68 __O__ Cramped quarters
4 __O__ Balancing	19 __X__ Handling	54 __O__ Cold	69 __O__ High places
5 __O__ Climbing	20 __X__ Fingering	55 __O__ Sudden temperature changes	70 __O__ Exposure to burns
6 __O__ Crawling	21 __O__ Feeling	56 __O__ Humid	71 __O__ Electrical hazards
7 __X__ Standing	22 __X__ Talking	57 __O__ Dry	72 __O__ Explosives
8 __O__ Turning	23 __X__ Hearing	58 __O__ Wet	73 __O__ Radiant energy
9 __O__ Stooping	24 __X__ Seeing	59 __O__ Dusty	74 __O__ Toxic conditions
10 __O__ Crouching	25 __O__ Color vision	60 __O__ Dirty	75 __X__ Working with others
11 __O__ Kneeling	26 __O__ Depth perception	61 __O__ Odors	76 __X__ Working around others
12 __X__ Sitting	27 __O__ Working speed	62 __O__ Noisy	77 __O__ Working alone
13 __O__ Reaching	28	63 __X__ Adequate lighting	78 ....
14 .... Lifting	29	64 __X__ Adequate ventilation	79 ....
15 .... Carrying	30	65 __O__ Vibration	80 ....

DETAILS OF PHYSICAL ACTIVITIES: 16—62316–1   ☆ U. S. GOVERNMENT PRINTING OFFICE

    Sits (90%). Reaches for blueprints, specifications, and designing

equipment. Reads blueprints and makes calculations. Stands and walks

10% to and from other personnel to assign work or to confer with them.

DETAILS OF WORKING CONDITIONS:

    Inside (100%). Works in constant contact with others in adequately

lighted and ventilated room.

DETAILS OF HAZARDS:

    None.

* Bureau of Employment Security, *Job Analysis* (Washington, D.C.: U.S. Government Printing Office, 1965), p. 74.

More detailed are attempts to specify particular types and degrees of mental characteristics. The following list is illustrative of characteristics that might be considered under this heading:

General intelligence
Memory for names and places
Memory for abstract ideas
Memory for oral directions
Memory for written directions
Memory for spatial relations
Ability to estimate quantities
Ability to estimate qualities

Ability to plan
Arithmetical abilities
Reading abilities
Scientific abilities
Judgment
Ability to concentrate
Ability to handle variable factors

3. *Emotional and Social Specifications.* Although the trend is by no means widespread, nevertheless there is a growing realization that perhaps the most important aspects of man requirements are those pertaining to emotional and social characteristics. Various studies have

shown that the technical requirements of most factory and sales jobs are not too difficult to meet. Moreover, other studies have shown that most labor troubles stem from poor emotional or social adjustment of employees. Since the human requirements seem to be a greater cause of trouble than the technical, a trend toward consideration of this factor has developed.

Specifying required emotional and social characteristics is, however, a very difficult task. Yet, as illustrated in the following excerpt from the job analysis form of a large retail establishment, some companies appraise the social factors in all jobs.

SOCIAL CHARACTERISTICS OF THE JOB (CONTACTS)

A. Requirements for social adaptability in human relationships:
   1. Limited social relationships in situations of minor importance.
   2. Limited simple social relationships of major importance.
   3. Frequent social relationships; must deal repeatedly with unpleasant attitudes and situations of minor importance with immediate adjustment.
   4. Constant delicate social emergencies of major importance.

B. Relationship that exists between this job and store reputation:
   1. None to very little; little opportunity for work results to affect opinion.
   2. Close relationship between manner of doing job and outside opinion of store efficiency, etc.
   3. Constant major effect of work results on public and/or employee opinion of store.
   4. Major responsibility is to mold and influence the reputation of the store in the minds of public and/or employees.

C. Personal appearance, including dress, posture, poise, features, and voice required by the job:
   1. Social relationships and type of work require only average personal appearance.
   2. Social relationships require above-average personal appearance.
   3. Outstanding personal appearance required as part of the job.

In most instances, however, about the best that can be done along these lines is to rely upon the interpretative judgment of executives who are aware of the significance of personality and social factors. For example, in one company the supervisors have been given short courses in elementary and applied psychology. They have been advised to note the personal problems employees encounter in their respective departments. By this means, at least a rough form of personal and social specifications has been developed in the minds of the supervisors. Such specifications are far from precise, but they are much better than nothing at all.

4. *Behavioral Specifications.* At higher levels, behavioral descriptions are increasingly being included in specifications. This approach seeks to describe the overt acts of people rather than the traits that cause or underlie the acts. For example, it is generally agreed that an executive should have, among other traits, judgment; or a research engineer, creativity; or a sales manager, teaching ability. But at present, descriptions of the amounts of such traits, let alone their definitions, reveal very little agreement either among practical men or among theorists.

Hence, attention is being directed in some quarters to how people should act on a given job and toward others. For example, as noted in Chapter 1, executives have an effect upon subordinates in terms of such overt relations as their physical behavior and dress, their use of various forms of authority, the use of various measures of success, and the degree of freedom allowed their staffs. Consequently, some companies are examining candidates for promotion in these as well as the traditional trait terms. Or in the case of creativity of research engineers, some companies are checking on the degree of nonconformity, "free wheeling," and innovations candidates have shown in past and present positions, whether or not directly in research. And in the case of teaching ability, evidence is sought in terms of such factors as interest in learning, concern for the problems of others, and sensitivity to the feelings of others.

Responsibility for Collecting Information

Most companies assign the task of preparing specifications to the personnel department. Its work is subject, of course, to approval of line executives. This is a logical assignment because the personnel unit is commonly responsible for selection, training, and salary administration, all of which are served by job specifications. In some instances, job analysis is assigned to the time-study or engineering departments because of the interest of these units in the operational aspects of jobs.

Two alternatives are available for staffing the unit which prepares specifications. Either trained help may be brought in from the outside, or members currently on the staff who seem to have abilities along these lines may be given special training in job analysis methods. The advantage of the former alternative is that competent specialists are secured at once, but its disadvantage is that outsiders must learn the personality of the company and its special problems. The latter alternative reverses the merits and demerits. Most companies select analysts from their own ranks because it is easier to train such specialists than to find them in the labor market.

Methods of Gathering Data

Information for job studies is obtained in either of two ways—questionnaires or personal interviews.

In the questionnaire method a standard form is prepared by the job analysts and sent either to each worker or to the supervisors. Some companies prefer to gather job data from the workers, believing that they obtain more detailed information thereby, whereas others feel that the supervisor is a better judge of what should be included for each job. After the completed questionnaires are returned, the job analysts group them by jobs and then examine the findings, job by job. As may be expected, it is possible to survey all the jobs and positions in a company much more quickly by this method than by the interviewing method.

Under the interview method the job analyst obtains information by personal conference with the workers or supervisors, and sometimes both. If he is well trained for his work, the job analyst can gather more relevant information by interviewing than is possible with questionnaires. Moreover, he carries away with him a personal impression of the job, which contributes greatly to the accuracy of the studies. Usually, personal interviews are more costly and time-consuming than questionnaires. Which should be used depends upon the value received and required as compared to the costs and time involved.

Writing Specifications

In writing specifications, a number of requirements must be met. On the one hand, there are language problems. It must be remembered that the written word, unless carefully chosen, may not convey to the reader what the writer intended. Trade terms are particularly elusive and often colloquial; hence, when used, they should be defined in nontechnical language, if possible.

On the other hand, it is essential to avoid overestimating the requirements of jobs. The specifications should define the minimum acceptable standards for employment and performance on the job. Exceptional functions, only occasionally performed, should not be permitted to influence the overall description. Nor should specifications be colored by the personalities of or special skills exhibited by particular employees from whom job information may have been obtained.

In writing job descriptions, particularly when they are to be used in making work assignments, care must be exercised to minimize the chances of their becoming straitjackets. Thus, it is not uncommon for workers (1) to get into jurisdictional disputes over who is to do particular parts of jobs or (2) to claim that certain tasks need not be done because they were not included in the job description. Jurisdictional disputes may be reduced by seeing to it that two or more jobs are not assigned the same tasks. And avoidance of responsibility may be suppressed by including a catchall clause stating that management reserves the right to add or remove duties from particular jobs when circumstances (such as emergencies, changes in work load, rush jobs, or technological developments) dictate.

Further useful information regarding the preparation of job descriptions and specifications may be obtained by studying actual practice in these matters. Appendix A (p. 529) contains a detailed example. These materials merit close study because they illustrate the care that must go into the development of good job specifications.

To those who examine such materials as these for the first time, the procedures involved may appear unduly complex; but with practice, they become less formidable. Indeed, after practice along such lines, one wonders how any useful information was obtained previously.

QUANTITATIVE REQUIREMENTS

Methods of Estimation

Job and manpower requirements must be specified quantitatively as well as descriptively. In many companies, steps are taken to find replacements only after vacancies occur or are likely to occur. Although this method of estimating quantitative needs is simple, it possesses little else to commend it. On the contrary, its use aggravates interruptions to production and tends to result in hurried and hence poorly evaluated selection of replacements. Therefore, its continued use can probably be condoned only when replacements are few and far between.

The effectiveness of hiring can be raised by forecasting operative, technical, and executive requirements. Such forecasts may be based upon (1) production estimates, (2) past turnover records, and (3) expected technical and managerial needs.

Manpower Requirements and Production Estimates

Manpower requirements in some cases vary closely with fluctuations in production. Hence, forecasts of the latter are basic to estimates of the former. And production forecasts depend upon sales forecasts;

hence, sales forecasts are the basis upon which the estimates of manpower requirements are built. Thus, how much manpower is needed in a given department of a company depends upon factory schedules which, in turn, are worked out from sales forecasts and storage policies.

Inasmuch as sales ordinarily fluctuate more than is desired for purposes of production, most companies do not produce strictly to the sales curve. Instead, a production schedule is derived which levels out somewhat the peaks and valleys of sales estimates. The degree to which the production schedule is stabilized in comparison with the sales curve is largely dependent upon the storability of the products in question and their nonsusceptibility to the style factor. After factory schedules are computed, departmental work loads can be established. The departmental schedules provide the basis for determining labor needs in each department.

After manpower requirements are determined, it is then necessary to ascertain how much manpower of various kinds is available to produce the output scheduled for the period of time in question. These two classes of information can be compared to compute the manpower to be added to or removed from the payroll. In equation form, this computation resolves itself as follows:

TOTAL MANPOWER REQUIREMENTS *less* AVAILABLE MANPOWER *equals* MANPOWER TO BE ADDED (*or* REMOVED FROM) THE PAYROLL

The computation of available manpower begins with a listing of the present employees. From this is subtracted the estimated number who will leave for various reasons. This figure is then the net available figure which is introduced into the foregoing formula.

Labor Turnover

One of the oldest devices of estimating labor requirements is through labor turnover calculations. Inasmuch as vacancies are created by employees leaving the company, it is only wise to estimate statistically how many are likely to leave. Thus, it may be possible to learn about the number of job vacancies, even though who specifically is to leave cannot be ascertained. Such estimates are best made in terms of past turnover. Knowing trends of turnover is an excellent means of appraising how many vacancies are likely to occur in the future.

Labor turnover may be measured simply by relating accessions or separations during a given period to the average payroll for that period. For purposes of consistency and comparability, the month is the period commonly used. For example, if a company had an average payroll during a given month of 600 (585 at the beginning, plus 615 at the end, divided by 2), took on 50 employees, and 20 were separated from the payroll, then:

1. Based upon accession figures, turnover is calculated as follows:

$$\frac{50}{600} \times 100 = 8.33 \text{ percent}$$

2. Based upon separation figures, turnover is calculated as follows:

$$\frac{20}{600} \times 100 = 3.33 \text{ percent}$$

Depending upon whether a company expects a stable or a growing trend in the same month in the future, it can quickly determine what provisions must be made to fill manpower requirements.

Technical and Managerial Manpower Requirements

Increasingly, interest is turning to predetermining technical and managerial manpower needs. Waiting for vacancies to occur before seeking replacements of higher level employees is too risky in this highly competitive and complex age. So both small and large companies have turned their attention to filling future needs for executives and technicians. What may be done in this connection is described here in terms of positions covered and methods of expressing needs.

This area of manpower needs covers a wide range of tasks. First is the managerial category, which includes top executives, middle management groups, and supervisory levels. Second is the professional group, which includes such areas as engineers, chemists, accountants, economists, and lawyers. And third in the specialist group, which includes such personnel as technical maintenance men, research assistants, computer programmers, and commercial artists.

Calculating needs in all of these areas is difficult. Their numbers do not vary directly with production, as is the case with production workers. And estimating when incumbents are likely to leave is seldom subject to statistical averages in most companies. Nonetheless, useful attempts in these directions have been made. For example, Table 6–1 shows the replacements that are estimated to be necessary at all executive levels in a given company over a five-year period. And Figure 6–4 shows how a company estimates which engineers are promotable, thus obtaining a picture of those capable of filling advanced positions as well as those for whom replacements will have to be found.

TABLE 6–1

FIVE-YEAR EXECUTIVE REPLACEMENT PLAN*

Position	No. of Positions	Quits	Normal Retirement	Death and Early Retirement	Total	Cumulative Promotions
President..............	1	..	1	..	1	1
Executive staff........	13	..	4	..	4	5
General staff..........	39	..	11	5	16	21
Fourth level..........	115	6	40	14	60	81
Fifth level............	162	2	36	19	57	138
	330	8	92	38	138	246

*Briefly, we must be prepared (1) to produce at least one new top executive, (2) to produce two department managers per year, (3) to upgrade 22 people per year at the middle management level, and (4) to hire and retain annually 14 young people with good management potential.

FIGURE 6–4. An Example of a Manpower Audit

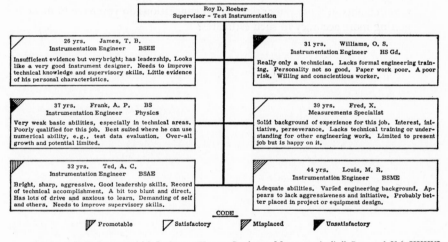

SOURCE: D. R. Lester and M. L. Owen, "How to Conduct a Manpower Audit," *Personnel*, Vol. XXXVI, No. 3, p. 49.

QUESTIONS

1. What is the difference between a job specification and a man specification? Which is easier to establish? Does this explain why the man specification is not so common as the job specification?

2. Why is a specification of job content fundamental to the procurement function?

3. What major steps should be taken in establishing and following a program of job specifications?

4. Why are emotional and social traits perhaps more important than technical characteristics on some jobs?

5. What is the difference between behavioral descriptions and trait descriptions? Which would you prefer, and why?

6. Select a job in which you are interested or one regarding which you can readily obtain firsthand information, and write a job and man specification following the illustrations and suggestions outlined in this chapter and in the Appendix. (Serviceman, bus driver, gas-station attendant, housewife, fraternity cook, stenographer, or clerk are just a few of the examples that come to mind.)

7. What are the advantages, disadvantages, and conditions of most favorable usage of the questionnaire and interview methods of studying jobs?

8. By what methods may estimates of quantitative requirements for labor be made? What are the advantages and disadvantages of each?

9. Why have labor turnover data been of such long-standing use in business? Of what use are such data? What pitfalls should be avoided in using turnover data?

10. What are examples of positions included in the technical and managerial categories of manpower requirements? Why is it difficult to estimate such requirements in these categories? What suggestions do you have to make for getting more accuracy in such estimates?

CHAPTER **7**

SOURCES OF MANPOWER SUPPLY

Variability of Sources of Supply

Suitable candidates must be attracted before the hiring procedure can be put into operation. To do this effectively requires a knowledge of sources of supply and how they may be tapped. These matters are the concern of this chapter.

Ordinarily, all of the sources of supply to be discussed here do not remain at a constant degree of usefulness but are affected by the general state of the labor market. For example, during war emergencies, sources such as older workers are utilized, contrary to normal practice, and sources such as casual applicants that had previously been satisfactory dry up.

Or looking into the future, as illustrated in Figure 7–1 by forecasts of national trends in employment, demands in higher level positions will place much greater strains upon manpower sources than will man-

FIGURE 7–1. Employment by Occupation, 1950–70

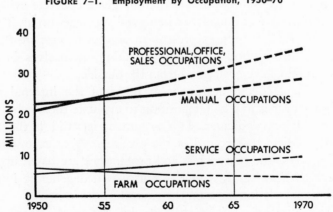

SOURCE: United States Department of Labor, *Manpower—Challenge of the 1960's* (Washington, D.C.: U.S. Government Printing Office, 1960), p. 10.

ual occupations. Hence a particular company must give consideration to local, statewide, and national conditions in studying sources of supply. Such surveys should concern themselves with the advantages, disadvantages, and conditions of most favorable usage of various sources of supply. ·

Types of Manpower Sources

Sources of manpower supply are commonly divided into internal and external sources. Internal sources refer to the present working force of a company. In the event of a vacancy, someone already on the payroll is upgraded, transferred, promoted, or sometimes demoted. Usually, the definition is expanded (and for understandable reasons) to include the following:

1. Those not on the payroll of a particular company but in the employment of affiliated or subsidiary companies
2. Those who were once on the payroll of a particular company but who plan to return or whom the company would like to rehire—for example, those on leave of absence, those who quit voluntarily, or those on production layoffs

All sources not included within the internal supply area, such as advertising, employment agencies, schools, floating labor, and those recommended by present employees, are external sources.

The Internal Source

1. *Advantages.* The internal source is often credited with being better than the external. This contention is based, in the first place, upon the argument that the morale of employees is raised by cultivating the internal source. Employees are thereby given concrete evidence that they are preferred over outsiders when good vacancies occur. This policy is commendable if it induces present employees to prepare themselves for transfers or promotions, thereby making themselves better than those who might have been hired from the outside.

Another and cogent argument in favor of the internal source is that the employer is in a better position to evaluate those who work for him than outside candidates. This argument is valid if the company maintains a satisfactory record of the progress, experience, and service of its employees, and if transfers and promotions are based upon measured merit. Otherwise, the internal source will degenerate into an undeserved monopoly for those on the payroll.

2. *Disadvantages.* The chief weaknesses of the internal source are twofold: danger of "inbreeding" and possible inadequacy of supply.

The first of these weaknesses arises out of the fact that the learner seldom has ideas or notions that differ widely from those of his teacher. As a consequence, he seldom contributes any startling innovations or makes suggestions, which are so important in our competitive economy. His company, therefore, is not likely to be known for its progressiveness and, indeed, may be left behind in the parade. Consequently, on jobs in which originality counts heavily, such as advertising, style designing, and basic research, the practice of always filling vacancies from within is seldom followed.

The policy of using internal sources also breaks down when there are numerous vacancies. During periods of rapid expansion, for example, the internal source is inadequate.

3. *Conditions of Favorable Use.* For most favorable use of the internal source of supply, then, conditions must be right. The number of vacancies to be filled must be within practicable limits, adequate employee records must be maintained, jobs calling for originality should not be assigned to present employees in blind adherence to seniority rules, and opportunities should be provided in advance for employees to prepare themselves for promotion. Much good will come, too, if publicity about well-merited transfers or promotions is carried in the company and local papers.

The External Source

Ultimately, of course, all vacancies must be filled from the outside. Even the company that prides itself upon its policy of filling vacancies exclusively from within must go to the outside to fill vacancies at the bottom of the promotional ladder. Hence, every company must be acquainted in some degree with the kinds of external sources. The major groups of external sources are employment agencies, advertising, floating labor, recommended labor, miscellaneous sources, and unions.

1. *Public Employment Agencies.* The employment agencies, particularly the public agencies, have grown in importance in the field of employment in recent years. The public agencies are discussed here first, and then attention is directed to private agencies.

a) Growth of Public Employment Services. The public agencies are represented by the United States Employment Service, commonly known as USES, and the several state employment services. Although the work of these groups has been closely intertwined in recent years, the state agencies are separate entities.

The USES came into existence when it was established as an independent unit in the United States Department of Labor. During

World War I, it acted as the sole recruiting agency for civilian workers in war industries. After the war, it was of negligible influence in the labor market.

The state services began their growth in the depression years of the thirties. The Wagner-Peyser Act of 1933 provided for financial benefits to states accepting the direction of the USES relative to a national system of employment offices. Growth took a spurt with the passage of the Social Security Act, which provided that laid-off workers, to be eligible for unemployment benefits, had to register with the state agencies. This gave the state agencies a roster of the unemployed—in a sense, the available worker supply.

The public agencies experienced further growth in World War II. Then they were given wide powers over hiring, classification of essential jobs, and job changes between companies by employees. During this time, the state agencies were merged into the USES. On November 15, 1946, the state agencies were returned to an independent status, though they are subject to various operational standards promulgated by the USES.

b) Services of State Employment Agencies. The state employment units are the agencies which operate directly in the employment field. What they do is exemplified by the work of the Ohio State Employment Service. Its basic job is to serve both worker and employer —and indirectly the community—by acting as a clearinghouse for jobs and job information. Its program includes a number of activities which serve to carry out this fundamental task.

The Ohio State Employment Service supports a full plan of employment counseling. The aim is to assist the applicant to make a suitable job choice based on facts about himself and the labor market. To do this, an analysis is made of the applicant's experience, training, education, interests, abilities, aptitudes, and physical capacities. His school record, tests, and physical capacity ratings are reviewed in a personal interview. He is given a picture of the labor market; of the kind and number of suitable opportunities; and of working conditions, salaries, required training, and promotional prospects in various jobs or establishments. And then he is helped to make a job choice or adjustment to labor market conditions, with actual referral to a job or an employer. The counseling service gives special attention to young and inexperienced workers, in recognition of the critical point at which these applicants find themselves in their working lives.

The Service has also interested itself in the use of psychological tests for personnel selection and employment counseling. Three categories of tests have been developed: proficiency or performance trade tests and oral trade questions, specific aptitude test batteries, and a general aptitude test battery. The proficiency or performance trade tests are used to measure skill in typing, dictation, and spelling. The oral trade questions are used to test job knowledge of skilled workers in approximately 250 occupations. Specific aptitude test batteries are used in the selection of workers to be trained on any of several hundred entry jobs. The General Aptitude Test Battery, excerpts from which are shown in Figure 7–2, is used to assist individuals having a vocational-choice problem. There is no cost to employers or workers for these testing services. They are supported by employer contributions under state unemployment compensation laws.

The state service operates in close touch with other state units affiliated with the USES. Thus, 1,800 employment offices located throughout the United States and its territories are at the service of applicants and employees through their local office. Local employers may be helped to find qualified workers outside the immediate area, and workers may be given reliable information about out-of-town jobs and employment conditions.

Another service along somewhat similar lines is the labor market information gathered by the state services. Summarized from the reports of local offices is such information as the number of men and women seeking jobs in each community, which industries are hiring and which laying off, wage rates in each community, surplus and scarce occupations, and the kinds of workers needed. Such data are also useful to companies which are interested in plant location changes or in decentralizing operations.

The Service also offers a selective placement service for handicapped workers. In this regard, an analysis is made to ascertain the physical capacities possessed by a handicapped applicant. Analyses are made of jobs to ascertain physical demands. And the capacities of these applicants are matched with the physical needs of jobs. Help is also offered to employees to smooth the induction of handicapped workers into industry.

The Service also seeks to promote employment of minority-group workers at their highest skills. It attempts to broaden acceptance of minority groups by employers, labor unions, and community groups. And it provides technical information and advice on the orderly introduction, use, and integration of minority-group workers into a company.

Special help is also available to war veterans. In this connection the Employment Service secures and maintains current information as

FIGURE 7–2. General Aptitude Test Battery

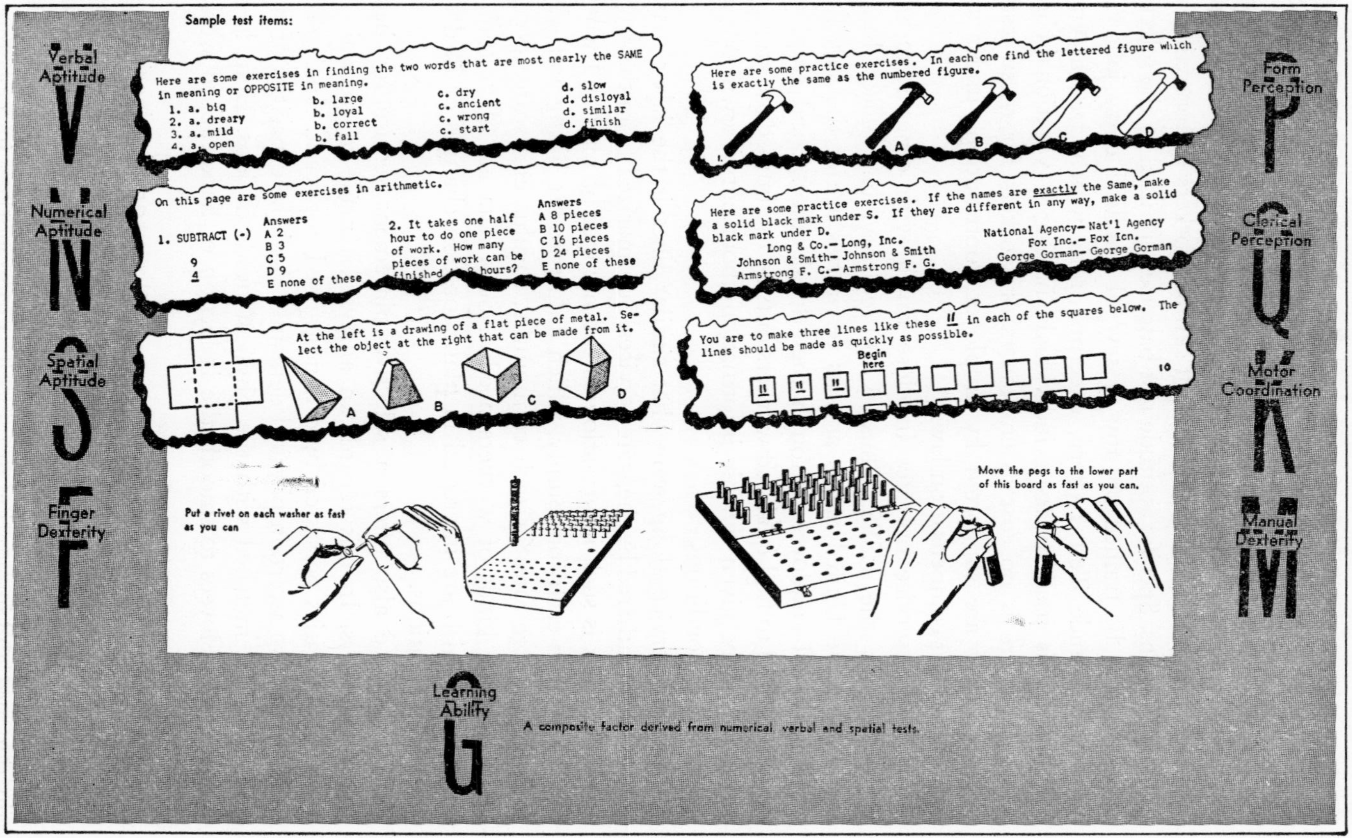

Sample test items:

V Verbal Aptitude

Here are some exercises in finding the two words that are most nearly the SAME in meaning or OPPOSITE in meaning.

1. a. big   b. large   c. dry   d. slow
2. a. dreary   b. loyal   c. ancient   d. similar
3. a. mild   b. correct   c. wrong   d. finish
4. a. open   b. fail   c. start

N Numerical Aptitude

On this page are some exercises in arithmetic.

                     Answers

1. SUBTRACT (−)   A 2
                B 3
   9   C 5
   4   D 9
                E none of these

2. It takes one half hour to do one piece of work. How many pieces of work can be finished in 24 hours?
         A 8 pieces
         B 10 pieces
         C 16 pieces
         D 24 pieces
         E none of these

S Spatial Aptitude

At the left is a drawing of a flat piece of metal. Select the object at the right that can be made from it.

F Finger Dexterity

Put a rivet on each washer as fast as you can

P Form Perception

Here are some practice exercises. In each one find the lettered figure which is exactly the same as the numbered figure.

Q Clerical Perception

Here are some practice exercises. If the names are exactly the Same, make a solid black mark under S. If they are different in any way, make a solid black mark under D.

Long & Co.— Long, Inc.
Johnson & Smith— Johnson & Smith
Armstrong F. C.— Armstrong F. G.

National Agency— Nat'l Agency
Fox Inc.— Fox Icn.
George Gorman—George Gorman

K Motor Coordination

You are to make three lines like these = in each of the squares below. The lines should be made as quickly as possible.

Begin here

10

M Manual Dexterity

Move the pegs to the lower part of this board as fast as you can.

G Learning Ability

A composite factor derived from numerical, verbal and spatial tests.

to various types of available employment, interests employers in hiring veterans, maintains regular contacts with employer and veteran organizations, and promotes the employment of veterans.

The Service has interested itself in the employment problems of college graduates. Although the registration procedure for college graduates and other applicants is the same, the Service has taken steps to help college students in additional ways. Representatives of the Service arrange meetings on college campuses. Interested students can schedule interviews for the purpose of asking questions about employment matters and seeking guidance on their possibilities for placement or on the need for adjustment. The Employment Service can also give useful advice on working toward promotions and on possibilities of promotions.

The Service is also responsible for being prepared to carry out the aims and objectives of defense manpower mobilization. In peacetime, it serves to expand defense production, relieve labor shortages, and increase the fullest possible use of available labor in critical areas. In wartime, as noted earlier, the Employment Service becomes a paramount agency in the labor market.

2. *Private Employment Agencies.* Private employment agencies have also grown apace with other sources during the recent years of labor shortages. These groups have tended to serve employees either in the technical and professional areas or in the relatively unskilled fields. In the former case, private employment services usually specialize according to such groups as office and clerical help, accountants and statisticians, engineers, salesmen, and executives. As a result of such specialization, they presumably are in a position to interpret effectively the needs of their clients, to build up a list of technicians upon whom they can readily draw as needed, and to develop proficiency in recognizing the aptitudes and abilities of specialized personnel. The ability of such agencies to be of service is also increased when local agencies organize into national associations through which interregional information and needs can be exchanged.

Some private employment agencies have, as noted above, restricted their clientele to the lower levels of worker skills. In such instances, they serve to attract applicants in numbers that the employer himself could not. This is particularly true of companies that have seasonal problems or are located away from the larger labor markets. Thus a company that has a seasonal logging operation, for example, may need quickly, but temporarily, a large but miscellaneous crew, including such workers as cooks and carpenters as well as lumberjacks. By turning to the employment agencies in larger cities, the employer can gather and ship out a group of floating workers that could scarcely be recruited in any other way.

In essence, then, the private agencies are brokers, bringing employers and employees together. For this service, they are compensated by fees charged against the employee or, more rarely, against the employer. The fee is usually computed as a percentage of a week's, two weeks', or a month's pay.

Charging for this service is of course legitimate, but the practice has led to abuses which, for a time, cast suspicion upon almost all private employment agencies. Such abuses led to state and local control being exercised over private agencies. Many of the employment agencies themselves, through their trade association, led in the fight to remove unscrupulous operators.

For a time after the USES had strengthened its position in the labor market, some felt that the day of the private agency had ended. Perhaps some of the weaker units were forced out, but the remaining ones certainly seem far from finished. Indeed, the competition has served as a tonic because the services of the private agencies have improved in the past several years. Some private agencies are no longer content merely to bring employer and employee together but are utilizing testing devices to classify and evaluate applicants, are adopting scientific counseling services to interpret the abilities of their clientele, and are employing advanced techniques of vocational guidance to increase the probabilities of correct placements. These advances have made private agencies even more attractive to employees who prefer their more personal and selective characteristics.

3. *Advertising for Labor.* Advertising in various media is also a widely used method of attracting labor. How much advertising is done usually depends upon the urgency of the demand for labor. Sometimes the classified sections of metropolitan newspapers have been well filled with such advertisements. On the other hand, this source is scarcely used when other channels supply sufficient candidates. The main shortcomings of this source are its uncertainty and the range of candidates that are attracted. Perhaps some of this is due to poor copy work, because most ads are uninspired, uninteresting, and not clear. Even when an advertisement is properly written and timed, the employer cannot be sure that it will pull the desired number of applicants. Moreover, he finds that he must cull the lot very carefully, since a good proportion of those who do present themselves are unqualified.

On the other hand, such advertisements should not be expected to do more than any advertisement can do—that is, attract attention and create a desire, which must be followed up by other appeals and selective methods. That many employers are aware of this is seen in the fact that they continued to use newspaper advertising during the war years, even when all hiring had to come through the USES. In these instances the advertising was intended to create a desire upon the part of available workers such that they would ask the USES to refer them to a particular company. When the medium of advertising is chosen carefully, the attention of desirable applicants can be attracted with a high degree of selectivity. For example, advertisements placed in trade journals or professional magazines can be directed so that only specific groups will be reached.

4. *Casual Labor Sources.* Most companies rely to some extent upon the casual labor which daily applies at the employment office or gate. Here again, the source is uncertain, and the candidates cover a wide range of abilities. Although it cannot be relied upon and does call for very careful screening, few companies care to shut off this source. In the first place, it is an inexpensive source; the applicant comes to the door of the employer of his own accord. Second, there always is an occasional good find that makes up for the expense of culling. And third, some companies believe it is good public relations—those in consumer goods industries particularly (bakeries, food products, public utilities, etc.)—to receive cordially all who come to the company premises, whether or not jobs are or will be available.

When it is desired to rely upon this source of supply, the physical facilities of employment should be made attractive and convenient. More will be said in this regard later in this chapter, but it is worth noting that an inviting waiting room, conveniently located to a main street and easily reached, is necessary. Sometimes, one wonders whether employers are trying to discourage applicants when one sees the untidy waiting rooms provided for casual applicants. In some cases, applicants must wait outdoors, even during unfavorable weather.

5. *Recommended Labor.* Recommended labor refers to all applicants who come to the employer on the direct suggestion of a present employee or other employers. Some employers cultivate this source, feeling that it provides a preselected class of applicants. When an employee recommends a friend for a job, it is likely that he does this with some degree of care. On the one hand, he knows that to recommend someone who is unsatisfactory will reflect upon his own good judgment; and on the other hand, he recognizes that his friend will not appreciate a lead that does not materialize in a good job.

6. Recruitment Practices. During periods of general labor scarcity, or in connection with scarcity of applicants for specific occupations, positive steps of seeking employees must be taken. What may be done is discussed in terms of usual factory or office jobs, highly skilled jobs, and technical and professional positions.

a) General-Run Jobs. Industry has taken a particularly active role in seeking employees during periods of a tight labor market. For example, during a concentrated program of inducing people to enter war work, in the relatively small city of New Britain, Connecticut, a total of 2,341 housewives were recruited in forty days. A complete campaign was worked out that included newspaper advertisements, posters, movie trailers, and shop-window displays. But of unique interest was a house-to-house canvass by women actually in war work.

A plant at Asheville, North Carolina, recruited blind workers for such jobs as sorting rough pieces of mica. The blind by touch alone were able to do as well as or better than those with normal vision who used a micrometer. Such discoveries of new uses in industry for the special skills of handicapped workers have been made through increased research in the field.

In some areas, intercompany and community exchanges of labor supply were carried out. By pooling information regarding projected hiring and discharges, it was found in some communities that employees could be exchanged in a mutually satisfactory manner. Thus, when a given company determined that a certain number of employees with particular skills had to be laid off, this was called to the attention of other companies that were expanding and in need of such skills. Good workers were thus assured of relatively steady employment, and the industries of the community helped themselves by keeping good workers from migrating.

b) Highly Skilled Workers. The foregoing cases also serve to illustrate methods of recruiting highly skilled workers. Also noteworthy is the plan of dividing complicated jobs into relatively simple operations; although not a source of labor in itself, it is a means of taking advantage of available or trainable sources. When, for example, the shortage of skilled toolmakers became dangerously acute, many companies found it desirable to divide this work into its components. Then, trainees were assigned to the simple aspects of the toolmaker's job, while the craftsman retained the complicated operations himself. Thus, his specialized talents were utilized to the highest possible degree and spread over the largest number of jobs possible. This plan has the desirable characteristic of making it possible to use lower levels of skilled and semiskilled employees, who are numerically larger than the highly skilled.

c) *Technical and Professional Positions.*   Many companies have turned to the schools to look for desirable applicants for such positions. They send representatives to college campuses to seek the cream of the

FIGURE 7–3

COLLEGE RECRUITING INTERVIEWING PROCEDURE

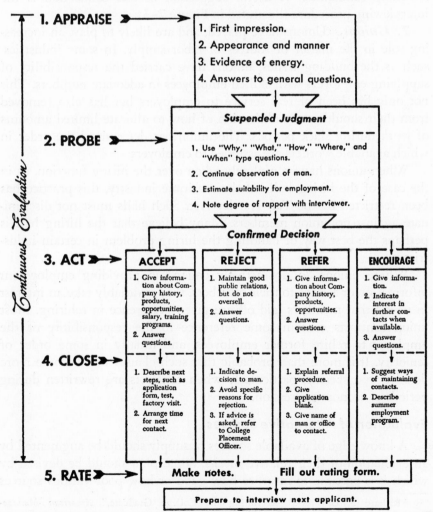

SOURCE: Richard S. Uhrbrock, "Recruiting the College Graduate," *American Management Association Bulletin,* 1953.

graduating classes. In a few cases the practice has been to offer summer employment to outstanding juniors and even sophomores with a view to permanent employment later. This practice enables the employer to try out the students and thus be in a better position to evaluate their potentialities. And the students not only gain useful work experience but also can better judge the desirability of making a permanent connection. Some college recruitment programs have been extended to the point that companies are willing to pay for postgraduate training of students in particularly scarce, specialized job areas. In all cases of college recruitment, it is highly desirable to be very careful in screening candidates.[1] A useful suggestion in this connection is the interviewing procedure illustrated in Figure 7–3.

7. *Unions.* Unions have played, and are likely to play, an increasing role in the matter of sources of labor supply. In some industries, such as the building trades, unions have carried the responsibility of supplying employers with skilled employees in adequate numbers. This not only has been of real service to employers but has also removed from their shoulders the obligation of how to allocate limited amounts of work during slack periods. The union has determined the order in which available workers are assigned to employers.

When unions have completely taken over the hiring function, as in the case of the hiring halls of the maritime industry, this practice has been restricted by the Taft-Hartley Act. Such halls must not discriminate against nonunion members. Many believe that the hiring hall is perhaps the best way of handling the hiring problem in certain industries.

Where unions do not actively engage in providing employment information or service to their members, they invariably take an interest in seeing that members laid off are given preference in rehiring. Most union contracts contain some reference to the responsibility of the employer to rehire former employees, and usually in some order of seniority. It is more than probable that such clauses will become more detailed and specific, particularly when contracts are rewritten during periods of economic recession.

Evaluation of Alternative Sources

A knowledge of available sources of supply should be augmented by an evaluation of their relative merits. Some plan should be devised by which it is possible to measure how good or how poor various sources

---

[1] Richard S. Uhrbrock, "Recruiting the College Graduate," *American Management Association Bulletin,* 1953, p. 11.

have proved to be. Some reference has been made in the foregoing discussion regarding the advantages and disadvantages of various sources, but such generalized conclusions should in particular cases be checked by objective measurements whenever possible.

Perhaps the most accurate way, though by no means indisputable, of evaluating the effectiveness of sources of manpower supply is to run statistical correlations. In this manner, it is possible to relate the factor of success on the job with the factor of particular sources of supply. A simple illustration of how this is done is shown by the study made in one company which, among other things, wanted to know how well people from various parts of the city in which it was located succeeded on the job. The map of the community in question was divided into

TABLE 7–1

SOURCE OF HIRING

	GATE HIRING		REFERRED BY PRESENT EMPLOYEES		REHIRING OF LAYOFFS		TOTAL	
	No.	%	No.	%	No.	%	No.	%
January	27	71	5	13	6	16	38	100
February	15	60	4	16	6	24	25	100
March	12	70	2	12	3	18	17	100

parts that had somewhat common characteristics—for example, purchasing power, nationalities, and schools. The records of employees selected from these areas were then correlated with the degree of job success as measured by the plan of employee rating operated by the company. It was found that the employees who came from certain areas rated higher than those who came from other areas. As a consequence, it was decided to restrict hirings to those candidates who came from the areas from which the better employees had come in the past. It was recognized that as a result of this policy, a few good employees from the restricted areas would be passed up, but it was felt that this loss would be less than that which would be incurred by hiring from the low-rated areas.

A simpler plan of evaluating alternative sources of supply is to use such measures as turnover, grievances, and disciplinary action. For example, by classifying turnover data according to the original sources from which employees came, it is possible to contrast the relative merits of sources of supply. The same result may be obtained by tabulating grievances and disciplinary action according to classes of hiring sources.

Table 7–1 provides an illustration of such a tabulation. Such studies are not conclusive, but they do throw light upon a subject that otherwise is beclouded by personal opinions and even prejudices.

Of interest in the matter of evaluating sources are general studies made of recruitment practices and attitudes toward selected employment agencies. In Table 7–2 are shown the results of the recruitment

TABLE 7–2

PERSONNEL RECRUITMENT PRACTICES OF 325 SELECTED COMPANIES

	Yes		No		No Answer	
	No.	%	No.	%	No.	%
1. Are any new employees furnished by an outside source?	180	55.5	129	39.7	16	4.8
2. Do you make a general practice of securing applicants through the United States Employment Service (State Employment Service)?	182	56.0	132	40.6	11	3.4
a) Do you use this service exclusively?	2	0.6	256	78.8	67	20.6
b) Do you use this service occasionally?	270	83.0	9	2.8	46	14.2
c) Do you avoid this service?	16	4.8	237	73.0	72	22.2
3. Do you make a general practice of securing applicants through schools and colleges?	186	57.2	124	38.2	15	4.6
a) Do you use these sources occasionally?	265	81.6	15	4.6	45	13.8
b) Do you avoid these sources?	0	0.0	229	70.5	96	29.5
4. Do you make a general practice of securing applicants through private (fee) employment agencies?	92	28.3	220	67.7	13	4.0
a) Do you use these sources occasionally?	221	68.0	41	12.6	63	19.4
b) Do you avoid these agencies?	38	11.7	136	41.8	151	46.5
5. Do you make a general practice of securing new employees through labor unions?	30	9.3	285	87.6	10	3.1
a) Do you use this source occasionally?	68	20.8	137	42.2	120	37.0
b) Do you avoid this source?	94	28.9	94	28.9	137	42.2
6. Do you make a general practice of securing applicants through your foremen, employees, friends, and other miscellaneous sources?	253	77.9	64	19.6	8	2.5

SOURCE: W. R. Spriegel and R. F. Wallace, "Recent Trends in Personnel Selection and Induction," *Personnel*, Vol. XXV No. 2, p. 79.

practices of 325 companies. Examination of this table shows that public agencies, private agencies, schools, and recommendations are most frequently used to attract candidates. Unions, in this study, were least commonly used. On the other hand, in particular geographical areas and for some jobs, union sources outweigh all others.

Another example of an evaluation study is shown in Table 7–3. This summarizes the study of public employment agencies, private employment agencies, and company employment departments. In this sample, seekers of employment had better results from company employment departments than from public or private agencies.

TABLE 7–3

SURVEY OF OPINIONS REGARDING AGENCIES OF EMPLOYMENT

Question 1: *How did you get your present job?*

	Private	Public	Company
All workers questioned:			
City A, 1946 (N = 284)...........	18%	7%	75%
City A, 1948 (N = 393)...........	19	3	72
City D, 1948 (N = 299)...........	16	8	76
Workers using all three agencies:			
City A, 1946 (N = 106)...........	28	10	62
City A, 1948 (N = 109)...........	40	6	52
City D, 1948 (N = 98)...........	25	6	69

Question 2: *In your opinion, which offers the best opportunity for getting work, the private employment agency, the public employment office, or the employment department of companies which hire their own workers?*

	Private	Public	Company	No Opinion
All workers questioned:				
City A, 1946 (N = 261)..............	24%	7%	58%	11%
City A, 1948 (N = 394)..............	19	7	55	19
City D, 1948 (N = 299)..............	22	7	61	10
Workers using all three agencies:				
City A, 1946 (N = 102)..............	34	8	52	6
City A, 1948 (N = 104)..............	34	3	57	6
City D, 1948 (N = 98)..............	39	6	55	0

SOURCE: I. G. Nudell and D. G. Patterson, "Attitudes of Clerical Workers toward Three Types of Employment Agencies," *Personnel,* Vol. XXVI, No. 5, p. 331.

Layout and Location of Employment Office

The physical layout and location of the employment office has an indirect, though nonetheless important, effect upon the attraction of suitable candidates. An office with comfortable furnishings and a pleasing appearance leaves a favorable impression upon applicants and adds to the efficiency of the employing staff. Also, one that is conveniently located is more likely to attract candidates than one that is not so easily reached. Indeed, this matter of location has become so important during recent years that some unique experiments have been conducted to make employment offices more accessible. For example, one company established branch employment offices in downtown locations, from which applicants found suitable were taken to the plant by station wagon. Other organizations have also employed auto trailers as added means of reaching and attracting labor. When the labor market is exceedingly tight, recourse to such methods is justifiable, though it might prove too expensive as a regular practice.

The layout and appointments of the employment office require careful consideration. The main problem here is that the volume of hirings varies so widely that it is difficult to arrive at a satisfactory compromise as to size. Usually, the employment office is too large or too small. Some examples of office layouts are shown in Figures 7–4, 7–5, and 7–6. It will be noted that all of the plans are designed to facilitate an efficient flow of applicants through the hiring process.

FIGURE 7–4.   Employment Office of a Small Plant

REST ROOM

FILING ROOM

EMPLOYMENT
MANAGER'S OFFICE

RECORDS ROOM

CLERK

WAITING ROOM

INTERVIEWER'S OFFICE

INTERVIEWER'S OFFICE

FIGURE 7–5.   Personnel Layout of a Medium-Sized Company

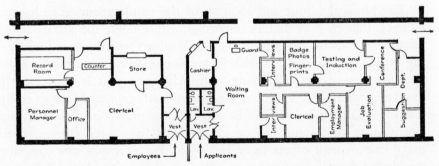

SOURCE: Cyril T. Tucker, "Three Ways to Lay Out a Personnel Department," *Factory Management and Maintenance*, Vol. CI, No. 9, pp. 154–55.

FIGURE 7–6. Personnel Layout of a Large Company

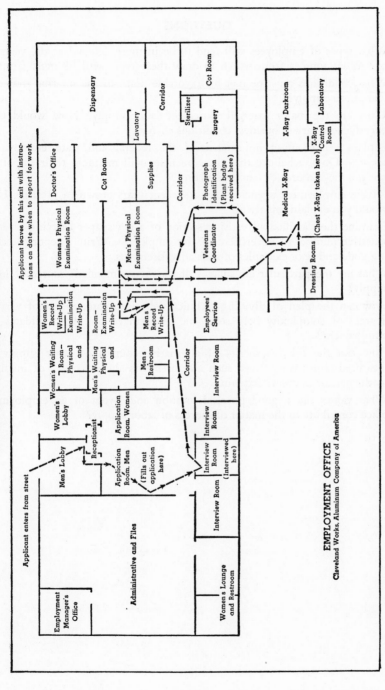

EMPLOYMENT OFFICE
Cleveland Works, Aluminum Company of America

SOURCE: Stanley R. Kuhns, "Making Job Applicants Feel They Belong," *Factory Management and Maintenance*, Vol. CIII, No. 10, pp. 98–99.

QUESTIONS

1. What types of employees will tend to be in more demand as the years go by? What sources from which to draw these types will be most fruitful?
2. What conditions must be met for favorable usage of the internal source of manpower supply?
3. What are the major external sources of labor supply? How would their effectiveness vary as business conditions change?
4. Explain the growing importance of the federal and state employment services. Do you believe that these agencies will maintain their important positions as a source of labor? Explain.
5. Private employment agencies have in recent years grown in prestige. How would you explain this trend?
6. Examine the classified advertising section of a newspaper carrying a representative number of advertisements for employees. Write a report describing good and poor examples of such advertisements.
7. What are the particular advantages of the "recommended" source of labor supply?
8. How can the plan of dividing technical jobs into components of varying degrees of complexity help solve the problem of finding candidates for employment?
9. How can the relative merits of alternative sources of labor supply be measured objectively? Need such measurements always consist of involved mathematical analyses? Explain.
10. What values can a good physical location and layout of an employment office contribute to the matter of sources of labor supply?

CHAPTER 8

THE SELECTION PROCEDURE

Major Stages

The selection procedure is the sequence of functions adopted in a given case for the purpose of ascertaining whether or not candidates possess the qualifications called for by a specific job or for progression through a series of jobs. The procedure cannot be effectively placed in operation until, as noted in earlier chapters, three major steps have been taken:

1. Requirements of the job to be filled have been specified
2. Qualifications workers must possess have been specified
3. Candidates for screening have been attracted

With these steps completed, it is then the task of selection to match the qualifications of candidates with the requirements of the job. Undesirable candidates are screened out and the qualified retained.

Selection processes of companies differ widely. Some companies are content with a cursory personal interview and a simple physical examination. At the other extreme, elaborate series of tests, examinations, interviews, and reference checks are employed.

Although there are differences in detail, almost all selection procedures include the following broad steps:

1. Designing procedural and structural relations
2. Initiating the selection process
3. Gathering information about candidates
4. Interpreting findings
5. Making decisions and recording results
6. Inducting successful candidates

Design of Procedural and Structural Relations

The selection procedure is like a sequence of hurdles. Successful candidates leap over them and arrive at the finish line; the unsuccessful do not. This is well illustrated in Figure 8–1. Three important questions must be answered in connection with these hurdles. First, how shall the hurdles be arranged? Second, who is responsible for checking the candidates as they try to go over the hurdles? And third, what are the characteristics of a good procedure of selection?

FIGURE 8–1. Summary of a Selection Procedure

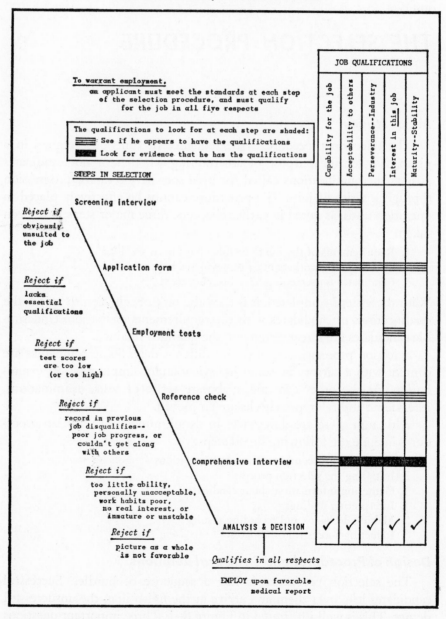

SOURCE: Milton M. Mandell, *The Employment Interview*, Research Study No. 47 (New York: American Management Association).

1. *Procedural Arrangements.* Procedural design encompasses a number of factors. Attention must be directed first to the number and kinds of hurdles to be included. Specifically, a decision must be made as to how many of such hurdles as the following are to be used: application blanks, reference letters, psychological tests, interviews, personal observations, and physical examinations. Second, and perhaps more difficult, is the matter of how detailed such tools are to be made. Shall application blanks, for example, be comprehensive, and shall interviews be in depth and conducted by several executives? And third, in what sequence shall investigations be made? For example, should psychological tests be given before or after personal interviews?

How thoroughly these questions are answered depends in part upon the significance placed upon procurement as a phase of personnel management. Those who feel that good selection is at the heart of employee productivity and good human relations will spend more time and money on it than do those who feel otherwise. It is argued here that the former are wiser. When good employees are hired, subsequent functions of personnel management and supervision are much easier to exercise. But casual hiring leads to higher costs of training, dealing with, motivating, and supervising subordinates.

How these questions are answered depends, too, upon other factors. For example, business conditions are important. When labor is scarce, a company which sets high standards of selection will be unable to hire as many people as it needs. Conversely, in a depression, standards can be raised very high. Cost is another factor affecting the design of hurdles, particularly in relation to the sequence of arrangement. Thus, it is usually desirable to give extended psychological tests only after some less expensive, preliminary steps have weeded those that are obviously unqualified. Nor would it be desirable to have higher executives interview candidates until lower levels have performed some screening operations. And finally, tradition is a factor affecting procedural design. For example, physical examinations were once conducted by the town doctor and so had to be given last. Nowadays, the physical examination is given on the premises of most companies and could therefore be moved up in the procedure. Yet, for tradition's sake, it is kept at the end.

2. *Organizational Relationships.* Very significant in the design of selection procedures is the matter of sharing responsibility for accepting or rejecting candidates by line and staff executives.

To begin with, to the personnel department is usually assigned responsibility for operating the selection procedure. In this capacity the personnel department, as a staff unit, assists the line departments; it does not dictate to them. First, unsuccessful candidates should be eliminated by the staff so that the time of the line executives is not spent needlessly on such people. Second, candidates who can meet line requirements should be made available promptly as required.

Such assistance does not relieve the line executive of responsibility or authority. The line executive should supply the personnel department with information needed for good hiring. For example, the sales manager should help to establish good job and man specifications for each of the positions under his jurisdiction. He should also hold himself in readiness to participate in particular phases of the selection process—such as technical interviewing—when that is required. And the ultimate authority of the sales manager, let us say, to accept or reject a candidate must not be contravened by the personnel department. The latter has the right to offer what it considers good candidates, but the sales manager must have the right to accept or reject (subject, of course, to review by higher authority, but not subject to the dictates of the personnel department, which has the right to petition for such a review). Thus, each executive complements the other in this vital task.

3. *Characteristics of a Good Procedure.* A number of characteristics must be built into a procedure if it is to be rated as a good selection plan. Of course, the essential feature of a selection procedure is that it produces results effectively and economically. To do this, each step in the selection sequence must be assigned a place so that it may contribute its fullest share to the final result. Moreover, each step or phase of the selection procedure must be equipped and manned to a degree commensurate with its importance. For each step, too, it is necessary establish (*a*) standards of performance and (*b*) means of allocating and determining responsibility for results. In designing the procedure, care should be taken to make it reasonably flexible, on the one hand, so that it can manage effectively temporary changes in volume, and, on the other hand, to make it sufficiently stable so that it is not subject to whimsical changes. The selection process should have definitely established starting and finishing points, so that unauthorized or dangling procedures will not be in operation. And finally, each step should give due consideration to cost, time taken, tradition, and legal requirements. These suggestions, in general form, apply to any procedure and hence possess a universal usefulness.

Initiation of Selection Procedure

The selection process is placed in operation by means of a release of authority to fill an existing or expected vacancy. How such authority is released, by whom, and to whom differs from company to company. In

FIGURE 8–2. An Employment Requisition

EMPLOYMENT REQUISITION

NUMBER REQUIRED — DATE OF REQUEST

DEPARTMENT — POSITION

DUTIES AND RESPONSIBILITIES

ADDITION TO PRESENT FORCE — PERMANENT — TEMPORARY — IF TEMPORARY HOW LONG?

REASONS FOR ADDITION

REPLACEMENT — PERMANENT — TEMPORARY — IF TEMPORARY, HOW LONG?

IF REPLACEMENT, GIVE NAMES OF EMPLOYEES REPLACED

RATE OF PAY — PER HOUR — PER WEEK — IS APPLICATION FOR BOND REQUIRED? — YES — NO

AGE LIMIT - MINIMUM — MAXIMUM

EDUCATION REQUIRED

ELEMENTARY SCHOOL — HIGH SCHOOL — COLLEGE OR UNIVERSITY

SPECIAL TRAINING

OTHER REQUIREMENTS

EXPERIENCE

KIND	YEARS DESIRED	KIND	YEARS DESIRED
TECHNICAL		CLERICAL	
TYPING		MECHANICAL	
STENOGRAPHIC		SPECIAL	

REPORT TO (SUPERVISOR) — LOCATION — DATE — TIME — A. M. / P. M.

REQUESTED BY — DEPARTMENT

APPROVED BY — DEPARTMENT

REMARKS

(NOTE TYPE IN DUPLICATE ORIGINAL TO PERSONNEL DEPT DUPLICATE FOR YOUR FILE.)

PLEASE ANTICIPATE YOUR WANTS AS FAR IN ADVANCE AS IS POSSIBLE AND GIVE SUFFICIENT DETAILS SO THAT THE PERSONNEL DEPARTMENT CAN MAKE AN INTELLIGENT SELECTION OF APPLICANTS.

TELEPHONE REQUESTS MUST BE COVERED BY A WRITTEN REQUISITION WITHOUT DELAY.

its simplest form, where the company is small and the line form of organization structure is in use, each executive decides for himself when vacancies should be filled.

As an organization grows, release of authority is clothed in formalized records and systems. Very common in such instances is the use of a form called the hiring requisition, issued to the employment office. Some companies permit first-line foremen and supervisors to issue hiring requisitions for any vacancies that occur. Other companies grant this right to supervisors in regard to direct help, such as machine operators, but require higher approval in the case of indirect or so-called "nonproductive" help, such as truckers, messengers, and clerks. Still other companies require all requisitions made out by foremen and supervisors to carry the signatures of higher executives. The purpose of such requirements is to control more closely the number of hirings and thus reduce the possibility of needless employment.

Hiring or labor requisitions differ in the kind and amount of information they carry. Under conditions in which the employment officer is personally acquainted with the job in question and the needs of the various departments, as is true in smaller companies, a short, simple form serves the purpose of initiating the selection process. In cases where such information is not personally known by the employment officer or his assistants, which would be true in large organizations, a more detailed statement is needed on the labor requisition, as illustrated in Figure 8–2. Here, the specifications are stated in coded as well as descriptive terms, so that reference may be made quickly to more complete specifications of job and personnel requirements.

As requisitions are received, they may be recorded in a labor journal or register, so that the status of unfilled requisitions may readily be ascertained and controlled. Employment requisitions are then assigned to employment assistants, who acquaint themselves with job and labor specifications and thus prepare themselves to check on available candidates.

Gathering Information about Candidates

The task of gathering information about candidates may be viewed in terms of (1) what information is sought, and how, and (2) how the information is interpreted after it is collected.

1. *Information Sought.* A variety of information may be gathered from and about candidates for vacancies. The efforts exerted in gathering such information may be studied in terms of (*a*) the information which is sought and (*b*) the means of deriving desired information. In the first of these divisions, the general classes of information include the following:

   a) Training, experience, and general background
   b) Mental ability and level of intelligence
   c) Physical condition, aptitudes, and skills
   d) Moral and emotional characteristics and skills
   e) Psychological and sociological aspects

Under the second of these divisions, the general groups of means of gathering information include the following:

a) Interviews
b) Tests and examinations
c) Personal observation
d) Application blanks, references, and similar reports
e) Union sources

In the present section the discussion will be restricted to application blanks, references, personal observation, and union sources, inasmuch as the use of tests, examinations, and interviews for collecting desired information is treated more thoroughly in the next few chapters.

a) *The Application Blank.* The application blank is undoubtedly one of the most common tools of selection. It invariably occupies a leading role because information gathered in this manner provides a clue to the need of and a basis for other selective processes. Its design differs widely from company to company, but the following general classes of information are sought in practically all cases:

1. Identifying information, such as name, address, telephone number, and social security number
2. Personal information, such as marital status, dependents, age, place of birth, birthplace of parents, number of sisters and brothers, etc.
3. Physical characteristics, such as height, weight, health, defects
4. Education
5. Experience, usually through the last three or four employers only
6. References, personal and business
7. Miscellaneous remarks and comments, such as hobbies, membership in organizations, financial status, and insurance programs

Details included under the foregoing headings may be noted by a study of the form illustrated in Figure 8–8 (pp. 139–42).

In determining what information is to be asked for on an application blank, it is invariably necessary to reach a compromise between what is wanted and needful and what can be obtained effectively on such a form.

The application blank is seldom used as the sole basis of hiring decisions. Its main usefulness is to provide information for reference checking, good interviewing, and correlation with testing data. Of course, when an applicant discloses a lack of needed training or experience, the application blank may serve to reject him.

The design and form of the application blank also deserves mention. On the one hand, it must be designed from the viewpoint of the applicant. In this connection the use of such devices as the following have been found helpful: grouping similar questions in adjacent blocks of space; using "yes" and "no" questions, as well as questions that can be checked, whenever possible; and using legible print. On the other hand, it must be designed with the company's purpose in mind. It should be relatively easy to handle in the employment office. This calls for consideration of such matters as ease of filing, durability throughout frequent handling, and prominence of the most pertinent information. In addition, it may be desirable to adopt two or more types of blanks so that they will fit the various classes of personnel to be selected—for example, general factory employees, general office employees, and executive and technical employees.

b) *Use of References.* The use of references is also common to most selection procedures. This practice places reliance upon the evaluation of former employers, friends, and professional acquaintances. Inasmuch as most people are reluctant to make reports that may hinder the chances of others, their opinions are not likely to result in accurate appraisals unless carefully controlled. For example, the probability of

FIGURE 8–3. A Sample Reference Form

_____, Social Security No._____,
has applied to us for a position as_____. Applicant claims to
have been in your employ from_____to_____. Having
had an opportunity to observe above applicant as an employee, your frank answers
to the questions on the reverse side of this card will be valuable to us, and would
be greatly appreciated. *We assure you that your replies will not be revealed to the applicant, or anyone else, under any circumstances.*

(*Reverse*)

1. When was he in your employ? From_____to_____.
2. What position did he hold?_____
3. Was his attendance regular? Yes_____No_____. If not, what was the cause
   of his absences?_____
4. Was he liked by his co-workers (well-liked, acceptable, sometimes criticized)?
   _____
5. Was his rate of progress slow, average, above average?_____
6. Was he asked to resign, or did he resign voluntarily?_____
7. Would you re-employ for a similar position? Yes_____No_____
   If not, why?_____
8. In view of your knowledge of his character, ability, and dependability, how
   would you rate him as an employee? Below average_____Average_____
   Above average_____
9. If you prefer, we will call you on telephone No._____

SOURCE: C. W. Brooks, "Checking Applicants' References," *Management Review*, Vol. XXXVII, No. 9, p. 465.

receiving an accurate appraisal is increased when a personnel officer seeking information knows and has the confidence of the personnel officer whose company has been given as a reference. Such close acquaintants are found in localities in which associations of personnel executives have been formed. Or if a reference form, such as that shown in Figure 8–3, is used which requires specific answers, the chances of getting unbiased references are increased.

The usefulness of references is also dependent upon the speed with which they can be checked. During times when the need for labor is great, decisions may have to be made about candidates very quickly. In urgent cases the telephone and the telegraph are employed.

c) Personal Observation. Despite the increased use of various types of formal tests, and despite the high probabilities of error due to personal prejudice or ineffectiveness, personal observation is undoubtedly widely used and weighs heavily in reaching decisions in the selection process. Certainly, interviewing, which essentially is a form of personal observation, has been credited with a higher role in selection since its operations have been studied more scientifically in recent years.

Indeed, interviewing is proving such a useful tool that its principles are worthy of description, which is the subject of a later chapter. In any event, much useful information can be obtained by talking to and sizing up candidates. It would be unwise to forgo its inclusion in the selection process simply because it can be easily misused. After all, any tool can be mishandled; the moral is that users should be properly trained to use such tools.

d) Union Sources. Information may also be obtained from local union offices regarding the preference to be given candidates. Indeed, in some instances, as noted earlier, the union hall would be the first and perhaps the only source of supply of labor. In such cases the union would sift out the candidates for employment. And it seems probable that as time goes on, the union office is likely to take a greater interest in who among their members is hired, in their competency to hold jobs, and in the company's tests of selection.

2. Interpreting Findings. The next major step in the selection process is to interpret findings and make decisions. Of course, this is a phase of selection that takes place at all stages of the process. Inasmuch as the selection process is also a rejection process, some candidates will fall by the wayside after each step. Some candidates may be rejected before they are even permitted to fill out an application blank, others will be rejected because of information received on the application blank, and still others will not fail until a final survey of all evidence is made.

This task of separating acceptable from nonacceptable candidates is very difficult, particularly in "twilight" cases and in cases where the candidates succeed in passing the preliminary hurdles. Let us assume that on a test used in connection with a particular job, the minimum passing grade is 75, and that a candidate gets 74. What should be done if his personal qualities, as well as his training, experience, and references, are satisfactory? The tendency is to accept the candidate in such instances in spite of the test score. But what if the test score is 73 or 72 or 71 or 70? When does the weight of the test outbalance the other factors? Most companies leave this to the personal judgment of the employment officer, or to his superior in important cases.

Reports and Records

1. ***Rejections.*** As decisions are reached regarding applicants, it is necessary to make out reports and records. These records may be classified according to whether the candidates are rejected, are not hired but would be desirable employees if vacancies were available, or are hired.

Keeping records of candidates not hired may seem a useless gesture, but it is not necessarily so. In the first place, if considerable study has been made of a candidate and he is found unsuitable, records of the case will prevent a restudy if the applicant should later present himself

FIGURE 8–4. Acceptance or Rejection Form

NOTICE OF ACCEPTANCE or REJECTION OF APPLICATION FOR EMPLOYMENT

TO SAMUEL MARKUM DEPT. HEAD PAUL SMITH DATE 10-1 1966

THIS IS TO ADVISE YOU THAT THE APPLICATION OF:

NAME JOHN DOE ADDRESS 1754 South Sixth St. PHONE Wa. 2046

HAS BEEN ACCEPTED / ~~XXXXXXX~~ FOR ~~XXXXXXXX~~ / PERMANENT EMPLOYMENT. (IF ACCEPTED - DATE STARTS TO WORK 10-5-66)

IF REJECTED - GIVE REASONS FOR REJECTION ______

THIS GOES TO FOREMAN AT TIME OF INTERVIEW AND MUST BE COMPLETED AND RETURNED TO SUPERINTENDENT'S DESK FOR REVIEW.

(THIS FORM TO BE SIGNED AND RETURNED DIRECT TO SUPERINTENDENT'S DESK) ______ FOREMAN again, as sometimes happens. Since microfilming has come into use, such records can be kept in a minimum of space. Figure 8–4 illustrates a record that could be used for rejected candidates. In the second place, a record of reasons for rejection is highly desirable in cases in which a company might be accused of unfair labor practices. This factor grows in importance as rules governing fair employment practices become formalized in state laws.

Practically all companies maintain a file of information on candidates who would make desirable employees if vacancies existed. The usefulness of such a file depends on the economic position of the industrial and business community. In a tight labor market, applications filed by candidates are usually found to be useless as a source of supply unless followed up within a day or two. On the other hand, during recession periods, applications may be a useful source even after weeks of being filed.

2. *Records of Hired Employees.* As to candidates who are hired, the systems of recording fall into three major groups. First, some companies place all hiring information for each employee in a folder. As time goes on, additional data, such as merit ratings, job and rate changes, educational accomplishments, and disciplinary cases are also placed in the folder.

Second, some companies compile, in addition to the folder, a card recapitulating important information in the folder. The card is filed separately from the folder and becomes the working scource of information about the employee. Figure 8–5 illustrates such a card. References to the card can be quickly made without disturbing the detailed materials in the folder.

And third, some companies have turned to data-processing equipment to keep personnel records. In some cases, records are stored in computers into which information is fed as it becomes available and from which it is retrieved as needed. This system is adopted when the number of employees results in voluminous records. Sometimes, tabulating cards, as illustrated in Figures 8–6 and 8–7, are used for this purpose. The former are sorted manually and the latter by machine.

Careful planning of personnel records will make it possible to maintain them at minimum expense. It is reported, for example, that in one case the personnel records of nine hundred employees are kept by one clerk.[1] Another interesting example of a personnel record for a smaller

---

[1] R. D. McMillen, "Personnel Records," *Factory Management and Maintenance,* Vol. CV, No. 6, p. 109.

FIGURE 8–5

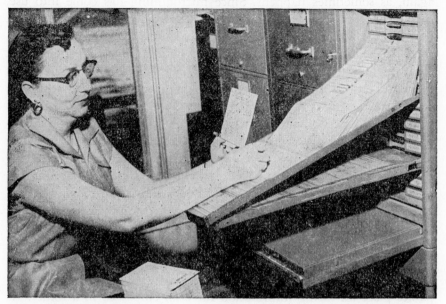

Kardex equipment makes personnel records available quickly at point of use

Supporting papers are kept in insulated files for reference when needed

SOURCE: Robert D. Johnson, "Personnel Files," *Systems*, July-August, 1954, p. 8. Reproduced by permission. Courtesy of Remington Rand.

PATHFINDER PUNCH PERSONNEL RECORD

(1) NAME: (LAST) (FIRST) (MIDDLE)

ADDRESS: STREET AND NUMBER — CITY

(1) EMPLOYEE NUMBER
SOCIAL SECURITY NUMBER
RESIDENCE ZONE NO.
TELEPHONE NO.

EMPLOYEE NAME OR NUMBER

(2) DATE OF BIRTH		
MONTH	DAY	YEAR
12	23	04

PLACE OF BIRTH: CITY — STATE OR COUNTRY

(3) CITIZEN OF: U.S.

(4) RACE: White

HEIGHT: 5 FT. 9 IN. **WEIGHT:** 164 LBS.

DESCENT: Scottish

HAIR: Brown **EYES:** Gray

(9) HANDICAPS: (DESCRIBE) None

IDENTIFYING MARKS: None

(10) OWNS HOME? Yes **OWNS CAR?** Yes

(11) UNION: (IF ANY)

(8) MALE ✓ / **FE MALE** no

SPOUSE WORKING? no **LOCAL NO.**

(5) MARITAL STATUS:

	MONTH	DAY	YEAR
SGL.			
MARRIED ✓			
WID.			
SEP.			
DIV.			

(6) BIRTHDATES OF CHILDREN UNDER 18

NO.	MONTH	DAY	YEAR
1	3	23	1933
2	8	16	1935
3			
4			
5			

(7) ADULTS OVER 18 LEGALLY DEPENDENT ON EMPLOYEE

NO.	RELATIONSHIP
1	Father
2	
3	
4	
5	

LOCAL BOARD ADDRESS: STREET AND NO. — CITY

LOCAL BOARD NO. 719

DRAFT ORDER NO.

DRAFT CLASSIFICATION RECORD

DATE	(12) CLASS	(13) EXPIRES
6 30 44	2B-H	

EMPLOYMENT RECORD — ORIGIN?

(15) DEPARTMENT	JOB TITLE	(16) CLASSIFICATION NO.	RATE	(17) SHIFT	(18) TERMINATED	(14) DATE
Tool Design	Draftsman	153	115	1		9 16 44
			120			12 4 44

(15) REMARKS

JOB CLASSIFICATION

THOUSANDS — HUNDREDS — TENS — UNITS

(19) RE-HIRED (18) TERM-INATED (17) SHIFT (16) JOB CLASSIFICATION

OFFICE DEPARTMENT (15) TENS UNITS TENS UNITS (14) YEAR DATE EMPLOYED MONTH

FIGURE 8-7. A Personnel Tabulating Card

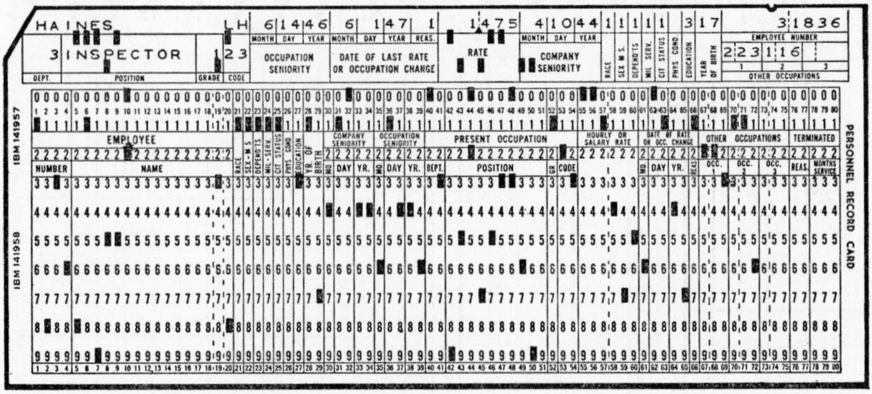

SOURCE: International Business Machines Corporation, *I.B.M. Accounting.*

company is the multipurpose form illustrated in Figure 8–8.[2] It may be used in the following ways:

a) Application blank (pp. 1 and 2)
b) Interview rating, test record, and reference checkup (p. 3)
c) Basic payroll record (pp. 3 and 4)
d) Medical examination form (p. 4)
e) Record of other personnel data, such as attendance, salary or job changes, and efficiency rating (p. 4)

Induction of New Employee

The final step in the selection process is that of inducting the new employee into his new surroundings and placing him on his new job. In many companies, this stage of an employee's tenure is handled very superficially. But there is a strong movement in the direction of handling this stage with great care because turnover among new employees is higher than among workers with greater seniority.

The stage of induction should take into account two major aspects: (1) acquainting the new employee with his new surroundings and company rules and regulations, and (2) indoctrinating him in the "philosophy" of the company and its reasons for existence. More companies build their programs around the first of these aspects than the second.

1. *Getting Acquainted.* In acquainting the new employee with his new surroundings and company regulations, practice tends toward giving introductory materials and instructions away from the working

<hr/>

[2] J. S. Kornreich, "Personnel Records for a Small Company," *Personnel,* Vol. XXIX, No. 5, pp. 431–36.

FIGURE 8–8. A Multipurpose Personnel Form

EMPLOYMENT APPLICATION

DATE:

FILL IN BOTH SIDES COMPLETELY

NAME: (Last) (First) (Initial.)

SOCIAL SECURITY NO.:

SEX: HEIGHT WEIGHT

ADDRESS:

U.S. CITIZEN: YES ( ) NO ( ) MARRIED ( ) SINGLE ( ) SEPARATED ( ) DIVORCED ( ) WIDOW(ER) ( )

NO OF DEPENDENTS CLAIMED FOR INCOME TAX EXEMPTIONS:

TELEPHONE NO

DATE OF BIRTH:

CHILDREN ( ) PARENTS ( ) OTHERS ( )

AGES OF CHILDREN:

IF FEMALE AND MARRIED STATE MAIDEN NAME

IF YOU HAVE NO TELEPHONE, THROUGH (Give name WHOM CAN YOU BE LOCATED? & Tel. No.)

DO YOU OWN YOUR OWN HOME? YES ( ) NO ( )

DESCRIBE PHYSICAL DEFECTS, IF ANY:

DO YOU HAVE ANY INCOME OTHER THAN WHAT YOU GET FROM WORKING? YES ( ) NO ( ) IF YES, WHAT?

MILITARY EXPERIENCE: FROM _____ TO _____

BRANCH OF SERVICE

HIGHEST RANK OBTAINED

HONORABLE YES ( ) DISCHARGE: NO ( )

IF IN RESERVES: ACTIVE ( ) INACTIVE ( )

ARE YOU A FORMER EMPLOYEE? WHEN? WHY DID YOU LEAVE?

NAMES AND RELATIONSHIP OF RELATIVES WORKING HERE:

MACHINES YOU CAN OPERATE:

POSITION DESIRED: SHIFT DESIRED: WAGES EXPECTED: WHEN CAN YOU BEGIN WORK?

RECORD OF EDUCATION

	No. of Years	NAME OF SCHOOL	DID YOU GRADUATE?	DATE YOU LEFT	COURSE	AVERAGE GRADE	DESCRIBE COLLEGE OR OTHER TRAINING—
GRAMMAR							
HIGH							
TRADE							

RECORD OF PREVIOUS EMPLOYMENT — SHOW PRESENT OR LAST POSITION FIRST

STARTING DATE	NAME AND ADDRESS OF COMPANY:	NAME OF SUPERVISOR
LEAVING DATE	TYPE OF WORK DONE:	REASON FOR LEAVING:
STARTING DATE	NAME AND ADDRESS OF COMPANY:	NAME OF SUPERVISOR
LEAVING DATE	TYPE OF WORK DONE:	REASON FOR LEAVING:
STARTING DATE	NAME AND ADDRESS OF COMPANY:	NAME OF SUPERVISOR
LEAVING DATE	TYPE OF WORK DONE:	REASON FOR LEAVING:

WAGES RECEIVED (×3)

(Page 1)

SOURCE: J. S. Kornreich, "Personnel Records for a Small Company," *Personnel*, Vol. XXIX, No. 5, pp. 431-36.

FIGURE 8-8 (Continued)

FAMILY INFORMATION (HUSBAND, WIFE, FATHER, MOTHER, BROTHERS AND SISTERS)

RELATIONSHIP TO YOU	PRESENT OR LAST OCCUPATION	CITY WHERE NOW LIVING	RELATIONSHIP TO YOU	PRESENT OR LAST OCCUPATION	CITY WHERE NOW LIVING

HOW LONG HAVE YOU LIVED AT YOUR PRESENT ADDRESS? _____ IF LESS THAN ONE YEAR GIVE PREVIOUS ADDRESS: _____

WHAT TRANSPORTATION WILL YOU USE TO GET TO WORK? _____

I DO ☐
DO NOT OWN AN AUTO ☐   IF YOU OWN AUTO, STATE MAKE AND YEAR: _____

REFERENCES GIVE THREE REFERENCES WHO KNOW YOU WELL. DO NOT GIVE RELATIVES OR FORMER EMPLOYERS.

1. _____ (NAME)   _____ (OCCUPATION)   _____ (ADDRESS)

2. _____ (NAME)   _____ (OCCUPATION)   _____ (ADDRESS)

3. _____ (NAME)   _____ (OCCUPATION)   _____ (ADDRESS)

GIVE NAMES OF PEOPLE WORKING HERE WHO KNOW YOU VERY WELL: _____

Additional Remarks and Information
(DESCRIBE OTHER EXPERIENCE, RELATED HOBBIES OR SPECIAL QUALIFICATIONS)

_____

READ CAREFULLY →

I UNDERSTAND THAT IF EMPLOYED, FALSE STATEMENTS ON THIS APPLICATION SHALL BE CONSIDERED SUFFICIENT CAUSE FOR DISMISSAL.

_____ (Applicant's Signature)   SIGN HERE →

APPLICANT — DO NOT WRITE BELOW THIS LINE

(Page 2)

FIGURE 8–8 (*Continued*)

INVESTIGATION

DATES	DATES	DATES
ATTENDANCE	ATTENDANCE	ATTENDANCE
WORK RECORD	WORK RECORD	WORK RECORD
REASON FOR LEAVING	REASON FOR LEAVING	REASON FOR LEAVING
REHIRE	REHIRE	REHIRE

TEST SCORES AND INTERPRETATION

PHYSICAL EXAMINATION	DATE	RESULTS:—		
BY DR.				
INTERVIEWED BY	DATE		GENERAL COMMENT	
1.				WORK ATT.:
2.				ALERTNESS:
3.				APPEARANCE:

STARTING DATE:	STARTING POSITION:	DEPT.:		SHIFT OR WORK HOURS:
STARTING WAGE:	AUTOMATIC INCREASE: PROMISED? YES ( ) NO ( ) AMOUNT?	DATE?	APPROVED BY	

(*Page 3*)

FIGURE 8-8 (Continued)

MEDICAL EXAMINATION

DATE _____ HT. _____ WT. _____

GENERAL APPEARANCE:

EYES: (R. (L.

EARS: HEARS WATCH (R. (L.

NOSE

THROAT

TONGUE

TEETH

NECK

CHEST CONTOUR

HEART

PULSE

BLOOD PRESSURE

LUNGS

ABDOMEN

EXTREM. (U. (L.

ING. REG.

G. U.

URINE

SPINE

SKIN

NOTES:

PAST MEDICAL HISTORY

SIGNED: DR.

PERSONNEL RECORD (Attendance, Salary or Job Changes, Efficiency Rating, Awards, etc.)

DATE	ACTION	EXPLANATION	DATE	ACTION	EXPLANATION

(Page 4)

center. Either a classroom lecture, a movie, or a group conference is used by a member of the personnel department. In any event, such subjects as the following are covered:

a) Company history, products, and major operations
b) General company policies and regulations
c) Relation of foremen and personnel department
d) Rules and regulations regarding:
    (1) Wages and wage payment
    (2) Hours of work and overtime
    (3) Safety and accidents
    (4) Holidays and vacations
    (5) Methods of reporting tardiness and absences
    (6) Discipline and grievances
    (7) Uniforms and clothing
    (8) Parking
    (9) Badges and parcels
e) Economic and recreational services available:
    (1) Insurance plans
    (2) Pensions
    (3) Athletic and social activities
f) Opportunities:
    (1) Promotion and transfer
    (2) Job stabilization
    (3) Suggestion systems

It is ordinarily not expected that much of the foregoing will stick in the minds of the inductee, but this preliminary step does serve to prove that the company is taking a sincere interest in getting him off to a good start. Moreover, booklets and pamphlets may be supplied which provide a permanent record of the materials that have been seen and heard.

After preliminary sessions in the personnel department, the new employee is conducted to his working center. At one time the employee was given oral instructions and left to find his way himself, and some companies still use this system. Better practice, however, is to have either a representative of the personnel department act as a guide or someone from the operating department come over and take the new employee in hand.

Upon arriving at the assigned department, the inductee is introduced to his supervisor and fellow workers. The supervisor or a key employee then instructs the employee on such matters as to how to ring in and out, where the lockers are, departmental rules, and how his job is to be done. It is better practice to have the supervisor handle this phase of induction so that he can personally prove at a critical time management's desire to build a friendly and helpful relationship.

After an employee has been placed on his job, good induction practice also involves periodic follow-up. Either by reports or, better, by personal visits from the supervisor or a representative of the personnel department, the status of the new employee is ascertained after a couple of periods of 30 or 60 days. This serves to check whether the employee has been properly placed, whether the promises the company made to him have been kept, and whether any problems have arisen that require attention.

2. *Indoctrination.* The induction stage provides an excellent opportunity to develop attitudes of new employees toward their new employment and surroundings. Hence, more and more companies are taking advantage of this opportunity to sell their philosophies, the whys and wherefores of private enterprise, the advantages of the capitalistic system, the need for productivity, and the reasons why the firm operates as it does. This approach to induction should be taken by both the personnel department and the line supervisors.

Perhaps the essence of indoctrination is to convince the employee that what is good for the company is also good for the employee. If the company honestly practices this philosophy, indoctrination is not to be criticized. If the approach is concerned, however, only with the best interests of the employer, the indoctrination is built on sand. Indoctrination based on mutual self-interest, moreover, must be a continuous process, beginning when a person is hired and persisting throughout the relationship.

QUESTIONS

1. Define the term "selection procedure." How does this differ from selection functions?
2. In what order should a company place the various hurdles included in its selection procedure, and how high should they be placed?
3. What tests would you apply in order to determine whether or not a specific selection procedure is a good one? Apply these tests, if possible, to the procedure of some company.
4. What are the various ways in which action of the selection procedure may be initiated?
5. What classes of information are ordinarily sought from candidates for employment? By what methods is the information sought?
6. Of what usefulness is the application blank in hiring?
7. How much confidence can be placed in the average reference letter? How can the level of confidence in such letters or reference requests be raised?
8. Why is personal observation a widely used method of gathering information

about candidates for employment? Does the reliability of this method justify its wide use?

9. Why is the induction of new employees such an important matter? What are some of the reasons why new employees are "critical"?

10. Upon whom, and why, would you place the greatest burden for the induction of new employees? Would you permit the use of indoctrination here?

CHAPTER 9

INTERVIEWING AND COUNSELING

The Role of Interviewing and Counseling

The interview is one of the most commonly used methods of seeking information from job applicants. It is a face-to-face, oral, observational, and personal appraisal method. Usually, it is more than a means of getting information. It also involves (1) giving information that will help the applicant make up his mind about the company and (2) giving advice or suggestions that may serve to change the attitude, mental or emotional, of the interviewee.

The subjects of interviewing and counseling are taken up at this point because they are of significance in the procedure of hiring. However, these techniques are also important in handling grievances, taking disciplinary action, vocational guidance, handling employees being separated from the payroll, assisting employees with personal problems, handling transfers and promotions, and conducting training sessions.

Good interviewing is not easily executed. It must be based upon sound rules and applied by skilled personnel. How this may be done can be seen by examining the following aspects of the subject:

1. Purposes
2. Types
3. Technical factors
4. Procedures
5. Rules

Purposes

As already noted, interviewing has uses in a variety of personnel areas. It is desirable, therefore, to note what purposes interviewing is intended to serve in the important areas of employment, training, human relations, and labor relations.

1. *Employment.* Viewing employment in the broadest sense, interviewing has a contribution to make in selecting, inducting, placing, and terminating the tenure of employees.

Interviewing has been the most universally used tool in selection. The employer, by means of talk and observation, seeks to determine the degree to which the applicant possesses desired qualities. He attempts to appraise the applicant's mental, physical, emotional, and social qualities —potential or developed. Thus, his primary purpose is to select the candidate who will best advance his business objectives.

But the interview is not all one-sided. The applicant usually hopes for more than a job—he wants a good job. So the employer in the interview must also serve the purposes of the applicant. He must give information and convey an attitude that will help the applicant decide whether or not to accept a job if it is offered to him. The selection process is therefore a rejection process by the candidate as well as the employer. And it is far better for an applicant to turn down an offer that would result in an unsatisfactory situation in the long run even though there may be short-run advantages.

A particularly difficult area of interviewing is that concerned with counseling those who have taken psychological tests. An excellent ex ample of suggestions which executives should follow in such cases is seen in the following excerpt from a test interpretation manual prepared for each personnel manager of branch plants and divisional units of a large company:[1]

Introduction

Most persons who have been tested are intensely curious about their results. At the same time they are frequently apprehensive. They may come to the interview somewhat tense and nervous, and everything possible should be done to put them at ease.

The test profiles are arranged so that the interest patterns are discussed first, ability and aptitude second, and personality characteristics last. This sequence is followed because it is believed to be most conducive to free discussion.

Nothing at this time, not even skilled test interpretation, is so important as a genuine human interest in the individual. This implies an understanding, noncritical attitude which encourages talk. Avoid cross-examinations in regard to test findings and do not use test results as a basis for criticism of job performance. If *he* wants to discuss any problems which the tests bring out, let *him* take the initiative.

---

[1] Hubert Clay, "Experiences in Testing Foremen," *Personnel,* Vol. XXVIII, No. 6, pp. 466–70.

Interest Patterns

The discussion of interests provides an easy opening to the interview because nothing threatening to the individual is involved. His scores in an interest area can be either high or low and he is not upset. By the time he has gone through his interest scores and agreed or disagreed with them he is usually relaxed and far better able to accept anything unfavorable which may come up later in the interview. The interviewer, too, has a chance to "size up" the individual and his reactions during this warm-up period and thereby handle the balance of the interview more smoothly.

Ability and Aptitude

The discussion of ability and aptitude has to be carefully handled, especially in the case of an individual whose scores are below the average. This is particularly true of low general ability scores. Avoid using the terms "intelligence" and "IQ." It can be pointed out to the individual that one reason for reporting the results in letter grades is that some persons get too concerned over differences in numerical scores, even when the differences are too small to be significant.

It may be advisable to stress to the interviewee the research nature of the project and to say quite frankly that we do not know yet how much a given score means as far as supervisory success in our company is concerned. It should be emphasized particularly that the best men do not necessarily get the highest scores.

An important aspect of ability testing is the fact that while we can measure a man's ability we cannot measure his willingness to use that ability. Many men of high ability fail to succeed at a high level because of a lack of persistence, initiative, and other hard-to-measure qualities. ›

Personality

The discussion of personality is left until last because it often results in the individual "opening up" or unburdening himself of some problem or problems. It is a great advantage to be able to continue such talk, as mentioned earlier.

It should be remembered that scores on a personality questionnaire depend upon the individual's willingness and ability to rate himself frankly and honestly. Some persons merely answer the questions the way they think they should be answered rather than the way they actually feel. It is always well to inquire whether the scores agree with the individual's estimate of himself. For example: "Do you believe that you have more energy than the average man, as this score indicates?" or "This score suggests that you tend to be oversensitive and rather easily hurt. Is that an accurate picture of you?"

Certain personality traits cannot always be accepted literally. The individual's behavior actually may be a cover-up for the opposite tendencies. Aggressiveness, for example, may be an artificial role which a man assumes to cover up feelings of inadequacy and insecurity. This kind of aggressiveness is quite different from a wholesome aggressiveness expressed by a really confident person. Personality scores should always be compared, if possible, with observations of the individual in his everyday living.

Turning now to induction, the interview both in the personnel department and by the supervisor is a desirable way to give the new employee information on company objectives, policies, procedures, and details pertinent to his position. But perhaps more important is the opportunity to communicate an attitude of friendliness toward and interest in the inductee. For this purpose, the interview is a particularly effective tool.

Similarly, interviewing has a real contribution to make when employees are placed on a job, transferred, or promoted. A well-planned interview can serve to impress the employee with the opportunities of the job, to compliment him on the reasons why he was selected, to indicate dangers he should avoid, and to suggest avenues of advancement. Placement is a particularly favorable occasion for talk and discussion. A person is at a stage of achievement and also in a mood to receive a message.

But employees also leave their jobs. The interview can serve to determine why the separation is taking place. Discussions may point to some shortcomings on the part of the company or sources of irritation to employees. Such interviews are helpful to the company in indicating what it needs to do to increase its effectiveness in dealing with the labor factor. They are helpful to the employees who remain because of the improvements which follow. And they may be helpful to the employee who is leaving because (*a*) he may stay on after a constructive interview and (*b*) he may clarify his own thinking and improve his behavior on future jobs.

2. *Training.* The interview is a very useful tool in training. In such instances, it sometimes goes under the name of "coaching." The interviewer or coach seeks to transmit "know-how" and "know-why" by talk, example, and demonstration. Coaching has very desirable features. It can put a man at ease, reduce his tensions, and thereby release the powers within him to perform at his best. Mistakes can be readily corrected, answers quickly provided, and assurances of good progress immediately given.

The interview is obviously a good training tool. But far more than that, it can serve to develop loyalty toward management. The employee who has been coached toward success will unconsciously if not openly cooperate with the person who gave him needed help. Hence, if an executive is serious about gaining the confidence and respect of his subordinates, there are few ways that will pay higher dividends than training, and few tools of training that are better than personal coaching.

An interesting example of interviewing as a training device (and also for selection) is the "stress-type" interview. Here, the candidate is exposed to a variety of difficulties, obstacles, embarrassments, rudeness, and accusations. He then is evaluated on how well he handled himself under these circumstances or how long it took before he broke under them. Obviously, such interviewing would be justifiable only where the job specification called for qualities to meet highly unusual and severe stresses and strains.

3. *Human Relations.* Using the term "human relations" in the more restricted sense of encompassing personal problems and difficulties, interviewing has a particularly useful sphere of application. In this connection, interviewing often goes by the name of counseling. The intent is to help employees help themselves in solving problems with which they are perplexed, or simply to provide an environment in which unsolvable problems can be borne with some grace and courage.

The problem areas may be company- or noncompany-caused, as illustrated by such cases as the following: An employee is having marital difficulties; he has lost a loved one; he is not making satisfactory job progress; he is drinking excessively; he cannot seem to get along with his superior; or he is frustrated or bored. No matter what the source, the problems obviously will affect the employee on the job. For that reason, some companies try to be helpful no matter what the source. Other companies restrict their attention to company business.

In either event, counseling may be helpful in a number of ways. For example, an appraisal interview can be useful to the subordinate who wonders why he is not making satisfactory job progress. He can thereby be shown his strong and weak points and what he has to do to gain favorable consideration for promotions. Or counseling may help a person find the sources of his personal difficulties. Telling a person he ought to quit excessive drinking, for example, is seldom effective. But counseling may be helpful in uncovering why the man is drinking; then the employee can make a logical attack upon his problem and not feel that he is a hopeless case.

4. *Labor Relations.* Interviewing is an invaluable tool of disciplinary action, grievance handling, and relations with unions. These phases will be examined more fully in later chapters. Worthy of note in passing, however, is the point that labor relations sometimes involve deviations from desired practice or differences of opinion. In disciplinary action, for example, an employee has departed from a desired course; in grievances the company has not confirmed the expectations of employees; and in collective bargaining, there are differences regarding

standards of wages, hours, or working conditions which should be maintained.

The contributions of interviewing in such instances may be fourfold. First, good interviewing can help to determine the truth: i.e., to what extent the employee or the company was in error and what fair wages, hours, and working conditions are. Second, interviewing can serve as a platform from which to convey the good and honorable intentions of management and, for that matter, of the other parties concerned. Third, interviewing can help management to learn directly the attitudes, reactions, and viewpoints of its employees and of the representatives of its employees. And finally, interviewing can disclose the areas of personnel management regarding which the skills of executives need improvement and increased attention.

Types of Interviewing

The attainment of the foregoing purposes may be sought by any of a number of types of interviewing. In actual practice, there are undoubtedly as many types of interviewing as there are interviewers. By and large, much interviewing has been unplanned and unskilled. In such cases the interviewer may have some notion of the information he desires or the purpose he hopes to accomplish. Beyond that, he relies upon spur-of-the-moment questions or insight to guide the actual interview. Such practices are not very successful, nor do they serve to contribute to a student's understanding of good principles and practices of interviewing. Much more can be learned from study of the following methods:

1. Planned interview
2. Nondirective interview
3. Depth interview
4. Group interview

1. *Planned Interviews.* Many interviewers have improved themselves by following definite plans of action. Before entering into the actual interview, they work out in their minds, if not on paper, what they hope to accomplish, what kinds of information they are to seek or give, how they will conduct the interview, and how much time they will allot to it. During the interview, deviations from the plan may be made; but when the interviewer deviates, he does so with knowledge of what he is doing and how far off he is from his intended track. Although there is some formality about such a plan, flexibility is one of its major advantages.

A more formalized type of planning is that illustrated by the patterned interview. It is based on the assumption that to be most effective, every pertinent detail must be worked out in advance. And equally important, the interviewer must be skilled; he need not be a trained psychologist, but he must cultivate the uncommon faculties of common sense and interpretative ability.

A set of specific questions is used in patterned interviewing. These are prepared from three sources. First, job and man specifications provide a guide to important questions. Second, information that may be derived from application forms and references provides a clue to what should be asked. And third, experience with past interviews will indicate useful types of questions. The result is a formal list, such as the excerpt illustrated in Figure 9–1.

Thus the formal list of questions is but a device to aid the memory of the interviewer. He follows through his check list and devises additional questions to amplify his knowledge of the candidate wherever needed. This is the point at which the psychological skill of the interviewer comes into play. As he gathers information from the candidate, he must interpret it in the light of his understanding of normal standards of human behavior and attainments. Should he find from his questions on recreation habits, for example, that a given candidate seems immature for the job in question, the interviewer will be more vigilant when other classes of questions are asked, in order to ascertain whether or not the clue to immaturity is substantiated.

2. *The Nondirective Interview.* In recent years, much interest has been shown in the nondirective interview. As its name implies, the applicant in such an interview is not directed by questions or comments as to what he should talk about. While the interviewer may intersperce brief phrases, these should be noncommital, so that the candidate determines the trend of conversation.

The theory of such interviews is that a candidate is thus more likely to reveal his true self than when he answers set questions. With set questions, the candidate tends to respond as he thinks the interviewer wants him to, or with favorable answers, whether they are true or not. But in the nondirective approach the candidate obviously does not know how to slant his replies or commentary. As he talks, he will reveal by what he includes and what he does not state much about his goals, interests, and competency.

As in the case of the patterned interview, a major step of the nondirective technique is to study the requirements of the job to be filled and then learn as much as possible about the candidate from such sources as the application blank, reference letters, and tests. From such

FIGURE 9–1. Excerpt from Patterned Interview Form

DOMESTIC AND SOCIAL SITUATION

Married   Single   Widowed   Divorced   Separated   Date of marriage
                                                    Are he and his wife compatible?

Living with wife?   Yes   No   (If no) Specify   Dependents: Number

Ages   What plans do you have for your children?
Do dependents provide adequate motivation?

What difficulties or serious arguments have you had with your wife?   Financial?   Social?   Personal?

Have you been married previously?   Yes   No   (If yes) How many times?

When and what was the reason for end of marriage or marriages?   Death   Divorce

Separation   (Unless death) What were the reasons?
Do his domestic difficulties indicate immaturity?

Of what lodges and clubs are you a member?   Officer?   Does he show leadership?

What do you do for recreation?   What hobbies do you have?
Does his recreation show maturity?   Will his hobbies help his work?

To what extent do you and your wife entertain?   Does he seem socially well-adjusted?

When did you last drink intoxicating liquor?   To what extent?   (Doesn't drink)
Is this sensible drinking?

What types of people, racial or religious groups or nationalities do you actively dislike?
Is he biased?

SOURCE: Robert N. McMurray, "Validating the Patterned Interview," *Personnel*, Vol. XXIV, No. 6, p. 266.

studies the interviewer ascertains what he must listen for while the candidate is talking.

Such interviews are started by putting the candidate at ease by the usual introductions, courtesies, and idle talk. Then the candidate is requested by an appropriate statement or opening question to talk about his personal history. After the candidate starts talking, the interviewer must keep the candidate talking. Suggested aids to do this are as follows:

a) Give your entire attention to the applicant.
b) Listen attentively, and resist the temptation to talk.
c) Never argue.
d) Do not interrupt or change the subject abruptly.
e) Use questions sparingly, but for purposes of keeping the candidate talking, filling a gap in the story, obtaining more specific information, and checking conclusions.
f) Allow pauses in the conversation, but interject some nondirective comment if the pause becomes uncomfortable.
g) Phrase responses briefly.
h) Keep conversation at a level suited to the applicant.
i) Try to appreciate the applicant's underlying feelings.
j) Diplomatically and carefully talk to applicants who seem to be withholding information.[2]

The task of the nondirective interview is to determine what kind of person the candidate really is. The interviewer must be skilled in measuring the story the candidate tells against the normal standards of human behavior, attitudes, and attainments. In terms of how the candidate conducts himself, from his disclosures of training and experience, and from his statements on recreational and social activities, the interviewer must appraise the candidate's qualifications to fill the job in question.

3. *The Depth Interview.* Although not strictly a distinct type, the depth interview is worthy of special note. It is used to go into considerable detail on particular subjects of an important nature, the idea being that intensive examination of a candidate's background and thinking is indispensable for correct evaluations and decisions.

As a case in point, assume that a candidate for employment has noted that one of his hobbies is sailing. In the common types of interviewing, this subject will not be pursued much further, if at all; the interviewer will undoubtedly reach a conclusion based on his stereotype

---

[2] N. A. Moyer, "Non-directive Employment Interviewing," *Personnel,* Vol. XXIV, No. 5, pp. 383–87.

of amateur sailors. In a depth interview, however, the subject might be chosen for exhaustive analysis. The interviewee would be asked when he got into sailing, and why; where he sails, and why; with whom he sails, and why; how often he sails, and why; how much time and money he invests in his hobby, and why; what types of equipment he owns and prefers, and why; in what kinds of weather he prefers to sail, and why; and what kinds of friends he selects for his crew, and why. The emphasis is upon the "why," and, if possible, the why of the why. Of course, the questions are not asked crudely and belligerently. Finesse is required. It is felt that only through such exhaustive analysis can one get the true picture of a candidate. And as far as time, resources, and skill permit and conditions warrant, the investment in interviewing in depth will yield much revealing information.

4. *The Group Interview.* An interesting departure is to interview groups rather than individuals. This may be done either by having one or more executives question a group of candidates or by having a group of executives observe a number of candidates talking over some assigned questions or problems. Such an approach has two major advantages. First, the time of busy executives is conserved because all candidates are interviewed at one time. And second, it is possible to get a better picture of candidates when they have to react to and against each other.

Technical Factors

The effectiveness of any type of interviewing is basically dependent upon the skill with which certain factors common to all interviewing are utilized. These factors are language, the senses, and mechanical aids.

1. *Language.* Interviewing takes place largely through the use of words. Words are representatives of ideas, thoughts, and feelings; they are not the actual ideas, thoughts, and feelings. Unfortunately, words are not precise and universally accepted representatives. Hence a given word such as "union" does not mean, signify, or denote the same thing to every user. Indeed, to a top executive, it might denote a dastardly conspiracy; while to a worker, it might connote a bond of security and friendship.

The good interviewer does not, therefore, take it for granted that his ideas will be conveyed to another simply because he chooses words which have a given meaning to him. He becomes instead a student of the meaning of words. He knows that words not only have sounds— phonetics—but also, as noted in an earlier chapter, shades of meaning— semantics. He thereby learns to avoid words which are likely to arouse needless antagonism and doubt, and to select words which are likely to convey his thoughts precisely and with a favorable reaction.

Appropriate selection of words thus helps to clarify exchanges between interviewer and interviewee, and serves to minimize undesirable reactions. But going further, appropriate usage of language can avoid embarrassment and mistakes, and can lead conversations along desired channels. On the one hand, words whose meanings are not known to the listener should be avoided. If polysyllabic verbiage which the interviewee does not understand is used, he seldom, if ever, will reveal his ignorance; so the exchange of information is not achieved as desired by both parties. And on the other hand, the interviewer who can ask suggestive questions, use descriptive terms, and draw clear word pictures will get full answers. He will reduce the number of "yes-no" answers, and particularly answers which the interviewee thinks the interviewer wants to hear.

2. *The Senses.* The interviewer must use his senses to good advantage, especially those of sight and hearing. By careful practice, the interviewer can improve his observational skills. He can note the behavioral patterns of the interviewee. What mannerisms or expressive movements does he have, such as excessive hand movements, ear pulling, and nervous jerking? How does he control his physical posture during the interview? Do his face and eyes show unusual changes as questions become more intensive or border on the personal or embarrassing? Are there evidences on the clothing or hands of poor personal habits or lack of cleanliness? Observation of such items will provide some clues as to how a man acts.

Hearing, too, is deserving of special attention. Most people believe they are good listeners, but that is far from the truth. Only through conscious practice can one become a good listener. In the first place, there is a psychological barrier that must be circumvented. People can generally receive (listen) about four to five times as fast as they can send (talk). It is hard, therefore, to concentrate attention under such circumstances. In the second place, a good listener must listen. He must avoid talk until the time is ripe for it. He should restrain the desire to talk that almost everyone has. He does not argue, interrupt, or disapprove without due cause. In the third place, a good listener listens with sincerity, interest, and apparent attention. He gets involved in the problem, exercises his mind in grasping the ideas being expressed, and applies his logical faculties to the case at hand. And in the fourth place, the good listener, through his behavior and expressions, conveys to the interviewee his undivided concern for what is being said.

3. *Mechanical Aids.* The efficacy of interviewing is also being raised by the use of mechanical aids. Recorders of various types are being used to obtain transcriptions of interviews. The record can be replayed as often as needed to verify and evaluate the information so obtained. In a few instances, movies have been taken, so that a visual record is also obtained. Of interest as an observational aid is the use of window glass which is unidirectional. A number of people can observe an interview without themselves being seen. If a hidden microphone is used, the observers can also hear the conversations.

It would not be amiss to note the contribution of surroundings to good interviewing. An appropriately equipped room which is private is very desirable. This may seem to contradict what was said in the foregoing paragraph about recordings and hidden observers. In some instances, it may be defensible and useful to refrain from telling the interviewee about the hidden observers. But in most cases, he should be informed of the reasons for their use, and his permission for their use should be obtained.

Procedures of Interviewing

From what has been said thus far, it can be seen that interviewing involves (1) establishment of the purposes of interviewing; (2) design of a plan to gather, record, and analyze information and reach conclusions thereupon; and (3) development of skillful interviewers. Enough has been said on the first of these points. Attention is now directed to the second and third points.

1. *Gathering and Interpreting Information.* Since interviewing is largely a looking and listening technique, information may be easily forgotten or distorted with the passage of time, unless recorded. While a few companies use sound recordings for this purpose, by far the greater number employ the printed and written word to preserve pertinent data and findings. An excellent example is contained in Figure 9–2. This form succinctly records (*a*) the areas of information that are to be considered, (*b*) the interviewer's findings by areas, (*c*) his interpretations of findings by areas, and (*d*) his total detailed evaluations.

The final test of interviewing and counseling is, of course, whether or not they achieve established goals satisfactorily. It may be noted that interviewing was once considered to be an unreliable tool of selection; and to this day, it remains so when performed in an unplanned and unregulated manner by unskilled executives.

However, in those instances in which interviews have been carefully planned by skilled personnel, the results have been highly successful.

FIGURE 9–2. Interview Form
(First Page)

FORM 69
(9-1-44)

INTERVIEWER'S EVALUATION OF APPLICANT

DATE *6-27-19 4 4*

NAME OF APPLICANT *Helen Frances Davis*   LOCATION *1631 Arch St., Okla.*

JOB CONSIDERED FOR *Telephone Operator*   INTERVIEWER *Stella Burns*

AREAS TO CONSIDER	FINDINGS	INTERPRETATION OF FINDINGS
I VOICE, MANNER & APPEARANCE		
1. VOICE AND SPEECH (PLEASANT, CLEAR, DISTINCT, NO ACCENT)		
2. MANNER (COURTESY, SPEECH, GESTURES, FACIAL EXPRESSIONS)		
3. APPEARANCE (POISE, DRESS, CLEANLINESS, FEATURES)		
4. PHYSIQUE (WEIGHT, HEIGHT, REACH, STRENGTH, HANDEDNESS)		
5. VISION AND HEARING		
6. PERSONAL CHARACTERISTICS (COOPERATIVENESS, FRIENDLINESS, ADAPTABILITY, TEMPERAMENT, AGGRESSIVENESS, NERVOUSNESS)		
II WORK HISTORY		
1. KIND OF JOB OR HOME DUTIES (APTITUDES, SKILLS AND COOPERATION REQ'D)		
2. WORKING CONDITIONS (HOURS, HAZARDS, SURROUNDINGS, SUPERVISION)		
3. REASON FOR LEAVING JOB (INCOMPETENCE, INSTABILITY, TEMPERAMENT, FRICTION WITH SUPERVISION, LAY OFF)		
4. ATTENDANCE RECORD		
5. MILITARY EXPERIENCE (DATES OF SERVICE, BRANCH, STARTING AND FINAL RANK, DUTIES AND RESPONSIBILITIES, KIND OF DISCHARGE)		
6. EMPLOYER REFERENCES (DATES OF EMPLOYMENT, TYPE OF WORK, PAY, WOULD HE RE EMPLOY)		
III SCHOOLING		
1. FORMAL SCHOOLING (AMOUNT AND KIND, DATES)		
2. SPECIALIZED TRAINING OR ON JOB TRAINING		
3. MILITARY TRAINING		
4. BEST AND LEAST LIKED SUBJECTS (IN SCHOOL)		
5. REASON FOR LEAVING SCHOOL		
6. ATHLETIC AND SOCIAL ACTIVITIES, SPECIAL INTERESTS (IN SCHOOL)		
7. SCHOOL REFERENCE REPORT (STANDARD AND TESTS, CLASS STANDING, ATTENDANCE, PERSONAL RATING)		
IV SPARE TIME ACTIVITIES		
1. HOBBIES		
2. CHURCH ACTIVITIES		
3. COMMUNITY ACTIVITIES		
4. TYPES OF READING		
5. SOCIAL ADJUSTMENT FACTOR (GREGARIOUSNESS, SECLUSIVENESS, PARTIES, SOCIAL HABITS)		

SOURCE: N. A. Moyer, "Non-directive Employment Interviewing," *Personnel*, Vol. XXIV, No. 5, pp. 391–92.

Results of studies made by Robert N. McMurray are rather conclusive in this respect. For example, as may be noted in Table 9–1, interviewers' ratings of prospective employees correlated very closely to the employees' ultimate success on the job as measured by foremen's ratings. In another study of truck drivers (selected excerpts of findings are tabulated in Table 9–2), he again finds a good correlation between

FIGURE 9–2 (Continued)
(Reverse Side)

AREAS TO CONSIDER	FINDINGS	INTERPRETATION OF FINDINGS
V HOME & FAMILY BACKGROUND		
1. CHILDHOOD AND ADULT FAMILY LIFE (CONDITIONS EXPOSED TO AND ADJUSTMENTS MADE)	Five other children; one in Navy, four in school.	Co-operative attitude required
2. FINANCIAL STATUS (APPLICANT'S STANDING, INDEBTEDNESS, SOURCE OF INCOME)	Father, claim adjuster for many years.	
3. FAMILY'S ATTITUDE TOWARD TELEPHONE COMPANY AND JOB	Good home and religious training	Good conduct and integrity likely.
4. HOME VISIT REPORT (FAMILY CONSISTS OF, ATTITUDE OF FAMILY TOWARD JOB AND COMPANY, ADJUSTMENT OF APPLICANT IN THE HOME, OTHER INFORMATION)	Parents favorable to Company	Parents will help insure permanency and effort
5. CREDIT INVESTIGATION REPORT		
VI HEALTH		
1. HEALTH AS A CHILD AND PRESENT STATE OF HEALTH	Childhood diseases, measles, mumps, and whooping cough.	Health satisfactory.
2. WIFE OR HUSBAND'S AND CHILDREN'S HEALTH (IF MARRIED)		
3. OPERATIONS, SERIOUS ILLNESSES, OR ACCIDENTS (IF ANY)	Family insures good health habits.	
4. HEALTH AS INDICATED BY DRAFT STATUS OR MILITARY DISCHARGE (IF DISCHARGED FOR MEDICAL REASON)	Family healthy	

EVALUATION OF FINDINGS*

JOB QUALIFICATIONS	JOB SPEC.	I	II	III	IV	V	VI
COMMON QUALIFICATIONS (ALL JOBS)							
AGE (SATISFACTORY)	√	✓	CHECK FROM APPLICATION BLANK				
GOOD HEALTH AND APPEARANCE	√	✓		✓			✓
COOPERATIVENESS	√		✓	✓	✓	✓	
PERMANENCY (DESIRE FOR)	√			✓			
GOOD CONDUCT	√				✓	✓	
INDUSTRY	√						
DEPENDABILITY	√			✓			
INTEGRITY	√					✓	
MOTIVATION	√			✓			
SPECIAL QUALIFICATIONS							
PHYSICAL:							
A APPEARANCE (PLEASING)							
B STRENGTH							
C. SIZE (WITHIN NORMAL LIMITS)							
D VOICE (PLEASING NO DEFECTS ETC.)	✓	✓					
E. HEARING (NORMAL)	✓	✓					
F VISION (NORMAL ACUITY)	✓	✓					
G. RIGHT HANDED							
H. ARM REACH (SATISFACTORY)	✓	✓					
WORK EXPERIENCE (STATE):							

JOB QUALIFICATIONS	JOB SPEC.	I	II	III	IV	V	VI
EDUCATION, KNOWLEDGE, AND PROFICIENCIES							
A. MINIMUM FORMAL EDUCATION OR EQUIV. {IN SCHOOL YEARS 8	✓			✓			
B. MATHEMATICS	✓			✓			
C. PHYSICS							
D PRINCIPLES OF ELECTRICITY							
E. HANDWRITING AND PRINTING (NEAT)	✓		LOOK AT APPLICATION BLANK				
F TYPING							
G. STENOGRAPHY							
H MECHANICAL DRAWING							
APTITUDES:							
A. INTELLIGENCE				✓			
B. PLANNING							
C ANALYSIS							
D. OVER-ALL PHYSICAL COORDINATION				✓			
PERSONAL CHARACTERISTICS:							
A EASE AND QUALITY OF CONVERSATION		✓					
B EMOTIONAL STABILITY OR TEMPERAM'T	✓	✓					
C ADAPTABILITY	✓			✓	✓		
D TACT							
E. INTERESTS (STATE).				✓	✓		

*UNDER "JOB SPEC" INSERT A CHECK MARK (√) FOR EACH REQUIREMENT LISTED ON THE JOB SPECIFICATION UNDER 'EVALUATION' INSERT, WHEREVER THE FINDINGS INDICATE IT
A CHECK (√) TO INDICATE QUALIFIED'
A CROSS (X) TO INDICATE "NOT QUALIFIED"

INTERVIEWER'S RECOMMENDATIONS	CHECK OVER-ALL CLASS. FOR SPECIFIC JOB	
Appears to meet all requirements of job. Unable to verify school history at moment because schools are closed.		1 WELL QUALIFIED ☑
		2. INTERMEDIATE ☐
		3 POORLY QUALIFIED ☐

interview ratings with "pass-fail" criterion. And in selecting salespeople by use of the chronograph, it was reported that in one company no one now sells less than 65 percent of standard, as compared with a low figure of 35 percent before the new technique of interviewing was used.[3]

[3] Lester Smith in the *Wall Street Journal*, February 16, 1948.

TABLE 9–1

COMPARISON OF INITIAL INTERVIEW SCORE WITH SUCCESS RATING
(Men and Women Combined)

FOREMEN'S SUCCESS-ON-THE-JOB RATING	INTERVIEWERS' RATINGS			
	1	2	3	4
Outstanding	6 (35.3%)	8 (47.1%)	3 (17.6%)	....
Above average	2 (1.2%)	88 (53.0%)	75 (45.2%)	1 (0.6%)
Below average	....	13 (6.6%)	175 (88.8%)	8 (4.6%)
Very poor	....	....	4 (14.8%)	23 (85.2%)

SOURCE: Robert N. McMurray, "Validating the Patterned Interview," *Personnel*, Vol. XXIV, No. 6, p. 270.

TABLE 9–2

COMPARISON OF DRIVER INTERVIEW RATINGS WITH
"PASS-FAIL" CRITERION

	INTERVIEWERS' RATINGS			
	1	2	3	4
Still in service (successful)	6 (75.0%)	15 (38.5%)	12 (26.1%)	2 (13.3%)
Left service any reason (failures)	2 (25.0%)	24 (61.5%)	34 (73.9%)	13 (86.7%)
Total number originally interviewed	8 (100%)	39 (100%)	46 (100%)	15 (100%)

SOURCE: Robert N. McMurray, "Validating the Patterned Interview," *Personnel*, Vol. XXIV, No. 6, p. 270.

In connection with nondirective interviewing, the following results are claimed in one case:

1. The percentage of turnover cases which could be ascribed in whole or in part to faulty selection, while the labor market was growing tighter, has declined steadily.
2. The department supervisors say they are getting people better fitted for the work. Follow-up studies bear this out.
3. Interviewers who have used both the questionnaire and the nondirective method say the latter enables them to make more effective appraisals.
4. Applicants frequently tell interviewers they liked the interview because it did not seem like an interview. They had expected to be asked a lot of questions; instead, they just had a pleasant chat.

5. Other companies in the Bell System that have adopted this method report similar results.[4]

These few studies could be supported by others indicative of similar results. They are sufficient to show the value of good interviewing practices. It is to be noted that such practices are not perfect, but they are far better than poor practices.

2. *Developing Skillful Interviewers.* It has already been noted that an important element in interviewing is the skill of the interviewer. This suggests the need for careful selection and training of interviewers.

In selecting interviewers, practice varies considerably. Some companies select for such work only those who are college trained in psychology and psychiatry. Others place emphasis upon mature experience in the type of work for which people are going to be interviewed. But allowing for variations, a list of qualifications would include the following:

a) A suitable background of experience similar to that of those who are to be interviewed

b) Maturity of action and viewpoint, so that the others unconsciously tend to assume an attitude of confidence and cooperation

c) Experience and training in sizing up people from their behavior and actions (as opposed to mere physical build or appearance)

d) A combination of an objective viewpoint and an appreciation of human feelings and attitude

e) Good judgment, so that the "chaff may be separated from the wheat" during the interview, and so that the proper weight is assigned to information obtained from the interview in relation to other sources of information

f) An ability to work through organizational channels with supervisors and other executives

g) An ability to plan the work of interviewing and to see the total as well as individual implications

Individuals with such capacities or potentials for their development are not too difficult to find in most companies. Usually, the main thing to be done is to train available talent properly. A review of such training programs is therefore in order.

The practices of training interviewers and counselors are varied[5] Some companies use the conference method to conduct training sessions. Others give trainees the opportunity to attend evening courses at local colleges. Some prepare instruction manuals which cover such

---

[4] Moyer, *op. cit.*, p. 396.

[5] Policyholders Service Bureau, Metropolitan Life Insurance Company, *The Employee Counsellor in Industry* (New York), pp. 21–22.

points as factors common to all interviews, subjects to be covered during interviews, how to conduct follow-up interviews, and how to counsel employees. Interviewers have also been helped by giving them firsthand experience in various shop and office departments.

In one company the training given interviewers consists of ten lessons:

1. Establish tentative job qualifications
2. Review application for employment
3. Preparation for conducting practice interviews
4. Conducting practice interviews
5. Recording the findings
6. Interpretation of the findings
7. Introduction of job specifications
8. Evaluation of findings
9. Closing the interview
10. Practicing the complete interview[6]

In addition, trainees study plant operating departments and write job specifications. Later, follow-up training is given interviewers as specific cases require.

Another good training device is a check list, which is used by the interviewer to review his own methods. One such list includes the following suggestions:[7]

a) Take the interviewee's point of view.
b) Examine and discount your own prejudices.
c) Help the interviewee to be at ease.
d) Deserve and gain the interviewee's confidence.
e) Listen.
f) Allow time enough without dawdling.
g) Take pains to phrase questions so that they are easily understood.
h) Avoid implying answers.
i) Avoid impertinence and embarrassment on the part of the interviewee.
j) Encourage the interviewee to qualify or explain answers.
k) Achieve something definite.
l) Make subsequent interviews easy.
m) At the close of the interview, watch for casual leads.
n) Separate facts from inferences.
o) Record all data at once.

Rules of Interviewing

This discussion can best be closed by summarizing a number of rules of good interviewing. They have been developed largely by trial and error, although it is encouraging to note that research is beginning to

[6] Moyer, *op. cit.*, p. 395.
[7] An excerpt from training materials of the Ohio State Employment Service.

make contributions. Adoption of these rules does not provide an unfailing high road to successful interviewing but serves to increase the probability of a useful exchange of information or views. Nor does a mere listing provide anyone with automatic tools; they must be practiced in order to gain proficiency.

1. Perhaps the basic rule of interviewing is to respect the interests and individuality of the interviewee. Unless one conveys a sympathetic understanding of the other fellow's point of view and desires, it is difficult to develop a feeling of confidence, which is essential to getting or giving information. On the one hand, one should be sensitive to the ideas and feelings of others. And on the other hand, one should not underestimate the intelligence of employees, display an attitude of superiority, or use trick questions.

2. It is also of high importance in interviewing to preestablish clearly the objectives to be gained or purposes to be served by interviews. Until this is done, it is impossible either to plan an interview effectively or to act convincingly during one. A practical difficulty, however, is that many interviews must be conducted on the spur of the moment. The pressure of other jobs may make it impossible to schedule interviews so that allowances may be made for preplanning time. This excuse should seldom be used in employment interviewing, but lack of time often affects the interviewing that takes place between executives at various levels and their subordinates.

3. There is no principle of interviewing that has been more frequently stated—and deservedly so—than that of making the interviewee feel at ease. To this end, the interviewer must act and be relaxed and at ease himself. Any failure in this respect, particularly where grievances or disciplinary action are concerned, results in an atmosphere of tension and belligerence unconducive to a free exchange of ideas. In the employment interview, too, the feeling of newness that obstructs the interview must be reduced by placing the interviewee at ease. As good a way as any to attain a relaxed discussion is to start slowly with some topic known to both parties. No matter how busy the interviewer is, he must give the impression at the outset that sufficient time for an unhurried discussion is available. When time is short, it is preferable to postpone the interview.

4. Another principle of good interviewing is to allow—indeed, to encourage—the interviewee to talk copiously. In the case of grievances, for example, this practice serves not only to draw out the whole complaint but also to cool off the aggrieved party. Only by encouraging a full discussion is it possible to lead the interviewee to unburden himself to the point that nothing important or relevant is left unsaid. Fifteen- or

twenty-minute interviews, for example, scarcely allow ample opportunity for full expression. Indeed, hours are to be preferred.

5. An important suggestion to the interviewer is that he be a close student of the meaning of words, i.e., of the field of semantics. He must be sure that he knows what meaning an applicant gives to such words as "capitalism," "profits," "rights," and "merit." He must guard against using words that might arouse unnecessary antagonism or reservations, such as "low intelligence," "boss," "governmental interference," or "psychoneurosis." And although it is very difficult to do, he must try to ascertain how words used by a particular individual may be colored by past working experiences or charged with the emotionalism of personal experiences.

6. The interviewer should keep his views and opinions to himself unless they are of significance to the interviewee or until the latter has had sufficient opportunity to express himself. Even though keeping quiet is difficult, he must develop this virtue. Moreover, should he make up his mind as to what is to be done, he should not end the interview abruptly but should close it diplomatically, so that the interviewee feels satisfied that a full hearing has been accorded him. In the case of a job refusal, for example, the applicant may otherwise feel that the decision was hasty or based on an incomplete picture of the facts. Or in the case of a grievance, the interviewee may gain the impression that the company was prejudiced from the start.

7. In regard to concluding an interview, the interviewer should know how to draw it to a close and should be prepared to state his views or decisions clearly and concisely and, if possible, conclusively. A final and positive answer need not be made; but if such an answer is possible, so much the better. If an answer cannot be given with finality, it is a good rule to indicate what other steps are to be taken, and why. In addition, a definite time schedule for a decision or another meeting should be set. In this way the interviewee is more likely to feel that the interviewer is capably and reasonably seeking a fair solution.

8. Physical conditions and layout should be selected that are suitable to the purposes of the interview. Insofar as practicable, quiet and secluded (out-of-hearing, if not out-of-sight) surroundings should be available. Few interviewees, whether looking for a job, airing a grievance, or being rebuked, want to be overheard by others. Most of us like to have others hold the opinion that we are accepted members of the group; an open interview may give evidence to the contrary. An unobtrusive location also makes it possible for the interview to proceed without interruption and with a minimum of distracting influences.

9. It is well to note that the use of interviews should be considered

part of an effective and economical plan of exchanging information. For example, where or how should the following type of question be posed: "What financial obligations do you have?" The matter raised is of such a personal nature, however, that it is likely to prove less embarrassing to a candidate if it is asked during an interview when the reason for asking it can be given. Some go so far as to say that interviews should be used to gather personal and qualitative information, whereas other devices, such as application blanks and tests, should be used to secure quantitative information. This suggestion has some merit, although it is often difficult to draw a clear boundary line between qualitative and quantitative information. Perhaps a more practical rule to follow is to gather as much factual and biographical data as possible on the application blank and then follow up in the interview with detailed questions on those subjects which appear, in a particular case, to have potentialities for adding useful clues. Thus, in nine cases out of ten, there may be no reason for following up the answers that applicants give regarding hobbies, let us say; but occasionally, the listing may provide a basis for further personal questioning.

QUESTIONS

1. What are the purposes for which interviewing is useful?
2. Prepare a set of "patterned interview" questions for hiring a stenographer. Try out the list with a fellow student, and report how the original list could be improved.
3. Try out a nondirective interview before the class on a student who is tardy, in order to determine why he came in late. Do your difficulties give a clue to the kinds of problems for which this type of interviewing cannot and can be used? Explain.
4. Do you expect the nondirective method to be used widely in business? The depth interview? Why, or why not, in each case?
5. What is the objection to taking notes during an interview? How else may the interviewer be sure of remembering exactly what he should remember? In what types of interviews may note taking be desirable and permissible?
6. What qualifications should an interviewer possess?
7. What suggestions can you offer to a person who desires to become a better and more effective interviewer?
8. It is said that allowing interviewees to talk freely is a desirable way to settle many problems. How can the average executive find time to give employees unhurried discussions?
9. Suggest ways in which an interviewer may draw an interview to a close gracefully, yet conclusively.
10. Suggest ways in which appropriate physical arrangements for interviewing may be provided for supervisory interviews in the shop.

CHAPTER 10

TESTS

Popularity of Tests

Perhaps no subject in the field of selection has received as much study and attention as that of testing. Since World War I, when psychological tests were adopted by the United States Army as a means of aiding in the placement of army personnel, much has been written about tests, their development, application, and usefulness. But even now, usage has not come up to the volume of writings.

The limited usage is not, however, a serious reflection upon the desirability and feasibility of testing. Nor is the fact that some companies have discontinued the use of tests a sign of inherent weaknesses. Some companies do not care to invest the time and money needed to build a successful testing program. Others became discouraged because tests did not solve their hiring problems, a conclusion they should have reached before seeking a cure-all. And others think that their selection problems are susceptible to more understandable solutions.

As experimentation continues, refinements are bound to lift testing above such objections. The use of tests requires much study and skill, however; and for these reasons, it has perhaps lagged in adoptions. And for similar reasons the complexity of the subject will permit no more than a generalized discussion of testing, which is taken up here under the following headings:

1. Basic concepts and assumptions of testing
2. Areas of usage
3. Types of tests
4. Operating a testing program
5. Rules in testing

Basic Fundamentals

It is desirable to understand at the outset that a test—any test—is a process of measurement. By such measurement, it is hoped to determine how well a person has done something or may do something in the future. The measurement may be in intangible or quantitative terms. Thus, upon being introduced to someone, we decide immediately or soon after that our new acquaintance is a "right guy" or perhaps someone who should not be trusted. Our judgment is qualitative, since we do not specify how right or how untrustworthy he is. Nevertheless, in our own fashion, we have given a test and reached a conclusion regarding his future performance.

On the other hand, our conclusions may be expressed quantitatively. As a result of a formal intelligence test, a definite score would be obtained for each person—e.g., an intelligence quotient of 102. Of course, a quantitative score is better, in the sense that it can be communicated to others more readily, yet it is not necessarily any more accurate than qualitative scores or verbal descriptions.

Tests are thus invariably based upon samples. This need not destroy one's confidence in them. So long as steps are taken to see that given samples are representative of the areas of which they presumably are samples, their usefulness is not questionable on that score.

Tests, it is to be noted, provide measures of past aspects or predictors of future events. Test results must therefore be used with care. On the one hand, the score of a test, which is intended to reveal how much experience, training, or ability along particular lines one has acquired, does not disclose unerringly what may happen in the future. This is so because it is difficult to estimate with how much enthusiasm the skills may be applied as time goes on.

On the other hand, tests which are intended to provide predictions about the future are as yet more accurate in their negative implications than in their positive significance. For example, if candidate A receives a high score on a battery of tests and candidate B receives a low score, the resonable deduction is that B is not likely to succeed if hired and hence should not, other things considered, be hired. As for A, it is plausible to expect him not to fail, but the contention at the present stage in the development of tests is not that he will succeed in proportion as his grade is high.

But even the most enthusiastic supporters of tests do not insist that decisions regarding applicants or employees be reached solely on the basis of test scores. They should add to the sum of information gathered from such sources as application blanks, references, and interviews. Yet, the potential of tests has been well expressed in the following commendatory words: "The most important results of our six years' experience [with tests] is to enable me to say without hesitation that it is beyond anyone's power to do as good a job of employment without tests as can be done with their careful use."[1]

Areas of Usage

Tests have been used in a variety of areas. To illustrate this, examples will be cited in the areas of selection, guidance and placement, and training.

1. *Selection.* Testing has had its widest application in the area of selection. Its success there has been highest in connection with shop and clerical jobs and less so—but still on the promising side—with professional and executive positions.

Looking first at operative jobs, an example of successful testing is found in a company that compared 88 hirings with testing and 45 without testing during a five-month period.[2] Percentages of those who subsequently failed on the job were 7.8 for those tested and 49 for those not tested. Based on a minimum cost of $55 to train a replacement, $990 was lost by not testing the 45. This figure was computed on the assumption that testing the 45 would have eliminated the unfit from this group as successfully as it did with the 88. In that event, only four would have had to be replaced, instead of 22, as was the case. The saving in 18 replacements at 55 would have amounted to $990. On the other hand, if the 88 had been hired without testing and if 49 percent had failed—as was true of the nontested group—the loss would have been $2,035 ($55 × 37).

An example of how effective a single test can be is shown by an analysis of the production record of workers whose vision differed. It was found that average hourly earnings of employees who met visual standards were 20 percent more than of those who did not.[3] Moreover, the quality of workmanship of the former was found to have increased about 8–15 percent.

Turning to the executive area, much study is being devoted to it, although the surface has been little more than scratched. One conclusion that stands out is the necessity of combining ratings and interviews with selected batteries of tests, to be able to screen potentially good from inferior executives. Thus, to results of tests on such factors as interests, emotional stability, general intelligence, and personality must

---

[1] Edward N. Hay, *Inaugurating a Test Program,* Personnel Series, No. 43 (New York: American Management Association), p. 26.

[2] A. R. Michael, "Tests Help Cut Turnover Rate 74% in Five Months," *Factory Management and Maintenance,* Vol. CIX, No. 5, pp. 78–80.

[3] N. Frank Stump, "Vision Tests Predict Worker Capacity," *Factory Management and Maintenance,* Vol. CIV, No. 2, pp. 121–24.

be added opinions on such factors as training, experience, social responsibilities and relationships, productive record, and hobbies.

As a case in point respecting supervisors, one company installed a selection procedure heavily weighted with psychological testing, interviewing, and performance analysis.[4] It reported that before installation, one out of every two foremen failed, on the average. In the first year after installation, one of its factory units had 33 successes out of 35 promotions to the supervisory level.

The right combination of selection factors is even more significant at higher executive levels. This is so because no one combination of factors and personal characteristics has been found to describe all successful executives. Hence the establishment of a man specification of the "ideal" executive is as yet impossible. If tests are devised to select candidates with ideal qualities, this will eliminate those who do not meet the standards but who might otherwise have developed into successful executives. Moreover, such specifications open the way to conformism because the smart candidates will slant their answers and behavior to approximate the predetermined ideal.

Turning now to the technical area, a case of testing sales engineers is noteworthy. One company has employed tests of vocational interest, mental maturity, personality, and mechanical aptitude with other selection devices. It feels that its selection and placement of its sales engineers may be improved by 10–20 percent by the use of psychologcial tests.[5] This conservative estimate contains an important moral: A selection device should not be judged by whether it provides perfect results but rather by its capacity to make a reasonably significant improvement in results.

2. *Guidance and Placement.* A significant use of tests is found in connection with guidance and placement. When it is realized that most young people do not know for what field of endeavor they are best suited, it can be seen what a vast field of service for testing is available. All that can be done here is to note some contributions of testing to guidance in the business field.

One study has some interesting comments on vocational predictability. Recognizing the limitations of the samples studied and the importance of "other things not being equal," a number of tests have been found useful (by no means perfect) in predicting occupational success. In the case of accounting, for example, tests of arithmetic reasoning,

---

[4] Matthew Radom, "Picking Better Foremen," *Factory Management and Maintenance,* Vol. CVIII, No. 10, pp. 119–22.

[5] James Onarheim, "Scientific Sales Engineers," *Personnel,* Vol. XXV, No. 1, p. 34.

reading comprehension, and reaction speed tended to discriminate between above-average and below-average accountants.[6] This study reported that a spatial relations test was the best discriminator among engineers and a reading comprehension test was useful in the case of managers. On the other hand, this study reported that none of its tests were of use in predicting success in wholesale or insurance selling.

An interesting example of test usage in placement is found in the case of a company that compared apprentices selected with and without tests. In this case, 24 applicants for the course were given tests. The results were then compared with scores of five apprentices who had been hired without tests but were given the battery of tests later. Eleven of the applicants outranked all of the original apprentices, and 20 outranked all but three. This shows strikingly that job placements were not only expensive for the company but also unfair to the apprentices who were on jobs in which they were not apt to achieve a satisfactory degree of success.[7]

FIGURE 10–1. Relationship between Scores on a Finger-Dexterity Test and Average Learning Cost to the Plant in Minimum Makeup Pay

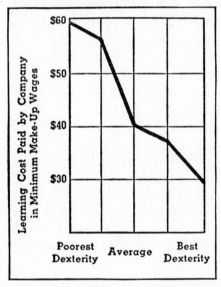

SOURCE: C. H. Lawshe and Joseph Tiffin, "How Tests Can Strengthen the Training Program," *Factory Management and Maintenance*, Vol. CII, No. 3, pp. 119–21.

3. *Training.* Tests have also been useful in strengthening training programs. An interesting example of this is reported in using tests to determine who should be trained, where training should begin, and whether training has been adequate. It was found that the learning cost of employees who had scored lowest on a finger dexterity test, as measured by a simple pegboard, averaged $59.00 before they earned the minimum hourly rate on a piecework basis. On the other hand, those with the highest finger dexterity incurred a learning cost of $36.40 before making the rate. Figure 10–1 illustrates these relationships. Obviously, savings in training costs would more than offset the cost of such selection tests.

This report also showed that tests can save training costs by deter-

---

[6] R. L. Thorndike, *Who Will Be Successful 10 Years from Now?* Personnel Series, No. 163 (New York: American Management Association), pp. 3–14.

[7] C. A. Drake, "Aptitude Tests Help You Hire," *Factory Management and Maintenance*, Vol. XCV, No. 6, p. 57.

mining where training should begin. On a simple measurement question asked about an illustration showing some blocks adjacent to a scale, it was found the 70 percent of 650 applicants were unable to read to one thirty-second of an inch. Obviously, training would be wasted in these cases unless the training were started at a level low enough to teach measuring fundamentals.

The question of whether training has been adequate is also of significance. Figure 10–2 illustrates the relation between scores on an electrical information test and hours of instruction. By preestablishing a measure to indicate when a person has sufficient knowledge to handle a particular job, it is possible to determine how many hours of training are ordinarily required to attain the desired score. Thus, if it is decided that anyone who has a grade of 80 may be turned loose on a job, then, by the use of such a chart as that in Figure 10–2, it may be noted that training would be needed for about two hundred

FIGURE 10–2. Relationship between Length of Training Period and Scores on an Electrical Information Test

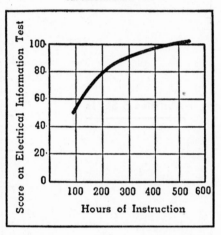

SOURCE: C. H. Lawshe and Joseph Tiffin, "How Tests Can Strengthen the Training Program," *Factory Management and Maintenance*, Vol. CII, No. 3, pp. 119–21.

hours. Obviously, any figure above or below this would be wasteful either by overtraining or by poor production due to undertraining.

Types of Tests

Having seen the uses to which tests have been put, it would now be desirable to examine various kinds of tests. Time and space preclude this because estimates show that tens of thousands of tests have been developed. Some good can be derived, however, by describing and illustrating tests under the following headings: (1) characteristics tested and (2) individual tests and batteries of tests.

1. *Characteristics Tested.* The characteristics measured by tests fall into four major categories: physical, abilities and skills, interests, and personality. As suggested in Figure 10–3, each of these is divisible into more specific characteristics. Almost everyone has some acquaintance with physical tests such as those of height, weight, strength, eyesight, and hearing. Hence, this group need detain us no longer.

The area of abilities and skills is not so well known. It has reference

FIGURE 10–3. Measures of Human Characteristics

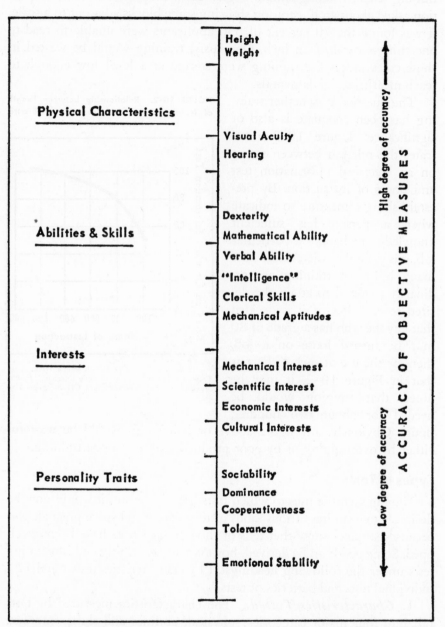

to competence in getting things done. But competence can be viewed in two ways: (*a*) one may already be proficient in getting things done, or (*b*) he may merely possess the potential. The first is referred to as proficiency or achievement; and the second, aptitude. Tests that fall in this grouping are illustrated by the following:[8]

a) Tweezer dexterity tests are used to determine whether a candidate possesses sufficient finger performance and control to handle small parts efficiently and without undue fatigue.

b) A test of mechanical ability may be obtained by checking the speed with which a candidate can assemble oddly shaped jigsaw blocks.

c) Another test used to determine mechanical ability is the spatial relations test. This serves as a measure of a candidate's ability to visualize the shape of physical objects.

d) Tests of machine skill have been designed in which the operator is checked (1) for speed and accuracy in controlling two cranks turned at different speeds and in different directions, and (2) for hand-eye co-ordination in turning a crank while following with the eyes a line drawn on a revolving drum.

e) A test used to screen candidates for fine assembly work has been based upon dexterity in handling small parts.

f) Inspection tests are usually made up of sample jobs which check visual acuity and finger dexterity.

g) Technical intelligence has been measured by the use of pictorial multiple-choice questions, as has mechanical comprehension to understand various types of physical relationships.

h) A classification and placement test designed to measure individual performance in twelve basic skills of seeing is incorporated in a testing instrument called the "Ortho-rate."

These skills are not as pure as their names might indicate. Intelligence is a case in point. To begin with, it is perhaps irrevocably mixed up with other phases of human characteristics, such as learning, experience, background, personality, mechanical ability, executive talent, sales ability, and interests. Moreover, intelligence can be further divided into such elements as numerical memory, verbal memory, reasoning, imagination, and spatial memory. Hence, in the design of tests, it is necessary first to specify what particular aspects of a trait such as intelligence are to be measured. Otherwise, a general measure, such as the IQ, must be interpreted not as a pure score but as one covering a variety of similar characteristics.

Testing of abilities and skills alone is invariably ineffective in predicting success because interest and motivation as well as skill are

[8] Richard S. Uhrbrock, "The Expressed Interests of Employed Men," *American Journal of Psychology*, Vol. LVII, No. 3, pp. 317–70; Vol. LVII, No. 4, pp. 537–54.

important. Tests have been devised to measure interest, but not much has been done as yet with the motivational factor. A sample taken from a test to check interests is shown in the following:[9]

In checking the interests of people, the samples following are illustrative of the types of tests which have been employed.

  a) Below are names and accomplishments of persons who have attained fame. If the life and work of a man interest you, circle the L before his name; if you are indifferent to his accomplishments, encircle the I; if you dislike the type of activity he stands for, encircle the D.

    L I D 1. Johann Gutenberg—movable type for printing presses
    L I D 2. Hervey Allen—author of *Anthony Adverse*
    L I D 3. George Corliss—valve gear for steam engines
    L I D 4. Thomas Edison—incandescent lamp

  b) Below are listed several paired occupations. Suppose that each occupation pays the same salary, carries the same social standing, and offers the same future advancement. Place a check ($\checkmark$) in front of the one occupation of each pair which you would prefer as a life work. BE SURE TO MARK ONE OF EACH PAIR.

1. Research chemist
   Factory superintendent
	6. Sales manager
	   Advertising manager

2. Budget director
   Sales manager
	7. Research chemist
	   Personnel director

3. Office manager
   Construction engineer
	8. Factory superintendent
	   Office manager

4. Research chemist
   Sales manager
	9. Design engineer
	   Sales manager

5. Personnel director
   Office manager
	10. Budget director
	   Design engineer

Personality also conditions the application of abilities and skills. Tests in this category have been perhaps least successful in measuring what can be expected of a person. This is due to the fact that:

  a) The degree to which personality is important in various occupations has not been established with certainty.

  b) The components of personality have not been defined to the satisfaction of all concerned.

  c) Personality is more nebulous than other human characteristics and therefore harder to measure.

The truth of this can be seen by even a casual glance at the following listing of categories of traits used to describe and measure personality:

  a) General level of activity—e.g., active, vigorous, calm, alert, elated, jumpy, jittery, and compulsive behavior

---

[9] *Ibid.*

b) Attitudes toward life, individuals, and society—e.g., contented, bewildered, immature, cautious, tolerant, submissive, belligerent, prejudiced, and realistic

c) Control and intensity of feelings,—e.g., extroverted, stable, self-sufficient, worried, depressed, alienated, masculine, paranoic, and schizophrenic

2. *Individual Tests and Batteries of Tests.* Tests may be part of a group or battery, or may be given singly. A battery of tests is considered to give much better results. This does not mean that a candidate must receive high grades on all the tests given. On the contrary, some of the tests included in a battery may be given with a view to finding what things a candidate is neither equipped to do nor interested in doing. This tends to strengthen conclusions reached on the positive tests included in the battery. A few examples follow:

a) In checking the usefulness of tests for time-study men, the following battery of tests was employed:[10]
  (1) Otis Employment Test (general mental ability)
  (2) Bennett Mechanical Comprehension (mechanical comprehension)
  (3) Moore Arithmetic Reasoning (quantitative thinking)
  (4) Minnesota Paper Board Form (visualizing bidimensional objects in relation to space)
  (5) Guilford-Martin (working with and getting along with others; objectivity, agreeableness, co-operativeness)
  (6) Kuder-Preference (major interests; mechanical, computation, scientific, persuasive, artistic, literary, music, social service, clerical)

b) A battery of tests given to supervisor included the following:[11]
  (1) Strong Vocational Interest Blank for Men
  (2) Kuder-Preference Record
  (3) Wonderlic Personnel Test
  (4) Classification Test for Industrial and Office Personnel
  (5) How Supervise
  (6) General Clerical Test
  (7) Test of Mechanical Comprehension
  (8) Guilford-Zimmerman Temperament Survey

c) A battery of tests used in a selection procedure for salesmen included the following:[12]
  (1) PRI Classification Test
  (2) Purdue Adaptability
  (3) Minnesota Paper Board Form
  (4) Cardall Test of Practical Judgment
  (5) Sales Selector

---

[10] Charles A. Thomas, "Special Report on a Test Analysis of a Group of Time Study Men," *Advanced Management,* Vol. XVIII, No. 8, pp. 13–14.

[11] Hubert Clay, "Experiences in Testing Foremen," *Personnel,* Vol. XXVIII, No. 6, pp. 466–70.

[12] Erwin K. Taylor and Edwin C. Nevis, "The Validity of Using Psychological Selection Procedures," *Personnel,* Vol. XXX, No. 3, pp. 187–89.

      (6) Allport-Vernon Study of Values
      (7) Guilford-Zimmerman Temperament Survey
      (8) Strong Vocational Interest Test

Operating a Testing Program

Since it has been impractical to analyze even a part of all tests in use, some useful suggestions regarding any tests may be provided by commenting upon (1) staffing and organizing a testing program, (2) recording and interpreting test results, and (3) measuring the accuracy of tests.

1. *Staffing and Organizing.* Undoubtedly, a most important requirement of a good testing program is that of assigning it to competent personnel. Immediately, there comes to mind the psychologist, trained in the theory of tests, their construction, their uses, and their meaning. When possible, such a person should be given responsibility for operating the testing program. However, it is not always possible to utilize full time the services of a professional psychologist. A part-time consultant may be employed in such cases, or it is possible to assign some individual with the required potential and have him study in this field himself. Many a case is on record of executives who have become proficient in operating a testing program after study of and experimentation with tests.

From an organizational point of view, a number of suggestions are in order. To begin with, the top executives must be convinced of the desirability of testing. Until and unless they are "sold," the battle with the lower levels of an organization will be eventually lost or hard-won. Next, top management should be kept abreast of the developmental stages of the program. And it should be kept informed of progress by means of reports illustrating the success of the testing program.

Those on lower levels of an organization will also have to be convinced of the usefulness of testing. Unless one wants a forced acceptance—and consequently, an unstable position—it is best in these levels to go slowly. Usually, only a department or two should be selected as the area of installation. Results here should then be so self-apparent that the program will expand of its own accord. The following statement illustrates convincingly how this actually works out:

By the third year we had developed enough confidence in one or two department heads so that they were willing to allow us to test some of their employees. After a time one of these department heads sent us, gradually, most of the 200 employees in his department, and subsequently he never made a promotion or transfer without consulting me and inquiring about test indications.

The influence of tests on selection and promotion was thus being extended and gave us an increasing number of opportunities to "sell" supervisors and employees on the value of tests. This job of selling is never finished. By now we are not merely tolerated; our testing program is taken for granted in most departments, and in some it is regarded as an essential aid to the supervisor. There are departments, nevertheless, where, even yet, testing employees is impossible. Such departments challenge us to further effort in establishing clearly the value of psychological methods, including testing.[13]

FIGURE 10–4. Visual Patterns Desirable for Electric Soldering Operations, and the Actual Score Made by One of the Employees in the Highest Hourly Rating Group. Scores in the Darkened Area Are Undesirable

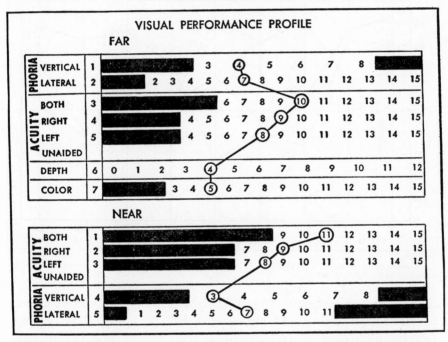

SOURCE: N. Frank Stump, "Vision Tests Predict Worker Capacity," *Factory Management and Maintenance*, Vol. CIV, No. 2, pp. 121–22.

2. *Recording Test Results.* Another operational aspect worthy of consideration is that of recording test results. Such records can be expressed simply in arithmetic or verbal terms, or they may be displayed graphically. Arithmetic or verbal terms have simplicity and ease of recording in their favor, but they lack the desirable characteristic of visualization. For example, Figure 10–4 illustrates the graphical method of displaying test results in regard to visual measurements. The "profile," or line connecting various test scores, quickly and clearly

---

[13] Hay, *op. cit.,* p. 27.

reveals to the reader the coordination of given operators as compared to desirable limits.

On a broader scale, the value of profile recording may be seen in Figure 10–5. Here, test scores on nine tests are recorded. The tests were

FIGURE 10–5. Inspection Test Profile

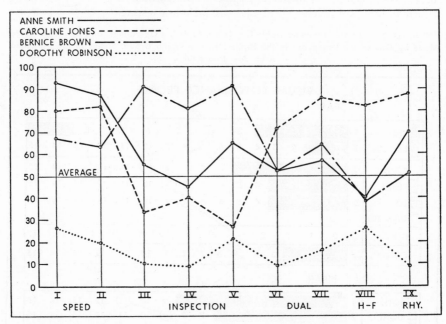

Source: C. A. Drake and H. D. Oleen, "The Technique of Testing," *Factory Management and Maintenance*, Vol. XCVI, No. 3, pp. 77–78.

as follows: (*a*) pinboard, (*b*) right-right turning, (*c*) special inspection, (*d*) case sorting, (*e*) visual perception, (*f*) controlled turning, (*g*) right-left turning, (*h*) hand-foot coordination, and (*i*) rhythm. The profiles of the four candidates shown in Figure 10–5 make it possible to draw conclusions much more quickly than if the scores had merely been expressed arithmetically.

3. *Measures of Accuracy of Tests.* Tests are usually measured in terms of their validity and reliability. On the one hand, tests are obviously developed and designed to test something—e.g., intelligence, temperament, finger dexterity, or reading ability. The degree to which a given test does this is a measure of its validity and is commonly expressed by means of the statistical device of coefficient of correlation. Simply, this refers to a measure of the degree to which those who have high, average, and low scores also have high, average, and low production records, as illustrated in Table 10–1.

TABLE 10–1

ILLUSTRATIONS OF TEST VALIDITY

JOB PERFORMANCE	TEST SCORES		
	Low	Middle	High
Diagrammatic illustration of perfect validity:			
High..	0	0	100
Middle..	0	100	0
Low..	100	0	0
Diagrammatic illustration of zero validity:			
High..	33	34	33
Middle..	33	34	33
Low..	33	34	33
A more "realistic" illustration of validity:			
High..	5	30	65
Middle..	20	50	30
Low..	65	25	10

SOURCE: "Basics of Testing," *Personnel*, Vol. XXXII, No. 6, pp. 550–51. Adapted from a manual prepared for the Navy Department by the United States Civil Service Commission, Washington, D.C.

An example of a simple determination of validity is provided by the following case of selection of office employees:

After administering five different tests we found two which predicted success to a fairly high degree. The critical score on each test is such that, of the 20 best operators, 15 made good scores; and of the 20 poorest, only 5 made good scores; or, in other words, if we had discharged all the operators with scores below the critical point of either test, we would have lost 25 percent of our best operators, but no less than 75 percent of our poorest.

This is not as high a degree of correlation between test scores and performance as is often obtained; we believe we can improve it by further experimentation with other tests.

The correlation indicates, however, the probability of a very substantial degree of success in selecting operators who will subsequently prove satisfactory. As a matter of fact, of 5 operators employed in the last three years as beginners, that is, without experience, 4 are now among the 20 best girls and only 1 is in the lower group. That one is well up in the lower 20 and, we think, will move higher after a little more experience.[14]

In other words, the higher the validity of a test, the more accurately can a prediction be made about those tested. This is shown in Table 10–2 in terms of chances of improvement increasing as validity increases.[15]

[14] *Ibid.*, p. 32.

[15] Bernard Hanes, "How Psychological Tests *Can* and *Can't* Help," *Factory Management and Maintenance*, Vol. CXV, No. 11, pp. 152–53.

On the other hand, a test which is supposed to measure something should yield approximately the same answer for the same person at different times (allowing for the memory factor and improvement on the job because of experience). The degree to which a given test does yield consistently the same scores is a measure of its reliability and is also commonly expressed as a coefficient of correlation.

TABLE 10–2

How Tests Take the Gamble out of Personnel Selection

Validity Coefficient of Test	Percent Improvement over Chance
.20	2
.30	5
.40	8
.50	13
.60	20
.70	29

An example of a simple determination of reliability is provided by the following case in which pupils who had been given a test in blueprint reading were later retested:

Months later, people were retested at random, the same test being used. There was an improvement in the scores, but not more than 7 points. Seven points out of 100 is a negligible figure which could be charged to remembrance or practice. Theoretically, we could say that each person hit his own level again on a retest, and that the test was reliable. Or, in other words, that each time it was used one could depend on getting accurate results. The reliability of a test can be bettered by lengthening it. This should not be done to extremes because the element of writing fatigue may void any good results. Employment tests should not run more than 30 minutes to be practical.[16]

Rules of Testing

This discussion can perhaps best be summarized by noting some rules of good testing practice. Such rules may be grouped under the headings of (1) human relations aspects, (2) operational suggestions, and (3) uses of test scores.

1. *Human Relations Aspects.* The user of tests must be extremely sensitive to the feelings of people about tests. Most people are relatively concerned about whether tests will disclose fairly their real capacities or will be used fairly in appraising them. It is well known by test administrators that people will often try either to give the "right" answers or slant their reactions. As a consequence, insofar as possible,

---

[16] R. W. Gillette, "Tests Help You Hire Right," *Factory Management and Maintenance,* Vol. XCIX, No. 10, p. 80.

tests must be constructed and administered so as to minimize the probabilities of getting distorted results.

On the other hand, steps must be taken to reduce the reasonable fears and suspicions of people. Careful explanation of the purposes and uses of tests are helpful. Pointing out that tests alone are not the sole criterion in making decisions is desirable. Explaining that high scores on all factors are not required is useful. Stressing the fact that tests are not intended merely to seek out weaknesses is reassuring. And above all, proving through actions subsequent to testing that one takes cognizance of the whole man—his strengths and his weaknesses—serves to bring out favorable reactions to tests.

2. *Operational Suggestions.* Several operational suggestions are in order. It is highly desirable to make careful job and position studies as a basis for building tests. Job analysis is essential in order to determine the skills, aptitudes, or other characteristics for which tests must be designed. Until this information is obtained, the selection or development of tests can only be based on guesswork.

Moreover, it is generally agreed that tests should be selected or developed with a view to particular jobs in a particular company. Although there are tests which may have general reliability, such as the general intelligence test, specific adaptations are invariably called for. Local conditions, variations in jobs (even with the same title), and differences in company policies and operation methods are sufficient reason for making individual adaptations.

Another operational rule is that reliance should not be placed solely upon tests in reaching decisions. Tests are most useful when they are given a part in the task of selection, placement, or training of employees. Other devices such as application blanks, interviews, and rating scores should be given a prominent role. There is a danger that one's initial enthusiasm for tests may tend unwarrantedly to relegate these other instruments to a small role. When this first flush has passed, there is equal danger that tests may be discarded for failing to provide all the answers.

There also are operational rules related to testing. On the one hand, adequate time and resources must be provided to design, validate, and check tests. Any attempt to hurry is an almost inevitable invitation to ineffectual results. On the other hand, the effect of time upon people must be considered. Most people change with time. Hence a test used to select for initial employment should be used only to judge a candidate for that job. If it is desired to test for promotability or potential, interest and aptitude tests are in order. The latter, it must be remembered, are less accurate than trade tests. The accuracy of tests of both aptitude and proficiency is not of such a high order that they can be applied indiscriminately.

3. *Uses of Test Scores.* Some comments on the use of test scores are also in order. Care must be exercised in determining the critical score of a test. This is the point at which unsuccessful candidates are to be cut off, and is illustrated in Table 10–3. But it is well to establish

TABLE 10–3

HOW A CRITICAL SCORE SEPARATES GOOD
AND POOR WORKERS

Test Score	Poor Employees	Good Employees
100		1
90		4
80		6
70	2	5
60.....Critical Score.....0		4
50	7	2
40	8	
30	6	
20	4	
10	2	
0	1	

SOURCE: Bernard Hanes, "How Psychological Tests *Can* and *Can't* Help," *Factory Management and Maintenance*, Vol. CXV, No. 11, pp. 152–53.

upper as well as lower cutoff points. A person may eventually prove unsatisfactory if he is too intelligent for the job in question.

Care must also be exercised to interpret and use correlation figures correctly. A high validity rating does not mean that the given test can be used with impunity. For example, an individual may score low on a test of high validity. Yet, through high personal motivation, he may more than make up for, let us say, a minimum of technical skill. On the other hand, a test with a low validity rating may nevertheless give a valuable clue to a particular applicant's strength or weakness.

Organizationally speaking, some rules on test usage are worth noting. Only the expert—the psychologist, consultant, or staff specialist—should be allowed to design, select, and interpret tests. He should be the keeper of the tests, scores, and related information. Others have an interest in them and have a right to the benefit of testing. So the line and staff executives and supervisors should cooperate in the use of tests, but it should be a relation of doctor and patient. The expert should be recognized as the authority; and he will be if, like the doctor, he proves his worth in supplying needed help.

In the final analysis, tests must be judged in terms of their contribution to the solution of problems of selection, placement, and training.

Such judgments might not be too difficult to arrive at were it always possible to try out various tests by comparing test scores with the production records of employees. But unlimited resources are seldom provided for such research. As a consequence, most tests must be devised and evaluated within time limits and budget expenditures that do not allow all the latitude that might be desired.

QUESTIONS

1. If testing is, among other things, a sampling process, how does one know when one has an adequate and representative sample?
2. What are the fundamental assumptions that underlie the use of psychological test in employment?
3. Look up the meaning of the words "diagnostic" and "prognostic." What relation do these terms have with the use of tests?
4. Assume that an applicant for a job receives a score of, let us say, 69 on a battery of tests for which the passing grade is 70. What would your decision in this case be, and why?
5. Explain the difference between tests designed to measure acquired skills and those designed to measure aptitude.
6. What relationship is there between organization structure and the development and use of tests? How does this relationship change as a company grows from small to very large size with decentralized branch office or factory operations?
7. Visit a few companies using tests, and write a report covering such points as how long it took to get reasonably good results, obstacles that had to be overcome, and what tangible proof they have of the effectiveness of testing.
8. Indicate what is meant by validity and reliability of tests. Describe how measures of validity and reliability may be obtained.
9. In what respects must human relations be given consideration in developing and operating a testing program?
10. In order to minimize misuse of tests, what advice would you underline in preparing a report to a company that is proceeding to install a new program?

CHAPTER 11

TRANSFERS AND PROMOTIONS

Scope of Transfers and Promotions

Many vacancies are filled by internal movements of present employees. These movements are termed transfers and promotions. The former term refers to changes in which the pay, status, and job conditions of the new position are approximately the same as of the old. In the case of promotions, the new position has higher pay, status, and job conditions as compared with the old.

Handling a program of transfers and promotions requires attention to a number of details, which are discussed here under the following headings:

1. Purposes of transfer and promotion programs
2. Operational aspects
3. Practical limitations
4. Seniority aspects

Purposes

The primary purpose of a transfer or promotion is to increase the effectiveness of the organization in attaining its service and profit objectives. When an employee is placed in a position in which he can be most productive, chances for successful results of the organization for which he works are consequently increased. It should be the aim, therefore, of any company to change positions of employees as soon as their capacities increase and opportunities warrant.

Another significant purpose of transfers and promotions is of a personal nature. Job changes provide an opportunity for present employees to move into jobs that provide greater personal satisfaction and prestige. Being transferred to a new job may open up new avenues of advancement or add the spice of variety to daily routines. Often, too, prestige is a factor, in that the person transferred is publicly recognized for his accomplishments. Of course, not all employees want to be transferred or promoted. Many like the assurance of a settled security; yet, most like to feel that opportunities for transfer or promotion are available.

Operational Aspects

Transfer and promotion systems are either informal or formal. Under the informal plan, decisions as to who should be transferred or promoted usually await the occurrence of a vacancy. Moreover, the bases upon which decisions are made vary from vacancy to vacancy and from time to time. As a consequence, no one knows what his status is or is likely to be under this system. But its use is often justified because of its simplicity or because of the infrequency of job changes.

The informal plan gives way, as a company grows or as the losses in morale flowing from it become evident, to some formal program. The plan may be based upon a system of pertinent job and man information or upon the seniority of employees. In this section, attention is directed first to the informational systems and then to seniority plans.

A systematic plan of transfers and promotions which pretends to be complete must contain the following:

1. A plan of job relationships
2. A plan and policy for selecting appropriate employees
3. A plan of records and reports

1. *Plan of Job Relationships.* The basic step in building a plan of transfer and promotion is that of determining the horizontal and vertical relations between jobs. Thus, for each job a schedule must be provided of the jobs (*a*) to which transfers may be made and (*b*) to which promotions may be made.

Job analysis is an indispensable tool for making such determinations. It provides information on the skill, experience, training, responsibility, and environmental factors involved in each job. Comparing such information for various jobs serves to disclose which jobs are related because of similar job requirements. Then, on each job specification, as illustrated in Figure 11–1, the jobs from and to which changes can logically be made are listed. Here, it is shown that a molding machine operator may be promoted to a divider man, promoted from a pan greaser or a molding machine helper, or transferred to a cake-baker helper or wrapping machine helper.

Establishing such job relationships does not imply that lines of transfer and promotion are unbending. If it happens that a particular

FIGURE 11–1

JOB SPECIFICATION

Job Title: <u>MOLDING MACHINE OPERATOR</u>   Department: <u>MAKE-UP</u>

EMPLOYEE QUALIFICATIONS

MALE:<u> X </u> FEMALE:<u>   </u> ENGLISH S:<u> X </u> R:<u> X </u> W:<u> X </u> Race:<u> W </u>

EDUCATION: Public<u>   </u> High<u>   X   </u> or Baker's<u>   </u>

EXPERIENCE: 2 months Pan Greaser and Molding Machine Helper.

PHYSICAL REQUIREMENTS: No contagious or venereal disease; pass physical examination of food handler; normal eyesight.

MISCELLANEOUS: Worker must be careful, honest, co-operative, dependable, and alert. Must have fine sense of touch and good memory. Must have ability to move hands rapidly and skillfully to twist pieces of dough.

CONDITION OF WORK

Machine<u>   X   </u>   Hand<u>   </u>   Heavy<u>   </u> Light<u>   </u> Medium<u>   X   </u>

Stand<u>   X   </u>   Sitting<u>   </u>   Stooping<u>   </u>   Hazard<u>   X   </u>

Rough<u>   X   </u>   Accurate<u>   </u>   Inside<u>   X   </u>   Outside<u>   </u>

Dusty<u>   X   </u>   Hot<u>   X   </u>   Cold<u>   </u>   Dirty<u>   </u>   Greasy<u>   </u>

Quick<u>   X   </u>   Slow<u>   </u>   Humid<u>   </u>   Sticky<u>   X   </u>

Miscellaneous:

EMPLOYEE INFORMATION

RATE OF PAY: $2.40 hr.; time and ½ for overtime.

HOURS OF WORK: 8-hr. day, 48-hr. week, Sunday to Friday; longer hours overtime.

WORK SHIFT: 1 P.M. to 9 P.M.

VACATION: One year, one week; five years, two weeks.

PROMOTIONS: May be promoted to Divider Man.
May be promoted from Pan Greaser and Molding Machine Helper.
May be transferred to Cake Baker apprentice or Wrapping Machine Helper.

PERSONAL EFFECTS REQUIRED: White uniform, hat, and apron.

DUTIES

1. Under general supervision of Divider Man to properly mold all bread into cylindrical form.
2. To uniformly twist pieces of dough together.
3. To put into pans twisted pieces of dough.
4. Supervise Pan Greaser and Molding Machine Helper to see that proper types and amount of pans are greased prior to beginning of run and to see that panned bread is properly racked.

person filling a job has the qualifications, as often happens, to jump into another line of progression, this should be permitted. However, this is a matter of personal qualifications and does not destroy the validity of natural job relationships.

When job relationships have been fully explored in this manner, it is desirable to construct promotion and transfer charts, samples of which are shown in Figures 11–2, 11–3, and 11–4. Such diagrams may

FIGURE 11–2. A Progression Chart

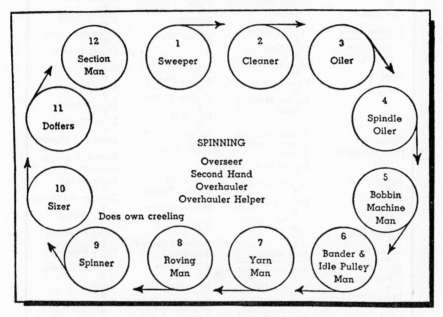

SOURCE: "Training New Employees Quickly," *Textile World*, Vol. XCIII, No. 7, p. 60.

appear to be complicated, but study of them quickly provides an answer regarding the jobs to which changes can be made. Moreover, such diagrams are superior to the images of job relationships that exist merely in the minds of executives and employees. And such images are seldom identical.

2. *Selecting Candidates for Promotion.* The next important part of a transfer and promotion plan is that by which employees are selected for available job vacancies. The significance of this to employees cannot be overestimated. In their eyes, this is the crucial test of the fairness of a company's plan. Hence, care should be exercised to select employees according to agreed-upon standards and not upon personal whim. Where a union is involved, such agreement will usually

FIGURE 11–3. Upgrading Sequence Chart for Job Classifications in a Cotton Textile Plant

Carding:
Section Hand
↑
Card Grinder
↑
Card Tender
↑
Card Stopper
Slubber Hand and Fly Frame Tender
↑
Can Turner
↑
Transfer Hand
Draw Frame Tender
↑
Oiler

Spinning:
Fixer and Section Man
↑
Doffer
↑
Sizer
↑
Spinner
↑
Roving Man
↑
Yarn Man
↑
Band and Idle Pul. Man
↑
Spindle Oiler
↑
Oiler
↑
Cleaner

Upgrading sequence chart for job classifications in a cotton textile plant.

Spooling:
Section Man
↑
Section Man Helper
↑
Spooler Hand
↑
Yarn Man
↑
Piece Rocker
↑
Yarn Cleaner
↑
Tailing Machine Hand

Warp Twisting, Warping and Winding:
Section Man
↑
Twister Tender
↑
Twister Creeler
↑
Twister Doffer
↑
Oiler
↑
Reel Hand
Warper Tender
↑
Warper Helper
↑
Warper Creeler
Winder Tender
↑
Winder Helper

Filling Twisting:
Section Man
↑
Doffer
↑
Creeler
↑
Filling Helper

Slashing:
Section Man
↑
Slasher Tender
↑
Size Man
↑
Slasher Helper
↑
Beam Man

Beaming:
Beamer Tender
↑
Beamer Helper

Drawing-in and Tying-in
Section Man
↑
Drawing-in Hand
↑
Drawing-in Helper
↑
Tying-in Operator
↑
Tying-in Helper

Weaving:
Loom Fixer
↑
Weaver
↑
Tying-on Warps
↑
Laying-up Warps
↑
Pick-out Hand
↑
Smash Hand
↑
Battery Hand
↑
Taking-off Cloth
↑
Filling Hauler
↑
Oiler
↑
Cloth Hauler
↑
Loom Blower
↑
Loom Cleaner
↑
Overhead Cleaner

Baling, Trading, Burling:
Folder Hand
↑
Brander and Sewer
↑
Press Booker
↑
Head Pressman
↑
Press Helper
↑
Baler and Sewer
↑
Grader
↑
Remnant Hand
↑
Calender Hand
↑
Burler

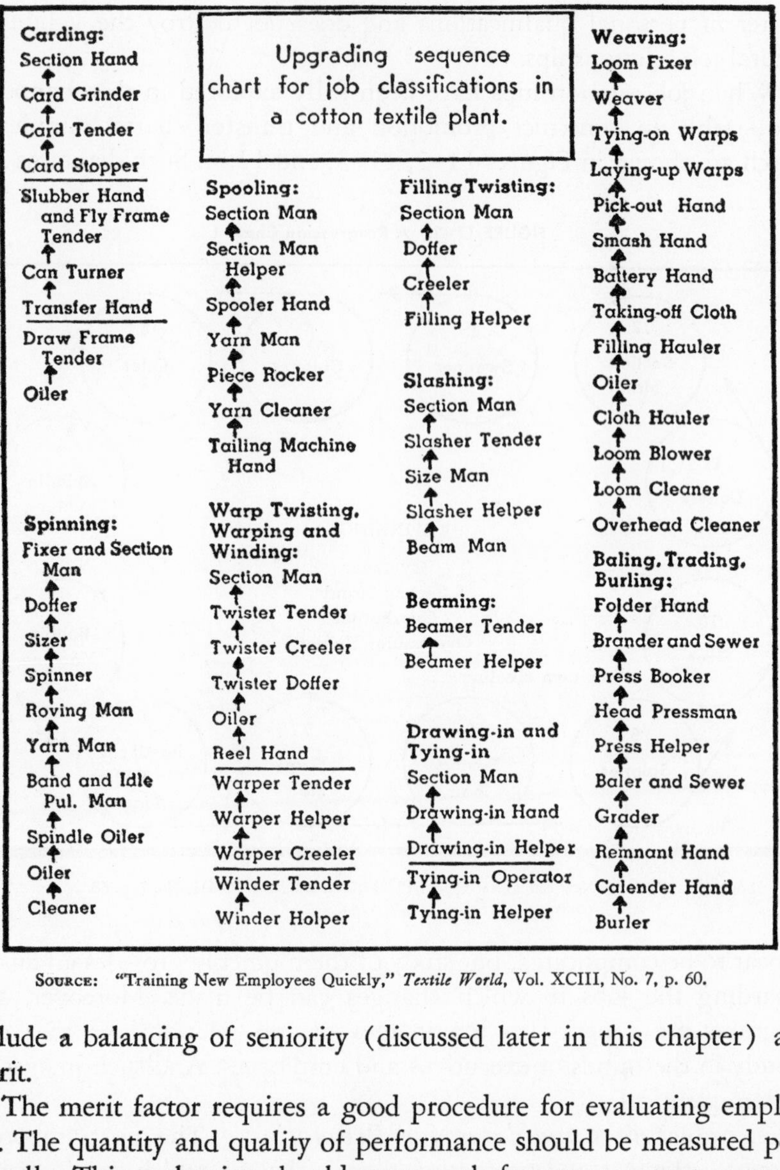

SOURCE: "Training New Employees Quickly," *Textile World*, Vol. XCIII, No. 7, p. 60.

include a balancing of seniority (discussed later in this chapter) and merit.

The merit factor requires a good procedure for evaluating employees. The quantity and quality of performance should be measured periodically. This evaluation should cover such factors as output, cooperation, willingness to accept responsibility, degree of initiative, and ability to get along with others. An excellent illustration of how this may be done in connection with supervisor positions is shown in Figure 11–5. Evaluations are discussed more fully in the next chapter.

The plan of employee evaluation should include an arrangement for

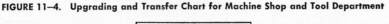

FIGURE 11–4. Upgrading and Transfer Chart for Machine Shop and Tool Department

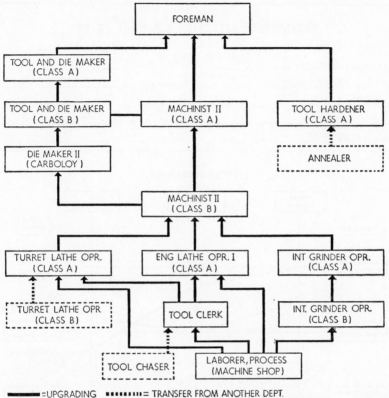

consultation and perhaps vocational guidance. By discussing a person's strong and weak points before vacancies occur, a two-edged weapon is employed. Those who are ambitious can get suggestions on how to improve themselves. On the other hand, a record of such discussions can be cited to those who did not get a desired job because they failed to follow suggestions. When discussions with employees take place only after transfers or promotions are not received, it is difficult to convince disgruntled employees that they were fairly treated. This is an example of the principle that, to be acceptable, standards should be discussed before as well as after application.

3. *Records and Reports.* A third important part of a transfer and promotion plan is that of designing adequate records and reports. The system should include the following:

a) Forecasts of job vacancies
b) Central reporting of vacancies
c) Locating qualified employees

FIGURE 11–5

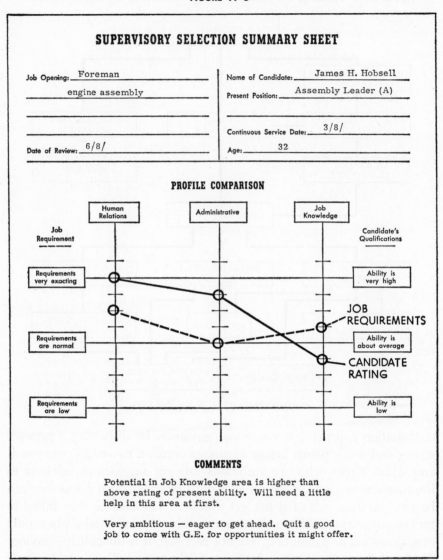

d) Notification of all parties concerned
e) Follow-up of transferred and promoted personnel

a) *Forecasting Vacancies.* Efforts should be made to determine how many vacancies are likely to occur during coming periods on various jobs. Advance preparations can then be made to locate qualified employees. As a consequence, the stability of the organization can be maintained. Moreover, the danger of overselling present employees on the probabilities of advancement will be minimized. It is indeed destruc-

FIGURE 11–5 (Continued)

JOB REQUIREMENTS OF POSITION TO BE FILLED

1. CHARACTER OF GROUP TO BE SUPERVISED

Consider:

Size of group 25 men - 3 women
Ratio—male to female

Age distribution 18 to 40 - mostly young

Educational levels mostly H. S. Grads

Special problems (such as
turnover, training, etc.)   new group, but training requirement
not high (Vestibule training school)

Supervision—direct or
through assistants.

3 group leaders

2. ADMINISTRATIVE RESPONSIBILITIES

Consider nature and
amount of:

Planning
Paper work   Close coordination of flow of parts
Coordination required. Must handle payroll, rework,
and production records.

Consider special
requirements in Group incentive system
regard to:

Quality   Quality (workmanship requirement
Quantity   very high - Air Force project - Inspection
Cost   very demanding.)

3. GENERAL NATURE OF OPERATION

Consider:

Tools   Mostly hand tools - no big equipment
Equipment

Processes   Assembly of large parts - semi-skilled
Skilled or unskilled   and unskilled

Manufacturing or assembly

Mass production or job shop   Mass production assembly line
Working conditions   good
Fluctuations in work load   steady

tive of morale when employees are led to expect job changes that do not materialize.

Such forecasts are not overly difficult to make, provided that information on future sales volume and personnel turnover is available. As noted in Chapter 6, "Job and Manpower Requirements," it is then possible to estimate with a practical degree of accuracy how many vacancies will have to be filled. For example, in a company that has forty supervisors at present, turnover of supervisors has been 10 percent

FIGURE 11-5 *(Continued)*

CANDIDATE'S QUALIFICATIONS IN RELATION TO JOB REQUIREMENTS

1. POTENTIAL ABILITY IN THE HUMAN RELATIONS AREA

(Ability to gain respect and cooperation of others, motivate others, handle relations with superiors and staff, etc.)

Consider:
Maturity
Effect on others
Attitude towards others
Other personality characteristics

Very good personality for supervision. Very successful as a working leader. A lot of successful leadership experience. This is his strong suit.

2. POTENTIAL ABILITY IN THE ADMINISTRATIVE AREA

(Ability to plan, organize, delegate, make decisions, handle paper work, etc.)

Consider:
Work habits
Application
Education and training
Verbal and numerical abilities
Motivation and interests

According to indications based on his present work habits he should be very good in this area. A good organizer. Scores well above average in mental tests. Interested in assuming more responsibility.

3. POTENTIAL ABILITY IN THE JOB KNOWLEDGE AREA

(Familiarity with jobs to be supervised, Company policies and procedures, etc.)

Consider:
Work experience
Technical competence
Abilities or aptitudes important to success in the work

Experience limited to assembly work. Not familiar with all types of assembly work. However, he scored very high on test of mechanical comprehension, and he has had one year of engineering school (M.I.T.) so he should be able to pick this up very easily.

annually, and increases in volume of business are expected to increase the supervisory force by about 5 percent annually; hence, six vacancies will have to be filled in the supervisory ranks during the coming year.

Another effective way of forecasting vacancies is to show the ages of executives on the organization chart. This can be done graphically by using different colors for different age groups—e.g., red for ages 50 and over, orange for 40–49, blue for 30–39, green for 20–29, and brown for 19 and under. Such an organization chart will immediately show the

FIGURE 11–5 (Continued)

SUMMARY RECOMMENDATION

Generals

      Should make a very good first-line supervisor.

Recommendation as to his major training needs:

      Needs more diversified job experience.

Estimate of Future Growth:

      With technical experience (know-how) has potential
      to advance to higher supervisory levels.

If not appointed to a supervisory job, this candidate
Is best qualified for what other type of work (if any)?

      Leader - present job. Perhaps special
      assignments where working with people is important.

This Summary Evaluation Made by ____H. Dorner_____

general areas which may be out of balance in terms of age groups and in which steps should be taken to provide for transfers or promotions. In what areas training of executives for transfer and promotion should be undertaken may also be disclosed.

b) Reporting Vacancies. Central reporting of vacancies is an essential of a good transfer and promotion plan. Otherwise, some vacancies will be filled from the outside rather than from within. As a consequence, employees will tend to lose confidence in the company's interest in them. The procedure which suggests itself here is (1) to have all hiring done on a requisition basis and (2) to have all requisitions pass through the hands of a transfer and promotion section in the personnel department. In this way, requisitions can be reviewed with an eye to filling vacancies from within before outside sources are explored. This may result in some delay during rush periods, but it is offset by better employee confidence in management's consideration of employee interests.

c) Locating Candidates. Locating qualified (whether by merit or seniority) employees requires a search of personnel records. This is a formidable task when files of written records must be examined personally. But the use of tabulating equipment or electronic computers to store and search for information speeds up the process immeasurably. Reference to such records was made in Chapter 9. See also Figure 11–6.

Of course, a record should also be maintained of employees who specifically request or are recommended by their superiors for transfer or promotion.

Another method of locating candidates is that of job posting. Under this method, notice of vacancies (as illustrated in Figure 11–7) is posted on bulletin boards and on the time clock or is announced through the company newspaper or some other form of communication. Such posting may be limited to the department or division in which the vacancy occurs, or it may be posted on a company-wide basis. The notice may be posted for some limited time—e.g., a week or ten days—or it may remain posted until the job is filled, no matter how much time is needed. This practice of posting has grown out of union desires that present employees be allowed an opportunity to bid on good jobs before outsiders are given a chance at them.

d) Authorizations and Notifications. Another important aspect of a procedure of transfers and promotions is that of proper authorizations and notifications. On the one hand, the central unit responsible for locating qualified workers should not be permitted to initiate transfers of its own accord. It should request superiors of qualified employees to authorize a job change. It may have to "sell" its requests, but this is better than staff interference with line authority. Then, too, the personnel department should be ready to suggest replacements to the superior who is losing a good man. Such practices will tend to gain line cooperation.

On the other hand, the system should provide for proper notification of all concerned. The person to be changed is usually best informed by

FIGURE 11–6. Employee Information Card

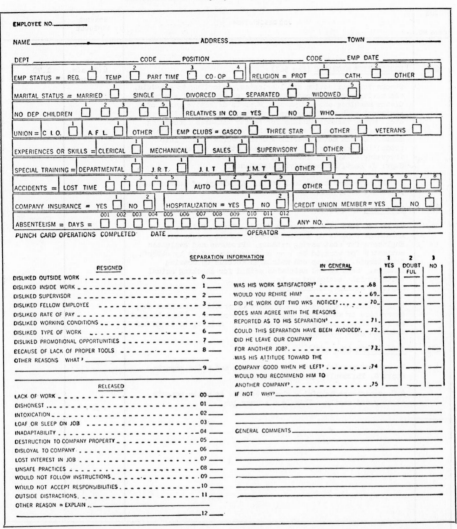

his own superior. In that way, line authority is not divided. In addition, subordinates are impressed favorably by executives who show signs of looking after the interests of employees. The approval of the new superior under whom the employee is to work must also be obtained by the personnel department. In this way the staff position of the personnel department does not intrude upon the authority of the line department served. And finally, notices of the change should go to the payroll department, personal history section of the personnel department, and any other sections that keep records of employees.

FIGURE 11–7. Job Postings

JOB CODE NO.	JOB DESCRIPTION	WORKING SCHEDULE	JOB RATE
283	**LUBRICATION MECHANIC** (Req 567) Checks for lubrication and lubricates, according to schedule, the moving parts or wearing surfaces of mechanical equipment. Cleans machines and equipment. Reports defective parts of equipment such as worn belts, worn bearings, loose flywheel, etc. Makes recommendations for safety measures concerning equipment on which he works. Makes simple bearing replacements. Checks motor bearing spacing, works to fit into production schedule. Makes recommendations for change in frequency or type of lubrication. Supv: J. Lunt, Preventative Maintenance. Should have good mechanical sense. Knowledge of lubricating procedure essential.	6:00 a.m. 2:30 p.m.	1.70
252	**ESTIMATOR** (Req 622) Estimates cost on all jobs in Machine Shop. Sets up and maintains records on all estimates. Checks prints with Engineers for cost saving methods. Procures and evaluates estimates for work to be done on breakdown orders by other departments. Sets up and maintains records on drawing changes. Sets up and maintains method for checking actual costs against estimated costs. Supv: R. Wilkins, Machine Shop. High School or equivalent - 2 years in practical machine shop experience or mechanical estimating experience. (Must be good at figures and have neat hand writing.) Ability to learn and maintain good office procedures.		420/mo Group 15
253	**Q.C. TESTER** (Req 457) To conduct special tests, evaluate data and write reports. Supv: G. Thibeault, Quality Control. Q.C. experience helpful - should be able to write reports clearly and easily. This is a summer job.	8:00-4:45	1.60

It is our general policy to fill job openings from within the company when there are qualified candidates among our own people. If you are interested in any of the above jobs, please tell your supervisor or contact Personnel *immediately*. Jobs will be posted for three days before being filled. Occasional exceptions may be made when particular speed is necessary in filling the vacancy, and recent postings of similar jobs have brought no response. The details of how the Job Posting System operates are contained in Personnel Instructions 52-12 which your Supervisor can show you.

POSTING DATE: 7/10/56

SOURCE: H. G. Pearson, "Pros and Cons of Job Posting," *Personnel*, Vol. XXXIII, No. 3, p. 274.

e) Follow-up. The final step of a good transfer and promotion plan is that of follow-up. After an interval of a month or two, a brief interview would suffice to determine whether all is going well or whether some form of corrective action is in order. This form of feedback is similar to that recommended for new employees. After all, the changed employee is a new employee in his new job, even though he is an old employee in the company.

Some companies allow the feedback to come from the employee himself in the form of a grievance or complaint. This assumes that all employees will air their dissatisfactions, which is not true. Moreover, it places upon the employee the responsibility for a function that is largely managerial, and management should not shirk its responsibilities.

Limitations

Whether or not, and to what extent, a transfer and promotion plan can be put into operation depends upon a number of factors. Obviously, there must be sufficient vacancies to warrant investment in an involved plan. That is why a small company or one in which turnover is very low would be foolish to waste time and resources on a formal plan. The objectives to be gained would not be worth the effort.

If there is danger of "inbreeding," a plan of filling the better positions from within should not be adopted. In organizations where new ideas, initiative, and originality rate a premium, outside hirings are to be preferred. Otherwise, replacements are bound to be made with employees who know little more, if anything, than those whom they replaced. The result is bound to be unsatisfactory in a highly competitive situation.

Again, a plan of transfers and promotions should be circumscribed if satisfactory horizontal and vertical job relationships cannot be readily established. Thus, where jobs in a factory or office differ radically, it may not be possible to establish job sequences which make it possible for a candidate to progress readily from one job to another. In such cases a plan of training must be established so that those who deserve transfers or promotions can be prepared for job changes.

Perhaps the most serious problem of transfer and promotion plans arises out of the difficulty of measuring the overall qualifications of employees. It is a formidable task to measure and weigh together such factors as quantity and quality of output, cooperation, acceptance of responsibility, and aptitude for progress. Nor is it easy to explain the results to those who are affected by such measurements. To face up to the development of a good measuring plan or to accept the simpler but less logical plan of seniority is a choice of perplexing difficulty.

Seniority

Length of service—or seniority—is a governing factor in matters of transfers and promotions in many companies. It is also of particular significance in collective bargaining, which is discussed in Chapter 25.

Attention to this important subject is directed here to the following aspects:

1. Calculating length of service
2. Balancing merit and seniority
3. Privileges affected by seniority
4. Areas of application

1. *Calculating Seniority.* The method of calculating length of service is an important part of a seniority plan. It should provide for the following factors: (*a*) when seniority starts to accumulate, (*b*) effect of various interruptions to employment, and (*c*) the effect of transfers and promotions upon seniority calculation.

a) *Accumulating Seniority.* When there are no outside factors involved, seniority begins to accumulate as soon as an employee is hired. This should be specifically stated, particularly when a company undertakes collective bargaining. Otherwise, there is a possibility that the seniority of employees hired before a contract goes into effect may be dated from the date of the contract. Also, in the case of union contracts, it is important to note whether or not new employees have seniority rights during their period of probation and whether or not the probationary period will be included in the calculation of seniority. Again, where large numbers of employees are hired on the same date, a question of seniority may arise unless a basis for priority is established. In such instances, priority may be established upon such an arbitrary basis as order of clock numbers assigned or alphabetical listing.

b) *Interruptions to Service.* After seniority begins to accumulate, there are a number of interruptions to service for which provision should be made. Ordinarily, interruptions that are due to the company's actions or are relatively short are customarily not deducted in calculating seniority. For example, time off for short personal absences, layoffs, and sick leaves are included in seniority accumulations. However, extended leaves of absence, layoffs beyond designated periods of time, and extended sick leaves are often deducted in computing seniority. These aspects of calculating seniority will not cause difficulty so long as they are recognized and provided for.

c) *Job Changes and Seniority.* More difficult to handle is the effect of transfers and promotions upon seniority calculations. For example, workers may be unwilling to accept or may even refuse transfers if the change means a loss of seniority. Or workers who have been promoted to a supervisory position and later demoted have sometimes found themselves at the bottom of a seniority list. Except in a few industries, such as the building trades, where the seniority of foremen is protected, the seniority status of supervisors and transferees is not protected traditionally unless specifically stated by company policy or union agreement.[1] Hence, it is desirable, when questions of this type are likely to arise, to specify what the seniority privileges will be. Perhaps the fairest provision is to allow demoted supervisors the seniority they had before the promotion took place. In the case of transferees, it would seem fair to allow them to retain their seniority if they return to their old jobs and to have some measure of adjusted seniority if they remain on their new jobs. Otherwise, only the most adventuresome will be willing to transfer.

Exemptions from seniority rules may also be desirable for technical and professional employees and for trainees. In order to avoid discriminatory practices in connection with such groups, unions sometimes require that the number of exempted employees must be limited to some percentage of nonexempted groups. In any event, to prove its fairness to all employees, it is well for management to define specifically exempt jobs and positions, and to restrict the conditions under which the exemptions shall apply.

2. *Merit versus Seniority.* A second important part of any seniority plan is the matter of balancing seniority in relation to merit. This will occasion much debate unless carefully defined. It might seem that a statement such as the following would be clear and fair: "As between two employees with equal ability, the one with the greater seniority will be given preference." To begin with, does ability refer to the minimum required for the job or to relative abilities of candidates? Employees usually argue for the former, while management argues for the latter. Moreover, there is the usual conflict about the accuracy of management in measuring ability.

Whatever hope a company may have to work out a plan balancing merit and seniority will depend, therefore, upon a number of factors. First, a set of job and man specifications should be carefully prepared, so that claimants for jobs can be shown that requirements are objective and not capricious. Second, a complete and thoroughly understood transfer and promotion plan should be promulgated. Third, a good system of employee merit rating should be installed. Merit must be measurable, or its proponents have built their house of arguments upon sand. This system must consider the views of the union, and ratings

---

[1] Giving a person such as a supervisor, shop stewart, or committeeman preference in layoffs or rehirings without regard to service is also termed superseniority or preferential seniority.

under it should be subject to some set plan of review. Fourth, performance standards should be set as objectively as possible, so that measurements of employee productivity and cooperation may be more readily acceptable by all. And lastly, a well-thought-out grievance procedure should be established which is acceptable to employees and to the union, if employees are so represented. These requirements are not easily met; until they are, there is little use in arguing for merit in place of seniority.

3. *Employment Privileges Affected.* The relative weight that seniority will have upon various classes of employment privileges also should be carefully defined. For example, it may be completely controlling in such matters as length of vacations and choice of vacation periods; or it may be controlling in choice of work periods, shifts, or runs in the case of transportation services. On the other hand, it may be only partly controlling in such matters as transfers and promotions. Similarly, in the matter of discharges and layoffs, seniority may be given part or total weight. In any event, the effect upon these employment aspects should be considered individually if disagreements are to be minimized.

Moreover, how seniority shall apply in each class must also be determined. For example, limitations must be placed on senior employees who replace or "bump" junior employees. Senior employees may be required within a given period of time to demonstrate that they can competently perform the jobs of employees they bump, or junior employees may be protected if they hold special types of jobs or if they have been with the company for a specified number of years.

On recall of employees after a production layoff, seniority rules vary. In some companies, no new employees may be hired until all available laid-off employees are recalled. In other cases the company may have some discretion in hiring new employees as compared to layoffs. In addition, the sequence of recalling senior employees should be carefully indicated in terms of area of work to which their seniority applies and in terms of its importance relative to merit.

4. *Area of Application.* Finally, the application of the seniority principle should give consideration to the area to which it applies. For example, it is unwise to give seniority company-wide application in such matters as transfers. Otherwise, the result will be that workers unqualified for vacancies will nevertheless apply for them if they have company-wide seniority. Hence, it is important to select carefully the area over which, or the occupations within which, seniority of given classes of employees will apply.

The usual areas of application are the department, the occupation (the "family" classification), or the company. No one of these of itself is without disadvantages. As noted above, the company-wide plan unduly favors the senior employee who wants to bump more qualified employees in departments outside the immediate experience of the senior employee. In the case of departmental plans, very capable and key employees may be lost because they cannot replace less qualified employees with less service in other departments. And the occupational plan may be affected by the disadvantages of the departmental or company-wide plan, depending upon how narrow or wide the job family in a given occupation happens to be.

To minimize disadvantages arising out of seniority areas, it may be desirable to establish restrictive rules. For example, company-wide seniority may be applied to all unskilled and semiskilled jobs, departmental seniority may be applied to skilled jobs, and occupational seniority may be applied to certain highly specialized classifications. Another restrictive rule, of course, is that of applying merit qualifications to such seniority areas.

Summary

In summary, the seniority plan of determining employment changes has the advantage of apparent simplicity in its favor. However, as may be deduced from the foregoing discussion, extreme care must be exercised in writing the seniority clauses; otherwise, troubles will arise that may be more bothersome than those it had been hoped to avoid. The major disadvantage of the seniority plan is that merit and ability tend to receive a minor place in reaching employment decisions.

Yet the position taken by some unions in favor of seniority is readily understandable. For one thing, one can scarcely argue about such a definite matter as the date on which an employee started to work with the company. On the other hand, merit ratings and interpretations of the relative abilities of employees to advance are subject to some debate, even when the best of systems is employed. So a union cannot be blamed for refusing to embroil itself in such arguments. For another thing, though less justifiable, there are the traditional arguments, which some unions still uphold, that all employees in a given occupation or unit of work are to be treated alike. If individual differences were recognized, this would lead to arguments within the union itself. This internal debate would weaken the solidarity of the union's bargaining power with the company. Hence, it is more sensible for the union to forgo theoretical accuracy in order to enhance membership solidarity.

Unless more definite and acceptable methods of calculating ability and merit are applied, however, seniority may be expected to retain, if not to gain, a higher place as a tool for measuring employment preferences.

QUESTIONS

1. What are the purposes of transfers and promotions?

2. Why is a good plan of employee evaluation so important in operating a transfer and promotion plan? Are employees likely to be more trustful of executives when a rating plan is in use?

3. An employee is dissatisfied because he has not received a transfer he considers should have been his. How would you go about convincing him that the right decision has been made?

4. How do you think an organization chart showing the age range of executives would be received by the executives? If they objected, what would your course of action be if you thought such a chart was desirable to point out future personnel needs at the upper levels?

5. If any company in your community is using job posting, ask one of their executives how the plan is working out. If a union is involved, try to get their opinions, too. How do the two sets of opinions agree?

6. Assume that a given supervisor is opposed to recommending transfers or promotions of his employees because he contends that he would thereby be faced with the task of replacing skilled workers with untrained employees. What arguments would you give in rebuttal?

7. Under what conditions would you advise against transfers and promotions as means of filling job vacancies?

8. Develop a plan for calculating length of service. To what factors must consideration be given in making such calculations?

9. Indicate the extent to which seniority should be weighed as compared to merit in relation to such matters as transfers, promotions, demotions, choice of vacation periods, and choice of working shifts.

10. Discuss the merits of seniority plans that are job-wide or apply to a family of jobs, as opposed to those that are company-wide. What problems arise in each case?

CHAPTER **12**

MERIT EVALUATION

Evaluation Programs

As noted in the preceding chapter, employment privileges may be earned by superior performance. In such cases, some plan of evaluating performance must be used. The plans go by such names as merit rating, service appraisal, progress rating, performance evaluation, and merit evaluation. And they have such other uses as in counseling, training, compensation, and handling grievances and disciplinary cases.

Evaluation of employees is one of the oldest and most universal practices of management. It is applied formally or informally to all employees—operative, technical, professional, and executive. Most companies have used formal plans primarily in connection with operative employees. However, a good rating program should encompass all employees of a company, as does that illustrated by Figure 12–1, used in connection with engineers. Hence the discussion in this chapter will give consideration to suggestions which are useful for all levels and categories of employees.

Some managements have given up—or have been forced to give up—formal plans in favor of the seniority plan for determining rewards and privileges. They were discarded because of some defect in the design or use of the plans. The moral is that formal evaluation plans will not, in and of themselves, operate effectively.

The superiority of formalized plans of evaluation can be claimed only when they are planned, operated, and controlled with care. How this may be accomplished is discussed here under the following headings:

1. Objectives
2. Fundamental issues of evaluation
3. Design of rating forms
4. Accuracy of evaluations
5. Rules of evaluation

FIGURE 12–1. Engineer Appraisal Form

BELL & HOWELL COMPANY

NAME _____ CLOCK NO. _____ POSITION _____ DATE _____

APPRAISED BY _____ DATE INTERVIEWED _____

		UNSATISFACTORY	FAIR (Somewhat below average)	GOOD	EXCELLENT (Somewhat above average)	OUTSTANDING (Well above average)
		1 2 3	4 5	6 7 8	9 10 11	12 13 14 5
1.	INITIATIVE Enterprises; drive; capacity for independent action; degree to which he assumes responsibility when orders are lacking; degree to which he follows through on a job despite obstacles.					
2.	COOPERATIVENESS The trait of working wholeheartedly both with and for others in an open-minded objective fashion; possession of the qualities of tact, courtesy, friendliness and tolerance.					
3.	EXPRESSION Facility in expressing ideas both orally and in writing. This implies the ability to communicate ideas in a logical, coherent fashion and the ability to summarize.					
4.	QUANTITY OF WORK Amount of useful output in the light of the opportunities afforded by the job. The output may be written or otherwise.					

5.	QUALITY OF WORK The general excellence of all kinds of output, including written material, with consideration given to the difficulty of the job. Accuracy, thoroughness and dependability of output should be considered, but not quantity. In the case of supervisors, this trait includes skill in directing and guiding others.													
6.	CREATIVENESS Originality, including imagination and inventiveness.													
7.	ENGINEERING OR TECHNICAL JUDGEMENT Skill in analyzing situations and arriving at sound conclusions from available facts even though the available data may be incomplete or seemingly contradictory.													
8.	VERSATILITY & ADAPTABILITY Willing and capable of doing successfully several lines of work, as need arises.													
9.	GENERAL COMPANY INFORMATION The degree of understanding of procedures of major and minor company policies and conformance to them. (See Inst. 3 B)													
10.	BUDGET AND/OR SCHEDULES Ability to perform within budget limitations and/or according to schedules and commitments.													
11.	PROFESSIONAL INTEGRITY Degree of willingness to face facts and follow course of action indicated.													

Objectives of Evaluation

Any of a number of objectives may be sought by means of rating programs. First and foremost is the simple objective of determining more accurately which employees should receive pay increases, which should be given transfers or promotions, and which should be given preferred status. Second, when disputes arise over such matters, the availability of a series of ratings (particularly if they have been discussed with the employees concerned) provides management with information that will help to satisfy the aggrieved persons. Third, from the viewpoint of management, supervisors and executives who know that they will be expected periodically to fill out rating forms (and be prepared to justify their estimates) will tend to be more observant of their subordinates and hence to become better day-to-day supervisors. In the fourth place, when supervisors follow uniform rules of rating, the treatment received by all employees will be more consistent throughout the organization. And lastly, an evaluation program recognizes and seeks to make appropriate adjustments for the existence of individual differences.

An evaluation plan need not encompass all these objectives. Indeed, by union agreement, it may be decided that merit shall have little or nothing to do with choosing candidates for transfer or promotion, let us say. Yet, merit rating could serve as a basis for counseling employees about their strengths and weaknesses or for improving supervisory-employee relations.

This discussion of objectives would be incomplete without the admonition that rating plans must not be used for purposes beyond their capacities. To be specific, some plans have been wrecked by using them to grant general or individual compensation increases that really stemmed from labor market conditions and not from individual merit. When the news gets around that a supervisor has granted someone an increase so as not to lose him, others soon demand the same treatment. Such misuse of merit rating makes everyone a participant in a crooked game that leads to mistrust not only of merit rating but also of other personnel practices of management.

Fundamental Issues of Evaluation

Perhaps the best place to begin a description of merit evaluation is with the fundamental issues raised by evaluation. These include (1) the basic theory of evaluation, (2) the bases of comparison involved in evaluation, and (3) the question of whether or not evaluation should be discussed with employees.

1. *Basic Theory of Evaluation.* As already noted, evaluation is the act of estimating the relative worth of employees in order to determine the rewards, privileges, or advantages that should be given to or withheld from each. One measure of relative worth is the contribution made by each employee. In simple form, this may be diagrammed as follows:

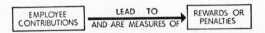

However, it is not always possible to measure employee contributions. Or when it can be done, it nevertheless may be desirable to advise employees how their contributions may be increased. In such instances, it is necessary to ask: What is there about the individual that caused the contribution? For example, individual characteristics, instead of contributions, may be used as the basis of rewards and penalties, as shown in the following diagram:

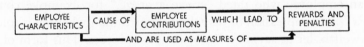

Let us assume that employees A and B receive $2.00 an hour on a given job and are being considered for raises. Their respective contributions to service objectives should be weighed because the contributions that anyone makes to the ultimate customers of a company are the justification for compensation. But if, in the first place, it is impossible to measure such contributions because an individual's work is intermixed with that of others, ratings may be made of the characteristics that caused the contributions. Or second, if it is desired to tell each employee why his contributions are as they are, a rating should be made of employee characteristics as the basis for such suggestions.

2. *Basis of Comparison.* Another fundamental issue of rating concerns the bases of comparing personal characteristics or contributions. When it is said, for example, that employee A is better than employee B, the comparison may be based upon any of the following:

a) The two employees relative to each other
b) A and B as compared to other workers
c) A and B as compared to an ideal worker
d) Arbitrary yardsticks of various factors

Perhaps there is no more common method than that of comparing two or more people in a given situation. To be sure, this practice suffers from the lack of a common and unvarying standard, but it is simple. Hence, some of the earliest attempts to rate employees were based upon a simple ranking of workers. The names of all employees were placed on cards, and the cards were sorted in order, from highest to lowest.

A more modern version is the paired-comparison method. Cards are prepared with two names on each, every employee being paired with every other one in a given unit. The supervisor (or two or more raters) checks on each card the name of the employee he considers to be the better one. A tabulation can then be made showing which employee has received the most checks down to the one who has received the least. These methods do not indicate the relative differences in employees, and the ratings depend upon who is on the payroll at a given time. At least, the rater has put himself on record and is therefore likely to be more careful in his estimates.

Accuracy of ratings may be advanced by comparing all employees with selected employees who are considered to be representative of the best, above average, average, below average, and the poorest. In this way, an employee who rated "above average," for example, could be given a better impression of his relative worth than when he is told that he is twelfth, let us say, in a list of forty employees. This form of man-to-man rating may be improved in two ways. First, several factors may be used in rating man to man. For example, an employee may be compared to a five-man standard in terms of such factors as initiative, cooperation, and dependability. These factor ratings are then arranged to establish an overall grade. Second, instead of using actual employees as standards for best, above average, and so forth, ideal descriptions may be developed. This avoids changes in standards that occur when employees who have been used as models leave the department or company.

While some companies use refined systems of man-to-man rating plans, the trend has been toward plans in which measuring sticks of factors common to all employees are used. For example, Figure 12–2 illustrates a form in which raters evaluate subordinates by checking along lines divided into various lengths to indicate degrees of contribution or personal characteristics. Such graphical methods have gained in favor because qualitative differences are easier to visualize.

3. *Consultations with Employees.* Another important question is whether or not results of evaluations should be discussed with employees. The decision not to do so may be reached for two reasons. First, some companies feel that rating discussions lead to needless controversy and recrimination. And second, in connection with the forced-choice

FIGURE 12-2

EMPLOYEE PROGRESS RATING

NAME OF EMPLOYEE _____ POSITION TITLE AND LINE NO. _____

REPORT BY _____ Date _____ DEPARTMENT _____

LENGTH OF SERVICE: 1. ON THIS JOB _____ 2. WITH COMPANY _____ PREVIOUS RATING _____

GRADING SCALE

1. QUANTITY OF EMPLOYEE'S OWN WORK

How much work does this employee complete as compared with other employees who are doing or have done similar work?

40	50	60	70	80	90
More than 33% under average output. Cannot or does not keep up to acceptable minimums of output. New on job ☐	From 10 to 33% under average output. Works slowly or in short spurts, but produces enough to get by. New on job ☐	Actual output equals output expected after normal training and experience.	From 10 to 33% above average output. Does more than his share. Works rapidly and consistently.	Over 33% above average output. Recognized as a top worker. Consistently top performance.	

Rating ☐ × Weight ☐ = Factor Score ☐

2. QUALITY OF EMPLOYEE'S OWN WORK

How well is his work performed? Consider here the degree of completeness or the number of errors, mistakes and rejections.

40	50	60	70	80	90
More than 34% under quality average. Workmanship very poor. Output has an excess of unacceptable units. New on job ☐	From 10 to 33% under average quality. Quality is occasionally poor and unacceptable. New on job ☐	Quality of work equals that expected after normal training and experience.	From 10 to 33% fewer errors than average. Covers almost all details of work thoroughly.	Over 33% better quality than average. Does a complete and thorough job in all respects.	

Rating ☐ × Weight ☐ = Factor Score ☐

3. INFLUENCE UPON THE WORK OF FELLOW-WORKERS

How does this employee affect directly the output of fellow-workers?

40	50	60	70	80	90
Reduces output of others very much. Is surly or inconsiderate, upsets morale, and makes trouble. Can't seem to cooperate.	Reduces output of others somewhat. Visits or gossips excessively. Plays practical jokes. Or just fails to click with others.	Neither improves nor harms output of others. Fits in without hindrance Cooperates as requested.	Works helpfully and pleasantly with others. Tones up work. Cooperates on own initiative.	Brings out the best in others. Helps and teaches others willingly. A strong force for good morale.	

Rating ☐ × Weight ☐ = Factor Score ☐

4. INFLUENCE UPON THE ATTITUDE OF OUTSIDERS

How does this employee affect directly the attitude which customers or other outsiders have toward the company?

40	50	60	70	80	90
Often antagonizes others. Personal appearance, manners, habits, or language are annoying. Often complained about. New on job ☐	Occasionally antagonizes others. Lacks tact or a desire to be helpful. Occasionally complained about.	Does work impersonally and meets people with unimpressive politeness. Rarely criticized or complimented by outsiders.	Has sincere interest in others and shows it. Usually makes them feel at ease and satisfied.	Invariably impresses others with work, manners, and attitude of helpfulness. Very often complimented.	

Rating ☐ × Weight ☐ = Factor Score ☐

5. TECHNICAL SUPERVISION REQUIRED

How much instruction does this employee require? How often must this employee be checked on the technicalities of his work?

40	50	60	70	80	90
Must be instructed and followed-up often. Very easily confused. Slow in grasping the obvious. New on job ☐	Understands only simplest routines, must be checked on others. Sometimes confused. Overly cautious. New on job ☐	Handles routine jobs without training or supervision. Needs help on more difficult tasks.	Handles routine jobs and some difficult jobs on his own. Needs help on some difficult jobs.	Very skilled and resourceful. Can work on all jobs without supervision. Very keen and quick to understand.	

Rating ☐ × Weight ☐ = Factor Score ☐

6. HUMAN SUPERVISION REQUIRED

How much supervisory attention does this employee require of a personal point of view?

40	50	60	70	80	90
A problem employee. Has groundless grievances. Disciplined frequently. Supervised more or less constantly.	Must be prodded at times. Stays in a rut. Resents suggestions. Has little enthusiasm.	Cooperates as instructed. Neither dull nor overly reliant. Seldom complains or disciplined.	Needs very little attention. Can be stimulated easily. Makes no trouble. Accepts personal advice and suggestions.	Very loyal and reliable. Works harmoniously with superior. Never nags or causes any trouble. Self starter.	

Rating ☐ × Weight ☐ = Factor Score ☐

7. USE OF COMPANY RESOURCES AND PROPERTIES

How efficiently and carefully does this employee utilize or safeguard machines, tools, materials, supplies, or other properties?

40	50	60	70	80	90
Consistently misuses materials, tools and machines, extremely careless and inefficient. New on job ☐	Occasionally misuses materials, tools, and other properties. Sometimes careless. New on job ☐	Care in use equals that expected after normal training and experience. Neither noticeably careful nor careless.	Seldom wastes or misuses materials or tools. Obviously careful with supplies and equipment.	Does work with a minimum of waste or damage. Handles tools and materials with craftsman's ability.	

Rating ☐ × Weight ☐ = Factor Score ☐

8. FUTURE POSSIBILITIES OF THIS EMPLOYEE

Does this employee have potentialities for growth, special skills, or aptitudes that can be utilized in the future?

40	50	60	70	80	90
Lacks interest, ambition, or training. Has no particular skill and education. Little chance of improvement. New on job ☐	Lacks interest and initiative, otherwise, has good skill and education. Never makes suggestions. Not apt to do better New on job ☐	Interested in work and has aptitudes which must be developed by training or experience. Occasionally makes suggestions	Displays interest in self-improvement. Taking additional training. Very alert. Notices ways of improving methods.	An exceptional prospect for technical or leadership position. Has excellent record of suggestions. Superior to requirements of present job. Capable of filling better jobs.	

Rating ☐ × Weight ☐ = Factor Score ☐

Sum of Weights ☐

Total Factor Score ☐ ÷ Final Score ☐

plan of rating, to be described later, it is necessary that the method of scoring the rater's opinions be kept secret.

Although there may be occasions when ratings should be withheld from employees, it seems better to work toward a relationship of frank discussion between employer and employee. If grievances exist, or if employees have shortcomings, they cannot be reduced or removed simply by waiting. Sooner, or later, the matters must be discussed. The question is one of timing: When is it most appropriate to open discussions? Of course, after a rating program has been installed, the first ratings will raise what appears to be a hornet's nest of controversy. Once these are cleared up, subsequent ratings will result in fewer controversies.

The periodicity of rating which most companies follow is indicative of the fact that ratings tend to reduce rather than increase disagreements. It is rather common to rate new employees more frequently than old. Thus, in one company, new employees are rated after one month, three months, six months, and a year. Thereafter, they are rated annually. This practice recognizes that newer employees are more likely to be sources of trouble than older employees who have had advice on their progress or lack of progress. Some companies that have started rating plans placed them on a quarterly basis. It was decided later that semiannual or annual ratings would suffice. This, too, recognizes that after years of unplanned attack upon sources of trouble, many grievances and problems will have piled up that, for a time, will require extra attention.

Designs of Evaluation Forms

The term "theory" has been used several times in connection with rating, for the reason that there is no one way of rating that has been proved completely superior to all others. In the following discussion of rating designs, more attention will be paid to the graphical method because up to the present it has been the one most widely used.

1. *Design of Graphical Forms.* The use of rating forms can lead to excellent results, provided that practical rules of design are adopted. In the following are listed and described some of the more significant rules:

a) Perhaps the most important step, at least initially, in the design of forms is to determine precisely the objectives of the program. As noted earlier, there are two major uses of evaluation: (1) as the basis for rewards and penalties, and (2) as the basis for explaining to employees why they are or are not making progress. If the first of these objectives is sought, the rating form should include factors that measure as closely as possible employee contributions. Figure 12–2 is an example of such selections, in that, except for the last item, all factors relate to production or efficiency in production.

b) Having determined the type of factors to be rated, the next step is to determine which factors, and how many, should be selected. This problem is not too difficult when evaluation is restricted to productivity. For example, the factors in Figure 12–2 are very inclusive, covering all aspects of a given individual's work; yet the number of factors to be rated is not unduly large.

Evaluations that delve into personal characteristics present a more difficult problem. To begin with, even a brief review of the following list of personal characteristics reveals differences in specificness and problems of overlapping:

Personality	Honesty	Persistence
Character	Initiative	Imagination
Dependability	Industriousness	Enthusiasm
Attitude	Leadership	Aggressiveness
Adaptability	Judgment	Loyalty
Appearance	Cooperativeness	Creativeness

In selecting the factors to be rated, it has been found that not more than nine to twelve traits should be used. Some investigations have shown that as few as three or four traits are sufficient to give good results. However, until various groups of executives are taught to give up their belief that there is safety in numbers, it is easier to get their cooperation when a higher than a lower number of traits is used.

As to the traits to be selected, a better choice can be made if the following rules are watched:

1. Select traits that are specific rather than general; e.g., honesty is more definite than character.
2. Select traits that can be defined in terms understandable in the same way by all raters.
3. Select traits that are common to as many people as possible.
4. Select traits that raters can observe or be taught to observe in the day-to-day performance of employees.

c) Since all factors usually do not have equal weight in all jobs, it is also necessary to determine how much importance should be accorded to each one. This can be accomplished by conference with interested line executives. Some companies provide space for the weights on the form itself, whereas others contend that it is better to omit the weights in order to avoid confusing the raters. In the latter case the weighting is done by the personnel department.

d) In the physical design of rating forms, an important question is that of how to arrange the factors and the spaces for rating. This involves (1) the order of arranging factors and (2) the particulars of rating. There is no general rule that is followed in arranging factors; some arrange them from specific to general, and others reverse this; some like to list factors easy to rate and then go on to the more difficult; and still others adopt a considered disorder.

In the matter of particulars of rating, there is a diversity of practice, much of which is mere whim. When the graphical plan of rating is to be used, adoption of the following suggestions may be desirable:

1. Do not number all scales in the same direction from high to low or low to high. To do this encourages the tendency of raters to evaluate all factors as they do the first, irrespective of warranted differences.
2. Use of scales of varying length, as shown in the following design, also serves to reduce the influence of the rating of earlier or subsequent factors:

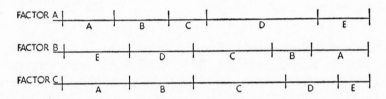

3. Use descriptions to indicate varying degrees of each trait instead of grades and numbers, and omit division points along the scales. As a consequence, the tendency of raters to fit each employee to the scale rather than to concentrate on the employee will be avoided. For example, some raters tend to check the following scale in the center or edge of each grade, depending upon their personal bias:

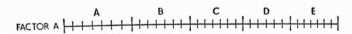

The following type of scale tends, however, to take the mind of the rater off the scale and make him concentrate on the employee:

e) The description of factors and degrees of factors, already mentioned, deserves special attention. Some of the hypothetical illustrations used in the foregoing would, if adopted, be weak because descriptions are not given. To use such terms as "excellent," "above average," "average," and so forth, to describe varying degrees of factors is undesirable because each rater must make up his own mind as to their meaning. As a result, varying standards are used to rate employees. Much to be preferred is the practice illustrated in Figure 12–3 of providing raters with space under each factor wherein raters can enter comments or significant incidents.

f) And finally, consideration should be given to general rules of form design. That is, size of type, color and weight of paper, size of form, and so forth, should be chosen to conform with such matters as who is to use the form, how long the forms are to be kept, where and how long forms are to be filed, and whether or not information is to be transferred to other records. Unless these matters are also kept in mind, rating forms will be designed, as many have been, that are difficult to handle at various stages of the rating procedure.

g) These recommendations, it is important to note, need not be followed to the letter in every case. Indeed, it is often unwise to insist upon some of these rules when such insistence would lead to objections from executives who must finally approve the program, but who are as yet not sufficiently educated to appreciate the finer details of design. In one case, for example, the personnel director had to violate rules of which he was aware because he knew that to insist upon his views might jeopardize the whole rating program. Wisely, he calculated how far he could go in designing a good system and yet get it approved. He did not confuse top executives with technical details, because he knew that once the program began to show results, he could get the changes that were desirable. Knowing how fast to push the extension of various personnel programs is an absolute requirement if a personnel director expects to be successful, personally as well as professionally.

2. *Design of the Forced-Choice Method.* The forced-choice method of rating has been developed in an attempt to improve the accuracy of ratings by reducing the biases, intentional or not, of raters. Under the graphical method, for example, a rater may give a particular employee high ratings because he wants that person to receive a raise. Under the forced-choice method, the rater, when making his choices, cannot tell how the final rating is going to turn out.

This is accomplished by providing the rater with from 30 to 50 sets of statements from which he is to choose in each set the one that is most and the one that is least descriptive of the person being rated. Examples

FIGURE 12–3

RATING FORM FOR SUPERVISORY CANDIDATE
(For Use In a Rating Interview)

Name of Candidate *Jas. H. Hobsell* Evaluator *H. Homer*

Name of Individual Interviewed *W. Schmutz* Date *6/8/51*

Position *Foreman of Assembly Section*

Information sought   *Suggested questions for the interviewer*

1. PERFORMANCE AS A WORKER

A. TECHNICAL COMPETENCE IN THE PROPOSED SUPERVISORY JOB
—Understand most of the work well?
—Would he be able to answer technical questions?
—Does he often have to get help from supervisor?
—Do others respect him for his technical competence?

Below Average | Above Average

Seems to understand work fairly well, but lacks experience on all jobs in assembly. Picks things up quickly.

Tell me something about his performance as a worker? (How would you describe him in general?)

How well does he know the different parts of the job? (i.e.; his technical competence)

What parts of the job does he do best? Poorest?

B. WORK HABITS
—Hard worker?
—Turn out good quality work?
—Organize his work well?
—Safety conscious?
—Good housekeeper?
—Thorough?
—Cost conscious? Watch scrap, etc?
—Tend to emphasize one aspect of the job at the expense of others? *No.*

Below Average | Above Average

Eager - hard worker. Very good organizer.

Neat, thorough, efficient.

Tell me something about his work habits, such as the kind of work he turns out, how he organizes his work, and the like?

How about the amount of work he turns out? Is he the kind of guy who finds work to do, or does he wait until a new job is assigned?

2. MENTAL AND PHYSICAL QUALIFICATIONS

A. MENTAL ABILITY
—Catch on quickly to new things?
—Does he look ahead to catch things before they happen?
—Use good judgment? Make wise decisions?
—Ever suggest new approaches to problems?
—Could he keep records and write reports if he had to?

Below Average | Above Average

Catches on quickly. Uses his head - looks ahead.

How well does he catch on to new things? Can he be switched to other jobs easily?

How about his ability to make decisions?

Does he look ahead to catch things before they happen, or is he apt to wait until something has to be done?

B. PHYSICAL CHARACTERISTICS
—In good health?
—Out sick a lot?
—Any defects which would handicap him in a high-pressure job?
—Regular in attendance? (If poor, is it due to sickness?)

Below Average | Above Average

O. K.

Good attendance.

How about his health?

Does he have any physical defects which would handicap him in a high-pressure job?

Courtesy: General Electric Company

FIGURE 12–3. (Continued)

3. PERSONALITY CHARACTERISTICS

A. MATURITY

  —Apt to indulge in too much horseplay?
  —Show childish reactions (pouting, tattletale, etc.)
  —Stand up well under pressure?
  —Willing to accept responsibility? (Handle problems or duck them?)

Below Average   Above Average

How about his personality? Would you describe that in some detail?

Is he always very mature in his actions, or is he sometimes a little childish in some ways?

Very mature. Good sense of responsibility

B. SOCIAL EFFECTIVENESS

Effect on others—
  —Others have confidence in him?
  —Enjoy working with him?
  —Others take their troubles to him?
  —Express himself well?
  —Too much of a "swell guy"? (others take advantage of him)

Below Average   Above Average

What effect does he have on others? Would he gain the respect and cooperation of others?

Others enjoy working with him "One of the best leaders we've had."

Attitude toward others—
  —Interest in people?
  —Cooperative?
  —Fair and objective, or inclined to be prejudiced?
  —Tend to blame others for his own mistakes?
  —Tend to treat junior members of group as inferiors?
  —Inclined to be "cliquish"? (Might have favorites)
  —Good reaction to authority? A good follower? Resent criticism? Likely not to obey a rule when it's easier not to?

Tell me something about his attitude toward others?

Does he always seem to be thinking of the other person, or does he sometimes tend to be a little self-centered?

How does he react to authority?

Very helpful with new men - seems to have a lot of interest in others.

a good follower. Welcomes constructive criticism.

C. MOTIVATION

  —Is he eager to advance?
  —Interested in a career with the Company?
  —Understand Company polices and regulations well?
  —Can he be counted on in emergencies?

Below Average   Above Average

How would you describe his attitude toward his work and the Company?

Very eager. Has high hopes to get ahead in G. E.

SUMMARY BY RATER

Assets— *a natural leader.*

All things considered, what do you consider this man's major strong points to be?

Liabilities— *Lacks experience.*

What are his major shortcomings?

Overall recommendation— *Would be an excellent supervisor.*

How would you rate his chances of success as a supervisor?

Recommendations regarding his future in other lines—

Could use a broader experience background - a chance to acquire more technical "know-how."

If he were not considered to be qualified for a supervisory job, can he advance along other lines?

FIGURE 12-3. (Continued)

SUMMARY RATING BY EVALUATOR

SUMMARY OF ASSETS—

Good personality for leadership
Eager - hard working.
Bright - uses his head.
        Good organizer.

SUMMARY OF LIABILITIES:—

Lacks experience.

OVERALL SUMMARY—

Evidently is excellent supervisory material.
Could use additional technical experience.

SUMMARY RATING (Based on contact with this Rater only.)

A POOR prospect for supervisory work.	About AVERAGE as a candidate for supervisory work.	An EXCELLENT prospect for supervisory work.

EVALUATION OF THE RATER

How well does he know the
candidate?   *One year*

Does he seem to be objective?
Any biases or prejudices?   *Seems to be very objective.*

Is there anything in his personal
make-up (habits of work, interests,
personality, attitudes, etc.) that
would be likely to affect his
judgment of others?

How would you rate him as a judge
of this candidate?

Below   Above
Average   Average

from the United Parcel Service plan, as reported by Eileen Ahern of the American Management Association, are as follows:

Most	*Least*	
A	A	Would be very difficult to replace
B	B	Lets difficulties get him down
C	C	Alert to new opportunities for the company
D	D	Tries to run things his own way
E	E	Tends to delegate things which will not reflect credit on him

Most	*Least*	
A	A	Not willing to make decisions unless he has very complete information
B	B	Makes snap judgments about people
C	C	Has not demonstrated up to now that he has the ability to progress further
D	D	Very valuable in a new operation
E	E	Good for routine supervisory job

Some of these statements sound favorable, and some do not. But from previous research, it will have been found that some of the favorable ones are really meaningful and count for a person if checked; the same is true of the unfavorable. The rater, however, does not know which of the "favorable" ones are really favorable, and which of the "unfavorable" are really unfavorable. So the rater cannot by choice favor his friends and purposefully harm those he dislikes. He therefore must choose the respective phrases in each set which best tend to describe the person being rated.

The forced-choice plan has a high potential of accuracy not only because bias is reduced but also because the raters do not have to interpret trait terms nor determine how much weight to give to various traits. The plan, however, has two shortcomings. First, it is practically useless for counseling purposes because it is impossible to explain simply why a person was rated as he was. Second, its construction involves a great deal of work to arrive at discriminatory as well as neutral, but seemingly discriminatory, statements. A brief statement of how this may be done is suggested in the following procedure:

a) Gather actual words and phrases used in describing supervisors.
b) Cull them for observability and universality.
c) Scale them for their degree of attractiveness or unattractiveness.
d) Determine how well each discriminates between good and poor supervisors.
e) Determine the score that each gets in adding up the total score.
f) Verify the scoring system set up by check experiments.[1]

---

[1] Reign Bittner, "Developing an Employee Merit Rating Procedure," *Personnel*, Vol. XXV, No. 4, p. 290.

Accuracy of Evaluations

Unless the accuracy of evaluations is checked, they will be unacceptable to employees and useless to the company. Accuracy may be tested by checking the *validity* of evaluations, that is, how well ratings really measure the factors they set out to measure. Thus, if a plan purports to measure (among other things) initiative, it is valid if this trait is really appraised. Second, accuracy must be concerned with *reliability,* or the consistency with which ratings are made. Thus, if a supervisor gives an employee a rating of "very good," let us say, on two successive evaluations of his dependability, and the employee deserves this rating, the ratings are said to be reliable. And third, accuracy of raters, one to another, may be checked.

1. *Validity of Evaluations.* Measuring the validity of evaluations is not easy because criteria are seldom available against which to check ratings. When an employee is rated for such a factor as personality, for example, the very fact that he is being rated for it is usually an indication that a better method of estimating it is not available. Yet, by comparing ratings with various aspects of an employee's employment records and performance, adequate checks of validity can be obtained.

Perhaps the simplest overall check of validity is to compare ratings with the performance of employees. For example, when ratings of personal traits compare favorably with ratings of performance, a smooth progression should be obtained when the data for all values are arranged from high to low. The existence of the "halo effect" is also a sign of low validity of ratings. This can be determined by examining ratings to note whether there is a tendency for raters to rate all other factors the same as some one factor about an employee with which they were particularly impressed, favorably or unfavorably.

A check on validity can also be obtained by comparing estimates of two or more raters on the same employees. For example, if two raters, A and B, rated a given employee as shown in Figure 12–4, the validity of one or the other, or both, is in error. The lines connecting the scores for each factor by each rater are called "profiles" and are commonly used because they aid the eye in interpreting the ratings. Such differences in estimates are common because most raters tend to be somewhat easy or harsh. Hence the tendency of each rater must be discovered and either corrected by instruction or allowed for if given raters are too set in their ways.

The critical-incident technique is an interesting plan for increasing the validity of ratings. It provides for the collection and classification of

FIGURE 12-4. Comparison of Profiles

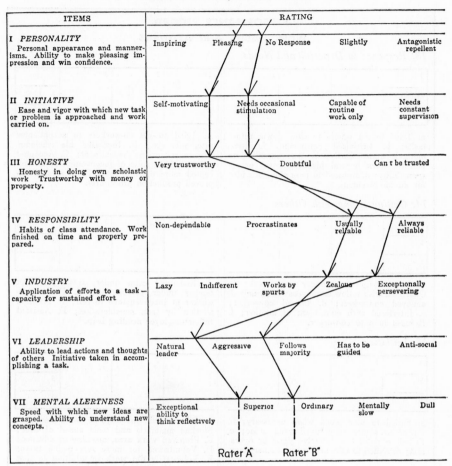

ITEMS	RATING				
I PERSONALITY Personal appearance and mannerisms. Ability to make pleasing impression and win confidence.	Inspiring	Pleasing	No Response	Slightly	Antagonistic repellent
II INITIATIVE Ease and vigor with which new task or problem is approached and work carried on.	Self-motivating	Needs occasional stimulation	Capable of routine work only		Needs constant supervision
III HONESTY Honesty in doing own scholastic work Trustworthy with money or property.	Very trustworthy		Doubtful		Can t be trusted
IV RESPONSIBILITY Habits of class attendance. Work finished on time and properly prepared.	Non-dependable	Procrastinates		Usually reliable	Always reliable
V INDUSTRY Application of efforts to a task — capacity for sustained effort	Lazy	Indifferent	Works by spurts	Zealous	Exceptionally persevering
VI LEADERSHIP Ability to lead actions and thoughts of others Initiative taken in accomplishing a task.	Natural leader	Aggressive	Follows majority	Has to be guided	Anti-social
VII MENTAL ALERTNESS Speed with which new ideas are grasped. Ability to understand new concepts.	Exceptional ability to think reflectively	Superior	Ordinary	Mentally slow	Dull

Rater "A"   Rater "B"

SOURCE: Excerpt from a form used at Ohio State University.

reports of behavior which represent significant examples of success and failure. The supervisor is first given instruction on traits to be observed and samples of behavior descriptive of successful and unsuccessful application of the traits. Then, he must note when such incidents actually take place. An excerpt from a form for recording the incidents is shown in Figure 12–5. The theory of the plan is that the rating really consists of observed experiences rather than opinions about behavior; like a production report, it shows what happened and not an opinion about happenings.

2. *Reliability of Evaluations.* The reliability of evaluations is ordinarily checked by comparing the ratings of given raters from period

FIGURE 12–5. Excerpt from a Critical-Incident Rating Form

PERFORMANCE RECORD
WORK HABITS AND ATTITUDES

13. Response to Departmental Needs

4	3	2	1		1	2	3	4
5								5
6								6

a. Tried to get others to slow down, refuse tasks; b. Criticized equipment, facilities, methods unnecessarily; c. Was unwilling to perform work beyond his assignment or responsibility; d. Refused to pass along his idea for an improvement.

A. Tried to get co-workers to accept new rate, job, etc.; B. Increased his efficiency despite co-workers' resentment; C. Accepted extra work in spite of inconvenience; D. Accepted more difficult jobs; E. Suggested improved production procedures.

14. Getting Along with Others

4	3	2	1		1	2	3	4
5								5
6								6

a. Became upset or angry over work; b. Quarreled with fellow employees; c. Criticized, annoyed co-workers; d. Bossed co-worker; e. Interfered with equipment of another; f. Refused help to co-worker.

A. Remained calm under stress; B. Kept temper under provocation; C. Helped co-worker at inconvenience to self; D. Avoided friction by tact, consideration; E. Assisted fellow employee needing help.

15. Initiative

4	3	2	1		1	2	3	4
5								5
6								6

a. Failed to plan work when necessary; b. Failed to obtain tools until need arose; c. Failed to point out defective parts or operation; d. Failed to take action in an emergency.

A. Planned efficient ways of doing work; B. Stocked materials and tools ahead of time; C. Prepared work area, machine in advance; D. Volunteered for more responsible tasks; E. Voluntarily did work in addition to that expected; F. Pointed out defects on the line.

16. Responsibility

4	3	2	1		1	2	3	4
5								5
6								6

a. Passed up chance for more training; b. Passed up chance to learn more about the job; c. Gave misleading, incorrect instructions; d. Poorly directed work in foreman's absence.

A. Got additional information on his job, department; B. Took additional outside training; C. Got information on improving work; D. Planned a schedule for others; E. Trained, instructed other employees; F. Got cooperation between employees.

SOURCE: John C. Flanagan, "Principles and Procedures in Evaluating Performance," *Personnel*, Vol. XXVI, No. 5, p. 383.

to period. If an employee has improved in certain aspects or remained the same, the ratings should have increased in value or remained the same, as the case may be. When such comparisons are made for the first time, it will invariably be found that most raters have not made the necessary adjustments in their estimates. Discussions with supervisors at this time will serve to clear up mistakes in using the rating form and in interpreting the various terms and descriptions. It is unwise to rely too heavily upon such comparisons as a check on the accuracy of ratings because employees are bound to change from period to period. Hence, checks should be made also with other measures which indicate the relative changes in employees from period to period. For example, records that show how an employee's performance has changed can be used to determine whether or not sufficient allowances have been made in the ratings from period to period. Some companies also compare the estimates of a number of raters for the same ratees as a check on their reliability. There is some question whether this is a test of validity or reliability, or both. In any event, its use is advisable for the good it will do in calling attention to variances in raters.

3. *Accuracy of Raters.* It is also desirable to determine (*a*) which raters are more lenient than others and (*b*) which have a tendency toward the halo effect. Leniency of raters can be determined simply by averaging the ratings of each and then getting an average of the averages. Any rater whose average is significantly off the average should be checked for leniency or undue strictness, as the case may be. Another check on leniency can be obtained if two or more raters rate the same employees. Significant deviations can be readily checked.

In the case of the halo effect, as noted earlier, ratings are influenced by a particularly impressive characteristic of an employee. For example, a given supervisor may be impressed by the neatness of a particular employee. Unconsciously or consciously, the supervisor proceeds to overrate the worker on matters of dependability, initiative, cooperation, etc. Sometimes this tendency can be discovered by a simple examination of ratings. At other times, interviews will be necessary to ascertain the degree to which given supervisors are susceptible to such errors.

The foregoing checks of validity and reliability may be made by simple observation or by means of statistical correlations. As noted earlier, for example, a simple diagram of the estimates of two raters is sufficient to bring out the need for corrective measures. On the other hand, more complex measures can be derived by correlating statistically various aspects of ratings.

Rules of Evaluating

Forms of rating are only tools that must be used properly if desired ends are to be attained. Skill and understanding must be applied in rating employees. Hence, it is now appropriate to suggest a number of rules which, if followed, will increase the contributions of evaluations.

First of all, it is important to select raters carefully. In some companies, two raters, usually the immediate supervisor and his superior, evaluate each employee. The purpose of the double evaluation is to derive a check on the ratings and to induce higher executives to keep in closer touch with lower levels of the organization. This practice is, however, debatable. To be sure, the purpose of the double check is admirable, but it is unwise to ask an executive to make estimates about employees with whom he seldom associates or cannot associate without neglecting his regular duties. Ordinarily, it is better practice to place the burden of rating on the person best able to assume it—the immediate supervisor.

Second, rater should be thoroughly instructed in the purposes and values of the program. Hence, it is desirable to hold conferences in which the reasons for the program, the part supervisors are to play, and the advantages to all concerned are carefully explained. Such conferences also can increase the prestige of the supervisor and his own feeling of worthwhileness by showing him how important he is to the success of the program.

Third, all factors, degrees of factors, and terms should be meticulously explained to raters. Both verbal and printed explanations are worth using. In this way, there is greater assurance that all raters will interpret all terms in the same way and hence produce ratings that are based on the same standards.

Fourth, it is imperative to recognize the sensitivity factor in rating. Any plan which purports to evaluate employees runs into the feelings of people about what may happen to them. They become concerned about the fairness of the rater. They may even question the right to "measure" any human being. Hence the plan should give assurance that no arbitrary decisions will be reached. Indeed, it might be well to forgo such words as "measure" and "evaluate." In their place, it would be well to substitute such phrases as "how we are getting along" or "what is happening to performance."

Fifth, along similar lines, rating should be viewed in its psychological and sociological as well as technical framework. This merely is a recognition that any rating affects the attitudes of individuals as individuals and as members of groups. The person rated can easily react unfavorably even to a fair rating if he feels the system of rating exposes him to a reduction of his status in the eyes of fellow workers.

Sixth, several suggestions can be made that will improve the accuracy of ratings. To begin with, raters should be impressed with the need for observing workers in terms of the factors in which they are to be rated. In this way the task of rating will not be a chore or a matter of guesswork. Raters should also be advised to guard against allowing recent events or isolated cases to influence unduly their decisions. In this connection, the practice of recollecting examples of individual performance and traits is desirable. Then, too, raters should be advised to allow enough time and find a relatively quiet office for the rating job. Interruptions tend to reduce the accuracy of ratings. And finally, it has also been found advisable to rate all employees one factor at a time because the consistency of rating is thereby increased.

QUESTIONS

1. In designing a merit-rating form, why is it essential to state as precisely as possible the objectives that are to be sought in the use of the plan?
2. If employee contributions could always be measured accurately, would there be any need to measure employee characteristics? Explain.
3. What are the pros and cons of discussing evaluations with employees? What is your stand on the position?
4. By what methods is it possible to minimize the "halo effect" and the tendency of raters to be influenced by the rating form rather than by the employee?
5. Why is it undesirable to use merely the names of factors or simple grades such as "above average," "average," and "superior" on an evaluation form?
6. Some rating forms provide space wherein the rater provides specific examples to illustrate the grading he has made on particular factors. What is the advantage of this practice?
7. What is the theory behind the forced-choice method of rating? Is this not an implied indictment of executives? Explain.
8. Why is it desirable that ratings be both valid and reliable? Which, in your opinion, is more difficult to achieve? Why?
9. Who should rate operative employees? Is it desirable for an employee's supervisor and the supervisor's superior to evaluate an employee?
10. What rules would it be desirable to follow in evaluating employees?

CHAPTER 13

TRAINING OPERATIVE EMPLOYEES

Training and Education

This chapter and the next three are devoted to a study of training and education in business. The term "training" is used here to indicate any process by which the aptitudes, skills, and abilities of employees to perform specific jobs are increased. This task may be contrasted with that of increasing the knowledge, understanding, or attitude of employees so that they are better adjusted to their working environment. The term "education" is used here to denote the latter task.

To clarify these terms, the example of a trainee on a drill press may be considered. Teaching him how to operate the drill press is training, whereas giving him a course in economics is education. The two may go hand in hand, as in the case of a supervisor who, while showing an operator how to seal a package, also talks about the sales policies of the company and their importance to each factory employee.

Although education in attitudes is often undertaken at the same time as training, and wisely so, it is better for discussional purposes to take up the two phases of learning separately. Hence, in this chapter, operative training will be discussed, and training of executives will be taken up in the next chapter. Following that, educational programs will be taken up under the chapter headings of "Morale and Attitudes" and "Communications."

In the present chapter, training of operative employees is taken up under the following major headings:

1. Justification and scope of training
2. Courses and programs of training
3. Factors in a training program
4. Evaluation of training programs

JUSTIFICATION AND SCOPE

One of the first questions that must be answered regarding training is whether or not the cost is justified. The simplest argument in favor of a formal program is that a company pays for training whether it has a program or not. Some executives conclude that they do not have any training costs because they have no training program. But are all their employees hired with skills and aptitudes equal to the jobs to be done? Do their employees learn nothing while they are working? Whose machines, materials, and facilities are employees using while their skills improve? Answers would show that the employees learn on the job by themselves, but the company unwittingly foots the bill.

Viewed positively, the values of training are not far to seek. First, training serves to improve employee skill, which in turn increases the quantity and quality of output. Second, the relative amount of equipment and material required to produce a unit of output is decreased. Third, executive effort will tend to shift from the disagreeable need of correcting mistakes to the more pleasant tasks of planning work and of encouraging expert employees. Fourth, the various increases in productivity will find a reflection in increased returns to employees. And last, the general tenor of relations between employers and employees, as well as their individual satisfaction, will tend to be more wholesome, resulting in more pleasant and satisfactory working conditions. All these objectives, it is worth repeating, may be sought without adding to company budgets. The money is being spent, so it may as well be spent wisely.

Although all employees should undergo training, all need not be trained to the same degree, and seldom can all be trained at the same time. Company facilities for training are rarely sufficient to undertake such a broad program. Hence the guiding principle should be that of attacking training problems where the needs are greatest. After urgent needs are taken care of, those with lower priority should be served.

As yet, standards as to the amounts of training that should be provided on various types of jobs are practically nonexistent. Even in the field of apprentice training, practice differs considerably. In some trades the apprentice period is two years; and in others, it is as high as seven. But compared to this, length of training among other job areas is variable beyond mention. Each company must work out time standards of training for itself, changing them as its experience warrants. Standards should be set for such matters as:

1. Total hours of training time
2. Calendar spacing of the total hours
3. Parts of the day assigned to training
4. Scheduling of retraining sessions

COURSES OF TRAINING

Many approaches to training are being used in industry. To describe and examine them all is beyond the scope of this chapter. However, the more common methods of training operative employees are taken up now. The types of training are not mutually exclusive but invariably overlap and employ many of the same techniques. For example, Figure

FIGURE 13–1.   Graphic Presentation of the Approach to Nonsupervisory
Training Programs in the Automotive Industry

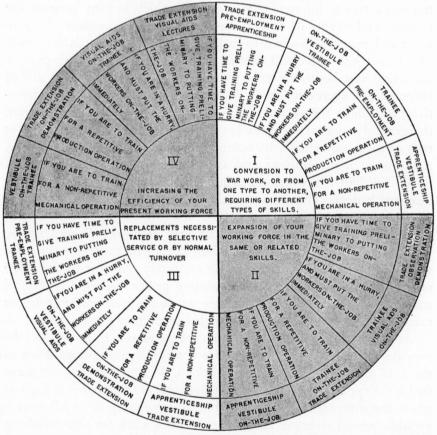

In the center circle are listed the problems generally faced; in the second circle, the different situations involved; and in the outer circle, the methods recommended to meet the specific problem.

Source: Automotive Council for War Production, *Training and Upgrading* (Detroit), p. 6.

13–1 illustrates graphically the types and methods of training that may be used to serve various purposes under various conditions. A few of the more common types are examined more fully in this section.

On-the-Job Training

Undoubtedly, training is most commonly done on the job. It requires no special school, the student is being trained at a point where no changeover will be required, and his output adds to the total of his department. These are favorable points for a training plan that is simple, too.

Since on-the-job training is commonly used and is likely to continue to be, the requisites of a good program are now described. In the first place, what the learner is to be taught, and how, should be determined and preferably set down on paper, at least in major outline. Second, the instructor should be carefully selected and trained. Such courses as "job instructor training," to be discussed in the next chapter, should be given to trainers. It is well for the supervisor to do the training himself if time will permit, because it will give him a favorable opportunity to get acquainted with the new worker and to "sell" himself and the company to him. When time does not permit the supervisor to do this work, the next best practice is to have a departmental trainer. When this is not practical, a seasoned and understanding worker should be appointed to teach the new worker. But it is well to pay such part-time instructors a bonus for each learner trained, so that they will not hurry this responsibility in order to return to their own duties on which incentive payments may otherwise be lost. And third, a definite follow-up schedule should be provided, so that the results of the training and the progress of the learner can be established. In this way, all instructors will be more likely to do their work effectively.

Vestibule Training

In "vestibule" training, employees are taken through a short course under working conditions that approximate actual shop or office conditions. It gets its name from the resemblance of the school to a vestibule through which one passes before entering the main rooms of a house. Such a course usually takes from a few days to a few weeks at the most and is used where only a few skills are to be acquired. Thus, training may be given to newly hired comptometer operators. As a result, they will be able to do the work required of them when they step into the departments for which they were hired.

Vestibule training has the advantage of training relatively large numbers of people in a short period of time without disturbing the flow of shop or office routines. Moreover, the employees can be adjusted to actual conditions under guided direction and gradually speeded up as they gain confidence. In addition, misfits or poor practices can be eliminated before actual production conditions are encountered.

Vestibule training, however, requires the duplication of shop or office facilities in a school area. Consequently, it must be limited to types of instruction in which the machinery used is not too expensive to install in a school or which can be used, on and off, as employment demands, without excessive overhead cost. It is also limited to those jobs in which there is high turnover or a continually increasing demand for workers.

Apprenticeship Training

Apprenticeship is followed in trades, crafts, and technical fields in which proficiency can be acquired only after a relatively long period of time in direct association with the work and under the direct supervision of experts. A partial list of areas in which such training is practiced includes the following:

Barbers	Die sinkers	Jewelers	Plumbers
Boilermakers	Draftsmen	Lens grinders	Printers
Carpenters	Electricians	Millwrights	Shipfitters
Coppersmiths	Engravers	Molders	Stonemasons
Coremakers	Furriers	Painters	Toolmakers

The federal government and the unions have had an impact upon apprenticeship training. The federal government has interested itself in apprentices because of wage rates, training subsidies, and standardized practices. If an employer desires to pay apprentices less than amounts prescribed by wages and hours laws, apprenticeship agreements must be covered in writing and submitted to administrators of these acts in order to obtain a certificate of exemption. Apprentice courses are subject to federal regulation when learners are subsidized by the government. And the federal government, through its Federal Committee on Apprenticeship, has also cooperated with state apprenticeship councils to standardize apprenticeship practices regarding amounts of training, wages, and measures of progress.

Unions, too, are concerned with apprenticeship programs. On the one hand, they are interested in establishing apprentice quotas in order to prevent undue displacement of fully trained workers by learners. Second, they have used such programs to restrict entry into a trade or industry. And third, they have bargained over wage rates and conditions of employment of apprentices.

Internship Training

Internship training refers to a joint program of training in which schools and businesses cooperate. Selected students carry on regular school studies for periods ranging from three to nine months and then work in some factory or office for a designated period of time, alternating in this fashion until the course is completed. The training is usually conducted in connection with highly skilled or professional types of training. Trade and high schools often cooperate with industry in this way to train various vocational workers. And it has been employed by industry and colleges for training for management and engineering positions.

By such training, it is hoped to gain a good balance between theory and practice. In addition, students may gain a better appreciation of their school studies by having a practical background against which to visualize classroom principles. Moreover, the students who have a definite vocation or profession in mind are likely to be better motivated because they can see the practical side of their objectives being achieved. From the company's side, the gain is in a better balanced employee and one who has already been interned to its practices.

Internship has its disadvantages. It is such a slow process as to try the patience of the student as well as the instructor or supervisor. It takes so long that one or both of the parties involved may become discouraged. It suffers when business depressions call for layoffs; and under it, present employees feel that the interns are being favored at their expense.

Outside Courses

A number of agencies and groups have cooperated with industry in the solution of its training problems. Vocational, correspondence, trade, and evening schools have been a constant source of supply of semi-skilled, skilled, and technical workers. Such training must be sufficiently broad to qualify graduates for any one of a number of employers.

The federal government, through a number of agencies, has assisted industry in its training work. Vocational training is given particular support by providing for contribution of federal funds to match contributions by the states. The Smith-Hughes Act of 1917 apportioned $7 million annually for such programs. Subsequent amendments in 1934 (the George-Ellsey Act) and in 1936 (the George-Deen Act) increased the federal contribution. Federal support is also given to vocational training of the handicapped and veterans. And the Manpower Development and Training Act of 1962 has been helpful to those who need retraining and upgrading because their old jobs have been lost in the march of technological change.

The federal government also gives assistance in apprentice training through its Apprentice Training Service, established in 1937 as a section of the Division of Labor Standards, United States Department of Labor. Agencies interested in such vocational education are illustrated in Figure 13–2. A brief outline of its cost-free services is as follows:

FIGURE 13–2. Federal-State-Local Relations in Vocational Education

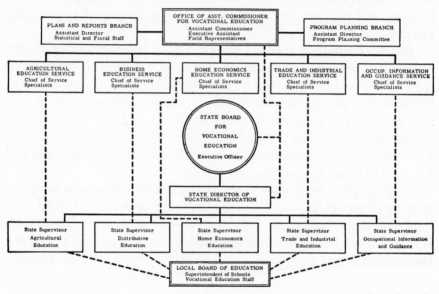

Source: Division of Vocational Education, Office of Education, Federal Security Agency.

1. *Training Apprentices.*   Assistance is given in improving or inaugurating apprenticeship programs and providing suggestions on methods and techniques relating to the operation of such programs.
2. *Training Advancing Workers.*   Advisory assistance is provided regarding the training of advancing workers. These are workers being trained for skills beneath the journeyman level but requiring a fairly high degree of skill. The period of training for such workers is shorter than for apprentices, but the problems of training are comparable.
3. *Labor Relations Affecting Training.*   Assistance is provided in dealing with labor problems encountered with the operation of on-the-job training programs. Typical problems applying to training include seniority rights, wages, number of persons to be trained, hours of work, establishment of training schedules and breakdown of operations, establishment of shifts, standards of selection, and supervision of trainees.

4. *Supplementary Labor Agreements.* In plants where employees are organized, assistance is provided in preparing supplements to established bargaining agreements where the existing agreement is not sufficiently flexible to cover such situations as war training and employment.
5. *General.* In many instances, assistance is also provided with regard to employment requirements of federal or state laws and problems of production as they relate to training.

During the war the federal government also performed yeoman service through its efforts in advanced training and education. Its work in connection with the Training within Industry program was particularly successful and will be discussed more fully in the next chapter.

Teaching Machines

Until recently, learning has normally been associated with a human teacher. Coming into play is the use of mechanical devices to aid the learner. Through audiovisual mechanisms, instruction has been carried on in such fields as company organizations, product knowledge, sales completions, office forms, and technical language. These are more or less routine areas, although developmental efforts are being conducted in more creative-type areas.

With the use of such a mechanism—or programmed instruction, as it is better called—material to be learned is fed into a machine. Each bit of information is imprinted on an individual frame. The machine projects some informational item, after which the student is asked on a succeeding frame to respond to a question or problem pertaining to the preceding informational frame. The student's response is fed into the machine by selecting from a choice of button switches, or by making a check mark. If the response is correct, the machine turns up a new frame with additional information, to which the student again responds. If the response is wrong, the machine repeats the original information in the same or a new form. Until a satisfactory response is obtained from the student, he is not given new and more complex informational bits.

Such mechanical programming is expensive to construct but has impressive advantages. The instruction is individualized, and a person can go as fast as his capbilities permit. The material is presented in small segments; this operaies on the principle that small-dose learning is best and that small errors can be more quickly unlearned than large ones. Such programming must be constructed with extreme care so that a logical and rigorous lesson plan is provided. And since a student is immediately told whether he is right or wrong, his successes reinforce the learning process, and his failures lead to immediate corrections.

Retraining and Upgrading

Curiously enough, either a shortage of labor or an excessive supply may necessitate retraining. The case of shortages is well exemplified by war conditions. A need for such training was created because most companies had to change from civilian pursuits to war work and yet increase their output at the same time. Hence, on the one hand, employees who had skills for making automobiles, let us say, had to be retrained to make tanks. And on the other hand, many who were performing semiskilled tasks had to be given additional training so that they might be upgraded to skilled jobs. Their jobs, in turn, were filled by upgraded unskilled workers, and these were replaced by learners, many of whom might be women with no industrial experience whatsoever.

Courses in upgrading and retraining are much the same as other training methods discussed thus far. Their unique feature lies in the fact that otherwise experienced workers are given additional training to handle new and more difficult assignments. The problem is to pick and choose course material so that trainees can take on their new jobs relatively quickly. For example, one company that took 48 months on its toolmakers' apprentice course, selected parts from it so that operators could be taught to perform a few skilled jobs in from six to 18 months. Such intensive training in which students spent approximately 25 percent of their time in class and 75 percent on machine operations built up a working force that could meet war production demands on time.

The case of excess labor bringing about retraining is illustrated by the recent increase in unemployment brought on by automation. This has become very serious in some areas. As a consequence, the federal government enacted the Manpower Development and Training Act of 1962. This authorized the government to spend $435 million in the period from 1962 to 1965, and additional sums thereafter, to provide free retraining for those with obsolete or inadequate skills.

This retraining program has a number of qualifications. First, it is aimed at the unemployed. And it is particularly concerned with heads of households who have been workers not less than three years in the past, unemployed youths of age 16 or older, and certain workers in farm families. Second, it provides cash allowances to some trainees. Heads of families may receive an amount equal to the average weekly unemployment compensation payment of the state in which the trainee lives, for a period up to fifty-two weeks. Youths in the 19–21 age bracket are limited to not more than $20 a week.

This type of training is conducted outside of the business enterprise. As such, it represents a departure which may well be a new trend in training. The government makes studies to determine what skills are needed in various areas. Then, it provides facilities and instruction to the unemployed who do not have these skills. In this manner the unemployed are brought back into the labor market and thereby taken off relief and the unemployment compensation rolls.

FACTORS IN A TRAINING PROGRAM

The operation of a successful program requires that due consideration be given to a number of factors. These include (1) the organization of a training program, (2) the planning of the program, (3) the selection of trainees and instructors, and (4) adherence to rules or principles of learning.

Organizational Aspects

A training program has a much better chance of being effective if it is well organized. To begin with, one person or unit in the organization should be made responsible for training. In a small company, this means that a line executive will have to be given this responsibility. In larger organizations the personnel manager or a training director should be assigned the task of planning, organizing, and evaluating the program. Such division of responsibility should be made with the clear recognition that the foremen, supervisors, and other executives assisted by the designated teaching officers possess ultimate authority over and responsibility for training within their respective units. As an example of this, Figure 13–3 shows the various types of training for which a training co-ordinator in one company was made responsible for planning and coordination. Fig. 13–4 shows how the execution of some of the training work was actually assigned to the shop departments.

Second, unless the interest and prestige of the administrative levels support a training program, it will be accepted with reluctance by the lower levels. Top management is best convinced by facts that disclose the results that can be expected from training. And it has been found desirable to give top management a condensed version of the training so that executives can personally visualize its practicality.

And third, it is well to consider the role of the union in the organiza-

FIGURE 13-3

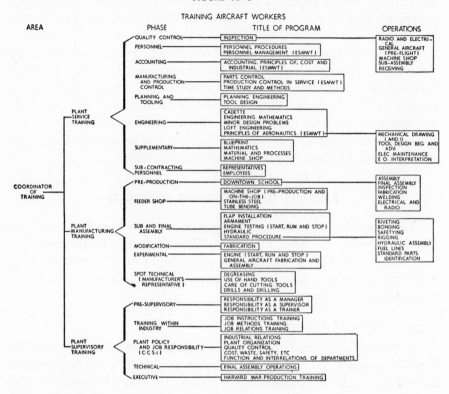

TRAINING AIRCRAFT WORKERS

tion for training. This may include such matters as courses of training, responsibility for selecting or restricting candidates, and evaluation of training work. These matters may be handled through collective bargaining, through joint committees, or informally. In any event, it is probable that with the passing years, union interest in training is likely to grow because of its effect on job placements and wage rates.

Planning the Program

Along with good organization, careful planning is a most important prerequisite of training. When such aspects as where, who, how, what, and when are preplanned in a training program, the result will be fewer mistakes and better trainees when the program gets under way. An excellent example of this is seen in Figure 13–5, which illustrates the results obtained from a careful study that led to the building of an effective training program. The lower curve in this chart shows how much progress may be expected in a year from "normal efficiency

FIGURE 13–4. Training Organization Chart

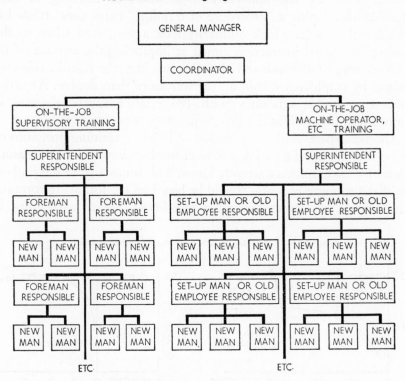

FIGURE 13–5. Learning Curves

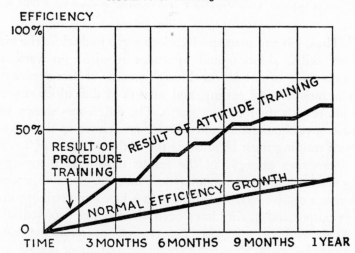

Source: E. F. Wonderlic, *Procedure and Attitude Training*, Personnel Series, No. 47 (New York: American Management Association), p. 50.

growth," meaning the happenstance methods of learning in most offices. By developing a "procedure of training," employees attained in three months results which ordinarily took a year. And when to this training was added instruction aimed at improving the attitude of the employee toward his work and his fellow workers, the relative efficiency attained by employees within a year was more than double. Anything which can double efficiency with the relative inexpensiveness of planned training, such as this program, certainly proves its value.

Another aspect of planning is that of building training programs on a good foundation of (1) job and man specifications and (2) measurements of what employees actually know. This follows from the proposition that a training program should be based on the following formula: What should be known *less* what one knows *equals* what must be

FIGURE 13–6. Training Results from the Analytical Method

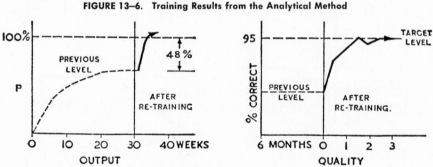

SOURCE: G. H. Ladhams, "A New Method for Training Operators," *Personnel*, Vol. XXVIII, No. 6, p. 477.

learned. Thus, job and man specifications serve to disclose the kind and degree of skills, abilities, and aptitudes required on various jobs; whereas checking of employees through records of past experience and education, interviewing, testing, and surveys of difficulties encountered on the job reveals their current status. The differences shown by these two broad investigations should provide an answer to the question of how much training must be allowed for in the program of a company.

An interesting example of the results of careful planning is the training system known as the analytical method. By close attention to the positive, negative, and skill factors in a job, some striking improvements in output and quality have been obtained, as depicted in Figure 13–6. As shown here, otherwise "experienced" operators increased their performance by about 50 percent in output and about double in better quality after such training. As noted, the analytical method requires attention, first, to emphasis upon positive factors on a job, which include the following:

1. The need to earn a living
2. The wish to master and to progress in a job
3. The sociological fact that it is normal to be employed

Second, negative factors on a job such as the following must be reduced:

1. The perplexing task of trying to acquire several skills and abilities simultaneously
2. The difficulty of settling down in a new group of people or those who have more proven skills than the learner
3. The problem of adjusting to an atmosphere where production predominates

Third, emphasis must be upon skills rather than duties. The difference is illustrated in Table 13–1, which shows the job breakdown for the job

TABLE 13–1

OPERATION: GARMENT MAKING (SEWING MACHINE)
JOB BREAKDOWN AND ANALYSIS

Orthodox Method

(Description of Movements)
1. Pick up piece of fabric with each hand from 2 piles (L. & R.).
2. Bring pieces together and superimpose corners to correspond.
3. Raise machine Foot (Use knee).
4. Position R.H. top corner in machine $\frac{1}{8}$" beyond edge of Foot.
5. Lower Foot.
6. Stitch along fabric edge to next corner, both hands guide fabric to maintain accurate stitching line (feet control machine speed).
7. Continue similarly with remainder of garment . . . etc.

Analytical Method

A. Description of movements similar to opposite.
B. Analysis of main requirements for operator. For example:
Senses chiefly involved:
  Touch ("feel" of fabric, etc.).
  Vision (Concentration but general awareness).
  Movement (Muscle sense).
Mental capacities:
  Judgment
  Anticipation
  Perception
  Coordination (hand, foot, eye, bimanual).
  Correct rhythm and tempo.
  Correct movement pattern.
Muscular activities:
  Finger, wrist, hand dexterities.
  Arm movements and body rhythm.
  Leg, knee and foot movements.
Development and integration of the above leading to:
  Absolute control of machine at speed.
  Correct control of fabric in motion.
  Manipulative control and coordination of movements, etc.

SOURCE: G. H. Ladhams, "A New Method for Training Operators," *Personnel*, Vol. XXVIII, No. 6, p. 475.

which, when taught to the workers, resulted in the improvements reported in Figure 13–6.

Selection of Trainees and Instructors

Another basic factor in training is to select trainable employees. Inasmuch as training costs money, expenditures are warranted only for those from whom the greatest returns will be received. Thus, higher production results are obtained sooner at a lower training cost. Employees may also be preselected for various types of training by having detailed knowledge of their past experience and training. An example of a form which has been used to obtain this information is illustrated in Figure 13–7. In this connection, testing programs are highly worthwhile. As noted in an earlier chapter, employees selected by tests learn faster and better than nontested employees.

The selection and training of instructors also is significant. Here is an excellent opportunity for supervisors. The supervisor who becomes skilled in training methods can show the employees his interest in their welfare better than all the words in the world. By working with them to help them better themselves, he will gain their loyalty and their confidence. If lead men or gang bosses are used as trainees, they also deserve careful preparation, if training time and effort are not to be wasted. In the case of regular full-time instructors, special care should be exercised to see that such individuals not only know the rudiments of instruction but also like to teach and have an interest in the student.

Rules and Principles of Learning

Although the subject can be little more than scratched, it is desirable here to note some rules and principles that should be followed if a training program is to be effective. To begin with, in planning a program, it is wise to determine how frequently instruction should be given, and the effect of recency, types of materials, and visual and audio devices upon the learning process. The conditions and atmosphere of instruction are also items to be considered.

More specifically, industrial training is more effective when shop instruction is correlated with classroom instruction. This follows not only because the learner can see the improvement he is making in actual production, but also because of the principle that the more specific and concrete the material of instruction, the better the learning. All of this suggests, too, that it is imperative to select trainers who can stimulate the learners to exert themselves. An otherwise admirable plan

FIGURE 13–7. Experience Record

EXPERIENCE RECORD

NAME: _____   CLOCK NO._____

ADDRESS:_____   S.S. NO._____

For the purpose of determining the qualifications and experience of the employees as to their mechanical experience for defense work, the questions below are submitted:

1. Grade completed in school_____

2. Have you completed a school course in:
   (1) Arithmetic _____   (4) Trigonometry _____
   (2) Algebra _____   (5) Shop (Mach.) _____
   (3) Geometry _____

3. Have you served an apprenticeship as:
   (1) Machinist_____ (2) Toolmaker_____   (3) Diemaker_____ (4) Any other_____

4. Can you read blueprints?_____

5. Can you read micrometers?_____

6. Can you read a Vernier?_____

7. Have you had experience operating the following machine tools?:

	Prod.	Tool-room	Specify Type			Prod.	Tool-room	Specify Type
(1) Lathe	___	___	___	(10) Diamond Boring Mach.		___	___	___
(2) Multiple Turning Machine (Bullard, etc.)	___	___	___	(11) Auto. Screw Mach.		___	___	___
				(12) Hand Screw Mach.		___	___	___
(3) Milling Machine	___	___	___	(13) Chucking Machine (New Britain, Cleveland, etc.)		___	___	___
(4) Drill Press	___	___	___					
(5) Drill Press (Multi)	___	___	___	(14) Gear Cutter		___	___	___
(6) Grinder External	___	___	___	(15) Broaching Mach.		___	___	___
(7) Grinder Internal	___	___	___	(16) Semi-Automatic Lathe		___	___	___
(8) Planer	___	___	___					
(9) Shaper	___	___	___	(17) Any other		___	___	___

School   Practical

8. Have you had any training in mechanical drawing or design? _____ _____

9. Have you had experience as·
   (1) Mach. shop foreman _____   (7) Cutter grinder _____   (14) Instructor-Machine Shop _____
   (2) Mach. shop inspector _____   (8) Tool hardener _____   (15) Indicate experience, if any, on manufacture of ordnance parts; if so, what parts _____
   (3) Toolmaker _____   (9) Machine repairman ___   (10) Welder _____
   (4) Diemaker _____   (11) Boring mill (toolroom) _____
   (5) Machinist _____   (12) Layout (bench) (Surface Plate) _____   (16) Any other (use reverse side if necessary)_____
   (6) Tool and gage grinder _____   (13) Patternmaker _____   _____

10. Please indicate any other mechanical qualifications (use reverse side if necessary)_____

11 Indicate class of work you prefer_____

12 Indicate class of work best qualified for_____

Your answers will be supplemented by further practical examination and demonstration

SOURCE: *Factory Management and Maintenance*, Vol. CI, No. 10, p. 117.

of training will almost inevitably fail to achieve desired results if this principle of instruction is violated.

Also of interest is the fact that in teaching, it is sometimes best to start describing the middle steps of an operation rather than the first or last, as is usually done. Students who are pushed at the most rapid rate of which they are capable do better than when a more leisurely pace is maintained. It is also well to alternate lectures, demonstrations, and actual shop practice at carefully worked-out time intervals to get the best results. And to cite one more principle of this nature, the instructor should stand beside the student when demonstrating, so that the student will not have to reverse the images he receives, as is true when the instructor stands facing him.

Another category of rules pertains to the media and mechanics of instruction. These are so numerous that only a few suggestions can be mentioned here:

1. Use graphical, illustrative, and sample materials freely and frequently. Such matters as charts, drawings, and models increase the effectiveness of teaching and learning.
2. Use good classroom facilities, and select the best possible shop areas for instruction purposes.
3. Determine the best time for classroom work. Lectures ordinarily should not be longer than 50 to 60 minutes; discussion periods can be longer, provided that intermissions of about 10 minutes are provided after 45 minutes.
4. Examinations or tests should be scheduled at appropriate intervals in order to check the student and provide him with a sense of progress.
5. Groups in training together should seldom be larger than thirty persons if discussion is to be encouraged and if instructors are not to be over-worked.
6. Questions should emphasize "how" and "why" rather than "yes" or "no."
7. The use of pictures, whether shown by movies, slides, strip slides, or other methods, cannot be overstressed. It has been discovered that thereby:
    a) Interest of students may be increased up to 40 percent.
    b) Their range of immediate understanding may be increased up to 25 percent.
    c) Their time for completing a course may be decreased up to 25 percent.
    d) Their retention of information may be increased up to 35 percent.

EVALUATION OF TRAINING PROGRAM

Although it is contended here that training programs are well worth their cost, it is nevertheless argued that the activities of training should be evaluated. This will not only result in getting more for the training dollar but also make it possible to improve training techniques and practices. In the final analysis, the savings and improvements resulting from training must be set off against the cost of training to determine the extent of positive advantage. Such comparisons must be made on a month-to-month, company-to-company, or interdepartmental basis, to establish worthwhile conclusions.

The types of evidence which may be gathered to show savings and improvements include the following:

1. Production factors:
    a) Increase in output
    b) Decrease in scrap
    c) Decrease in unit times and unit cost of production
    d) Reduction in space or machine requirements
2. Labor factors:
    a) Decrease in labor turnover
    b) Decrease in absenteeism
    c) Decrease in number and severity of accidents
    d) Betterment of employee morale
    e) Decrease in grievances and disciplinary action
    f) Reduction in time to earn piece rates
    g) Decrease in number of discharges or quits

FIGURE 13–8. The Relation between Efficiency and Weeks of Training or Experience for Trainees and Beginners in the Operation of Disc Cutoff Machines

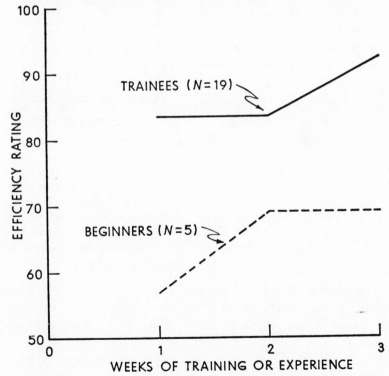

When such information is gathered, the value of training will seldom be taken for granted or questioned. Yet, it is not an onerous task to collect these data. In gathering them, care should be used to bring out the results of training by comparing the records of trainees with those of employees who were not trained. How this may be done is illustrated in Figure 13–8. There is a striking contrast between the efficiency of trainees and those who learned on the job. Such data establish strongly the desirability of planned training.

Another way of evaluating training programs is that illustrated in Figure 13–9. Here is shown the progress made by two trainees, one who

FIGURE 13–9. Learning Curves

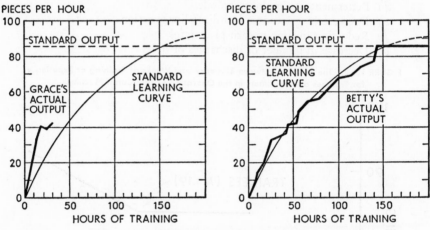

SOURCE: A. R. Knowles and L. F. Bell, "Training Curves," *Factory Management and Maintenance*, Vol. CVIII, No. 6, p. 115.

GRACE WAS TOO GOOD	BETTY? JUST RIGHT
Too good, that is, for this particular job. From the start, her progress (*heavy line*) was far better than standard. She'd worked before on repetitive jobs, and was glad to be transferred to the machine shop.	It paid to train her. Her learning curve (*heavy line*) practically coincides with the standard curve. She reached full production on the twenty-first day, and consistently met standard without difficulty.

is "too good" for the job and one who is just right. Certainly, when it is possible to ascertain the future prospects of employees so early in their employment tenure, the tool which helps is deserving of favorable support.

A few words on evaluation also are in order from a legal and professional point of view. Some training programs may have to be measured in terms of legal requirements. For example, a company that desires to qualify war veterans under an approved learner or apprentice course must meet minimum standards on such matters as quantity and quality of instruction. In cases in which a company seeks exemptions under the Wages and Hours and Walsh-Healey acts, this information must be available. Even when not mandatory, establishing such standards is desirable in order to keep the planning of courses on a definite schedule and to stipulate times for evaluating training results.

If the quantity of training is relatively unstandardized, its quality is even less so. To be sure, where federal or state agencies supervise vocational, learner, apprentice, and rehabilitation training, some review of the quality of courses and instructors is made, but this is as yet largely personal and variable. There is little doubt, however, that the quality of training has improved in the last few years. A favorable sign is the formation of the National Association of Training Directors and local associations of training directors, with the raising of standards of industrial training one of their major purposes.

QUESTIONS

1. Is it desirable to separate training and education in actual practice? Explain.
2. How would you go about justifying the cost of a formal training program for an industrial plant?
3. Although on-the-job training is used more widely than any other plan, does this mean that it is the best plan of training operative employees? Explain.
4. Why do such groups as unions and governmental agencies concern themselves with apprenticeship training in industry and business?
5. What are the merits and demerits of the internship plan of industrial training?
6. What are teaching machines? Why is their use increasing?
7. What training plans should be established in order to serve the needs caused by (a) rapid but short-run expansion and contraction of business and (b) long-run changes in volume and technology?
8. To whom should organizational responsibility for training be assigned?
9. What rules and principles of learning would it be desirable to follow in a training program?
10. How would you proceed to evaluate the effectiveness of a training program?

CHAPTER 14

EXECUTIVE DEVELOPMENT

Significance of Executive Development

One of the most encouraging trends in recent years is the recognition given executive development. Earlier, few companies either considered formal training necessary or gave it any thought whatsoever. Too commonly, it was felt that those who were appointed to the management ranks at the supervisory levels or those who were moved up the executive ladder either possessed leadership aptitudes and know-how or could acquire needed skills by experience. Moreover, managerial aspects of an executive's job were not given much consideration because technical competence was viewed as being of overriding importance.

The practice in most companies has been to select for supervisory positions those who have exhibited the most proficiency in technical work. Thus the best salesman, for example, is made the supervisor of his department when a vacancy occurs. Yet the skills which led to his selection are usually of little value in managing salesmen. There is a significant difference between a being-managed position and a managing position. Yet the manager has been expected to learn managing skills on his own.

Nor do those who move up the managerial ladder have a happier experience when they must educate themselves. It is one thing to supervise operative employees and another to supervise executives. The task of planning, organizing, directing, and controlling minor areas differs in important degrees, if not in kind, from that assumed by major executives. Yet the acquisition of needed skills, knowledge, and attitudes in higher levels has often been left to individual effort and the laws of chance.

But an encouraging change has been accelerating. More and more companies are giving increased attention to executive development at all levels, from supervisory through middle management levels to the top.

To survey such developmental efforts, the materials in this chapter are divided into the following parts:

1. Planning executive development
2. Types of programs at various executive levels
3. Content of developmental materials
4. Follow-up and evaluation of developmental results

PLANNING EXECUTIVE DEVELOPMENT

Executive development is the program by which executive capacities to achieve desired objectives are increased. The implications of this definition may be noted by commenting briefly about each of its terms. The word "program" implies that development must be concerned with a number of interrelated subjects, factors, and needs. "Executive capacities" implies consideration for (1) various personal abilities, (2) potential as well as current jobholders, and (3) all managerial levels. "Desired objectives" implies consideration for the goals of the company, of the executives, and of those being managed. And the term "increased" implies that a change must occur in the executive and, through him, in his subordinates.

This overall view of the concept of executive development provides the basis for discussing the planning of a developmental program. In this section, attention is directed to the fundamental questions of the executive capacities that need to be developed, who should be included in the program, and what conditions affect development. Later parts of this section take up examples of specific programs and of their evaluation.

Executive Capacities

Students of management are generally agreed that an executive's effectiveness depends in large measure upon his knowledge, skills, attitudes, and behavioral patterns. How much of each and in what proportion for various executives are debatable; but even here, there is much agreement on specific aspects of each.

Knowledge refers to what an executive must know about the subjects with which he deals and the functions he must perform. He must be knowledgeable in the technical area in which he manages. Such areas as production, sales, finance, accounting, engineering, and research are examples. He must have knowledge in managerial areas—i.e., in planning, organizing, directing, and controlling the work of others. He must have knowledge of people; such disciplines as psychology and motivation come to mind. And he must have knowledge of the environments in which he works; these include such areas as social, cultural, political, and ethical.

Knowledge must be applied, which calls for skills. Broadly speaking, he must have skill in solving problems; in making decisions; in dealing with things, ideas, and people; and in making his own personal adjustments to conditions and people. More specifically, the foregoing require such skills as communicating (listening as well as talking), reading, writing, creating, being sensitive to others, concentrating on tasks, and utilizing various tools (such as logic, statistics, mathematics, and psychological principles).

Attitudes are an influential factor affecting leadership. How does one perceive his job, his superiors, his subordinates, and his company? How does one perceive oneself personally, in relation to others, and in relation to future hopes and ambitions? How does one view challenge, change, and responsibilities? Almost everyone has some answers to these vital questions, but how well they are evaluated is another matter.

And finally, an executive's behavioral pattern is a part of his capacity for good or evil. On the one hand, his overt actions of dress, speech, and way of acting in various situations are seen by and affect others. The way he cooperates with others, the bases on which he decides about people, the manner in which he uses authority, and the way he allows (or does not allow) empathy to develop are examples of what those with whom he associates discern very quickly and therefore adjust their actions to his.

Candidates for Development

Obviously, all executives must possess the foregoing capacities. Equally obvious is the fact that a developmental program must be based upon some policy of who needs training most and which capacities require attention. Some needs are greater than others. High-priority needs should be taken care of first. Later, others will be included. Thus, development is recognized as an ongoing responsibility, yet one with properly evaluated timeliness. Priorities must be established by (1) a guiding principle and (2) needs of organizational levels, particular vacancies, and specific individuals.

1. *Guiding Principles.* The foundation for a developmental program is laid on the simple proposition that needed capacities *less* availa-

ble capacities *equals* capacities to be developed. For each executive position a specification of needed knowledge, skills, attitudes, and behavioral patterns would have to be established. For each person who holds or aspires to an executive position, a statement of his level of knowledge, skills, attitudes, and behavioral patterns would be derived. Then the difference between what capacities a person should have and does have constitutes developmental needs. A form used in this connection is illustrated in Figure 14–1.

If this formula were applied to every position and person, the developmental program, if fully implemented, would in practically every company call for unavailable amounts of time, money, and skills. Hence, how much can be built upon the foundation laid in the preceding section calls for the exercise of judgment. Where shall the resources which are available be applied? In any company the answer would have to be made after some evaluation of particular needs. All that can be done here is to comment generally on organizational and personal needs.

FIGURE 14–1. Form for Estimating Developmental Needs

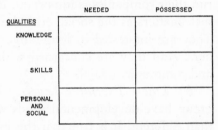

Source: W. J. E. Crissy, R. M. Kaplan, and L. H. Grossman, "Matrix Models for Planning Executive Development," *Business Topics,* Vol. XIII, No. 2, p. 22.

2. *Needs of Organizational Levels.* "Executive development" has been applied here to all managerial levels. To some, the term is used only in connection with top-level administrators. Lower levels are encompassed by such terms as "middle management training" or "supervisory training." Each of these will be considered here.

a) Administrative Levels. Not too many years ago, a developmental program for top-level executives would have been placed at the bottom of a priority list, were it placed there at all. But since then, there has been almost a complete reversal of opinion in many companies. Presidents and vice-presidents, as well as major divisional administrators, are including themselves among those needing development.

A number of reasons may be cited for this change. Significant is the fact that going back to school does not imply ignorance nor a reflection upon one's status. Once upon a time, a president would have been the butt of the silent scorn of his subordinates and the open ridicule of his friends if he had taken part in an executive development program. Indeed, he himself would not have admitted that he needed development after having worked his way through the "school of hard knocks."

But now the positive value of participation is openly recognized (and even is a status symbol). A profound influence has been the growing recognition that a top executive is essentially a manager. His prestige depends upon how well he can manage various experts, not upon his expertise in technical matters. And growth and dynamic changes in companies make even more imperative his concentration on managerial tasks. So, increasingly, he has recognized that to keep abreast of his profession—management—he must take advantage of developmental programs.

Executive development has also appealed to top executives because of the broader roles and implications they see in their jobs. How they run their companies is important. But they also see the need to explore such matters as the social, ethical, and political roles of their decisions. They are interested in long-range planning in this dynamic world of ours. And they are concerned with their relations with human forces and community affairs.

b) Lower Executive Levels. Levels below the top management group have developmental needs which are fundamentally more alike than different. It is true that the job specifications for middle management executives are somewhat different than those for supervisors. The middle manager has to take a broader view of his responsibilities. He still has to pay close attention to the completion of various specific projects. But he must think of them in terms of overall company objectives and plans. And he must be aware of the need for interdivisional cooperation. So emphasis of executive development for middle managers has in part tended to direct attention to company-wide factors.

Development of middle managers follows the same pattern as that for supervisors when it comes to specific, on-the-job performance and to preparing members in either group for promotion. In both cases, developmental efforts have been concerned with increasing managerial effectiveness. Perhaps the supervisor has received more attention in this respect because he is the one who made the most drastic change when he first moved into the managerial ranks. Then the individual's whole outlook as well as ways of operation had to change. The middle manager has received less developmental attention because he has already received some executive training at the supervisory level.

In the case of both groups, promotional objectives must be considered in a developmental program. Some supervisors must be prepared for movement into the middle management group, and some middle managers must be prepared for top management positions. Usually, promotional objectives are achieved by stressing on-the-job performance skills and then evaluating closely progress made on the job. The assumption is that those who make progress in managing current assignments because of training are most likely to succeed when promoted to higher jobs.

3. *Needs of Particular Individuals or Positions.* Development needs may also be ascertained by interpreting the needs of particular individuals or of expected job vacancies. Instead of making overall studies of organizational needs, many companies make their decisions in terms of pressures of current shortages. Expansion of business or loss of key personnel makes it obvious that there are not enough executives or that available executives need training. There then is a hurried program to prepare those at lower levels for promotion or to expand the capabilities of current jobholders to meet expanding opportunities. Such developmental planning is justifiable in smaller companies or in those caught in unexpected changes.

But more sophisticated methods of developing programs may be used. As noted in Chapter 6, "Job and Manpower Requirements," forecasting business and personnel changes can provide a basis for better estimates of training needs. It is possible in many cases to calculate for coming periods of time, within small degrees of error, how much business is to be done and, therefore, executive requirements. And it is possible to estimate turnover of personnel at various levels and, as a consequence, how many executives will have to be replaced. Schedules of personnel needs thus arrived at are an effective means of determining who has to be developed and to what degree.

Conditions of Executive Development

The foregoing discussion has stressed a number of factors that enter into the composition of an executive development program. In describing who has to be trained, how much, on what aspects, and with what resources, vital dimensions of such programs have been covered. But it would be negligent to overlook the environmental factors involved in and group interactions affected by development programs.

Turning first to environmental factors, it must be noted that executive development takes place in a complex atmosphere. The learning process is, as already noted, largely concerned with the economic success of an enterprise. It is restricted by the dollars available to carry on programs and justified by the dollar outputs it can eventually bring forth. But it also affects and is affected by the feelings of people as individuals and as members of groups. Hence, executive development is conditioned by psychological and sociological overtones. It must give due consideration to how people feel about programs, their perceptions of the rewards and obligations which flow from participation in them, and the changes which may take place in their status and roles.

In short, what goes into and comes out of a development program is affected by individual and group feelings, customs, and standards. Placing a seasoned executive into a classroom is different from enrolling a student in a college course. In the former case the marks of the teacher-student relationship must be removed, or resistance to the learning process will be informally significant, if not openly evidenced. The values of the development program, moreover, must be made as directly and immediately apparent as possible to the executive. Otherwise, he will conclude that it is below his dignity as well as a waste of his valuable time. He is not a student but a practitioner. He wants the value of the program to be as apparent to others as to himself.

This brings us to the point of interactions of people involved in executive development. A participant in a program must have assurance that as a result of his participation, there will be favorable relations with his superiors, his peers, and his subordinates. Some programs have suffered because the lessons learned in a program are not supported by the practices or opinions of one's superiors. This condition is most frustrating after one returns to the job. Or if one's peers believe that favoritism or special treatment is accorded a participant, a less than satisfactory relationship will result in cross-horizontal contacts and co-operation. And if one's subordinates perceive the program as a means of getting more out of them without compensating returns, the participant finds that his development experiences bring forth undesirable resistance.

If, then, an executive development program is to achieve desired changes, it must be adapted to the various conditions and people involved in it. To change successfully an executive's knowledge, skill, attitudes, and behavior, it is necessary to know how various people will be affected by and relate to the changes. Action will bring reaction. And the reactions will be along personal lines of attitudes, feelings, perceptions, and reasoning as well as technical lines.

TYPES OF DEVELOPMENT PROGRAMS

Having reviewed the implications and general planning of executive development, it is now appropriate to comment on some of the more common types of such programs and their coverage.

On-the-Job Development

Most executive development is accomplished on the job. The trainee learns the job under actual fire. He can size up his subordinates, and in turn be appraised by them, without artificial support or backing. He can demonstrate independently his latent leadership aptitudes. Some have argued that the best executives will naturally rise to their opportunities without formal training. And it is also claimed that this path up the executive ladder does not build up false hopes in understudies or destroy the initiative of those not specifically being groomed for promotion.

Undirected on-the-job training, however, has serious disadvantages. One no longer expects such experts as chemists, accountants, or designers to learn on their own. Inadequate programs for managers are equally unjustifiable. Moreover, on-the-job training is costly and time-consuming relative to its effectiveness. And finally, such training is wasteful, in that the lessons learned by one generation are not transmitted efficiently to succeeding generations.

It is admitted, of course, that the actual working situation—whether executive, professional, or operative—will always be an important learning situation. But sole reliance on it is defensible only in small companies, or when emergency or expanding conditions preclude other expedients. In most instances, however, it should be buttressed by more formal programs, some of which are now discussed.

Understudy Plans

Executive development by means of understudies also has its proponents. Under this plan, each executive is assigned an understudy who, in addition to his regular duties, acquires some familiarity with the responsibilities of his superior. The understudy is thus expected to be prepared to take over his superior's work when the latter is away. And he presumably will have been prepared to move into his superior's position when the vacancy occurs.

This plan has a number of advantages. Training-wise, learning takes place in the atmosphere and position in which the executive will be expected to perform. And from the executive's point of view, an excellent opportunity is opened to prepare himself for advancement.

The understudy system suffers, however, from some disadvantages. First, aspirants for promotion other than the selected understudy may feel that their chances are so remote that it is useless to exert themselves. Second, understudies themselves who have to wait a long time for vacancies may become discouraged, particularly when they see vacancies fortuitously open quickly for understudies in other organizational lines. And third, some superiors, jealous of their positions, refrain from opening their store of knowledge to potential replacements. Because of such real and practical limitations, many companies prefer to place the race for promotions on an open and unpreselected basis.

Short-Term Courses

A popular type of executive development is that of the short, intensive school program. Executives are brought together for periods of a few days up to a month for training on well-defined topics. These short courses, or workshops, as they are also known, are conducted by companies themselves, by trade and professional associations, and by universities. They are usually restricted to qualified executives and professional staff members. Their purpose is to provide refresher courses as well as instruction in new developments. Specific topics covered in such schools include work in counseling, testing, job evaluation, use of computers in decision making and systems building, and various aspects of collective bargaining. In some cases the subjects covered are very general in nature, such as basic economics, political forces, literature, and social factors.

In addition to the value of the course materials, the opportunity for discussion by small groups of executives with common interests and problems is an advantage of this form of training. A possible shortcoming, which can be minimized by scheduling the courses during seasonal lulls, is that they take executives away from their desks for a relatively extended period of time.

Since such short courses often rely upon guided discussions by small groups of conferees, it is desirable to comment briefly on the features of this phase of these programs. To be most effective, conferences call for the following:

1. A competent conference leader or instructor
2. A preplanned outline of what the group is to cover and how it is to be conducted
3. A well-equipped conference room
4. A limit to the number of conferees, preferably not over fifteen
5. An interesting beginning, spirited and pointed discussions, and a good summarization

Position Rotation Plan

Another plan of training which has had some acceptance in industry, perhaps influenced by assignment shifts in military organizations, is that of rotating key and promising executives and subordinates. The assumptions of such plans are threefold: (1) that by job rotation, executives will tend to think in terms of managerial principles rather than the technical aspects of particular functional fields; (2) that rotating will permit good executives to determine the functional fields in which they would prefer to manage; and (3) that by gaining a broad view of interdivisional problems, the top positions in the company can be filled by better qualified appointees. Against these values must be cited the disadvantages of the disturbances caused in inaugurating the plan and in the periodic changes of leadership in various departments and divisions.

Multiple Management

An interesting development in the training of the group of executives in between the supervisory and top level of an organization is that inaugurated in 1932 by McCormick & Company of Baltimore. Under this plan, known as "multiple management," three boards supplement the senior board of directors. These boards are the factory executive board, the sales board, and the junior executive board. Interest here is in the last of these.

The theory of the plan is that by working on managerial problems in much the manner that a board of directors does, the executives on the junior board will gain useful education. The board works on such problems as those pertaining to bonuses, wages, working conditions, and company plans and policies submitted to it by employees. In carrying on its discussions, and in reaching its decisions, the board has access to all company records. The solutions and suggestions adopted by the board, if approved by the senior board or the president of the company, are made company rules and regulations.

The organization of the junior board provides for rotation of members and stresses the advancement of promising executives. Membership on the thirteen-man board is by elections held every six months, at which time at least three of the current members must be replaced. Each member in turn sponsors an apprentice for two months. The thought is to guide, encourage, and indoctrinate employees who have been hired within the preceding two years and who seem to possess executive ability. And the junior board members by their own work are aware that their activities may lead ultimately to selection for the senior board, membership in which is dependent, for one thing, upon service on one of the boards mentioned earlier.

This plan has much to commend it. Executives in the middle group are given the opportunity to tackle significant company problems, to discuss them freely and openly, to exhibit their judgment and originality, and to meet with senior officers on matters of significance to them. They can develop a sense of worthwhile contribution to the solution of over-all problems of the company. Above all, to themselves personally, they know that opportunities for promotion are available and that their chances depend upon their own performance, open to the view of their colleagues as well as superior officers.

Training within Industry

An outstanding contribution to training of supervisors was made during World War II by the Training within Industry program (TWI) of the War Manpower Commission. Its work was so outstanding that the methods it refined and developed have continued to be used ever since by some companies. This program considered it important to develop the following needs of a supervisor:

1. Knowledge of the work
2. Knowledge of responsibilities
3. Skill in instructing
4. Skill in improving methods
5. Skill in leading

To develop these skills and knowledge, the program covered the following subjects in four ten-hour time allotments with sessions of two hours each:

1. Job instruction training:
   a) Prepare the worker.
   b) Present the operation.
   c) Try out performance.
   d) Follow up.
2. Job methods training:
   a) Break down the job.
   b) Question every detail.
   c) Develop the new method.
   d) Apply the new method.
3. Job relations training:
   a) Get the facts.
   b) Weigh and decide.
   c) Take action.
   d) Check results.
4. Program development training:
   a) Spot a production problem.
   b) Develop a specific plan.
   c) Get the plan into action.
   d) Check results.

Other Supervisory Programs

TWI provided but one plan of supervisory training. A few other plans are now mentioned out of the long list of attempts to train this particular level of the executive group. Since many supervisors start out as group leaders with the primary responsibility of training and some simple supervision, an example of training for this initial stage of leadership is desirable. In one instance a program has been developed in which trainees are given a three-month course under the guidance of trained instructors and under shop conditions. The trainees are given assignments that are intended to provide working knowledge along technical lines in the application of leadership qualities to improve production, in the workings of various line and staff departments, and in principles of supervision.

In another program, emphasis is laid upon the development of better relations between supervisors and the upper levels of management. This is accomplished by bringing small groups of foremen into a series of full-day meetings, lectures, and conferences with top management. By means of a carefully planned schedule and a topical outline, various aspects of company and supervisory problems are explained to and discussed with the supervisors. In this way the policies of the company can be instilled, and the association of top and supervisory officials leads to more friendly relations. After the foremen return to their jobs, a series of meetings is conducted with their immediate superiors and leaders of associate departments. Thus, from the top levels to his own department the supervisor gets a feeling of working relationships that is most helpful to him and to the "family" for which he works.

Another supervisory program is based upon guided reading of published literature. Books, bulletins, and magazine articles dealing with good foremanship are distributed to the supervisors. At intervals, conferences are held to discuss particular views, and tests are given to determine how much has been read and how well.

Decision-Making Training

Of great interest are attempts to train executives in decision making. Of course, executives have always made decisions. But the processes of decision making have been, and still often are, considered to be beyond the realm of structured training. Some attempts along this line have been made under the general head of problem solving. This has amounted largely to presenting to executives such well-known stages as stating the problem, making hypotheses, gathering data, testing alternatives, selecting and applying a given alternative, and following up the results.

More recently, decision-making training has taken more rigorous and sophisticated approaches. Logical thinking, mathematical models, electronic computers, and creativity analysis have been explored with a view to reaching a better understanding of how decisions can be improved. Thus, it is not enough, for example, to use case problems as a teaching aid in this area. Instead, it is more important to examine such matters as how one goes about in his thinking from the known to new insights into the unknown, how to relate various dimensions of a problem, how to utilize various mathematical and computer aids in thinking, and how to establish criteria for optimizing results when interacting objectives must be sought. Practically, such training has been conducted by simulating various kinds of decision-making situations (games, for example) and then conducting intensive reviews on how and why various strategies were selected.

Business Games

An interesting development in executive training is that of business games. This amounts to the design of a simulated situation in which decisions must be made as various events occur. The decisions are made by groups of players. The groups compete with each other in the sense that the one whose decisions bring about the optimum results is the winner. Playing this game is intended, of course, to provide a learning experience, not merely to see who wins.

The value of this type of training may be seen in how the game is constructed and played. A situation is established in which decisions must be made in—and which interact on—all divisions of the company. Such things as the current financial condition, the market situation, production facilities, and available personnel and funds are postulated. Then, at specified periods the players make decisions on how they would spend their money on such items as sales promotion, research and development, personnel services, production facilities, etc. These decisions are recorded on forms provided for the purpose and collected by umpires, who calculate the impact of the decisions on the company. The results are returned to the players, who then make new decisions. These, in turn, are collected and evaluated for impact, and returns are made to the players. This continues for the length of the session—which may be for a period of three or four hours, or longer. The umpires presumably have preestablished criteria for determining the impact of various decisions on the business.

The learning process is enhanced by conducting a critique session. To begin with, the umpires review the game strategies and results of the various teams. Each team reviews its own decisions and reasons therefor in relation to the results obtained. The team benefits also by evaluating what it might do differently were it to replay the game. And a general discussion by all concerned is helpful in summarizing what various members have learned from the process.

Role Playing

A method that has in recent years received much favorable attention is that of "role playing," which was first introduced as the psychodrama or sociodrama. Under this method a group of supervisors meets in conference, and two are selected to act out some situation which is commonly encountered or is causing trouble. For example, the situation might be that of an employee who is seeking a transfer. Then, one of the supervisors is assigned the role of the employee, and the second becomes the supervisor. A few pertinent facts are decided upon, and then the two, without rehearsal, act out how the supervisor and employee would react.

As the two act, the members of the conference observe, make mental notes, and evaluate the performance. After the drama is completed, others may be selected to act out the same situation, or a general discussion of the acting thus far may be reviewed. Often, a recording is made, so that the actors can review their own performances.

The desirable features of this method are centered in the fact that the learner learns by doing. He can observe, sometimes for the first time, his own actions in a critical way, particularly when sound recordings are used. There is a subsidiary value in improving the supervisor's ability to speak effectively and secure acceptance of his ideas. But the method does take a lot of time which many find too costly to make available.

Sensitivity Training

Another area to which executive training has been directed in recent years is that of sensitivity to those with whom one must deal. This is an outgrowth of the realization that executives get work done through others and with others. No matter how much an executive knows about the technical phases of his work, he will not achieve the highest possible degree of success unless he is aware of his own feelings, attitudes, and needs, and those of his superior, his subordinates, and his associates.

Such awareness may be increased by training. For a long time, executive training has recognized this only within a narrow spectrum. Thus, training has often been directed with a view to improving speaking skills. But other skills are now receiving attention. Does one know how, for example, to listen? To what degree is he aware of the feelings of various classes of people? How does the nature of a particular project or company goal affect the attitudes and desires of various people? How should arguments, orders, discussions, counselling, etc., be communicated? Training along such lines is a rightful recognition that in interacting with others, it is important to work out how to interact as well as the "what" of the interaction.

CONTENT OF DEVELOPMENT PROGRAMS

The foregoing has covered the most important types of executive development programs, and has also noted various techniques and tools used in connection therewith. It is now pertinent to examine the subject matter which is covered in such courses. This might seem a relatively easy assignment, but actually it is most difficult, for the simple reason that so little is known about what makes for successful leadership. And this is, of course, the essence of management. Some programs seek to improve and develop leadership capacities, and some satisfy themselves with the various problems a manager, executive, or supervisor is likely to encounter. Attention is given first to the latter type of content, and then leadership qualities are examined.

Perhaps the obvious and simplest approach to the matter of content is to take up tasks the executive is most likely to encounter. Of interest is the fact that most executive development programs, from this angle, take up various subjects connected with handling people—the so-called "human relations" problem. Such subjects as the following are discussed:

1. Present-day labor-management philosophy and policies
2. Working with others through organizational channels
3. Communicating up and down organizational channels
4. Employment policies and practices
5. Training and education policies and practices
6. Discipline, grievances, and rules and regulations
7. Employee services and recreation
8. Transfers, promotion, merit, and seniority policies
9. The union contract—its meaning and implications
10. Community agencies and institutions

On the other hand, a more basic approach is to try to develop content, which has reference to the basic characteristics a leader should possess, irrespective of the specific tasks performed. Unfortunately, there is as yet no agreement as to what these characteristics are. However, much study is being devoted to this problem, and it is likely that agreement among students will consequently develop. To illustrate the characteristics that have been included in executive development programs, the following list is of interest:

1. Ability to think
2. Ability to organize
3. Ability to handle people
4. Ability to plan
5. Ability to lead
6. Ability to get and interpret facts
7. Loyalty
8. Decisiveness
9. Teaching ability
10. Ability to solve problems
11. Courage
12. Self-motivation
13. Desire for achievement and prestige
14. Social balance and understanding
15. Sense of responsibility
16. Emotional balance and poise
17. Ability to influence people, individually and in groups
18. Attitudes toward subordinates and associates
19. Attitude toward community associations
20. Attitude toward economic and political systems

This list is by no means complete, but it does illustrate the wide range of subjects that have been considered basic leadership traits.

An interesting illustration of the training desirable for leaders may be deduced from Figure 14–2. This depicts the fundamental responsibilities of executives and, in the case cited, the approximate percentage of time spent in performing the duties. Certainly, if the content of a job can be so determined, the next step in appropriate training is more easily taken.

Since there is so much variation in content, the best practice for any company in establishing its own program is to give consideration to outside practices, but to build its program in terms of its own needs. This can be done by taking the following steps:

1. Determine as precisely as possible the major objectives or tasks the company faces.
2. Inventory present executive capacities.
3. Compute the shortages of executive capacities as compared to major needs.
4. Establish the content of training required by individual executives to bring them up to desired standards.

By tailoring content to suit individual needs, it is possible to arrive at a program which will invariably prove valuable. Moreover, such an approach usually achieves better executive cooperation in the program because the executives themselves must help in developing it. And where participation is involved, there is a greater desire to make the

FIGURE 14–2. Executive Responsibilities

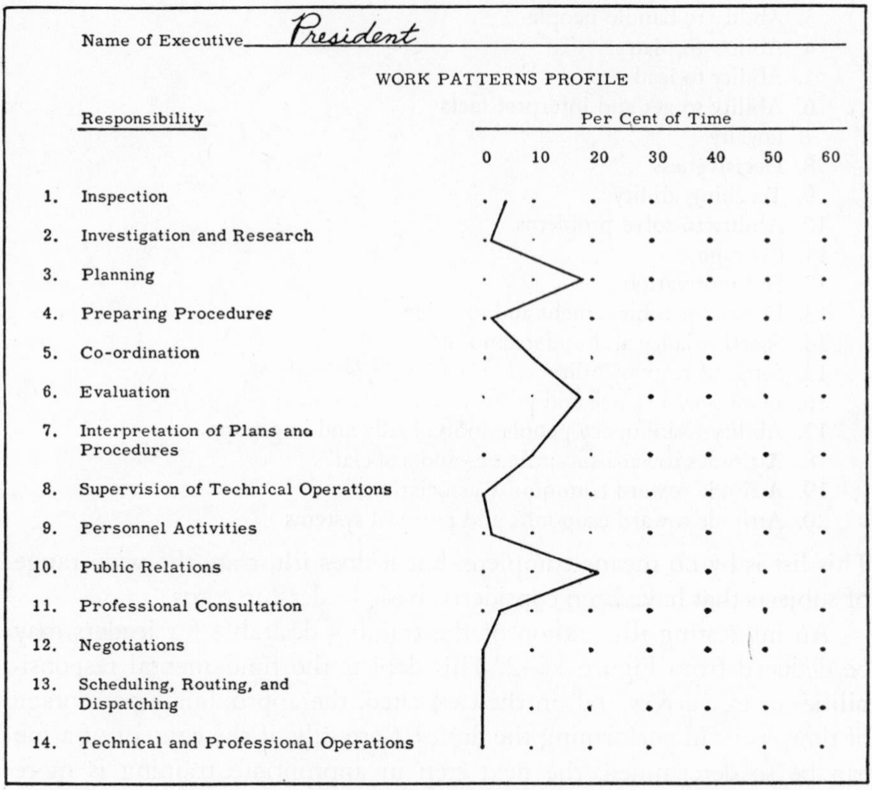

SOURCE: C. L. Shartle, "Leadership and Executive Performance," *Personnel*, Vol. XXV, No. 5, p. 371.

program work. In the final analysis, this in itself helps to develop a better leader because an executive who seeks to improve himself possesses a sound feeling of service to others—a desirable quality of true leadership.

FOLLOW-UP AND EVALUATION

Follow-up and evaluation of executive development programs are particularly difficult because it is almost impossible to determine which results of executive efforts are attributable to training and which to other causes. Nevertheless, it is desirable to make an attempt in this direction because a partial answer is better than none. Examples are available of measurements which have been made of training results. In the case of TWI, a study of six hundred plants gave the results shown in Table 14–1.

TABLE 14–1

TRAINING RESULTS

KIND OF RESULT	PERCENTAGE OF PLANTS REPORTING RESULTS			
	Under 25%	25–49%	50–74%	75% and Over
Production increased.............	63	16	1	20
Training time reduced..........	52	25	7	16
Manpower saved................	89	9	1	1
Scrap loss reduced..............	89	5	5	1

Interesting results in individual plants are shown in the reports illustrated in Figures 14–3 and 14–4.

An interesting summary of the results that should flow from a good program is contained in the following listing (certainly it is a broad-gauge test of this subject, as well it should be):

1. Increased executive management skills
2. Development in each executive of a broad background and appreciation of the company's overall operations and objectives
3. Greater delegation of authority because executives down the line are better qualified and better able to assume increased responsibilities
4. Creation of a reserve of qualified personnel to replace present incumbents and to staff new positions
5. Improved selection for promotion
6. Minimum delay in staffing new positions and minimum disruption of operations during replacements of incumbents
7. Provision for best combination of youth, vigor, and experience in top management and increased span of productive life in high-level positions
8. Improved executive morale
9. Attraction to the company of ambitious men who wish to move ahead as rapidly as their abilities permit
10. Increased effectiveness and reduced costs, resulting in greater assurance of continued profitability[1]

Evaluation of Trainees

Another approach to evaluation is that of determining how well executive trainees have learned. On the one hand, they may be tested and rated after their courses of training. Thus, in some of the plans mentioned in the foregoing, supervisors, and higher executives as well,

---

[1] E. W. Reilley and B. J. Muller-Thym, "Executive Development," *Personnel,* Vol. XXIV, No. 6, p. 412.

FIGURE 14–3

TWI OUTSTANDING "RESULT OF THE WEEK" IN DALLAS DISTRICT

Result was noted and reported to us on (Date) *May 3, 1945*

Result of: J.I.   *x*   J.M.   *x*   J.R.   *x*   P.D.

---

1. Kind of establishment (name of product or service)   *Shipbuilding*

2. Name and location of plant   *"X" Company*

      May we use company name?   Yes   *x*   No

---

3. Number of employees in plant   *18,749*

---

4. Number of employees affected   *15,000*

---

5. Just what happened in "before and after" terms:
   (State evidence in facts, figures, man hours, etc.)

During the past 4 years four different types of vessels have been built. When the yard opened only 2% of the workers had previous shipbuilding experience. About 50% had no previous experience in any related industry.
The average employment during this 4 years has been 18,000. The number of certificates issued in the three TWI "J" programs are:

              J.I. 2850
              J.M. 800
              J.R. 540

Mr. Newell Hogan, Training Director, and Mr. James D. McClellan, Production Manager, reported the following beneficial results from TWI programs:

        Increase in production..............45%
        Reduction in training time...........78%
        Reduction in scrap.................69%
        Reduction in tool breakage.........75%
        Saving of manpower...............45%
        Reduction of accidents..............70%

These results were arrived at by comparison of production department records, based on the construction of the first 50 destroyer escorts as compared with the last 50. The credit for these beneficial results is largely attributed to the successful continuous use of TWI programs.

All levels of supervision in both the yard and the office have been processed in one or more of the "J" programs. This accounts for the large number of employees affected.

SOURCE: War Manpower Commission, *The Training within Industry Report* (Washington, D.C.: U.S. Government Printing Office, 1945), p. 94.

are rated as to their promise for further training. In addition, regular examinations are scheduled to ascertain how well various phases of technical and descriptive materials have been absorbed. Such tests should be given with care in order to avoid the development of a feeling on the part of trainees that a "school" is being operated; most executives

FIGURE 14–4

TWI OUTSTANDING "RESULT OF THE WEEK" IN DENVER DISTRICT

Result was noted and reported to us on (Date) *April 16, 1945*

Result of: J.I. *x* J.M. *x* J.R. *x* P.D.

1. Kind of establishment (name of product or service) *Rubber products*

2. Name and location of plant *"X" Company*

    May we use company name? Yes *x* No

3. Number of employees in plant *5,000*

4. Number of employees affected *40*

5. Just what happened in "before and after" terms:
          (State evidence in facts, figures, man hours, etc.)

   Before "J" Programs:
     In one clerical department, where 46 were employed, 375,000 units were produced in one year.

   After "J" Programs:
     By applying the three "J" methods conscientiously and continuously, 450,000 units were produced by 40 workers.
     This is an increase of 20%, or 75,000 units, in output by a work force reduced by 13%, or 6 workers.

   The quality of the work was also greatly improved.

   Note: Most credit is given to J.I. and J.R., as the work force has always been method-improvement minded.

SOURCE: War Manpower Commission, *The Training within Industry Report* (Washington, D.C.: U.S. Government Printing Office, 1945), p. 93.

like to feel that the "little red schoolhouse" is a part of their past.

More informal plans of follow-up include conferences and discussions by superiors with those who have taken training work. In this way the supervisors can obtain some measure of the value of the training received, and the trainees will prepare themselves more carefully, knowing that such talks are to take place. An added value of such informal talks is that they bring various levels of leadership together more frequently, giving each the opportunity to get better acquainted with the other.

An inversion of follow-up which has desirable points is that in which trainees are asked to express themselves on the quality or results of training. In one company, for example, executives are asked to sign and comment upon the quality and usefulness of each conference they attend. This acts as a double-edged weapon: (1) The conference leader and training school are alert to build and conduct better sessions, and (2) the conferees must be more attentive in order to be able to express pertinent interpretations and criticisms. In another company, executives who take various forms of training are required to fill out weekly reports indicating progress in various aspects of their work. All that is required is a simple check (without quantitative estimates) opposite any of the following items: reduction of indirect labor, indirect cost, daywork operations, materials, or supplies; and increase or improvement in processes, quality, personnel relations, or suggestions. Here again, knowledge that the training is expected to produce results will keep the trainees alert to see how training material can be applied in various phases of their work.

QUESTIONS

1. Why has the adoption of executive development programs accelerated in recent years?
2. What capacities do developmental programs for executives seek to upgrade?
3. Indicate what differences in training programs might be found in the case of lower levels of executives, middle groups, top executives, and staff executives.
4. What environmental factors and group factors are involved in or affect executive development efforts?
5. What is your appraisal of on-the-job training plans for executives?
6. What are the advantages of "business-game" training for executives? How does this training tie in, if at all, with decision-making training for executives?
7. "Role-play" with another student a situation in which you pretend to handle an employee who refuses to take a promotion to a higher job because of his fear of failure. What difficulties do you encounter in this practice session, and what must be done to overcome them?
8. What is your opinion of sensitivity training for executives?
9. Some have contended that conferences serve merely to waste time, delay decisions, and increase organization politics. How may these pitfalls be avoided?
10. By what methods may executive development sessions be evaluated? What are the difficulties standing in the way of such measurements?

CHAPTER 15

MORALE AND ATTITUDES

Scope of Discussion

Education as well as training are essential to effective performance by well-adjusted people. Education serves to influence favorably the understanding, perceptions, and attitudes of people at all organizational levels. Operative employees, for example, work more effectively when they understand what management is doing, when they feel that management's objectives are significant and fair, and when they agree that management's practices are justifiable. And executives, in turn, can lead more effectively when they understand the motives, needs, and thinking of employees. Through such understanding comes (1) appreciation for one another's interests and problems, (2) adjustments in their thinking and action, and (3) fair compromises in their plans and interactions.

If management is to educate labor effectively, it must determine what labor knows, feels, and believes. It must be aware of the morale and attitudes of the lower levels of an organization. Hence, this chapter is devoted to practices by which such needed information is communicated upward. In the next chapter, attention will be directed to downward and horizontal flows of information. Thus is established the two-way flow of communications which is indispensable to the education of both management and employees.

In this chapter the upward phase of communications is taken up under the following headings:

1. Meaning of morale
2. Theory of morale development
3. Factors of morale development
4. Measuring morale and attitudes
5. Steps in developing morale
6. Rules of morale determination

Meaning of Morale

Definitions of morale are many. A review of them all would show that they define it in terms of what it is, what it does, where it resides, whom it affects, and what it affects. Thus, to use the foregoing classification, morale is composed of the following:

1. What it is—an attitude of mind, an esprit de corps, a state of well-being (or unwell-being), and an emotional force
2. What it does—affects output, quality, costs, cooperation, discipline, enthusiasm, initiative, and other aspects of success
3. Where it resides—in the minds, attitudes, and emotions of individuals as members of a group
4. Whom it affects—immediately, employees and executives in their interactions; ultimately, the customer and the community
5. What it affects—willingness to work and to cooperate in the best interests of the enterprise and, in turn, of the individuals themselves

Simply stated, then, morale is a state of mind and spirit, affecting willingness to work, which in turn affects organizational and individual objectives. Morale may range from very high to very low. It is not an absolute but is subject to change, depending upon management's plans and practices.

This simple definition emphasizes willingness to work. This is important. A person may be so contented with his lot that he does only enough to get by. Another person works hard because he is dissatisfied. He wants to better himself. Good morale would scarcely be a condition of the former person; it could well be of the latter. Dissatisfaction of a group need not be a sign of poor morale when it is associated with a desire to improve through cooperation with organizational goals. Dissatisfaction with management could, however, well be a sign of poor morale.

The foregoing implies that morale is a group manifestation. A particular person may have a favorable attitude toward his own work and supervisor. But the group with whom he works may take a very unfavorable stand against certain company practices. The unfavorable group reaction may well offset the effect of an employee's personal opinions.

One more point about this definition: It infers a relation to organizational success. But it also makes reference to individual satisfaction. When morale is low, employees evidently have been driven to this sad state by some poor practice of management or by a mistaken interpretation of a good practice. To develop good morale, management need not conclude that a battle with labor is inevitable. On the contrary, employees are as interested in good morale as is management—perhaps more so, because they suffer not only from the results of but also from the state of poor morale.

Theory of Morale Development

In undertaking any program, it is desirable to have a good theory—a sound explanation—of how the program works. A morale development program is no exception. Unless one has a logical and defensible theory, his management of morale may be worse than if no program at all were operated. It is suggested here that such a theory should give consideration to the following:

1. Logical sequence of development
2. The essence of morale
3. Effects of good morale

1. *Sequence of Development.* If morale is a state of mind, to use this brief phrase for its other facets, how does it come about? What causes this state of mind? It might be stated, simply, that management, the environment, or what the company does causes it. But to continue the questioning, why might these cause it?

To begin with, management only does what is logical when it runs a company. It seeks to earn a profit by producing a product or service at a competitive price. And this it hopes to do through the proper utilization of labor, tools, materials, machines, and other resources. So it hires enough workers at going rates and expects from them the skills and talents labor possesses. No more of people does it ask—so it seems—than of the materials which are purchased. The materials have certain qualities which are needed and so does manpower.

But of all the resources management buys, labor has a set of characteristics peculiar and unique unto itself. It is "used," to be sure, as are the other factors of production. But in addition, it thinks and feels how it is being used, why it is being used, whether its compensation is satisfactory, and particularly how it compares with other factors and with its own members. In short, it reacts to, as well as acts in, its environment.

This does not imply that people are unduly selfish. Employees may react very favorably when they conclude that the company's objectives are good, significant, and widely admired. Indeed, to cite an extreme case, the highest form of unselfishness is exhibited by those willing to give up their lives for their country. In business affairs, such sacrifices are not called for, yet employees may exert themselves for the company's good and their own good when they respect the goals of the company.

The sequence in which company goals and individual goals are related is highly significant as far as morale is concerned. In cases of good morale the employees work for the company first and then get their reward. In cases of poor morale the employees want assurances of pay first, and then the work is rendered. While the interests of both parties are intertwined, in the former case the logical sequence for effective relationships is in effect, but not so in the latter case. But when people mistrust each other, they cannot logically be blamed for taking an illogical course.

Unfortunately, objective and factual explanations in economic terms are seldom adequate. Who can explain in a company of 40,000, let us say, why a particular individual deserves to get precisely $3.50 an hour? Without doubt, the answer is that no one can do so.

Thus, much understanding is based upon other factors. Employees feel that compensation is right or wrong by:

a) Gossip they hear from other workers
b) Profit reports they read in the papers
c) Salaries of executives they read about
d) Treatment they get from superiors
e) Claims and arguments of union representatives
f) Working conditions, in particular and in general
g) Intelligence or education they themselves possess
h) The way they feel about their fellow workers

Obviously, almost anything may affect understanding and, in turn, attitude of mind or spirit.

2. *The Essence of Morale.* Morale is, in essence, conditioned by a group's understanding of the relation between personal interests and company interests. Employees who conclude that their interests are being served fairly when they contribute to the organization's interests develop a favorable attitude of mind. Conversely, their attitude is poor when they perceive an unfair treatment of their interests.

A critical aspect of thinking about contributions and compensation inheres in the nonstorable character of manpower. The time, skill, and energy of people must be used and rewarded here and now, or they are forever lost. So employees are keenly aware of the need of immediate and fair decisions in their behalf.

Essentially, then, morale develops out of a mutual satisfaction of interests. In the case of labor, it understands that to gain its goals, it must help the company achieve its goals. And labor must also believe that the share it gets is fair in relation to what it and others contribute. If the interests of all parties to a group endeavor are, in their respective minds, fairly served, their morale will be high. So morale development takes place through the process of successfully integrating interests.

3. *Effects of Good Morale.* This discussion of the theory of morale can best be summarized by noting the possible effects of good morale. These effects may be classified as immediate and ultimate.

Immediately, good morale has some very important results for management and for employees. Management finds that subordinates are willing to follow their requests and commands with enthusiasm and respect. Indeed, work is done without the need of commands or supervision. This is a very pleasant condition for the executive. Moreover, he will find that employees will work hard in the face of difficulties. When overtime or holiday work is called for, the response will be quick and understanding. And most of all, employees openly show the respect for and confidence in their leaders which is so satisfying to the leaders themselves.

Good morale has immediate effects upon employees, too. They work with satisfaction and pleasure. The hours of work go by in an atmosphere of relaxed effort. Nothing seems to drag, the days are not empty and boring, and a feeling of insignificance is absent. It is, in short, good to be at work and in association with one's fellows and one's superiors. Work—as much as it can be—is a pleasure and not a misery.

These immediate effects cause some desirable ultimate effects. To management, there is higher output of better products at lower costs. And in turn, there will be more consistent, higher profits. To employees, there are higher wages, more secure employment, and a higher standard of living. And to society in general, there are more goods and services obtained more effectively from the limited supply of resources.

These effects do not all flow from morale itself. Morale should not be looked upon as the only source of success. Even the best employee cannot make bricks without straw. But the best employee can do much, much better with what he has than the worker whose morale is low.

Factors of Morale Development

It is now pertinent to note the factors which have an effect upon employee morale. As a broad statement, anything can influence the attitude of employees; the factors are infinite. A more useful approach to this matter of factors is to classify them according to their source, as follows:

1. The employees themselves
2. Management practices
3. Extracompany forces and factors

1. *Employee Factors.* The quality of morale is definitely influenced by the type of employees. As already noted, understanding has a significant effect upon morale. And understanding is dependent, in part, upon the ability of people to understand. If, then, the ability of employees to understand reasonable explanations is low, management, try as it may, will not be able to get across its messages. Thus, in its hiring policies, a company should seek not only people who are capable of doing their jobs but also those who can grasp the logical relationships and rewards involved in group effort.

The status and roles of employees have a bearing upon the possibilities of morale development. Employees may be members of a union. In that case, they will invariably take on attitudes and reactions because of their membership. This does not mean that such attitudes will necessarily be negative. But it does mean that management will have to deal with a group which is not so easy to convince of the views it considers correct. Even when not organized, labor may take on particular attitudes because of such things as the labor-management history in a given community or the manner in which labor looks upon itself in the factory.

2. *Management Practices.* The most important group of factors affecting morale are those falling within the province of management. Included here would be (*a*) the various subject matters regarding which management normally makes decisions and (*b*) the manner in which management acts in carrying out its various duties.

In regard to the first of these categories, a brief outline is sufficient to indicate their significance upon the morale of employees. Few employees, indeed, would be unaware of or disinterested in how the following were decided:

a) Objectives—to what extent the goals of stockholders, customers, and labor are to be served
b) Policies—the basic guides established in a company relating to such questions as wage levels, seniority versus merit, promotional channels, working conditions, and union-management relations
c) Procedures—steps to be taken in handling such matters as grievances, disciplinary action, employee services, and counseling
d) Communications—the extent to which and the channels through which information is to flow back and forth between organizational levels

These listings are sufficient to illustrate the impact such decisions can have upon the morale of employees. Any one of these areas has more than enough powder to blow up relations between labor and management. Conversely, they can be the source of great good, as illustrated in Figure 15–1, which summarizes the opinions of the employees in one company toward two levels of management.

But morale is affected not only by what management does, but by how it does what it does. Thus an executive may be absolutely fair in his decision in selecting a particular man for promotion. But to other interested candidates the selection may appear the rankest kind of favoritism. This happens when the executive is secretive about the stand-

FIGURE 15–1. Report of Employee Opinions of Management

YOUR SUPERVISOR

Please tell us how you rate your *immediate supervisor* on:

Explaining and teaching the work:
44.8 He's a good teacher.
35.7 He gets by.
9.0 He can't teach.
10.5 He doesn't try to teach or explain.

Treating people fairly:
36.1 He's always fair.
38.9 He's fair most of the time.
15.7 He's fair about half the time.
7.2 He's not often fair.
2.1 He's never fair.

Letting you know the news:
50.5 He keeps me posted.
49.5 We don't get much news from him.

Giving a hand when there's trouble:
52.1 He's good about helping you out.
29.2 He does about what he's supposed to do.
18.7 Don't expect much help from him.

Giving Orders:
73.9 He tells you to do a thing in a way that makes you feel like doing it.
26.1 The way he tells you to do things makes you mad.

Upgrading:
62.4 He usually picks the best people to move along.
12.3 He makes poor selections.
25.3 I think he plays favorites.

Letting you know how you're doing:
48.5 He lets me know in a nice way how I'm doing.
11.1 He lets me know in a poor way how I'm doing.
40.4 He doesn't let me know in any way.

Being a good leader:
36.5 He's a good leader.
42.4 He's an average leader.
21.1 He's not a leader.

　　　　* * *

We are happy that, generally, TP supervisors are given a pretty fair rating. There is room for improvement in the areas of letting people know how they are doing, and in passing along instructions.

BOY, WHAT AN ASSIGNMENT!

GOOD GUY!

LET ME BUZZ YOUR EAR!

C'MON GANG— FOLLOW ME!

YOUR DEPARTMENT FOREMAN

Will you please answer the same questions about your *department foreman,* the man to whom your supervisor reports:

Explaining and teaching the work:
35.1 He's a good teacher.
24.2 He gets by.
5.3 He can't teach.
12.2 He doesn't try to teach or explain.
23.2 His job doesn't call for him to teach or explain.

Treating people fairly:
33.2 He's always fair.
35.4 He's fair most of the time.
17.6 He's fair about half the time.
10.1 He's not often fair.
3.7 He's never fair.

Letting you know the news:
36.7 He keeps me posted.
63.3 We don't get much news from him.

Giving a hand when there's trouble:
40.0 He's good about helping you out.
23.5 He does about what he's supposed to do.
22.4 Don't expect much help from him.
14.1 His job doesn't call for him to help.

Giving Orders:
72.4 He tells you to do a thing in a way that makes you feel like doing it.
27.6 The way he tells you to do things makes you mad.

Upgrading:
57.5 He usually picks the best people to move along.
14.9 He makes poor selections.
27.6 I think he plays favorites.

Letting you know how you're doing:
39.2 He lets me know in a nice way how I'm doing.
9.1 He lets me know in a poor way how I'm doing.
51.7 He doesn't let me know in any way.

Being a good leader:
37.7 He's a good leader.
40.6 He's an average leader.
21.7 He's not a leader.

　　　　* * *

You gave both foremen and supervisors a good rating on their fairness. That foremen as a group did not rate quite as high as supervisors may be explained by their less frequent contacts with employees due to the nature of their duties. We wish that both foremen and supervisors would give you more news.

Courtesy: Thompson Products, Inc., Cleveland, Ohio

ards used to evaluate the various candidates, when he gives his preferred choice special privileges or opportunities to gain needed experience, or when he refuses to discuss the matter with those passed over.

The behavior of executives is particularly significant as a morale factor. Some executives are autocratic in their attitude toward subordinates. Others imply a feeling that they are better than their subordinates —that the latter are second-class citizens. Others are suspicious of the motives and actions of employees and openly indicate their lack of confidence. Others avoid, if not despise, the company of their workers. And still others are contemptuous of the intelligence of employees. Such attitudes are quickly noted. Obviously, it is natural for employees to return a negative attitude of mind. To reverse these behaviorisms serves to enhance the morale of employees.

3. *Extracompany Forces and Factors.* Morale may also be affected by forces and factors outside the company itself. The union is a significant example, and various community and family relationships are another.

The union is so closely intertwined, and becoming increasingly more so, with company affairs that it may be incorrect to classify it as an extracompany agency. But legally it is, if not in other relationships. Certainly, it is a potent morale factor. How employees feel toward their company is significantly determined by the indoctrination they receive from their unions. And at times—such as during a strike—their attitude seems to be totally swayed by this force.

This is not intended to imply that the union is to be viewed as a foe of management, that it inevitably is opposed to whatever management stands for. There is no doubt that there are those in management—and those in labor—who take this position. A fairer view seems to lie elsewhere. The union, in its best role, is a guardian of the fair interests of labor. It should be concerned with a fair share for labor, not an unfair share. It should seek logical, factual, and scientific answers to labor-management problems, not dogmatic, prejudiced, or expedient answers. In its rightful role a union need not be construed as a negative morale factor. It can well contribute to the willingness of employees to work hard and to cooperate effectively.

Other extracompany forces affecting employee morale are numerous. Though it may not be company business, an employee's attitude toward his work is affected by a variety of things, such as:

a) How well he gets along with his wife, children, and relatives
b) The nature of his associations with friends and neighbors
c) The state of his health or of his family

d) Whether or not he has picked a winner in politics, in his favorite team, or in the last football pool

e) Environmental factors in the community, such as parking and traffic conditions, housing conditions, and smoke conditions

To what extent management can divert his attention from these matters during working hours is conjectural. Sometimes, they are so strong that it would seem better to close down the shop for all the good that is being done. On the first day of the hunting season, during the World Series, at a critical election time, or when everyone is a bull in the stock market, willingness to work seems to be at its nadir.

It might seem a herculean task to cope with such an infinite variety of morale factors. This is not so. Not all are effective at the same time. But to work with any of them, management should be able to determine which ones are effective at particular times. A check list, expanded from those suggested in the foregoing, will be helpful in that connection.

Nor should a manager be pessimistic because some of the morale factors seem to be out of his jurisdiction. Perhaps an executive cannot make a direct attack upon such morale factors as unions or family relations. But something can be done. Education can be a powerful tool to help an employee make a better appraisal of the arguments presented by his union. And counseling aid may help him solve his marital problems. Efforts in such directions are time-consuming and divert executive time and resources from company business. But they are justifiable if they ultimately result in higher productivity and better cooperation.

Determination of Current Morale

With this background of the meaning and theory of morale, it is now appropriate to discuss ways and means of working toward morale development and improvement. The action to be taken can be simply expressed by the following formula:

Desired morale *less* current morale *equals:*
1. Deficit to be made up or
2. Excess to be protected

Before plans can be developed, it is significant to determine the current state of morale. The present section is devoted to a description of how this may be done, by taking up (1) measures of morale and (2) methods of measurement. In the following two sections, plans of improving morale and follow-up of morale plans will be discussed.

1. *Measures of Morale.* Unlike temperature or distance, morale cannot be measured directly. It is as yet impossible for all practical purposes to delve directly into the minds or feelings of people. As a consequence, morale measurement must be based upon indirect units or interpretations.

Indirect measures of attitude are of three types: experimental measures, personal measures, and results. The first of these has to do with psychological attempts to measure attitudes. Clinical studies are made in a variety of ways to get a person's reactions, outlook, physiological changes, and ideas. From measurements of mental, emotional, and physical differences, variations in different people to the same situations or stimuli are noted. Such measures are useful at present only in particularly difficult situations where the high cost may be offset by important results.

More practical measures may be obtained from personal manifestations of various types. For example, the behavior of employees is very revealing. Are they surly or cheerful, despondent or happy, listless or enthusiastic, dull or alert? These overt actions are excellent, though qualitative, measures of morale. This is particularly true when changes in behaviorism can be detected. Another group of personal measures is that of verbal expressions. Employees express opinions or attitudes concerning such things as company policies, executive behavior, working conditions, or other matters. Whether or not their expressions really reflect their true morale is something that must be carefully checked by management in one way or another. This problem of methods will be touched on in the next few pages. A third group of personal measures is obtained through noting complaints or expressions of unwillingness to work. Records of such things as grievances, disciplinary cases, absenteeism, tardiness, and refusal to work overtime will quickly reveal trends in morale changes.

Actual results of one kind and another are also useful, if indirect, measures of morale. What is the trend of individual and group productivity, quality of work, unit costs, machine breakdowns, material usage, and the like? Undesirable trends would merit investigation. Assume, for example, that productivity in a given department has fallen 10 percent during a particular month. An investigation shows that no technical changes were made during this period. The only change has been the assignment of an engineer to the position of assistant supervisor. Upon further investigation, it is found that employees are fearful that the appointment was made to establish tighter output standards. Whether their fears are justified or not is beside the point for the moment. The fact is that the output figures did indicate a possible explanation for the lowering of morale.

2. *Methods of Measurement.* A number of methods are available by which measures of morale may be obtained. The major ones are observation, interviews, questionnaires, and record keeping.

a) Observation. Observation can be one of the best methods to measure morale. Perhaps its very simplicity lulls executives into ineptitude. They look, but they do not see. Or they are so overloaded with details, important tasks, or an overextended span of control that they have no time to look. Or they may foolishly pride themselves on an ability to size up individuals with the merest glance. Or they may be afraid to look lest they find something wrong. Suffering from these failings, any executive will get no use from observation, and he may get actual misinformation.

To use observation, an executive must practice observation and then do it consciously and systematically. He will be aware of morale and morale changes of employees if only he will watch their behavior, listen to their talk, and note their actions. People "tell" us constantly how they feel. They tell us by a shrug of the shoulder, a change of facial expression, a shuffling of feet, a nervous fluttering of hands, a tonal expression, a change in work habits, or an avoidance of our company. An observing executive will make note of these. Any departures or deviations from normal will put him on immediate notice that something may be wrong.

But how far from normal must an employee deviate before the deviation is worthy of executive action? While this is difficult to answer, there are few leaders who do not state—after a change has been pointed out to them—that they noticed the change earlier but did not think much about it or forgot about it, though they intended to look into it. The point is that since executives do acknowledge such deviations afterward, they could as well consider taking action about them earlier.

b) Interviewing. Interviewing is another useful method of morale measurement. And again, it is a tool any manager could learn to apply with great profit to himself. Interviewing provides for a face-to-face, personal, and verbal exchange of information, ideas, and points of view. But it is not something that will be satisfactory if done in a casual, unplanned, or careless manner. This is the way it is usually done. And that is why it is generally useless as a morale measurer.

But interviewing can be very effective. The interviewer must adhere to a few basic rules. These were reviewed in an earlier chapter, so reference to them is all that need be noted here. A few other ideas are, however, in order. Employees either must be made to feel free about coming in for interviews or must be sought out at times that will give a good sampling of their attitudes.

One seldom encounters a successful plan of employee-initiated interviews. To be sure, many companies announce an open-door policy. A study of those who come through the doors voluntarily would reveal few takers. A few may go to the top and more to their own superior or the personnel department if they are "burned up" about something. But as a method of measuring morale, particularly in initial stages of change, such interviews have little to commend them.

Employer-initiated interviews are to be preferred if interviews are to be relied upon as a method of measuring morale. In such instances, some plan for sampling opinions is desirable. Thus an executive may plan to talk informally to a given number of employees every week or month. Or he may use some anniversary, such as a hiring date, to contact his subordinates conveniently. If staff members such as personnel department representatives or counselors participate in the interviewing, they may schedule interviews in particular departments or among certain types of workers. In this way, trends in particular areas may be determined and compared with those in other areas or past periods.

c) Questionnaires. A popular method of measuring morale is that of the questionnaire. Employees are asked to express their opinions on a printed form to specific or open-end questions. In the first type an employee may be asked such questions as the following: Do you get a satisfactory answer from your supervisor when you ask him about wages? Then a specific list of answers is provided from which a choice can be made as follows:

Always; usually; sometimes; seldom; never

This type of questionnaire makes it easy for the employee to answer and for management to collate and compare answers. But it does restrict the employee, or it may cause him to supply answers to questions about which he has never thought.

An open-end question has no terminal limitations. Of this type is the following question: What do you dislike most about your work? Here, the employee is restricted neither in what he may say nor in how much he says. It is difficult, however, for management to collate and compare the answers. And many employees do not like to take the time to write out full answers or cannot express themselves satisfactorily.

In either type the questionnaire may cover only selected subjects, or it may "cover the waterfront." The latter type suffers from excessive length but is useful in isolating particular subjects which may be causing discontent. The former can serve to obtain quickly the views of employees on particular topics. Then, from time to time the questionnaire can be repeated to determine what the trend is on the particular subjects.

d) Record Keeping. It is also desirable to design and operate a good system of record keeping if such results as output, quality, and costs are to be used to measure morale. Output and quality records should be kept by individuals and departments. Absenteeism and tardiness should be recorded on personnel summary cards and recapitulated on departmental record sheets. Similarly, records should be kept on any other measures which may denote morale changes, such as grievances, disciplinary action, suggestions made, and merit ratings.

Plans for Improving Morale

The current state of morale having been ascertained according to one of the methods suggested in the foregoing, steps may then be taken to improve morale—if a deficit exists. A deficit may be readily apparent when something is obviously wrong. When negative morale is "written all over" the attitudes or actions of particular individuals or departments, there is no problem of where action must be taken. But when it is simply desired to raise morale, what will constitute a reasonable increase becomes a matter of judgment or guesswork.

In broad outline, a program to develop morale would consist of the following:

1. Divide and locate responsibilities for morale upon:
   a) Line and staff executives
   b) Administrative and operative executives
2. Determine the relationships that exist between:
   a) Company objectives and personal objectives
   b) The factors which cause good morale and the results which flow from it
3. Determine the extent to which good morale exists in terms of:
   a) Effectiveness of the organization in attaining its objectives
   b) The attitudes of employees toward various phases of the company
4. Develop and install plans for:
   a) Counteracting the forces leading to poor morale
   b) Strengthening the forces leading to good morale
5. Follow up and evaluate morale-building programs:
   a) By periodic audits of specific programs
   b) By periodic audits of all personnel activities

This outline is not expanded here because, in essence, it is the outline of the entire text.

Rules of Morale Determination

Several suggestions are worth noting if the flow of information relative to morale is to be valid and reliable. Perhaps the foremost requirement for morale development and maintenance is the realization that these are high responsibilities of management. If management is to protect and enhance its desired prerogatives of leadership, it will do well to take the time and effort to improve the morale of its supposed followers. If management does not, neither it nor anyone else should be surprised when the allegiance of employees attaches to outside groups rather than internal management. And even though management may take the financial risks of operating a business, that in itself does not convince labor that its loyalty should be on management's side.

In the second place, a careful division of responsibilities regarding morale must be made between the staff and the line executives. To the personnel division may be assigned such tasks as developing personnel programs into which morale-building phases have been constructed, making morale surveys, and testing the morale implications of various operating plans and procedures. But to the line executives must be assigned the major responsibilities for morale building and maintenance.

Top management's plans and policies determine the whole course and personality of a company. But it is the supervisor or foreman who influences the employee day in and day out, no matter what top levels may be thinking. Hence the policies of the supervisor become the policies of the company to the employee. If top management wants its policies carried out, it is imperative that supervisors be directed and controlled along desired lines. Only then will there be consistency in management's efforts to affect the attitudes and actions of employees.

In the third place, it is desirable for management to support its opinions about morale with tangible evidence. Most executives, to a greater or lesser degree, like to think they are good judges of what is on the minds of their subordinates. If they were as good as they think they are, the task of measuring employee attitudes would require little more than passing attention here. But the evidence is to the contrary.

How far wrong management can be in its interpretations of what workers think may be deduced from a survey in which foremen and employees were asked to rank various morale factors. The results are summarized in Table 15–1. Here, we see that the employers' emphasis upon fair pay, job security, interesting work, and promotion, to mention but a few factors, is not shared in equal degree by the employees. The latter, surprisingly enough, placed promotion, working conditions, and job security at the bottom of the list. When management's sights are so far off the mark, something should be done to correct its aim.

In the fourth place, attitude measurement should not be viewed as a single-process program. No company contemplates taking just one inventory of materials, nor should it be satisfied with a single inventory of

TABLE 15–1

RANK ASSIGNED VARIOUS FACTORS BY FOREMEN AND EMPLOYEES

Job Goal	Ranked by Workers	Ranked by Foremen
Full appreciation of work done...................	1st	8th
Feeling "in" on things...........................	2d	10th
Sympathetic help on personal problems............	3d	9th
Job security.....................................	4th	2d
Good wages......................................	5th	1st
"Work that keeps you interested".................	6th	5th
Promotion and growth in company.................	7th	3d
Personal loyalty to workers......................	8th	6th
Good working conditions.........................	9th	4th
Tactful disciplining..............................	10th	7th

SOURCE: *Foreman Facts* (Newark, N.J.: Labor Relations Institute), Vol. IX, No. 21; reproduced in *Management Review*, Vol. XLIII, No. 6, p. 362.

attitudes. Such a program should provide for continuous measurements at definite times. This will provide significant indications of trends as well as information of use at particular times.

In the fifth place, employees must feel completely assured that none of their statements are used to their disadvantage. Otherwise, it is improbable that they will ever express their opinions voluntarily to management. When questionnaires are used, every precaution should be taken to preserve anonymity. This is not possible in the interview; hence, it is important for the interviewer to convince the employee that his confidences will in no way be violated. Along similar lines, the results of attitude testing should not be used to establish rules which will work to the detriment of the employees.

In the sixth place, it is necessary to be aware of errors that should be avoided. It is essential to accept with reservations the views that employees express, since people are reluctant to reveal, and often hold back unknowingly, their true feelings. It is essential to know the time, place, and conditions under which answers were given because these and the effect of recent events color replies. And it is essential to avoid simple and generalized conclusions, since people are complex beings with varying degrees of satisfactions and dissatisfactions that cannot easily be disassociated.

And finally, it must also be recognized that even though morale is slow to develop and difficult to maintain, it can be lost overnight. It seems to be a human trait to remember the bad and forget the good, to believe the rumors and shy away from logic and facts, and to pursue heroes one day and cast stones upon them the next. For example, not long ago during an arbitration hearing a representative of labor claimed that piece-rate data could not be trusted because the company had cut some rates twenty years earlier. Although the company representative contended and the the labor representative agreed that no cuts had been made since that time, labor was still skeptical. Such evidences are striking in the lesson they teach: Eternal vigilance is the price of good morale.

QUESTIONS

1. Define the term "morale." What are the factors affecting morale? What are the effects of good morale?
2. What is meant by the process of morale development? What stages are included in this process?
3. Analyze critically the term "prerogatives of management." Are the interests of employees and employers identical, opposed, or partly both? Explain.
4. What management practices and factors are particularly relevant to the morale of employees?
5. What right has a company to delve into an employee's opinions about himself or about his social, political, and ethical attitudes?
6. What measures may be useful to interpret the morale of employees?
7. Conduct a survey on some subject such as "What do you think of unions?" or "Should management prerogatives be protected by law?" Include in your sample some students who have worked in industry and some who have not. Do background differences reflect themselves in attitudes? What is the moral?
8. Discuss the advantages and disadvantages of interviewing as a method of learning the attitudes of employees.
9. Why do most persons think they are good judges of people? Can you cite any evidence that contradicts this good opinion that people have about themselves?
10. What rules would you recommend be followed in order that flows of information relative to morale be valid and reliable?

CHAPTER **16**

COMMUNICATIONS

Scope of Discussion

After the successive managerial levels have learned the attitudes and opinions of employees, the communication process can then be reversed in direction. Upward have come ideas, comments, reactions, attitudes, and reports through all levels from the very lowest. Now, downward must flow clarifications, interpretations, orders, instructions, and policies.

This two-way flow completes the circle of a well-rounded communication process. Each direction of flow should stimulate and be stimulated by the other. In fact, several exchanges, up and down, may be needed to complete the education on some subjects. For this reason, the phrase "sharing information" is perhaps a clearer term of best practice. Certainly, the downward flow is apt to be better designed and much more effective when it is based upon a clear understanding of what employees are thinking (or not thinking) abour various subjects.

What is said in this chapter should constantly be viewed, therefore, in terms of what was said about the upward flow in the preceding chapter. In this discussion of the downward flow the subject will be taken up under the following headings:

1. Communication through the several managerial levels
2. Content and conveyors of education and communications
3. Organizing the communication program
4. Rules of education and communication

Communication through the Several Managerial Levels

If the education of the employee is to proceed satisfactorily, the leadership of ideas must stem from the top of the organization down through the intervening managerial levels. Hence, it is advisable to review communication practices through (1) top management, (2) middle management groups, and (3) supervisory levels.

1. *Top Management Groups.*   One of the most significant movements in recent years has been that concerned with top-level executive development. This is a most encouraging trend because good communications must be based upon an intelligent leadership. Moreover, it takes real courage for any executive to concede that he needs to learn more about his job. Particularly is this true of those who have reached the top. After all, has not the top-level group reached those heights because of ability and skill? Although this is true, there has nonetheless been a widespread acceptance of the idea of continuing education for higher executives.

Of particular interest here are the labor-related subjects which might well be included in top-level executive programs. A variety of topics suggest themselves. Until top management seeks definite answers to questions such as the following, it can scarcely expect lower levels of management to know how to communicate with workers.

   a) What are the social responsibilities of management?
   b) To what extent is business liable for the various risks which endanger employees?
   c) What is an optimum balance between reasonable profits and fair wages?
   d) Can workers be loyal to both the company and the union?
   e) What are realistic policies toward political activities on the part of the company?
   f) How do the roles of management and workers interact?
   g) To what extent, and how, should employees participate in managerial decisions of importance to them?

These are significant questions. Anyone who assumes that he alone is gifted enough to answer them or has derived final answers to them is "riding for a fall." So the movement of top executives to take counsel on these matters represents a most wholesome advance in labor-management relations.

2. *Middle Management Groups.*   Preparing middle management groups for their communication responsibilities usually involves the following three major areas of education:

   a) To learn precisely the educational plans of top management
   b) To coordinate horizontally the educational responsibilities of various line and staff units
   c) To transmit specific educational plans to lower supervisory levels, and ultimately to employees

The nature of these educational responsibilities is readily apparent, so that brief comments concerning them will suffice here. If it is significant for top levels to continue acquiring an education, it is equally important, if not more so, for those who are as yet moving up the line. Moreover, since the middle groups stand between the top and the bottom, they occupy a strategic position affecting labor-management relations. They must be adequately prepared to transmit accurately, and to control constructively, the plans, policies, and ideas of the top levels.

The middle management groups determine also the degree of consistency and uniformity with which employees in the various divisions of a company will be educated. Hence, co-ordinated educational sessions are particularly needful here, so that production and personnel units, let us say, take the same views on how the ideas of top management are to be carried out. When such units operate at cross purposes, even though with the best of intentions, the destructive effect upon employees is beyond measure.

This crosswise interchange of ideas leads some to conclude that organizational communications are essentially three- rather than two-dimensional: up, down, and across. The evidence favors such a conclusion. Even though the main flows may be up and down, crosswise coordination is increasingly important as a company grows. The various functional and staff units must be brought into a common plan of thought if the top and the bottom are to work together effectively and harmoniously.

3. *Supervisory Levels.* In the thinking of many, the education of supervisory levels of management is critical in affecting employee communications. Without doubt, day in and day out the supervisor is in closer contact with workers than any other management level or unit. In the formal organization structure, it is the foremen and supervisors who are "management" to the workers. And even informally, workers tend to feel that the supervisors determine how well they will or will not be treated as individuals. And when channels of communication are followed, it is through the supervisors that most information will be channeled downward and upward. Indeed, they may be bottlenecks, misinterpreters, and deceivers—or the reverse—depending upon the kind of education to which they are exposed by upper managerial levels.

Granting the truth of these contentions, any neglect of supervisory education is to be condemned. Moreover, such education is greatly needed because few, if any, supervisors learn anything about the educational phases of their jobs before they become supervisors. They step into their managerial responsibilities with practically no knowledge of what is expected of them or how their obligations are to be performed. Therefore, it is manifest that this group must be educated not only in the various subject matters top management considers important but also in how to get such subject matters across to the worker.

Communication Content and Conveyors

The key point of communications is, of course, the message. Through the message the executive hopes to educate the employee. And thereby are to be changed the attitudes, opinions, the information, and —ultimately—the behavior of the employee. But since message content must be transmitted through some agent (human or mechanical), it is important to give consideration to this aspect of communications. Hence the content and the conveyor are discussed together here, because they are so closely related.

In the space of this section, only excerpts and selected illustrations of communication content and conveyors can be given. It is not possible to examine the extent to which such content should be developed or the pros and cons of usage of various conveyors. It is hoped that the examples will serve to disclose typical content and usage. The materials in this section will be grouped under the following headings of typical subject matter, and incorporated under these headings will be examples of communication conveyors:

1. Major topics included in communication programs:
    a) Company history, objectives, and services
    b) Company organization, finances, and operations
    c) Personnel objectives, policies, and practices
    d) Economics and the American system
    e) Political and community relations
2. Major groups of communication conveyors:
    a) Individualized personal contacts
    b) Group personal contacts
    c) Written media
    d) Demonstrations and displays
    e) Radio, television, films, and recordings

1. *Company History, Objectives, and Services.* The significance an employee feels is in part due to the importance he and his associates attach to the company. If he knows nothing of a company's history, objectives, and services, he can take little pride in his company. It is wise, therefore, to give him such information. A number of plans may be cited in this connection.

The induction program for new employees is a common way of communicating the message of company history, objectives, and services. Part of the personal conferences of new employees with staff members of the personnel department and with their respective supervisors may be devoted to such subjects. At this time, too, some companies have used films to highlight the story of how the company was founded, by whom, and some of the early trials and tribulations. The story can be brought up to date to show the present position of the company in the industry.

Booklets are often used to cover these subjects. They are relatively inexpensive for presenting the story of a company's origin and growth. Moreover, they have a degree of permanence which films, for example, do not have, as far as ready reference to them is concerned. But to induce workers to read them is a problem. In this connection, well-designed, excellently illustrated, and carefully worded copy is helpful. An interesting case of stimulation is provided by one company which developed a quiz game, based upon plant publications and meetings, to be played during the lunch hour. Winners were given free lunches for answering correctly questions about the company's history, products, and personalities.

Plant publications are also used to provide information about the background of a company. These cover such subjects as how management has sought to provide job security, the importance of quality production for company success, and reviews of various company operations internally and in relation to customers.

Product display boards are also used to help employees visualize their contributions to the final product. Cutaway models serve to show various parts of a product and something about their purposes. Some companies display competitors' products so that employees may gain some insight into the task facing their own company in maintaining its position in the industry and in the market.

2. *Company Organization, Finances, and Operations.* This area of subject matter receives a great deal of attention from many companies. The reason is that it is necessary to help an employee see how he fits into the structure and operations of the company. Group meetings have been widely used to explain current problems of the company to employees. One company holds regular monthly meetings in which various executives take turns in explaining the cost and profit position of the company. Supervisors are briefed before the meetings so that they will be in a better position to carry on with the explanations in their own departments.

A variety of methods have been used to communicate information in this general area. Television, for example, has been employed to highlight a company's operations to a wide audience. The comic-book format has been used to present a company's annual report to employees.

Some companies use the public-address system to inform employees about such items as new customer orders or cancellations, available training courses, and contemplated expansion programs. And some companies have used conferences to discuss with employees various phases of company operations and plans.

3. *Personnel Objectives, Policies, and Practices.* Of immediate interest to employees is, of course, their financial and nonfinancial returns and possibilities. It is understandable, therefore, why many companies concern themselves with communications in this area. Practically all companies do some explaining of wages, hours, and employment conditions during the induction process. But it would be foolhardy to stop there, because interest in these subjects continues throughout an employee's tenure with a company.

Every conceivable conveyor has been used for communications in these areas. Undoubtedly, the best one is the supervisor. He can give the personal attention practically everybody prefers to impersonal or mass media of communication. And when the competency of the supervisor in this regard is upgraded, this serves to make him a more confident leader, with a reward not only to himself but also to the members of his group.

Personal interviews are often employed in this area. This approach provides a desirable personal touch. In one case, for example, each supervisor reviews with each of his subordinates his personal situation with respect to salary, available benefit plans, profit sharing, vacations, and holiday arrangements. Another company uses interviews to discuss safety practices on specific jobs. Interviews are used by another company to be sure that employees know all aspects of their jobs, how they are getting along on them, what the future has in store, and whether or not they are using all the help their supervisors can give them.

Even though the supervisor is well qualified to communicate in this area, the use of other media is also desirable. Booklets, for example, have been used to answer questions frequently asked about company retirement plans and pension arrangements. Employee forums—of large as well as small groups—are sponsored by one company at which subjects of interest are covered by company or outside speakers. Another company uses informal dinner meetings at which written questions are answered by a panel of company executives.

Interesting examples of communications may also be cited in connection with questions of job security and union-management relations. Many companies have taken pains to show how job security is tied in with competitive leadership and high productivity. From the positive side, employees are told such things as: "The success of a company depends greatly on you." "Job security and job opportunity depend on satisfying the customer." "The security of your job is wrapped up in improvements of quality, reliability, and reputation." And when layoffs are likely, it is well to advise employees on prospects for reemployment in terms of:

a) The company situation, so that damaging rumors among employees are minimized
b) What is being done to reduce the numbers of layoffs
c) The order of layoffs, should they come
d) The probable length of layoffs
e) What employees laid off should do to keep the company informed of their availability for recall

As to union-management relations, much is being done to improve mutual understanding. For example, union and company officials have taken joint tours of their own plants as well as those of competitors to promote a better understanding of their own positions and problems. Other companies are using columns of their periodicals to give union news, views on union relations, and explanations of contract clauses. Many companies also use conferences and meetings with supervisors to gain their views and to clarify their understanding of labor-management problems. Thereby the ability of supervisors to transmit the messages to employees is improved.

4. *Economics and the American System.* One of the most interesting phases of education has been along lines of increasing economic understanding. The movement has gained strength, particularly in the last several years, because of the belief that an employee who does not comprehend how our economic system works cannot feel confident about the fairness of his wages, the reasonableness of profits, or the significance of the capitalistic system. Hence, industry and various public and private institutions have interested themselves in disseminating economic knowledge.

Interesting as these efforts are, space permits only the citation of a few examples of various types of efforts along these lines. For example, the Inland Steel Company and the Borg-Warner Corporation developed a series of four films which attempted to show the following:[1]

---

[1] These films have since been taken over by the American Economic Foundation for purposes of general distribution.

  a) How We Got What We Have
  b) What We Have
  c) How to Lose What We Have
  d) How to Keep What We Have

After each of the films is shown, a discussion period is devoted to an examination in detail of the particular subjects.[2]

The Du Pont Company developed a conference method program with a board type of presentation in this connection. This conference concerns itself with the features of the American economic system, its accomplishments, the place of competition, the place of individual freedom in the system, and the place of the company in our system. A trained conference leader first conducts an appreciation session over the whole subject matter. Then, he leads three 1½-hour discussion sessions, based on a broad presentation. He also trains others to conduct conferences on the program. The technical aspects of the program have since been made available for general distribution through the National Association of Manufacturers.

The Republic Steel Corporation also uses a conference program, but on a more extensive basis. Its program contains fifteen sessions and in the first year was restricted to supervisors. The conferences are built around lectures, discussions, and visual aids. This program is now available for general distribution through the University of Chicago, and has as its objectives the following:

  a) Raising the level of knowledge and understanding about the economic system, and how the corporation fits into it
  b) Providing a framework for analyzing and appraising economic proposals and problems
  c) Developing in individuals an appreciation of the role of the corporation and the economic system
  d) Developing confidence in the corporation and the system
  e) Encouraging desirable changes in attitude and behavior both on and off the job

5. *Political and Community Relations.* In addition, some industries have worked closely with various community agencies and groups to make education a community project. An example of such cooperation is illustrated in Figure 16–1. The instruction in such in-

---

[2] A very useful survey of various programs similar to this may be found in Dillard E. Bird, *Survey of Economic Education* (Dayton: Foremanship Foundation, 1951).

FIGURE 16–1. Organization Chart of Community Groups

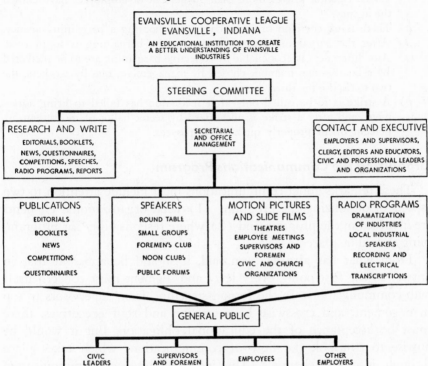

SOURCE: Thomas J. Morton, "Public Relations Job," *Factory Management and Maintenance*, Vol. XCVI, No. 12, p. 40.

stances has been intended to support the following propositions and procedures:

a) Every citizen benefits from industry's growth.

b) You are entitled to the facts.

c) Collective bargaining is the one practical means to assure fair wages, reasonable hours, and satisfactory working conditions.

d) All employees, as well as management, benefit by improving productive efficiency.

e) Citizens should be protected in their right to work.

f) The American system of industry is best for everybody.

g) Management and wage earners have mutual interests and need close personal relations.

h) Management is obligated to give a square deal to every employee in the shop.

i) Adherence to the letter and spirit of the law avoids strikes except after all means of peaceful adjustment have been exhausted.

j) Demand for recognition as sole bargaining agency only after an impartial election proves more than 50 percent of employees have chosen the agency.

k) There is no coercion or intimidation in choosing a bargaining agency.

l) After the bargaining agency is chosen, the bargaining is to proceed.

m) Any differences irreconcilable by collective bargaining are to be mediated by a board—one member chosen by management, one by workers, the two to choose the third.

n) A strike is to be called only after mediation has failed to bring agreement, and after a strike is authorized by secret ballot of more than 50 percent of all properly qualified employees.

Organizing the Communications Program

These remarks about communications must include attention to two aspects of organizing the program: (1) what organizational elements are involved in the program and (2) where responsibility for programming should be placed.

From what has already been said, it should be apparent that in answer to the first point, every level and segment must concern itself with communications. In the formal structure, from supervisors to top management, and crosswise between line and staff executives, there must be acceptance of the educational obligation. But it would be unwise to overlook the flow of communications which takes place through informal channels. The informal lines of communication should be used, but with subtle care so that they do not go underground because of fear or misunderstanding. Also, the extraformal structures of union channels should be employed to communicate information upward and downward.

But when everyone is responsible, turning now to the second point, there is grave danger that no one will be responsible. Hence, specific delegation of authority for leadership of an educational program is desirable. The personnel division is a natural choice here. It should provide leadership of ideas but should always submit program proposals to the appropriate line executives for suggestions and approval. The latter, with line authority, will then spearhead the execution of approved plans using the help supplied by the personnel division. Moreover, the personnel division can seek out help on communications matters from management consultants, educational institutions, professional societies, and business and trade associations. Such an organizational setup would serve to insure proper design of programs, minimum conflict between organization units, a strengthening of the work and support of line executives, and advantageous use of all communications resources and opportunities.

Rules of Communications

From all that has been said thus far, it might seem that good communications are not difficult to achieve. It is true that effective attention to lines, purposes, content, and conveyors of communications is not too difficult. Were this all, it would be hard to see why communications fail so often and generally cannot be graded much higher than just fair.

But there is more to communications than the matters that have already been discussed. Communications must be applied. And application must give careful consideration to certain principles and overcome certain obstacles that are inherently difficult and complex. Among these are the following:

1. The factor of change—resistance to change
2. The educational process—difficulties of teaching
3. The individual—obstacles in reaching people
4. Semantics—the mystery of words
5. Classes—obstacles of stereotypes
6. Degrees—questions of how much

1. *The Factor of Change.* The need for communications perhaps arises basically out of the difficulties associated with change. Putting in a new office procedure, establishing a new vacation policy, or starting a new appraisal system—as examples—meets with varying degrees of resistance. To gain acceptance of the particular change requires communication—some before, some during, and some after the change. People involved in the change want to know the mechanics of the new setup. But more importantly, they want to know how they will be affected. Their security is involved.

If business operations did not change, there would be little need for communications. But they do change. So employees must be convinced to make and accept the changes. They must be convinced for a number of reasons. In the first place, there is the normal human resistance to getting out of a habitual way of doing things. Communications can be helpful in reducing the psychological frictions of this type.

Much more significant, in the second place, is the resistance arising from feelings of insecurity. Almost any change arouses questions of its possible negative impact upon job security, wage levels, social and organizational status, and personal prestige. To counter such feelings calls for considerable communication.

Usually, the practice in such cases has been to explain the nature of proposed change as already decided upon by management. This does not do too much in allaying fears. So explanations of why changes are needed and why they are desirable are communicated. This is of some help if specific attention is directed to advantages accruing to employees. Better still are communications which raise the need of change, without specifying a course of action, but instead inviting suggestions as to what should be done. This approach involves employees in managerial decision making, which few companies have been willing to adopt. If managerial resistance to this change in decision making can be reduced, undoubtedly much progress can be made in reducing employee resistances to change.

2. *Educational Process.* Communication is thus for management a task of changing the thinking of employees—an educational process. Yet, frequently, management does not realize it is an educator. Many executives believe that education is a task of the schools. It is for people from 6 to 16, on the average. But business has the same "students" from 16 to 65, in theory if not always in practice—and at an age when maturity characterizes the students. During a man's working life, he will learn something—if not from management, then from others. And what he learns elsewhere may not be to management's liking. Hence, it must be concluded that the role of educator must be accepted as a significant part of the job of management, meaning every executive from the highest to the lowest.

As educators, management must be skilled in transmitting information and knowledge to subordinates. Each executive must therefore know the subject matter he must teach. This is not enough. A teacher must also be a preacher and a coach. He must be a preacher because convincing employees about the profit system, let us say, is more than a statement of cold logic. All of us learn best when the teacher is enthusiastic, transmits a feeling of conviction, and employs various devices to bring human interest into his lessons.

As an educator, the executive must apply the best techniques of coaching. He must always keep in mind that the employees are to play the game, not he alone. So he must teach them how to act in the situations in which they will find themselves. This involves insight into the problems to be met and insight into the reactions that people will have in meeting them. Yet, many an executive fails to get across his ideas as he would like because he does not cultivate such insight. It is too easy to forget, once we have learned how to perform some act, how much difficulty we ourselves had in learning. Unless the coach keeps this in mind, the students develop obstructions to learning which make the executive's task even more difficult.

Finally, education has its problems because it is a thinking process. In all human activities, thinking ranks highest in difficulty. It is hard to concentrate for more than short periods of time. And sequential, logical analysis demands intense concentration. To get employees (or executives) to apply themselves, various educational devices must be used. Simple doses, constantly repeated at properly spaced intervals, through the best of conveyors (such as pictures and diagrams), must be used.

FIGURE 16–2. A Difficulty in Communicating

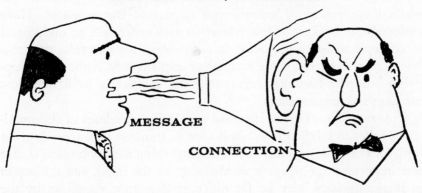

COMMUNICATOR

Urge
Purpose
Knowledge

RECIPIENT

Capable of Understanding
Willing to Listen

Courtesy: General Electric Company

Much could be learned in this regard from the comic books and movies of Walt Disney. He educates extremely well in a most interesting and painless manner.

3. *The Individual.* This last point about the thinking process leads naturally to a consideration of the difficulties of reaching individuals simply because of their human makeup. We assume that we shall not receive a busy signal when we call up. And we assume that the person has the technical equipment to receive the message which is sent. These assumptions are rarely warranted. And so communications based upon them are bound to be ineffective, as suggested in Figure 16–2.

If communications are to be successful, problems flowing from people as human beings must be solved. Do people want to know, for example, whether or not the profit system is fair to them? Of course they do, but only *when* they want to know. Most of the time, they do not want to be bothered with such details. Then, for one reason or another, employees get upset. Management tries to reach them with lessons on how our profit system works. But suspicion meets its efforts. It is important in this matter of communications to figure out how to intrigue employees when they would just as soon not be bothered.

Moreover, employees are often preoccupied with personal problems and interests. Management must compete with other demands upon the thoughts of employees. In this competition, it should use many of the fine ideas it employs in its advertising and sales promotion programs.

Finally, in communications, consideration must be given to the technical equipment of subordinates to receive the messages. Have employees the background in education and experience to understand the concepts to be transmitted? It does mean, for example, that employees must be given some accounting explanations if they are properly to interpret messages concerning the company's profit and loss statement and balance sheet.

4. *Semantics.* One of the most perplexing problems of communications arises in relation to symbols used to transmit messages. A given word, for example, may not mean the same thing to all who hear it. But more important, the image a word creates in the mind, and the action the image initiates, may be far different than that visualized by the transmitter. Nonverbal sounds, too, such as a factory whistle, may connote one thing to the employer and another to the employee. Or a picture of a new machine the company proposes to install may not convey the idea of job security, as the company intends, but rather the idea of technological unemployment and job insecurity. And finally, the actions and trappings of executives may raise in the minds of employees ideas and actions far different than those in the minds or expectations of executives.

This area of the effect of symbols upon the minds and actions of people is entitled "semantics." It is concerned with a study of the meaning of symbols used in communication. Obviously, such study is appropriate to all areas of human endeavor. Only very recently, however, has it received the attention it deserves in the field of business.

The trouble with symbols is that they seldom are singular in meaning and seldom uniform in the actions they cause. Take a word such as "profits" as a language symbol. It will undoubtedly mean to management something the company deserves to earn. To employees, it may mean the same; but more likely, it will suggest in part an excessive and undeserved return. Management consequently may be inspired to work harder, whereas labor may be affected negatively.

Thus, given words at the same time may have good and bad effects.

"Collective bargaining" and "unions," for example, are words which infuriate some executives but make employees feel good. On the other hand, "Taft-Hartley" arouses ill will in the minds of many workers, but is balm to the feelings of employers. And somewhat similar reactions, but perhaps not so violent, would be caused by such words as "security," "AFL–CIO," "National Association of Manufacturers," "automation," "management prerogatives," and "executive salaries."

The moral of all this to management is twofold: First, it should choose its words (and other symbols, too) carefully in preparing communications; and second, it should examine its own reactions and understanding of the words. This involves a good deal of study. A good place to begin is with past communications. What words were used? Were they simple or complex? Could they have been misconstrued? Then, some studies of employee reactions are called for. How do employees react to such words as "job," "profits," "boss," "work," "pay," "order," "service," and "business"?

5. *Classes.* Another difficulty in communications that must be overcome is the obstacle created by the class attitude taken by various groups. Thus, in many instances, workers feel that as a class, they are opposed to the class of executives. It is their duty, then, to refrain from accepting the views expressed by management. This is uniquely illustrated by the employee who gets a promotion to a supervisory position. While he is an employee, various fellow workers come to him because he is their natural informal leader. They believe whatever he has to say and take whatever action he suggests. After he becomes boss, the visits stop, and such messages as he initiates are scorned or questioned. Yet, both before and after, the man in question holds—or so he thinks—the same feelings toward his fellow workers. But now he is in another class, and he takes on the characteristics, viewpoints, and motives of that class,

Such typing of classes occurs in the executive levels, too. Staff people tend to categorize line executives as biased, relatively ignorant, and noncooperative individuals. The line people return the compliment by classifying staff people as impractical visionaries, who are constantly scheming to take control of their departments. And upper level executives generally are suspicious of lower level supervisors, feeling that the latter are not company-minded, take the side of labor, and generally lack needed managerial qualities. The lower levels have their own picture of the upper levels, viewing them as a group which is simply profit- and cost-minded, with little or no regard for the daily problems of getting work done and for the human factor in the shop.

On top of these organizational stereotypes, there may be overlappings of political, racial, religious, color, and job groupings. It is unwise to group all employees as being under the political influence of Democrats, Republicans, or labor unions. To address communications in terms of one grouping alone will certainly antagonize the others. And similarly, it is unwise to assume that all employees hold the same views on race, color, and creed—even those of the same race, color, and creed.

All of this means that management must design its communications with these class groupings in mind. In part, too, the communications should be designed to minimize some of these class distinctions. There should be little justification for employees to feel about executives the way they do, or for other classes to take the positions they hold. There is a vast difference, of course, between what should be and what is. Unfortunately, employees have often been given good reason to characterize executives the way they do. Similarly, the other classes often are on sound ground for their evaluations of the other groups.

The design of communications to minimize class distinctions must begin, therefore, with a revision of acts which tend to raise class barriers. Management, for example, must live so that employees will not consider executives as natural enemies. Similarly, staff people should not act as if they alone are repositories of all that is good; line people should have confidence in their own abilities and not reflect characteristic manifestations of an inferiority complex in relation to staff people; upper management should put more managerial responsibilities upon lower supervisors; and the lower levels should take a broader company view and seek to earn the confidence of upper executives.

Thus, good communications really begin with action. The way we live speaks louder than words. But if our actions are good, the words we speak—if carefully chosen—will effectively convey our messages to various selected recipients.

6. *Degrees and Quality of Communications.* But how much communication is necessary? All of the preceding would seem to imply that management should spend most of its time communicating. To be sure, this would be impractical. It is imperative that enough thought, time, and skill be given to this phase of an executive's job so that the other phases will not suffer. For it will avail an executive little if he does a good job of planning, organizing, directing, and controlling the work of others, let us say, but fails in transmitting his ideas to others. He can be a successful executive only to the degree that his team does what he wants it to do. And this depends as much upon communications skill as upon skill in preparing the materials to be communicated.

Perhaps as significant is the ethical quality of communications. To management, education has a utilitarian and selfish purpose. Communications with employees are intended ultimately to raise the productivity of the workers. Presumably, their efforts will be more effective because they are better adjusted to their working environment.

As long as employee development proceeds along such lines, the communications program has substantial justification. But what if the development of the employee is intended to change or clarify his basic economic, social, or political ideas? For example, a program may be undertaken to convince him that private enterprise is better than any form of government ownership, that a system of private investment is better than socialism, that the profit system is superior to national planning, that union membership will bring no lasting benefits, and that management leadership is fairer and more democratic than union or political administration of industry. Such phases of communication may be termed "indoctrination." To some, this may mean propaganda or possibly unfair twisting of the truth. Such opinions or criticisms are based not upon the type of education, but upon its fairness, accuracy, and validity. And those who voice them may themselves indoctrinate or propagandize, but see nothing wrong in it because they believe the content of their programs is right and just.

Hence the right to indoctrinate or propagandize is not the issue. Since capitalists ("management" is too often used incorrectly as a synonym for this term) have so much at stake in a business enterprise, they should have the right to protect their investments by all legal and ethical means. This would include their right to instruct their managements to carry on programs of indoctrination and propaganda in such matters as the principles and the desirability of capitalism. But to go beyond the borders of fairness in such efforts by employing high-pressure tactics and partial truths is not ethical. The question, however, of what is fair, ethical, and accurate is one that is difficult to answer in many cases. Nevertheless, this should not be a reason to remove the rights of management (or for that matter, of unions, political groups, or other agencies) to indoctrinate.

To sum up, whether the communication is intended to provide information or change the attitudes of employees (even to the extent of indoctrination or propagandizement), the efforts of management are justified. But the premise of fairness, honesty, and ethical standards is assumed and must be protected. Without this, counterforce will be built up that will result in loss of faith, confidence, and loyalty.

QUESTIONS

1. What is the relation between upward communication and downward communication in a business? Which takes place first?

2. With what subject matter is education of top management primarily concerned?

3. What is the task of education for the middle management group of executives?

4. Why is such significance generally attached to the role of the supervisor in employee-employer relations? Do you think that the supervisor actually has as significant a role in this connection as some would have us believe? Why, or why not?

5. What is the key factor in communications downward? What is it supposed to accomplish?

6. What are the major topics included in communications programs? What are the major conveyors used to transmit messages downward?

7. Why is the comic-book type of conveyor of communications so effective? Does this necessarily imply anything about the mentality of the average employee?

8. Why is there so much interest in communications concerned with economics and the American system? Why does business not concentrate on the task of producing and distributing goods and services, and leave such education to the schools?

9. To what aspects of an educational nature must a good communication give consideration?

10. What has the subject of classes to do with a communications program?

CHAPTER 17

REMUNERATION POLICIES

Significance of Remuneration

Scarcely any subject is as important to all levels of employees as financial remuneration. Certainly, many grievances are related to compensation. In part, this may stem from the fact that employees sometimes express their discontent with management practices by complaining about compensation. But in large measure, complaints have their source in the feeling that compensation is unfair. Moreover, all employees are continually reminded of compensation by the race between expenditures and the next payday—a matter of purchasing power. And how an employee feels about compensation is significantly affected by what his neighbors think about his spending power—in a sense, a status symbol.

The Problems of Remuneration

Such sensitivity is not, however, the critical factor in remuneration. The trouble lies in the lack of a measuring device which can establish to the satisfaction of all concerned what an employee is worth in financial terms. To be sure, many measuring approaches are being used. But all are subject to some question by both the businessman and the recipient. Yet, payments of wages and salaries must be made in the present; neither management nor employee can await the day when a perfect measuring device is invented.

This is not necessarily a pessimistic outlook. Reasonably good remuneration plans and policies can be established. They must be based, however, upon careful consideration of a number of factors. Insofar as management's role in remuneration is concerned, close attention should be directed to the following:

1. General remuneration theories and issues (the subject matter of this chapter)

2. Determination of rates for specific jobs and positions (the subject matter of Chapter 18)
3. Provisions for variations within given job and position rates (the subject matter of Chapter 19)
4. Remuneration allowances in various benefit arrangements (the subject matter of Chapter 20)
5. Consideration of factors related to financial remuneration (the subject matter of Chapter 21)

Scope of Present Discussion

The amount an employee receives on payday is significantly influenced by his company's program of wage and salary administration. And this program, in turn, will have been vitally influenced by the answers the company derived to the following basic questions:

1. What is the economic basis of remuneration?
2. How can economic factors and forces be measured?
3. What is the influence of unions and collective bargaining?
4. What is the impact of governmental influences?
5. What safeguards can serve to minimize mistakes in wage programming?

Economic Explanations

In a world in which various groups have recourse so often to the use of force in gaining desired goals, the effect of economic principles often seems negligible. But sooner or later, the millstones of economics grind out their truths to the disadvantage of those who did not obey its precepts. Hence an understanding of economics is needed by both line and staff executives. Although this is not the place to delve into detailed aspects of economic wage principles, some of the more important ones will be touched upon.

1. *Wages as a Price.* Without forgetting the human aspects of labor, it is nevertheless necessary at the outset to recognize that the term "wage" is a particular kind of price, that is, the price of labor. As such, it is subject to the same type of analysis as any other price. Assuming, for the moment, the absence of frictions, political regulations, and pressure groups (either managerial or labor), wages are set at the point where the demand curve for labor crosses the supply curve of labor.[1] Hence, to

---

[1] This oversimplified statement has the merit of making it possible to discuss, in a limited space, a topic that otherwise would have to be left untouched here.

act rationally in setting wage policies, it is necessary to determine the curves for demand for and supply of labor.

Although this is extremely difficult, if not impossible, in most cases, nevertheless an understanding of the theory of demand and supply determination is very useful. At least, the manager who studies the forces behind demand and supply will not overlook some very influential factors when building his compensation program.

2. *Demand Curve.* The demand for labor (to begin with this factor) has two major aspects. First, each company has a demand for labor, that is, the quantities of labor that it is willing to hire at varying prices. Ordinarily, these quantities go downward, as indicated in Figure 17–1. The downward trend is due to the decrease in productivity of any

FIGURE 17–1

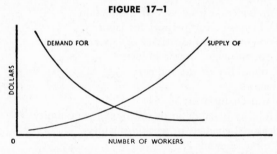

group of workers, as explained by the general principle of diminishing productivity. Every company should be able to produce a reasonably accurate chart of its labor requirements, or demand curve, at any given time. Second, for every company, there usually is a community or industry demand curve, depending upon the number and type of competitors for labor in the area in which a company is operating. This type of demand curve is difficult to produce exactly; but it, too, has a downward trend, as depicted in Figure 17–1. A simple way of doing this is to estimate the types and quantities of labor that all users of labor require at different rates of output.

3. *Supply Curve.* The supply curve, on the other hand, has an upward trend, as indicated in Figure 17–1. This is a recognition of the fact that ordinarily it takes increasing quantities of dollars to lure larger numbers of workers into the employment market. Here again, there are company and area supply curves. Most companies have a supply of labor that is loyal to them irrespective of general wages or competition. And then, there is a general supply curve representing quantities that can be drawn upon or lost by a particular company, depending upon the wages it is willing to pay. Supply curves are difficult to draw, although here, too, more or less accurate estimates can be made by counting the population by sex and age groups and by getting estimates of types of skills available in the community.

4. *Forces Affecting Demand and Supply.* To estimate demand and supply curves at any particular time, it is essential to ascertain as accurately as possible the factors that influence such curves. In outline, the following are factors commonly of importance:

A. Demand factors
   1. Short-run changes in:
      a) Company production schedules
      b) Competitors' production schedules
      c) Seasonal production
      d) Consumer demands
   2. Long-run changes in:
      a) Fundamental processes of production
      b) Demands of competitors for labor
      c) Fundamental productivity of labor
      d) Growth or decline of industry
      e) Profitability of the industry
B. Supply factors
   1. Short-run changes in:
      a) Mobility of labor in or out of the community
      b) Seasonal changes in working habits
      c) Union demands
   2. Long-run changes in:
      a) Cyclical depressions or periods of prosperity
      b) Influx of new industries or departure of old
      c) Family size and other population characteristics
      d) Costs and standard of living
      e) Trends in union strength and governmental regulation

5. *Noneconomic Factors.* But people are more than economic creatures and factors of production. When a society achieves a productive capacity beyond the mere subsistence level, the participants will seek a share in the affluence. What they gain will depend in part upon bargaining and political power and in part upon the understanding of businessmen of the need of people for a higher standard of living.

Hence the role of noneconomic factors in compensation matters cannot be overlooked. Economics may set limits on wage and salary levels above which the result may well be bankruptcy. But political, social, and union forces may set limits below which levels may not be set but which might otherwise have been justified on purely economic grounds. It is now appropriate to examine various ways in which economic and noneconomic factors are considered in solving compensation problems.

Calculating Economic Forces

Although the economic mills grind out the truth, they seem to do so too slowly for most practical purposes. Employees must be paid in the present. No one wants to wait for the completion of supply and demand calculations. So it is not unnatural to seek a formula which returns quicker answers and which still has some relation to the supply and demand of goods produced.

1. *Employee Contributions.* A logical approach seemingly is to remunerate employees for the contributions they make to salable goods and services. Thus the company sells the goods and then shares the monies so received with—among other groups—labor. But employees invariably receive wages and salaries before (often months before) goods are sold and sometimes when the finished goods cannot be sold at all. It is obvious, then, that remuneration must be calculated and paid before labor's contribution to sales can thereby be measured. Moreover, it is a difficult—if, indeed, not impossible—task to determine what contribution a specific employee, let us say a typist, makes to a product such as an electronic computer.

If contributions cannot be measured directly, are there factors which influence contributions, and can they be measured? No involved cogitation is needed to conclude that as far as employees are concerned, their contributions to a company's success are dependent upon the following:

a) Time spent at work
b) Energy and skill expended—physical, mental, emotional, and social
c) Willingness to cooperate

These can be measured with varying degrees of accuracy. Time, of course, is readily ascertainable. Energy and skill call for judgmental evaluations. And willingness to cooperate is undoubtedly the most difficult to measure. Yet, anyone who has worked or watched people work soon realizes that willingness to expend energy is perhaps the most important factor for which people are paid wages.

The proof of this is immediately seen in cases of method changes. Let us assume that energy and skill can be expressed in units and that management improves job methods with the following results:

	Old Method	New Method
Output per hour	100	200
Energy and skill expended by labor	30	20

If the principle of cause and effect were invoked to support its claim, management presumably should be given credit for the increase in production. Indeed, to follow the argument to its logical end, wages should be decreased, because labor is spending less energy in working and is taking no more time.

But in all likelihood, wages will have to be raised! And this despite the claim that management might make that it caused the increased output by devising the improved method. Labor would argue that it too contributed to the result. Having noted that output has now been doubled, it would simply conclude that it should share in the increase and just as simply refuse to cooperate if a share were not forthcoming.

The control labor exercises in withholding its services reaches an extreme in the case of strikes, but slowdowns on the job are often as destructive a form of unwillingness to cooperate. And yet the cooperation expenditures called for may actually be smaller because of improved methods of doing the work!

In short, workers must be compensated for their willingness to cooperate, as well as for their time, skill, and energy. How to measure willingness is a difficult matter and is largely left to rule-of-thumb methods. For example, many follow the precept of Frederick Taylor that wages should be increased from 15 to 30 percent when output is increased—even when it is doubled or tripled. The reason Taylor chose this figure is that he believed that larger increases at any one time spoil workers rather than stimulating them to greater effort.

2. *Monetary Conversions.* While it is possible to measure the foregoing factors, the measurements are not expressed in monetary terms. How convert eight hours of work, fifty units of energy, and sixty units of cooperation into dollars and cents? One way is to see what others in the same community or in the same line of business are paying for such employee contributions. Another is to establish a job evaluation plan by which varying degrees of such factors are given monetary values. Both of these approaches are discussed more fully in a later chapter. For the present, it is sufficient to note that conversions into monetary terms are invariably based upon opinions. Yet, such opinions, when expertly made, can provide reasonably accurate answers to the wage determination problem.

Influence of Unions and Collective Bargaining

Increasingly, the right to make wage determinations is being shared by management with unions. It is therefore desirable to examine some of the concepts which have been given a significant place in remuneration determinations because of union activity. Of particular interest are the concepts of administered wages, productivity increases, ability to pay, cost of living, "lump of work," "equality of workers," and bargaining strategies.

1. *Administered Wages.* There are some who ascribe little practical weight to economic forces as wage determinants. Instead, they contend that representatives of labor and management in the collective bargaining process set wages—administer wages. Presumably, these parties have the power (and exercise it) to determine rates irrespective of supply and demand factors. There is ample evidence that wage rates and fringe benefits have been increased when labor market conditions would have indicated a reverse action. So it sometimes appears that those in positions of power, rather than economic forces, are the real determiners of wage levels.

To the extent that monopolistic conditions exist, such determinations have current and practical significance. But even the parties to administered wages cannot completely ignore economic forces. The union, for example, must determine how many jobs it is willing to sacrifice if wage demands are set at an unduly high level. And managerial representatives are not unaware of the fact that some sales will be lost if high labor costs result in high sales prices. In the mining industry, for example, marginal workers and marginal mines were removed from that industry when wage rates were established several years ago at levels considerably above those that had previously prevailed. Sooner or later, adjustments to supply and demand must be made when wage rates are administered, so long as the administrators cannot also control the buyers.

2. *Productivity Increases.* An interesting development in wage determination has been the productivity increase, as espoused by a number of unions and as used by the federal government as a guide line to noninflationary wage increases. This is based on the fact that overall productivity in this country has tended to increase on the average about 3 percent a year. So the unions in some industries have gained the concession that employees should share in the annual average increase —and this though there may actually be no increase in some years or in the industry in question.

When management makes such a concession, it is economically justified only when labor makes a contribution to the productivity increase. To accept the conclusion that labor in a given company should be given an annual productivity adjustment because national averages have shown a certain percentage increase is scarcely logical. To do so would result in overcompensation in some cases and undercompensation in others. Much more defensible would be a productivity factor based (*a*) on what improvement there has been in a specific company, (*b*) on the degree to which labor caused the increase, and (*c*) on a definition of productivity giving consideration to company contributions to improved efficiency.

3. *Ability to Pay.*   Another basic issue which has been given prominence since the rise of union strength is that of ability to pay wage increases demanded by labor. The unions contend that increases should be given by those who can afford them. Management contends that ability to pay has little if anything to do with current wages. The debate between the two can be endless because both are partly right as well as partly wrong.

Simple analysis is enough to show that the contentions of the parties are dependent upon the influence of time on wages. In the short run, the economic influence on wages of ability to pay is practically nil. All employers, irrespective of their profits or losses, must pay no less than their competitors and need pay no more if they wish to attract and keep workers. For example, if those who are operating unprofitably cut wages because of losses, they would soon find that their employees were leaving them, provided that other jobs were available.

In the long run, however, productivity is of vital influence. When industry in general is able to pay high wages, individual producers who wish to take advantage of the tide of prosperity have to bid for labor to help carry on profitable operations. And the limit to their bidding—which, of course, they hope is not approached too closely—is their increased ability to pay. Conversely, when a depression hits, wages and/or employment must be cut because funds are not available.

4. *Cost of Living.*   The relation of cost of living to wages is another basic question in establishing remuneration policies. Its significance has increased because many companies have agreed to tie in wage increases (and decreases, too, in some instances) with changes in cost of living as reflected in cost-of-living indexes such as that compiled by the Bureau of Labor Statistics. For example, adjustments in wages are made monthly or quarterly as the index changes. How much of a wage adjustment will be made depends upon the agreement between labor and management as to the percentage of wage change that is to be made for each percentage change in the cost-of-living index.

Such practices seem to have a logical appeal. Yet, analysis will show that cost of living has an indirect, not a direct, bearing upon wages. The reasonableness of cost-of-living clauses, or "escalator clauses," as they are sometimes called, lies in the fact that wages and cost of living tend to go up and down at the same time. For example, in the rising phase of a business cycle, all prices tend to rise. Thus the items labor buys go up in price. And wages of labor do, too. In the case of labor, its requests for increases are then met, for the very simple reason that the supply of labor is relatively less than the demand for labor. The supply-demand relationship also favors price increases in the goods that labor buys in its standard of living.

This analysis would hold true on the down side of a business swing. Then, of course, cost of living and wages would tend to move lower.

So, any way one looks at it, cost of living and wages seem to be related directly, particularly to those who work for wages which are used to buy their "cost of living." The relation is not, however, causal; each goes up or down because of general market and competitive conditions. It is like a cloud and a sailboat moving in the same direction. No one would say the cloud is pushing the sailboat. Rather, the wind would be recognized as the causal factor in the case of cloud and boat. Similarly, with wages and cost of living, the "wind" is the force of supply and demand.

Since cost of living and wages tend to move together, it may be practical to use the former as a measure of the latter. But this should be done with a clear statement that the cost-of-living indexes are an expedient, not the real measure of wages.

But even when used as expedients, the practice of tying wages to cost-of-living indexes eventually runs into one or more difficulties. In the first place, the tie between wages and living costs is usually made during periods of rising prices when employers are not reluctant to grant wage increases. But during deflationary periods, employees are irritated by the periodic (even though small) readjustments of wages that are made as living costs go down. Second, arguments eventually are raised as to how cost-of-living indexes should be computed. In one case, opinions differed as much as 100 percent in regard to how much costs had risen. Finally, a vicious circle would be induced if all employers followed this practice. Thus a price rise would call for a wage increase, which would increase costs, which would lead to an increase in prices, and so on, bringing about an inflationary spiral detrimental to all.

5. *Lump-of-Work Theory.* Another aspect of union activity which has influenced wage determination is the belief that workers should take it easy on their jobs if they wish to avoid working themselves out of jobs. This is the "lump-of-work" theory, which assumes that there is just so much work to be done and no more. So the policy is pushed—either openly or covertly—to limit the amount of work that will be done for a given rate of pay. Or for each employee or number of

employees, a helper, assistant, or standby must be provided. At its worst, featherbedding, or being paid for not working, is the result.

Such a theory has an apparent soundness when business falls off. Employees can readily see that no more work will be forthcoming if they finish the orders on hand. So they tend to restrict output to protect their jobs in a depression. They continue the practice in a prosperity period because wages can be increased because of the "shortage" of labor to do the available work. But if there are possible losses to some workers if they do work themselves out of a job, there are greater losses by not working effectively. Eventually, the higher labor costs will affect the company adversely and result in fewer hirings than would otherwise be made.

6. *Equality-of-Workers Theory.* There is encountered occasionally the principle that all workers are economically equal on given types of jobs (presumably because they are born politically equal). A common application of this principle is that of paying all workers in a given class of work the same rate, irrespective of individual merit. Its application is desirable for the union because it eliminates the troublesome controversies between workers of varying ability as to the rates they should receive. The union can then concentrate its attention upon other matters than that of reconciling intraunion differences. Such supposed equality is the basis of seniority rules for granting wage increases which otherwise have little validity.

7. *Union Strategies.* It is also imperative for management to be aware of the strategies unions may be pursuing in relation to wage matters. For example, union strategy may call for asking for more money than the workers expect to get, by putting out a wage demand in order to get something else, or by placing wages last on a list of demands to that management, in its eagerness to get to wage questions, may be more lenient on other demands. Of course, management may counter with proposals that tend to offset the strategy of labor; but to do this, it must be aware of the extent to which labor is using wages as a bargaining tool. When labor in a given case asks for a 30 percent increase in wages, what does it really want? Until an answer is attempted, management cannot intelligently set its counterproposals at the most advantageous point.

Wages are used by unions to control or affect their internal affairs as well as relations with employers. For example, wage rates have been bargained for that will retard the flow of learners into a trade. In addition, levels of wages between different grades of work are often closely watched so that members do not quarrel among themselves over relative wages. In some instances, wage adjustments have been sought to offset the introduction of laborsaving equipment. And most unions nowadays estimate closely the possible effect upon employment of the levels of wage increases they seek.

Governmental Regulations

If the unions have had an impact upon remuneration practices, so too has the government. The federal government has been particularly influential in the matter of minimum wage controls, as exemplified by the Fair Labor Standards Act, the Walsh-Healey Act, and the Bacon-Davis Act. Since state regulations, in cases where they have been enacted, tend to follow federal laws in such instances, only the latter are described here.

The Fair Labor Standards Act

The Wages and Hours Law was enacted in 1938 and subsequently amended for the dual purpose of helping to spread employment and to outlaw unsatisfactory wage rates. The latter purpose is accomplished by establishing a minimum pay level of $1.40 an hour, rising to $1.60 on February 1, 1968. The former purpose is achieved by penalizing employers who work their employees beyond forty hours a week by requiring them to pay 50 percent more for the excess hours. This is where the term "time and one-half for overtime" is derived, the actual overtime being paid for at the rate of one and one-half times the regular base rate.

Pertinent, too, is the Equal Pay Act of 1963, which was signed by the President on June 10, 1963. This Act prohibits wage differentials based on sex after June 10, 1964, for workers covered by the Fair Labor Standards Act (FLSA).

1. *Coverage of the Act.* The FLSA covers all businesses and employees, with stated exceptions to be noted later, who engage in interstate commerce or who produce goods that enter interstate commerce. While the Act defines "interstate commerce" in broad terms, in test cases the courts have defined it so stringently that any business which is not strictly intrastate should be prepared to follow its provisions. Thus, companies that ship only a small percentage of their goods across state lines have been judged to be affected by the law. If only a small percentage of one's business is interstate, let us say anywhere up to 10 percent, it is highly desirable, if possible, to segregate employees working on interstate business, since the others may then be legally excluded from the provisions of the law.

2. *Exclusions under the Act.* There are three classes of exclusions under the Act. First, completely exempt are strictly intrastate activities, except for the following:

a) Retail or service activities when annual gross sales are $1 million or over
b) Gasoline service stations when annual sales are $250,000 or over
c) Local transit companies whose annual sales are $1 million or over
d) And all others, not mentioned above, whose annual sales exceed $1 million

Second, exempt from overtime requirements for specific periods are the following:

a) The first processing of various agricultural and livestock products for the first 14 weeks of a seasonal period
b) Any seasonal industry, if specified as such by the administrator of the Act, and then for 14 weeks only
c) Employees under certain types of work guarantees and as specified in a union contract

Third, exempt for limited periods from the minimum-wage provisions are apprentices, learners, handicapped workers, and messengers.

3. *Employee Exemptions.* It is important under this Act, and the Walsh-Healey Act, too, that the coverage of the term "employee" be clearly understood. Generally speaking, an employee is one who is subject to the directions of an employer or his managerial representatives regarding what is to be done, and how. Having the right to discharge also serves to separate employers from employees. More specifically, owners, executives, and independent contractors are examples of those considered to be employers. Of particular interest here are the tests by which it is determined whether or not particular employees may be included in the following exempt groups: executives, administrative employees, professional employees, certain sales employees, and a miscellaneous group.

a) *Executive Exemptions.* In general, the nature of the work and the salary received determine executive exemptions. More specifically, an executive is considered to be one whose primary duty consists of managing an establishment or a recognized department or subdivision thereof. He must also customarily direct the work of others (at least two subordinates), have authority to fire or recommend discharge or promotions, and exercise discretionary powers. He must devote not more than 20 percent of his hours worked to performance of duties not related to managerial duties. And he must be compensated (exclusive of board, lodging, or other facilities) at a rate of not less than $100 a week.

If the executive in question receives at least $150 a week and meets all other requirements except the 20 percent rule, he shall also be deemed to be an exempt executive.

b) Administrative Exemptions. Administrative exemptions are also related to nature of work and salary received. Exemptions are granted to those who perform office or nonmanual work that is concerned with management policies or general business operations. The work must require exercise of discretion and independent judgment, be of a specialized or technical nature, and be performed only under general supervision. Not more than 20 percent of the time must be spent on tasks not related to administrative work as defined. And the salary received (exclusive of board, lodging, etc.) must not be less than $115 a week.

If the administrative employee receives at least $150 a week and meets all other requirements except the 20 percent rule, he shall also be deemed to be an exempt employee.

c) Professional Exemptions. The professional tests are similar to those of the administrative employee in respect to the $115 minimum salary under a 20 percent rule, or $150 a week without this rule. Definitions of duties are of course different. A professional employee is one who performs intellectual and varied duties as opposed to routine, manual, or physical work. He must exercise discretion and judgment. His education must have been in a field of science or learning customarily acquired by a prolonged course in specialized and intellectual study, as distinguished from general academic training, apprenticeships, or trade courses. Or the work may be in a recognized artistic endeavor dependent upon invention, imagination, or talent as opposed again to work calling for general, manual, or broad training and ability.

d) Sales Exemptions. In addition to retail exemptions noted earlier, "outside" salesmen may also be exempted. Such salesmen must, to begin with, make personal calls at the customer's place of business. Mail or telephone sales are not exempt unless they are an adjunct of the personal call. And not more than 20 percent of the time must be spent on such activities as clerical work, attending sales conferences, making incidental deliveries or collections, and traveling.

e) Miscellaneous Groups. As noted earlier, apprentices, learners, handicapped workers, and messengers are the principal classes eligible for exemption from minimum-wage provisions.

For apprentices to be exempted, their training agreement must be in writing, and it must cover the following points:

1. Provide for not less than 4,000 hours of reasonably continuous employment
2. Provide for participation in an approved schedule of work and at least 144 hours per year of related supplemental instruction

3. Set forth the proportion between the number of apprentices and the number of experienced workmen in a given job classification
4. Specify the relation of apprentice rates at various periods to the rates paid experienced workers
5. Be approved by the state apprenticeship council or other established state authority, if state authority exists

In the case of handicapped workers, learners, and messengers, sub-minimum wage rates may also be paid. This cannot be done, however, until certificates of exemption noting the specific reductions permissible are obtained from the federal agencies.

4. *Contractual Exemptions.* Under certain types of collective bargaining agreements, exemptions are permitted. Under the Belo-type contract—named after the case in which this clause was legalized—the employer need not comply with overtime requirements. However, he must guarantee a certain sum each week, no matter how many hours are worked.

Such agreements have further conditions. No employee shall be employed more than 1,040 hours during any consecutive 26-week period, or more than 2,240 hours in 52 weeks. In any event, hours over 60 a week are entitled to overtime pay.

5. *Records.* Although the FLSA does not require that specific forms of records be kept, rulings of the administrator indicate that certain types of information should be recorded. First, for each employee, such personal data should be kept as name, address, date of birth if under 19, and occupation. Second, time records should be kept regarding the standard workweek, hours worked each day and each week, and absences. Third, payroll records should cover dates of payment, pay periods, daily and weekly earnings, basis on which payment is made, bonuses earned, and any deductions from wages paid. And fourth, if the company hires employees who work at home, detailed records should be kept on the foregoing, as well as the amount of work distributed to and collected from each such worker.

6. *Penalties.* Employers who violate this Act may be punished in a variety of ways. By injunction, an employer may be forbidden to ship goods interstate, to pay less than minimum wages, or to keep inadequate records. By criminal prosecution, if an employer is convicted of having willfully violated the Act, he can be fined up to $10,000 or imprisoned for a term of not more than six months, or both. And if an employee has not been paid his due under the law, he may sue to recover the wages due, plus an equal sum as liquidated damages, plus attorney fees and litigation costs. It is not necessary that the employer's failure to pay be willful.

The Walsh-Healey Public Contracts Act

The Walsh-Healey Act differs from the FLSA in two important respects. First, the overtime provisions are set on a daily (eight-hour) as well as a weekly (forty-hour) basis. Second, the minimum wages are based upon prevailing community rates, as determined by the Secretary of Labor after public hearings.

1. *Coverage under the Act.* The matter of coverage is also important under this Act. In general terms, it covers those parts of an employer's business which come into contact with federal contracts of $10,000 or more. For example, the following firms would be covered:

a) Those dealing with any federal agency
b) Those that supply or manufacture contracted articles
c) Those that accept subcontracts from the prime contractor with a federal agency, or work with him in the execution of a contract
d) Those that ship goods on behalf of a regular dealer

The more important exemptions include the following:

a) Various transportation and communication facilities
b) Construction contracts
c) Personal service contracts
d) Perishable commodities
e) Stock on hand

The definitions of employees under this Act are much like those of the FLSA. The following are the principal exemptions:

a) Employees not engaged in work directly connected with the manufacturing, fabrication, assembling, handling, or shipment of articles, supplies, and equipment
b) Office, custodial, and maintenance employees
c) Executive, administrative, and professional employees

2. *Methods of Computation.* Methods of computing time and pay for overtime are much the same for the Walsh-Healey Act as for the FLSA, except that the day as well as the week must be considered in computing overtime. To illustrate, assume that two employees whose hourly rate is $3.00 (which is the established rate for the area) work the following daily hours in the same week:

Employee #1—12, 8, 8, 8, 6, or a total of 42
Employee #2—8, 8, 8, 8, 8, 8, or a total of 48

Their pay would be computed as follows:

Employee #1—42 × \$3.00 = \$126 plus 4 × \$3.00 × ½
$$= \$6.00, \text{ or a total of } \$132$$

This takes into account the four hours' overtime on the first day which is greater than the overtime calculated only on the weekly basis.

Employee #2—48 × \$3.00 = \$144 plus 8 × \$3.00 × ½
$$= \$12, \text{ or a total of } \$156$$

This takes into account the eight hours' overtime over forty for the week.

3. *Required Records.* The records required by this Act are much the same as by the FLSA. The Walsh-Healey regulations require the same personal data as the Wages and Hours Law, plus these two additional items:

a) The sex of each employee
b) The number of each contract each employee works on, and the dates when the work is performed

Except for the overtime column, payroll records under both the Wages and Hours and the Walsh-Healey acts may be identical. The reason for the exception is that the Wages and Hours Law requires overtime pay only for hours worked over 40 per week, whereas the Walsh-Healey Act requires overtime pay for hours worked over eight per day or 40 per week, whichever is greater.

Firms covered by the Walsh-Healey Act also must keep a record of the "injury frequency rate" in their establishments on a quarterly basis. The injury frequency rate is calculated by multiplying the total number of "disabling injuries" which occur during each three-month period by one million and dividing that sum by the total number of man-hours actually worked within the same quarterly period.

4. *Penalties for Violations.* The penalties for violations of this Act may be very severe. They are as follows:

a) Money damages for child or prison labor
b) Wage restitutions
c) Cancellation of contract
d) Blacklisting

Perhaps the most effective method of enforcement of the Walsh-Healey Act is that which provides for the assessment of money damages against the contractor.

If the contractor violates the minimum-wage or overtime stipulations, he has to pay the wages due, equal to the amount of any unlawful deductions, rebates, refunds, or underpayments.

Failure to comply with the stipulations of the Walsh-Healey Act, which are a part of the contract, constitutes breach of contract by the contractor. As in other instances of breach of contract, the penalty is cancellation of the contract. In addition, he can be made to pay any increased costs if the government gets someone else to complete the contract.

The Comptroller General is required to distribute a blacklist to all government agencies. The persons or firms whose names appear on this list cannot be awarded any government contract for a period of three years following the date upon which the Secretary of Labor determines that a breach occurred, unless the Secretary recommends otherwise. Obviously, to be placed upon this list would be a serious penalty in many cases.

The Bacon-Davis (Public Construction) Act

The Bacon-Davis Act is similar to the Walsh-Healey Act, since it too regulates minimum wages on governmental contracts. It relates to contracts in excess of $2,000 for the construction, alteration, and repair of public works. All mechanics and laborers must be paid at least the prevailing rate as established by the Secretary of Labor.

If contractors pay more than prevailing rates, they do so at their own risk, since such additional costs are not reimbursable. If contractors pay less, they are subject to any of the following penalties:

1. The Secretary of Labor may withhold accrued payments due to the contractor from the federal government.
2. The contracts held by the contractor may be canceled outright by the government.
3. The contractor's name may be placed upon the Comptroller General's ineligibility list for further contracts.

Safeguards in Wage Programming

This discussion of remuneration can best be closed by making a number of suggestions regarding wage programming. In the first place, it should be perfectly obvious that anyone who is convinced that he has a perfect answer to wage problems and can correctly set wages is merely deluding himself. There is as yet no method of such perfection available. To believe so merely establishes a block in the road that otherwise leads to intelligent compromise.

In part, the explanation for the belief that wages can be set accurately derives from false deductions relative to the use of time-study methods. In this connection, one often hears the phrase that such methods lead to the determination of a "fair day's pay for a fair day's work." Time-study methods are useful only in regard to the latter half of this phrase; they can be used to determine standards of output with a high degree of accuracy. But having established, for example, that on a given job a well-selected, trained, and experienced worker should be able to produce 800 units a day, all that can be expected from time-study methods has been derived. What the wage value of the 800 units is cannot be determined by time-study methods. To be sure, time-study analysts proceed from there to set value rates, but they are using other yardsticks or techniques in doing so, not time study. Since the time-study man does the rate setting, many incorrectly conclude that his slide rule also is capable of deriving economic values.

The use of time-study methods is not criticized here but rather their misuse. To claim for them results that they cannot yield is a serious error, which is cited here as evidence of the belief held by many that unimpeachable wages can be set. If management is to make intelligent progress in its wage policies, it must convince others of its understanding of the complexity of the subject by refusing to take an unbending or narrow attitude toward it. Certainly, unions in many cases have become vigorous opponents of time-study methods because of misuse in setting rates.

In the second place, management's wage policies should be based upon a full account of all factors—economic, legal, union, and social—that have some effect on wages. To do this, it is absolutely essential to determine as precisely as possible how these factors exert their influence. Such factors as cost-of-living indexes, union demands, changes in population structure, competition, and federal regulations all have their place in the wage structure. However, some work directly and others indirectly, some work slowly and others rapidly, and some are positive in wage determinations and others negative. Unless the direction and force of the composite of factors is determined, grievous errors will be committed in establishing wage policies.

For example, a personnel manager must properly evaluate short-run influences and long-run influences if he is to help his company reach correct wage decisions. Moreover, companies which foolishly raise arguments that apply in the short run but not in the long run, or vice versa, merely weaken themselves in the eyes of their employees when the truth is known. When economic forces are against him, the employer should be the first to admit it and not confuse the issue. This does not mean that he should not seek to protect his interests by legitimate means, but to do so by ignorant claims is folly. The employees' confidence in the judgment of the employer is thereby lost.

Finally, and perhaps most important of all, wage policies should be viewed as an integral part of the structure of a personnel program. Wages are undoubtedly the keystone to the arch of this structure, but not the structure itself, as some employers seem to believe. Indeed, some have been so preoccupied with wages that unions have taken advantage of this bias to gain unwarranted and ill-advised concessions on working conditions and rules. The ill-advised seniority rules accepted by some companies, which they must follow thereafter to their regret, are a case in point.

When wages are given their proper place in the personnel program, they are neither overemphasized or underemphasized. Wages alone cannot bring about higher production, better morale, and better relations with employees. Nonfinancial incentives, proper handling of grievances, good working conditions, availability of various services, and development of confidence in workers are examples of other matters that can add to or detract from the efficiency of the wage program itself.

QUESTIONS

1. Can wages be measured precisely? If they cannot, what hope is there of ever minimizing wage disputes?
2. What is the economic explanation for wages?
3. For what are employees basically paid?
4. Would you ascribe the strength of unions in wage matters to their convincing explanation of economics, to their political power, or to their bargaining power? Are not the latter two inadequate in the long run if not based on sound economics?
5. What is the appeal of "administered" wages? Is it not built on unsubstantial grounds?
6. Assume that company A has made a profit of $1.5 million this year, but expects to lose $250,000 next year, while company B has lost $500,000 this year but expects to make $1 million next year. What effect should these data have upon wages in these companies?
7. If a company wishes to make wage adjustments in line with changes in the cost of living, what advice would you give this company, and against what pitfalls would you suggest that it provide safeguards?
8. What is the purpose of minimum-wage laws? What are their presumed benefits? In what way might they be harmful to employees?
9. In what respects, if any, do the overtime provisions of the Walsh-Healey Act differ from those of the FLSA?
10. What can time-study methods contribute to the determination of wages? What should not be expected of such methods?

CHAPTER 18

JOB EVALUATION AND WAGE CLASSIFICATION

Introduction

As noted earlier, relative even more than absolute compensation is of critical importance in affecting employee morale and effort. It is surprising to see the change in an employee who, seemingly satisfied with his remuneration, learns of the higher earnings of a fellow worker whom he considers his inferior. Hence, it is imperative, if a company wishes to minimize such occurrences, to determine what each job is worth and, if a range is allowed on each job, what each individual is worth. Determining job values comes under the heading of job evaluation and wage classification (which is the subject of the present chapter); and determining the value of employees (which has been discussed in Chapter 12) is known by a variety of names, such as merit rating, employee rating, and service rating.

Job evaluation is essentially a process of measurement. Factors considered of importance in determining the value of jobs are measured by the use of arbitrarily designed yardsticks. The quantities for the factors are summed up for each job, and the totals are converted into dollar values. Thus, each job is assigned a monetary value that has a definite relation to other jobs, since all have been measured by the same yardsticks.

Various methods have been designed to make such measurements. In major outline, all follow the same general pattern, which includes the following major steps:

1. Establishing organizational responsibility
2. Determining jobs to be evaluated
3. Making the job analysis
4. Evaluating the jobs
5. Preparing wage and salary classifications

Organizational Aspects

Almost without exception, those who have had experience with job evaluation programs have concluded that such programs should have the approval and sponsorship of top executive levels. Particularly in the initial stages, a major committee, of which the president or executive vice-president is chairman, should guide the development of job evaluation. This is desirable in order to convince any doubting Thomas that top management is convinced of the permanent value of the program. After the program is well under way, periodic conferences should be scheduled with top executives so that they may be kept informed of results and may have the opportunity to offer constructive criticisms.

1. *Organization Responsibility.* Responsibility for job evaluation is usually assigned to the industrial engineering section, a wage unit of the personnel department, or some interested operating executive. There is much sense to its assignment to industrial engineering because of the professional interest, competency, and activity in this area. Its placement in the personnel division has much to commend it, too, particularly since a total wage and salary administration program is often its responsibility. The "interested executive" assignment is usually made in smaller companies or when it is wise to avoid jurisdictional disputes over its placement in personnel or industrial engineering.

2. *Staffing the Unit.* Wherever in the organization the job evaluation program is assigned, provision must be made for staffing it with competent help. In some companies, trained and experienced help is hired from the outside. In others, members of the staff are given special training. By the former method, competent help is secured at once, but it takes some time for the outsiders to become acquainted with the characteristics and policies of the company and its employees. Under the latter method the staff selected for the job is acquainted with the company, its executives, and its employees, but it must acquire skill in carrying out job evaluation. Both plans have been used successfully, so the choice in any particular case depends upon which can be installed most economically and effectively. In any event, the staff should be a permanent one, with opportunity provided for continuing study and experience in order to improve its competence.

3. *Approval of Evaluation Plans.* Where authority rests in approving and using job evaluation data should also be specified if all organizational aspects of the program are to be properly considered. Since the personnel department is a staff department, it obviously cannot enforce the program, the development of which has been assigned to it. Hence, approval of the plan must be in the hands of some top-line

executive. Even when this is provided for, the personnel department must solve the problem of securing full cooperation of unions and the using departments. More and more, job evaluation has become subject to collective bargaining. Thus, consultation, if not direct cooperation, with unions at all stages of development and use seems desirable. Moreover, building satisfactory relations with foremen and supervisors is an essential part of the organizational problem. Even though top management approves a job evaluation program, the supervisors can delay or even sabotage its development if they withhold their cooperation or give it grudgingly.

Selection of Jobs to Be Evaluated

Few companies have included all jobs and positions in their evaluation programs. Ordinarily, the program is limited in most companies to shop jobs or office work. In some instances, sales and executive positions have been evaluated, too. It might seem at first glance that all types and levels of jobs should be included. Usually, there are practical difficulties in the way of an all-inclusive study. It would take too long, and at the outset the staff is usually not sufficiently sure of itself to tackle the nonroutine jobs. Moreover, such jobs are not ordinarily the ones from which the cries of discontent arise. Executive, professional, and technical jobs are usually excluded, at least in the beginning. The line of demarcation has been conveniently set in some instances by excluding all jobs receiving more than a set amount a year in salary—in some cases as low as $4,000 and in others up to $15,000. Or a particular level in the organization chart is used; for example, all jobs below the first line of supervision may be included.

Such exclusions should not, however, be made permanent. When time and conditions permit, all positions should be brought into the plan. Otherwise, there will be groups of discontented employees because of discrepancies between evaluated and nonevaluated jobs. When selling jobs are separated from nonselling, or engineering from technical shop jobs, for example, in order to get an evaluation program done quickly, grievances of those in the nonstudied jobs will be difficult to handle. Indeed, the latter may become more vociferous when they see changes being made in studied jobs but not in theirs, as has happened with engineers in some companies who have favored becoming unionized as a consequence.

Moreover, when companies try to include previously excluded jobs in the program, they find that the new jobs can seldom be fitted into the existing scheme. The alternatives are to have two evaluation programs, which do not quite match, or to start all over and reevaluate the old jobs under an overall program. Either course is unsatisfactory and can be avoided if the evaluation plan is developed with a view to including all jobs ultimately, though at the outset only particular groups of jobs are to be evaluated.

Making the Job Analysis

The basic material of job evaluation is provided by job analysis. Since the nature and scope of job analysis have been described in an earlier chapter, it is necessary here merely to note the information which is secured by job analysis and which is essential to subsequent steps of job evaluation. The following information is usually collected:

1. Job title or titles, including trade nicknames
2. Number of employees on the job, and their organizational and geographical locations
3. Names of immediate supervisors
4. Materials, tools, and equipment used or worked with
5. From whom work is received and to whom it is delivered
6. Hours of work and wage levels
7. Conditions of work
8. Complete listing of duties, with an estimate of time spent on each group, classified according to daily, weekly, monthly, and occasional
9. Educational and experience requirements
10. Skills, aptitudes, and abilities required
11. Promotional and transfer lines from and to the job
12. Miscellaneous information and comments

Job Evaluation Plans

After the foregoing preparations have been made, measurement of jobs in nonfinancial terms may be undertaken. This step, to repeat, is based on the assumption that to develop correct financial relationships between jobs, it is first necessary to set forth quantitative relationships based upon arbitrarily constructed yardsticks. In simple terms, this means that if it is found that job A is worth two units on a predetermined scale and job B is worth four units on the same scale, then, whatever A is worth in dollars, B should be worth twice as much. How the jobs are quantitatively related to each other depends upon the system employed. The following systems of evaluation are described here:

1. The simple ranking plan
2. The job classification method
3. The point system
4. The factor comparison method

1. *The Simple Ranking Plan.* Under the simple ranking plan of evaluation, jobs are arranged in order of increasing value in accordance with the judgment of the arrangers. This is first done on a departmental level by a committee of job analysts and supervisors, and then on interdepartmental levels by a committee which also includes higher line executives. In all cases of ranking the committee members read the job descriptions or, if descriptions are not available, examine their mental pictures of the jobs and grade the jobs in terms of their individual interpretations of the relative amounts of such elements as the following:

  a) Difficulty and volume of work
  b) Responsibilities involved
  c) Supervision given and received
  d) Training and experience requirements
  e) Working conditions

After all jobs have been ranked, they are grouped into a small number of classes, usually from six to ten. Wage and salary rates are established for each of the classes, either arbitrarily or by job-rating methods to be defined later. All jobs are then paid within the dollar range established for each class.

This plan is obviously simple, can be done quickly, and does not require a large staff; but it has many disadvantages. The reasons why jobs have been ranked as they are, are locked in the minds of the rankers, whose scales of value vary from one time to another and whose individual concepts of jobs differ. The rankers are ordinarily inexperienced in such work, so that their decisions are uncertain and largely a series of compromises. When it comes to interdepartmental ranking of jobs, their inexperience is even more apparent, because few raters are acquainted with all jobs. Under the circumstances, the job-ranking plan should be used when time or resources to employ a better method are not available or as a check on the accuracy of other methods.

2. *The Job Classification Method.* The job classification method is a refinement of the ranking method. Under it, major job classes or grades are first established, and then the various jobs are assigned by rankers to these grades. Figure 18–1 illustrates a gradation of five classes, designated by a title label and increasing in value. The raters read the job descriptions and, depending upon their personal interpretations of the relative difficulty of tasks, responsibilities involved, and knowledge and experience required, decide in which of the classes each job should be placed.

This method, too, is relatively simple to operate and to understand, does not take a great deal of time, and does not require technical help. Although it represents an advance in accuracy over the ranking method, it still leaves much to be desired, because personal evaluations by executives unskilled in such work establish the major classes and deter-

FIGURE 18–1

DESCRIPTION OF JOB CLASSIFICATION

Third Class Clerk: Pure routine concentration, speed and accuracy. Works under supervision. May or may not be held responsible for results.

Second Class Clerk: No supervision of others; especially skilled for the job by having exhaustive knowledge of the details. Person: close application, exceptional accuracy and speed.

First Class Clerk: Must have characteristics of 2nd class clerk. Assume more responsibility.

Senior Clerk: Technical, varied work, occasionally independent thinking and action due to difficult work, which requires exceptional clerical ability and extensive knowledge of principles and fundamentals of business of his department. Not charged with supervision of others to any extent, work subject to only limited check. Person: dependable, trustworthy, resourceful—able to make decision.

Interpretive Clerk: Those handling or capable of doing a major division of the work. Complicated work requiring much independent thinking, able to consider details outside control of supervision or routine.

---

mine into which class each job shall be placed. In this case, as in job ranking, it is difficult to know how much of a job's rank is influenced by the man on the job. Although the job and not the man should be evaluated, the foregoing methods provide practically no safeguards against this form of error. The job classification method should be used when an organization is small, when jobs are not too complex or numerous, or when time and resources to use another method are not available. It will produce better results than the ranking method without great increase in time or cost.

3. *The Point System.* The point system of job evaluation is the most widely used and, according to its proponents, yields accurate results without undue expense or effort. In simple outline, it values jobs

by means of yardsticks, one for each factor that is considered to be common to all jobs. By summing up the readings of the several yardsticks, a quantitative expression is derived for each job. These sums are point values, which must then be converted to dollar values.

In applying the point system, the following steps are taken:

a) Establish and define a list of factors common to all jobs that are being covered.

b) Construct a measuring yardstick for each factor.

c) From the job description, prepare a schedule showing qualitatively to what degree each job possesses the various factors enumerated above.

d) Apply the yardstick to convert the qualitative descriptions to quantitative units.

e) Sum up for each job the readings obtained for the individual factors.

f) Rank the jobs in accordance with the scores obtained in the foregoing steps.

g) Determine the dollar value to be assigned to relative positions in the job ranking.

a) *Job Factors.* Job factors are characteristics that are common to all jobs to be covered in the program. They can be readily determined by making a survey of representative jobs. Ordinarily, no more than six to nine major factors with appropriate subheadings should be used; otherwise, the ratings will be subject to useless controversy.

The factors and subfactors that are found most commonly in job evaluation programs are responsibility, skill, effort, education, working conditions, and experience required. The factors of the widely used plan of the National Metal Trades Association (NMTA) are shown in Table 18–1 and those in a plan devised by the National Office Management Association (NOMA) are shown in Table 18–2.

TABLE 18–1
POINTS ASSIGNED TO FACTORS OF NATIONAL METAL TRADES ASSOCIATION PLAN

Factor	1st Degree	2d Degree	3d Degree	4th Degree	5th Degree
SKILL					
1. Education	14	28	42	56	70
2. Experience	22	44	66	88	110
3. Initiative and ingenuity	14	28	42	56	70
EFFORT					
4. Physical demand	10	20	30	40	50
5. Mental or visual demand	5	10	15	20	25
RESPONSIBILITY					
6. Equipment or process	5	10	15	20	25
7. Material or product	5	10	15	20	25
8. Safety of others	5	10	15	20	25
9. Work of others	5	10	15	20	25
JOB CONDITIONS					
10. Working conditions	10	20	30	40	50
11. Unavoidable hazards	5	10	15	20	25

TABLE 18–2

POINTS ASSIGNED TO FACTORS OF NATIONAL OFFICE
MANAGERS ASSOCIATION PLAN

1. Elemental—250 points

2. Skill—500 points
   a) General or special education............................160
   b) Training time on job.................................... 40
   c) Memory.. 40
   d) Analytical.. 95
   e) Personal contact...................................... 35
   f) Dexterity... 80
   g) Accuracy... 50

3. Responsibility—200 points
   a) For company property................................. 25
   b) For procedure..125
   c) Supervision.. 50

4. Effort—physical factors—50 points
   a) Place of work... 5
   b) Cleanliness of work................................... 5
   c) Position.. 10
   d) Continuity of work.................................... 15
   e) Physical or mental strain.............................. 15

SOURCE: National Office Management Association, *Clerical Job Evaluation*, Bulletin No. 1 (New York).

In the case of evaluation plans for managerial positions, the following factors and subfactors have been used in a number of companies:[1]

Know-How:
   Requirements of duties
   Knowledge
   Planning required
   Mental application
   Understanding required

   Administration
   Original thinking
   Creative ability
   Managerial techniques

Responsibilities:
   Initiative
   Accountability
   Effect on profits
   For personnel relations
   For policy making
   For policy interpretation

Relationships:
   Supervision exercised
   Demand for leadership
   Influence
   Influence on policy making
   Influence on methods

b) Measuring Yardsticks. After the factors to be used are determined, yardsticks must be established by which increasing importance in each of the factors may be measured. This is usually done in two stages. First, the total points that any factor or major subheading of a factor may have are established. Such assignments of points determine the relative value of the various factors. For example, in the NMTA

[1] R. E. Sibson, "Plan for Management Salary Administration," *Harvard Business Review,* Vol. XXXIV, No. 6, p. 108.

plan, skill has a maximum of 250 points and responsibility 100; and in the NOMA plan, skill has a maximum of 500 points and responsibility 200; so in both cases the ratio between the two factors is 2½ to one. Second, varying degrees of each major factor are than assigned an increasing number of points within the total established for it. For example, in the NOMA plan, 160 of the 500 points for skill are allotted to general or special education, which is divided into three levels, each receiving a share of the 160 points. Thus a job that requires the maximum education would receive 160 points, one that required high school training would receive 92 points, and one that required grammar school training would be given 40 points.

These determinations are arrived at through the pooled opinions of line and staff executives. Cross checks of various kinds can be employed to compare the accuracy of major divisions and point assignments within divisions. The NMTA plan, for example, has been adopted in numerous companies, so that its allocations have weathered the most difficult of tests. In any event, after the points have been allocated, they, along with verbal descriptions of major classes and grades within classes, should be formally written up, so that all may use and interpret the system similarly. The NOMA plan cited here is an example of how this may be done in simple yet relatively clear terms.

Although yardsticks are arbitrarily determined and vary in "value" from company to company, this does not impair their accuracy. As long as the yardsticks in each company are carefully designed and adhered to in measuring jobs, the relative values of all jobs can be established with accuracy. For example, if company A and company B have a maximum total of 300 points and 450 points, respectively, for responsibility, then, on a similar job, if A gives it 100 points, B should give it 150 points. And if the total points received by the job are 400 by company A and 600 by company B, this does not mean that the job is worth 50 percent more in company B, but it means that the yardsticks in company B are 50 percent longer. In each company, similar jobs will be in relatively the same position, as may be seen in the following table:

	Company A (Points)	Company B (Points)	Ratio
Job X..............	400	600	150.0
Job Y..............	500	825	150.0

Some companies use as few as 400 points as the maximum, and others go into the thousands. What figure to use is not so important as accuracy in the allocation of the points among the factors and grades in the factors.

c) *Rating Jobs.* After the job factors and measuring sticks have been established, the task of evaluating individual jobs can begin. The first step is to translate the job descriptions for each job into a written statement of the various job factors contained in each job. Thus, if the first factor to be measured is education, the amount of education required should be listed on a work sheet for each job. The next step is to apply the education yardstick to the amount of education specified on each job. For example, if a given job calls for four years of high school and the points assigned to that level of education are 92, this amount is written on the work sheet for the job in question.

And so on, in order, each factor of each job is measured until points have been assigned to all. The points for each job are then totaled to get its point rating. Obviously, these steps of rating are largely routine. The big tasks are preparing acceptable job descriptions and yardsticks. When these have been done, the function of applying the yardsticks to each job is relatively easy.

d) *Monetary Conversions.* The point values assigned to jobs at this juncture are, to repeat, stated in point values which are nonmonetary units. Through such measurements, it has been determined how jobs rate relative to each other. To be of practical use, the relative positions accorded jobs by the point system must be expressed in monetary terms. To accomplish this, two major steps are usually taken. First, a plan is established for determining how nonmonetary units are to be converted into dollar units. And second, a decision is reached as to how jobs of increasing importance are to be grouped into wage classes.

The task of conversion is usually based on a comparison of present company salary rates with those being paid in the community for comparable jobs. By making a check with other employers in the community, the data for such a comparison are derived. The comparison need not be made for all jobs; a limited number of selected jobs that are representative of several points on the job list is sufficient. Let us assume, for example, that data on community and company rates, as shown in Table 18–3, are collected for selected jobs.

Study of such figures would indicate that company rates in this case are well in line with community rates. Hence a conversion of point values to dollar values could be undertaken. If company and community rates were not in line, decisions would have to be made as to how rates out of line would be reconciled with community rates.

Careful analysis of these two sets of weekly rates (particularly if charts were prepared) would indicate that company salaries increase in an arithmetic progression, whereas those in the community follow a percentage increase. This provides a clue to two possible bases of conversion—the arithmetic and the percentage bases. In the foregoing case the company salary increase is approximately $4.75 for each 20-point increase, whereas the community increase is about 5 percent for each 20-point increase. The arithmetic plan results in a straight line when point values are set off against dollar units on a chart. The percentage plan results in a line that curves upward.

TABLE 18–3

Selected Jobs	Point Values	Average Company Salary per Week	Average Community Salary per Week
A...................	400	$ 65.50	$ 70.75
B...................	420	70.25	74.50
C...................	460	79.50	82.00
D...................	500	91.00	90.75
E...................	540	99.25	100.50
F...................	560	104.00	105.00
G...................	600	115.00	115.50
H...................	660	130.50	133.50

The arithmetic plan has simplicity in its favor, but economic principles favor the percentage plan. It has been found, for example, that most companies without a considered wage plan tend to overpay the lower jobs and underpay the higher jobs. Yet the supply of labor available to fill the lower jobs is invariably relatively more plentiful than that to fill the higher jobs. Hence, in developing a salary curve, it is preferable to select the percentage plan of increase. In this way, jobs in the higher point ranges will be accorded a wider dollar range than those in the lower point ranges.

e) Job Classes and Rate Ranges. In most job evaluation plans, it is felt to be undesirable to establish a salary curve in which separate dollar values are assigned to each unitary increase in point values. Instead, a number of job classes are established, increasing in point values, with all jobs in each class being paid the same salary base. It might be decided, for example, that all jobs would be grouped and paid as shown in Table 18–4.

As may be noted in Table 18–4, the brackets of one class may overlap somewhat those in the ones below and above it. Indeed, the top rate for the 400-to-439 class, for example, is above that of the lowest rate for the 440-to-479 class. Such overlapping is a recognition of the fact that each class includes a number of jobs of varying point values. Moreover, it provides an opportunity for employees within a given class to obtain base rate increases if their work and length of service merit them.

The range within each class depends in part upon arbitary decision and in part upon the number of classes. The ranges in the cases cited

TABLE 18–4

Point Value Range	Salary Base	Fixed Range ($8.00)	Percentage Range (20%)
400–439	$ 70	$ 66–$ 74	$ 63–$ 77
440–479	80	76– 84	72– 88
480–519	90	86– 94	81– 99
520–559	100	96– 104	90– 110
560–599	110	106– 114	99– 121
600–639	120	116– 124	108– 132
640–679	130	126– 134	117– 143

above were based upon a fixed rate of $8.00 and of a 20 percent difference, respectively. The arithmetic base might have been set at more or less than $8.00, and the percentage might have been set at some figure other than 20 percent. The range in each class is usually set somewhere between 20 percent and 50 percent of the minimum figure; or the percentage is divided by two, and the range for each class is established by adding and subtracting the percentage amount from the average salary rate for each job class. On the other hand, the class range depends upon the number of classes. Thus the more classes there are in a given plan, the narrower is the bracket for each class. An example of a wage chart is shown in Figure 18–2.

After the wage brackets are established and jobs are assigned to their respective classes, comparisons will ordinarily show that actual salaries in some cases exceed the maximum for their job class and others fall below the class minimum. These are sometimes called "red circle" rates because they are marked in color to call attention to needed corrections. The usual practice is to raise gradually the underpaid jobs and to allow time to take care of the overpaid employees. The latter will eventually leave the payroll or be promoted to higher job classifications commensurate with the rates they are receiving.

4. The Factor Comparison System. The factor comparison system is also widely used. It is similar to the point system in that jobs are evaluated by means of standard yardsticks of value. It differs from the latter by using key jobs as the basic yardsticks. Otherwise, the same steps are taken in making preliminary job descriptions and in bringing together the expert opinion of trained specialists and line executives. The major steps in the program consist of the following:

a) Determination of key jobs.
b) Ranking of key jobs
c) Valuing of factors into which key jobs are divided
d) Comparison of all jobs with key job ratings
e) Establishment of dollar value of all jobs

The first step in this plan is to determine the key jobs. For this purpose, jobs are selected that cover the range from low- to high-paid jobs. Moreover, the jobs must be ones over which job analysts and executives do not disagree on the amount of pay. The jobs, too, must be definable in accurate and clear terms. Usually, from 10 to 30 jobs are picked at this stage.

FIGURE 18–2

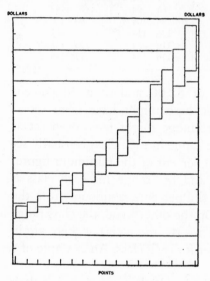

SOURCE: For this chart and much of the material in this chapter, the author is indebted to M. J. Jucius, H. H. Maynard, and C. L. Shartle, *Job Analysis for Retail Stores* (Columbus, Ohio: Bureau of Business Research, Ohio State University, 1945).

Next, the key jobs are ranked. This is first done on an overall basis. Then the jobs are ranked, factor by factor, somewhat similarly to the point system. Here, too, salient factors must be selected, such as mental requirements, skill requirements, etc. An example of how this may be done is shown in Table 18–5. The five key jobs are ranked in the following order for mental requirements: job No. 1 is first, job No. 35 is second, job No. 20 is third, job No. 75 is fourth, and job No. 120 is fifth. On physical requirements, however, the ranking is almost reversed.

After the key jobs are ranked factor by factor, the base pay for each job is allocated to each factor. As may be seen in Table 18–5, the base pay of job No. 35, for example, is divided in the following way:

Mental requirements.....................................$0.62
Skill requirements....................................... 0.66
Physical requirements................................... 0.60
Responsibility.. 0.44
Working conditions...................................... 0.30

Next, all jobs, one at a time, are compared with the table of key job values as just established. This is done by determining for each job the key job to which it is most similar, factor by factor. Assume, for example, that job No. 27 is being checked against Table 18–5. Assume further that it is found to have the following characteristics:

Similar to:	For:
Job No. 1.............................	Mental requirements
Job No. 20............................	Skill requirements
Job No. 35............................	Physical requirements
Job No. 35............................	Responsibilities
Job No. 20............................	Working conditions

The final step of dollar evaluation can now be taken. The individual jobs are then given the factor values, factor by factor, of the jobs to

TABLE 18–5

TABLE OF KEY JOBS

Rankings and Factor Values

Job	Total Base Rate	Mental Requirements		Skill Requirements		Physical Requirements		Responsi-bilities		Working Conditions	
		Rank-ing	Rate	Rank-ing	Rate	Rank-ing	Rate	Rank-ing	Rate	Rank-ing	Rate
No. 1	$2.94	1	$0.74	1	$1.00	5	$0.50	2	$0.50	5	$0.20
No. 20	2.78	3	0.50	2	0.80	3	0.66	1	0.60	4	0.22
No. 35	2.62	2	0.62	3	0.66	4	0.60	3	0.44	2	0.30
No. 75	2.46	4	0.48	4	0.62	2	0.80	5	0.30	3	0.26
No. 120	2.30	5	0.32	5	0.44	1	0.86	4	0.36	1	0.32

which they are similar. In the instance just cited, the rate would be $2.80 an hour, which is the sum of the factor values of $0.74 for mental requirements, $0.80 for skill requirements, $0.60 for physical requirements, $0.44 for responsibility, and $0.22 for working conditions.

In carrying out the comparison plan, the various steps included are much more detailed than outlined above. For example, after the key jobs are selected, ranked, and rated, it is usually found desirable to include other jobs, in order to establish a comparison table against which all jobs are to be checked. Thus, to the dozen or two jobs that constitute the master list, there are added up to 50 or 100 supplementary jobs, so that enough detail will be available to fit, without argument, all the other jobs into the table. Moreover, as the rating of jobs progresses, it may be found desirable to make some changes in the master key jobs because some are found, for one reason or another, to be out of line with other jobs. These changes obviously take more time than anticipated at the outset, but they do reduce errors in the plan.

5. *Internal and External Consistency.* This plan calls for a great deal of work because it is essential to develop consistency not

only in the rankings of the key jobs but also in the allocations of the base rates of the key jobs to the various factors. This two-way check, in the eyes of the proponents of the factor comparison system, makes it superior to the point plan. They admit that their system involves more time and effort but insist that the internal consistency of rates is increased by the methods of checking and cross-checking which they employ.

The external consistency of this plan is obtained in the same fashion as in the case of the point rating plan. As noted in connection with the latter, it is necessary to compare company rates with community or industry rates for comparable jobs. Through such a comparison, a smooth progression of rates, from key job to key job, can be obtained. In the case of the comparison method, company rates are related to outside rates before the final selection of key jobs is made, whereas in the point plan the company rates are usually related to outside rates after the point values have been established.

Outside comparisons are particularly useful in checking on executive compensation. One such survey has found that subordinate executives receive the following as a percentage of the president's salary in selected companies:[2]

Position	Percentage
Company president	100%
Executive vice-president	72
Top marketing executive	56
Top financial executive	55
Top production executive	52
Top industrial relations executive	38

Such information provides a check on relationships within one's own company.

Summary

To conclude this discussion, a number of comments are in order regarding the accuracy of job evaluation plans. In the first place, such plans do not eliminate wage controversies. When questions arise—for example, asking why job X received 87 points and not 89—it is possible to present the analysis by which the decision was made. Attention can be directed to specific factors as proof that thought, not whim, was the basis of evaluation. But the parties to the disagreement can

---

[2] Kenneth Henry, "The President's Pay Check," *Dun's Review and Modern Industry*, Vol. LXXI, No. 3, p. 40.

concern themselves with examining a system rather than unsupported opinions.

In the second place, it must be kept in mind that the factors of a job evaluation plan sometimes do not adequately take account of the marketplace, in spite of what may be done to assure external consistency. Although a particular job may rate only $2.50 an hour according to the evaluation plan, an extreme shortage of help or union bargaining in that category may require the payment of $3.25 an hour. Some companies will insist on fighting for the $2.50 rate to maintain the integrity of the job evaluation plan. Others accept the $3.25 rate, but only as an exception which will not be permitted to affect the relative rates of other jobs. There is no way of proving which course of action is right. Circumstances and managerial discretion are controlling elements in what will or can be done.

Perhaps this suggests, in the third place, that it is well for a company to work with a union, when one is involved, in developing and operating a job evaluation plan. If the union is informed after a plan is adopted, there is a natural objection because it was not consulted on the development. When its cooperation is sought from the start, there may be disagreements, but the final product becomes a "baby" that will be protected as much by the union as by management.

QUESTIONS

1. What are some of the problems encountered in staffing the job evaluation department? How may they be solved?
2. In what respects is the job classification method of job evaluation an improvement over the simple ranking method?
3. How are the yardsticks for measuring job factors developed? Inasmuch as all companies that use the point system do not employ job yardsticks of the same length, is their accuracy not doubtful? Explain.
4. The use of yardsticks results in determining how many points are to be assigned to each job. What do these points mean? How may they be converted to monetary values?
5. What are the relative merits of the arithmetic base and the percentage base in calculating wages for jobs with low point values? With high point values?
6. What policies seem most reasonable in dealing with the wage rates of jobs that are found to be above or below the rates set by the wage curves of the evaluation plan?
7. What is the factor comparison plan of job evaluation? Why do its proponents claim it to be the most accurate of evaluation plans? What are its disadvantages?

8. A particular person's job falls into a job class whose upper wage limit is $2.25 an hour, whereas if it had received one more point, the job would fall into the next job class, whose upper limit is $2.50 an hour. He argues that on the factor of skill alone, his job is worth at least one more point. How would you proceed to discuss this case?

9. What is meant by the terms "internal consistency" and "external consistency"? What is their relevance to job evaluation?

10. How do job evaluation plans take into account, if at all, the influence of the marketplace?

CHAPTER **19**

PLANS OF REMUNERATION

Introduction

In addition to determining how much employees are to be paid, it is necessary to select a method for calculating compensation. Two companies may have approximately the same wage and salary schedule, yet each may apply different methods by which compensation is computed. Thus, one company may employ the piecework plan and the other a timesaving bonus plan. Or one company may pay its salesmen on a straight commission plan, and another may use a combination plan of drawing account and commissions. The result in salaries may be approximately the same. Yet, in both of these cases the individual companies may be highly pleased with their selections and would not consider changing to the plan of the other. And each may be justified in concluding that a change would be undesirable.

A compensation method cannot be selected wisely unless the management knows the workings, advantages and disadvantages, and conditions of best usage of available plans. It is the purpose of this chapter to describe and examine the more common types of wage and salary plans for production employees, clerical and sales employees, and executive groups. The plan that should be adopted in a specific case may then be better determined.

The discussion here is taken up under the following headings:

1. Basic kinds of plans
2. Tests of a wage plan
3. Specific wage plans
4. Remuneration of salesmen
5. Executive compensation

Basic Kinds of Plans

There are two major kinds of wage and salary payment plans. In the first category are plans under which remuneration does not vary with

335

output or quality of output. Instead, they are computed in terms of some time unit. Since it once was common to pay workers by the day, time plans of shopworkers are referred to as "daywork," even though the hour is now the standard time unit of calculation. In the case of office and executive employees, the time unit may be the week, the half-month, the month, or rarely the year. Time plans are nonincentive in the sense that earnings during a given time period do not vary with the productivity of an employee during the time period.

The second category is composed of incentive plans, or those in which remuneration depends upon output or factors related to output during a given time period. It is to the benefit of an employee to bestir himself to produce more, to sell more, to reduce costs, or to utilize various resources more effectively, as the case may be. There is a direct financial stimulus in incentive plans that is lacking in time-computed remuneration plans.

Under these broad plans a number of specific plans have been developed. There is no one plan that is best under all circumstances. A plan (or plans, in some cases) must be selected to do the job that has to be done. Before describing and evaluating in more detail the more common types of compensation plans, it is therefore desirable to outline the tests by which the feasibility of particular plans may be ascertained.

Tests of Wage Plans

The apparent purpose of a wage plan is to remunerate employees for the work they perform. This is only one side of the story because it gives the impression that output is a function of wages alone. Wage plans do more than this; the nature of the plan itself may or may not appeal to workers. Hence, it is important to know what characteristics of wage plans appeal to employees so that they are stimulated to exert greater efforts. The following are desirable qualities in a wage plan:

1. Easily understood
2. Easily computed
3. Earnings related to effort
4. Incentive earnings paid soon after being earned
5. Relatively stable and unvarying

1. *Understandability of Wage Plans.* Obviously, all employees like to know how their wage plan works. If they do not, they become fearful that they are not getting what is justly due them. Hence, it is desirable to select a simple wage plan; or if a complicated one is chosen, all employees should be instructed in how it works. For example, a supervisor in one company was asked to explain to a group of foremen

his company's wage plan. He took about 15 minutes in his attempt, but succeeded only in confusing everyone. Obviously, if a supervisor cannot describe the basic outlines of a plan in 15 minutes, it is scarcely conceivable that any of the employees understand how it works.

2. *Ease of Computation.* Somewhat similar to the characteristic of understanding is that of ease of computation. Most employees like to be able (*a*) to compute daily, from time to time, what they are making; and (*b*) to check the accuracy of their pay envelopes. If they can do neither without help or without taking too much time, they tend to lose confidence in the plan. The effect upon their output will be adverse. Thus a wage payment plan should be sufficiently simple to permit quick calculation, or arithmetic tables should be supplied by reference to which calculations can be quickly made.

3. *Effective Motivation.* A pay plan should also provide for incentive within the work range of a particular job. To begin with, standards should be set so that they are attainable by competent workers. Obviously, if par is beyond the capacity of employees, they will not try. However, a par standard attained without trying is equally poor. Again, if quality of workmanship is significant in particular cases, a wage payment plan should not be selected that will stimulate output and affect quality adversely. Or if it is desired to stress output, a wage plan should be selected that pays a high premium at the upper levels and penalizes—or at least does not overcompensate—low production. And finally, if quantity and quality are to be stressed at the same time, a plan should be selected that will not unduly influence the worker to work too fast or to become careless of quality.

4. *Relation between Effort and Payday.* Incentive wage plans, if adopted, should provide for remuneration to employees as soon after effort is exerted as possible. In this way the reward or penalty is fixed in the minds of the employees in connection with the work they did. Payment at the end of each day would be best from this point of view, were it not for the undue cost of distributing a daily payroll. A weekly period is customary and serves this purpose, provided that the payday is not too distant from the work to which it applies. An interval of three or five days, at most, should be sufficient to calculate and distribute the payroll.

5. *Stability of Wage Plans.* Finally, a wage plan should be relatively stable and unvarying. Frequent tinkering with wage plans gives the impression that the management is seeking to defraud the employees. Hence, it is imperative thoroughly to consider available plans, so that need for subsequent changes or tinkering is eliminated. But

incentive plans particularly, though stable in appearance, may be made variable or given the appearance of variability by rate cutting, changes in time standards, or changes in the value of money. As will be noted later, rate cutting has been an evil that has made the piecework plan suspect in many quarters.

Types of Wage Payment Plans

A large number of wage plans have been devised, but relatively few have been used to any significant degree. Various surveys have disclosed that daywork and piecework are used to pay about 90 per cent of all industrial workers. The others are paid under a miscellany of plans, with some variant of the timesaving plan predominating. Hence, only the following plans, which include the more widely used and are representative of various types, are discussed here:

1. Daywork
2. Measured daywork
3. Piecework
4. Timesaving plans
5. Efficiency bonus plans
6. Group plans
7. Profit- and revenue-sharing plans

In the formula of the wage plans the following symbols are used:

$$W = \text{Wages earned}$$
$$H = \text{Hours actually worked}$$
$$S = \text{Standard time}$$
$$P = \text{Percentage}$$
$$R = \text{Rate per hour in dollars}$$
$$U = \text{Rate per unit in dollars}$$
$$N = \text{Number of units produced}$$

1. *Daywork.* Daywork is not only the oldest but the most common way of remunerating employees. It refers to all time-payment plans used in paying workers, although the hour is the time unit most commonly employed. Wages are computed under it by multiplying the number of hours worked by the rate per hour, as follows:

$$H \times R = W$$

For an employee who works overtime and is paid extra for the overtime, either of the following formulas may be used, assuming H to be the total hours worked, H_n the nonovertime hours, and H_o the overtime hours:

$$(H \times R) + (H_o \times R)50\% = W$$
$$(H_n \times R) + (H_o \times R)150\% = W$$

If an employee worked 52 hours in a given week and his basic rate was $2.00 an hour and he received overtime allowance over 40 hours, using the latter formula his pay would be calculated as follows:

$$(40 \times \$2.00) + (12 \times \$2.00)150\% =$$
$$\$80 + \$36 = \$116$$

The daywork plan has been widely adopted for several reasons. It is simplicity itself to compute and to understand. Also, it is unnecessary to set quantity standards as the basis for computing wages. It is also strongly supported by many unions because the plan does not stimulate speedups or penalize the average or less-than-average worker. And under it, quality is not sacrificed because it does not stimulate workers to concentrate on production alone. On the other side, the major disadvantage of daywork is its lack of motivation, which is very serious if high production is desired. It is also undesirable from the point of view of cost accounting because unit costs are more difficult to compute than under such plans as piecework.

The adoption of daywork is generally advisable under the following conditions:

a) When standards of output cannot be readily or accurately set
b) When output is mainly made up of odd-lot jobs differing one from another
c) When quality, material and machine costs, and workmanship are more important than quantity
d) When output can be controlled by management or conveyors and is not subject to individual influence
e) When employees insist upon its use

2. *Measured Daywork.* The advantages of daywork may be gained and the disadvantages minimized by the system known as measured daywork. Under this plan, employees are paid under the daywork system, but hourly rates are revised periodically in accordance with measures of their overall qualifications. The following steps are taken under this plan:

a) The base rate for each job is carefully established by means of job evaluation.
b) A table of values is prepared to show the percentage to be added to the base rate on each job because of varying degrees of personal performance in regard to productivity, quality, dependability, and versatility.
c) Each worker is rated periodically (the period varies in practice from three to six months) on his productivity, quality, dependability, and versatility.
d) Each worker is then paid during the next work period at the base rate plus the percentage as determined by his rating and the table of values.

For example, in a given installation, it has been decided to allow up to 30 percent above base rate for superior personal performance in productivity, quality, dependability, and versatility. A table of values is established so that ratings of 70 percent or less earn the base rate, whereas higher ratings earn an addition to the base rate for the coming period. For example, employees who rate 80 percent are allowed an additional 10 percent; those who rate 90 percent are allowed 20 percent; and those who rate 100 percent are allowed 30 percent.

The advantage of this plan is that wages may be easily computed, yet employees are provided with a motive for improving their performance. Moreover, earnings are not dependent upon one factor, such as output, but are affected by quality of output, dependability, and versatility. In addition, this plan provides supervisors with an opportunity to point out to employees specifically which aspects of their jobs can be improved. Management thereby assumes a job which is often shifted to the workers themselves by other plans.

The major disadvantages of this plan are twofold. First, it is not easy for employees to understand why various factors have been assigned particular weights, or why the base rate and the maximum amount that may be added to the base rate are, let us say, 30 percent, as in the case just cited. Unless employees have confidence in the fairness of a company, these matters may be questioned. Second, the incentive value of the plan is not particularly strong from day to day because rate changes are made at relatively infrequent periods. Hence, on any given day the employee may let down and feel no remorse because the effect on the rate for the next period is somewhat remote.

The conditions under which this plan would be most plausible include the following:

a) When overall performance is important in measuring employee worth
b) When specific output standards cannot be accurately set, yet some incentive for better production is desirable
c) When gradual and stable improvement in workers is desired rather than variable day-to-day performance
d) When supervisors are to be impressed with the need for more careful observation of employees and the need for better guidance, training, and improvement

3. *Piecework.* The most widely used incentive plan is piecework. As its name denotes, wages are determined by the number of pieces or units of work that are completed. Each piece is given a prescribed value, which is known as the piece rate. Rates are commonly set by time study, although in the past and in some companies in the present, rates have

been set by using past experience on similar jobs, or even mere guess-work. The formula for wage computations under this plan is as follows:

$$N \times U = W$$

Thus, if on a particular day an employee produced 1,080 units on a given job, the rate for which was $0.01 a unit, his earnings would be:

$$1,080 \times \$0.01 = \$10.80$$

His earnings consequently vary with output. When employees are working on small lots, making more than their hourly rate on some and less on others, it is the usual practice to add the piecework earnings together for a particular period, sometimes for a day but in no case for more than a week, to determine whether total piecework earnings exceed daywork. If they do not, it is customary to pay the day rate. Under this practice, piecework is called guaranteed piecework. In most cases, too, output is inspected to determine how many parts have been spoiled, because these are not included in calculating the operator's earnings.

Incentive value, simplicity in calculation, and understandability are the most commanding advantages of this plan. While there may be misunderstandings about the content of a piecework system, the form of it never gives trouble. Piecework is also favorable from a cost account-ing point of view because the labor cost of each unit of output is the same, irrespective of output.

The major disadvantage of the plan derives from its misuse. Over the years, many employers, either selfishly or to correct mistakes in setting rates, have cut rates time and time again. To the employee who is at the receiving end of such cuts, it looks like a scheme to get more production at his expense. After this happened to him or his fellow workers, a resistance movement would develop along the following lines: (*a*) workers would loaf while being time-studied, and (*b*) they would not earn over an amount which would encourage the manage-ment to cut rates.

Another disadvantage of piecework is that the standard for a job is expressed in monetary terms which makes it subject to changes in the value of money. Thus the standard must be changed as the dollar changes in value. During a period of increasing prosperity, for example, piece rates have to be revised upward (and downward during depres-sions), although the time taken to do the job still remains the same. Finally, the piecework plan, with its uniform progression of earnings as output varies, does not provide sufficient incentive at higher outputs when the effort required is greater.

4. *Timesaving Plans.* One of the oldest incentive plans is the timesaving plan. Under it, an employee is paid for the time he actually puts it on a task plus a bonus based upon a percentage of the time saved under the time set for the tasks on which he works. Under this plan the following formula is used:

$$(H \times HR) + [(S - H)R]P = W$$

Thus, if a worker whose rates was $2.50 an hour took eight hours on a job on which the standard allowance was $12\frac{1}{2}$ hours, and the percentage was $66\frac{2}{3}$, his earnings would be:

$$(8 \times \$2.50) + [(12\frac{1}{2} - 8)\$2.50]66\frac{2}{3}\% = \$27.50$$

When the plan was first developed, time standards were loosely set. Hence the percentage of time saved which went to the employees was rather low, usually $33\frac{1}{3}$ percent. As standards have been set with greater accuracy, the percentage allotted to the workers has steadily gone up, so that in some installations of this plan, employees are receiving as much as 100 percent of time saved. The increase in the percentage does not necessarily mean that workers earn more than before. The effect of the increased percentage may be offset by the decreased time allowed in the time standard. For example, in the following, the earnings are the same, although the time standards and percentage allowed vary:

$$(8 \times \$2.50) + [(12\frac{1}{2} - 8)\$2.50]66\frac{2}{3}\% = \$27.50$$
$$(8 \times \$2.50) + [(12 \quad - 8)\$2.50]75\% \quad = \$27.50$$
$$(8 \times \$2.50) + [(11 \quad - 8)\$2.50]100\% \quad = \$27.50$$

Timesaving plans have two major advantages. First, since the standard upon which earnings are based is expressed in time units, it is not subject to the random fluctuations of the dollar. If adjustments must be made in earnings, the hourly rate can be changed, leaving the time standard unaffected. Thus the employees are not inclined to lose faith in job standards. Second, since the bonus is based upon time saved, the attitude of employees is conditioned by the positive factor of gaining through saving. This has a better psychological effect than that produced by the pressure of piece rates, for example.

5. *Efficiency Bonus Plans.* Another type of incentive is the efficiency bonus plan. Under it, the relative efficiency of each employee is computed weekly and a bonus paid of varying degree, depending upon the efficiency attained. This plan calls, first of all, for establishing a table of values for increasing degrees of efficiency. Selected values taken

from one plant in which bonuses start at 66 percent efficiency are shown in Table 19–1.

For each job a standard time allowance is established, by time study or by reference to records of similar jobs completed in the past. At the end of each week, each worker's efficiency is derived by dividing the

TABLE 19–1

Efficiency	Percent Added to Basic Earnings
66	1%
70	4
75	5
80	8
85	11
90	15
95	20
100	25

time allowed on various jobs by the time taken. To his base wage is then added a percentage for his relative efficiency. For example, a worker who took 40 hours to complete jobs on which the allowance was 36 hours would be paid $115, computed as follows:

$$(H \times R) + (H \times R) \text{ selected } \% = W$$
$$(40 \times \$2.50) + (40 \times \$2.50) \ 15\% = \$115$$

The major advantage of this plan lies in its emphasis upon efficiency. Comparisons can readily be made from week to week or between employees; thus, personal efficiency tends to rise because of the competitive factor. The plan has two disadvantages: (*a*) The plan is expressed in terms which are not readily understandable, and (*b*) employees tend to complain about the standards they must surpass in order to earn a bonus.

The plan has the most favorable conditions of use when it is desired to educate workers in the need of efficiency and to bestir them to compete in raising their relative efficiency.

6. *Group Plans.* The foregoing plans have been discussed on the assumption that each individual is remunerated in terms of his own efforts. In addition to such individual or "straight" calculations, plans may be placed upon a group basis. Earnings of individuals are thus computed by prorating the bonus or premium produced by the group. For example, Table 19–2 shows how the individuals in a group would share (prorated on the basis of hours worked and rate per hour) a bonus of $32.50 they had earned as a unit.

In summary, there are numerous plans from which it is possible to select one or more that will fit one's requirements. Significant, in any event, is the importance of calculating basic standards fairly and equitably. But perhaps most important of all is the need for determining how much remuneration should be provided to attain varying degrees of employee efficiency. To this aspect of wage plans, there is no simple answer except the advice that intense study is indispensable.

TABLE 19–2

Employee	Hours Worked	Rate per Hour	Basic Wage	Prorata Share	Bonus	Total Wage
A..............	40	$1.80	$72.00	$ 72.00/ 266.64	$8.78	$80.78
B..............	36	2.00	72.00	72.00/ 266.64	8.78	80.78
C..............	38	1.88	71.44	71.44/ 266.64	8.69	80.13
D..............	32	1.60	51.20	51.20/ 266.64	6.25	57.45
			$266.64	266.64		

Whether or not incentive plans should be used is not examined here for the simple reason that unless unions or conditions prevent, incentive plans are ordinarily superior to nonincentive plans, not only for the employee but also the employer. It is scarcely conceivable, for example, how the record of production displayed in Figure 19–1 could have been attained, had not the company in question used an incentive plan. Of course, such a plan is not easy to install in intermittent and nonstandardized types of work; but even here, successful plans may be found. Maintenance jobs, for example, once thought of as daywork jobs, are increasingly being paid on some plan of incentive. The key in all of these instances is careful determination of standards of production and careful establishment of a unit of output.

7. *Profit- and Revenue-Sharing Plans.* A final group of plans related to compensation is characterized by some form of sharing in profits or revenues. These include (*a*) sharing directly in profits, (*b*) sharing through stock ownership, and (*c*) sharing through royalty provisions.

a) Profit-Sharing Plans. Sharing of profits with employees has been used with varying success as a means of compensation. A number of companies have tried it and discarded it because the employees or employers were dissatisfied with the results.[1] Yet, other companies have

---

[1] P. A. Knowlton, *Studies in Profit Sharing* (Long Island City: Profit Sharing Research Foundation, 1953). This contains an excellent analysis of discontinued (as well as successful) plans.

been more convinced that profit sharing is useful in building productivity and better employee relations. This much can be said, however: A company must have a fairly stable history of profits, or the plan is

FIGURE 19–1. Total Annual Compensation per Employee, Lincoln Electric Company and Six Selected Major Corporations,* 1934–50, and Sales Value per Employee, Lincoln Electric Company and Electrical Manufacturing Industry, 1934–49

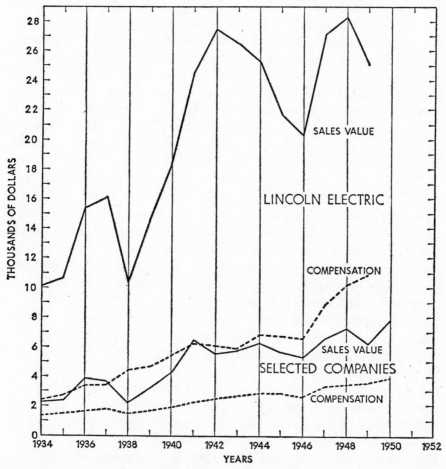

* General Electric Company; Westinghouse Electric Co.; Sylvania Electric Products, Inc.; Allis-Chalmers Mfg. Co.; General Motors Corp.; and U.S. Steel Corp.

Source: Adapted from James F. Lincoln, *Incentive Management* (Cleveland: Lincoln Electric Co., 1951), pp. 258–63.

bound to fail. Employees cannot be stimulated to greater effort or expected to increase their loyalty to a company when there are no profits to divide.

Moreover, plans that rely upon profit sharing to stimulate individual efficiency are proceeding against two fundamentals of wage incentive plans. First, remuneration is spaced too far from the effort of employees.

A plan in which profits are shared in February will scarcely possess much stimulating power in July, let us say. Second, the connection between reward and effort is scarcely discernible. An employee may work very conscientiously and get no share in profits because there are none in some years. Or he may see a fellow worker loaf and get just as much as he does in prosperous years. Hence, profit sharing is not always a stimulant to production.

On the other hand, as a means of developing team spirit and for educating employees in the risks and interdependencies of business, profit sharing has much to be said for it. Some companies have noted such favorable trends as the following after experience with profit sharing: a sharp decline in labor turnover, a greater loyalty to the company, a better spirit of cooperation with fewer petty grievances, and a generally improved tone of relationships and understanding between employee and employer. And it is difficult for an employee to complain about excessive profits when he shares in them, too.

Finally, profit-sharing plans will not succeed as a substitute for other personnel practices. The companies that have had the most success with their profit-sharing plans are those that stress their other personnel plans. Thus, they note their high wages, savings plans, good supervision, recreational and educational facilities, and grievance-handling machinery as parallels of a successful profit-sharing plan. Satisfied with good wages, employees are then stimulated to higher efforts by the prospects of sharing also in profits.

b) Employee Ownership of Stock. From time to time, interest in employee ownership of stock waxes strong as a means of improving employee and employer relations. The usual practice is to allow employees to purchase stock at prices more or less reduced from current market levels. The purchases must usually be made on a time basis, to encourage the thrift idea and to prevent employees from selling at higher prices. Also, the number of shares an employee may buy is restricted by seniority or earning power clauses. If an employee leaves the company before the stock is paid for, most plans provide that the employee will receive the amount of the payments plus interest, usually computed above current rates.

Stock plans are preferred by some because employees are made partners of the business in name as well as in fact. It is felt that since employees share in losses as well as profits, they become more conscious of the problems that beset their companies. As a consequence, they become more tolerant and loyal.

Unfortunately, the risks of stock ownership sometimes result in large losses to employees. For example, it is obvious what happened when a stock sold to employees at $30 went up to $150 and then tobogganed to $1.50. Employee morale, in this instance, for a time was not worth the proverbial plugged nickel. As a consequence of such experiences, many have concluded that the risks of stock ownership plans exceed the possible advantages. Moreover, employees can gain little feeling of self-assurance or of contribution when they watch stock prices go up and down for no obvious reasons.

c) Royalty Provisions. Labor, in its organized endeavors, is seeking to gain a greater share of industry's earnings by royalty demands. These consist of payments, usually to a union organization of employees, based on a levy for each unit of output. The funds thus collected are to be used for a variety of purposes—for example, to aid the unemployed, to supplement payments to those injured on the job, and to support various other welfare activities.

Among the first of these royalty arrangements was made by the American Federation of Musicians. It arranged for the payment of royalties on radio and television transcriptions and phonograph records according to frequency of broadcast. The funds so collected are to be used for the relief of unemployed musicians. In 1946, John L. Lewis created a furor in the coal-mining industry by demanding a royalty of 10 cents on every ton of coal mined. He then gained a 5-cent royalty, which has since been raised to 40 cents in soft coal and 50 cents in anthracite. The proceeds are used by the union to compensate injured miners and their families. Other unions are also considering the advisability of seeking royalties, and it is almost certain that the demands in this direction are bound to take a sharp upturn.

Management cannot be exceedingly happy over this development as a personnel practice, for it represents a practice over which it has no control and from which it can seemingly derive no benefit. Perhaps the most significant lesson that management can learn from these demands is that it must anticipate the reasons for which royalty demands are likely to be made, and it must be prepared to rebut them. If labor can prove that royalties are needed to serve welfare needs which management could but does not carry, public sympathy will be on the side of labor. And management will have to pay for, but will lose control of, another prerogative.

Remuneration of Salesmen

Remuneration of salesmen may be by straight salary or some form of incentive compensation. Since the salesman's job is usually more variable than the average factory job, the problem of establishing a stable and satisfactory unit of output is much more difficult; some even conclude that it is impossible. Nevertheless, various incentive plans have been devised that have had varying degrees of success. Although details vary, all plans can be grouped under one or more of the following headings:

1. Straight salary
2. A commission based upon units sold
3. A commission based upon factors affecting sales other than units sold

1. Straight Salary Plans. Straight salary plans include those in which salesmen are paid strictly in accordance with the time they spend on their jobs. The week is the common time unit. This plan finds favor with those who contend (*a*) that the salesman in the particular case has little or no control over how much he sells and (*b*) that the number of factors which are important in affecting sales is so large that it is impossible to give due consideration to all of them in any incentive plan. Some also favor straight salary because they have seen commission plans misused to the point that no one retains confidence in them. Where the foregoing conditions prevail, the use of commission plans is obviously questionable.

2. Unit Commission Plans. Straight salary plans, in and of themselves, contain no incentive value. Hence, when the amount of sales depends largely upon the calls that are made and supervision itself cannot spur salesmen to take the necessary initiative, commission plans are desirable. Under these plans, salesmen are paid a set commission for each unit sold, a commission that varies as output increases, or a commission that begins only after a set quota has been sold. The bases for commissions are so numerous that space does not permit full descriptions. However, two opposing theories are worth citing. In some companies the rate of commission decreases as sales increase, and in others the rate increases. In the former case the belief is that salesmen who make too much will lose their zest for work. In the latter case, it is recognized that large volumes are harder to make, yet add greatly to the profit of the company. Hence, it is concluded that increasing commissions are needed to attain the high volumes. Which theory should be followed depends, among other things, upon the nature of the sales problem, the type of salesmen required, and the type of sales executives directing the sales. But in any event, the existence of such opposed theories illustrates the need for care in selecting an appropriate plan.

3. General Commission Plans. Because selling often involves much more than repeated calls to get more business, some incentive plans are based upon other factors as well as volume of sales. For example, bonuses may be computed in terms of such factors as the following:

a) The quantity of various products sold, graded by their profitability to the company
b) New business obtained
c) Service calls made
d) Repeat orders obtained
e) Sales expenses reduced
f) Cash business obtained relative to credit accounts
g) Percentage of bonuses obtained from new or highly competitive areas
h) Complaints received on old customers' list

Such plans call for important decisions regarding the weights the various factors will have and how they are to be measured. This is very difficult; yet, if the factors are of importance and the salesmen's attention should be called to them, the work necessary to the development of standards will have to be done.

4. *Characteristics of a Good Compensation Plan.* Of interest in this connection are the findings of the Dartnell Corporation, which surveyed 1,800 plans. It was concluded that successful compensation plans allowed for the following payments to salesmen:

a) Security money, in the form of a basic salary or drawing account against commissions
b) Incentive money, over and above base pay, earned by putting forth extra effort
c) Opportunity money, earned through promotion to more profitable territories or branch managerships
d) Loyalty money, which allows in the base salary for length of service or special contributions to the welfare of the business
e) Practice money, to encourage testing of new sales ideas which might otherwise adversely affect regular income sources[2]

Executive Compensation Plans

The compensation of executives, although paid to a relatively small number of employees, nevertheless affects many, many more. For example, all employees are more or less interested in what the boss gets. If the earnings are out of line with their standards, however arrived at, they become disgruntled, and then the undesirable results of industrial unrest become apparent. In addition, if executive salaries are exorbitant,

---

[2] "Trends in Salesmen's Compensation," *Management Review*, Vol. XLII, No. 11, pp. 663–64.

they may cut into the share employees receive. This is usually a negligible amount, however. One company illustrates the relation of executive salaries to employee wages by stating that were all salaries of top executives distributed to employees, the latter would gain the equivalent of a package of cigarettes a week.

And executive compensation is, of course, of interest to the executives themselves, who, like the employees, are desirous of receiving as much as possible for their service. The question is raised, then, and as yet is unanswered, as to how much should be paid to executives in order to obtain their services. It is easy to say that they should be paid what they are worth, but some violent controversies have raged as to whether or not any executive is worth $1 million a year, as some have been paid. One side argues that without the leadership of the executive who received such a salary, the company would not have been so successful as it was, nor could it have employed as many workers at the wages that it did. The other side retorts that the same results could have been attained without such munificent compensation to the executive in question, since a lesser amount and the prestige of the position would have been sufficient compensation. Executive talents are not so scarce, add the opponents, that a few isolated individuals possess a monopoly.

All of this leads to the conclusion that great care must be used to set compensation for executives, since such decisions affect the attitudes of others in addition to the efficiency of the executives. It is desirable to describe executive compensation methods so that the relative merits of available plans may be noted. This is done here under two headings: (1) major executives and (2) minor executives.

1. *Major Executives.* Straight salary, bonuses, stock purchase plans, and profit sharing are used to compensate major executives. Straight salary is undoubtedly the most common method. It is often adopted because the task of managing is made up of many variables and imponderables, the direct measurement of which would be a herculean task. Hence, as is true of any job whose units of work cannot be readily defined or measured, the only alternative is the daywork or time interval principle. With top-level executives, the month or the year is commonly used.

However, many companies hold the opinion that the full measure of executive effort cannot be obtained unless some stimulant is applied. In such cases, indirect measures of accomplishment are used to determine how much effort executives have exerted beyond that which is normal for the job and which is compensated for on a salary basis. The most common measures are profits, sales, and expenses. Using these as a base, bonuses are paid in addition to the salary. Thus, one company pays its top executive a percentage of the profits the company earns. Another establishes a quota of profits which must be earned before executives share in profits. And a third establishes a sliding scale of percentages related to sales (a fourth ties this to expenditures) by which the base salary will be increased.

Another plan of compensating executives is that in which stock is offered to them at a nominal figure or at a figure that leaves ample room for speculative profit. The executives are thus given a stake in the business, which can redound to their benefit if their efforts are skillfully applied to its operation. Usually, these plans make handsome rewards possible. For example, an executive who took charge of an ailing business was given the option to buy 100,000 shares at $12 a share. Within a year the stock rose in value to $16, yielding the executive a paper profit of $400,000. Had the stock not risen in price, however, his efforts would have been rewarded only by a small salary. Hence the probability of small earnings as well as of high profits makes such plans highly stimulating. Indeed, the plan is criticized by some on the ground that executives become so conscious of the market price of the stock and the short-run factors that affect prices that they do not pay attention to the fundamentals that make for long-run stable growth of a business.

The theory in these cases is that profits are correlated to executive efforts and thus are an accurate measure of executive contributions.[3] The theory is weak because profits are sometimes made no matter how unwisely executives act and losses are incurred despite the best possible judgment. Prosperity periods and depressions leave in their wake results for which no individual should take credit or be penalized. This condition should be recognized in any plan in which executive compensation is based upon results; otherwise, executives will from time to time be overpaid or underpaid. That the theory is weak is not offered as a reason for not using incentives for executives. It is mentioned so that a plan is not idly adopted, thus inviting the chance of yielding undesirable consequences to all concerned.

All the foregoing methods of compensating executives result in taxable income. Since tax rates take a large part of such increases, there is a trend for companies to pay for a variety of expenses incurred by executives. The range of such payments, or "fringe benefits," to executives includes the following:

---

[3] The favorable incidence of the capital gains tax as opposed to the higher personal income tax is also important.

a) Medical care

b) Counsel and accountants to assist in legal, tax, and financial problems

c) Facilities for entertaining customers and for dining

d) Company recreational areas—golf course, swimming pool, and gymnasium

e) Membership fees in clubs and business associations

f) Costs of education and development of executives, scholarships for children of employees, and business magazines and books[4]

Such benefits are tax-free to the recipient. Were he to pay for them himself out of salary, his income would have to be increased a minimum of 30 percent for lower income executives and much higher for executives in the upper tax brackets. Obviously, this is a form of executive compensation that merits favorable consideration.

2. *Minor Executives.* Most minor executives are paid on a salary basis, although incentive plans of one form or another are used in a minority of cases. The proponents of the salary plan expound the usual claims for it and make the usual charges against incentive plans, which need not be repeated here. The discussion will be limited to a description of typical plans for incentive compensation of minor executives.

Perhaps the oldest form of compensating supervisors and foremen on a basis other that straight salary is that of paying them a bonus, depending upon the incentive earnings of their subordinates. For example, in one time saving plan the supervisor shares in part of the time saved by his subordinates. Thus the latter receive $66\frac{2}{3}$ percent of the time saved, and the supervisor (who presumably helped them indirectly to be more productive) receives the remaining $33\frac{1}{3}$ percent. Such practices are commendable because they stress the fundamental responsibility of the supervisor to lead a more effective group of employees.

Another type of incentive plan is based directly upon departmental productivity or cost reductions. Under such plans, it is necessary to take the following steps:

a) Define in quantitative terms the factors to be included in the plan

b) Establish standards by which to measure varying degrees of success

c) Establish a sliding scale of bonus percentages for increasing degrees of accomplishing the factors specified in the plan

For example, in simple outline, the plan of one company is based upon attainment of production schedules. This plan requires careful review of production standards, machine methods, and sales requirements, so that extraneous factors will not affect the supervisors unfairly or too leniently. Then the schedule for each job during a particular

---

[4] *Business Week,* June 20, 1953, pp. 183–84.

period is set. Actual completion dates are then compared with scheduled dates, to arrive at a percentage of success. Supervisors receive a bonus, depending upon their effectiveness in meeting schedules. This company stresses meeting of schedules because delivery to customers is a prime factor in its success.

In another plan, reduction in expenditures is the key to supervisory bonuses. A flexible budget is established for each department, depending upon its expected rates of output. If actual expenses of a department are less than budgeted figures, the supervision receives a bonus varying with the percentage of the saving. In the so-called "Scanlon plan," such cost savings are also shared by operative employees. Some unions have strongly supported the Scanlon plan as a fair method of compensation.

Other plans of supervisory bonus payments are more complicated. For example, one company weighs the following factors:

a) Attainment of budgets
b) Scrap reductions
c) Direct laborsaving
d) Efficiency in output
e) Savings in materials used
f) Savings in maintenance costs

Under this plan, standards are established for each of the foregoing factors, their relative importance is determined, and a scale of values for overall achievement is established. The value of all this work, it must be noted, goes beyond the effect upon supervisory efficiency; it has the added value which careful planning brings forth. Although such plans may require a great deal of preliminary thought, the calculations a supervisor must make to compute his earnings can be simplified by preparing statistical tables from which foremen can, at a glance, determine the bonus they have earned.

Records

A significant problem in all wage plans is the effect they have upon record keeping. It has been noted from time to time that some plans aid the work of cost accounting, for example, whereas others are not so simple to handle. The same holds true for payroll computations. Hence, plans should be weighed in terms of the effect they are likely to have upon the work of payroll computations. Of course, the whole problem of payroll calculation has been complicated by the extra records required by the Social Security Act, the Wages and Hours Law, and various deductions, such as "pay-as-you-go" federal income taxes and bond purchase plans. As a consequence, it is desirable to design forms that will make this work as speedy and economical as possible. Illustrative of practices that employ mechanical devices is the growing use of tabulating-card equipment.

QUESTIONS

1. Differentiate between a wage plan, a wage incentive plan, and a job evaluation plan.
2. Evaluate the various wage plans by checking each against the desirable characteristics a good plan should have. What plan or plans are the best by this test?
3. If the advantages of the piecework plan are so strong, why is it so often viewed in such a poor light?
4. If a high percentage were allowed in the bonus in the portion of time saved, would it necessarily mean that the employee would therefore earn more because of this? Explain.
5. When employees share in a group piecework system, what factors enter into the calculation which determines how much each will receive from the total group earnings?
6. What is the royalty plan of payment, and how does the employee receive this payment?
7. What is the essential factor that serves to explain why incentive plans are more difficult to establish in the case of such employees as salesmen and maintenance workers than in the case of production workers?
8. For what factors other than sales output may a salesmen be compensated?
9. If profit-sharing plans and stock purchase plans find favorable usage among executives, why are they not equally good for operative employees?
10. How would you determine what a fair salary is for the president of a company? Indicate the factors to which you would give consideration in making this determination.

CHAPTER 20

FRINGE BENEFITS

Scope of Discussion

In addition to the compensation an employee receives directly, a number of benefits accrue to his advantage. A few examples are insurance programs, pension rights, vacations and sick leave with pay, and separation allowances. In a sense, they are delayed forms of compensation, paid in the event of prescribed occurrences or contingencies.

At one time, such benefit allowances were a very small percentage of take-home pay. Hence someone ascribed to them the apt term "fringe benefits." With the passage of time the percentage has increased substantially, so that the term, although generally used, is not correctly descriptive of the amount or importance of the benefits.

Attention is directed here to this important aspect of compensation under the following headings:

1. Overall coverage and amounts
2. Insurance plans
3. Pension plans
4. Unemployment compensation plans

Fringe Benefits

In recent years, there has been a trend on the part of unions to make demands which increase the return to employees in ways other than direct wages. Examples are vacations with pay, sick leave with pay, establishment of funds to assist employees injured in accidents, and provision of medical services. These wage supplements provide employees with services or returns they otherwise would have to finance themselves. Since they are in a sense an indirect payment, they are popularly called "fringe" benefits.

The cost of fringes is by no means insignificant. In a survey conducted by the Chamber of Commerce of the United States, the cost averaged 25.6 percent of the direct labor payroll. This amounts to 68.8 cents per payroll hour, or $1,431 per employee per year, as seen in Table 20–1. Fourteen years earlier, the annual bill for fringes, according to a Chamber survey, was $819.

TABLE 20–1

NONWAGE PAYMENTS AS PERCENT OF PAYROLL
OF 1,150 COMPANIES, 1963

Items

Employer's share of compulsory old-age insurance, unemployment compensation, and workmen's compensation.................	5.6%
Employer's share of agreed-upon payments for pensions, insurance programs, separation pay allowances, and miscellaneous payments to employees..	7.8
Pay for rest periods, lunch periods, washup time, etc..............	2.7
Payments for vacations, holidays, voting time, National Guard duty, time off for personal reasons, etc...........................	7.8
Bonus, profit sharing, special awards, etc..........................	1.7
Total...	25.6%
Nonwage payments as:	
Percent of payroll..	25.6
Cents per hour worked..	68.8
Dollars per year per employee.................................	$1,431

SOURCE: Chamber of Commerce of the United States, *Fringe Benefits, 1963* (Washington, D.C., 1964), p. 9.

So employers should be prepared to expect increasing demands for fringe payments. One of the jobs of the personnel department should be to anticipate the direction of fringe demands, and it should be prepared to submit recommendations concerning their justification. Management can then react intelligently to requests of labor.

The best preparation is to make studies of various possible demands, so that if they are presented, a reasonable reaction can be established immediately. For example, the demand that employees be paid for sick leave or that their sick-leave allowances be increased cannot be deflected by words alone. Such countercharges that the cost of the program would be excessive or that malingering would be increased excessively must be supported by facts. Displaying a chart such as that illustrated in Figure 20–1 will carry weight in support of a claim that an increase in sick-leave allowance will tend to increase malingering. Information gathered in advance, analyzed for principles and aptly illustrated, is the substantial basis upon which management can fight fringe demands, anticipate them, or agree gracefully that they are warranted, when once presented.

It may be argued, too, that management should attempt to have some fringe plans or parts thereof paid for by the employees themselves. This makes sense, on the one hand, because some employees would be better off if they underwrote the plans which best fitted their individual needs. For example, employees do not benefit from a pension plan if they leave a company, yet not to leave restricts their mobility. Or some employees with good health records may feel that they indirectly support but gain little from health insurance programs. It would be better in such cases if the company were to support a basic minimum

FIGURE 20–1. An Analysis of Sick Claims

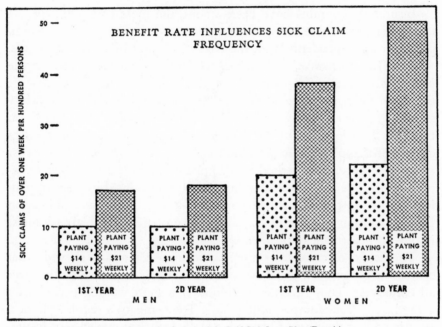

SOURCE: General Motors Corp., *An Analysis of the Paid Sick-Leave Plan* (Detroit).

program, while the employees added at their own expense such additions or plans as they thought best for themselves.

On the other hand, and of greater import, is the fact that as costs of current fringe plans rise, and as more plans are added, some companies will find the burden competitively difficult to bear alone. Hence, it is advisable to work toward a division of responsibility. Some plans would be underwritten by the company and others by the employees. The former would include plans generally assumed by business and the latter those which employees wanted in addition to the basic group. The company could well help in finding ways and means by which the latter plans could be obtained at reduced cost to the employees.

This approach makes sense also because only through shared responsibility and participation can fringe plans serve the needs as well as benefit the employees. As long as employees are given various benefits, there is little reason to expect anything in return. Yet, business must earn the wherewithal through increased productivity to cover the expenditures it incurs on behalf of its employees. One of the most convincing arguments to employees that productivity supports expenditures is to gain their participation in sharing some of the expenditures.

Insurance Programs

Insurance programs have been among the most common types of fringe benefits. These serve to provide financial protection to an employee or his dependents from the risks of death, illness, and accidents.

1. *Life Insurance.* Life insurance has long been included in the programs of many companies. This is explainable in part by the fact that such financial protection seemed to be an obligation a company should accept for the long service of loyal employees. It was an obligation that had been initiated by companies which paid the funeral expenses of deceased employees. As insurance companies began to offer low-cost group insurance, this method has supplanted the uncertain funeral expense plan. The cost of the insurance has been assumed by the companies. And the forthright acceptance of a contractual insurance obligation provides employees with positive assurance of their company's interest in one of their financial problems.

The range of company-supported insurance plans is so wide that only a few general comments are in order here. Such plans usually cover all employees. They become eligible after a short waiting period after being hired—for example, ninety days. The company's regular physical examination at the time of hiring is usually sufficient evidence of insurability.

The amount of insurance for each employee is related to salary and age. Salary-wise, amounts increase with the level of earnings. Lower levels are insured at minimum amounts, with insurance increasing as the base salary increases. Thus, minimum amounts may be $1,000 or $2,000, whereas the upper limits may be established at the five-figure range. As age increases, most plans provide for a lowering in the insurance. This is based on the assumption that an employee who survives into advancing years does not have the same family obligations he would have had earlier. He has had time also to make some savings for such obligations as he does have.

Most insurance plans are supported entirely by the company. Some have provisions whereby employees may increase their insurance by contributing to the insurance premiums. This opportunity is often offered to executives. And many plans give an employee the right to convert the group plan to an individual policy without further physical examination if his services with the company are terminated; but in such a case the ex-employee pays the premium. Some plans include an employee in the group insurance program after he retires or suffers a permanent disability before retiring.

2. *Health and Accident Insurance Programs.* Growing in popularity are insurance programs covering financial losses due to illness and accidents. Of course, the employee is protected from losses incurred in connection with company business and operations. These are covered by state industrial compensation laws and are commented upon in Chapter 23. But non-company-incurred losses to an employee, or those to his dependents, have long been considered to be matters of his own concern. There is, however, a trend toward company aid and assistance in such areas.

First steps toward company assistance came in the form of making it easier and cheaper to procure protective insurance, but at the expense of the employees themselves. Blue Cross is an example. Employees in such instances pay the premiums but at lower rates because groups of employees participate in the program. The company provides the group for which group rates can be gained. As time has gone on, some companies have undertaken to share the costs of such insurance, and some now shoulder all the costs themselves. Sharing or full responsibility has in some cases been assumed voluntarily as a gesture of good human relations and in some cases been accepted because of the pressures of collective bargaining.

The risks and benefits included in these programs are varied, but a few comments will serve to provide a general picture. If an employee cannot work because of an accident or illness—noncompany-incurred —he is subject to two losses. First, there are medical and hospital bills to be met. The appropriate insurance can indemnify him for these expenses. Hospital costs for a room, medication, nursing services, technical equipment, and operating facilities will be covered up to specified limits. And payment of the doctor's fee is also insurable within given amounts and for given services.

Second, there are losses of wages while not working. These, too, may be covered by insurance. The amount received, the duration over which benefits will be paid, and the stated waiting periods vary, depending on the contract which is written.

The dependents of an employee may also be included in some of these insurance coverages. Thus, certain hospital, surgical, and medical expenses of one's family may be covered. And the insurance would apply to expenses due to illness, accidents, or obstetrical and maternity care.

Pension Plans

Pensions have come to be an important type of fringe benefit. The private plans are of course normally a fringe benefit. But even pension plans under the Social Security Act are underwritten in part by the employer and, to that extent, are a fringe benefit to the employee.

1. *Private Pension Plans.* Private pension plans were once relatively few in number. They were underwritten voluntarily by some companies which took a farsighted view of the need for protecting the employee when he retired. Or some, in a paternalistic attitude, felt that pensions were good for their employees.

But the gates for private pensions were opened wide in October, 1948, by the United States Supreme Court in the Inland Steel decision. Here, it was ruled that pensions were not bargainable only if the union contract expressly excluded pensions from bargainable subjects. As a consequence, union after union—which had previously thought that it was precluded from bargaining about pensions—demanded and won pension benefits for its members.

Since private pension arrangements have increased in importance, it is desirable to survey the following points covering the operation of such plans:

a) Who is eligible for pensions?
b) What is the amount of benefits?
c) How are pensions financed?
d) Who contributes to the financing?
e) What if death occurs before retirement?
f) How is the plan administered?

a) *Eligibility.* Since pensions are paid to retired employees, the significant question to working employees is: Am I eligible to receive a pension? This depends upon eligibility rules, which usually cover waiting period, length of service, age, work factors, and nature and amount of compensation.

First, most pension plans establish a waiting period before employees become eligible. This may be anywhere from one to five years. The longer period tends to penalize floaters and perhaps reduce turnover. The shorter period tends to give the newer employee a feeling that he is a part of the total program of his company.

Second, the length of service affects eligibility. This is particularly important as far as the amount of the pension received is concerned, provided that other tests of eligibility are met. Thus a minimum number of years of service must be completed at a before-retirement age if full benefits are to accrue. Lesser service results in smaller payments.

Third, the question of lower and upper age limits must also be answered. Some companies limit eligibility to those over 25 or 30 years of age, because the clerical cost of administering the plan for such employees offsets any possible advantages the plan might have for the company or the employee. The upper limit, on the other hand, raises important problems. To include older employees raises the cost of the plan, but to exclude them either may arouse employee antagonism or may fail to qualify the plan under the requirements of the Internal Revenue Service.

Fourth, the working situation may also determine eligibility. Employees in certain types of work or locations may be excluded. Or only salaried, clerical, and executive ranks may be included. Or again, nonunion employees may be excluded from a plan negotiated by a union. In any event, exclusions should be logically justifiable; or again, employee enmity may be incurred, or the approval of the Internal Revenue Service may not be forthcoming.

Fifth, the nature and amount of compensation may be determining factors in eligibility. Salesmen on commission, part-time employees or those earning less than some set figure—$3,000 a year—and all hourly rated employees may be excluded. The general trend is, however, away from such compensation exclusions. Certainly, collective bargaining has improved the position of hourly rated employees, who were once rather generally excluded.

b) Amount of Benefits. Another matter of major concern is the level and amount of benefits. To the employee, this is significant because it determines what he will receive—and perhaps contribute, if the plan is contributory. And to the employer, it is significant because it determines in part how costly the plan will be.

Private pension plans have in recent years frequently been tied in with social security payments. In that event, an employee may be entitled to a pension, let us say, of $300 a month. The company makes up the difference between $300 and the amount the pensioner receives from social security payments.

c) Financing. Before discussing who contributes to paying for a pension plan, it is desirable to note the various ways in which provision is made for assuring payments. The simplest plan of providing funds is the current expenditure method, in which payments are made out of general cash at the time employees retire. How much must be paid out can be quickly ascertained by listing the pensioners and the amounts due to each. The plan has disadvantages: Cash or assets may not be available when needed, tax advantages may be lost, and the actuarial basis of pensions may not be followed. So, with few exceptions, a plan of advance provision or underwriting of funds is adopted. These are the so-called "funded methods" and include insured or trusteed plans.

Insured plans are those in which future pension liabilities are assumed by a commercial insurance firm upon payment of premiums to it by the company. Such plans have the usual advantages of having a specialist assume the liability. Under trusteed plans the employer acts, in a sense, as his own insurance company or pays over each year's fund accumulations to a trustee. Such plans are preferred by the larger employers, who feel that they are equipped to do the work the insurance companies do in such matters, thereby saving some of the overhead cost which is loaded into the premium charged by an insurance company.

d) Contributions to Cost of Pensions. Funds may be accumulated by joint payments of employees and employers (the contributory plan) or by payments by the company alone (the noncontributory plan). Which plan should be used has been subject to debate, and it is improbable that universal agreement will ever be reached.

Proponents of the noncontributory plan argue that this is a cost business should assume. Where unions are concerned, they insist on this point and are gaining it increasingly in collective bargaining. Proponents of contributory plans claim that in sharing costs, employees become more interested in the plan and, indirectly, in other affairs and problems of the company.

e) Benefit Payments to Survivors. When death occurs before retirement, benefit payments must take another form. Either a lump sum or an annuity may be paid to survivors or the employee's estate. This must be provided for, or again the plan will not be qualified by the Internal Revenue Service, which requires that a pension plan be for the benefit of employees or their beneficiaries. The employee has the right to select his beneficiaries, and his wishes must be respected. If the employee has selected no beneficiaries, the plan may provide for an order of priority as follows: the employee's wife, his children, his parents, his brothers and sisters, and his estate. The company cannot be a beneficiary in this listing and still qualify the plan, under Internal Revenue Service regulations.

The amount of payment will vary with the particular nature of the plan. This should take into consideration the age of the deceased, length of service, earnings, the employee's contributions, company contributions, interest factors, and rulings of the Internal Revenue Service.

f) Administration. The administration of a pension plan involves a number of phases. First, consideration must be given to legal requirements. Tax laws and directives must be observed; otherwise, important income tax privileges will be lost. The Taft-Hartley Act requires joint representation of employer and employee with respect to plans in which the union or its appointees are directly involved in fund administration (insured or trusteed plans may sometimes be exempt). And plans must conform to the registration requirements of the Securities and Exchange Act, the insurance and trust provisions of state laws, the wage provisions of the Wages and Hours Act, and various estate and inheritance tax laws.

Second, provision must be made for adequate representation by various interested parties. Company executives, union executives, private insurance company executives, and various state and federal agencies may all have a direct or indirect role to play. And the services of such technical specialists as lawyers, accountants, actuaries, tax experts, labor relations experts, corporate and financial experts, investment counselors, and statisticians may also be required.

Third, adequate records must be kept in detail. These will include information on the following:

1. Accession of new employees
2. Voluntary severance of old employees
3. Disability severance of old employees
4. Employees going on retirement rolls
5. Earnings of employees
6. Changes in positions or wage rates of employees
7. Various details of fund investments, changes, and earnings
8. Premium payments
9. Pension and supplementary benefit payments
10. Tax computations
11. Costs of operating the plan

And finally, a pension plan should be designed with the assistance of qualified advice on a number of salient points. It should be adequate to meet retirement needs, and it should be fair to employee and employer. It should be actuarially and legally sound. It should be built with due consideration to a firm's place in the industry and the market, and to its future possibilities. Perhaps above all, it should be an integral part of a company's total objectives and programs, not just an adjunct tacked on because of outside pressures or what seems good for employees.

2. *Federal Old-Age Assistance.* Approved by the President on
August 14, 1935, and with several subsequent amendments, the Social
Security Act provides, among other benefits, for old-age and survivor
benefits.

This aid is financed by means of taxes shared equally by the employee and the employer, or paid entirely by the self-employed. The tax
is variable and is collected on earnings up to $4,800 a year. The taxes
serve to pay the benefits and the cost of administering the program. The
employer collects the taxes and pays over the sum to the Internal
Revenue Service. This payment is credited to the account of each employee, to whom has been assigned a social security number.

Retirement benefits are payable to the wage earner and his (her)
family upon retirement at the legal age. Survivor benefits are payable to
the insured's family, no matter what the age is at death. Disability
benefits accrue to the worker if the insured becomes totally disabled
between the ages of 50 and 65.

The exact amount of benefits cannot be calculated until a claim is
filed, being dependent largely on average earnings, period of contributions, and the particular type of claim. By way of illustration, however,
Table 20–2 shows payments (rounded to the next lower whole dollar
figure) to various classes of beneficiaries.

TABLE 20–2

BENEFICIARY	AVERAGE MONTHLY EARNINGS AFTER 1950			
	$150	$250	$350	$400
For retirement at 65	$ 73	$ 95	$116	$127
For disability at 50	73	95	116	127
For retired woman worker starting at age 62	58	76	92	101
For one surviving child	54	71	87	95
For retired couple, wife starting at age 62	100	130	159	174
For widow under 62 and one child *or* two dependent parents	109	142	174	190
For widow under 62 and two children	120	190	232	254
Maximum family benefit	120	202	254	254
Single lump-sum death payment	219	255	255	255

If a person becomes entitled to benefit payments based on the social
security account of more than one person, the amount received will be
no more than the larger of the benefits. For example, a woman who is
eligible for retirement benefits on her own account as well as those of
her husband would receive no more than the larger of the two accounts.
Or her children would receive the benefits of one, but not both, of the
parents.

In the event an insured person becomes totally disabled for work between the ages of 50 and 65, he (she) becomes eligible to receive insurance benefits. The amount will be the same as the old-age benefit would be if the insured were already 65. The amounts can range from $33 to $127 monthly. Dependents, however, do not get any payments while the insured is receiving insurance benefits. But benefits become payable when the insured becomes entitled to old-age insurance, or if he should die.

Unemployment Compensation Plans

Another, and very significant, area of fringe benefits is that relating to compensation when an employee is laid off either temporarily or permanently. Concern here is with plans arrived at by negotiation to provide unemployment benefits, governmental plans of unemployment benefits, and plans of compensation upon an employee's severance from the company payroll.

1. *Negotiated Plans.* In the early 1950's the unions began to press for a guaranteed annual wage. They achieved partial success in 1955, when agreements were reached in the automobile industry to provide supplemental unemployment benefit (SUB) payments. Subsequently, agreements were similarly reached in other industries. The success is partial in that, with a few exceptions, benefit payments are for 26 rather than 52 weeks, as desired. Moreover, limitations as to employees covered and amounts to be paid have been established.

The supplemental aspect of the plans derives from the fact that they are usually tied in with state unemployment compensation plans. For example, one plan provides for the payment of $25 a week while an employee is receiving state benefits. The payment is increased to almost $50 after state benefits are exhausted. In another company an amount (not to exceed $30) is added to the compensation received from the state, so that a person's weekly benefit would amount to 65 percent of his after-tax, straight-time wage.

The SUB plans also contain specific rules on eligibility for payments. First, some period of seniority is usually required. For example, an employee covered by some of the automobile industry plans must work a year before he can acquire benefit credits. Second, the amounts to which an eligible employee is entitled will vary. The credits to an account are granted in accordance with a formula related to time worked. Thus, in one plan an employee is granted a credit unit for each two full weeks of work. In a full year, he would accumulate twenty-six units and thus be eligible for twenty-six weeks of supplementary benefits. It is also common to give shorter service employees a lower credit than longer service employees. This is done so that the former—who would be the first to be laid off—would not exhaust accumulated funds and thus leave the latter unprotected.

Obviously, fund accumulation is significant, particularly during the earlier years of a SUB plan. The usual method has been to have the employer contribute to the fund by a standard amount for each hour of work—e.g., 5 cents per man-hour. Moreover, the benefit payments are normally scaled down until the fund is built up to a satisfactory amount.

2. *Governmental Plans.* The federal and state governments have also taken steps to stabilize income through a plan of unemployment insurance. The unemployment title of the Social Security Act gives the federal government authority to administer an unemployment insurance plan in cooperation with the states. The Federal Unemployment Tax Act authorizes the collection of a payroll tax for this purpose which amounts to 3 percent of the payroll up to $3,000 per employee. But the federal government does not pay benefits. This can only be done through the states. To collect funds for benefits, the states tax the employers. This might seem like double taxation. But in states with federally approved insurance plans, employers may deduct (credit) to the state up to 90 percent of the tax paid to the federal government. All states have passed appropriate laws to take advantage of this credit.

With these funds the states have provided for varying benefits. The benefits vary according to amount, length of time paid, and individual employee records. The maximum payable for a week of unemployment (excluding allowances for dependents, provided by eleven states) ranges from $26 to $55. The maximum weeks of benefits range from 18 to 39. And the qualification of individuals for benefits depends (*a*) upon how long he worked in covered employment before becoming unemployed and (*b*) upon his registration with the state employment office for suitable work, should it become available.

Obviously, this program does not establish wage stabilization. It does provide a buffer while the unemployed are looking for work. Moreover, it indicates the type of program that government may be asked to expand, as some already are demanding, if periods of unemployment should become severe.

3. *Severance Benefits.* Severance payments refer to the fact that after a certain number of years or after a certain age, or both, an employee acquires a right to a payment, now or in the future, even though he should leave the company before the regular retirement age. This right is referred to as a vested right or a vesting of benefits.

The vested right depends upon the method of contributing. It is generally agreed that an employee's contributions are returnable upon severance. Whether or not interest should be paid, and how much, is a matter of company policy. As to the employer's contributions, practice varies. Some companies provide for full vesting (and immediately) of company contributions. This is done to set at rest any rumors that the company will discharge eligible employees just before the retirement age. Others provide for delayed vesting; leaving employees may receive, at what would have been their retirement age, the pension to which they would have been entitled, or receive a paid-up insurance policy. And in some companies, those who leave of their own accord lose all benefits of company payments. The latter plan is followed by only a very small minority.

The advantages of forfeiture are that it discourages turnover and that when severance does occur, the cost to the employer is reduced. On the other hand, forfeiture may make some employees fearful of and hence less loyal to management and may make the plan disallowed under the provisions of the Internal Revenue Service.

QUESTIONS

1. Assume that the employees in your company, through their elected representatives, place before you a demand for a particular fringe benefit that would amount to 15 cents an hour for each employee. How would you handle this situation?

2. What, if anything, can management do to make employees feel more related to and identified with the company when such fringe demands as paid vacations, pension programs, and health insurance plans are granted? Or must the union always get credit for such benefits?

3. Life insurance programs have been supported by business for a long time. Why have these programs had an appeal, whereas such programs as health and accident insurance have been late in arriving?

4. How do you explain the recent trend toward private pension plans? What lessons does this have for personnel managers?

5. What effect do you feel the extension of pension plans, both private and public, is likely to have upon the hiring of older employees? What can be done about this?

6. As a personnel manager discussing with employees the question of amount of pensions, what would you tell them is a reasonable pension? How would you prove your contention?

7. What phases and factors must be given due consideration in the administration of pension plans?

8. What is the purpose of SUB plans? To what are they supplemental? Who finances them?

9. How is unemployment insurance handled through governmental programs? Who pays for these programs?

10. What is the relation of vesting to severance payments? What trend do you think will take place in this relationship?

CHAPTER 21

RELATED COMPENSATION PROBLEMS

Introduction

Two subjects related to compensation have thus far been ignored but may now be given attention. The first is how time is related to wage and salary administration. The second is concerned with the possibilities of guaranteeing remuneration.

TIME PROBLEMS

Variables

How long should an employee work? This simple question involves numerous problems that are not easy to solve. For example, within the memory of many who are still working, the average workweek has decreased from around 70 hours to 40 hours. Some contend that a decrease to 35, or even 30 hours, is justifiable. And the working day has decreased from one of dawn to dusk to an average of eight hours, with some companies on a six-hour day. Then, too, such practices as the five day week, vacations with pay, rest periods during the working day, and reduced hours for female and child labor are relatively recent innovations that have not necessarily been standardized beyond change.

As already suggested, the question of the work period resolves itself into a series of questions, depending upon the particular time periods under consideration. The day, the week, and the year are major time periods, and each in turn raises problems. Within the week interval, there are matters of working days, shift changes, and paydays to be considered. And during the year, weeks to be worked, vacation periods, and holidays must be determined.

How these matters should be resolved can easily be stated in principle. The length of working periods should be such that the maximum productivity is derived, at the least cost, with due regard to the health and welfare of the employees. Its application is something else again. Management, unions, employees, governmental agencies, and other groups have disputed and continue to dispute these matters vehemently from time to time. And it may be well to point out at the outset that no final solution is likely because the problems are affected, on the one hand, by social and political as well as economic conditions and, on the other, by the conflicting views various groups bring to bear upon their solution.

Daily Time Problems

At the present time, the eight-hour day is rather general throughout the United States. A number of companies exceed this figure, but only a small percentage work fewer hours. Ordinarily, when a day of less than eight hours is worked, it is usually due to the fact that no time out is taken for lunch—the employees eat while working. A few companies have tried a six-hour day. This practice makes it possible for four shifts to be employed, each shift working six hours without a break for lunch. As the productivity of industry increases, there is no reason why the length of the working day may not be decreased to or below six hours, just as in the past it has been decreased from the fourteen-hour day once worked.

1. *Starting and Stopping Time.* Although the length of the working day for particular classes of workers is usually the same in particular communities, considerable variation is found in other aspects of daily hours. For example, starting time in some companies is as early as 6:30 A.M. and in others as late as 9:30 A.M. Stopping times differ in like manner. These variations may be explained as follows:

   a) Some trades, such as service industries, must start earlier to be ready to meet the needs of other industries.
   b) Employee preference; in one company that asked its employees to note their wishes, a starting time of 7:00 A.M. was selected.
   c) Staggered starting times are encouraged to permit transportation and restaurant services to handle loads without burdensome peaks.
   d) Tradition or growth without plan.

Even within the same company, starting and stopping times may differ for shop and office workers and sometimes between divisions of shop workers. This is done to prevent overloading of various facilities and services or as a form of perquisite of office workers. Of course, maintenance workers usually have to arrive early to get the plant ready for operation.

2. Lunch Periods. Lunch periods constitute another problem of daily working hours. Practice here is varied. As in the preceding instance, office workers often have a longer lunch period than shopworkers. In their case, periods up to 1¼ hours are occasionally found, while an hour is the maximum for shop workers.

While employees seem to prefer a shorter lunch period because their overall working day is decreased, there is danger that sufficient time may not be available for getting back to work on time. Employees will then tend to "jump the gun" in starting their lunch period. A short lunch period may also result in the harmful practice of eating too hurriedly.

3. Rest Periods. Whether or not rest periods should be provided constitutes another problem of daily working hours. Almost without exception, this practice has been found to have favorable effects—fatigue, loitering, visiting, accidents, and spoilage are reduced, and productive efficiency is increased. Breaks of eight to twelve minutes in the morning and again in the afternoon are found to be effective. Except where the nature of operations prevents, the only obstacle to the universal adoption of this practice is the reluctance of employers to try it. They do not like to break with traditional practice, or they fear that employees will demand a shorter day instead of the rest periods.

4. The Coffee Break. Closely related in nature to the rest period is the coffee break. Either formally or informally, the practice is growing, particularly among office and technical workers, to allow time to obtain a snack or a drink during working hours. Proponents of the practice contend that the coffee break provides a desirable energy booster as well as a rest period. These advantages are usually worth the time taken provided the interval is not allowed to become overly extended and provided the breaks are not repeated too often.

5. Overall Working Day. And finally, what constitutes the overall working period must be defined for pay purposes. Ordinarily, the stated hours of starting and stopping constitute the limits of the working day. This must be understood by the employees, particularly where time clocks are used and employees must stamp their time cards on the clocks. In such instances the cards will be punched before the starting time and after the stated stopping time by employees who are on time and do not quit early. The times as thus recorded are not used to calculate hours worked but to check an employee's on-time arrival and departure. For example, in the following case the employee would be paid for eight hours of work and not for eight hours and sixteen minutes:

	Stated Time		Time Card Punched	
	Starting	Stopping	In	Out
Morning.............	8:00	12:00	7:52	12:01
Afternoon............	12:45	4:45	12:40	4:47

Portal-to-Portal Issues

Reaching one's assigned station and departing from it sometimes consumes so much time that compensation must be given either because of union demands or because of legal requirements. For example, the coal miners have won such concessions. And federal rules were incorporated in the Portal-to-Portal Act of 1947, the provisions of which were included in the revisions made in 1949 in the Wages and Hours Law.

Federal legislation spells out what is excluded as well as included in compensable time. Thus the law specifically excludes the time an employee spends going to a workplace, starting his "principal activity," and returning from the workplace. Such activities as going to work, reaching one's station, checking in and out, washing, changing clothes, and getting one's pay check are not compensable. However, if any one of the foregoing is not for the convenience of the worker but is really an integral part of the job, it is compensable.

More specifically, activities compensable as part of an employee's principal activity include:

1. Waiting to begin or resume work for reasons beyond an employee's control—such as waiting for materials
2. Getting instructions before going on a shift, or getting materials
3. Remaining on call on the employer's premises, where the employee is not free to leave the plant (except for scheduled sleeping time)
4. Preparing reports required by the job
5. Getting medical attention during working hours
6. Eating meals where the employee must remain at his working post
7. Rest periods under twenty minutes
8. Time spent in handling grievances, under an established plan in effect in the company
9. Attending business conferences or schools in connection with work duties

Weekly Time Problems

1. *Total Hours a Week.* The weekly time interval also raises a number of problems. First, there is the question of the total hours to be worked. During normal times the workweek in most companies is

about forty hours. Of course, during peak periods the workweek is extended. On the other hand, the standard workweek of 25 hours has been negotiated by the electrical workers in the New York City area. This illustrates the desire of some unions to get a shorter workweek so as to spread work in the face of the effects of automation upon employment.

During normal times the overtime pay provisions of the Wages and Hours Law militate against a workweek of over 40 hours. Obviously, a 50 percent increase in labor costs will not be assumed unless offsetting reductions or customer demands warrant. During the war, on the other hand, it was a question of how long the workweek should be extended. The experience of the British seemed to indicate that a week of 56 to 60 hours was satisfactory; but that beyond this, various losses outweighed the gains. However, in this country, a 48-hour workweek seemed to be best. Very likely, it will always be hard to determine what a workweek should be because of the effect of what employees become accustomed to.

2. *Working Days a Week.* The number of days to be worked is also of importance in the weekly picture. The five-day week is rather common throughout the United States. Certainly, the evidence during World War II indicated that employees disliked the six-day week more than they did longer hours. Even the 5½-day week is disliked by those who once have the opportunity to try the five-day week. From the employer's point of view, the effectiveness of employees on the half day is not always worth the cost. When the employer can be persuaded, therefore, that no significant loss of business will be incurred, he will close on Saturday.

There is a movement in the making to bargain for a four-day week. This is intended as another way for labor to share in the increased productivity of industry. As automation comes on, the four-day week— or even the three-day week—may well be one way of sharing in its fruits.

3. *Shift Arrangements.* Of course, when the nature of operations or rush of business demands, the workweek may have to be extended and extra shifts of workers employed. The matter of shifts has debatable alternatives. Beyond mentioning the alternatives, space here does not permit a statement of the advantages and disadvantages of each. The matter of shifts may be handled in the following ways: (*a*) Each group of employees is set permanently in a given shift position; and (*b*) each group rotates shift positions at weekly, monthly, or other periods.

Yearly Time Problems

In the yearly interval the major problems revolve about holidays and vacation periods. There is a discernible trend toward paying shop as well as office workers for several holidays a year. Hence, what holidays will be recognized should be specifically stated. Holidays may be important because many companies pay time and one-half or even double time to those who have to work on these days. To avoid possible arguments about premium days, therefore, these days should be established in advance. Since absenteeism after holidays by those who

FIGURE 21–1. Comparing Vacations Plans

MASS VACATIONS	STAGGERED VACATIONS
ADVANTAGES	
Using the slack season to close the plant for paid vacation period can help avoid the unpleasantness of seasonal layoffs. Especially useful for highly seasonal industries.	Continuous deliveries to regular customers, and all normal services, are possible the year around. Interruption might play into competitors' hands.
Capacity operation is easier for 50 weeks of the year. Efficiency isn't cut by vacation absences.	New orders can be accepted at all times and completed on schedule. A maker of cardboard boxes could take a rush order any time, give it priority (or overtime) and complete it even with 20% of his force on vacation.
Extensive repairs, equipment installation, and inventory taking can be done during the vacation without slowing output or causing lay-offs.	Rapid processing of perishable goods on hand is assured. Continuous manufacturing would prevent spoilage of goods.
It's easier to schedule work. There's no more need to keep making allowance for employees away on vacation. So every department's output is easier to predict.	Employees have a wider choice of vacation time. Those who want to take their time off during the hunting or fishing season—or in the winter —can be accommodated.
All workers are treated the same. This simplifies the foreman's job of scheduling vacations, and the accounting department's job of issuing vacation pay. It also stops complaints that "Bill got his vacation in July, why must I take mine in May?"	Good community relations are preserved. The load on recreational and travel facilities is spread more evenly.
DISADVANTAGES	
The expense of closing the plant down and of reopening it two weeks later may be high.	Production may slow down because of operation with a reduced labor force.
Some maintenance operations and routine services must be kept going even while the plant is closed. Don't forget their cost.	Bottlenecks may be created by the absence of even a few people—particularly in small plants or in departments with small staffs where the effect of absences is felt more strongly.
You might miss some business. And some customers may be inconvenienced.	Poorer supervision and short-range planning may result when an assistant takes over during the key man's vacation.
New employees not eligible for vacations will lose income during the shutdown—unless you can find work for them in the plant.	Work may pile up for specialists, who will then have a heavier-than-ever load when they return.
Some employees may be eligible for longer vacations than the shutdown period.	Resentment and friction may arise among employees if too many want off at the same time. Since it is impossible to satisfy all requests, management is forced to refuse some.
Vacation facilities may be overloaded in the area if too many employees are off at once.	Costs can run high for training temporary replacements and for overtime work made necessary by vacation cuts in the work force.
Employees may not like to have vacation periods fixed for them. It's tougher to tie in with plans of relatives or friends—or with game seasons.	

Source: J. B. Bennet, "Vacations—Mass or Staggered," *Factory Management and Maintenance*, Vol. CVIII, No. 6, p. 128.

worked on and received double time for holidays is excessive, one company reduced this by providing that pay would be calculated at straight rather than double rates for holidays in the event of unexcused absences following them.

Vacation periods are also of growing importance, since more and more companies are granting vacations with pay (because of collective bargaining in many instances) to shop as well as office workers. Two problems must be decided here: (1) the length of vacations and (2) the time of taking vacations. Office workers generally get two and in some instances three weeks, and shop workers get one or two and increasingly three weeks, depending upon seniority. All vacations may be taken at the same time, which has the advantage of avoiding conflicts about vacation selection and the need of replacing key employees. Or they may be staggered, so that business can be conducted as usual right through the year. Which plan should be used may be determined by checking in a particular case the advantages and disadvantages in the list provided in Figure 21–1.

STABILIZATION PROGRAMS

Employees are interested not only in fair wages but also in uninterrupted wage opportunities. Unfortunately, various seasonal and cyclical disturbances disrupt continued earning power. Many believe that nothing much can be done to secure employees against such risks. Yet a number of programs have been devised to provide some degree of protection against such losses of income.

This is not the place to debate the issue of income stabilization. All that can be done here is to note what has been done by industry and government in this respect. The programs fall into two major categories:

1. Job stabilization, which seeks to provide continuous work opportunities and thereby assures employees of steady earnings
2. Wage stabilization, which provides steady wage payments, whether or not employees are actually working

Job Stabilization

To all concerned, stabilization of jobs would be a real boon. The employer seeks job stability because it leads to production efficiency, which means, in turn, that excess capacity, with its high costs, can be reduced to a minimum. And to employees, the assurance of steady employment is of real significance, dependent as they are on a steady source of income. Unfortunately, cyclical and seasonal fluctuations are formidable obstacles to these hopes. The effect of these fluctuations must be reduced or removed, if possible, if stabilization of jobs is to be attained. Attempts to do this may be classified as follows:

1. By individual companies:
   a) By adoption of sales practices that stabilize production
   b) By adoption of production practices that stabilize production
   c) By adoption of personnel practices that stabilize production
2. By intercompany cooperation in regard to:
   a) Sales practices
   b) Production practices
   c) Personnel practices
3. By governmental regulation and assistance:
   a) Unemployment compensation regulations
   b) Assistance of employment services
   c) Assistance of informational service

Individual Plans

The basic question a company must answer when considering job stabilization is: Is the program worth the cost? Although it has been contended that such is the case, nevertheless any proposals offered by the personnel department should carry schedules of (1) losses due to job fluctuations, (2) costs of programs aimed at reducing fluctuations, and (3) the gains to be derived therefrom. To make such estimates, it is first necessary to examine statistically the seasonal and cyclical fluctuations that have and are likely to beset the company. Only after this has been done can the size of the stabilization job be appreciated and the desirability and flexibility of alternative plans for solving it be considered.

1. *Sales Practices.* Most stabilization programs start with the sales area, since anything which will stabilize sales will obviously stabilize production, and hence jobs.

On the one hand, much can be done by companies themselves to eliminate practices that tend to destabilize sales. Unplanned sales programs are cases in point. For example, salesmen may receive no instructions regarding products to be pushed, types of sales to be avoided, or what promises may be given on shipping dates. As a consequence, production bulges are extended, or opportunities to fill in production valleys are missed. All this suggests that a simple and early step toward job stabilization can be taken by developing and adhering to planned selective sales programs.

On the other hand, customers should be induced to become more stable buyers. First, in the case of seasonal items, buyers may be encouraged to send in advance orders by allowing special discounts, guaranteeing against price declines, offering exclusive rights of distribution, offering exclusive selection of styles, and permitting purchase on consignment. Second, in the case of items that are being ordered in small lots, buyers may be induced by methods suggested above to place a large order, with deliveries to be made periodically. And third, by inducing the ultimate consumer to use around the year some items that he is now using only at certain seasons, all the distributors back to the manufacturer will tend to become more stable buyers. Perhaps no better example of success in this regard can be found than that of sellers of soft drinks, who market almost as much of their product in winter as they do in summer months.

2. *Production Practices.* Production practices and policies should also be studied with a view to stabilizing employment. One of the most useful practices in this respect is that of producing to stock during seasons of low sales. This is not a cure-all because it is not universally feasible. When the following conditions prevail, its use should be given favorable consideration:

   a) Parts or products can be stored:
       (1) With a minimum of loss due to deterioration or evaporation
       (2) At a minimum cost of handling, storing, and financial investment
   b) Minimum losses will be incurred because of:
       (1) Style changes while goods are stored
       (2) Declines in price during storage

Such products as locomotives and construction equipment fall outside this class because of the physical problems of storing and the cost of carrying the items. On the other hand, many consumer items which are regularly purchased can be stored within the foregoing requirements.

Another practice which has much to commend it is that of "dovetailing" or producing different items for different seasons. This is usually difficult because facilities that are economical for the production of one type of product are ordinarily uneconomical for others. However, diversification should be considered because it may provide a way of balance production.

A variety of other production practices has been devised with a view to stabilizing production. Production control methods, for example, have much to offer here. Available work may be routed and scheduled to provide a stable work load. Another practice that has desirable features in this connection is to defer work of certain kinds to slack periods. Maintenance work, construction jobs, and scrap handling are cases in point. Another useful idea is to design products so that various parts are interchangeable, irrespective of exterior style or variations in size. In that way, sales of particular products may fluctuate, yet production can be stabilized by producing to stock, if need be, or by producing to a plan of production control that has, as far as the workers are concerned, removed some of the vagaries of size or style factors.

3. *Personnel Practices.* Job stabilization may also be favorably affected by planned personnel practices. More accurate analysis of labor requirements, development of versatility of employees, and planned placement of work loads are the major ways in which this may be done.

a) Stabilizing Hiring Practices. Lack of information regarding labor needs and hiring is a major cause of instability. When such poor employment practices are permitted, foremen in departments in which the work load is increasing will hire extra labor to handle it, not knowing that the load is temporary and that layoffs will soon be in order. Even when it is known that work loads are temporary, some companies proceed to hire willy-nilly, not caring about the disturbing influence to the labor situation. If, then, job stability is a desirable goal, the first and easiest step any company can take in attaining it is to forecast the labor requirements as accurately as possible and, on this basis, to lay down stabilizing rules of hiring. Indiscriminate, inconsistent, and temporary hirings may then be reduced to a minimum.

b) Developing Versatility. The development of versatility in workers also has much to be said for it because varying work loads then can be handled by a smaller number of employees. The theory of this practice is that workers who are kept on the payroll can be shifted, with a minimum loss of effectiveness, from jobs on which output is falling to those on which output is increasing. This makes it unnecessary to hire one worker for the first job, lay him off, and then hire another specialist for the second job, who in turn would have to be laid off when the work load in that area declines.

Versatility may be attained in two major ways—selection and training. By seeking candidates who have all-around abilities, employees selected can be shifted to other jobs as work loads require, thus adding a link to the chain of job security. Training of workers is also a desirable practice in the development of versatility. To be effective, training programs must be started and continued far enough in advance of actual need to allow employees time to gain new and added skills.

c) Leveling Work Loads. A third important way of stabilizing jobs by means of personnel practices is to level work loads. For example, hours of work may be adjusted so that available work is shared by all employees. Ordinarily, this will be practicable on the downward side of the business cycle, so long as reductions in hours of work do not reach the point at which all workers are on starvation wages. When this point is reached (what it is, is a variable depending upon employee opinion and standards of living), employees with seniority lose their desire to share the work with the younger employees and insist that the latter be released. On the upward side, taking care of peak loads by means of overtime, without hiring extra workers who must before long be laid off, depends upon the willingness of employees to give up their leisure and upon their efficiency as the factor of fatigue takes effect. However, within the practicable limits, adjustment of hours is a simple way of stabilizing jobs.

A good system of transfers is also effective in this regard. If work loads of varying amount are scheduled in different departments at different times, transfer programs can be worked out so that employees may be shifted between departments without need for layoffs. This practice can be adopted, however, only if, in addition to the requirements of sales and production tie-ups suggested in the preceding paragraph, employees possess versatility.

Intercompany Cooperation

In a competitive society, no one company can install practices the cost of which will place it in an unfavorable position as compared to other firms. Job security is a goal the attainment of which involves some practices that, if adopted, call for intercompany action to be successful. Great progress in this direction has been made by a number of groups. Favorable results have been achieved by such groups as local and state chambers of commerce acting in behalf of their areas, trade associations working for the benefit of particular industries, and national business associations such as the National Association of Manufacturers and the more loosely knit Committee of Economic Development, acting for the benefit of all businesses. Such diverse groups as the American Legion, church bodies, and unions have also interested themselves in ways and means of stabilizing jobs.

A variety of sales, production, and personnel practices have been developed on an intercompany basis. Perhaps the most important contribution in this respect is the collection and dissemination of various types of information. Certainly, information on such subjects as inventory positions, buying potentials and trends in various markets, new developments in materials and machines, trends in employment, and price fluctuations is highly useful in keeping employers from making mistakes that lead to overemployment and the inevitable layoffs. Inter-company cooperation in gathering such information may be obtained through their own bureaus of information or outside bureaus subsidized to carry on this work.

In addition to the contributions to the ability of individual companies to make better decisions which aid in stabilizing producton, inter-company cooperation can lead to the elimination of destabilizing practices. For example, fluctuation of output in the automobile industry has been reduced by changing the time of introducing new models from the spring to the fall of the year. And the agreement of various industries to avoid extravagant claims, excessive discounts, and high-pressure salesmanship has tended to reduce unsettling results in the market and thus, in turn, to stabilize employment. More positive action has been taken by industries that have sought on a cooperative basis to educate customers in more stable buying methods.

An intercompany practice which has been successful in stabilizing production is that of interchanging workers as slack periods develop in one company while a peak load must be carried by another. Of course, such interchanges are the responsibility of workers in most markets, but the results of individual search are not always satisfactory to the workers, nor do the companies always get back desirable workers. When companies in a community get together to discuss their work loads, however, employees may be shifted from company to company with a minimum of lost time and effort to the employees. Some interesting problems, such as effect upon seniority, must be worked out; but their solution seems to be a small price to pay compared to the losses that are avoided thereby.

Governmental Influences

Job stabilization has also been influenced by governmental regulation and assistance. Regulatory influences have come chiefly from the Wages and Hours Law and the unemployment compensation laws, while the work of such agencies as the Employment Service and the United States Departments of Commerce and Labor has been of an assisting nature.

1. *The Wages and Hours Law.* As noted earlier, one of the fundamental purposes of the Fair Labor Standards Act (FLSA) is to encourage the sharing of available work by penalizing employers who work their employees more than 40 hours a week. Obviously, an employer who has to increase his labor costs by 50 percent for overtime will consider very seriously the advisability of hiring additional workers.

If he does, the objective of stabilizing employment in the overall sense by reducing unemployment will be attained.

More direct encouragement of employment stabilization is also provided in Section 7(b) of the FLSA by the exemptions from overtime payments granted to companies that establish employment guarantees by collective agreement. To qualify, no employee shall be employed more than (a) 1,040 hours in any period of 26 consecutive weeks or (b) 2,240 hours in any period of 52 consecutive weeks. In the case of seasonal industries, overtime need not be paid except after twelve hours in a workday or 56 hours in a workweek.

2. *The Social Security Act.* Another encouragement to stabilized employment stems from the unemployment compensation provisions of the Social Security Act. Under Titles III and IX of this Act, employees of industry, in states that have approved plans, are compensated for periods up to thirty-nine weeks, depending on the legislation of the states in which they reside. The funds for compensation are obtained by taxes computed as a percentage of individual payrolls. Records are kept of the contributions of each company and of compensation paid out against the individual accounts. In most states, adjustments are made in the taxation for particular companies if the withdrawals from the fund, because of a low record of layoffs, are at a minimum. The amount of the adjustments depends upon the system of merit or experience rating particular states have adopted. Obviously, it is to the benefit of companies operating in states in which rating may lead to reduction in taxes to reduce fluctuations in employment whenever possible.

3. *Assistance of Federal Agencies.* Other federal agencies have lent an assisting hand in reducing job instability. The United States Departments of Commerce and Labor have collected a variety of data which are useful to employers in reaching more intelligent decisions regarding business problems, thereby reducing mistakes that lead to layoffs and employment fluctuations. Also, the United States Employment Service and the state employment services assist employers in the selection of workers who are better suited to their jobs; consequently, layoffs due to misplacements are reduced.

WAGE STABILIZATION

Scope of Plans

Programs of wage stabilization are based on the proposition that wages and salaries should be continued at a more or less constant rate when it is impossible to stabilize production. A variety of such plans have been developed. The key points of difference pertain to:

1. The employees covered by guarantees
2. Guarantee periods and amounts
3. Examples of voluntary plans
4. Conditions of favorable usage

Employee Coverage

Most plans are limited to certain classes of workers. Length of service, type of work, and a calculated number of employees are used to establish limits. Length of service is undoubtedly the most popular method for determining the employees who are to participate in wage stabilization plans. It is, of course, easy to calculate and understand and, moreover, has the actual advantage of the test of time—since the company has been able to retain the workers for a length of time, probabilities are in favor of being able to continue their employment. The service requirements of some plans are as low as six months and as high as five years, with a period of one year being favored.

Job classes are also used by some companies because the retention of employees on certain key jobs is highly desirable. Technical, professional, supervisory, and maintenance employees are examples of those to whom guarantees are extended.

And finally, some companies establish the number of employees to whom guarantees can be extended by calculating labor requirements for a future period of time. After this figure is determined, seniority by job classes is then employed to determine which of the employees will be included in the number of employees to whom the guarantee can be extended. This method has the advantage of protecting the company against excessive guarantees, but it has the disadvantage of making some key employees uncertain about income stability.

Guarantee Periods and Amounts

All plans establish a definite period of time during which guarantees apply or are calculated. In most instances the year is the base period, although some plans limit the time to as low as three months. Obviously, if a plan is to give employees assurance of steady income, it should at least aim toward the annual basis. This provides a sufficiently extended period so that employees are not disturbed by what is going to happen to their income in the near future. Of course, from the company's point of view, guarantees beyond a year's time are full of danger because economic conditions and prices beyond its control and its powers of foresight may lead to impossible financial burdens. However, most companies should be able to forecast within reasonable limits of accuracy the sales they will make during a year's time and hence be able to establish this period as a limit to their guarantees.

Although questions of who is to be covered for how long may be answered with relative ease, how much is to be guaranteed is a much more difficult question. The variations in this regard in actual practice show that differences of opinion are wide. Guarantees differ in terms of liability of payments and amount of payment.

With rare exceptions, most companies limit their guarantees or establish rules for counterbalancing overpayments or underpayments. A common way of doing this is to establish a basic workweek and a basic pay check for each week. If the actual earnings of employees are less than the basic check, the differences are recorded and must be made up in future weeks when overtime hours raise actual earnings above the basic check. The basic pay check may be based on a standard workweek of 40 hours (or upon some lesser figure) if actual hours from week to week fluctuate around 40. If the period within which shortages must be made up is definitely stated, let us say a year, as some plans provide, the liability of employers is minimized, yet the wage plan may be termed a guaranteed wage plan.

Many companies limit their liability by agreeing to advance employees, for specified periods of time only, an amount sufficient to make up the difference between the amount earned and the guaranteed weekly pay check. These advances are continued only for a limited period of time or up to the pay for a given number of hours. Should these limits be reached, the makeups are stopped. And as noted earlier, the advances must be made up by the employee when workweeks exceed the basic week or some percentage of a basic week.

Examples of Voluntary Plans

A number of companies are widely recognized for their contributions to wage stabilization programs, and a brief description of their plans is in order.

Procter & Gamble, for example, has been a pioneer in this field. This plan is essentially an employment guarantee plan. Permanent factory workers are guaranteed employment for at least forty-eight weeks of the year. To make the plan feasible, the company had (1) to redesign certain key manufacturing operations so that year-round instead of seasonal operations could be carried on and (2) to revamp its distribution methods so that retailers purchased on a periodic rather than a casual basis. The work guarantees are given to employees with two or more years of consecutive service. Workers also are subject to job changes as work loads of various divisions dictate.

The Nunn-Bush Company, noted for its plan of fifty-two checks a year, is another pioneer in wage stabilization. This company, too, has worked out very carefully the conditions under which wage guarantees can be made. It has found that the amount that can be paid to employees is about 20 percent of the value of production. Hence, by forecasting sales for any year, it can determine what its payroll will be. Jobs throughout the company have been evaluated, and each employee included in the plan may draw one fifty-second of his annual rate each week. At the end of four-week periods, adjustments are made if actual earnings are above or below drawings. Only workers who are in an "A" group, consisting of those whose seniority and ability merit it, are included in this weekly pay check plan; the other or "B" workers are paid on an hourly basis without any guarantees. The guarantees in this case are not a fixed amount but a fixed percentage of whatever business the company gets.

The Hormel Company of Austin, Minnesota, has also been in the vanguard of the movement for wage stabilization. Employees receive fifty-two pay checks a year, with a minimum of 38 hours at the hourly rate in any week. In weeks of over 40 hours, no overtime at premium rates is paid. Overages and underages are balanced at periodic intervals. At the end of the year, employees earn bonuses based upon the earnings of the company and upon production in excess of estimated quantities. Thus, this plan includes a profit-sharing feature.

The elements of the plans of a few other companies that illustrate some variations in practice are also worth citing as follows:

The William Wrigley, Jr., Company pays a percentage of regular earnings to employees laid off. Payment is made to employees of six months' service or more, and continues for four to thirty weeks, depending upon service.

The Armstrong Cork Company will make up the pay of employees up to 48 hours for any two weeks at its own expense and will prepay wages between 60 percent of standard earnings and actual earnings, which difference must subsequently be repaid by the workers.

The Sears, Roebuck and Company plan pays its employees a regular weekly amount fifty-two weeks a year, requiring workers to work whatever number of hours, up to but not beyond reasonable limits, is needed to get the work done. Earnings in excess of weekly guarantees during the year are paid to employees. Payments in excess of earnings are absorbed as a loss by the company.

Conditions of Feasible Usage

Wage stabilization requires favorable conditions. Desirable though it may be to employees and employers, it is not something that can be established or not, as the whim dictates. To begin with, wage stabilization is practically limited to periods of a year or less. Hence, as a stabilization of cyclical forces, it is an aid, not a cure-all. And even within the yearly or seasonal period, many companies are unable to do much about wage stabilization. For example, those whose swings of business are violent and unpredictable—the so-called "producer goods industries" are a case in point—cannot undertake such programs.

On the other hand, those whose business is in the consumer goods field and who are more or less depression-proof (meaning more resistant than others) may adopt such plans. A review of the names of companies that have installed them soon indicates the predominance of consumer-type industries. And finally, industries which can economically store parts or finished products are in a better position to stabilize wages than others. Thus, anything a company can do to reduce seasonal fluctuations, to increase the storability of products, and to increase the versatility of employees makes wage stabilization more feasible.

The variations in these conditions explain why some companies can be more liberal in their guarantees than others. Whereas some can guarantee weekly pay checks of fixed amount without repayment features in the event of overpayments, others must restrict their guarantees to little more than wage advances that must sooner or later be repaid. In any event, the steps taken by any company in this direction serve to reduce one of the most serious threats to labor's security and peace of mind.

How far this movement will go is conjectural. Guaranteed wages have an appeal, however, that is difficult to resist. And it must be granted that most companies never have laid off all their employees at any time. At least, guarantees of this amount could be feasible. So it is safe to conclude that negotiations for such guarantees are not likely to abate. How many employees will be covered and the extent of guarantees will depend upon economic conditions, the type of industry, the strength of union bargaining power, the strategy of union drives, and the facts that management can marshall about its industrial situation.

QUESTIONS

1. How would you answer the question of how long an employee should work in any given time period?

2. What are the arguments for and against the provision of rest periods during the working day? What are the practices in your community in regard to rest periods in business?

3. What is an effective workweek? What do you expect the workweek to be five years from now? Why?

4. How may the shift problem in industry be handled? Discuss the advantages and disadvantages of the fixed- versus the swing-shift plan.

5. What types of economic fluctuations cause employment fluctuations? What is the probability of eliminating them? Of minimizing them?

6. Why is it that a single company, acting alone, can seldom do much about job stabilization? Is it not true, however, that some companies have scored singular successes in stabilizing jobs? What conditions are present in such cases?

7. If work is stabilized in some departments of a company but not in others, is this likely to lower morale in the latter departments? If so, would it be better to forgo job stabilization until the entire company can be included in the plan? Explain.

8. Although training is likely to increase the versatility of employees, will not training also increase unrest because employees will become dissatisfied if new opportunities are not opened to them?

9. What are the key points that have to be covered in a wage stabilization program?

10. Under what conditions is wage stabilization preferred to job stabilization as a means of providing economic security?

CHAPTER **22**

SERVICE AND PARTICIPATION PROGRAMS

Scope of Plans

Over the years, there has been offered to employees a miscellany of plans which fall outside the borders of affairs strictly pertinent to business. Some, such as athletic programs, seem well removed from the business of producing and selling goods. Others, such as medical plans, are more closely related, in that they provide services which might otherwise be unavailable. And still others, such as company periodicals, may indirectly affect employee morale, teamwork, and productivity.

How far a company will go in establishing such programs depends upon its basic philosophy, community factors, union relations, and forces pressing for or against particular plans. All that can be done here, therefore, is to comment upon various programs and some guide lines for their operation. This is done under the following headings:

1. Recreational, social, and athletic programs
2. Participation programs
3. Services of convenience or personal necessity
4. Organization of programs
5. Rules of adoption and operation

RECREATIONAL, SOCIAL, AND ATHLETIC PROGRAMS

Purposes of Programs

Recreational, social, and athletic programs have a double purpose. They make for a well-rounded life for employees, and they serve thereby to build employees who are better equipped to perform their daily tasks. What specific plans should be provided requires careful consideration of objectives, morale, and environmental factors. For example, answers to such questions as the following should be sought:

1. Are any objectives of the company being missed because facilities for recreation are not available?
2. Does the community provide adequate and usable recreational facilities?
3. Is a union offering such plans or facilities?
4. Is employee morale, and hence willingness to cooperate, weak because of a lack of adequate recreational facilities?
5. If recreational plans are established, will the employees in sufficient numbers take advantage of them?

Recreational and Social Programs

Assuming that favorable answers are derived, a wide range of programs is available from which to make selections. In describing these plans, only a superficial attempt is made to group them in recreational, social, and athletic categories. After all, such plans as bowling leagues have aspects of all of these: They provide physical exercise—the athletic aspect. They provide a change in the tempo of living that brings renewed vigor to employees—the recreational aspect. They encourage gregariousness among employees—the social aspect. Or a company symphony orchestra for example, may be to one individual a recreational opportunity and to another a social event. Hence the groupings here are for purposes of convenience rather than being indicative of exclusive categories.

1. *Social Get-Togethers.* Occasional events such as company-sponsored dances and picnics are the usual way in which recreational and social programs are initiated. Whereas dances may be operated with relative ease because participation of those who attend the event is assured, such programs as picnics and outings call for a good deal of planning and organizing. Games and contests should be planned for all age groups and for both sexes. The events should be scheduled so that they neither drag nor overlap. Small prizes, too, are a desirable feature for winning contestants. And it is important that the executives attend and participate with unconcealed enjoyment.

Parties organized to suit the season serve to promote interest. Beach parties in the summer, Halloween and Thanksgiving parties in the fall, and Christmas and New Year's parties in the winter are examples of such occasions.

2. *Informal Associations.* Other recreational activities are pro-

vided by informal get-togethers of employees in clubrooms of their own. During rest periods, lunch hours, or before or after going to work, employees may gather in the club for refreshments or dancing. More elaborate arrangements provide facilities for athletic activities of various kinds.

3. *Musical Groups.* A miscellany of other recreational plans has been adopted. The employees of one company have been unusually successful in organizing a symphony orchestra. This activity began with the formation of an orchestra for playing popular music, which evolved after a few years into a symphonic group. Of interest is the fact that this orchestra has been a success not only for the participants but also for nonparticipating employees who have learned to enjoy classical music. More popular among musical activities are dance bands, glee clubs, and military bands.

4. *Drama Clubs.* Many companies also have drama clubs. These seem to be very attractive because they provide employees an opportunity to produce and stage plays as well as act in them. Such groups have given plays on the stage and also have presented radio dramas. Thus, this activity provides a variety of opportunities to attract employee participation.

5. *Flying Clubs.* Flying clubs have been organized by the employees of some companies. This is a relatively expensive activity, but the cost for the individual can be reduced considerably by the formation of clubs. Ordinarily, such clubs can be organized only in large companies. The number of potential fliers must be large enough to support a continuing turnover of learners and participants.

6. *Flower and Garden Clubs.* Gardening, from time to time, has proved of wide interest. During the war years, vegetable gardening was a very successful employee service. Such programs can be made more effective by planning shows at which vegetables and canned goods are to be displayed and judged. Some companies have also had success on a more permanent basis through smaller scale flower clubs. Here, too, periodic shows help to stimulate employee interest and activity.

7. *Noon-Hour Programs.* The noon hour provides a real opportunity for providing employees with recreation. Horseshoe pitching and softball are popular in many companies. Other companies prepare elaborate programs of noon-hour entertainment, occasionally using professional talent from the entertainment world, famous figures in the sports world, and visitors of public renown. The latter type of program, on a large scale, can ordinarily be established only by the large company. The inexpensive nature of some of these programs is illustrated in

FIGURE 22–1

Production Area during Working Hours

Courtesy: North American Aviation, Inc.

Recreation Area during Lunch Hour

Courtesy: North American Aviation, Inc.

Figure 22–1, showing how production space and aisles are used for noon-time recreational purposes.

8. Special Interests. Groups with special interests may also be served. Chess and checkers clubs, camera clubs, and bridge clubs are examples. These groups, though small, will nevertheless be found to be among the most active that can be established.

9. Physical Facilities. Recreational and social plans must often be implemented by physical facilities. When community facilities are adequate and conveniently located, it is desirable to take advantage of them. However, it will ordinarily be found necessary to provide some space on or near the company premises. Arrangements for social events can be provided with relative ease when company restaurants are designed for all types of occasions. Thus the restaurant building of one company is used for dances, parties of all types, educational meetings, and meetings to pass out rewards for seniority and suggestions. In some cases the recreation building is separated from the company building. This has the advantage of removing the employee completely from the working atmosphere. Unusual facilities for various sports and social gatherings are provided by the 180-acre park established by the National Cash Register Company of Dayton for these purposes. Such arrangements are, of course, the exception.

Athletic Programs

1. The Popular Sports. Athletic programs are widely used to engage employees in after-hours activities. Bowling and softball, in season, are particularly popular with many companies. The former has grown widely in employee acceptance because it is a good mixer sport and can be enjoyed by the tyro as well as the expert. Softball teams have grown in popularity, too. Some companies stress intramural teams, whereas others sponsor intercompany leagues. The former provides opportunity for a large number of employees to participate in athletics, while the latter gives employees an opportunity to cheer for their company, thus encouraging institutional pride. Basketball teams require more skilled participants and are usually restricted to intercompany competition, but they do provide much spectator entertainment. The merit of these programs sometimes has at least one serious detraction. As one company official noted, the costs of industrial compensation for accidents were higher in the case of recreational programs than for factory operations.

2. The Minor Sports. A variety of other athletic sports is also sponsored. Tennis and golf tournaments or parties are planned by some companies. In a few instances, skeet, trapshooting, and pistol ranges have been provided. Swimming facilities are also provided by some companies by renting community facilities at stated times and under qualified supervision. Gymnasiums may also be rented under similar conditions in some cases. In a few instances, companies have built such facilities for the exclusive use of employees.

Horseshoe pitching is also of interest to some employees. This game possesses possibilities in any program because facilities can be provided easily and the playing time of the game is relatively short. Hence, it furnishes an excellent sport for the lunch hour. Continuing interest can be derived by keeping cumulative records and setting up interdepartmental teams. Other sports that have been established in a few instances include ice and field hockey, cricket, squash, and badminton. Because of the skill required by most of these sports, they have been less popular.

Enough enthusiasts can usually be found in most companies to organize a fishing club. In addition to organized outings, meetings to discuss fishing and outdoor recreation and to swap "lies" may be planned.

Music in the Plant and Office

Although music in business is a twilight case of a recreational or social program, it is included for discussion here because music does have an aesthetic or emotional appeal that is more related to the recreational or enjoyment capacity of the employee than to his physical nature.

For many decades, music, as well as other forms of discussion and entertainment such as the reading of stories, has been employed during working hours in various foreign countries. Until recently, such practices were almost nonexistent in the United States. But in the past several years, there has been a small but growing trend toward the use of music as a means of improving production by relieving monotony and by providing employees with a lift. Although the evidence is by no means conclusive, studies both here and abroad have claimed that production has been increased from 5 to 15 percent after the introduction of music. Quantity and quality increases as reported by the Muzak Corporation are shown in Figures 22–2 and 22–3. The results in terms of lessened fatigue, cheerier dispositions, and increased emotional stability are equally favorable, if not measurable.

The introduction of music in the plant had to await the development of satisfactory equipment. Modern developments now make possible the

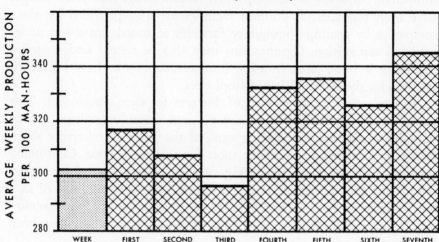

FIGURE 22–2. Effect of Music upon Quantity of Production

Source: Muzak Corporation.

distribution of music from central stations to strategically located loud-speakers at reasonably low cost. The musical equipment need not be located in the factory. Such services, in large communities, may be purchased from companies established solely for this purpose.

Another significant factor in the use of music is the building of programs that will not interfere with working rhythms and will appeal to employees. The music suitable for a punch press department may be

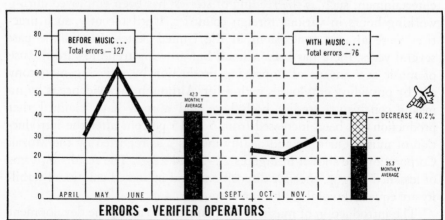

FIGURE 22–3. Effect of Music upon Quality of Production

Source: Muzak Corporation.

distracting to a central stenographic department, and vice versa. Usually, some experimentation will be necessary before programs suited to various departments are established. Similarly, experimentation will be necessary to select programs that the majority of employees prefer.

The equipment for sending music may also be employed to broadcast various messages. Although some companies frown upon this practice, others favor it. The latter use the system to make special announcements, to describe lost and found items, to welcome new workers, to send birthday and anniversary greetings, and to broadcast such public events as World Series baseball contests, football games, news reports, and addresses by the President of the United States.

PARTICIPATION PROGRAMS

Although the inclusion is somewhat arbitrary, company periodicals and suggestion systems are discussed here in connection with employee services because both attempt to relate the employee to his working environment. Either might be dispensed with, as some companies have done, on the grounds that periodicals are ineffective and suggestion systems are likely to bring about disputes and controversies between employees and employers. On the other hand, the supporters of such plans see much good in them as means of improving the ties between the two groups.

Company Periodicals

Company periodicals are publications such as newspapers or magazines issued regularly to employees. Their widespread use is seen in the fact that three out of four companies with assets of $5 million and over have such publications.[1] They are discussed here because their content in most cases is devoted to social and personal items of interest to employees. But they also are used for instructional purposes of a general nature and to disseminate information regarding company products, policies, rules, and regulations. However, the latter must be heavily sugarcoated with personal items, or they are not likely to be read.

1. *Objectives.* The fundamental purpose of company publications of this type is to bring employee and employer closer together. The larger organizations, in particular, have recourse to such devices in order to personalize employee-employer relationships. Employees become better employees, so the theory of company magazines goes, because they

---

[1] According to an address of Dr. Claude Robinson before the American Association of Industrial Editors (*Personnel,* Vol. XXIX, No. 5, p. 452).

have been recognized publicly as a significant part of the organization.

Publication of company rules and of explanations of procedures and plans also can serve indirectly to make employees feel that they are an important part of the organization. In the first place, they are taken into the confidence of the company; and second, their ignorance regarding various aspects of company operations is removed. Hence, when properly handled, which means writing from the employee's viewpoint, company news can be as effective a morale builder as personal items.

2. Layout and Form. To be effective, company periodicals must be made up with care. Much thought and study should be given to such matters as technical form, content, periodicity, method of distribution, and staff for gathering and editing materials. Some companies invest very small amounts in mimeographed sheets, whereas others publish magazines that compare favorably with the finest magazines found on the newsstands. In either event, the important point is to determine carefully what type of magazine will serve the conditions and needs most appropriately.

Several points are well worth noting in regard to the technical composition of periodicals. The size of magazines should be such that they are easy and convenient to handle. Type should be selected that is easy to read, and headings should both attract and guide the reader. And perhaps above all, the style of writing should be somewhat on the breezy side, interesting and appealing to the average employee.

3. Content. In regard to the content, it is generally agreed that personal items, social events, and recreational and athletic news should make up the greatest part of a magazine. Some contend that nothing else should go into a publication intended for employees. Perhaps it would be better to argue that nothing should be included unless it is written or translated for employees. After all, the opening of a new office building, for example, may be company business, but it is also of real interest to employees. So, too, is news about products, processes, and organization changes.

News of personal interest, however, should lead all the rest. New additions to the staff, transfers and promotions, marriages and births, unusual happenings to employees, hobbies and activities, awards and recognitions, leaves of absence, and serious illnesses are examples of items that should be reported. A liberal sprinkling of pictures, particularly of children, is also desirable. After this, social events of personal interest, both within the company and within the community, such as dances, parties, and gatherings, should receive attention. Then, too, the various sports activities of employees, such as standings of teams, personal performances, and game schedules, should be highlighted.

Although some people may state that they do not care whether or not they get their names in the paper, there are few indeed who actually do not like such mention, insignificant though the occasion for it may be. The old rule of the small-town newspaper that each subscriber's name should be mentioned at least twice a year in the paper also holds true of the company periodical.

4. *Periodicity and Distribution.* How often magazines should be issued and how they are to be distributed must also be considered carefully. In most cases, magazines are published once a month. Periods of greater or less time are selected infrequently. A month provides a convenient interval as well as one that whets the employees' interest and does not overwork the publication staff.

The question of how often is comparatively easy to answer, but the question of distribution is difficult. There is wide difference of opinion as to methods. Some companies prefer to mail the magazines to the homes of employees. In this way, there is greater assurance that the families will read the magazines. Some pass out the magazines as the employees punch the clock, and others distribute them through the departmental supervisors. The last two methods are used primarily because of their convenience and secondarily because each employee is given his own copy on the company premises, providing another direct contact between employee and employer.

The real problem is, of course, to have the magazine read; otherwise, it may as well not be issued. This can be accomplished by including various features such as puzzles, rewards for those who notice special items scattered through the magazine, and contests for such suggestions as names of new sections of the magazine or comic characters that are used to depict safety lessons and other instructions that may be run in the magazine from time to time. Emphasis on personal items serves to promote reader interest.

5. *News Gathering and Editing.* Finally, arrangements must be made for gathering and editing the content of magazines. A popular method is to hire a full-time magazine editor and to rely upon selected employees from various departments to gather and report the news. This arrangement has the advantage of expert direction and of employee participation, but it suffers from the possibility that the employee reporters will not do a thorough job of news gathering. This may be circumvented by frequent staff meetings in which the departmental reporters are made to feel the importance of their jobs and, at the same

time, are instructed in what news to gather and how to do it. In some companies a full-time staff to do all of the work is hired, members being selected from present employees or from sources outside the company. In this way the technical competence of gathering and preparing news items is assured. Whether or not a sense of employee participation is lost depends upon how closely reporters get in touch with employees and how well they ferret out and report their activities.

Suggestion Systems

General education and communication may also be improved by means of a good suggestion system. Although some companies have had unfavorable experience with suggestion plans, favorable results are more common.[2] To be effective, however, suggestion plans should be designed with care in regard to the following aspects:

1. Objectives of suggestion plans
2. Procedures for collection and evaluation
3. Policies of compensation

It is invariably necessary to precede the inauguration of a suggestion system with a campaign of publicity designed to acquaint employees with the values of the system and how it is to operate. Specific notes should be made regarding the gains to the employees. In this connection, it is important to stress that laborsaving suggestions will not result in layoffs.

Then, it is important to publicize the procedures of the system, as illustrated, for example, in Figure 22–4. In particular, employees should be informed as to how suggestions should be made, where they should be deposited, and how they are to be judged. Every effort should be made to indicate how the employee who makes a suggestion is to be protected in any rewards or recognition which may arise from the suggestion. In this connection, some companies have found it desirable to establish judging committees made up of employees as well as executives and technical assistants.

Rewards for acceptable suggestions are a matter of argument. Some companies frown upon any rewards except expressions of congratulation. Others conclude that some form of financial compensation is indispensable. In the latter event, practice varies. Some companies establish maximum rewards of $25 to $50, whereas others use formulas by which employees may be paid up to 25 percent of the first year's savings

---

[2] The proponents of suggestion systems have been numerous enough and enthusiastic enough to form a group known as the National Association of Suggestion Systems.

FIGURE 22-4. Suggestion-Processing Flow Chart

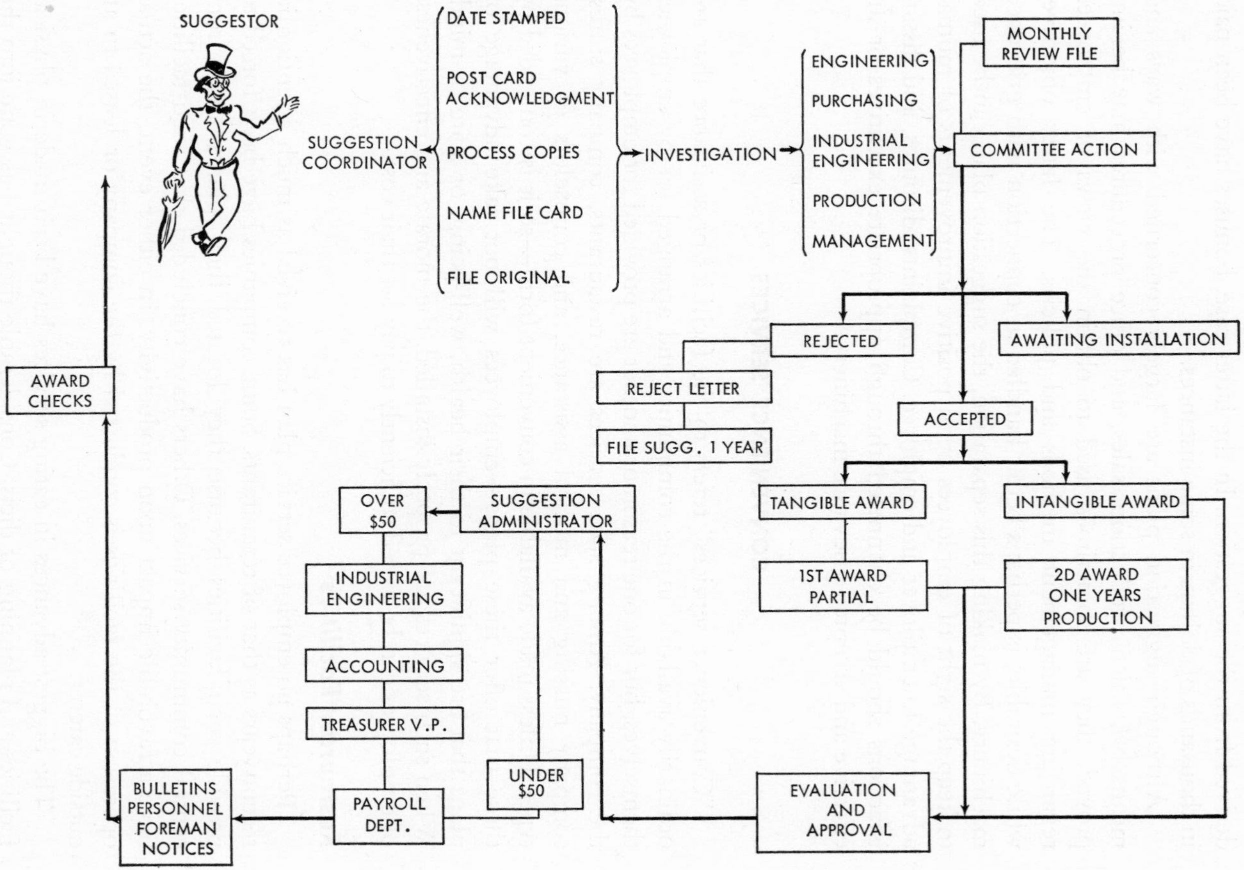

SUGGESTOR

DATE STAMPED
POST CARD ACKNOWLEDGMENT
PROCESS COPIES
NAME FILE CARD
FILE ORIGINAL

SUGGESTION COORDINATOR

INVESTIGATION

ENGINEERING
PURCHASING
INDUSTRIAL ENGINEERING
PRODUCTION
MANAGEMENT

COMMITTEE ACTION

MONTHLY REVIEW FILE

REJECTED

AWAITING INSTALLATION

ACCEPTED

REJECT LETTER

FILE SUGG. 1 YEAR

TANGIBLE AWARD

INTANGIBLE AWARD

1ST AWARD PARTIAL

2D AWARD ONE YEARS PRODUCTION

EVALUATION AND APPROVAL

SUGGESTION ADMINISTRATOR

OVER $50

UNDER $50

INDUSTRIAL ENGINEERING
ACCOUNTING
TREASURER V.P.

PAYROLL DEPT.

BULLETINS
PERSONNEL
FOREMAN
NOTICES

AWARD CHECKS

derived from the suggestion. In the latter case, bonuses have been paid in thousands of dollars in some instances.

Although suggestion plans are largely concerned with ways and means by which production, sales, and office procedures may be improved, they are sometimes used to obtain the views of employees regarding management methods and policies. The latter objective, while desirable, is perhaps better handled in connection with grievance machinery. By making this separation, the suggestion plan can be used to keep the sight of employees upon positive improvements of mutual advantage to employer and employee. Complaints, disputes, and dissatisfactions should be channeled through appropriate executives or an effective and accepted grievance machinery.

CONVENIENCE SERVICES

"Convenience services" refers to the facilities or assistance that are ordinarily available in the community and arranged for by employees themselves, but for one reason or another are provided for employees by the company. Among such services are restaurants, company stores, company nursing and medical assistance, and counselors of various types. Unless made available in convenient form—so it is contended by those that offer these plans—employees will not take advantage of plans that are significant to their health, well-being, or state of mind. When such services are properly installed, the morale and effectiveness of employees can be raised sufficiently to pay for their cost.

Restaurant Facilities

Perhaps no employee service plan has received as much attention in recent years as that of restaurants. Some companies have been forced to provide such facilities because they located their plants away from central community services. Others have concluded that such facilities have a favorable impact upon productivity. In either event, the actual operation of the facilities is conducted by the company or leased to an outside caterer.

The biggest advances in eating services have been made in physical facilities and planning of diets. Considerable thought has gone into the design and location of restaurants and eating facilities. The technique of layout planning is being adapted to the design of company cafeterias. In addition to fixed restaurant sites, more and more companies are adopting mobile and automatic food-dispensing units. These units are used by some companies to serve employees who are located at inconvenient distances from the regular restaurants of the company. Other companies use these devices to reach workers during working hours and provide them with soft drinks, milk, candy, and sandwiches.

Careful study has been made of the dietary needs of workers. Industrial dietitians and nutritional experts have become permanent members of the personnel staff of many companies. The dietitians must plan meals that not only are well balanced but also will be selected by the employees. To induce good selections, a popular method is to offer the planned meals as "specials" at a relatively low price. One company has gone so far as to serve free meals to employees, so that they have no problem of "selling" the balanced diet. Another method is to feature items, such as salads, that are deemed good for the diet. One company took all soft drinks out of the restaurant so that milk would not have that competition. Another company has used the idea of contests among employees to attract attention to balanced menus. Employees have responded not only by offering menu suggestions but also by buying more of the balanced menus than they did when the company alone decided what the menus were to be.

A final word on nutrition has reference to the practice of some companies of supplying employees with vitamin pills as a supplement to possible dietary deficiencies. Of course, the practice of providing salt tablets to those who work under very hot conditions has for a long time been known to be desirable in replacing body salts lost by perspiration.

Company Stores

Company stores in some localities have had some adoptions. In communities where retail stores are inadequate, company stores perform a needed service. The offerings to employees can be wide, covering food, clothing, sports equipment, automobile supplies, and household furnishings. Many of these items may be available on the store premises. Others may be offered through discount arrangements with dealers, only samples being shown at the store.

In some instances, company stores have acquired a poor reputation. They have been used as a means of making excessive profits. They have also been used to keep employees in debt, thereby assuring the company of little, if any, labor turnover. These instances, although infrequent, occurred often enough in the past that unions at times raise the issue in collective bargaining negotiations. Moreover, the wages and hours administrator has laid down rules governing how employees shall be paid so that they will not fall victims to unscrupulous company-stores practices. Company stores have also been opposed by community retailers, who feel that such profits logically should go to them. And some states have outlawed them.

The charge that company stores are exacting excessive profits can be avoided by turning over their operation to employees. In one company the store is run by the employees for the purpose of financing various employee activities. The profits are used to support various recreational, social, and athletic activities. As a consequence, these programs are run and supported by the employees themselves. The company lends a minimum of support by providing store space at a minimum charge.

Credit Unions

Facilitative services include a variety of plans, only a few of which can be mentioned here. An interesting example is the credit union, which has had a phenomenal growth in the United States. The credit union is essentially a small-loan institution operated by employees for their own benefit. Its purpose is to have a source from which short-term loans may be obtained for personal needs at rates far below those that are charged by the "loan sharks." Since some employees are hard pressed for funds occasionally, the credit union offers a worthwhile service to them. And to the employees who invest in the credit union, it offers a combination savings and interest-earning plan, and also a life insurance program based upon the savings and age of the member.

The losses in credit unions are remarkably low, having averaged less than 20 cents per $100 loaned. In the first place, the officers of credit unions review applications for loans from a restricted group with whom they are well acquainted, since they are all fellow employees. Hence, losses are reduced at the source by careful screening of applications. In the second place, most plans have established an upper limit above which loans will not be made to any given individual. In this way, risks are spread over a large number of borrowers. In the third place, credit unions are subject to state and federal regulations, depending upon how the unions are established. Since 1907, when the first state law was enacted, forty-four states have enacted legislation governing the operation of credit unions; and in 1934, provision was made for federal incorporation.

Some idea of the pace with which credit unions have grown may be seen in the fact that there were about 5,000 credit unions in 1936 and over 22,000 in 1965. In that year, loans outstanding amounted to over $8.5 billion. The majority of these unions are in the industrial states, with California, Illinois, Michigan, New York, Ohio, Pennsylvania, and

Texas each having over 1,000 credit unions. In California the membership exceeds 1.8 million.

Home Purchasing

Assistance to employees in purchasing homes is also a popular plan
of employee service. Such assistance is usually provided by a building
and loan financial plan. This combines a savings plan, for employees
who want to invest their savings, with the loan feature, for those who
wish to build or buy homes. The borrower then repays to the loan
association a fixed amount each month or payday. In other cases the
company itself provides the financial assistance and deducts a fixed
amount, covering principal and interest, each payday. Both plans make
it possible for employees who so desire a procure long-term loans at
reasonable rates with a minimum of red tape. Indeed, some companies
make the loans at extremely low rates as an encouragement to home-
ownership, believing that such acquisitions make for stable employees.

Miscellaneous Services

An unusual type of employee service is exemplified by the practice
during war years of providing nursery service, to encourage more
women with preschool-age children to seek war work. By supplying
space, facilities, and trained attendants for children, a service was provided that was expedient to the war effort and helpful to the families of
servicemen. In many cases, women with young children could not
otherwise accept war work. Unless they could leave their children in
safe and capable hands, their entrance into war employment was out of
the question. And until company nurseries were opened, baby and
children "sitters" were simply not to be had.

Medical Services

In recent years, there has been a tendency for more and more
companies to provide employees with medical service. Such service
usually has started with visiting-nurse service for sick employees. It has
gradually been extended so that varied medical service is available not
only to employees but also to their families. Thus, hospital and surgical
facilities are available in some companies for all types of illness and
operations. Also, the services of dentists and optometrists are offered in
some cases.

Consultative Services

Included among the facilities offered by some companies are consul-
tative services of various kinds. For example, some companies have

opened their legal departments to the personal problems of employees. In most instances, this is restricted simply to giving initial advice as to what to do if threatened with legal suits, for example, or what rights one has in various difficulties that may present themselves. In other instances, help is given in instituting a suit, in selecting legal counsel if protracted court action is necessary, and in suggesting the nature of action to be taken. Of course, except in minor cases or actions, the legal departments are not offered to carry on court actions or extended cases. However, limited service is highly desirable because most employees do not have the slightest conception of what to do or what not to do when faced with legal difficulties. Hence the availability of this service will be of great aid to them, at very little cost to the company, unless perchance it should have an unusual number of troublemakers on its payroll.

Other companies have made arrangements whereby employees may discuss various problems with vocational guidance experts, psychologists, psychiatrists, and family relations experts. Such services, too, can do much to find and eliminate sources of trouble that disrupt an employee's ease of mind and, therefore, his capacity to produce efficiently and effectively.

Retirement Consultation

An interesting type of service is that related to easing the transition of employees into retirement. Three phases of retirement may be noted: preretirement, actual retirement, and postretirement.

In the preretirement phase, it has been found desirable to discuss with employees and executives their approaching retirement. Problems they are likely to encounter in readjusting, possible plans they may make, and financial changes that will be forced upon them are examined. Each is counseled to consider the new way of life he and his family will soon be facing. And help may be given to plan for new hobbies, to investigate possible activities, and to prepare for changes gradually.

In the actual retirement stage, it has been found desirable to establish a formal program of leavetaking. Such affairs as banquets, with their gifts and speeches, at which are gathered associates and executives, show the appreciation of fellow workers and the company. Making the rounds of one's associates, particularly when accompanied by a high executive, adds to the prestige of the individual and his pride in the significance attached to this tradition by the company. And a careful explanation of the formal plans and services to which the pensioner is now entitled should also be made at this time.

In the postretirement stage, various activities may be undertaken which serve not only to tie in the pensioner with the company but also to build good will throughout the organization. Literature such as house organs, letters, and periodicals should be sent to pensioners. Participation in social and recreational clubs should be encouraged. Use of company facilities, advisory services, and medical aids should be extended. And the right to visit the plant or office may well be granted. Indeed, in this latter respect, some companies have found it very useful to continue key employees or executives as consultants on a part-time, extra-fee basis. A few have provided special areas where pensioners may continue to work part time or which they may use for their private hobbies.

ORGANIZATION FOR SERVICE PLANS

In most companies the various service plans are operated under the jurisdiction of the personnel department. Within this department a section is established to inaugurate and direct the service plans. This section is often called the employee service department, but it is also known by such names as the welfare department, the recreation and athletic department, the insurance department, and the benefits department.

In performing its duties, this unit may rely upon the assistance of others. Thus, in the establishment of pension plans, for example, the service department would call upon the legal, financial, and statistical departments for advice on technical aspects of pensions. And in the operation of the recreational plan, for example, it would rely in most companies upon the help and cooperation of formal committees or organizations of employees.

Example of Service Organization

To illustrate how the company organization ties in with employee organization, it is well to describe the plans in use by a few companies. Of interest, to begin with, is the plan used by a company employing ten thousand workers in a large city location.

In this case a recreation club, operated by the employees, serves as a nucleus for all social and athletic events within the company. All employees may join, the dues being 25 cents a month. The management of the club is in the hands of officers who are elected by the members. Activities include baseball, bowling, golf, skeet shooting, model auto

racing, roller skating, dances, and other social affairs. Annual Halloween and New Year's parties are sponsored. The annual Christmas party
is an outstanding event, being given for the children of employees.

The officers are advised and assisted by an activities director, who is
on the staff of the personnel division. The director also plans and
operates special entertainment and activities for the company. Noon-
hour entertainment is an example of such activities. The activities
director also has charge of the distribution of tickets for special events
held outside the company, such as operas, sports events, and circus
performances. Thus, much of the work done here is by the company,
but the employees are made to feel that they are running the show.

Organizational Plan under Decentralized Operations

In another case an employees' club has been established at each of
the several plants operated by the company. The general plan of organization is the same at all of these, but the program and activities of each
plant are determined by the people located in them. Each of the clubs is
made up of departmental groups averaging from about 50 to 100
members, thus providing a well-knit working unit. The supervisor of
the department is a member, but he can neither vote nor hold office.

In each department, employees elect their own president, vice-president, secretary-treasurer, social chairman, athletics chairman, and welfare chairman. It is noteworthy that the greatest interest is in the social
activities—dances, parties, picnics, and the functions of hobby and
special interest groups. The athletics committee plans activities the
employees desire most—archery, table tennis, basketball, softball, golf,
swimming, etc. Bowling, by the way, has proved the most popular
sports activity. Among the activities the welfare committee carries on
are building a fund to buy flowers for hospital patients, distributing
Christmas baskets, and organizing first-aid or home-nursing classes.

The departmental presidents are then organized into the executive
council, and the departmental chairmen into councils for the plant.
Thus the social chairmen form the social council, and so on. Each
council elects its own officers and meets once a month.

Dues vary from 10 to 50 cents a month, as the members of each
department determine. The funds go into the departmental treasury. In
addition, a central club fund, administered by the club's executive
council, is built up from vending-machine profits, admission to central
club dances, cafeteria profits, and other plantwide social or athletic
events, as well as company contributions. Most club affairs are therefore

self-supporting. Any employee, however, whether or not a member of the club, may attend any of the central parties or dances.

At most of the plants the employee club has a clubhouse or rooms—one has an auditorium, a kitchen, a game room, a reading room, and one or two meeting rooms. The company provides and owns this property and buys all permanent facilities. The funds of the club are used only for current expenditures.

These clubs, like those in most companies, are not incorporated. Hence, to insure officers against the unlimited liability which may accrue from such organizations, the company has arranged to protect the officers from damage suits by means of a rider on the company's public liability insurance policy.

Company Experts

Another case of organization is illustrated by an employees' club in which the company supplies expert advice and guidance. A member of the staff of the industrial relations department, who is known as the activities director, helps organize and counsels the employee organizations which are a part of the employees' activities association. This is a nonprofit association, organized and supported by the employees. Membership begins automatically for every employee at the time of employment. No dues are paid, the organization's activities being financed by the profits from vending machines.

A board of directors governs the association. It is composed of one representative from each club or activity represented in the association; the activities director, who is an ex officio member; and one other appointed by the president of the company. The latter appointee is an accountant who keeps the books and serves as treasurer of the association.

Whenever at least fifty employees participate in an activity, a petition may be made to the board of directors for representation in the association. Among the activities represented are a band, baseball, basketball, bowling, boxing, a camera club, chess and checkers, fishing, riding, golf, a gun club, horseshoes, a mixed chorus, and tennis. The company provides and maintains an athletic field with night lighting, where baseball and softball games are played. It also provides a darkroom for the camera club and facilities for the gun club and the casting club. It also pays the salaries of the activities director and his secretary, and allows for time spent by the other company representatives on work of the employees' association. Beyond these expenditures, the employees carry the financial burden. The management feels that employee interest in recreational and social activities has a direct relationship to the extent to which employees plan, manage, and support their own activities.

The activities director also counsels the girls' club, to which all women employees belong automatically and which raises money through social activities for charitable purposes; the employees' relief association, a mutual benefit association; and the employees' credit union.

Rules of Operation

If such plans are to yield the fullest returns, several suggestions are in order regarding the plans and their operations. Worthy of careful consideration are the following points:

1. *Primacy of Wages, Hours, and Working Conditions.* In the first place, service plans will do little good if a company's wages, hours, and working conditions are not considered satisfactory by the employees. These are the foundation, without which all else is futile. Employee service plans cannot support a weak or unfair structure of wages, hours, and working conditions. Hence the first principle in establishing service plans is to review the basic values of employee relationships. Until any questionable features are removed, the installation of service plans should be delayed.

2. *The Factor of Need.* In the second place, employee service plans should not be installed unless there is a real need for them. They should not be viewed from the moralistic angle of being good for the employees. Rather, the question must be: Do the employees want the services? To establish playgrounds, athletic fields, and recreational facilities, for example, just because some executive feels that these will turn employees away from the corner saloon to the good life will almost inevitably lead to failure. Of course, a company should not install features that would lead to moral deterioration, but neither can it succeed in making employees tread the straight and narrow path.

3. *Employee Support.* In the third place, a service plan should not be sponsored unless the employees are willing to support it with their time, effort, and (sometimes) money. To give employees facilities is dangerous to long-run success for the simple reason that those things that are easily obtained are seldom appreciated. But when employees help to build facilities, such as softball diamonds or vegetable gardens; to manage activities, such as dances or parties; or to finance activities through monthly dues, for example, their attitude changes from that of

an outsider to one of personal ownership. Hence, it is invariably wise to provide for employee participation—whether by contributions of time, effort, or money should be determined by the particular circumstances.

4. *Stimulating Employee Interest.*   In the fourth place, the company need not wait for employees to need particular service plans or to display willingness to participate in them. Steps can be taken to suggest, directly or indirectly, the desirability of various plans. One company, for example, has contended that all its plans have been established at the request of its employees. However, it has not been averse to dropping hints where they will do the most good. In one case the company was "surprised" by the request of employees for financial aid in building low-cost housing; but its surprise was only superficial, because company executives had hinted months before to a few key employees that low-cost housing would be a desirable thing for many employees. The idea was subsequently presented at a meeting of the employees' club and soon snowballed into a company-aided program. Such steps must of course be taken with caution, lest any sign of company interference undermine the employees' feeling of possession.

5. *Overall Coverage.*   In the fifth place, service plans should be developed so that all employees have some service or facility in which they have an interest. Not all employees want to participate in or watch softball games, bowling, or fishing, for example. However, if opportunities are provided in a variety of fields, most employees will find some service plan that will interest them. Unless breadth of offerings is sought, the result will be that only a few employees will participate. The service plans in that case are useful only to a restricted part of the payroll. For example, varsity athletic projects have that shortcoming. These should be strengthened by encouraging employees to be spectators at contests or by providing intramural sports that will permit mass participation.

6. *"Soft-Pedaling" Expenditures.*   In the sixth place, it is desirable to operate plans with a minimum of financial fanfare. Otherwise, there is real danger that employees will tend to wonder whether or not the plans are being financed at the expense of lower wages. If employees begin to ask such questions, it is usually certain that trouble is bound to follow. Although costs of such programs are invariably low, they may seem high to employees who note elaborate recreational and sports equipment. Moreover, expenditures for these affairs tend to become a subject of collective bargaining, with consequent loss of control over them by management. Hence, it is well to build facilities conservatively, to indoctrinate employees regarding their low cost, and to en-

courage employee participation in their management and financing. Under these conditions the facilities will be accepted rather than suspected.

7. *Relating Company and Personal Objectives.* And finally, service plans should be organized and operated so that employees become a more integral part of the company because of them. In other words, the bowling league should not only result in recreation and exercise but should also build company esprit de corps. Any activity or event should be designed so that a tie-in with company objectives and aims is made. This is not easy; but unless it is accomplished to some degree, the employee service plans will represent an unconnected appendage that serves no useful organizational purpose. And wholesome and enjoyable though some activities may be, if they are not related to company objectives, they have no reason for taking up company time, resources, or energy.

It is worth repeating in this respect that unions are increasingly interesting themselves in social and athletic programs. They are conducting parties and dances, organizing athletic teams, and operating recreational activities. Whether or not this trend will continue to an extent which will ultimately see unions assuming a predominant role is as yet uncertain. But if it does, management will have lost an opportunity of substantial proportions to build employee relatedness and loyalty.

QUESTIONS

1. As more and more service and participation programs are underwritten, how can the personnel manager be sure that the point of diminishing returns has not been passed? Have you any evidence that in some companies such a program has reached a state where the "tail wags the dog"?

2. In one company the policy is against having any parties or similar affairs for employees because of fear that drinking might become excessive, with the result that the affairs would get out of hand. Comment upon this policy. What suggestions have you to offer to avoid undesirable results if parties are to be held?

3. If a company sponsors such athletic programs as softball and bowling, should executives participate with employees? What are the advantages? What are the dangers? How may the latter be minimized?

4. Visit a company that has installed musical programs during the working hours. Report on your findings.

5. In one company, nothing except personal items and human interest subjects is included in the company newspaper. Do you think the company is getting its money's worth by eliminating references to company items and news?

6. Many companies provide restaurant services. Upon what ground is this justified? Do not community businessmen have a right to object to this type of competition?

7. When a company underwrites or provides medical, dental, and hospital services for its employees and their families, have socialized medicine and paternalism been attained indirectly? Explain.

8. When a company provides services such as those of psychiatrists, are not employees almost forced to use them whether they want to or not? Does this not lay the groundwork for revolt rather than for better relationships between employees and management?

9. When the personnel department is responsible for service plans, how can it gain the cooperation of the employees in operating them?

10. One company turns over all recreational and social affairs to the employees' club but makes available the services of a trained recreational and social counselor. What are the merits of such an arrangement?

CHAPTER 23

PHYSICAL SECURITY

Introduction

Of significance to both employer and employee is the sense of physical security which surrounds the employee. Working conditions, health, and safety are particularly important in this connection and therefore constitute the major areas of study in this chapter. To these subjects, various fields such as medicine, engineering, psychology, and management have devoted considerable attention. Space here, however, permits only a review of various pertinent practices and principles contributed by these fields to better working conditions, improved health, and increased safety. Before taking up specific aspects of these subjects, it is worth noting (1) the objectives of improved physical security and (2) the general trend of development in dealing with physical security.

Objectives

Numerous objectives may be attained by proper attention to working conditions, health, and safety. From the viewpoint of the individual, the value of these efforts can hardly be overestimated. For example, looked at, first of all, from the side of losses, how can anyone estimate the value of lives lost in industrial accidents? Or how can the loss to the individuals maimed in such accidents be estimated? Of course, insurance benefits may provide some financial relief to these individuals or their beneficiaries, but the personal sufferings and losses are inestimable.

And viewed positively, healthy and safe workers gain personal satisfactions which alone make the effort to improve health, safety, and working conditions worthwhile. A more cooperative spirit, higher morale, better workmanship, better use of materials and equipment, and better discipline are reflected in such workers. They not only gain more enjoyment from their work but also make the working day of their fellow workers and superiors more agreeable. And of course, what happens to the individual—either negatively or positively—is of interest also to his family, his relatives, his friends, and the community.

To the company the objectives are many and significant. As an example, a quarter of a million working days, and the production thereof, are lost annually by fatal and disabling industrial accidents, according to estimates of the Bureau of Labor Statistics. The corollary losses of idle machinery, working capital, and space, of extra efforts to rearrange schedules and working crews, and of delayed shipments are beyond calculation. In the face of these facts, it is easy to see why industry now places a high priority on the effort to meet the challenge of safer and healthier working conditions.

Trends

Despite these obvious advantages, positive impetus to the development of a real interest by industry in the physical well-being of workers stemmed originally from the passage of industrial compensation laws by the various states. Prior to that time, which centers around the turn of the century, industry paid little attention to these matters because their burden and cost fell largely upon the worker, his family, or the community. Although industry theoretically could be held responsible for accidents, practically there were enough legal loopholes to make it immune to unfavorable lawsuits. In the common law, under which earlier employee-employer relationships were determined by precedent of previous court decisions, industry could escape financial responsibility for accidents under any of the following conditions:

1. An employee's own carelessness (known as the "contributory negligence rule")
2. The actions of a competent fellow worker (known as the "fellow-servant rule")
3. The risk connected with the work which the worker was willing to take when he accepted employment (known as the "assumption-of-risk rule")

Of course, the employer was expected to operate his business in a reasonably safe manner, to provide reasonably safe working conditions, and to employ workers competent to perform the tasks assigned to them.

1. *Disadvantages of Common Law.* The results of such legal rules and administration were unsatisfactory. In the first place, when accidents just "happened," so that the cause could not be assigned to employer or employee, the latter had no recourse. Second, the loopholes

in the common law were so wide that there were few occasions when the employer could not escape through them. Third, since court actions were the only medium by which responsibility could be established legally, they often dragged out so that employees gained little, even in the event of a favorable conclusion. And last, industry itself never knew when a heavy judgment might be levied against it. Thus, unfavorable though common-law principles and procedures were to employees, they also had risks for the employer.

2. *Enactment of Statutory Legislation.* However, the demand for changes in legal rules came largely from labor, although some social-minded industrialists also favored changes. After much agitation, various states enacted laws covering compensation for accidents and illness arising from occupational hazards. These statutory enactments replaced the common-law decisions. By now, all states have passed some such legislation.

The fundamental advantage of industrial compensation laws is that, irrespective of what or who causes an accident, except in instances of outrageous disregard of safety rules, the employee is compensated for financial losses he incurs. Compensation is paid in a variety of ways. In the case of death, lump sums or weekly allotments may be paid to dependents. In the event of total or partial disability, the individual may be paid a lump sum and also provided with periodic subsistence payments. And in the event of accidents or illnesses which result in temporary losses of earning power, weekly allotments of varying amounts are provided.

3. *Financial Arrangements under Statutory Law.* The funds for such compensation are obtained by charges against the employer. This is done through payment of premiums to insurance systems of private ownership in some states and to state-operated systems in others. Administrative machinery is provided by which the amount of liability can readily be determined, though in all cases recourse may be had to the judicial branch in the event of disagreement with administrative rulings.

The charges against employers will tend to vary with the number and severity of compensable accidents and illnesses. Hence, it is to the interest of management to reduce them to the lowest possible number. Such efforts cost money, to be sure, but accident-reduction programs are nevertheless followed because of the principle that to make or save money, it is invariably necessary to spend money. Here is an important explanation of many safety programs that industry has promoted: It has been found that they are financially less costly than accidents.

4. *Merit Rating.* Further incentive to reduce accidents and hazards is provided by the practice of adjusting insurance premiums in accordance with merit ratings of health and safety practices and results. The most common way of doing this is to adjust an employer's insurance rate in accordance with his accident record. This is known as experience merit rating. Another plan is to adjust rates according to the degree of risk which is present on an employer's premises. Obviously, a factory or office which maintains and safeguards its equipment is likely to have fewer accidents than one in which the reverse is true. This system of adjusting rates is known as schedule merit rating.

WORKING CONDITIONS

General Considerations

When pictures or descriptions of factories as they existed prior to the turn of the century are contrasted with the physical arrangements of modern plants, there can be little doubt about the importance management attaches to good working conditions. These conditions are apparent, on the one hand, in the technical tools of production. Machines and equipment used directly in production are designed with a view to the comfort and effective employment of the skills of the operator. For example, levers by which operators make adjustments to the machines are placed with a view to anatomical features of the human body and not to mechanical demands alone.

And on the other hand, various features that might simply be said to add to the comfort of the worker are designed and installed with due care. Lighting and air conditioning, locker and personal facilities, and hazard controls exemplify the types of features management considers as indirectly affecting production and costs through their direct influence upon the comfort and physical well-being of employees.

Although the actual work of design and maintenance of working conditions is largely the work of the engineering and plant maintenance departments, nevertheless the personnel phases of such work are significant. To begin with, the personnel department has a stake in such matters because of their effect upon the loyalty and attitude of employees. This department should therefore have an advisory relation to the departments that may plan for and maintain physical conditions. In the second place, unions often make an issue of physical conditions. Hence the personnel department should be attentive to such matters, so that disputes or frictions do not arise. And third, the personnel department should keep abreast of new developments in order to be able to advise management on steps that might be taken so that desirable improvements will not be overlooked.

Phases of Working Conditions

This is not to imply that the personnel department must have technicians on its staff. Rather, it should be acquainted with technical working conditions merely to the extent that any shortcomings may be detected, corrections requested, and improvements suggested. In the following, attention is therefore directed to various important phases of working conditions.

1. *Material Handling.* Material handling is the source of the greatest number of injuries in industry. Hence the flow of materials in all of its phases should be carefully planned. First, handling of materials and parts at machines and benches should be studied, to the end that physical handling is reduced to a minimum and adequate protective devices are provided. Second, the flow of work between machines and departments should be facilitated by proper equipment, and should be provided with well-designed and well-marked storage spaces and aisles and roadways. An interesting example of how a study of hazards can be tied in with the design of flow of work is illustrated in Figure 23–1.

2. *Machine Guarding.* Protection of the worker by the strategic placement of mechanical guards and electronic controls is another essential of good working conditions. Various devices can be provided to protect workers (*a*) from the many parts of all equipment that transmit power and (*b*) from the hazards at the point of work. The dangers arising from the mechanical devices that surround the worker as well as the hazards arising from adjusting, inserting, and manipulating materials and tools should be considered here.

3. *Factors of the Work Place.* The comfort and efficiency of workers is also affected importantly by the physical factors at the work place. For example, the influence of chairs is not small. In one company, chairs in the factory have been designed that are adjustable to differing sizes of individuals. The chair seats can be moved up and down, the backs both up and down and in and out, and the footrests up and down. Moreover, the chairs have foam-rubber seats and backs. In another company the installation of chairs that can be easily moved on operations that require considerable stretching and movement has increased production 25 percent and decreased fatigue noticeably. Such adjustable chairs are particularly desirable when women as well as men are employed on similar operations.

Other factors of the work place that deserve mention are the level of

FIGURE 23-1. A Safety and Process Chart

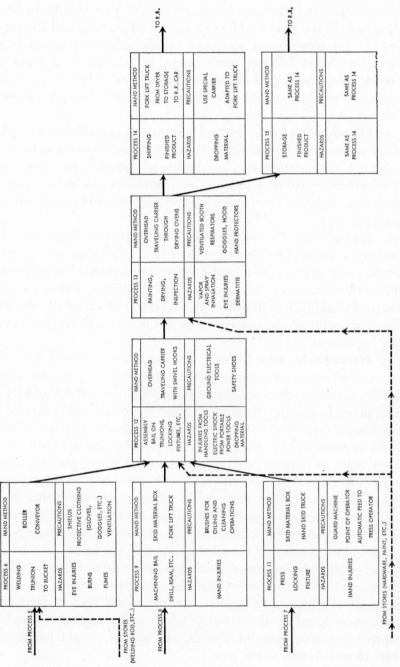

SOURCE: George Koller, "The Challenge of Post-War Safety," *Personnel*, Vol. XXII, No. 6, p. 65.

work surfaces and clothing or safety devices that should be worn. Adjustment of the level of the work surface to the height of the person using it, and provision of platforms or adjustable chairs, can reduce fatigue and hence increase productivity. In relation to clothing and safety devices, rules regarding these should be established with a view to employee comfort and tastes, or cooperation will be difficult to secure.

4. *Disaster Controls.* Hazard and disaster controls are also essentials of good working conditions. A well-designed system for detecting, inhibiting, and fighting fires is absolutely essential. In cases where explosions are possible, a program of control should include periodic inspections, isolation from other operations, and devices for reducing igniting factors.

5. *Radiation.* The nuclear age has brought to industry a new challenge to safety. The consequences of radioactivity are so severe that extreme measures must be adopted to protect employees from exposure. This involves such practices as appropriate buildings, warning devices, protective clothing, handling devices, and safety education. As the trend of nuclear energy accelerates, the needs in this area will become increasingly imperative.

6. *Heat, Light, and Noise.* The importance of heat, light, and noise control are commonly recognized. In the matter of atmospheric conditions, temperatures should be controlled between 65 and 85 degrees, depending upon the nature of the work and the season of the year. Unless otherwise required by work processes, relative humidity should be maintained in the range from 45 to 50 percent. Dust, fumes, vapors, and gases should be removed from work places, obnoxious work places isolated, or workers supplied with protective devices, such as masks, particularly when there is a possibility of occupational disease and illness. Temperature and air cleanliness control may require an air-conditioning system, but there is evidence that the value of maintaining personal efficiency during the summer months, for example, outweighs the cost of such equipment in most cases. The effect of lighting should also be carefully determined. Good illumination is a factor not only in productive efficiency but also in accident reduction. Hence, standards of illumination based on the advice of illuminating engineers should be adopted. Necessary goggles, shields, and glasses should be provided where there is danger to the eyes.

The factor of noise is also of significance in promoting employee comfort and efficiency. In factories the noise of many operations is at present seemingly beyond control. But it is possible to segregate excessively noisy equipment, to dampen vibration, and occasionally to redesign machines that are particularly annoying. In offices, however, much has been done to soundproof walls and ceilings as well as equipment and machines. The results in such cases have more than offset costs.

Since excessive noise can also lead to hearing injuries, which may be compensable under industrial compensation laws, noise measurement surveys are suggested if there is any question about noisy conditions. The threshold of painful noise begins around 110 decibels, the unit used to measure sound. An idea of sound and noise intensities may be gained from the following list of sound conditions:

Rustle of leaves	20 decibels
Average office	30
Stenographic room	60
Average conversation	60
Average machine shop	70
Newspaper pressroom	90
Subway train	110
Boiler factory	110

7. *Color.* Proper use of color may also have a constructive influence on safety and efficiency. One company reported that cost of accidents was reduced from $1.21 to $0.18 per employee after old machinery was painted to conform with safety recommendations instead of a uniform gray. A production increase up to 20 percent was also noted. Suggested colors are as follows: yellow or orange for dangerous materials or parts of machinery; green, white, gray, or black for safe materials; blue for protective materials; and red for fire protection materials and equipment.[1]

8. *Personal Needs.* Good working conditions also call for adequate provision of conveniences of a personal nature. Good drinking water, properly cooled and made available through well-located dispensers, should be supplied. Adequate toilet facilities that are well located, lighted, and ventilated, and carefully cleaned and disinfected, should be provided. Facilities such as shower rooms are also indispensable when working conditions may lead to skin diseases or contamination. And finally, dressing and rest rooms should be provided if women are employed.

9. *Factory Landscaping and Layout.* The outside of the factory should also be given attention in the matter of employee comfort and attitudes. First, the general appearance and landscaping cast an impression upon employees for good or for bad. Second, strategic arrangement and pleasing appearance of approaches, streets, sidewalks, gates, and

---

[1] *Management Review,* Vol. XXXVII, No. 5, p. 266.

entrances can be a part of good working conditions. And third, arrangements for parking of automobiles and areas for waiting for transportation—private or public—can put the employee into the right (or wrong) attitude toward his working day.

HEALTH

Pertinent Factors

The health of employees may be influenced by a number of factors. Off-plant living conditions and habits, medical services, environmental conditions, and past personal history are of vital significance. These phases are seldom considered within the domain of management influence and so are not treated here.

Health is also significantly influenced by working conditions and safety practices. This is discussed in other sections of this chapter, so no detailed mention of these phases need be made here. Of interest here are two commonly encountered health programs: (1) medical examinations and (2) various health services. Discussed in this section, too, is the matter of organizing medical services.

Medical Examinations

Most companies give due recognition to provision for and performance of adequate medical examinations. This may be seen by reviewing (1) coverage of examinations, (2) facilities for examinations, and (3) medical and health records.

1. *Coverage of Examinations.* A useful survey of the subject may be made by noting who may be examined, when, and how.

A list of those who may be examined would include the following:

a) Applicants for employment or reemployment
b) Employees who return from extended leaves of absence
c) Employees who are returning from sick leave
d) Employees who have been absent, excused or not excused, for a specified number of days, usually six to twelve days
e) Employees engaged in occupations with exposure to disease or illness
f) Employees whose work might endanger the life or health of customers or fellow workers
g) All employees, periodically or as new developments in medicine warrant

The periodicity of or frequency with which examinations may be given also varies. A list of the variations follows:

a) An examination of employees only when they enter the employment of the company

b) Nonperiodic examinations for those returning from sick leave, etc.

c) Periodic examinations:

    (1) Voluntarily assumed by the company for all employees or those engaged in hazardous or health-affecting occupations

    (2) Required by law for those engaged in occupations affecting the health or security of customers or patrons

A list of types of examinations which may be given follows:

1. Medical examinations of general physical condition
2. Examinations for communicable disease—e.g., syphilis or tuberculosis
3. Visual and dental examinations
4. Psychiatric examinations
5. Visits to the homes of employees

Of course, few companies include all of the foregoing in their examination programs, for the reasons that (*a*) opinions differ as to how far a company should delve into a person's physical and mental makeup, and (*b*) facilities and staff are not always available or are beyond the resources of some companies, particularly the smaller plants.

There is a strong tendency, however, toward expansion of such programs. To cite but one example, there is a growing interest in the benefits of psychoanalysis and psychiatry. Various companies have moved slowly and with satisfactory results in this direction. The aim here is not so much to eliminate the obviously unbalanced but rather to help employees and executives who have minor troubles to minimize blocks and obstacles to more effective and satisfying living. This approach has also been useful in dealing with problem drinkers, of whom it is estimated there are about 3 percent among the employee and executive ranks.

2. *Facilities for Examinations.* Most companies provide excellent facilities for physical examinations relative to their size and needs. Usually, facilities are provided adjacent to the personnel department office, since most examinations are given in connection with various personnel procedures—e.g., new employees, transfers, employees returning from sick leave, or those absent without permission who are returning to their jobs. This location is also desirable because it gives applicants an opportunity to get a favorable impression of the company. Moreover, it is sufficiently removed from busy traffic to make its location favorable for medical work.

Next to the medical and professional staff, equipment is invariably the most important part of the medical department. What it should contain depends upon the examinations to be given, the hazards that exist in the company, the policy of the company, and the number of workers to be served. Usually, facilities are provided for minor injury cases, chest X-ray pictures, syphilis tests, and urinalysis, as well as cursory eye, ear, nose, and dental examinations. Some of the larger companies also have completely equipped operating rooms and hospital units. A few have eye and dental dispensaries.

3. *Medical and Health Records.* All medical, health, and accident procedures should be properly implemented with adequate records and reports. Since vital decisions are based on them, it is doubly essential to gather and report information so that those who use them will be able to interpret them properly. The records which may be kept are so varied that no more can be done here than to list the major categories:

   a) Medical examinations
   b) Dispensary cases handled
   c) Reports of accident occurrence
   d) Investigations and surveys of working conditions
   e) Trends of accidents, occupational illness, and first-aid cases

Health Services

In addition to examining candidates and employees, health services may be expanded to include (1) surveys of plant conditions and (2) off-plant medical care.

1. *Plant Surveys.* Plant surveys are essential in order to maintain healthful working conditions. They serve to reveal sources of occupational disease, unsafe working conditions, and conditions conducive to the development of fatigue. The surveys should be made periodically or upon special occasions. They should be conducted by skilled technicians operating out of the medical department of the personnel division, since this will insure freedom from interference by or condonation of undesirable conditions by line executives. In addition, the skills of properly trained technicians and professional talent will be brought into play in this important work.

In order to appreciate the types of surveys and checks, some of the more common types will be noted. An important phase of such surveys is that of checking operations that tend toward occupational disease or illness. Examples are making dust counts in core rooms and checking the percentage of carbon monoxide in the air of certain baking rooms.

As important, but less obvious to the observer, are factors leading to the development of excessive fatigue. Surveys of noise, vibration, and material movements may be related to output, scrap, absenteeism, illness, and accidents. Such studies may serve to determine if these factors are present to an undesirable degree.

2. *Extension of Health Services.* In some companies the health and medical services, originally provided only to serve the internal needs of the company, are now being extended to the families of employees. Such extensions are not to be confused with health and medical service insurance, described in an earlier chapter, which provide for financial assistance to those who require such services from their own doctors. Medical facilities have been made available to employees and their families usually in cases where community facilities are inadequate or where company officials take the view that employees must be given such opportunities or they will not seek medical services, even when financially able, until too late.

The expansion of health services usually takes place by providing visiting-nurse service to employees away from work because of illness. After this, provisions are made for giving free physical examinations to all who desire them. Also, the services of company doctors or hospital facilities are made available in the case of emergency operations due to causes outside the employment contract. From these extensions, it is a simple step to provide free examinations and at-cost, or even free, service in connection with the prevention or cure of visual, aural, and dental problems, as well as general physical ailments.

Some health services are of an educational nature. For example, first-aid courses have been sponsored by many companies. Their effects have external as well as internal value, for the records are replete with cases in which lives have been saved and serious pain and losses prevented by those who had completed Red Cross first-aid courses. Home-nursing courses are another example of training along these lines sponsored by some companies. Company sponsorship has also extended to allied subjects, such as nutrition. Instruction material in this field includes the theory of good nutrition as well as practical applications, such as suggested menus.

Organization for Medical Services

In most large companies the medical department is made a part of the personnel division. Its work is so closely related to the objectives that are sought by the personnel function that the union is a natural one. Moreover, to keep an organization from having too many independent units which would overload the top executives, many units must be combined, even though there may be, on occasion, some reason for independent action. For example, some companies believe that the relation between doctor and employee is so private that the doctors should report to no one but the chief executive of the company. That the privacy of the relationship must be guarded is true, but to conclude that confidential information can be entrusted only to the chief executive is not. Such arguments reflect upon the ability and fair-mindedness of other executives, who, if they cannot be trusted to keep such matters confidential, should be discharged and replaced by more dependable men.

However, it is essential for the personnel director to have the utmost confidence in and respect for the opinions of the medical unit. For this condition to prevail, the medical staff should be selected and trained so that it understands the relationships involved in industrial medicine. It is necessary to define, therefore, the relations of the medical staff to the following groups:

1. To employees, with whom they should deal strictly in terms of matters arising out of the employment and industrial situations. If it is the policy of the company to offer services and aid beyond this, the doctor, the employee, and executives should be informed of the exact nature and extent of available services.
2. To community physicians and local health agencies, whose availability to workers should be respected and whose cooperation in attacking health problems should be sought, since outside factors are often as significant to physical well-being of workers as plant conditions. Local and state health departments, such agencies as the Red Cross, and medical doctors are as much in the fight for good health as company staff members.
3. To management, through whom the medical staff must frequently work to gain the cooperation necessary to "sell" health and accident programs, and whose proficiency can be increased in reducing hazards to health and safety.

This discussion does not imply that medical organization is a problem of large companies solely. Disabling injuries are about 50 percent higher in small than in large plants. While the smaller plants cannot individually support medical departments, there is no reason why several plants cannot employ doctors and nurses on a cooperative basis.

This is being done in several cases and is working out satisfactorily at a reasonable cost. One plan of cooperation provides for the establishment of a central clinic for three companies having a total of 800 employees. At the central clinic a doctor spends three hours a day, and a nurse five. The nurse spends an hour a day at each of the three plants. In another plan operated by eight companies having a total of 4,000 employees, a full-time nurse is employed in each plant, while a full-time doctor visits each plant each day.[2]

SAFETY

Importance and Scope

In no other phase of physical security has management shown greater application than that of accident prevention. The excellent attitude of industry generally toward safety work, when compared with the lax standards once maintained, would lead one to believe that accidents are relatively infrequent. Although great progress has been made, there is much room for improvement. For example, data on accident frequency and accident severity rates shown in Figure 23–2 are not commendable in some industries. Although the frequency rate was as low as 3.36 in the steel industry, it was 37.78 and 17.26 in the coal-mining and lumbering industries, respectively, in 1965. Mining also shows up poorly in the accident severity column. It is understandable, therefore, why union leadership in this industry has recently demanded that a fund be set up to take care of accident losses.

These trends, though improving, are evidence of why safety activities are still strongly supported by industry. To appreciate better the nature of such activities, the following phases are here studied:

1. Measures of accidents
2. Mechanical aspects
3. Human aspects
4. Organizational aspects

Measures of Accidents

As already noted in the foregoing sections, accidents and safety may be measured in indirect and direct terms. Indirect measures include such information as the effect upon various aspects of production as a result of accidents and illness. For example, data on losses to production, lowered quality of output, and increases in costs of absenteeism and turnover are commonly collected and reported.

The more direct measures are the frequency and severity rates of accidents. The frequency rate is determined by multiplying the number of lost-time accidents during any selected period by one million and dividing the result by the total number of man-hours worked during the

---

[2] *Factory Management and Maintenance,* Vol. CIX, No. 9, p. 122.

FIGURE 23–2. Injury Rates, Reporters to National Safety Council

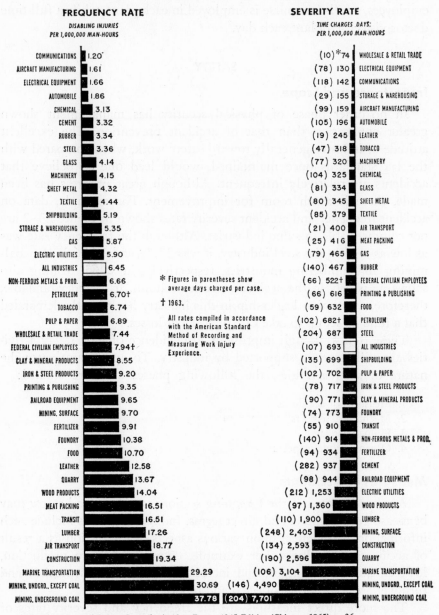

FREQUENCY RATE		SEVERITY RATE
DISABLING INJURIES *PER 1,000,000 MAN-HOURS*		*TIME CHARGES DAYS:* *PER 1,000,000 MAN-HOURS*

FREQUENCY RATE			SEVERITY RATE
COMMUNICATIONS	1.20	(10)*74	WHOLESALE & RETAIL TRADE
AIRCRAFT MANUFACTURING	1.61	(78) 130	ELECTRICAL EQUIPMENT
ELECTRICAL EQUIPMENT	1.66	(118) 142	COMMUNICATIONS
AUTOMOBILE	1.86	(29) 155	STORAGE & WAREHOUSING
CHEMICAL	3.13	(99) 159	AIRCRAFT MANUFACTURING
CEMENT	3.32	(105) 196	AUTOMOBILE
RUBBER	3.34	(19) 245	LEATHER
STEEL	3.36	(47) 318	TOBACCO
GLASS	4.14	(77) 320	MACHINERY
MACHINERY	4.15	(104) 325	CHEMICAL
SHEET METAL	4.32	(81) 334	GLASS
TEXTILE	4.44	(80) 345	SHEET METAL
SHIPBUILDING	5.19	(85) 379	TEXTILE
STORAGE & WAREHOUSING	5.35	(21) 400	AIR TRANSPORT
GAS	5.87	(25) 416	MEAT PACKING
ELECTRIC UTILITIES	5.90	(79) 465	GAS
ALL INDUSTRIES	6.45	(140) 467	RUBBER
NON-FERROUS METALS & PROD.	6.66	(66) 522†	FEDERAL CIVILIAN EMPLOYEES
PETROLEUM	6.70†	(66) 616	PRINTING & PUBLISHING
TOBACCO	6.74	(59) 632	FOOD
PULP & PAPER	6.89	(102) 682†	PETROLEUM
WHOLESALE & RETAIL TRADE	7.44	(204) 687	STEEL
FEDERAL CIVILIAN EMPLOYEES	7.94†	(107) 693	ALL INDUSTRIES
CLAY & MINERAL PRODUCTS	8.55	(135) 699	SHIPBUILDING
IRON & STEEL PRODUCTS	9.20	(102) 702	PULP & PAPER
PRINTING & PUBLISHING	9.35	(78) 717	IRON & STEEL PRODUCTS
RAILROAD EQUIPMENT	9.65	(90) 771	CLAY & MINERAL PRODUCTS
MINING, SURFACE	9.70	(74) 773	FOUNDRY
FERTILIZER	9.91	(55) 910	TRANSIT
FOUNDRY	10.38	(140) 914	NON-FERROUS METALS & PROD.
FOOD	10.70	(94) 934	FERTILIZER
LEATHER	12.58	(282) 937	CEMENT
QUARRY	13.67	(98) 944	RAILROAD EQUIPMENT
WOOD PRODUCTS	14.04	(212) 1,253	ELECTRIC UTILITIES
MEAT PACKING	16.51	(97) 1,360	WOOD PRODUCTS
TRANSIT	16.51	(110) 1,900	LUMBER
LUMBER	17.26	(248) 2,405	MINING, SURFACE
AIR TRANSPORT	18.77	(134) 2,593	CONSTRUCTION
CONSTRUCTION	19.34	(190) 2,596	QUARRY
MARINE TRANSPORTATION	29.29	(106) 3,104	MARINE TRANSPORTATION
MINING, UNDGRD., EXCEPT COAL	30.69	(146) 4,490	MINING, UNDGRD., EXCEPT COAL
MINING, UNDERGROUND COAL	37.78	(204) 7,701	MINING, UNDERGROUND COAL

✱ Figures in parentheses show
average days charged per case.

† 1963.

All rates compiled in accordance
with the American Standard
Method of Recording and
Measuring Work Injury
Experience.

SOURCE: National Safety Council, *Accident Facts—1965 Edition* (Chicago, 1965), p. 26.

same period. The severity rate is computed by multiplying the number
of days lost because of accidents during any selected period by one
million and dividing the result by the total number of man-hours
worked during the same period. The charting of such rates is shown in

Figure 23–3. Although it is contended by some that these formulas are arbitrarily established and that they do not reflect the real pains and losses of accidents, nevertheless they have the advantages of almost universal acceptance and of comparability.

FIGURE 23–3. A Chart of Accident Rates

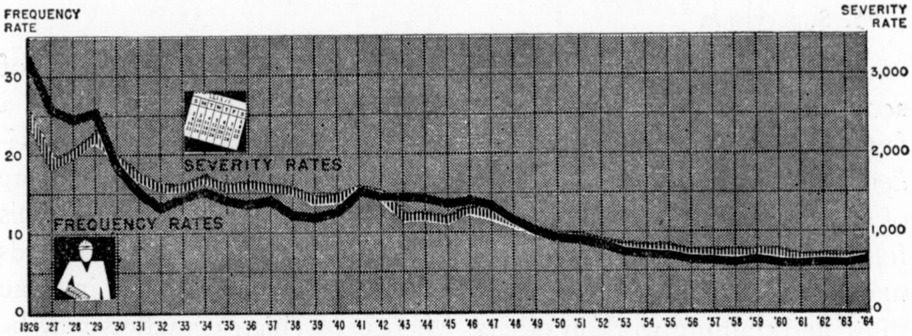

SOURCE: National Safety Council, *Accident Facts—1965 Edition* (Chicago, 1965), p. 28.

Mechanical Phases of Safety

Much has been done to make work mechanically safe. This phase of safety is largely the province of the engineering department, so the discussion here is limited to examples of what has been done along these lines. Some very ingenious devices have been developed to help protect workers. Examples are the use of handcuffs which automatically pull the operator's hand from the danger zone on the downstroke of the ram of a punch press, electronic devices that prevent machines from operating as long as hands or arms are in the danger zones, safety masks to save the wearer from serious and painful injuries when hot metals splash, portable air pumps to supply fresh air during the cleaning of large tanks, and safety shoes in which are built steel toeplates to guard against falling objects.

The emphasis upon safety in the design and use of devices of work is essential and commendable. High output with a minimum of accidents cannot be attained unless work places and tools are designed so that risk exposure is reduced. Hence the work of the engineering department must be carried on at all times with eyes wide open to matters of safety. That most companies have done this is a matter of record.

Human Phases of Safety

If mechanical aspects of safety work have been handled so well, why is the rate of accidents still relatively high and the financial loss so great? The answer is that employees, and supervisors particularly, are not sufficiently safety-conscious. To counter this through an effective safety program, the following aspects must be properly handled:

1. Accident-prone employees
2. Selection of employees
3. Training
4. Discipline
5. Supervision

1. *Accident-Prone Employees.* First, let us look at the record of accidents from the viewpoint of the individual. It is often found that a few employees in every plant have the most accidents. The term "accident-prone" has consequently been applied to an employee who, in spite of all efforts to educate him, continues to have more accidents than his fellow workers. What should be done about such employees depends upon the underlying factors. Perhaps discharge is the only cure in some cases, and training work in others; whereas psychiatric analysis may be necessary in still other cases. In any event, such employees should receive special attention and perhaps care.

2. *Selection.* An ideal approach to reduction of accidents is by elimination of accident-prone candidates in the selection process. It is possible to do some good through interviews and examination of work histories. Evidence can be gathered regarding the accidents candidates have caused or have been involved in during previous employment. Moreover, a forecast of safety proneness can be estimated by the use of psychological tests relating to such factors as physical capabilities and emotional stability. In one company in which interviews, tests, and medical examinations were used along these lines, it was estimated that preventable accidents were reduced by more than one half. To the savings of accident reduction can also be added those of reduced training costs, absenteeism, and sick pay. Hence, this ideal approach to safety has very practical advantages.

3. *Training.* High on the list of a good safety program is the function of training. This has a number of possibilities. Perhaps the best time to start safety training is when a new worker is being inducted. Through the use of carefully designed lectures, visual aids, demonstrations, and conferences, a lasting impact can be made upon the employee when he is in a very receptive frame of mind. How well this works out is seen in the experience of one company that reported a reduction in accident rates of 78 percent, as compared to the situation before such a program was in effect.[3]

[3] Asa P. Lombard and William D. Noa, "Cut New Worker Accidents 78%," *Factory Management and Maintenance,* Vol. CXI, No. 2, pp. 98–101.

Second, courses completely concerned with safety have been effective. Employees are lectured on or participate in conferences concerned with major causes and examples of accidents, ways and means of prevention, proper use of safety devices and clothing (see Figs 23–4 and

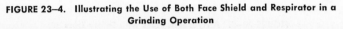

FIGURE 23–4. Illustrating the Use of Both Face Shield and Respirator in a Grinding Operation

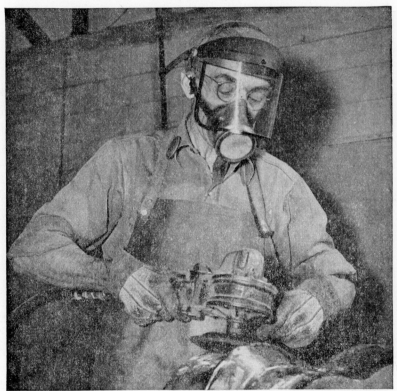

Courtesy: Curtiss-Wright Corporation

The worker is finishing a drop hammer die.

23–5), the services of the medical and accident departments, and what the individual can do to "build" safety in work.

In the third place, employees may be taught how to use such practices as job analysis in reducing accidents. With this technique the worker himself learns how to observe the job with a view of determining what aspects of methods, machines, tools, or the operator himself have dangerous characteristics. Then the worker himself suggests means by which the danger can be removed or minimized. Figure 23–6 illustrates a change suggested under this program.

In the fourth place, it is desirable to publicize accident records and safety programs. Talk or words alone are insufficient to bring home to all employees the full importance of accident prevention. Hence, most companies implement their programs by various techniques to dramatize their purposes.

FIGURE 23–5. A Hydraulic Press with Safety Trips

Courtesy: Curtiss-Wright Corporation

In using two operators, the hazard is eliminated by forcing both of them to utilize both hands to operate four trips, two on either side.

The devices employed have been so many and varied that space here permits only reference to a few. A rather common plan is to use large displays to illustrate the safety records of various departments or divisions of the plant. The theory of such displays is that a competitive attitude to keep down accidents will develop. Bulletin boards are also commonly employed to draw the attention of employees to unsafe working practices and desirable safety precautions.

Another device which utilizes the principle of competition is that of contests in which the best or worst departments are rewarded or penalized. Comical awards are made, such as pictures or statues of white elephants, intended to ridicule the losers and hence stimulate them to do better. In some cases, contests have been credited with reducing frequency and severity rates by 50 percent.

Other techniques are also used in connection with direct training in accident prevention. In recent years, sound movies have been increas-

FIGURE 23–6. A Safety Suggestion

JOB SAFETY ANALYSIS

Change in Protection

DEPARTMENT:___Furnace___ DATE:___August 2, 1954___

JOB:___Crane Operator___

OPERATION:___Checking crane prior to operation.___

POSSIBILITY:___Someone working on crane or runways.___

PRESENT PROTECTION:

1. Danger sign on main electrical switch.

PROPOSED PROTECTION:

1. In addition to the danger sign, a padlock should be used to inactivate the switch. If several crafts from the repair crews are working on the crane, each craft must place its own lock on the switch.

PREPARED BY: _____

CHECKED BY: _____

SOURCE: W. S. Walker and C. J. Potter, "Worker Participation in Safety through Job Analysis," *Personnel,* Vol. XXXI, No. 2, p. 147.

ingly employed for this purpose. They are particularly effective in presenting convincing, lasting, and easily assimilated lessons. The use of charts and graphs to illustrate safety training lessons is also effective.

4. *Discipline.* Another tool used in safety work is that of disciplinary action. It is particularly applicable in instances in which employees willfully break safety rules or in which an impartial penalty is preestablished as a warning to employees. As an example of the former, some companies assess penalties after analyzing the cause of an accident and

finding that an employee is at fault; the employee can be expected to be more careful only if penalized by such means as a layoff, loss of privileges, or demotion. At times, discharge may be resorted to, but this is an implied recognition that the offender can be cured only by complete removal.

FIGURE 23–7. A Spray Attachment Inserted in the Bomb-Bay Mechanism of an Airplane to Prevent Its Being Activated and Injuring Mechanic Working in the Bomb Bay

Courtesy: Curtiss-Wright Corporation

As an example of the latter, definite penalties may be posted in advance. Thus, it may become a company rule that employees who participate in horseplay with air-pressure guns shall be subject to immediate dismissal. Or those who fail to wear assigned safety goggles or clothes, let us say, shall be laid off for a specified number of days. And those who come to work under the influence of liquor shall be sent home immediately, or in some cases discharged.

5. *The Role of the Supervisor.* Perhaps even more culpable than the individual are the supervisor and his superiors. When management is lax in safety matters, its attitude is reflected all down the line. However, when management is strict in enforcing safety measures, the records improve strikingly. Indeed, workers who, through their own carelessness, have had accidents are often loudest in their criticism of

FIGURE 23–8. Operator Using Respirator While Spray Painting

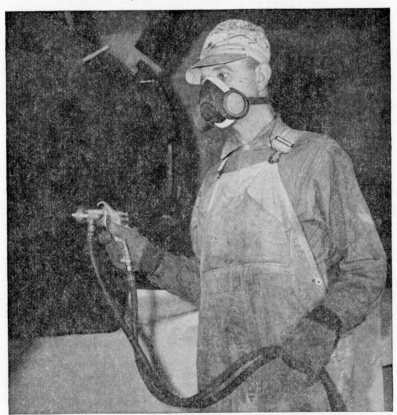

Courtesy: Curtiss-Wright Corporation

supervisors for having failed to make them toe the mark on safety practices. Thus the records, on the one hand, and the complaints of workers, on the other, bear witness that supervision is the key to the problem of accidents. All the work of the engineers and of the safety trainers are of little consequence if supervision is weak in these matters.

Obviously, the answer to this aspect of accidents is the development and maintenance of a high sense of safety-consciousness on the part of supervisors. To begin with, appointments to supervisory positions should not include candidates in whom can be detected a lack of appreciation for or a poor record of accident prevention. Second, all supervisors should be constantly impressed with the importance that top management places upon safety work. Third, not only should supervisors be given specially designed safety courses, but safety suggestions should also be incorporated in all of their training. Fourth, supervisors should be encouraged to show employees by example, by precept, and, indeed, with occasional dramatics, their intense belief in and demand for adherence to safety rules and practices. And last, supervisors who have excellent records for safety should be rewarded appropriately and openly, to prove to them that their efforts are appreciated and so that the recognition receives the benefit of public acclamation. If all these steps are followed, there is little probability that a company will have an excessive accident rate, no matter what other practices it fails to incorporate in its program.

Safety Organization

Finally, good safety work depends upon proper organization. On the one hand, this means that every company should have someone or some department to whom sufficient authority is given to carry out an effective program. In most companies a safety department in the personnel division is the answer to this question. On the other hand, intercompany cooperation and education calls for efforts by industry-wide organization. As a consequence, various industries have established safety committees in their trade associations to investigate unsafe conditions, to suggest methods of improvement, and to develop educational materials.

Perhaps most influential among the outside agencies is the National Safety Council, organized in 1911 as a nonprofit, nonpolitical, cooperative organization. Its purpose is to reduce the number and severity of all kinds of accidents. It covers the fields of industrial safety and health, traffic and transportation, other public safety, school and child safety, and home, farm, and general safety.

The Council serves as a national and international clearinghouse to gather and distribute information about causes of accidents and ways to prevent them. Through its headquarters and regional offices and its state and local units, it carries on a continuous and unified program of accident prevention.

The Council receives safety information from its members and through the constant research of its own staff of statistical, educational, and engineering technicians. These facts and figures are tabulated and broken down to show where, when, how, and why people are injured.

The information shows whether various safety measures are getting results and what needs to be done.

In regard to the particular field of industrial health and safety, the Council investigates and compares ways of making equipment and

FIGURE 23–9. Example of One of a Series of Safety Posters

working conditions safer. It helps the plant management, the foreman, and workers to locate hazards and guard against them, as well as to recognize and prevent occupational diseases. It outlines programs for stimulating and maintaining safety interest both on and off the job.

Safety information is disseminated in various ways. The Council prepares and distributes a wide variety of publications, pamphlets, booklets, posters, and other employer and employee educational materials. It also has worked out and supplies material on a complete accident prevention plan applicable to any industry or organization. In addition, the Council works with newspapers, radio and television stations, magazines, and motion pictures in presenting safety information.

Other outside agencies interested in safety work include such groups as the American Society of Safety Engineers, the International Association of Industrial Accident Boards and Commissioners, and individual industry and trade associations.

QUESTIONS

1. Can you prove that good working conditions are a good investment from a personnel point of view? In your own community, what is the correlation between working conditions and the quality of morale in various plants and businesses?
2. A given employee had a perfect safety record for ten years. One morning, while operating a machine, he cut off part of a finger. How would you go about determining the cause of this accident?
3. Why has statutory legislation been more effective in reducing industrial accidents than common-law rules?
4. What right has a company to prescribe a physical examination as a condition of employment? Is not this an intrusion upon individual privacy?
5. Are such health services as hospital and dental services to members of an employee's immediate family beyond the reasonable obligations of a company? What is your reasoning in this regard?
6. To whom should the medical staff in a given company report? What safeguards must be adopted to protect the professional status of doctors in a company?
7. Define the terms "frequency rate" and "severity rate," as used in connection with accidents. What shortcomings do these measures have?
8. Why is the supervisor a key man in safety work?
9. Why is the role of personnel management growing in safety work? What phases of personnel management are particularly pertinent to safety and accident prevention?
10. How may a company go about protecting itself from the accident-prone employee?

CHAPTER 24

AREAS OF SPECIAL PERSONNEL INTEREST

Scope

In this chapter a group of subjects of special personnel interest is considered. The subjects are taken up because their inclusion elsewhere would have been somewhat strained; yet, to exclude them would be to overlook some significant areas. The subjects include the following:

1. Minority groups
2. Handicapped workers
3. Older employees
4. Women employees
5. Technological innovations

Minority Groups

One of the questions that more and more companies are having to answer is what to do about various minority groups. Until recently, this was largely a voluntary matter. But now, both the federal government and more than a dozen states have passed laws of varying degrees of compulsion requiring employment practices to be free of partiality concerning race, color, creed, and sex.

In this brief survey of discriminatory practices, no attempt is made to evaluate the claims of those who wish to employ whom they please or of those who seek to eliminate discrimination. These are crucial matters but call for more space than is available here. The discussion is limited, therefore, to a description of discriminatory practices, examples of governmental intervention, and steps in introducing minority groups.

1. *Nature of Discrimination.* Discriminatory employment practices may be defined as those practices which result in decisions regarding the employability of people on the basis of race, color, creed, or sex

instead of skill, ability, and capacity. In the United States, Negroes constitute the largest minority group. In lesser degree, and varying with localities, such other groups as Jews, Catholics, Seventh-Day Adventists, Jehovah's Witnesses, Mexicans, Puerto Ricans, and immigrants from various small European countries are included within this category. The charge of discrimination is usually shown by comparing the percentage of employment of a particular group with the percentage of that group in the total population. Thus, in a given community in which Negro workers made up about 10 percent of the working population, a majority of the companies had less than this percentage of Negro workers, or none at all. And of those that had Negro workers, none had relatively equal percentages of Negroes and whites in all kinds of jobs. The Negroes held the poorer and less desirable jobs, were seldom given anything above a minor supervisory position, and were the last to be hired and the first to be laid off. Discrimination has also been noted in respect to wages, seniority rights, and union membership.

Ordinarily, such evidence as the following is cited as proof of discrimination on the part of an employer:

a) The policy of hiring members of a minority group as laborers or in custodial work only, regardless of their particular skills

b) The recruitment of a substantial number of skilled workers from a technical school with Jews and Negroes, but hiring a proportionately small number of Jews and no Negroes

c) Discharge of employees who refuse to salute the American flag or to stand during the playing of the national anthem

d) A preference for employees of a particular race to be entrusted with hiring

e) A refusal to hire a Negro craftsman unless he obtains a permit from a labor organization which bars him from membership on a parity with white craftsmen

f) Hiring under a quota system

2. *Governmental Intervention.* The federal and state governments have concerned themselves with discriminatory practices. The federal government, during World War II, by executive order forbade discrimination in public and private employment, and also ordered the administration of government-sponsored training programs to be free of discrimination. In other executive orders, it was required that contracting agencies of the government insert a clause in all defense contracts prohibiting contractors from discriminating against minorities in employment.

But the most important legislative action came in 1964 with the passage of the Civil Rights Act. This Act includes Title VII, the Equal Employment Opportunities Law, which went into effect in 1965. It prohibits employers in interstate commerce from discriminating against applicants or employees because of race, color, religion, national origin, or sex.

This title makes the following practices of an employer unlawful:

a) To fail or refuse to hire or to discharge a person, or otherwise discriminate with respect to that person's compensation, terms, conditions, or privileges of employment because of race, color, religion, national origin, or sex

b) To limit, segregate, or classify employees in any way that would deprive a person of employment opportunities or otherwise adversely affect an employee's status because of race, color, religion, sex, or national origin

c) To discriminate against a person because of race, color, religion, national origin, or sex in admission to or employment in any apprenticeship, training, or retraining program

d) To print or publish an employment notice or advertisement that indicates any preference, limitation, specification, or discrimination based on race, color, religion, sex, or national origin

e) To discriminate against a job applicant or employee because that person has opposed any unlawful practice under the Act, has made a charge of discrimination, or has testified, assisted, or participated in an investigation, proceeding, or hearing.

It is important to note that the Act makes an exception where religion, sex, or national origin are occupational qualifications reasonably necessary to the normal conduct of an employer's business.

The enforcement of the Act is entrusted to an Equal Employment Opportunity Commission. It works with state and local antidiscrimination agencies, as well as on its own initiative, to act on complaints submitted by job applicants, employees, and employers. If a complaint is not settled by conciliation, it is then taken to a federal court for appropriate consideration and action. The Attorney General of the United States may be invited to intervene in cases of general public importance.

Of the states that have passed such legislation, New York's Law against Discrimination, passed in 1945, is of typical interest. Its purpose is to guarantee every applicant for employment and every employee the right of equal treatment without regard to race, creed, color, or national origin. In administering the law, the State Commission against Discrimination has promulgated the rules that it shall be unlawful:

FIGURE 24–1.   A Guide for Questioning Applicants

INQUIRIES BEFORE HIRING	LAWFUL	UNLAWFUL
1. NAME	a. Maiden name. b. Name used if previously employed under different name.	Inquiry into previous name where it has been changed by court order, or otherwise.
2. ADDRESS	Inquiry into place and length of current and previous addresses.	Specific inquiry into foreign addresses which would indicate national origin.
3. AGE	a. Request proof of age in form of work permit issued by school authorities. b. Require proof of age by birth certificate after being hired.	Require birth certificate or baptismal record.
4. BIRTHPLACE OR NATIONAL ORIGIN		a. Any inquiry into place of birth. b. Any inquiry into place of birth of parents, grandparents or spouse. c. Any other inquiry into national origin.
5. RACE OR COLOR		Any inquiry which would indicate race or color.
6. PHOTOGRAPHS	May be required after hiring for identification purposes.	Request photograph.
7. RELIGION - CREED		a. Any inquiry to indicate or identify religious denomination or customs. b. May not be told this is a Protestant (Catholic or Jewish) organization. c. Request pastor's recommendation or reference.
8. CITIZENSHIP	a. Whether a U. S. citizen. b. If not, whether intends to become one. c. If U. S. residence is legal. d. If spouse is citizen. e. Require proof of citizenship after being hired.	a. If native-born or naturalized. b. Date citizenship received. c. Proof of citizenship. d. Whether parents or spouse are native-born or naturalized.
9. EDUCATION	a. Inquiry into what academic, professional, or vocational schools attended. b. Inquiry into language skills, such as reading and writing of foreign languages.	a. Any inquiry asking specifically the nationality, racial, or religious affiliation of a school. b. Inquiry as to what is mother tongue or how foreign language ability was acquired.
10. RELATIVES	a. Inquiry into name, relationship, and address of person to be notified in case of accident.	Any inquiry about a relative which is unlawful to ask an applicant.
11. ORGANIZATION	a. Inquiry into organization memberships, excluding any organization, the name or character of which indicates the race, creed, color, religion, or national origin of its members. b. What offices are held, if any.	Inquiry into all clubs and organizations where membership is held.
12. MILITARY SERVICE	a. Inquiry into service in U. S. Armed Forces. b. Rank attained. c. Which branch of service. d. Require military discharge papers after being hired.	a. Inquiry into military service in armed service of any other country. b. Request military discharge papers.
13. WORK SCHEDULE	Inquiry into willingness to work required work-schedule.	Any inquiry into willingness to work any particular religious holiday.

I. FEDERAL DEFENSE CONTRACTS: Employers having federal defense contracts are exempt only to the extent that otherwise prohibited inquiries are required by federal law for security purposes.

II. ANY INQUIRY IS FORBIDDEN WHICH, ALTHOUGH NOT SPECIFICALLY LISTED AMONG THE ABOVE, IS DESIGNED TO ELICIT INFORMATION AS TO NATIONAL ORIGIN, RACE, COLOR, CREED, RELIGION, OR ANCESTRY IN VIOLATION OF THE LAW.

a) For an employer to:
   (1) Discriminate in hiring, upgrading, or discharging employees because of race, creed, color, or national origin
   (2) Ask questions before hiring which directly or indirectly would disclose race, creed, color, or national origin
   (3) Print or circulate matter which directly or indirectly indicates discrimination because of race, creed, color, or origin
   (4) Discriminate against anyone who files a complaint or testifies in connection with the Law against Discrimination

b) For a union to:
   (1) Discriminate against members or applicants for membership because of race, creed, color, or national origin
   (2) Discriminate against employers on the same grounds

c) For an employment agency to:
   (1) Discriminate in registering or referring applicants
   (2) Ask questions before hiring which directly or indirectly would disclose race, creed, color, or origin
   (3) Disclose such information to employers
   (4) Print or circulate matter which directly or indirectly expresses discrimination because of race, color, creed, or origin
   (5) Discriminate against anyone who files a complaint or testifies in connection with the Law against Discrimination

d) For employees to:
   (1) Offer resistance to the hiring of anyone on grounds of race, creed, color, or national origin

e) For anyone to:
   (1) Compel, help, or incite or to attempt acts would lead to discrimination on account of race, creed, color, or national origin

As examples of what may or may not be lawful, Figure 24–1 illustrates the care which must be used in making specific inquiries of applicants in a state where a fair employment practices law has been enacted.

3. *Introducing Minority Groups.* In those instances in which companies have employed members of minority groups after strict enforcement of policies of exclusion, success attended the efforts only of those which followed a carefully developed policy of assimilation. This was necessary because the opposition of the existing working force had to be overcome and the natural belligerence of the minority members had to be prevented from coming to the surface.

The specific steps which have been found helpful in facilitating introduction of any minority group include the following:

a) Careful selection of the representative of the minority group to be introduced; characteristics of personality, emotional stability, and understanding of obstacles to be met are as significant as technical job qualifications.

b) Thorough indoctrination of the representative of what he is likely to encounter in going into the working situation and how he must handle himself therein.

c) Careful selection of the area or department into which introduction will be made; it is usually better to start slowly and thus show other areas that the introduction presents no unusual difficulties.

d) Counsel key employees regarding the contemplated introduction, indicate why it is necessary, and gain preliminary willingness to give it a trial.

e) It also seems better to initiate the program with only one representative, so that no group of minority members can form at the outset; after the ice is broken, more than one at a time can be employed.

f) Whether or not separate toilet facilities should be provided is debatable, although better practice here seems to be against separate facilities.

g) Follow up reactions closely to ward off trouble and to tackle unforeseen difficulties or obstacles.

Handicapped Workers

The handicapped worker also represents a problem that industry in general must face if charity is not to be the answer. Whether crippled, defaced, partially or totally blind, deaf, dumb, or otherwise handicapped, this group contains a source of labor which many companies have found to be very desirable. The case for handicapped workers is summed up very well in the following instructions which one office of the United States Employment Service issued to its employer service representatives, whose job it is, among others, to find jobs for handicapped workers:

TECHNIQUES IN SELLING THE EMPLOYER ON USE OF HANDICAPPED

a) In approaching an employer in behalf of a handicapped applicant the Counselor or Employment Service Representative never mentions the handicap first, as "I've got a one-armed man here, but he can do the work"; rather, he stresses the man's good points, building up in the employer a desire to hire the man. Then he can mention the limitation casually, adding that it does not hinder the applicant's performance on the job.

b) The Counselor and ESR use a specific name for the disability such as "lame" or "hard of hearing" rather than a general term like "handicapped," "disabled," or "a limited person," since the specific term does not produce a mental image of a person with a more serious handicap than that of the applicant and is less likely to arouse prejudice against him.

c) The Counselor shows by physical analysis of his applicant and physical-demands analysis of the employer's job that the applicant's limitation is not a work limitation. Thus, the employer may be led to conclude that he will hire qualified handicapped applicants for any jobs they can perform.

d) The Counselor or ESR stresses advantages in the employment of workers with certain types of handicaps for specific jobs; i.e., deaf workers may prove more efficient under noisy working conditions than persons with normal hearing.

e) He emphasizes the fact that disabled persons usually put forth more effort to hold their jobs, are less likely to leave their employment, and seem to be less prone to accidents.

f) The use of references from previous employers is often helpful because they cite specific examples of successful performance.

g) The Counselor or ESR develops a dependable relationship with the employer by referring only suitable applicants, whether handicapped or nonhandicapped. If this is done, the employer is more likely to accept the recommendations of the Counselor or ESR.

ANSWERS TO POSSIBLE EMPLOYER OBJECTIONS TO HIRING OF HANDICAPPED WORKERS

Counselors and ESRs should be prepared to reply courteously and intelligently to the objections against hiring handicapped workers which will be raised by employers.

a) *Objection.* The employment of handicapped persons means higher accident cost and compensation insurance rates.

Answer. Two factors are involved in a satisfactory answer to this question. First, employers usually assume that a handicapped person is more liable to a second injury than nonhandicapped persons. Various studies have found this not to be true in all cases.

Second, placement workers must be thoroughly familiar with the workmen's compensation law in their state in order to inform the employer of any special provisions which may have been made covering second-injury benefits for handicapped persons. In addition to any special provisions for second-injury benefits, it should be pointed out that the rate of compensation insurance for any employer is based upon the relation of accident cost to the total payroll.

b) *Objection.* The employment of handicapped persons will strain sick benefit or group insurance plans.

Answer. As regards sick benefits, the assumption here is that the handicapped are more liable to illness, injury, or accident than are nonhandicapped persons. This is not supported by evidence because, for example, in one study it was found that 60 percent of the nonhandicapped were absent during the period, while only 53 percent of the handicapped were absent.

In group life insurance, the rate is based solely upon the age and sex of the employees and not upon physical conditions. Companies issuing such insurance say that physical disabilities are not considered.

c) *Objection.* Handicapped workers are frequently absent because of weather conditions or illness. They cannot work regular hours.

Answer. This is similar to objection (*a*). The same answer may be used. Moreover, where the interviewer requires a medical statement to assist in determining the restrictions necessary to safeguard the health of the applicant, the employer who does not normally require examinations actually has better protection in employing handicapped workers than in employing other applicants who are not under medical supervision.

d) Objection. Disabled persons are not so efficient as normal workers.

Answer. In answering this question, the Counselor or ESR should stress that handicapped persons are referred only to jobs where they can compete satisfactorily with nonhandicapped workers. The interviewer has selected the applicant for the job because analysis of his capacities reveals he can meet the physical demands of the job.

e) Objection. Handicapped workers cannot be shifted so easily to other jobs in slack times.

Answer. The answer to this question must be determined by what the "other jobs" are. Within the scope of the physical qualification of the applicant, the answer is "yes"; otherwise "no," and no general answer can or should be given since everything depends upon the individual case.

In addition, in slack times, when the employer, after careful study, finds no suitable position open to which he can transfer the handicapped worker, he should feel free to let him go as he would any other worker in a similar position.

f) Objection. Other employees do not like to see them around; they make the office look like a charity concern; customers do not like to see them or ask them for service.

Answer. This is an expression of the social attitude which for centuries has denied handicapped persons an equal opportunity to develop their capacities. The feeling that other employees object probably looms larger in theory than in fact. When the handicapped person has a normal attitude, most people will become accustomed to him. The sales manager of a very successful New York department store uses a cane because of a limp, and finds no difficulty handling staff or customers.

g) Objection. Crippled persons need special attention; they expect special advantages and consideration from the employer.

Answer. There may be handicapped persons who have not been taught to develop self-reliance and who need special supervision in making a vocational adjustment. On the other hand, there are many disabled persons who have made good, who have been years with the same employer, who have been promoted to responsible positions, and who get along well with other people.

h) Objection. We provide for our own employees who become disabled and cannot, therefore, employ others.

Answer. The answer to this objection is that the applicants are placed on the basis of qualifications and are seeking jobs, not as charity, but on a competitive basis which is economically sound from the employer's point of view. Furthermore, if a person is disabled between jobs, or before his first job, such a policy would tend to keep him out of the labor market permanently, depriving employers of much qualified labor.

i) *Objection.* The entrance physical examination required by our company rules out all persons with physical disabilities.

Answer. The physical examination is commendable if used in a discretionary way to assure that applicants have no disabilities which prevent proper job performance, that they are in good health, and as a means of protecting the employer against future damage claims, such as for hernia which may have existed prior to the time of employment. On the other hand, to use the physical examination as a means of eliminating all but "perfect" physical specimens is an unfair discrimination against many who are in every way qualified for the job to be filled.

The Older Employee

The older employee during the depression years of the thirties threatened to become a serious problem to industry and society. Layoffs of older workers were exceptionally high. Younger workers were preferred for their future potential as well as current usefulness. Moreover, some employers may have felt that pension costs would be less if the older workers were laid off. Hence, one often heard during these years that the older worker was not as good an investment as the younger worker.

The experience of the war years and the removal of the fear of excessive social security payments have proved rather conclusively that the older worker is no more a problem than other groups of workers. Indeed, the record of the older worker seems to be better than that of younger groups. Whereas older employees cannot perform the heavy work that younger employees can, this is offset by the following:

1. Greater versatility, with an ability to handle a variety of jobs
2. Greater dependability, with a better record of absenteeism
3. Fewer accidents
4. Less volatile; hence, more stable
5. Fewer grievances and fewer occasions for disciplinary action

Thus, older workers make up in steady workmanship and craftsmanship what they may lack in ability to spurt for short periods or to handle heavy jobs. Inasmuch as our population pattern shows a change toward a higher percentage of older people, the place of the older worker in industry must be given more favorable attention. It is estimated that by 1970, two out of every five workers will be in the 45-or-older age group.

Employment of older workers should invariably be handled with thought, as should all employment matters. To begin with, a long-range program of hiring will serve to build a well-balanced force, so that a predominance of age groups of any bracket will not result. In the second place, a variety of procedures may be established for the older workers. Among these are the following:

1. Review of occupations best suited to accommodate employees of advanced years
2. Review of occupations that lend themselves with some modification to the accommodation of employees of advanced years
3. Training to increase and prolong the productivity of older workers within a given occupation
4. Training for other occupations more suited to those of advanced years
5. Adoption of a pension plan as a bridge between active employment and retirement
6. Arranging the pay of the employee in keeping with his productiveness and charging the balance to the pension account

Women Employees

Women as employees deserve the attention of personnel management because of their increasing numbers, misconceptions about their adaptability in business, and legal regulations. First, as to their numerical importance, the trend has been steadily upward. At one time in the United States, women were not hired in industry or business. Now the number of women working is estimated to be around 27 million. By 1970 the number is expected to increase to 30 million, the distribution of which by age groups is shown in Figure 24–2. Thus, about a third of the working force is made up of women. Obviously, the personnel aspects of such an important class deserve careful attention. Suggestions along these lines may be noted by commenting upon physical, mental, emotional, social, economic, and legal aspects of women employees.

1. *Physical Aspects.* Physically speaking, women are superior to men on some jobs and at a disadvantage in others. They are usually better at work requiring finger dexterity because their fingers are longer but their thumbs shorter than those of men. They are better on jobs that require circular rather than straight motions because they are relatively more knock-elbowed than men. And they are better on jobs calling for walking and picking up materials because their legs are relatively shorter than those of men. They do not possess, however, the relative physical strength of men. But industry has found that hiring weight lifters, whether men or women, is too expensive and that, therefore, such tasks are better assigned to machines.

2. *Mental Characteristics.* Concerning mental differences, women workers in general have no cause to feel inferior to the men. Studies have disclosed no significant differences. The woman worker is,

on the average, just as intelligent as the average male worker. This refers, of course, to native intelligence.

When it comes to acquired knowledge, the male worker has an advantage over the woman worker, but the superiority is not inherent. This means that with the same study and the same opportunity to

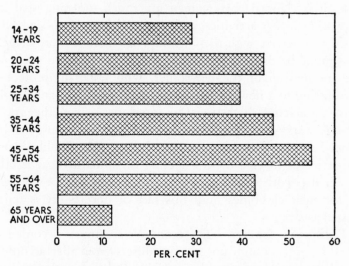

FIGURE 24–2. Percent of Women in Each Age Group Expected to Be in the Labor Force in 1970

SOURCE: United States Department of Labor, *Manpower—Challenge of the 1960's* (Washington, D.C.: U.S. Government Printing Office, 1960), p. 12.

acquire knowledge of technical matters, the knowledge of women employees would parallel that of men employees. Two deductions are worth drawing from this condition. First, men should generally be given preference to women on jobs in which technical knowledge is required. Second, the preference should be removed in cases in which individual women have caught up with the men.

3. *Emotional Aspects.* The emotional responses of women workers have been a subject of controversy. Most supervisors would say that they are more emotional than men on the job. However, there are no scientific studies which support this contention. Men may be more accustomed to the emotional outbursts of men, such as swearing, and not to the emotional outbursts of women, such as tears. But both are outbursts.

Women are newer to some jobs in business and industry, so they may be more sensitive and fearful. In such a stage, obviously there may be a tendency to react faster emotionally. But without doubt, as women become adjusted to their working environment, they are relatively as stable (or unstable) as men. The moral is that a temporary condition should not be construed to be a permanent trait that always requires special treatment.

4. Social Characteristics. Another characteristic that is considered to weigh more heavily in the case of women is that of social or group relationships. These relations may take a variety of angles. For example, it is claimed that women are much too interested in their fellow workers, their activities, and other subjects of gossip. All this is presumed to interfere with their work. That there is more or less truth in this cannot be denied. But again, such activities are evidence of a defense mechanism of the newcomer, who hopes to protect herself while adjusting to a new environment. And as long as any employee is given to understand that she is an interloper—even the gray-haired veteran of twenty-five years' service—she will act to protect her job.

Somewhat similarly, women employees get "clubby" or form groups. It serves to give them a feeling of solidarity that is otherwise lacking in the work situation. The women may not be aware of the reason for their clubbiness, but this fact of uncertainty is fairly well recognized as a cause.

5. Economic Aspects. The economic treatment accorded women in business often, though not always, differs from that accorded men. Women have, for a long time, been paid at lower rates than men for the same jobs. This practice has been condoned on the ground that women cannot work as effectively as men, or are not so dependable, or cannot perform all the duties that men can. When these charges are factually true in particular situations, the justice of lower compensation is indisputable. The difference in compensation, then, is ascribable not to differences in sex but to differences in capacities.

The trend in the economic treatment of women in business is, however, toward equality with men, both voluntarily and by legal compulsion. More and more companies are adopting the policy of equal pay for equal work, whether they have to or not. Some companies follow only the letter of this policy by claiming that women, even on the same jobs as men, do not do equal work because they must have help in lifting parts, adjusting machines, and meeting emergencies. But on the whole, the adoption of this rule usually leads to its being followed in the full spirit, sooner or later. Moreover, with the passage in 1963 by the federal government of the Equal Pay Act, women doing the same kind of work as men must be paid the same rates.

6. *Legal Aspects.*[1] Legislation relating to women in business is sometimes equalizing in effect and sometimes restrictive, as compared to that relating to men. As already noted, the Civil Rights Act of 1964 prohibits discrimination against women in employment on the basis of sex, and the Equal Pay Act of 1963 provides for equality of economic treatment. But it must be noted, as cited below, that some states have passed legislation which restricts the work or conditions under which work can be performed by women. Not every state has enacted legislation in each of the categories, and the standards vary widely, but the principal subjects regulated are as follows:[2]

1. *Minimum Wages.* Either by statute or by state wage boards, the base below which rates cannot fall is established for occupations or industries.
2. *Equal Pay.* Such regulations prohibit discrimination in pay because of sex, the principle being that the pay rate should be based on the job, and not on the sex of the worker.
3. *Hours of Work.* This category has reference to such aspects as maximum daily and weekly hours, days of rest, meal times, rest periods, and night work.
4. *Industrial Homework.* Regulations of this type establish restrictions or prohibitions on work done in the home in order to safeguard minimum-wage rate regulations.
5. *Employment before and after Childbirth.* This type of regulation establishes time periods before and after childbirth during which employment is prohibited.
6. *Occupational Limitations.* This category refers to occupations or industries in which employment is restricted or prohibited because working conditions are considered to be hazardous or injurious to health, safety, or morals.
7. *Miscellaneous.* These regulations refer to employment standards and plant facilities such as seats, weight lifting, lunchrooms, dressing rooms, rest rooms, and toilet rooms.

Technological Innovations

Of unique interest to personnel management is the increased tempo of technological innovations in production, offices, and distribution. Machines are replacing men and calling for changed skills of needed labor. Attention is directed here (1) to a brief description of new

---

[1] It may be noted that similar types of regulations are also usually found in many states and cities covering the employment of minors, whether male or female.

[2] United States Department of Labor, *1960 Handbook on Women Workers,* Women's Bureau Bulletin No. 275 (Washington, D.C.: U.S. Government Printing Office, 1960), pp. 121–32.

technology and (2) to a summary of the impact upon personnel management and labor.

In the past decade the trend toward mechanized processes has been accelerated. In particular, more and more operations are being automated. Processing of parts, material handling, assembly work, and inspection operations are being highly mechanized and made technologically self-regulating. Such machine control of machines has been made possible by "cybernetics." This is a coined term referring to electronic equipment by which mechanical processes can be automatically and continuously controlled, checked, and corrected. Carried over to the office, such equipment in the form of data-processing components makes it possible to process mechanically all types of quantitative and verbalized information. Even in such marketing areas as retailing, warehousing, and associated office work, automation and computers have made substantial inroads.

The impact upon work is startling. The machines can do routine work faster, more accurately, without tiring, and at less cost than can the human workers. As an example, office work that previously took weeks and even months can be completed in hours. But the machines do displace some workers and do call for new skills.

The matter of unemployment, to look at this first, is indeed challenging. To be sure, in the long run, the history of technological improvements shows that more jobs are created and society's standard of living is increased. But in the short run—and man must live in the "here and now"—technological unemployment causes severe losses to some. To meet this problem, a number of plans are being pursued, as follows:

1. Some companies agree not to lay off employees displaced by machines. These companies (*a*) rely upon natural quits, deaths, etc., to take care of the excess needs; (*b*) retrain employees for other jobs; and (*c*) expect expansion of business to utilize displaced personnel.
2. Some companies have more or less liberal severance pay plans whereby anyone displaced is given, in some cases, up to five years' pay.
3. The manpower retraining program of the federal government has compensation and training provisions for those who lose their jobs because of technological change.
4. Unions have bargained for financial and training benefits for displaced personnel, as well as for shortened hours, as a means of spreading available work over as many people as possible.

On the positive side, technological change will place more burdens upon personnel management. To begin with, the skills of the work force in any given company will be much higher. Drudgery and monotony will be minimized, and jobs will be more interesting. Personnel will be of a higher caliber, more alert, better trained, and more highly educated. Consequently, the job of human relations will have to be on a higher plane.

Briefly, the following shows the variety of subjects which will have to be reexamined or reemphasized:

1. Automation and cybernetics involve complicated equipment and processes. The need is great for highly skilled technical and maintenance personnel. Selection and placement techniques must be perfected to assist in securing capable employees who can operate such plants proficiently.
2. Redesign of plants will call for completely new job and man specifications. Job analysis and job studies will be prime necessities if selection, placement, and training are to be conducted successfully.
3. The importance of training will increase. More people will require longer periods of training. Engineers and other technical personnel will need supplementary training, maintenance workers will require additional skills and better technical background, and operative employees will have to convert to maintenance and control skills.
4. Automation will not eliminate the need of good relations with organized labor. Indeed, its cooperation will be needed in order to gain acceptance of layoffs and job changes and transfers.
5. The problem of compensation will have to be reviewed again all the way from basic theory to specific wage plans. The basis of incentives is likely to change from that of individual effort to that of overall results. Undoubtedly, too, supervisors will be included in the incentive plans.
6. It may be necessary to change from a line-and-staff type of organization to a functionalized scheme. The specialists who are required in such an operation must have a more direct control of operations.
7. Employee attitude changes must be expected. Better employee communications, idea sharing, and education are indicated. This will all place a bigger burden not only on the personnel department in designing better plans but also on the executives who must carry them out.
8. Automation should tend to reduce safety hazards, because machines will do the work, and because such devices as television can be used to view dangerous operations.
9. Better housekeeping will also be required in the automatic factory and office.

QUESTIONS

1. What is a minority group in industry? Upon what theory are laws passed that aim to prevent unfair employment practices?
2. Are discriminatory practices limited to race, color, and creed? Explain.
3. Some employers contend that they have no objection to hiring such minority

groups as Negroes but that many of their employees do so object. Is this a legitimate excuse? Explain.

4. In what respects are handicapped workers a problem in industry? In what respects are they not a problem?

5. Relate the contributions that job analysis, job placement, and job training make to the solution of the handicapped in industry.

6. In what respects have older workers proved themselves superior to younger employees? What policies should be followed in connection with older workers?

7. It is claimed that women cannot perform physical work on an equal basis with men. Should either they or men perform such tasks? Explain.

8. Are there any significant mental and emotional differences between men and women for working purposes? If not, why do men often complain that women are prone to break into tears when criticized?

9. What is meant by cybernetics, and what is its effect likely to be upon personnel management?

10. What problems will have to be solved when a business converts any of its processes to automation?

CHAPTER 25

UNION-MANAGEMENT RELATIONS

Scope of Discussion

Personnel management seeks to establish effective and satisfactory relations with employees. In general, its programs meet with relative success in most companies. Yet, from time to time, conflicts of lesser or greater degree disturb relations in all companies. "Labor relations" refers to the efforts to maintain satisfactory accommodations and to resolve disagreements between employees and management. Implied in the term are organizational arrangements, practices, and policies employed in such efforts.

A detailed examination of these efforts is undertaken in the two chapters that follow under the headings of "Handling Grievances" and "Disciplinary Action," respectively. Inasmuch as organized unions play a significant role in these matters, attention is first directed in this chapter to them, under the following headings:

1. General background of unionization
2. The Labor Management Relations Act
3. Stages of union-management relations

GENERAL BACKGROUND OF UNIONIZATION

The conditions under which and the stages through which management and unions conduct themselves are placed in better perspective by first viewing a number of pertinent aspects of unions themselves. Of importance are the following:

1. The role of unions
2. Historical aspects of union growth
3. Legal status of unions
4. Types of unions

The Role of Unions

In simple terms, an employee sells his skills, time, and willingness to work. The terms of this sales contract presumably are arranged by equals, subject to a free, competitive market. Such presumptions are unrealistic when a particular employee is arrayed against the average employer. To be sure, the employee can look elsewhere if he does not like an employer's offer. And the employee may have the weight of the labor market on his side when the demand and supply factors are favorable, as in a prosperity period.

Generally speaking, however, the employer usually has the advantages of better knowledge of the market, of the power to withhold employment, and of the economic strength to withstand the pressures of a particular individual. From a bargaining point of view, therefore, the employer in such instances is superior to the employee. And presumably, he has not been above arranging terms of sale more favorable to himself.

Obviously, the employee cannot be blamed if he seeks means of balancing the powers of bargaining. His recourse has been to join forces with his fellow workers. In short, in union there is strength. As a result, the power of the employer is balanced—and indeed, is sometimes outweighed—so that he must accede to wishes of his employees he might otherwise reject.

In bargaining, then, the role of the unions is to balance the economic power of the employer. In its simplest form, this role is played within the confines of a given company. The employees, through their elected representatives, negotiate the terms of employment with the company officials. The agreement thus reached by "equals" becomes the accepted mode of conduct between the parties for a designated period of time.

Much more complicated roles are assumed by unions (and by management) to achieve their goals. The unions (like management) seek the favor of public opinion, of governmental agencies, and of political parties. Legislation, for example, is sought which would protect and enhance the rights of labor, as will be noted in the next section. Moreover, individual unions combine to gain greater power.

So the union is more than an economic institution. It has political characteristics, seeking to use political power to influence governmental agencies in its immediate interests and sometimes on matters far removed from union-management relations. Indeed, at times, unions have been on the verge of forming a political labor party with a view to gaining their economic ends.

The core role of the union is, however, that of collective bargaining. Employees organize and elect representatives who bargain with management for the benefit of the employees. "Collective bargaining" is more complex than this. It is difficult to define because the extent, degree, and kind of bargaining and of "collective" effort depend upon the time, place, and parties of the bargaining process. The subjects over which labor and management will bargain also affect the definitions, and the methods and organizations used in bargaining powers vary from case to case and from time to time.

But broadly speaking, "collective bargaining" refers to a process by which employers, on the one hand, and representatives of employees, on the other, attempt to arrive at agreements covering the conditions under which employees will contribute and be compensated for their services.

To those who deplore the use of the word "bargaining" as indicative of a struggle between employer and employee, the relationship would be better stated by calling the process "collective cooperation." The role of the union becomes one of a beneficial and understanding partner.

Historical Aspects of Union Growth

Although labor unions have been in existence in the United States since the Revolutionary period, they have not been a significant factor in labor relations generally until recently. Prior to the Civil War, a few sporadic efforts resulted successfully in the formation of labor unions. Small-scale manufacturing was not conducive to and legal hindrances obstructed expansion of such organizations. After the Civil War, from which time modern industrial growth may be considered to date, labor agitation became particularly violent. Of particular interest in this regard was the Noble Order of the Knights of Labor, which flourished briefly but spectacularly during the two decades following the Civil War. Its programs and ambitions, however, were beyond its resources and the opposition industry could muster. As a consequence, it sputtered into insignificance and then extinction during the late 1880's.

This decade is important, however, because it marked the formation of the American Federation of Labor (AFL) in 1886. This group grew to the point that in the early 1930's, it stood as the country's major labor organization. In 1935 a number of unions affiliated with the AFL became dissatisfied with its organizing and jurisdictional policies, and withdrew from it. The new group chose the name Committee of Industrial Organization, which was subsequently changed to Congress of Industrial Organizations (CIO). In 1955 the two decided to join forces in a single group, the American Federation of Labor–Congress of Industrial Organizations (AFL–CIO). Present estimates of union membership of this group and independent unions vary from 15 to 18 million. This constitutes about a quarter of the working population. Union membership is relatively concentrated in the industrial areas of business. The office, sales, technical, and professional areas are not well represented, except in isolated cases.

Legal Changes and Status

The answer to why unions grow must be sought in large part in terms of legal strength. Thus, until the thirties, labor unions could gain little momentum because of the legal bulwarks erected against them. In the first place, business by and large had little to do with unions as long as their right to organize and bargain collectively was a matter of mutual consent and not compulsion. Second, legal injunctions could easily be obtained by business to halt a variety of union activities such as strikes, boycotts, picketing, and efforts to increase membership. And third, business could insist upon making employees, as a condition of employment, agree not to join unions (the yellow-dog contract).

Changes in the federal segment favoring unionization, however, started to come after the impact of the depression of the early thirties. The first important change came in 1932 with the passage of the Norris–La Guardia Act, which placed severe restrictions upon the use of court injunctions intended to curb or limit union activities, and outlawed the yellow-dog contracts. Then, in 1933, the National Industrial Recovery Act gave employees the right to organize and bargain collectively, and prohibited employers from using the yellow-dog contract. Union growth, as a consequence, accelerated.

Although the Act was short-lived, being declared unconstitutional on May 27, 1935, Congress passed the National Labor Relations Act, which was signed by the President on June 27, 1935. This Act not only gave employees the right to organize but made it mandatory for employers to bargain collectively with representatives of employees, if they so desired. The legal basis for collective bargaining was thus and finally laid in the United States. Subsequent federal legislation added protective measures in unionized relationships to both employees and employers. The Labor Management Relations Act in 1947 and the Labor-Management and Disclosure Act in 1959 are specific cases in point.

Types of Unions

It is now appropriate to note the different organizational forms used to carry on collective bargaining. Of particular interest are differences between representation plans and unions, between craft and industrial unions, and between miscellaneous groups, independent unions, and affiliated unions.

1. *Representation Plans.* The employee representation plan was once viewed as a promising contributor to better labor relations. Under this plan, employee committees were formed at the behest of management to submit the views and complaints of employees to management.

The National Labor Relations Act, as amended by the Labor Management Relations Act, made it unlawful, however, for a company to interfere with or assist in the organization of employees intended for purposes of collective bargaining. Where employee representation plans were in effect for such purposes, they became illegal because their formation had been assisted by management, in which case they had to be either disbanded or reorganized independently by employees. They had to operate independently of the employer. When so organized, the status of a legal union is attained.

2. *Craft and Industrial Unions.* The union is, therefore, the major vehicle by which employees bargain collectively with management. Although the one shades into the other in varying degrees in particular unions, the major types are the craft and the industrial.

The craft union is one in which membership is restricted to employees for a particular trade or craft. The employees may or may not be employed by the same company. For example, carpenters in a given community, irrespective of who employs them, may belong to the same union. Or all the carpenters of a given company may form a craft union and restrict membership to carpenters of the given company. The craft unions are older, more settled, and presumably more attentive to the particular problems and needs of given classes of workers.

The American Federation of Labor was essentially an association of craft unions. Each "local" or union of craftsmen was represented through a sequence of city, state, regional, and national craftsmen organizations, which, in turn, were affiliated with the AFL. The latter group acted as the agency that set national policies for the craft unions and served to protect the labor movement from influences beyond the control of local units. It was subject, however, to the regulation of the local units through the system of state and national representatives, elected by the locals to serve on the boards of the large organizational units.

Different in structure from the craft union is the so-called "industrial" union, which includes all types of workers in its ranks. Thus, all occupations would be eligible for membership in the same industrial union. Because of this policy of inclusion, it is sometimes referred to as the "vertical" type as opposed to the "horizontal" type of stratification employed by the craft union.

The CIO was the chief exponent of the industrial union. It came into existence largely because of dissatisfaction with the alleged failure of the AFL to pursue vigorously the organization of the mass of workers in American industry who had no particular skills to qualify them as craftsmen. The industrial unions contended that the crafts catered only to the "elite" of labor, disregarded the millions of workers who belonged to no craft, and had grown stagnant and conservative, if not outright reactionary.

These arguments have not been enough either to keep craft and industrial unions pure in form or to keep the two from combining. There are craft groups which include more than one craft and industrial unions that consist predominantly of one occupation. Moreover, the AFL and the CIO found it desirable to combine forces into the AFL–CIO. Presumably, the labor movement could be better served by bringing all types of workers under one roof. At the local level, craft and industrial distinctions may be retained; but unified direction is provided at the top policy-making level.

3. *Miscellaneous Types.* In addition to the AFL–CIO, a number of other unions are of interest. The railroad industry has long been a stronghold of the union movement. It is organized largely on a craft basis, with its various brotherhoods of trainmen, engineers, and other classes of railroad workers. The United Mine Workers (UMW), once led by the militant John L. Lewis, are also deserving of separate mention. They returned to the fold of the AFL after playing a leading role in the formation of the CIO, but are now acting independently. This union, made up of a miscellany of industrial workers as well as of miners, has been in the van of many drives to gain new and added emoluments for labor. And its leadership has displayed cunning in timing drives and choosing strategy so that success has attended its efforts much, much more than failure. Of interest, too, are the strong Teamsters Union and the organizations in the bakery fields which have separated from the AFL–CIO because of disagreements on ethical standards of union conduct.

4. *Affiliation versus Independence.* Finally, there is a group of unions that act independently and are not associated with any national group. For this reason, they are called independent unions. Ordinarily, they are formed by employees of a given company, exclusively from

which members may be selected, for the purpose of dealing solely with the company in question. Sometimes, they take members from a group of companies in a given locality. When an independent union is formed to bargain with a particular company, it may also be called a company union. This connotation must be distinguished from company-dominated independent unions, which are outlawed by the Labor Management Relations Act.

THE LABOR MANAGEMENT RELATIONS ACT

Scope of Act

As already noted, the Labor Management Relations Act (LMRA, or Taft-Hartley Act), which amended the National Labor Relations Act (NLRA) of 1935, is the federal legislation currently significant in organized relations and collective bargaining. It is based upon the power of Congress to regulate interstate commerce and applies, therefore, only to businesses which enter into or affect interstate commerce. In particular, Congress seeks through this law to reduce interferences to the free flow of such commerce caused by labor-management disputes. To this end, labor is given rights of organizing and collective bargaining. If management transgresses these rights, it is guilty, by definition of the Act, of unfair labor practices and is therefore subject to punitive measures. On the other hand, management is provided with certain protections against certain practices of labor organizations stated to be unfair.

The machinery of the Taft-Hartley Act has one purpose—to facilitate the process of collective bargaining. In other words, it does not prevent disputes or settle them. It serves to bring labor and management together so that they may resolve their difficulties and arrive at agreements as to how they shall work together. It requires all parties to bargain and confer in good faith.

If management is to conduct its labor relations affairs correctly, it must be aware of the prescriptions of this Act in regard to the rights of various parties, coverage, and modes of operation.

Rights of Parties

The LMRA, or the Taft-Hartley Act, as it is often called, establishes rights not only for employees but also for employers and for unions. Interferences with any of these rights may be construed as an unfair labor practice, with relief therefrom, or penalties, as noted in a later section.

Unfair labor practices of employers, as defined by the NLRA and the LMRA, include the following:

1. Interference, restraint, or coercion of employees in the exercise of their right freely to organize
2. Domination and interference with the formation or administration of a labor organization
3. Encouragement or discouragement of membership in a labor organization by discrimination in regard to hire or tenure
4. Discrimination because of filing charges or giving testimony under the Act
5. Refusal to bargain collectively with properly chosen representatives of the employees

The LMRA added protections for employees from certain union actions or relationships. The Act outlawed the *closed shop,* in which all workers eligible to belong to a union must be members in good standing and new workers must become, or be, union members at time of hiring. The *union shop,* in which all employees must join a union after hiring, is permissible only if the union can gain such a concession through the process of collective bargaining. Moreover, the Act leaves it to the option of the states, of which about twenty have so acted, to outlaw the closed and union shops, under the so-called *right-to-work* laws. The Act also permits deduction of dues from an employee's pay check and payment of the deductions by the employer to the union only if this is authorized in writing by the employee (the so-called *checkoff*). Employees need not pay excessive initiation fees. But nonpayment of initiation fees and dues is the only reason why a union can ask for a member's dismissal. And the Act permits an employee to take his grievances through the union up to management, or do it alone if he so desires, but any settlements reached individually must not undermine the union contract.

The employer has been given rights under the LMRA regarding protection from practices which might be unfair to him, as follows:

1. He may express himself freely about labor matters so long as no threat or coercion to employees is implied.
2. He may discharge, without obligation to rehire, employees who engage in illegal strikes, such as those intended to force employers to refuse to handle the products of another producer (the secondary boycott).
3. He may ask the National Labor Relations Board (NLRB) for a vote to be taken to determine whether or not a union claiming to be recognized as the bargaining agent has a majority of employees signed up.
4. He must bargain in good faith, but can now insist that the union also do so.

5. He can sue unions in the federal courts as entities, whose agents by their acts can be held liable.
6. He can set in force a sixty-day "cooling-off" period before a strike can be legally called, when a contract is due to terminate or be modified.
7. He is freed from "featherbedding," or rules requiring that pay be given for work not done.
8. He may refuse to bargain with unions representing supervisors.

The Taft-Hartley Act has undoubtedly imposed certain responsibilities upon unions, as to both management and workers. On the other hand, practically all the rights unions gained under the Wagner Act are still retained. To begin with, employees retained all rights to organize and bargain collectively through representatives of their own choosing. Moreover, the union has the right, under proper conditions, to:

1. Ask the NLRB for recognition elections
2. Ask the employer to bargain in good faith
3. Represent all employees who are eligible to vote
4. Maintain its status for one year without fear of jurisdictional disputes
5. Represent all employees who ask its assistance in processing grievances
6. File charges with the NLRB against unfair labor practices
7. Appeal to various government boards or the courts
8. Call strikes

Coverage of the Act

Not all companies and employees are subject to the provisions of the Act. There are three major tests of coverage relating to businesses, employers, and employees.

1. *Business Coverage.* As already noted, "interstate commerce" is the governing test for businesses that are included under the provisions of the Act. The Act does not specify which businesses are subject to it but includes all those "affecting" interstate commerce. The Supreme Court, in cases arising under the LMRA, and the National Labor Relations Board, in viewing its responsibilities, have interpreted "interstate" so broadly that practically all businesses are included. For example, the Act has been construed to cover such a wide range as transportation, communications, manufacturing, mining, public utilities, banks, brokers, and insurance businesses. Retailing has been included when there is some integration with interstate commerce, but purely local retail sales have thus far been construed as exempt.

2. *Definition of Employer.* The definition of "employer" is equally broad. It pertains not only to the general areas of management normally understood to be the employer group, but also to any person

acting as an agent of an employer, directly or indirectly. Hence the rules of agency apply, and an employer is liable for the acts of his agents.

In addition, no employer may move his plant to a new locality and then transfer it to a new and purportedly independent corporation without remaining the employer. He is still responsible for the unfair labor practice of the "independent" corporation.

3. *Definition of Employee.* The benefits of the Act are limited to all who normally would be considered employees. Of import is the status of strikers. Those who strike against an unfair labor practice of an employer are employees protected by the law against discrimination or replacement. Also, those who participate in an economic strike (in which a sixty-day notice of intent to strike has been given and during which time the status quo has been maintained) are employees. But those who participate in illegal strikes—e.g., boycotts, sympathetic strikes, jurisdictional strikes, and those to gain "featherbedding" rules— lose the benefits of the Act or may be enjoined by the courts to desist from such practices.

Several exceptions and exclusions are worthy of mention. Intermittent workers are excluded only if they actually are casual employees. Seasonal and part-time workers are not generally construed to be employees. Excluded also are agricultural labor, domestics in the service of a family or a person at his home, and persons employed by a parent or spouse. Of particular interest is the exclusion of supervisors, the attempted unionization of whom under the NLRA was opposed by many employers.

Operations under the Act

The operations of the LMRA are handled through the National Labor Relations Board and a general counsel. The Board consists of five members appointed by the President with the consent of the United States Senate. It acts as a judicial body—a labor court. The administrative functions of the Act are assigned to the general counsel. This individual, appointed like the Board members, is responsible for investigating charges of unfair labor practices, issuing complaints, and prosecuting unfair labor practices. But it is the Board which decides whether or not the law has been violated. In a word, the judicial duties are assigned to the Board and the administrative functions to the general counsel.

The Board cannot compel violators to obey its orders. To gain compliance, it must petition a circuit court of appeals in the area wherein an unfair labor practice is alleged to occur or wherein the person proceeded against resides or transacts business. The jurisdiction of the court is exclusive, and its judgment and decree are final except upon review by the Supreme Court of the United States.

RELATIONS WITH THE UNION

The basic objective of union-management relations is to establish an agreement regarding the conditions under which employees will render their services to the employer. These relations, as already noted, are governed in part by legislative rules. They are also subject to a variety of economic, administrative, and personal forces which the parties can bring to bear. When one of these parties is a union, the following are the stages through which management's relations with it tend to be conducted:

1. Preparing to negotiate agreements
2. Negotiating with unions
3. Subject matter of agreements
4. Living with the contract

Preparing for Negotiation

In many ways, preparing to negotiate a contract is the most crucial stage of union-management relations. What can be accomplished at the bargaining table depends largely upon what management brings to it. Blustering and obstructionist tactics are poor substitutes for solid facts and logical analyses about wages, hours, and working conditions. Good preparation calls for a considered program of information to be gathered, subjects to be studied, and assignment of responsibilities.

The foundation for negotiation is laid by fact gathering. To begin with, information should be collected, day by day, on how relations are progressing under the current contract. Such instances as grievances, disciplinary action, and disputes should be recorded under the sections or clauses to which they apply. Information should also be gathered on contract clauses of other companies in one's own community and industry. Estimates should also be made of the possible impact of economic and political trends. And finally, additional sources of information or access to experts should be provided for in the event negotiations take unexpected turns.

Preparation should include attention to appropriate subject matter.

FIGURE 25–1. Sample Page from a Clause Comparison Chart

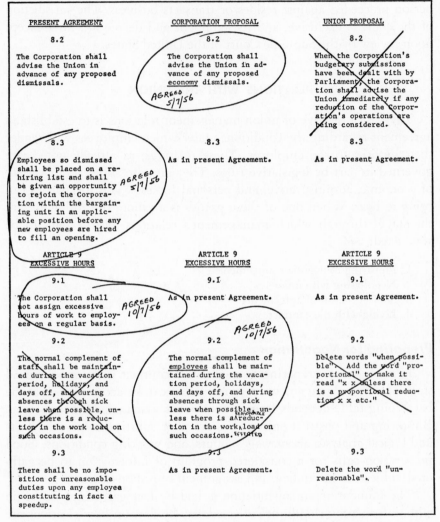

SOURCE: Clive B. McKee, "Know Your Climate—The Key to Effective Bargaining," *Personnel*, July-August, 1957, pp. 58–59.

Obviously, the current contract is a good place to begin. The present clauses should therefore be carefully reviewed, as illustrated in Figure 25–1. Then, current business literature, trade periodicals, and union publications should be closely scrutinized to ascertain what new subjects are likely to come up. The unions invariably give clues to the topics they may bring up. The guaranteed annual wage, for example, which led to supplementary unemployment benefits, was noised about for a few years before it was brought to the forefront of negotiations. A close

FIGURE 25–1. *(Continued)*

8.2
3r/6/56 Impossible. management
right to determine
size of work force.

8.2
.30/6/56 Union claims examination should be
permitted prior to
any economy
dismissals.

5/7/56 WITHDRAWN.

9.2
7/7/56 What is proportional? No
better than reasonable &
has implications.
Proposed "EFFECTED"

8/7/56 Agreed as in Corp.
proposals with amend-
ments as voted.

9.2
7/7/56 Union claims
workloads should
be reduced
mathematically.

8/7/56 Union agrees to
"effected" & "reasonable"
together.

study of business conditions also can throw light on the types of demands which are likely to be made or which the company may want to make.

And finally, careful assignments of responsibility should be made for gathering information, analyzing information and suggested proposals, and deciding upon the company's position. Supervisors and foremen, for example, are excellent sources of information on how the current contract is operating. They should be asked to submit regular as well as special reports on these matters. Staff members in the legal, personnel, commercial and economic research, and statistical departments should be assigned specific topics regarding which they are expected to collect pertinent information. Such materials should be funneled to one department or person who will be responsible for classifying, summarizing, and interpreting the findings. The personnel or industrial relations department would be the logical choice for this assignment. Of course, the ultimate authority for strategy to be pursued must rest with top management. If such departments do not exist, some line executive will have to assume this task.

Negotiating

For a number of years after the Wagner Act was passed, many top executives attempted to carry on the work of bargaining with unions. Although they recognized the need for experts in such fields as engineering, purchasing, sales, and production, they felt capable of handling personnel functions themselves. The results were to be expected. The unions, with full-time specialists on their staffs, gained many concessions unnoticed by the top executives, who seemed to think that wages alone were of importance in union negotiations. The advantages gained by unions in regard to such matters as grievance machinery, seniority rules, and discharge rules are evidences of the ineptness displayed by some top executives.

Again, personnel departments in some companies were little more than employment clerks and record keepers, so that they were in no position to advise management in negotiations. Indeed, the personnel manager seemed to be the last one to consult in such instances. Although lawyers were often called in, the company personnel department was invariably ignored. Only in recent years has there been a growing tendency to develop a strong labor relations division in the personnel department and to make it responsible for handling contract negotiations.

Although union-management relations are generally handled by each company on an individualized basis, there are instances in which bargaining and dispute settlements have been handled on an industry-wide or area basis. Cases in point are the steel and coal industries. For example, the UMW has carried on bargaining with the coal operators through their southern, northern, and anthracite producer groups. Agreements must be approved, however, by the individual companies and local unions with whom contracts are signed. Another interesting approach is found in the Mountain States Employers Council. This group, composed largely of employers in Wyoming, New Mexico, and

Colorado, provides such services as information on wages, personnel policies, and labor relations; a staff to assist in negotiations; management workshops and conferences; and bulletins and surveys.[1] Some of the larger airlines have also experimented with group talks, in an attempt to conduct mediation before troubles get far out of line and to negotiate on an informal basis.

Also of significance are attempts in various cities to bring all interested parties together with a view to better labor-management relations.[2] In such instances a committee is formed representing various community, civic, and business interests. It discusses current industrial problems, formulates policies, and helps settle disputes through available mediation, conciliation, and arbitration services. Variations of this program have been undertaken in a number of cities, including Boston, San Francisco, St. Louis, Buffalo, Minneapolis, Newark, Pittsburgh, Tacoma, and South Bend.

Subject Matter of Agreements

The range of subjects covered in union contracts does not differ significantly. These usually include:

1. Management prerogatives
2. Union recognition
3 Hours of work
4. Wages
5. Vacations and holidays
6. Seniority
7. Working conditions
8. Layoffs and rehirings
9. Arbitration and mediation
10. Renewal clauses

The details and treatment of these subjects differ so much that it is impractical even to begin to cite examples here. On the other hand, most of these subjects are discussed in preceding or succeeding chapters. In a sense, the union contract merely formalizes what should be good personnel practice on all these subjects. However, some comment is needed on management prerogatives, union recognition, renewal clauses, and intercompany cooperation.

1. *Management Prerogatives.* A clause of management prerogatives pertains to the rights, responsibilities, and areas of action which it

---

[1] *Business Week,* December 12, 1953, pp. 164–66.

[2] *Labor Law Journal,* Vol. III, No. 10, pp. 663–76.

retains, free from questioning or joint action by the union. It may be stated in general terms such as the following:

Except as otherwise in this agreement expressly provided, nothing in this agreement contained shall be deemed to limit the company in any way in the exercise of the regular and customary functions of management, including the making in connection therewith of such rules relating to operations as it shall deem advisable.

Or it may be more explicit, as in the following:

Nothing in this agreement shall limit the company in the exercise of its function of management, under which it shall have, among others, the right to hire new employees and to direct the working force; to discipline, suspend, or discharge for cause; transfer or lay off employees because of lack of work; to require employees to observe company rules and regulations, not inconsistent with the provisions of this agreement; to decide the number and location of its plants, products to be manufactured, and the methods and schedules of production, including the means and processes of manufacturing, provided that the company will not use these prerogatives for the purpose of discrimination. It is agreed that these enumerations of management prerogatives shall not be deemed to exclude other prerogatives not enumerated.

The former is preferred by some because it is general and all-inclusive. However, those who favor the latter statement argue that generalized clauses leave their meaning open to questioning by the union. But the latter is weak in the sense that what is not specifically reserved by management is presumably open to bargaining or union action. Some students also feel that all prerogative clauses are useless because labor will not countenance them if it feels its rights are injured. Moreover, labor is moving in on so many areas that were once construed to be out of bounds that there are few, if any, subjects that have not come within the scope of bargaining in some company or another.[3]

2. *Recognition of Union Clause.* Whereas clauses of management's prerogatives are not written into all contracts, clauses covering union recognition and prerogatives are invariably included. The recognition clause is necessary to indicate specifically the bargaining agency and the unit covered. Although not universal practice, the rights of unions and permissible activities are also included. Examples of clauses in this category are the following:

a) The company recognizes the union as the sole representative of its hourly and piece rate employees, including employees in the retail store, but

---

[3] Worth watching in this connection is the movement toward "codetermination" in Germany, where labor representatives by law are given a place on the board of directors. The exclusive rights of management are in such an event significantly diluted.

excluding executive supervisory employees, watchmen, office employees, and technical advisers, for the purpose of collective bargaining in respect to rates of pay, wages, hours of work, and other conditions of employment.

b) The company recognizes the union as the sole collective bargaining agency of the workers in those departments in which the union has a majority of the workers.

c) Union activities may be conducted by employees on the company property on the free time of such employees, but, except as provided herein under the subject of "grievances," the union shall not engage in any union business, discussions, or activities during working hours, and shall not solicit memberships, collect dues, or conduct organizing activities on the company property on the company time. The company will not permit any antiunion activities or discussions during working hours.

3. *Renewal Clauses.* The term of the contract and arrangements for renewals are also included in union contracts. Two examples of such clauses are shown in the following:

a) This agreement shall remain in force for one year from the date hereof and shall automatically renew itself from year to year, unless written notice of desire to terminate or to modify any portion or any of the terms hereof is given by either party to the other at least 30 days prior to the expiration of any such annual period.

If notice of desire to terminate or to amend shall have been given, negotiations for a new or amended agreement shall begin not later than 20 days prior to the expiration of the current yearly period and shall continue until an agreement has been reached. During such negotiations, this agreement shall remain in full force and effect, provided, however, that if negotiations continue beyond the termination of the annual period, either party may then terminate this agreement at any time upon 30 days' written notice to the other party.

b) This agreement becomes effective as of May 1, 19—, and shall remain in effect until May 1, 19—, and each year thereafter unless written notice of cancellation or changes desired is given 60 days prior to any yearly expiration date by any of the other parties of this agreement. If changes or amendments are desired, such written notice shall contain a complete list of the changes and amendments proposed. In that case, conferences shall be arranged to begin during the 15 days immediately following the 60 days' notice date.

Living with the Contract

An agreement, once reached, is not self-effectuating. It must, in the first place, be communicated to all affected levels. This means more than the printing of the union contract. On the one hand, meetings with supervisors, for example, are desirable to point out the significant features of the new contract. This not only makes the supervisors feel that they are important factors in labor relations but also prepares them to face employees with a greater feeling of assurance.

On the other hand, it would be desirable to hold extended training sessions based on the contract. Clause by clause, the various management levels could be shown the nature of the clauses, why they were adopted, what they really mean, and how they must be interpreted. Answers can be supplied to many questions which will be raised on the floor by the employees. And courses of action to be taken and executives to be consulted in the event of doubt can be suggested to help resolve difficulties that are apt to be encountered.

All of this prepares executives, in the second place, to handle labor relations matters day by day, as they pertain to or involve the union contract. The supervisor, in particular, will not only know his responsibilities and rights, but will also be more effective in communicating his arguments and the company's position. He will not make mistakes due to ignorance which the union might interpret as a prejudiced desire to undercut the union and to shortchange the employees in what is coming to them.

And in the third place, living with the contract involves knowing what to do about disagreements that arise but cannot be settled at the point of issue. Grievance channels, arbitration procedures, and provisions for mediation should be known, understood, and correctly practiced. These are merely mentioned here because they are discussed more fully in the next chapter.

In discussing these matters of union-management relations, no attempt has been made to pass judgment on the labor union movement. To some executives, it is an anathema. It is viewed not only as an interference with management prerogatives but sometimes as a parasitic if not corrupt blight upon civilization. An appraisal of such views is out of place here. And no matter what one's views are, business often must deal with unions. Consequently, it has been intended here to outline the basic considerations of which management must be aware in labor relations matters.

It may be noted, however, that both management and labor are made up of human beings—not one side solely of angels and the other solely of devils. Each can suffer from the ills of unethical, ignorant, and prejudiced motives. And as one studies union-management relations, it is equally clear that sound labor relations are essentially found in good personnel practices and human relations, whether in a unionized or a nonunionized setup.

QUESTIONS

1. As you view the history of labor-management relations in this country, do you think progress is being made? Why, or why not?
2. What is your philosophy of how collective bargaining should be conducted?
3. What attitudes and information must labor and management bring to the bargaining table in order to arrive at mutually satisfactory agreements? It it probable that such conditions can be practically approximated?
4. One of the objectives of the LMRA, as specified by Congress, is that interferences to interstate commerce arising out of labor disputes be reduced. How well do you think this objective has been attained?
5. What constitutes a threat under the LMRA? If an employer says that he will go out of business if his employees organize, is that an unfair labor practice? If it is, does not a ruling to prevent him from going out of business constitute a threat to his freedom of private property usage?
6. A foreman, after working hours, in his own home, and unknown to his company, condemns unions before a group of his workers. Would he subject his company to possible prosecution? Explain.
7. Why do you suppose some employers object so strenuously to the checkoff and maintenance-of-membership clauses?
8. What can first-line supervisors contribute to collective bargaining? Suggest ways in which their help and counsel can be obtained without undue waste of time and innumerable conferences.
9. What are management prerogatives? Some people claim that management has no prerogatives, only responsibilities. What do you think?
10. What phases must be given due consideration in the day-to-day living with a contract that management and a union have negotiated?

CHAPTER **26**

HANDLING GRIEVANCES

Employee Dissatisfactions

Perhaps the most common impression of labor-management relations is that they are generally unsatisfactory. This is questionable when it is seen that employee dissatisfaction as measured by time lost through strikes averages less than one quarter of 1 percent of total man-hours of work. But how measure what may be lost by dissatisfied employees who are at work, but who are not working to their full capacity? The general opinion is, however, that such industrial unrest causes high losses of productivity.

Hence, it behooves management to exert every effort to reduce employee dissatisfactions. Whether management proceeds on an individual basis or operates in conjunction with unions, it is argued here that the basic steps and principles of handling grievances—the particular subject of dissatisfactions discussed in this chapter—are much the same. Thus, grievance handling is taken up here first without reference to union relations. Then, note is made of some specific grievance procedures of interest when unions are involved. In either case, grievance handling is assumed to be as much a responsibility of line executives as of specialized staff personnel departments.

Specifically, the subject of grievances is discussed here under the following broad headings:

1. Basic considerations of grievance handling
2. Steps in handling grievances
3. Principles of handling grievances
4. Union-management relations in grievance machinery

BASIC CONSIDERATIONS

Meaning of Grievances

Although definitions are sometimes considered sophomoric, in few cases are definitions more useful than in the matter of grievances. This

is so because failure to recognize as grievances subjects that are grievances is almost certain to result in troubles going unnoticed until they
have become serious and difficult to handle.

Broadly speaking, a grievance is any dissatisfaction that adversely
affects productivity. But it is simply impractical to adopt such a broad
definition. No company has the resources, skill, or time to handle all
grievances.

To be workable, a definition must be more restrictive. Noncompany
sources usually have to be excluded because they are out of the control
of a company. Highly emotionalized grievances may well have to be
excluded because of the lack of skill to handle them. And unexpressed
dissatisfactions have to be excluded because of their nebulous character.
So it is common to define a grievance as a complaint expressed in
writing (or orally) on a company-related matter.

Implications of the Definition

Even this definition needs some explanation. In the first place, it is
presumed that there are, or will be, adverse effects upon productivity.
Some types of dissatisfaction are sources of good. Some of our greatest
advances have been made by dissatisfied people. The removal of such
motivators could scarcely be justified. But the irritants that reduce productivity are another matter. A company injures itself if it does not seek
to remove the obstacles to effective operations.

In the second place, the definition does not separate the subject
matter of the grievance from the undesirable attitude of the aggrieved.
Let us assume that an employee is disgruntled because he did not receive
a raise. Will giving a raise remove the dissatisfaction; or must something be done, in addition, about the wounded feelings? Obviously, the
two aspects need consideration; the term "grievance" must imply both
subject matter and personal attitudes.

In the third place, the definition must be accepted to mean that
anything—activity, policy, executive, or practice—in the company may
be the source of grievances. As a consequence, there is the implication
that a company is willing to correct whatever or whoever is causing
grievances.

In the fourth place, does the reference to expressed grievances imply
the exclusion of unexpressed grievances? Requiring an expressed statement may serve to formalize the grievance processes. But it would not
be wise to assume that no discontent exists unless it is stated in writing.
On the contrary, implied grievances are very dangerous because it is not
known when they may erupt. Moreover, the damage dissatisfied workers
do to productivity goes on unimpaired. Hence, such efforts as close

supervisory observation and attitude surveys should be employed to ascertain if there are smoldering areas of unrest.

And finally, the definition does not imply any judgment about the injustice, unfairness, rationality, or emotionality of the grievance. It implies, therefore, respect for the opinion of the aggrieved. To be sure, grievances based on misconceptions, lack of thinking, or emotionalism may be very hard to handle. But they may become harder to handle if the aggrieved is unsettled by being told of his weaknesses. Better by far to give a case every appearance of its being fully worthy of serious consideration.

Channels for Handling Grievances

Although a technical matter, channels for handling grievances should be carefully developed and information about them thoroughly disseminated. The labor relations department, various levels of executives, and the employees should know what relationships exist among them and how the various groups should work together. As noted earlier, it is assumed that grievances are handled by the company and the employees themselves, or through unions.

1. *Role of the Supervisor.* It is of course imperative that employees know the channels they may use in presenting grievances. Ordinarily, the supervisor should be accorded the first opportunity to handle grievances. Employees should be required to present their grievances to their supervisors, whether or not the grievances are finally disposed of by them. Unless this rule is established and enforced, supervisors will soon lose face with employees and become unimportant cogs in the organization. Allowing aggrieved employees to bypass supervisors and to take their complaints to higher executives or to the labor relations department weakens unnecessarily a key factor of management.

2. *Intermediate Agencies.* All grievances cannot be handled by supervisors because many of them involve issues or policies beyond the limits of supervisory authority or capacity. Hence, provision should be made for a second step in handling grievances. In some companies, this is done by providing that employees with unsettled grievances are to be sent to the labor relations department. Other companies specify that employees are to be sent to the next supervisor or line executive—e.g., the shop superintendent or the office manager, as the case might be. This stage provides the facilities of additional knowledge and authority, and will often be sufficient to resolve most of the difficulties that the first line of supervision cannot.

3. *Administrative Levels.* Since the second level of appeal will be incapable of handling some of the grievances involving company-wide issues or many groups of employees, machinery should provide for ready access to the administrative levels of the organization. Either the top executive of the company, by himself or in committee with administrative line and staff executives, should be established as a final court of appeal. To be effective, this court must prove itself in action and not merely brag of its open-door policy.

4. *Union Aspects.* And finally, the union may play an important role in how grievances are channeled to and from company- and union-organization levels. This phase of the subject will be discussed later in this chapter.

5. *Illustrating the Channels.* These channels of communication should be drawn up so that charts or pictures of them can be distributed to supervisors and employees. Figure 5–10 (p. 87) illustrates the use of a formal chart to serve this purpose.

STEPS IN HANDLING GRIEVANCES

Grievances must be handled in some systematic manner, the machinery of which is described in the last section of this chapter. No matter what the machinery, however, grievance handling calls for a number of common steps based on good ground rules. For convenience of discussion, steps are taken up in this section and rules in the next, although steps and rules are interdependent.

In handling grievances, the following steps should be taken:

1. Define, describe, or express the nature of the grievance as clearly and as fully as possible.
2. Gather all the facts that serve to explain when, how, where, to whom, and why the grievance occurred.
3. Establish tentative solutions or answers to the grievance.
4. Gather additional information to check the validity of the tentative solutions, and thus ascertain the best possible solution.
5. Apply the solution.
6. Follow up the case to see that it has been handled satisfactorily and the trouble eliminated.[1]

Describing Grievances

As stated, step 1 assumes that the grievance has been expressed. This section is concerned with (1) reliability of expressed complaints and (2) discovery of unexpressed grievances.

---

[1] Contrast these steps with those included in the job relations training program discussed on p. 254.

FIGURE 26-1

THE OHIO FUEL GAS COMPANY
INCIDENT REPORT

REPORTED BY _____

Name _____ Title _____ Position _____ TO _____

Name _____ Title _____ Location _____

DETERMINE OBJECTIVE — What I am trying to accomplish —

1. GET THE FACTS
(Be sure you have the whole story)

_____
_____
_____
_____
_____
_____
_____
_____
_____
_____
_____
_____
_____

2. WEIGH AND DECIDE
(Don't jump at conclusions)
(Possible actions)

_____
_____
_____
_____
_____

3. ACTION I HAVE TAKEN

_____
_____

RECOMMENDED ACTION FOR MY SUPERVISOR
(Don't Pass the Buck)

_____
_____
_____

4. CHECK RESULTS

Condition Found _____ Date _____
Condition Found _____ Date _____

HOW TO HANDLE A PROBLEM

DETERMINE OBJECTIVES

1.—GET THE FACTS.
   Review the record.
   Find out what rules and plant customs apply.
   Talk with individuals concerned.
   Get opinions and feelings.
   Be sure you have the whole story.
2.—WEIGH AND DECIDE.
   Fit the facts together.
   Consider their bearing on each other.
   What possible actions are there?
   Check practices and policies.
   Consider objective and effect on individual, group, and production.
   Don't jump at conclusions.
3.—TAKE ACTION.
   Are you going to handle this yourself?
   Do you need help in handling?
   Should you refer this to your supervisor?
   Watch the timing of your action.
   Don't pass the buck.
4.—CHECK RESULTS.
   How soon will you follow up?
   How often will you need to check?
   Watch for changes in output, attitudes, and relationships.
   Did your action help production?

DID YOUR ACTION HELP TO SOLVE YOUR PROBLEM? _____

If you were the employee involved, would you be satisfied with the action taken? _____

CHECK RESULTS _____ DID YOUR ACTION SOLVE YOUR PROBLEM? _____ HAS THIS INCIDENT BEEN HANDLED TO THE SATISFACTION
OF THE EMPLOYEE? _____ FOREMAN? _____ SUPERINTENDENT? _____ MANAGEMENT? _____ HOW OFTEN HAS THIS CASE BEEN FOLLOWED UP
BY YOU? _____ DAYS, WEEKS? _____ HAVE YOU SEEN ANY CHANGES IN OUTPUT, ATTITUDE, RELATIONSHIPS?
BETTER OR WORSE? _____
APPROVED: _____

Could this problem be avoided through the use of the foundations?

1. *Determining the Correct Grievance.* Many grievances, after being "settled," turn up again to plague management. The trouble in such instances invariably is that the wrong grievance has been handled. This could have been avoided if care had been taken at the outset to describe as accurately as possible the issue at the heart of the employee's complaint. As it is, superficial aspects of grievances are adjusted, while the fundamental cause of trouble remains untouched.

As a common case in point, employees often ask for raises when what really troubles them are such things as uncertainty about their jobs, a supervisor's failure to be polite, preference being given to a fellow worker, and an employee's dislike for the type of gloves the company is issuing. These matters are often difficult for the average employee to express in what he considers reasonable terms, yet they do irritate him. The irritation continues until he decides consciously or unconsciously to use wages as a basis for his complaint. And when the wage case is cleared, management is later surprised to find that something is still disturbing the ungrateful employee.

The chances of getting at the right grievances are increased if care is used in the initial contact with the employee. Encouraging a person to talk is one means of getting closer to the truth. And the practice of asking the aggrieved to put the case in writing is also desirable. A good example of a form for this purpose and one that would be useful for recording the entire history of a case is shown in Figure 26–1. This form could also be used in disciplinary cases.

2. *Unexpressed Grievances.* There are cases, however, when individual grievances go unexpressed and unexposed for long periods of time. If these were discovered earlier, the intensity of feeling which is ultimately generated would be largely minimized.

Various methods are useful in this connection. Statistical studies of turnover, complaints, transfers, earnings, and sources of suggestions and lack thereof can provide clues to actual or probable grievances. And skill in observation of the behaviorisms, attitudes, and habits of one's subordinates is particularly helpful in detecting signs of changes due to unexpressed grievances.

Gathering Facts

Having defined grievances as accurately as possible, the next step is to gather all relevant facts about the issue. It is important to know when the alleged grievance was first experienced, whether or not it has been repeated, how and where it took place, and the circumstances under which it transpired. This does not imply that grievances should be handled like law cases. It does mean that if the confidence of the employee is to be gained and held, he must be thoroughly convinced that management is completely sincere in seeing that justice is done. Such fact gathering or sifting requires a knack in interviewing and listening to employees, the principles of which were discussed in an earlier chapter.

1. *Nature of Facts.* Besides serving to convince the employee of the employer's sincerity, the step of gathering data is indispensable to a fair decision.

But what are facts, and what are opinions? Practically speaking, any claim which can be substantiated to the satisfaction of a reasonable person may be tagged as a fact; otherwise, it is an opinion.

In the matter of grievance handling, this raises two distinct problems. First, it is imperative to place the stated ideas of both employees and executives in their appropriate classes of either facts or opinions. This involves at times sensitive understanding of employee grievances and at times a selling job on the part of management to convince employees of its fairness. Second, when both sides have supporting "facts," it is difficult to prove which set of facts is weightier. Hence, management must guard against letting its opinions decide in favor of its facts; further analysis or perhaps compromise is in order.

It is well to note here that both labor and management tend to hold opinions or evaluate facts because of their respective roles in the business social world. Management should be aware of these predispositions. If it is, it will deal more carefully with grievances and consequently gain the confidence of employees which is so necessary in gaining acceptance of opinions that cannot be proved.

2. *Importance of Records.* Since fact gathering is not an easy task, after a grievance arises it is perhaps wise to develop a set of records and keep them up to date. For example, such records as merit rating, job rating, attendance records, educational and business records, and suggestions are invaluable. They serve to show in advance, for example, who should get a promotion, and to warn others why their chances of advancing are not good.

Establishing Tentative Solutions

After getting a clear picture of the grievance, the next step in the procedure calls for the establishment of tentative solutions or answers.

The method suggested here is similar to that employed by a scientist in the laboratory. The chemist, for example, does not carry on experiments willy-nilly. Instead, he sets up a tentative solution and then runs an experiment to see whether he is right or wrong. If the experiment fails, he has to start with another tentative solution, and he proceeds in this way until he finds the right answer. The significant point is that the experiments he runs are specifically set up to prove or disprove a tentative solution.

And so, too, in handling grievances, management must make a list of alternate solutions and later test them. In compiling possible solutions, management need not at the time make them known to the worker. It is usually better to reserve judgment until some opportunity is afforded to check them. Of course, if an immediate answer is required, the selection of the right answer will be dependent upon the experience, training, and good judgment of the executive involved.

But how are tentative solutions determined? In the first place, management has its own experience to fall back upon. Very likely, it will have had similar cases in the past, and these should provide it with the perspective required to figure out solutions applicable to the present case. In addition, it should have observed how other companies have handled similar grievances. In the third place, alternative answers may be collected from technical and trade publications. And if all the foregoing fail, the best possible guesses will have to be made. The important point is that a thorough search, commensurate with the importance of the case, should be made for alternative solutions.

Checking Tentative Solutions

Unfortunately, the executive cannot check his tentative solutions as the scientist can in the laboratory. He has two possible courses of action. First, he can rely on trial and error. He can check by applying a decision. This is a risky course; but often, it must be done because of the lack of time for further analysis. Second, he can evaluate alternatives on the basis of his own experience or the experiences of others. This presupposes that there exists information on past successes and failures with similar cases. And as an executive gains experience, and as a company compiles grievance records, there is good reason to believe that this method can be very useful in checking out tentative solutions.

Applying Solutions

Having reached a decision, it seems common sense that it should be applied. Yet, it is not uncommon to find executives who shrink from making an unfavorable, although warranted, decision. Indeed, some avoid making decisions favorable to employees for fear of "spoiling"

them or because it would signify that they themselves were wrong in the
first place. Yet, subordinates dislike supervisors who refuse to take a
definite stand, one way or the other. To be sure, all of us like to receive
favorable news, but that does not mean that employees will not accept
unfavorable decisions. On the contrary, they will, particularly when
they are certain that the decision is based upon a thorough study of the
facts and is passed on to them without vindictiveness.

The decision, having finally been reached, should then be passed
along in clear, unequivocal terms. After all, a grievance cannot be
handled just by listening to an employee's complaint; something must
be done about it. The ultimate decision is the tool of action.

Follow-up of the Grievance

It is unsafe to conclude that a grievance has been well handled until
a check is made to determine whether the employee's attitude has been
favorably changed. To assure themselves along these lines, executives
concerned need a timetable and a method of follow-up.

As far as a timetable is concerned, many executives rely upon their
memories to check on how grievances have been handled. This is
simple, but if there is any danger of forgetting, a written record should
be made. Records require paper work, but they do minimize serious
losses.

As for checking methods, several are available. Perhaps the most
common is casual observation—just see how the employee is taking the
decision, whether favorably or unfavorably. Next in order is to ask the
employee whether or not he is satisfied with the decision. Somewhat
similar in nature, but more subtle, is the practice of a general discussion
with the employee with a view to deducing indirectly his attitude. A
fourth method is to ask others about a given employee's reactions. This
latter is dangerous because it smacks of spying. However, when used in
the hands of an expert, it is desirable because it takes place away from
the particular person involved.

PRINCIPLES OF HANDLING GRIEVANCES

The foregoing steps will be little more than an ineffective routine
unless they are based upon well-considered principles. Such principles
are not absolute insurance of success in dealing with grievances because
laws of human behavior are nonexistent. However, principles do work
most of the time; hence, it is desirable to search them out and then rely
on them as guides.

In the field of handling grievances, a number of principles have
been distilled from the experiences of many companies. Grouping of

these for purposes of discussion is at best a makeshift. Thus the classification here merely lumps available suggestions under the general headings of interviewing, attitudes toward employees, attitudes toward supervision, and long-run rules.

Principles of Interviewing

In handling grievances, a considerable amount of time must be spent talking to employees, gathering data from them, and passing on various types of information. Such talks, to be most effective, should follow definite patterns and adhere to some well-tested rules. These have been discussed in an earlier chapter, so it is unnecessary to repeat the materials here.

Management's Attitude toward Employees

During the interview and afterward, and in other connections, the wise executive seeks to develop an attitude toward his employees that will result in gaining their confidence. Without this ingredient, grievances can never be handled with the highest degree of success.

To gain such confidence, the executive must have and must show the right attitude toward those who have (and also those who do not have) grievances. In the first place, he should not take the attitude that his subordinates are ignorant. No one, no matter how ignorant he is (and we all are, more or less, about different subjects), reacts favorably to those who deride his intelligence. Besides, sooner or later, the executive will underestimate the intelligence of some employee, to his own chagrin.

To develop confidence, in the second place, it is also wise to take the stand that employees are fair in presenting their grievances. This does not mean that care should not be exercised to guard against unwarranted or prejudiced demands. It does mean, however, that management should give the impression that the viewpoints of employees are considered to be fair unless proved otherwise.

And finally, in handling grievances, management should display a sincere interest in the problems of employees and a constructive willingness to be of help. Take, for example, the supervisor; he is the representative of management to employees, but he is also a representative of employees to management. If he does not accept the latter responsibility with a full spirit of helpfulness, the confidence and loyalty of employees will be difficult to attain.

Management's Responsibilities

In handling grievances, all executives must have confidence in themselves, be fully aware of their responsibilities, and be willing to carry these burdens. Such a positive attitude must be apparent to employees in order to gain their respect and cooperation.

An executive who lacks confidence in himself soon finds that his employees are aware of this and tend to be wary of him. Employees do not like to place their grievances in insecure or incompetent hands. They will tend to go around him or over his head. In either case the prestige of the executive and the effectiveness of his efforts suffer. Each executive should recognize that he is human and does have weaknesses; but he should also recognize that, granted reasonable qualifications, he is capable of handling his job. To be a bluffer is bad, but to have an inferiority complex because of ordinary shortcomings from which all suffer is perhaps worse.

Likewise, an executive should recognize the serious responsibilities he has undertaken. He has obligated himself in many ways for the success, happiness, and well-being of a number of fellow beings. Within his capacities and opportunities, he must seek to carry out those responsibilities. In dealing with grievances, he must give the impression of serious consideration. There must be no light-minded attitude or flippant remarks about the grievances of employees—they are no joking matter. They are important to the employee and an important part of the executive's job. By acting accordingly, the executive is much more likely to gain and hold the confidence of his employees when decisions have to be reached.

Long-Run Principles

In handling grievances, it is important that consideration be given not only to effects in the present but also to long-run and sometimes far-distant implications. Thus a decision reached today has an immediate effect and also very likely will have an influence upon the future relationship between employees and management. As a consequence, grievances should be handled in terms of their total effect upon the organization and not solely their immediate or individual effect.

1. *Long-Run Effects.* As an example, take the case of an employee who complains that he rather than someone else should have received a particular promotion. How this case is handled and what decision is reached will certainly have an effect upon the individual in question, but there will also be repercussions among other employees, both now and later. Others, too, will watch the case; they will note the decision and reach conclusions. And conclusions are guides to behavior. If other employees get the idea that it is useless to complain about promotions or that to get a promotion, deserved or not, one should "raise the roof,"

damage will be done for a long time to come. Hence a given case should be handled so that all parties, whether directly or indirectly interested, are convinced of the fundamental integrity of the management.

2. *Dangers of Losing Confidence.* Another truth to be remembered in the process of handling grievances is that it takes a long time to gain the confidence of employees and that, once gained, it can be lost overnight by a foolish decision or inept handling of a single case. In other words, eternal vigilance is the price of good labor relations. Every grievance must be considered important, no matter how irrelevant or insignificant it is. If an executive is tired, in a bad temper, or otherwise feeling out of sorts, he will be much smarter to ask for a postponement of a grievance hearing; but it should be done courteously, apologetically, and with an apparent attitude of regret. Although delays are undesirable, they are to be preferred to the risk of saying something that would incur the distrust or enmity of the aggrieved employee. It is harder to overcome the results of hotheaded blundering, for example, than those caused by delays.

3. *Human Nature.* In the long run, too, it is well to remember that human nature will not change much, if at all. People will become neither much better nor much worse. In handling grievances, people should be taken for what they are—their strengths and their weaknesses. In other words, to assume that grievances can be postponed until people see the light themselves; that harsh decisions are good for employees, as they will learn later on; or that being easy with them now can be made up for by cracking down later is to forget that people do not change a great deal. Fairness has been desired for ages past and will be for ages to come; hence the question will always be: "What is fair to all concerned?" It will be standards of fairness that largely change much more than the desire for fairness.

4. *Effects of the Past.* This leads to the thought that a long-run attitude should not only extend into the future but should also give consideration to what has happened in the past. Often, when an employee complains, the source of his complaint may actually not be found in present conditions. The source or cause may be something that happened in the distant past; but to make his complaint sound credible, he may blame some present condition. For example—and this has actually happened—an employee complained about his wages when what he really was angry about was the fact that six months previously he had been spoken to rather harshly by his supervisor. In short, grievances of today often have their roots in the acts of yesterday and their branches in the effects of tomorrow. The roots are sometimes

difficult to locate, and how the branches will grow is difficult to forecast. But hard though the task may be, it must be tackled as best one can; otherwise, grievance handling becomes grievance fighting.

MACHINERY FOR HANDLING GRIEVANCES

Appropriate machinery must be established to take the steps and to apply the principles discussed in the preceding sections. Responsibility must be assigned to given organization units and executives. And the systematic flow of grievances through various stages and units must be encouraged through appropriate procedural designs. Hence, grievance handling requires attention to organizational responsibility and procedures.

Organizational Responsibility

Organizationally, grievance handling is divided between and shared by first-line supervision, staff and middle management executives, top management, and labor union representatives (when involved).

1. *First-Line Supervision.* First-line supervision should be accorded the first opportunity to handle grievances. It should be empowered to pass upon grievances within policies, rules, and jurisdictional limits established by the company. And it is good practice to require employees to present their grievances to their immediate superior, even though the final disposition must await higher authority. Otherwise, supervisors are in danger of losing any importance in the organization and the respect of their subordinates.

2. *Staff and Middle Management Executives.* All grievances cannot be handled at the lowest levels because some involve issues or policies beyond their authority or capacity. Hence, responsibility is placed upon divisional, group, and area managers to handle grievance cases with broader implications. And these may be aided by a staff labor relations unit in three ways: The staff may supply line executives with advice or information on grievance handling; it may help executives in the processing of cases; or it may be given authority actually to settle certain classes of cases.

3. *Top Management Levels.* Top management has two large areas of responsibility in grievance handling. First, it must assume jurisdiction of cases which are company-wide in nature or significant as precedent makers. While the help of lower levels or staff units may be sought in such cases, they are of a nature the responsibility for which should not be evaded or delegated. Second, top management must establish the broad policies and rules upon which grievance handling in

the company will be based. Here again, top management may utilize the advice of a labor relations department, but the final decisions must be unequivocally accepted as its own.

4. *Labor Union Representatives.* And finally, in many companies, labor union representatives interact in the various organizational segments of the company. Shop and office stewards work at supervisory levels; higher level stewards and union agents work with upper management levels; and officials of union locals, business agents of unions, and representatives of national union offices work at key points of grievance cases wherever they develop.

Superimposed upon or paralleling the formal company organization structure is that of the union structure. The role the union plays often encompasses informal relations. Union representatives work out with their company counterparts decisions that bend contractual agreements or are based on timesaving shortcuts. But space here permits only touching upon formal relationships. These can be seen more clearly in the discussion of procedural aspects of grievance handling.

Grievance-Handling Procedures

Grievance handling usually involves a number of people, dealing with problems that often go through a number of stages, and sometimes extends over days to months of time. A well-designed procedure is needed if these variables are to be effectively coordinated. It must prescribe how various aspects of grievances are to be handled, by whom, in what order, and in what time periods. This section is concerned, therefore, with a discussion of such procedures and of arbitration, which is often an important part of such procedures.

1. *Design of Procedures.* Grievance-handling procedures are desirable whether a company is or is not unionized. In Figure 26–2 is shown a descriptive-type chart used in a nonunionized firm to illustrate its procedure. An interesting example of the procedure in a unionized situation is detailed in the following statement:

All disputes and grievances arising under the terms of this agreement shall be adjusted in the following manner:

The union grievance committee shall consist of five members, each of whom shall be responsible for grievances in a zone of the plant. The entire plant, for purposes of this Article, will be separated into five zones.

First Step. A grievance will be taken up by the employee and the shop steward or committeeman with the foreman of the department.

Second Step. If a satisfactory adjustment is not reached, the shop steward will refer the grievance to the member of the grievance committee responsible for that zone. This member of the grievance committee, with or without the shop steward, will take the matter up with the department superintendent.

FIGURE 26–2. Chart of Grievance Machinery

Third Step. If a satisfactory adjustment is not reached, the member of the grievance committee herein referred to will refer the grievance to the business agent of the union, who will present these grievances to the company each day at 10:00 A.M. The company at that time will return to the business agent of the union in written form any grievances which have been investigated.

The grievance committee of the union will meet with the labor relations manager or his assistant or someone of higher authority in the industrial relations department of the company each Tuesday and Friday to discuss grievances which the union feels require clarification and/or additional investigation.

Fourth Step. If a satisfactory adjustment is not reached, grievances may be referred in writing to arbitration.

Time limits on these procedures are as follows:

First Step.   One day or twenty-four hours
Second Step.   One day or twenty-four hours
Third Step.   Five days, or sooner if answers are available
Fourth Step.   One week for submission

Any dispute or grievance arising under the terms of this agreement which cannot be settled between the parties involved may be submitted by either party on written notice to the other party to an arbitration committee for their determination.

The arbitration committee shall consist of three representatives of the company and three of the union, the seventh and impartial arbiter to be selected by the six members designated.

If no agreement can be reached as to the seventh and impartial arbiter within three days after the first meeting of the six members of the committee, then they shall jointly petition the American Arbitration Association to make the appointment within five days after notification has been received.

The decision of the seventh and impartial member of the committee shall be final and binding upon both parties to this agreement. Every effort shall be made by the impartial arbiter to render his decision to both parties within ten days after the conclusion of the hearing.

The parties shall equally bear the expense of the impartial arbiter.

2. *Arbitration.* Ideally, the grievances of employees should be resolved by management and employees themselves. In practice, the two often cannot reach mutually satisfactory agreements. The alternatives then are a power struggle or arbitration. Obviously, the former is still often chosen. But the discussion here is with the latter, which is also often selected.

In arbitration, the services of an outside third party are sought to settle a grievance (or for that matter, other types of disputes, such as interpretation of contract clauses). The assumption is that an impartial, competent outsider can render a fair verdict not attainable from the parties themselves because of their prejudiced viewpoints or highly emotionalized stands. Moreover, by forgoing the costs of a power strug-

TABLE 26-1

COMPARISON OF PROCEDURES TO SETTLE INDUSTRIAL DISPUTES*

	How and by Whom Initiated	Procedure	Administrator	Who Selects Arbitrator, Mediator, Board, etc.	Decision	Appeals	Conclusion
Voluntary arbitration	By mutual agreement, or on demand of one party pursuant to prior agreement	Under rules chosen by the parties	The parties, themselves or AAA, or any other agency set up or chosen by parties	The parties, by mutual agreement	Award, based on evidence presented by parties at hearings and which parties agree in advance to accept	To court for enforcement or judgment, if good faith fails, or for correction of errors or misconduct	Execution of award in all but rare instances
Compulsory arbitration	By government agency or decree	As provided by government agency, or improvised by arbitrator	Whatever government agency orders the arbitration, or the arbitrator himself	Usually appointed by government agency	Enforceable award	To the courts	Acceptance of award, or strike or lockout, or seizure
Conciliation	By invitation of parties or in initiation of outside person or agency, or by conciliator, or government agency	Improvised—no set procedure	None	Named by government agency or outside person; parties may or may not agree to accept his services	None; result is compromise, agreement, or rejection	To public opinion	Compromise, agreement to arbitrate, or strike or lockout, or seizure
Mediation	By agreement of parties, or in initiation by outside efforts, or by government order or government agency	Improvised	The mediator, or the agency chosen to mediate	Named by mediation agency or chosen by parties	Compromise, or recommendation which parties are at liberty to reject	To public opinion	Compromise, agreement to arbitrate, or strike or lockout, or seizure
Fact-finding	By government agency or decree, or by agreement of the parties	As set by government agency, or the board	The Board	Government agency	Recommendation	To public opinion	Acceptance or recommendation, compromise, or strike or lockout, or seizure
Litigation	By summons of one party to other to appear in court	Rules of the Court	The Court	The Court	Decision of the court	To a higher court	Enforcement of eventual court decision

* Prepared by the American Arbitration Association.
Source: William Sheperdson, "When Reason Takes Over—Arbitration," *Modern Management*, April, 1946, p. 7. Reprinted by permission of the Society for the Advancement of Management.

gle, arbitration is not only a faster and less costly method of settling grievances, but is also one that reduces the chances of an escalation of the disagreement. Care must be used, however, in selecting a good arbitrator and in establishing rules governing his role in the grievance-handling procedure.

Arbitrators in a given case may be selected by the parties themselves or, upon their agreement, by some outside group. Thus, labor and management may themselves select an arbitrator. Or they may turn to the American Arbitration Association (a privately organized, nonprofit national organization founded in 1926) to recommend someone from its roster of accredited arbitrators. During disputes, the Federal Mediation and Conciliation Service may be called upon to exercise its good offices in bringing the parties together or to recommend an arbitrator. And an example at the state level is provided by the New York State Board of Mediation, which can offer mediation services or lend assistance in arbitration.

It is imperative to agree on the role and jurisdiction of the arbitrator. The agreement should be included as a clause in the union contract. It should specify how the arbitrator is to be selected and the term of his service. It should clearly state which grievances or aspects of grievances are arbitrable and which are not. It should prescribe how cases may go to arbitration. It should list the rules of procedure for hearing cases in arbitration. It should state whether the decision of the arbitrator is final or is reviewable in the courts. And it should specify how the arbitrator is to be paid, and by whom.

This section on arbitration may be summarized by reference to Table 26–1. This table lists various operational aspects of arbitration. And it is also of interest because it makes note of other devices for settling disputes. To those who contend that management gives up its rights of final decision to outsiders, no matter how experienced and impartial, when arbitrators are used, conciliation and mediation, for example, may be preferable. These are processes by which outside parties, usually governmental agencies, attempt to bring the conflicting parties together, to clarify issues, and to examine the various contentions. But they exert no powers of decision. As a consequence, this form of intervention appeals to some students of labor-management relations.

QUESTIONS

1. In a given company, a grievance must be written and presented by the employee to his supervisor. What are the arguments for and against such a plan?

2. If employees cannot take a grievance to the personnel department until it has been presented to their supervisors, what happens to grievances against supervisors, How would you handle such grievances?

3. It is said that some unions prefer to have all grievances reported to them so that they can build them up if necessary. What do you think of this accusation? What might the unions reply in rebuttal?

4. Suggest methods by which information about grievances may be obtained. Is an employee attitude survey likely to provide information about specific grievances or possible sources of grievances? Can there be group grievances as well as individual grievances?

5. Why is it difficult to obtain facts about grievances? If all the facts cannot be obtained in a given case, is it possible to reach fair decisions? What ingredient must be present when all the facts cannot be obtained if grievances are to be settled satisfactorily?

6. Why is it desirable to encourage employees with grievances to talk freely and fully? What must the executive not do if he wishes to encourage frank and complete talk? How are the executives to find the time to listen?

7. Can an interviewer avoid giving an employee a clue to how he feels about the merits of a grievance before a decision is actually expressed? Under what conditions might it be desirable to let an employee know before full discussion that a grievance is a good or a bad one?

8. Over what does a supervisor have authority to render decisions in regard to grievances? How about such subjects as wages, hours, and working conditions?

9. Distinguish between mediation, conciliation, and arbitration.

10. Investigate the work of the American Arbitration Association, and write a report on your findings.

CHAPTER 27

DISCIPLINARY ACTION

Introduction

Management's job would indeed be pleasant if employees never had any grievances against the company or the company never any complaints against employees. Such an ideal situation has never been known to exist. In the foregoing chapter, therefore, attention was directed to management's task in handling grievances of employees. The present chapter is concerned with disciplinary action, or what management must do when the employee is, or is alleged to be, at fault.

Since disciplinary action has the implication of penalties, and since dealing out penalties is full of dangerous possibilities, management must be fully aware of when, how, against whom, and why the disciplinary action should be taken. Only then will this action, however unpleasant, be likely to gain its purposes with a minimum loss of employee good will. Even when an employee fully deserves punishment, he invariably accepts it with some amount of ill feeling. Nevertheless, to forgo negative and drastic action when it is deserved is to ask for trouble. But to deal out penalties when they are not deserved or when the reasons therefor are not clearly understood is doubly dangerous.

In the discussion that follows, it has been deemed advisable to examine the meaning of discipline and disciplinary action. Second, the steps to be taken in disciplinary action are studied. Third, fundamental and practical principles to be followed in taking the steps of disciplinary action.

However, in the case of disciplinary action, as with grievances, management may deal in joint action with unions. Later in this chapter, therefore, mention is made of this phase of disciplinary action.

Disciplinary action in most companies is taken by line executives. The personnel department is responsible for taking final action on such serious penalties as discharge and for advising the line on desirable practices. Hence, in this chapter the discussion of methods and principles is pertinent to both line and staff executives.

Definition of Terms

A common complaint about employees is that they do not always do what they are told. Why do they fail to follow orders? There are several possible explanations. The employees may be ignorant; they may misunderstand orders and instructions; they may be careless; they may have little sense of responsibility; or they may purposely and with malice disobey orders or waste property.

These explanations indicate that employees approach their work with a variety of attitudes toward their fellow workers, management, and the company. Their attitude is summed up in the concept of discipline. Discipline is said to be good when employees willingly follow the rules of their superiors and their company. Discipline is said to be bad when employees either follow rules unwillingly or actually disobey regulations.

But how is discipline developed or attained? If discipline is good, it may be due to excellent handling of grievances or positive motivation of the workers, or it may be that cases of disobedience have been capably handled. Poor discipline, however, no matter what the cause, suggests the need for correction.

The type of correction depends, of course, upon the cause of poor discipline. If the attitude is unfavorable because the company is at fault, the action to be taken involves (1) removal of the cause and (2) convincing the employees of the desire of the company to be fair. Such correction comes under the heading of handling of grievances, general surveys of company policies and practices, and following up employee suggestions that pertain to such matters.

When the attitude is unfavorable due to faults in the worker, however, the action to be taken is known as disciplinary action. It involves warnings, suggestions, and other penalties by the company to the worker. The correction, it must be noted, implies some degree of force and penalty.

Although the two words are often used interchangeably, it is well to keep clear two ideas about discipline and disciplinary action. "Discipline," used as a noun and preceded by the adjective "good," means that the worker willingly abides by company rules and executive orders. When discipline is bad, it means that the worker, through some fault of his own, is not being obedient. Disciplinary action, or to discipline, means the steps taken to attempt to correct the disobedience and, if possible, the cause.

In handling disciplinary cases, there are two major aspects that must be watched: (1) the steps to be taken and (2) the principles to follow in each step. The two must be considered together in actual practice; but for purposes of discussion, it is simpler to take up each separately. Attention is now directed to the first of these aspects.

PROCEDURES OF DISCIPLINARY ACTION

Although it is not always possible or practical to follow a set routine in taking disciplinary action, nevertheless there are certain steps or stages to which attention must be directed at one time or another. These steps include the following:

1. Accurate statement of the disciplinary problem
2. Collection of full information on the case
3. Selection of tentative penalties to be applied
4. Choice of the alternative penalties
5. Application of the penalty
6. Follow-up of the case

Statement of Problem

Perhaps no more important step can be taken in the whole process of disciplinary action than to make absolutely certain about the problem that calls for discipline. There should be no guesswork in this step, or else mistakes accumulate through all the other steps.

In general, there are five questions that must be answered in arriving at a statement of a disciplinary problem:

1. Is this case one calling for disciplinary action?
2. Exactly what is the nature of the violation?
3. Under what conditions did it occur?
4. What individual or individuals are involved?
5. When or how often have the violations occurred?

1. *Determining the Nature of the Violation.* The first of the foregoing questions can seldom be answered first. Nevertheless, it is stated first because that question should run through all the proceedings. Falsely including a case under the heading of one calling for disciplinary action is bound to have unfortunate repercussions. Right from the start, it is a wise executive who does not jump at conclusions or misinterpret circumstances, for a slight delay in taking disciplinary

action is not so serious as delays in handling grievances. After all, if a subordinate is in the wrong, the case will keep; but if he is not and is falsely accused, the insult will smolder in his memory for some time. Insofar as possible, executives must assure themselves that a violation has occurred and that the violation is entirely or in part the fault of one or more subordinates.

2. *Stating the Violation.* With this in mind, the next step is to state precisely and objectively the nature of the alleged violation. The specific rule, regulation, policy, request, or order that was broken and the degree to which it was broken must be determined. There should be no generalities or vaporizing here; or certainly the less, the better. For example, the following statement, "My request that the materials on his workbench be moved immediately was not obeyed until the next day," is much better than "He didn't follow my orders." There is a specificness about the former that gives a quantitative as well as a qualitative measurement of the violation, which the latter lacks.

3. *Determining the Circumstances.* Of course, a violation may be excusable or not, depending upon the circumstances. In the example just cited, it might have been that the order was given shortly before quitting time. The worker might well have felt that he was not expected to work overtime but could finish the next day. Thus the worker might be excused for violating the order because the conditions, in the mind of the worker, justified quitting on time. After all, most employees leave their work places without reporting before leaving—in most instances, this is customary practice.

Moreover, in examining the circumstances, it might be desirable in serious cases to make a critical analysis of a person's background and makeup. This is done on the reasonable assumption that people are not inherently lawbreakers but that there may have been something that disposed a particular individual to break a rule. If the cause is found, its elimination will go much further in improving discipline than any penalty ever would. Viewed in this fashion, taking disciplinary action has a constructive and positive foundation rather than the negative force of punishment. It partakes somewhat of positive motivation, discussed in an earlier chapter.

4. *Individuals Involved.* It is also significant to know exactly what individual or individuals were involved in a violation. For example, if one individual has broken a safety rule, he alone should be punished; but if someone else has been involved in the case, he too should be included in the penalty. Thus a given employee may have cut himself, let us say, while sharpening a tool against company rules, which state that only a toolmaker shall perform this operation. Yet the toolmaker might have refused to do the job for one reason or another when requested to do so by the other employee. Of course, the injured employee had no right to proceed with the sharpening, but the toolmaker should also be included for possible discipline. Such multiple aspects of discipline must not be overlooked.

5. *Number of Repetitions.* And finally, it is desirable to state as precisely as possible when or how often the alleged violations occurred. Here again, the seriousness of a violation is dependent upon the number of violations. For example, a person who has been absent without excuse several times in a given month deserves a more serious reprimand than one who has been absent but once. Or again, if a violation occurs during a particularly busy or rush period, it should be weighed more heavily than one that takes place during a lull. However, these things will not be known unless specifically included; hence, time or times of violation should be cited.

To summarize, statement of the case requires careful examination of several aspects. It may involve some effort, but the results are worthwhile. First, the dangers of false or inaccurate accusations are reduced. Also, when presented with a clear statement of the case, employees learn that the superior is not making a hasty decision after a superficial examination but is desirous of being fair in dealing out penalties. In addition, the superior himself will feel more sure of himself in whatever decision he reaches. Moreover, a careful statement of the problem will indicate whether it is a case he himself should handle or whether it should be referred to his superiors. If the latter, a clear statement of the case will enable the superiors to take immediate disciplinary action with no lost time or waste motion in compiling the statement themselves.

Gathering Facts

Gathering facts is essentially supplementary to the preceding step as well as others to follow. Nevertheless, as in the case of handling grievances, pertinent data are essential. How these may be collected was discussed rather fully in the preceding chapter; hence, it is suggested that a review of that material be made.

It is worthwhile here merely to highlight some of the significant aspects of fact gathering. First, as noted in the preceding chapter, fact gathering is often a process of fact sifting. If opinions are mistaken for facts, it is easy to reach wrong conclusions. Second, a thorough examination of every case is suggested. When an executive has worked with a group over a period of time, he should know it well enough to expedite

the search for facts. Third, the facts of the case should be so well culled
that an executive should be willing to produce them should they be
called for. And fourth, management should be respectful of others
when gathering information to avoid losing the confidence of employees.

Establishing Tentative Penalties

Tentative alternative types of disciplinary action should now be for-
mulating themselves in the mind of the executive. The peremptory
adoption of a given course of action is invariably undesirable. It suggests a predisposition toward a prejudiced mind and may lead to incorrect discipline. Moreover, if the first disciplinary action is shown to be
inappropriate, a rehash of the case and a delay in its handling would
result.

1. *Types of Penalties.* At this juncture, it may be well to consider, at least in outline form, the various types of disciplinary action
that are available. Perhaps the most common type is the simple reprimand. This is sufficient in most instances to change the attitude of an
employee who has broken some regulation. After all, most of us do not
like to be criticized, no matter how gently, and will seek to avoid
incurring such disciplinary action. Indeed, with some individuals, it is
enough merely to point out their mistakes; they can be relied upon to
reprimand themselves.

Another form of discipline is the mild penalty, but nevertheless a
penalty. The penalties may be financial or nonfinancial. For example,
tardiness may subject the employee to a small loss of wage. Or an
excessive number of tardinesses or absences may remove the possibility
of a merit increase. On the other hand, nonfinancial penalties may
involve loss of preference for a transfer, various privileges, and assignment to favored jobs or tasks.

And finally, there are the more drastic penalties. These include
demotion, temporary layoffs, and outright discharges. As noted earlier,
such disciplinary actions are so serious that they require authorization by
the personnel department as well as the immediate executive. This does
not weaken the hand of the executive because an executive who has
carefully considered such a decision will seldom be overruled. Moreover, the best interests of the company may be better served sometimes
by transferring a man to another department rather than by outright
discharge. Removing him from his present department protects the
accusing foreman, and sending him to another department saves the
investment in the employee.

2. Standard Penalties. In the selection of tentative disciplinary actions, it is perhaps well (*a*) to have a list of all types of disciplinary actions permitted by the company, (*b*) to have a list of those types that various executive levels are permitted to take, and (*c*) to compile a list

FIGURE 27–1. Disciplinary Penalties

▶19. Posting or removal of any matter on bulletin boards or company property at any time unless specifically authorized by Industrial Relations Department.	1 day off	3 days off	Discharge		
▶20. Theft or removal from the premises without proper authorization of any company property or property of the government or of any employee.	Discharge				
▶21. Gambling or engaging in a lottery on company premises.	Discharge				
▶22. Misusing, destroying, or damaging any company property or property of any employee.	Discharge				
▶23. Deliberately restricting output.	Discharge				
▶24. Making of false, vicious, or malicious statements concerning any employee, the company, or its product.	Warning	3 days off	1 week off	Discharge	
▶25. Provoking, or instigating a fight, or fighting during working hours or on company premises.	1 week off or discharge	Discharge			
▶26. Drinking any alcoholic beverage on premises or on company time.	1 week off	Discharge			
▶27. Reporting for work obviously under the influence of alcohol or drugs.	1 day off	3 days off	1 week off	Discharge	
▶28. Engaging in sabotage or espionage.	Discharge				
▶29. Violating a safety rule or safety practice.	Warning	1 day off	3 days off	1 week off	Discharge
▶30. Immoral conduct or indecency.	Discharge				
▶31. Interfering or refusing to cooperate with Plant Protection officers in the performance of their duties.	Discharge				
▶32. Sleeping on job during working hours.	Discharge				
▶33. Entering restricted areas without specific permission.	Warning	3 days off	Discharge		
▶34. Refusal to show badge at the request of any member of supervisison or Plant Protection.	Discharge				
▶35. Leaving plant during work shift without permission.	1 day off	1 week off	Discharge		
▶36. Insubordination.	1 week off or discharge	Discharge			
▶37. Failure to observe parking and traffic regulations on premises.	Warning	1 day off	3 days off	1 week off	Discharge
▶38. Mistakes due to lack of knowledge.	Warning	1 day off	Demotion		
▶39. Leaving work area without permission before final whistle blows indicating end of shift.	Warning	3 days off	1 week off	Discharge	
▶40. Failure to report for overtime work without good reason after being scheduled to work according to overtime policy.	Warning	1 day off	3 days off	1 week off	Discharge

SOURCE: "Simplifies Discipline Procedure," *Factory Management and Maintenance*, Vol. CVIII, No. 10, p.458

that is pertinent and restricted to the case at hand. An example of increasing penalties as the number of repetitions grows is shown in Figure 27–1.

A list of all types of disciplinary action is a desirable tool. It can be used to make certain that no possibility is overlooked. Thus the executive involved can run down the list, actually written out or from memory, and see which might be pertinent. Having a list that divides penalties according to rank is desirable because executives will know which cases should be referred to others and which can be passed upon by themselves. For example, discharge is a very serious penalty and should be used only as a last resort. Moreover, a discharge may involve the company in a lawsuit, in which case the company as well as the supervisor would be affected. As a consequence, it is desirable for others besides the supervisors, for example, to pass upon such penalties.

The third list is the one that would be worked up for each case that seemed to call for disciplinary action. It could be developed very quickly after the other two were compiled. It need not, of course, be a written list, although this is desirable.

Choosing the Penalty

After a case calling for disciplinary action has been thoroughly examined and alternative penalties have been considered, the particular penalty to be applied should be chosen. The choice usually is made upon the basis of one's experience and a comparison of the case at hand with previous cases.

Also, it is wise to consult with others, particularly when a case evidently falls outside the jurisdiction of a given executive. But even on matters that come completely within one's scope, outside consultation can be very helpful. Thus the executive who talks over a troublesome case with his own superior, some other supervisor, or the personnel department gets the benefit of their advice, and he also gives himself an opportunity to recheck himself as he presents the case to the others.

In the choice of a penalty, it should be remembered that it will serve somewhat as a precedent if a similar case has never been handled. Employees are quick to compare current decisions with what has gone before. When the kind or degree of penalties to be assigned for particular types of disobedience, for example, is indeterminate, employees will conclude that management is wishy-washy and vacillating.

Applying Penalties

The next step, the application of the penalty, involves a positive and assured attitude on the part of management. If executives are to convey the idea that they are confident of the fairness of their decisions, their very attitude and conduct should be in accord with the decision.

In other words, if the disciplinary action is a simple reprimand, an executive should calmly and quickly dispose of the matter. When drastic action is called for, a forthright, serious, and determined attitude is highly desirable. On the one hand, the case is not overdone; nor, on the other hand, is the severity of the case minimized. In this regard, it is best to minimize one's personal feelings or desire to dramatize. Reprimands and penalties are always unpleasant to hand out; hence the quicker and more impersonally the matters are handled, the fewer the undesirable effects.

In taking action, too, this step should not be delayed. Penalties are most effective when the punishment is closely associated in the mind of the wrongdoer with the act that brought it on. If a penalty is delayed unduly, the employee involved may have forgotten the case or considered it closed, and therefore may conclude that the company is "picking on him."

Follow-up of Disciplinary Action

The ultimate purpose of disciplinary action is, of course, to assure good productivity by developing good discipline. Its aim is to make certain, as far as possible, that employees do not willfully or carelessly break rules or disobey instructions. The disciplinary action cannot repair the damage done. Hence, disciplinary action must be evaluated in terms of its effectiveness after it has been applied.

Too often, follow-up is a matter of assuming that disciplinary action has been effective as long as there is no recurrence of bad discipline. Of course, that is all right as long as rules are not being broken. A far better practice is to check closely employees who have been subject to disciplinary action. Their performance and attitudes should be subject to review, openly or with subtle casualness, as the seriousness of the case may suggest.

To be sure, employees who are being checked may resent it. However, since they did cause trouble, it will further serve the purpose of discipline for them to know that management's confidence in them has been shaken. This does not mean that management should "pour it on" indefinitely. In serious cases a checkup may be more or less formal; in less serious cases, casual checkups may be all that is desirable; and in simple reprimands, subtle observation ordinarily will be sufficient. If further repetitions are to be prevented, care obviously should be exercised at the points where difficulties have been encountered.

The personnel department should be informed of serious penalties, so that it, too, may follow up ultimate effects. A record of discipline cases should be filed here, so that severe penalties can be supported by evidence that misdeeds were of a continuing nature.

PRINCIPLES OF DISCIPLINARY ACTION

Although it is essential to know what steps should be taken in handling disciplinary cases, it is of equal importance to know the whys and wherefores of the steps being taken. Much remains to be learned about the underlying principles of disciplinary action. Yet, much useful experience is available in most companies. This may be seen by commenting on the desirability of disciplinary action, rules of dealing with employees, implications of disciplinary action, and union-management relations in disciplinary action.

Desirability of Disciplinary Action

At the moment disciplinary action is being taken, an employee may dislike being criticized, reprimanded, or discharged; but it may be good for him over a period of time. However, it should be good for the company both now and in the future.

1. *Responsibility of Line Executives.* Executives must be sold on the need of discipline from the company's viewpoint. After all, to be profitable, the company must be efficient. To be efficient, it must, among other things, have employees who do not excessively disregard rules, disobey orders, or work carelessly. Hence, to protect its own interests and those of the customers it serves, disciplinary action is essential to the company. Obviously, an employee who kills time is not helping the company; yet, he was hired to do a fair day's work, presumably at a fair day's pay.

2. *Responsibility of Personnel Department.* Executives should be convinced that disciplinary action is a tool that must be used for the company's benefit, even though it would be temporarily more pleasant if such action were not taken. Hence the personnel department can do much good by training executives not to shrink from taking disciplinary action when it is justified. That is one of their responsibilities as executives. It is one of their unpleasant duties and one for the assumption of which they are compensated.

3. *Confidence in Company Policies.* What if an executive believes that certain rules of the company are unfair? Several angles must be discussed regarding such a situation. In the first place, he should nevertheless continue to enforce it as though he had confidence in it. An executive who in any way leads employees to believe that he has no confidence in the company will soon find that the subordinates do not trust him. In the second place, he should make certain that he knows precisely why the rule was established. Often, we do not like what we do not understand, even though the lack of understanding may lie in our own failure to take steps to find out the meaning and reason for rules. If, after the second step, an executive is convinced that a rule is wrong, he should attempt to clear up the matter by presenting his side,

as he sees it, to his superiors with a view to suggesting a change. And finally, if a change is not made and the executive remains convinced of the inequity of the rule, he should either accept the rule notwithstanding or seek another position.

This does not mean that every time an executive disagrees with his superiors, he should resign. After all, no matter where or with whom one works, there will always be points upon which agreement is not unanimous. Hence, some disagreement does not mean disloyalty. But if after going through the steps outlined in the foregoing, an executive disagrees with some company rules, he nevertheless should follow them implicitly or give up his position.

Asking an executive to do this is no more than the executive asks of his subordinates. The reasonable executive knows that he may be wrong at times but that he must continue to do his job as best he can. And in this vein, he must attempt to explain rules and regulations to all subordinates. If his views are not seen clearly after reasonable effort, the executive must refer the case elsewhere or take steps to close the case himself. Similarly, in dealing with his superiors about company policy, an executive cannot expect to see through the implications of all rules.

4. *Developing Confidence in Employees.* These remarks about the attitude of executives toward company rules and policies have been somewhat extended because bad discipline is bound to result when executives do not have or fail to display confidence in company rules. Furthermore, it is inevitable that executives will fail to see clearly the need for some rules or penalties. Nevertheless, they must not permit an irreducible number of conflicts to ruin their attitude toward rules, at least in the eyes of their subordinates. For example, the supervisor who says to an employee, "Well, that rule was figured out by some brass hat who doesn't know what's going on down here," is doing an injustice to the company. He is also doing the employee, and himself particularly, a serious injustice. He is not only "passing the buck" but is also inviting other violations. The employees will be led to conclude that neither the supervisor nor the rules need be respected.

Attitude toward Employees

To confidence in company policies on disciplinary matters must be added confidence in the innate goodness of the worker. It is essential to believe that employees can be trusted even though they occasionally break rules. After all, even the best workers make mistakes of omission and commission. To be sure, it is hard to trust employees when, at times, a wave of rule breaking takes place. Unless a fundamental faith is held in the trustworthiness of labor, management will have little else to look forward to than a future of watching for and disciplining lawbreakers.

1. *Importance of Attitudes.* All of us influence people not only by what we do but also by the innumerable mannerisms that are inadvertent expressions of our feelings. In other words, our attitudes toward others show through our actions and behaviorisms. Hence, when an executive assumes that employees are untrustworthy, that attitude will be discovered by the employees, and they will return in kind.

The point is that even though some penalizing is inevitable, all employees should not be considered as inveterate lawbreakers. On the contrary, an underlying current of confidence in the fundamental integrity of employees must run through all disciplinary action.

2. *The Value of Disciplinary Action.* On the other hand, executives must be convinced that disciplinary action is needful and effective. In particular, they must feel that any penalties assigned in given cases were not only merited but were also beneficial to employees. If, in the future, wrongdoings are reduced, the resulting harmonious atmosphere can be in part ascribed to earlier instances of negative motivation. Such a happier state can be achieved because most people prefer to conform. The effectiveness of disciplinary action in attaining this goal can be increased by adding to penalties constructive suggestions on how transgressions can be avoided.

3. *The Use of Fear.* Good does not derive from correcting the damage done—that is a loss, more or less. It must come from a changed attitude toward the company's rules and regulations. It is too bad that some employees are willing to obey rules only for fear of penalties. But if it is to their benefit to have jobs, and if fear keeps them on the "straight and narrow," the use of reasonable penalties is of benefit to the employees themselves. It must be remembered that to some degree, fear rules the lives of all of us. The wise man can get along with a minimum of fear; yet, he too recognizes that it acts as a spur in his activities.

This brief comment upon fear, upon which penalties essentially rest, is not intended as justification for irresponsible employment of it. The role of fear should be restricted; nevertheless, when its use is called for, executives should be trained to employ it intelligently.

4. *Individual Differences.* Moreover, executives should be impressed with the fact that some people are very thin-skinned, whereas others have the hide of an elephant. As a consequence, it is essential to adopt disciplinary practices that fit the case. That is why such rules as "reprimand in private" are often cited. Not that some people should not

be penalized publicly. Rather, there is greater danger in using an occasional public reprimand than when private penalties are always assigned. Indeed, with some employees a good all-out airing in public works best, but one cannot always be certain that such a reprimand is best for the person in question. Hence, in dealing out penalties, it is wise to be conservative and gradually to step up the penalty, if need be.

Implications of Disciplinary Action

Disciplinary action can be successful only if an executive takes into account the implications of such action upon himself, upon others, and upon future relationships.

1. *Disciplinary Action as a Tool.* An executive must, to begin with, consider disciplinary action as a tool, not as a weapon of supervision. He should see penalties and reprimands in the same light as brakes on a car. They "slow down" employees when needed, they act as a preventive, but they cannot cure an accident.

Hence, when a penalty is applied, it should be in the manner of using a tool and not as a threatening gesture. The penalty is bad enough; the executive gains nothing—indeed, often loses prestige—when he becomes emotional or dramatic. Employees will accept penalties in good grace only when an executive does not gloat over the occasion, and they will tend to restrain themselves when they have confidence in the reasonableness of an executive's action. When disciplinary action is used as a club, an executive had better prepare himself for a period of intentional, willful, and perhaps vicious disobedience.

2. *Cooperation with Others.* Moreover, the executive's attitude toward disciplinary action can be seen in his attitude toward the efforts of fellow executives. Any indication of laughing at, ridiculing, or undermining the work of others will encourage repercussions from other executives and result in a loss of prestige in the eyes of one's own subordinates. When a man does not have respect for his own profession or those in his profession, he can look for little consideration for his own work in that profession. To destroy confidence in one's own efforts, one need only go about destroying confidence in those who are doing similar work.

3. *Aftereffects.* In taking disciplinary action, it is also imperative to remember that disciplinary action has its aftereffects. This comes about in two major ways. In the first place, a given penalty does or does not serve to change the employee's attitude toward company rules. This aspect has already been discussed. In the second place, a given penalty in a given case is considered as a precedent. In the future, therefore, when

similar cases are to be disciplined, the penalty should not be changed except for good reason.

As an example, if some infraction previously has been punished lightly, such as reprimanding a person found smoking in areas where smoking is not permitted, an extreme penalty such as discharge should be used with hesitation and with warning. It is far better to announce that thereafter the rule is going to be enforced strictly. Although the legal right to fire in such cases without warning seems to exist, some companies have found to their sorrow that an unannounced change in policy toward the enforcement of company rules has been considered a subterfuge by the National Labor Relations Board, for example, to obstruct collective bargaining. Thus, rules should be applied in the same way all the time, or there is danger of losing the confidence of employees or having some outside agency criticize the company and its management.

Union-Management Relations

Most companies take the stand that disciplinary action is a prerogative of management. They contend that management must have the unrestricted right to discipline employees, or else it will be impossible to produce the right quality of goods economically and effectively. In essence, the argument is that in accepting the responsibilities that go with operating a business, there must be a counterbalancing weight of authority. This attitude is held so strongly by some companies that they will neither relinquish any aspects of discipline to joint action with unions nor include any phase of it as a subject for collective bargaining.

On the other hand, there are companies which accept the offices of the unions in various aspects of disciplinary action. To begin with, some have agreed that the union may challenge cases in which it feels that punishment has been excessive, partial, or misdirected. In other cases, unions are given the right to participate in hearings in which the type of disciplinary action to be taken is being considered. And in still other cases the union itself may take disciplinary steps, such as layoffs or a reduction of status on a priority list. While direct participation in disciplinary action is not common, it does indicate how far some companies have gone in accepting union action in this area.

As time goes on, it is probable that unions will play a larger role in disciplinary matters. In the final analysis, such participation must be based on good principles and procedures. It is as much to the advantage of the union to be fair to employees as it is to management. Hence, if good principles must prevail eventually, it would seem to be the wise thing for management to adopt such plans and practices before they are forced upon it by outsiders. When outsiders force changes, they take credit for them; yet, it is management which must make them work.

QUESTIONS

1. What, if any, are the essential differences between the terms "discipline" and "disciplinary action"?
2. Why is the accurate determination and statement of the nature of a violation so important in disciplinary action?
3. If a number of employees are involved in an infraction of rules, should disciplinary action be taken individually or collectively? Explain.
4. What levels of penalties may be imposed? What essentially is the basic purpose of each?
5. What division of work would you suggest between the personnel department and line departments in the handling of disciplinary cases? How much would the division depend upon a definition of disciplinary matters?
6. What is the role of follow-up in disciplinary action?
7. A given supervisor complained to the workers that the policies of the company were unsound. What effect are such statements likely to have upon the supervisor? If you, as a supervisor, cannot understand certain policies in regard to disciplinary action, what should you do?
8. In your opinion, are employees essentially good or essentially bad? How must your relations to employees differ depending upon the stand you take?
9. On what grounds, if any, would you condone the use of fear as a tool of disciplinary action.
10. A given company takes the stand that disciplinary action is a prerogative of management and that it is in no way to be diluted by the union. Why might it take this stand? Should union help ever be sought in such matters? Explain.

CHAPTER 28

PERSONNEL RESEARCH AND EVALUATION

Introduction

At the outset of this text, it was noted that personnel management has to do with planning, organizing, directing, and controlling various tasks of procuring, developing, maintaining, and utilizing an effective work force. And throughout the foregoing chapters, principles and practices related to these functions have been described and examined. A useful review of the work of personnel management may be accomplished by emphasizing the research aspects of the function of planning and the evaluation aspects of control. Each chapter of this text could well have had sections on research and evaluation were space no object, but much duplication is eliminated by this final summary. It contains a point of view, however, which is fundamental to every function of personnel management discussed in earlier chapters.

The first section of this chapter is concerned with research, an activity without which planning must be based upon trial and error or upon what others have done.

The second section is concerned with evaluating personnel activities. One learns from the past only by reviewing what has been done. The lessons so learned can brighten the future. Evaluation has as its purpose, therefore, not recrimination, but rather the reduction of future errors and the maximization of future benefits.

PERSONNEL RESEARCH

Nature and Scope

Personnel research, defined simply, is the task of searching for and analyzing facts to the end that personnel problems may be solved or that guide lines governing their solutions may be deduced. Its scope is all-inclusive. There are no subjects in personnel about which so much is known that no further research is justified. On the contrary, our tested knowledge of basic relationships is so meager that it is a wonder that we get along as well as we do in working with people.

Even in fields in which business has been working for many years, a precise and indisputable basis of action is not available. Witness the following remarks on training:

> There is, then, little dependable research data published on industrial training. By dependable research data, I mean conclusions concerning a problem which are based on investigations which control, statistically or otherwise, all variables. This, of course, is not conclusive evidence that training men are not using a research approach. My contacts with industrial training, other than in my own organization, are not so broad as I would like. Yet these contacts have given me little evidence that an extensive use of research techniques is being made in industrial training.[1]

The absence of adequate research in every other field of personnel could similarly be observed. Hence the problem of research is to determine which of the many pressing problems should be studied first. It is a matter of determining how available resources and time can best be allocated.

Obviously, it is impossible here to survey the fields of needed research or what has been done. All that can be done here is (1) to comment briefly on some basic considerations in research and (2) to illustrate with an example or two the task and value of careful data gathering.

Basic Considerations

A number of comments are in order regarding how and why research should be carried on.

1. *Uses of Research.* The objective of research is the truth. This simple statement should be sufficient to support the claim that research is for the use of everyone concerned with a personnel problem. Labor, management, the general public, governmental agencies, and the consumer are its beneficiaries. Each gains, or none does. Unless this attitude is accepted by the researcher, whoever he may be, the results will be rejected on the grounds that "figures may not lie, but liars may figure." It is imperative, therefore, that in undertaking research, investigations

---

[1] William McGehee, *The Research Approach to Training,* Personnel Series, No. 117 (New York: American Management Association), pp. 32–33.

should be conducted in the hope of finding the correct answer—not the answer some particular group wants.

If research is conducted with a view to impartiality, each step of the research should be acceptable to and reviewable by any unbiased student. With this premise guiding one's research, the results will be useful to all concerned because they will be truthful.

More specifically, uses of research would be related to the following aspects of personnel management, human relations, and labor-management relations:

a) To measure and evaluate present conditions
b) To predict future conditions, events, and behavioral patterns
c) To evaluate effects and results of current policies, programs, and activities
d) To provide an objective basis for revising current policies, programs, and activities
e) To appraise proposed policies, programs, and activities

2. *Responsibility for Research.* The foregoing suggests, in turn, that research is not the sole responsibility or within the sole jurisdiction of any particular group, interest, or department. To be sure, for present purposes, it might be argued that a research section should be established in the personnel department of most companies. This is a fine practice because it serves to focus attention on research, to help establish a research program, and to provide for experts and facilities of research.

But others, too, can and should be brought into the fold. Line supervisors and executives at all levels can help with research projects as well as carry on their own projects. Where unions are in the picture, their help and cooperation should be sought. Nor should such outside organizations as educational institutions, private research groups, endowed foundations, and governmental agencies be overlooked.[2]

The importance of cooperation is evidenced by the growing use of operations research. This involves the solution of personnel problems by the use of teams of specialists who combine their talents, skills, and techniques in an interdisciplinary, scientific group effort. The group considers and weighs which among several alternative answers is best, giving due consideration to the dynamic character of the variables in a problem. Obviously, such cooperative effort provides a force of analysis which few, if any, personnel managers can hope to attain individually.

---

[2] Invaluable is the work of such organizations as the American Management Association, the National Industrial Conference Board, the Bureau of Labor Statistics, the Bureau of Foreign and Domestic Commerce, the National Office Management Association, and the Society for the Advancement of Management.

The extent of cooperation depends upon a number of factors. Some problems may be of an individual and confidential nature, whereas others may be of universal interest. The former may desirably be attacked on a private, individual, and intracompany basis. The latter may be attacked with all the outside help that can be obtained. In either event, most problems are so difficult that their solution demands the combined talents and resources of various specialists.

3. *Facilities of Research.* The suggestion is in order that extensive facilities, desirable though they may be, are not indispensable to carry on much useful research. The records of every company contain a wealth of information. All that is needed is the effort to examine them. For example, a simple survey, such as the question of why employees have left the company, will serve to improve personnel practices. In one company that made such a survey, it was found that a majority of quits occurred in two departments. Following up this trail by an attitude survey, poor supervision was discovered to be the cause. After this was cleared up by retraining the supervisors, the quits in these departments fell to a normal figure. Such research can be carried on without excessive cost or effort.

On the other hand, some research techniques involve high skill and considerable outlays for equipment. Some tabulating equipment falls into this category. Or linear programming, a mathematical and graphical method, is useful (but complicated) in arriving at decisions involving situations where several choices, with variations of degree in each choice, are available. And cybernetics, which employs sophisticated techniques of informational feedback and control, involves skills of a high order. But in complicated and important problems, decision making is dependent on such techniques.

4. *Importance of Pure Research.* One of the lessons that industry in general as yet must learn about personnel research is that pure research in this area is as useful as it is in physics and chemistry. It is not uncommon to read reports issued by various companies announcing the projected opening of new and complete facilities for research and testing in the physical sciences. But provision of facilities for research in personnel problems is rarely made. Yet, human problems of industry, it is generally agreed, are far more complex and numerous than physical problems. Unfortunately, research in human problems seems to many to be frosting on the cake, whereas technical research leads to direct results in the competitive battle for markets. Failure to learn how to handle labor problems, however, may eat up most of the profits technical research may be providing. A number of universities have in the past

FIGURE 28–1. Suggested Research Projects

Please check the areas which you consider worthy of research efforts.

Area

— a. Discovery of new principles of human relations
— b. Application of known principles of human relations
— c. Human characteristics and attributes
— d. Measurement of human characteristics and attributes
— e. Forecasting future of company with reference to its human relations position

— f. Personnel policies
— g. Labor market
— h. Job analysis and evaluation
— i. Recruitment, selection, and placement
— j. Individual testing

— k. Operator training
— l. Supervisor training
— m. Administrator training
— n. Performance rating
— o. Employee services

— p. Personnel records and reports
— q. Promotions, demotions, transfers, layoffs, and separations
— r. Health
— s. Safety
— t. Communications

— u. Employee attitude
— v. Adjustments and social relationships
— w. Wages and salaries
— x. Hours of work, rests
— y. Working conditions

— z. Production standards
— a'. Labor turnover
— b'. Absenteeism
— c'. Measures of effectiveness of personnel program
— d'. Legislation affecting human relations

— e'. Relationship with union
— f'. Collective bargaining
— g'. Clauses for union contracts
— h'. Grievance procedures
— i'. Mediation and arbitration

— j'. Other (*Please specify.*)

_____

_____

decade dedicated themselves to pure research in the personnel area, but substantial progress cannot be expected until industry joins ranks in examining human problems.

5. *Relation of Research and Collective Bargaining.* Another lesson that industry must learn is that it must undertake research if it is to bargain successfully with unions. The latter, in some instances, are so far advanced in their researches on wages, economic trends, bargaining processes, and labor relations that the efforts of management to refute labor's argument's are often pathetic. No other road will lead to stable labor relations but that which is paved with facts, information, and statistics. Until industry travels that road, it can look forward to nothing but emotional bombast, name calling, and pressure politics.

6. *Priority Lists.* Earlier, it was noted that establishing a priority of research projects is perhaps of greater practical significance than determining subjects of research. The tests of priority should be importance of problems and timeliness.

A useful way of developing such a list is to sample executive judgment. For example, a list such as that illustrated in Figure 28–1 could be sent to various executives. They could be asked to number, from the sample list, the first ten projects—or any other number—they considered most significant. The results would be most helpful in determining where money, talents, and time should be allocated.

7. *Attitude of Mind.* Research is conditioned, too, by attitude toward accepted principles and practices. Executives who do not question the way things have always been done are likely to make undesirable mistakes in working with their associates and subordinates. To illustrate, it is commonly held that high morale and high production go together. But the relation between morale and production has been found, as shown in Figure 28–2, to run in varying directions, depending upon the pressure exerted by supervisors for production. Commenting on this, it was noted as follows:

> Early in these studies, it was observed that leaders who are employee-oriented often have better records than production-oriented leaders, in the area of productivity as well as in the area of morale. On the other hand, it was later found that if a leader abdicates his interest in and responsibility for production it has an adverse effect on both productivity and morale. "Soft" leadership, over-emphasis upon consideration is not conducive to high morale. A moderate amount of emphasis on production is required to avoid both low production and low morale. But, beyond a certain point, higher productivity by means of pressure appears to be obtainable only at the expense of morale. How can a particular organization decide on the proper balance which best suits its needs? Can methods be found to increase emphasis on production (beyond the middle

FIGURE 28–2. The Relation of Productivity and Morale to a
Supervisor's Pressure for Production

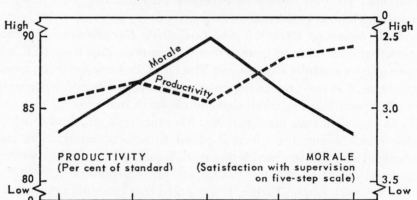

Source: Stanley E. Seashore, "Administrative Leadership and Organizational Effectiveness," in Rensis
Likert and Samuel P. Hayes, Jr. (eds.), *Some Applications of Behavioural Research* (Paris: UNESCO, 1957).
p. 58.

range which is essential for both production and morale), without damaging
morale? It will take much research to answer these questions.[3]

8. *Specialists and Their Techniques.*   And finally, a word more
is in order on the importance of looking to various fields and their tools
for help. To begin with, research emphasizes a search for facts. It is
therefore quantitative in nature. The most useful tools in this connection are mathematics and statistics. Hence, in the gathering, analysis,
and interpretation of data, reliance upon and understanding of statistical methods are indispensable. This does not mean that involved and
intricate formulas and calculations are the test of good research. It does
mean that relative to the nature of each particular research project, the
quantitative tools should be adequate.

And the range of specialists from whom help may be sought is broad
indeed. The assistance of psychologists has, of course, long been sought
and generally respected. And the statistician, too, has contributed much.
Recently, the services of others have proved most useful. For example,
the psychiatrist has been called in to help solve individual problems of
an emotional and mental character that were disturbing company efficiency and individual happiness. And increasingly, the sociologists and
anthropologists have carried on significant research and investigations
concerning group relations, customs, and status in industry.

---

[3] Stanley E. Seashore, "Administrative Leadership and Organizational Effectiveness," in Rensis Likert and Samuel P. Hayes, Jr. (eds.), *Some Applications of
Behavioural Research* (Paris: UNESCO, 1957), p. 59.

The moral is obvious; the field of research requires the services of numerous types of researchers and several kinds of tools. To seek answers through the methodology and principles of a single specialty is to build upon a weak foundation. Rather, research calls for a cosmopolitan attitude and interdisciplinary cooperation. The specialist who tries to build a fence around all aspects of research does himself and industry a serious disfavor.

EXAMPLES OF RESEARCH

To provide some substance to the foregoing discussion of personnel research, it is desirable (1) to show how research can contribute to a better understanding of a particular problem and (2) to note some recent contributors to personnel research.

Absenteeism[4]

The usefulness of research in reaching wise decisions and logical conclusions can be shown in connection with the problem of absenteeism. This discussion is taken up under the headings of importance, measurement, causes, factors, and control of absenteeism.

1. *Importance.* During periods when production is at a peak and labor is scarce, the absence of some workers from their appointed stations can be disruptive to production and morale. To illustrate, in a certain company, there were, in one department, eight absentees on one day after payday, and four others were sent home on the same day because of hazardous hangovers, making a total of twelve men (or 25 percent in this instance) absent from their work. In the chart in Figure 28–3, for example, absenteeism in the worst departments is about five times as high as in the best departments, and this unbalances production in all departments.

2. *Measurements of Absenteeism.* To combat absenteeism, it is necessary to determine its extent and causes. To do this, a definition of absenteeism should be established and records kept by departments for various causes of absenteeism by such divisions as seniority, sex, days of the week, and classes of jobs. Although there is no standard definition of absenteeism, the following definition of the Bureau of Labor Statistics is widely used:

"Absenteeism" is the failure of workers to report on the job when they are scheduled to work. It is a broad term which is applied to time lost because

---

[4] Tardiness is a problem similar to that of absenteeism. Its treatment might well follow the general pattern accorded absenteeism.

FIGURE 28–3. Chart of Absenteeism

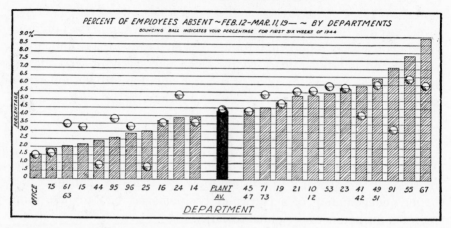

sickness or accident prevents a worker from being on the job, as well as unauthorized time away from the job for other reasons. Workers who quit without notice are also counted as absentees until they are officially removed from the payroll.

In order to have a common and comparable basis for measuring absenteeism in various plants, the Bureau of Labor Statistics suggest the following formula:

$$\text{ABSENTEEISM} = \frac{\text{MAN-DAYS LOST}}{\text{MAN-DAYS WORKED PLUS MAN-DAYS LOST}}$$

3. Causes and Distribution of Absenteeism. The specific causes of absenteeism are numerous and devious. To attribute absenteeism in a given case to illness, for example, may result in overlooking the fact that incorrect job placement may have led first to boredom, then to fatigue, and then to physical illness. Hence, in listing the following causes, no attempt is made to determine priority or immediacy of cause and effect. This can only be done by study of individual cases.

Among the reasons for absenteeism, the following list contains those cited frequently:

a) Ordinarily, illness is high on the list of absenteeism causes, running as high as 50 percent of the absenteeism in some cases.
b) Industrial accidents and occupational disease bring on much absenteeism. In one year the equivalent of the production of a million men for one year was lost due to industrial accidents.
c) Poor production and material control can result in absenteeism. Unless the flow of work between departments is balanced and maintained, workers may stay away from their jobs because they lose interest in their work and lose the feeling of the importance of being dependable.

d) Hours of work can contribute to absenteeism. Scheduled increases in overtime hours are sometimes almost entirely offset by hours of absenteeism. In one plant, men working seven days a week, 9½ hours a day, lost twice as much time as men working six days a week.

e) Lack of interest or of a feeling of responsibility and worthwhileness are fundamental causes of absenteeism. It has been found, for example, that campaigns intended to show employees the significance of their efforts have cut absenteeism as much as 50 percent.

f) After-payday sickness and hangovers contribute to absenteeism, particularly when combined with poor working conditions, lack of interest in work, and high wages.

g) A miscellaneous group of causes would include such factors as bad weather, lack of transportation, search for another job, personal business, oversleeping, and friends visiting from out of town (see Fig. 28–4).

h) Attitude of mind—caused by environmental factors, sociological factors, or opinions of neighbors—may condition some to develop a feeling of irresponsibility about coming to work.

4. *Factors in the Problem.* Study of the incidence of absenteeism will usually show some significant trends. In the first place, there seem to be absence-prone workers, just as there are accident-prone workers. From 10 to 20 percent of the workers will be found to be responsible for as high as 75 to 80 percent of the absences. Such workers may be more susceptible to illness, lack a sense of responsibility, or use absenteeism as their expression of vindictiveness. Second, such groups as women, new employees, and older employees are reported by some companies to have higher absence rates than other workers. This is not a general tendency because other companies claim that women and older workers are more dependable in this respect than the average worker.

Absenteeism is also related to the time factor. This first and last days of the week and the day after payday are usually the worst. Monthly trends are also discernible. November and December, with their year-end holidays, are usually the months with the poorest records, in some cases running two to three times as many absences as the average of the other months.

Departments or geographical areas also vary in their absence rates. Departments or locations distant from the homes of workers will usually have higher rates than others. There is occasional but not indisputable evidence that departments that call for heavy exertion or have monotonous operations and obnoxious conditions tend to have higher rates of absences. What the rates are in any company must be determined by statistical analysis.

FIGURE 28-4

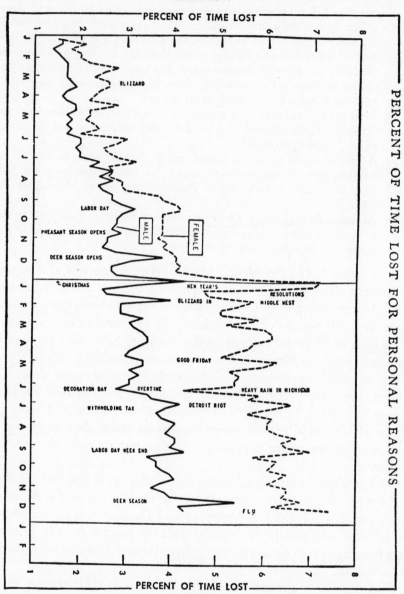

Source: General Motors Corp., *An Analysis of the Paid Sick-Leave Plan* (Detroit).

5. *Control of Absenteeism.* The control of absenteeism depends upon its causes. When these are uncovered by study and analysis, steps can be taken to eliminate them. Some of the cases are relatively simple to isolate and attack, but all are difficult to eliminate. For example, if it is discovered that illness of employees in a few departments is the major source of absenteeism, there is a real problem of how to combat the illness. Some companies have found vitamin tablets of use in such cases; others have insisted upon health examinations; and others have installed job rotation plans with success. In other words, there is no one sure cure for absence causes, once discovered.

All that can be done here is to list a variety of plans that have been used in this connection. The following are examples of control efforts:

a) Experiment with hours of work per day and per week to find the number at which absenteeism is reduced to reasonable limits.

b) Select employees with greater care to eliminate at the beginning the irresponsible, the illness-prone, and the unreliable.

c) Induct new employees in such a way that their critical attitude is reduced as quickly as possible and, with it, absenteeism from this source.

d) Plan the flow of production and materials so that workers do not on occasion find themselves without work.

e) Discipline chronic offenders by means of reprimands, layoffs, discharges, and loss of promotions and other privileges.

f) Provide rewards and bonuses for good attendance records.

g) Strengthen the hands of supervisors so that they know how to handle absenteeism.

h) Ridicule chronic offenders by publicizing names.

i) Interview all absent workers upon their return to determine causes and to impress upon them the seriousness of their absence.

j) Work with unions or labor-management committees so that the force of labor is applied against absenteeism.

In conclusion, it is interesting to compare rates of absenteeism among supervisors with those of operative employees. In the former group, among whom the feeling of responsibility ordinarily runs high, absenteeism will usually be near the zero mark, as compared to the usual 3 to 6 percent general average of absenteeism among the latter. Hence the moral is obvious: Develop in employees a sense of individual importance and worthwhileness, and their absenteeism will go down drastically. On the contrary, whatever causes employees to feel insignificant or useless will tend to increase the absentee rates.

Contributors to Personnel Research

As noted earlier, many disciplines have contributed to personnel research. All cannot be given space here. The debt of personnel management to psychology, psychiatry, medicine, statistics, and economics, for example, is large and well recognized. But such areas as sociology, group dynamics, operations research, and creative thinking are newer and deserve more than passing comment.

1. *Sociological Research.* The famous Hawthorne experiments are an example of research which illustrates the unpredictable sources of valuable information that may be uncovered. During experiments

conducted at the Hawthorne Works of the Western Electric Company to ascertain the effect of working conditions upon output, it was found that social and organizational relationships between employees are a most potent force in influencing employee output and morale. The status an employee enjoys because of the job he holds has much to do with his productivity, perhaps more than had ever been previously realized. Also, the roles which operators, supervisors, staff specialists, and union representatives assume have an impact upon interpersonal relations and group dynamics. Indeed, good human relations is often dependent on how groups feel about company policies and practices. All of these represent a sociological influence on the work of personnel management.

2. *Group Dynamics.* Of great interest recently has been the matter of how individuals work together and interact in small groups. This interest has been generated out of the recognition that people are associated in small groups either through geographical proximity or through project requirements. Since such is often the case, management should direct attention to how such groups can best work together. This implies concern with technical cooperation but, even more so, with what kinds of people should be associated together, how communications should be directed to them, how they should be motivated, and the consideration that should be given to leader-follower relationships. As yet, research here is in its early stages but has given evidence of becoming a rewarding form of investigation.

3. *Operations Research.* One of the greatest needs of personnel management is to derive quantitative support for the many decisions which must be made. Time and again, executives must make decisions upon the basis of judgment. To back up their judgments, they often have little more than a qualitative grasp of the factors in a situation. In part, this void has been filled by some statistical and factual analysis. Another contributor may be operations research.

Operations research, developed during World War II, is an intensive investigational method adapted since then to a number of fields, including that of business. It attempts to weigh the alternative courses of action that might be taken in a given situation and supply by mathematical analysis an answer to the most appropriate course of action. It often involves a team of experts to establish the factors in a problem, a model for describing how the factors interact, and a mathematical formula to evaluate the forces at work in the model.

While operations research in business has been utilized largely in connection with production problems, it has possibilities for use in the personnel area. For example, it has been used to analyze such problems as the optimum limits of executive compensation, when to work overtime, how to assign work to minimize labor costs, how best to word contracts, how much work should be done in how much time, the best incentive system for salesmen, and how to speed interplant communications. In the particular situations to which they apply—and operations research must be specific in its study of problems—it can provide personnel management with a quantitative picture of processes which previously has been unavailable to management. But it is obvious that it requires a great deal of time, expert staff, and money, factors which most companies as yet have been unwilling to spend on research in sufficient quantities.

4. *Creative Thinking.* Another aspect of personnel research of recent interest is that of the application of creative thinking. This has reference to the need of generating new ideas for the solution of personnel problems. Although getting its impetus in the field of applied sciences and advertising, creative thinking has much to offer to personnel research. When one considers the number of problems that confront management in such areas as selection, training, wages, motivation, and human relations, the contributions of creative thinking should be more than welcome.

As noted, creative thinking involves a planned attack on the generation of ideas to solve problems. It is intended to suggest ways and means for solving problems; the ways and means must then be tested. This is stressed because failure to solve problems is simply due in many cases to a lack of suggestions regarding alternative ways a problem might be attacked.

A particularly unique method of creative thinking is brainstorming. Under this plan a problem is presented to a group—let us say, how to increase the productivity in a particular department. Then the group is asked to suggest ways of doing this. The group is given two major instructions. First, ideas are to be expressed, no matter how inappropriate they may seem to be. And second, no ideas are to be evaluated or criticized during the idea-germinating period. After the brainstorming period is concluded, the ideas are explored for their plausibility. Some have found this technique to be particularly useful in developing new ways of solving problems. Others feel that individual thinking in isolation is still the best way of analyzing problems. Like almost all other techniques, this is still only a tool, not a universal cure-all, and should be viewed as such. It should be used when it seems to have a contribution to make, not in every problem-solving situation.

EVALUATION

Nature and Scope

Closely akin to research is personnel evaluation. It has to do with (1) measurement of the effectiveness of personnel programs and activities and (2) as a result of such measurements, determination of what should or should not be done in the future. Its effectiveness, as with research, is dependent upon information. And like research, its scope is as broad as the field of personnel management. The significant problem here, too, is what phases of personnel activities should be given priority. Available resources are seldom sufficient to permit an evaluation of all functions to an equal degree.

In this discussion of evaluation, it is impractical to examine various methods of evaluation. All that can be done is (1) to comment upon some basic considerations and (2) to summarize the subjects and methods of evaluation.

Basic Considerations

Evaluation of personnel and policies may be backward- or forward-looking. Since evaluation is concerned with a comparison of what happened with what was expected, there is a tendency to turn the process into faultfinding. The intent is that of finding scapegoats. Everyone expects to be called on the carpet. And as offsets, each begins to have alibis ready, to shirk responsibilities, to "pass the buck," and to mistrust others. Under such conditions, the evaluation has become worse than useless.

Forward-looking evaluation still has the determination of faults, mistakes, and errors in mind. But the purpose is not to assess penalties —although that may be done on occasions. The purpose is to find out what went wrong so that the mistake will not be repeated. In such an atmosphere the wrongdoer is as much interested in unearthing causes of failure as anyone else. With improvement being emphasized, pride in making progress is enlisted. The philosophy is positive, not negative.

Another consideration in evaluations is that of how often they should be made. A number of alternatives are available. Perhaps the most common plan is the annual evaluation or audit. At the end of the calendar or fiscal year a report covering such information as activities performed, results achieved, costs and expenditures, statistical displays, and comparison of objectives and accomplishments is presented. The reports are passed on to various executives and levels. Individual or group conferences are then held to discuss and appraise the contents.

Since too much water may pass over the dam before corrective action can be taken, other companies prefer monthly summaries of significant or exceptional developments. For example, the report illustrated in Table 28–1 provides much useful and current information on personnel activities. As a consequence, appropriate and timely action can be taken. Moreover, responsible executives are more likely to keep abreast of their personnel duties, so that undesirable exceptions will not have occurred to make such reports necessary.

In addition to periodic audits, there is the practice of conducting special studies as needed. For example, attitude surveys on particular topics may be conducted as occasion demands. Or special reports may be prepared on such matters as grievance cases, workings of seniority rules, or effect of overtime practices, for use in forthcoming bargaining sessions Or new legislation may necessitate a review of a company's practices to see what changes, if any, need to be made.

Along similar lines is the question of who should conduct evaluations and audits. Some hire outside consultants to make such reviews, whereas others perform this task themselves. The former course has the advantage of being conducted by disinterested specialists. They have no axes to grind and can evaluate a particular set of practices against a broad background of experience. They can present their findings without respect to fear or favor of any individuals. On the other hand, the outsiders are not always in the plant a sufficient length of time to get a complete and balanced picture of what is going on. And after they have presented their report, there may be no one to integrate their suggestions into future practices. However, the good in most cases outweighs the shortcomings, so that outside help is often used in conjunction with other plans, though seldom alone.

Most companies conduct their own audits. The examinations are most frequently assigned to the functional heads of the personnel division, although occasionally an audit and research unit is formed. The latter practice is limited to the larger companies. Under the former practice the employment manager reports on the achievement of hiring goals, the training manager on training accomplishments, and the labor relations manager on progress in collective bargaining. This seems to make the executive his own judge, but there are offsetting "juries." The conclusions of the various reports will be inconsistent and require reconciliation and explanation. Superior executives will find that reports

TABLE 28–1
SAMPLE PAGE OF PERSONNEL REPORT

INDUSTRIAL RELATIONS INDEX, OCTOBER	MONTHLY CUMULATIVE AVERAGE		MIDLAND
	Year to Date	Previous Year	Month
Employees, wages, and hours:			
Number of wage employees.........................	6,782	...	6,612
Total employees................................	7,618	...	7,470
Total man-hours (1,000).........................	1,334	...	1,595
Average weekly wage.............................	$ 85.34	...	$ 78.05
Average hourly rate (including overtime)..........	$ 2.16	...	$ 2.15
Premium overtime cost per hour...................	$ 0.07	...	$ 0.03
Premium overtime cost..........................	$81,728	...	$36,565
Employment:			
Applicants*....................................	42.8	...	8.4
Accessions*....................................	25.5	...	6.7
Separations*...................................	30.6	...	53.0
Percentage turnover rate per month................	2.7%	...	2.1%
Labor relations:			
Grievances pending first of month*................	4.4	...	5.6
Grievances filed during month*...................	1.0	...	1.5
Total grievances settled during month*............	0.7	...	0.4
At second step*.............................	0.1	...	0
At third step*..............................	0.3	...	0.1
At fourth step*.............................	0.3	...	0.3
Arbitration*................................	0	...	0
Grievances pending end of month*.................	4.7	...	6.7
Work stoppages—man-hours lost..................	8.9	...	0
Safety:			
Frequency rate.................................	1.54	...	1.69
Severity rate..................................	0.56	...	0.09
Compensation cost per 1,000 man-hours............	$ 3.76	...	$ 8.06
Supervisory training:			
Average hours in training........................	1.7	...	2.1
Suggestions:			
Received*.....................................	2.0	...	1.3
Adopted*.....................................	0.6	...	0.9
Declined*.....................................	2.0	...	0.9
Tangible savings...............................	$ 5,561	...	$ 6,723

* Per 1,000 employees (total).
SOURCE: Seward H. French, Jr., "Measuring Progress toward Industrial Relations Objectives," *Personnel*, March, 1954, pp. 338–47.

do not agree with their own interpretations of past events. And employees, through attitude surveys or expressed conflict, may enter counterevidence to the story told by reports.

But the personnel division need not be the sole appraiser of personnel practices. It is well to adopt the policy followed by some companies of having each line executive incorporate as a part of his annual or monthly report a section on personnel accomplishments and shortcomings. This has the advantage of underlining the sound premise that every executive is a personnel manager. It has the further advantage of interpreting personnel policies and practices at their most vital point, and not solely from the viewpoint of a staff bystander.

In short, evaluation can embrace the services of several groups and levels. The warning that must be called out here is: If many are made responsible, no one may tie all the loose ends together. Hence, whatever plan is followed, some one individual or organizational unit—senior vice-president or personnel manager or personnel evaluation division—should have the tasks of (1) bringing together all audit reports, (2) arranging meetings for their discussion, and (3) following up action taken on recommendations of such meetings.

Subjects and Methods of Evaluation

As in the case of research, there is no subject that is being performed so well that evaluation is unnecessary. Rather, all phases of personnel practice should be audited. In this way, it can be determined more accurately whether or not a company is getting the most out of the practices it is pursuing. But on the other hand, audits are desirable to ascertain whether all practices that might be of advantage to a company are being pursued. Each of these is now reviewed.

1. *Appraising Current Practices.* The field of evaluation is so broad that all that can be done here is to outline the areas and methods of evaluation. Merely by way of illustration, it is well to outline the field of coverage to be certain that nothing is overlooked, as follows:

a) Personnel functions to be evaluated:
    (1) Programming
    (2) Job analysis
    (3) Recruitment
    (4) Selection
    (5) Training
    (6) Rating
    (7) Transfers and promotions
    (8) Morale development
    (9) Health and safety
    (10) Employment stabilization
    (11) Wage and salary administration
    (12) Collective bargaining
b) Records and statistics to be used:
    (1) Time standards

(2) Cost records
(3) Test scores
(4) Training scores
(5) Interview records
(6) Work stoppages
(7) Numbers of medical reports
(8) Accident reports
(9) Grievance reports
(10) Turnover rates
(11) Unit labor costs
(12) Payroll data
   c) Methods of analysis:
(1) Comparisons between various time periods
(2) Comparisons between departments and with other companies
(3) Trend lines, frequency distributions, and statistical correlations
(4) Ratio analysis—e.g., labor costs per unit of output
(5) Classification of data by kinds of employees, products, departments, etc.
(6) Graphical or pictorial displays

An excellent example of evaluation is found in the Employee Relations Index (ERI) used by the General Electric Company. It is an attempt to measure the extent to which groups of employees accept, and perform in accordance with, the objectives and policies of the company. It is based on the following eight indicators, which were selected after detailed study of numerous aspects of employee behavior:

a) Periods of absence
b) Initial dispensary visits for occupational reasons
c) Separations from payroll
d) Grievances
e) Work stoppages
f) Number of suggestions
g) Disciplinary suspensions
h) Participation in insurance plans

The indicators are combined by means of the following multiple regression formulae to yield the ERI:

$$ERI = B_1K_1X_1 + B_2K_2X_2 + B_3K_3X_3 + B_4K_4X_4 + B_5K_5X_5$$
$$+ B_6K_6X_6 + B_7K_7X_7 + B_8K_8X_8 + C$$

where the B's refer to the weights for each element, the K's refer to constants depending on the level of the element in the plant, the X's refer to the respective indicators, and C is an overall constant for the plant or group in question.

Figure 28–5 shows how data are collected to compute the ERI, and Figure 28–6 shows a quantity summary form. The ERI is intended to

FIGURE 28–5. ERI Data-Collection Form

Fabrication; Jones, Foreman   Second Shift   12-31
Work Group   Shift   Summary for ERI Period Ending

Element	For the week ending: 10/3	10/10	10/17	10/24	10/31	11/7	11/14	11/21	11/28	12/5	12/12	12/19	12/26	Sum for 13 Weeks	Add Sum for Previous 13 Weeks	Score
Number of Employees	57	55	54	54	54	53	52	52	52	52	52	52	46	685		✕
Absentees	4	8	7	5	7	7	6	12	8	4	3	2	3	76		.11
Disciplinary Suspensions	0	0	0	0	0	0	0	0	0	0	0	0	0	0		0
Work Stoppages	0	c	0	0	0	0	0	0	0	0	0	0	0	0		0
Separations from Plant	0	0	1	1	0	1	1	0	0	0	0	2	4	10		.015
Separations from Work Group	0	4	1	1	3	2	1	0	0	0	0	2	8	22		X
Number "Bumped"	0	2	1	1	4	2	0	0	0	0	0	2	3	15		✕
Initial Occupational Dispensary Visits	5	1	3	2	3	1	3	2	1	2	3	1	3	30		.04
Grievances	0	0	0	0	0	0	0	c	c	c	c	0	0	0		.001
Suggestions	0	0	0	0	0	0	0	0	0	0	0	0	0	0		0
Group Insurance																96
Overtime	16	0	0	0	0	0	0	0	0	0	0	0	0	16		.02
Average Rate of Pay																2.45
Average Years Continuous Service																10.2
Average Number Dependents																1.8
% Male Employees																100
Average Age																38.3
% Union Dues Check-Off																89.2

SOURCE: Willard V. Merrihue, *General Electric Employee Relations Index*, Personnel Series, No. 168 (New York: American Management Association), p. 47.

help managers evaluate policies and practices, trace trends in employee relations, find trouble spots, perform their human relations duties more effectively, and control personnel costs.

2. Adequacy of Program. In the matter of determining whether or not a company is pursuing all practices which are of advantage to it, two major alternatives are available. First, outside consultants may be called in to review a company's program. This is highly desirable, because it is difficult for any company to examine itself. An outsider, however, who knows the practices of others, and particularly the breadth of programs found elsewhere, can do a good job of sizing up inadequacies, weak points, and gaps.

If a company desires to do this job itself, check lists such as the selected illustration shown in Figure 28–7 may be used. In this system of check lists, emphasis is placed upon the use of questions that may be answered either "yes" or "no." On the surface, this may appear to be an

FIGURE 28–6.   ERI Quarterly Summary Form

Work Group	No. Emp.	ERI	Absentees*	Disciplin. Suspens.**	Work Stoppages**	Plant Separations**	In. Occup.* Disp. Visits	Grievances**	Suggestions**	Insurance %	Overtime	Average Rate of Pay	Continuous Service	No. of Dependents	% Male	Average Age	Union Dues Check-Off	Shift
Test	43	107	11	0	0	13	3	0	2	93	51	$1.86	5.0	1.1	95.5	30	71.5	2 & 3
Insp. & Q.C.	21	96	6	0	0	4	2	4	73	100	115	2.19	18.2	1.5	100.0	45	66.7	1 & 2
Maint.	28	90	7	0	19	11	4	6	0	100	66	1.96	14.4	1.8	80.0	50	76.1	All
Maint.	28	101	8	0	27	11	3	1	3	100	126	2.04	8.3	2.3	96.0	46	100.0	1 & 2
Loading	17	105	17	0	0	9	3	2	0	100	182	1.74	9.5	2.7	100.0	45	81.4	1 & 2
Panel & Packing	30	117	5	0	0	3	5	0	3	100	177	1.85	17.0	1.8	93.5	47	63.3	1 & 2
Supply	30	111	10	0	0	10	5	0	0	100	91	1.74	11.1	1.8	93.5	42	63.3	1 & 2
Mach. Shop	35	82	24	0	0	24	6	4	0	100	22	2.40	13.1	1.9	100.0	40	100.0	Day
Mach. Shop	27	101	12	0	41	3	3	0	6	100	300	2.19	13.4	1.7	100.0	38	96.5	1
Mach. Shop	31	55	25	1	25	35	7	2	5	96	13	2.02	5.3	1.8	100.0	37	87.6	2
Fabrication	47	94	9	0	0	15	3	0	3	100	17	2.45	14.9	2.0	100.0	42	90.8	1
Fabrication	53	102	11	0	0	15	4	1	0	96	2	2.45	10.2	1.8	100.0	38	89.2	2
Fabrication	29	90	18	0	24	3	7	3	5	100	7	2.81	15.0	2.5	100.0	38	96.6	1
Assem.-Wire	48	112	12	0	0	8	3	0	2	98	72	2.42	11.3	1.9	91.5	36	89.4	1
Assem.-Wire	66	100	11	1	0	5	4	0	2	98	63	2.17	12.0	1.4	100.0	39	92.4	1
Assem.-Wire	51	115	6	0	0	3	5	0	9	100	3	2.18	13.2	2.1	100.0	40	99.7	1
Assem.-Wire & Paint	65	78	9	1	0	33	4	1	6	95	39	2.04	6.8	1.6	100.0	33	79.0	2
Supv. & Panel	44	100	9	0	31	12	3	1	0	100	13	2.22	12.3	1.7	97.1	35	100.0	1
Stockroom	38	102	10	0	0	20	4	0	2	95	76	1.67	6.1	1.3	100.0	34	89.5	1 & 2
Fab.	36	94	19	0	1	19	5	1	0	94	275	2.45	11.8	1.9	100.0	37	88.7	1
Fab.	18	92	15	0	20	21	5	0	0	95	58	1.96	5.4	1.4	100.0	32	94.5	2
Assembly	49	111	10	0	0	2	2	0	46	100	130	2.31	12.7	2.3	100.0	37	91.9	1
Assembly	10	115	8	0	0	0	4	0	23	100	145	2.36	9.0	2.3	100.0	36	91.0	2
Herkolite	18	104	13	0	0	12	5	0	8	95	112	2.44	16.3	1.7	100.0	45	89.5	1
Herkolite	8	97	19	0	0	20	1	0	0	88	24	1.85	6.9	2.2	100.0	36	100.0	2
Mean			13.0	.1	6.7	11.8	3.6	1.3	8.8	98.2	126.5	2.17	10.9	1.45	96.7	38.8	87.7	
Standard Deviation			8.0	.3	11.3	9.0	1.6	1.7	17.4	2.9	141.8	.3	3.7	.6	3.8	4.6	10.2	

*Expressed as per 100 employees per week.
**Expressed as per 1000 employees per week.

SOURCE: Willard V. Merrihue, *General Electric Employee Relations Index*, Personnel Series, No. 168 (New York: American Management Association), p. 48.

oversimplification. However, it must be remembered that problems cannot be solved or plans laid for their solution until they are uncovered. Hence the use of such audit forms is desirable, in that they serve to reveal areas of personnel practices in which improvements may be desirable. Once ascertained in this manner, the next step—and a very significant one, of course—is that of determining what is to be done about the practices in question.

Another interesting aspect of such check lists is that they focus attention upon the wide range of personnel policies and practices that various companies have found it desirable to include in their programs. The mere fact that these plans are cited in the check lists is sufficient to cause some employers to wonder whether or not they, too, should take a broader view in their personnel practices.

On the other hand, it is well to guard against unnecessary dissatisfaction with one's personnel program because of the use of such check

FIGURE 28–7

EXCERPT FROM A
CHECK LIST ON MORALE BUILDING

	Yes	No
I. Does the company—		
A. Explain to all employees the rules and policies of the company?		
(Necessary to prevent misunderstanding of rules and possible later disciplinary action. May increase employee participation in insurance, safety, health and other programs.)		
B. Explain the labor policy of the company?		
(To avoid misunderstandings and maintain better relations.)		
C. Show employees the importance of being at work every day as scheduled?		
(May prevent employee becoming an absentee.)		
D. Promote the feeling of employee's personal participation in work?		
(Every worker is an important cog in the production wheel.)		
E. Show all employees the use to which their products are put?		
(Employees are interested in final use to which products are put.)		
F. Appeal directly to workers by means of posters, bulletins and speakers of importance of their work?		
(These programs usually help in utilization of manpower.)		
G. Have a merit rating plan?		
(Employee is given an incentive to make a good record.)		
II. Does company have an organization for the sympathetic discussion of employee problems in order to help solve them?		
(Employee counsellors properly trained can analyze employee problems and propose programs to improve morale.)		
III. Are the following investigated as possible employee problems?		
A. Housing?		
B. Child-care?		
C. Transportation problem?		
1. Share-the-ride?		
2. Mechanical service to employee's car?		
D. A legal problem?		
E. A medical or dental problem?		
F. An eating facility problem?		
G. Fatigue due to too long working periods?		
H. Misunderstandings due to material shortages?		
(Lowered morale of employees is often caused by a problem on which employee needs advice.)		
IV. Does the company have program of providing recreation to employees such as—		
A. Morning and afternoon recess periods for women?		
B. Definite schedule of vacations?		
C. Interdepartmental baseball?		
D. Interdepartmental football?		
E. Interdepartmental basketball?		
F. Bowling team?		
G. Family picnics?		

lists. As one reviews his practices against a list which is a composite of numerous plans, it is easy to conclude that one's present program is inadequate. While it is well to have plans for future expansion, it is perhaps more undesirable to undertake an overly ambitious program which is likely to fail because of hurried installation than it is to proceed with a limited personnel program that is gradually expanded.

In any event, check lists do perform a function of indicating a type of practice that is useful in auditing personnel practices. It is simple, yet comprehensive. As a consequence, such a plan of auditing is more likely to catch the attention of busy top executives than extended descriptive reports.

SUMMARY

Perhaps it can be said in summary that research and evaluation reflect the philosophy of personnel management adopted by a company. In the last analysis, the particular attitude taken toward how problems of labor-management relations are to be solved will determine more than anything else the quality of a company's labor relations. This is so, but not because one's solutions are bound to be accurate—such an ideal state can scarcely ever be expected. It is so because others soon become impressed with the attitude management takes.

If the attitude is that of searching for the truth—let the chips fall where they may—the confidence and respect of employees will be increased. If the attitude is self-seeking, people will tend to return a similar attitude. These developments may be very slow in coming, but come they will. Perhaps that is why management so often despairs. It does what it considers good but sees no immediate results. It does not realize that in personnel management, time—much time—must elapse before we can reap what we have sown. But reap we shall; so, if a harvest is expected, the seeds must be planted early and cultivated with patience.

QUESTIONS

1. Inasmuch as no company can undertake all the research projects that it might desire, what tests should be adopted in order to determine which projects should be given priority?
2. Is there any significant difference between pure research and practical or applied research? Why is pure research in personnel not subsidized to the same extent as it is in the physical sciences?

3. How does the absentee record of executives compare with that of employees? How do you explain the difference? Could the same motivations that pertain to executives be applied to all employees?

4. A company reported that over half the male employees were absent on the first day of hunting one year. What would be your suggestion for handling this situation in the future?

5. Specifically, what contribution has sociological research made to personnel management? Relate the contributions to the managerial and operative functions of personnel management.

6. How does operations research fit into managerial decision making in the area of personnel matters?

7. Is creative thinking more applicable to long- or short-run problems of personnel management? To large or small companies? Is the same true of brainstorming?

8. A given company takes pride in the fact that its personnel policies and practices are audited once a year by an outside consultant. What is your opinion of this practice?

9. A personnel manager stated that he accompanied any proposed personnel plan with suggestions regarding its control and evaluation. What is your opinion of this practice?

10. Organizationally speaking, how should personnel research and control be established in order to get the most good out of such tasks with a maximum of cooperation from all concerned?

EXAMPLE OF A JOB ANALYSIS SCHEDULE

JOB ANALYSIS SCHEDULE

1. Job Title *POLISHER*	2. Schedule No.
3. Number Employed *30 (25-60)*	4. Establishment No.
6. Title of Verified Job 0	5. Date *November 17, 1958*
8. Alternate Titles *JEWELRY POLISHER*	Number of Pages *6*
(see VIII)	7. Industry *Jewelry*
10. Dictionary Title *BUFFER I*	9. Branch *Costume*
11. Code *6-77.020*	12. Department *Polishing*
13. Analysis Prepared by *J. O. B. Analyzer*	14. Field Office *Watucca*

15. JOB SUMMARY

Holds pieces of costume jewelry and manipulates them against the surface of laminated muslin, flannel, and wire polishing wheels which are power-rotated, to produce polished surfaces of various types on them before they are plated and painted.

MINIMUM QUALIFICATIONS FOR EMPLOYMENT

16. Sex *M*   Age   *18 to 60*

17. Necessary Physical Requirements (including height and weight): *Strong, dextrous hands to hold small objects while they are polished.*

18. Education: *S   R   W* English: Other: 0

19. Experience: *6 months in the same job, served within the past five years. (See VIII).*

20. RELATION TO OTHER JOBS

May be promoted from WASH BOY; JIGGER (See VIII).

May be promoted to FOREMAN (Polishing Room).

21. Supervision Received: General   Medium *X*   Close   By (Title)
    FOREMAN (Polishing Room)

22. Supervision Given: None *X*   No. Supervised   Titles

23. Seasonality: Industry *Peak: August to December. Trough: May to July*
    Job: *Same as Industry*

Supplementary sheets should include the following items: I. WORK PERFORMED; II. EQUIPMENT; III. MATERIAL; IV. SURROUNDINGS; V. HAZARDS; VI. SPECIAL INFORMATION; VII. DEFINI-TION OF TERMS; VIII. COMMENTS.

Supplementary Sheet

Schedule Number _____

Date   *11/17/58*

Sheet 2 of 6 Sheets

Job Title *POLISHER*	Per Cent of Time	Degree of Skill
I. *WORK PERFORMED*		

Note: The polishing work done here falls into six groups: (1) *oiling* (2) *gloss* (3) *cut and gloss* (4) *mat* (5) *satin* (6) *clean wheel.* By using different *polishing* wheels and *polishing compounds* varied results are obtained. Each POLISHER is expected to and at times does perform all of the six polishing operations but the POLISHING FOREMAN confines them as much as possible to one of the groups. The work in each case is essentially the same and is covered by the following description.

	Per Cent of Time	Degree of Skill
1. Prepares for polishing: Mounts a polishing wheel on the horizontal arbor of a *Polishing Lathe* and locks it in position with a washer and a nut; dresses the wheel to make its sections even and somewhat softer by starting the Lathe and holding a small hand *rake* and then an *emery stone* against the rapidly revolving wheel; holds a stick of compound against the wheel to make it more abrasive and smooths this off by holding a pad (usually a used wheel) against it to remove excess; repeats the dressing operation whenever the wheel wears unevenly; applies compound frequently.	10	2
Strong hands are required to dress the wheel and knowledge, gained through experience, is required to recognize when the wheel is satisfactorily dressed.		
2. Polishes metal jewelry: Receives trays of jewelry from the POLISHING FOREMAN with oral instructions regarding the surfaces to be polished; holds a piece of jewelry against the rotating polishing wheel by hand, with pliers, or with the aid of a *hook*; develops a polishing routine for the job and follows it for each piece, skillfully turning and shifting the piece to produce an evenly polished surface; makes a rapid visual inspection and, finding the finish satisfactory, lays the piece in the tray, using layers of paper to prevent scratching the pieces; carries the tray of completed work to the PAY ROLL CLERK.	85	3

Supplementary Sheet

Schedule Number _____

Date _____ *11/17/58* _____

Sheet 3 of 6 Sheets

Job Title *POLISHER*	Per Cent of Time	Degree of Skill
I. *WORK PERFORMED* (Continued)		
Strong and dextrous fingers, hands and arms and well-coordinated use of hands are required to hold the pieces of jewelry against the wheel; good vision is necessary to recognize spots requiring further polishing.		
3. Makes simple *forms* from wood and nails to facilitate holding particular pieces of jewelry while polishing, using hammer, saw, and knife.	5	1
II. *EQUIPMENT*		
Pliers; hammer; saw; and knife are supplied by worker.		
Polishing wheels: Usually laminated muslin wheels having the circles of muslin sewed together near the center but with the outer edges loose. A hole through the center of the wheel is provided for mounting it on the arbor of a Polishing Lathe. Muslin is used for oiling and cut and gloss operations. Other wheels are (1) felt, for a coarser finish called mat (2) wire wheel for a coarser finish called satin (3) special bristle brushes usually used for oiling operations.		
Polishing compounds of varying abrasiveness: Abrasive compounds which (in the order of their abrasiveness) are known as lea, tripoli, white diamond, and crocus are available in the form of sticks about 6 to 10 inches long and 2 inches in diameter. Lea is used to produce mat finishes. Tripoli is used for oiling (a cutting operation in which much oil is used.) White Diamond is used for light cutting and is advantageous because it is less oily than tripoli and the articles need not be cleaned after polishing. Crocus, which is a very fine abrasive, is used for polishing to a high gloss.		
Polishing Lathe: (Polishing Lathe, Bench Model, ¾ H.P., 3600 R.P.M., manufactured by the Diamond Machine Company, Providence, Rhode Island). A variable speed electric motor having an arbor extending from one side		

Supplementary Sheet

Schedule Number

Date   *11/17/58*

Sheet *4* of *6* Sheets

Job Title   *POLISHER*

II. *EQUIPMENT* (Continued)
on which interchangeable polishing wheels can be mounted. Different speeds are required for different polishing operations; 1700 R.P.M. being desirable for coarser finishes like mat and satin, and speeds as high as 3600 R.P.M. being used for the gloss finishes.

Rake: A simple tool made by driving many nails through a short length of wood so that their points project; this is used to dress the polishing wheels.

Emery stone: A piece of broken emery wheel used to dress the polishing wheels.

Hook: A steel wire hook with a wooden handle; by hooking this into a piece of jewelry, especially initials, it is possible to hold a piece that would otherwise be pulled out of hand by the polishing wheel.

Forms: Simple wooden jigs made by the worker to facilitate holding of the pieces of jewelry; some are made to hold several pieces at one time.

III. *MATERIAL*
None.

IV. *SURROUNDINGS*
There is a constant, noisy hum from the many Polishing Lathes and the exhaust system in the workroom. Each Polishing Lathe is hooded and is locally exhausted to draw off dust from the wheels. Despite these provisions the surroundings are quite dirty. The worker's hands and clothing are soiled by the compounds used.

V. *HAZARDS*
There is danger of injuring the hands when the article being polished catches in the revolving wheel and is pulled from the worker's hands. Slight burns from the heated articles of jewelry may be incurred.

JOB ANALYSIS SCHEDULE (Continued)

Supplementary Sheet

Schedule Number _____

Date   11/17/58

Sheet 5 of 6 Sheets

Job Title   *POLISHER*

VI. *REGISTRATION AND PLACEMENT AIDS*

Basic Requirements: Some polishing experience is required, in which the worker has learned the "feel of the wheel" sufficiently to be able to control the pressure against the wheel to produce the desired surfaces.

A knowledge of polishing compounds and the polishing operations for which they are appropriate is required.

Must be able to distinguish between shades of color or luster to produce evenly polished surfaces.

Variable Requirements: Determine:

What kinds of metal worker will polish.
(Brass, silver, gold, aluminum and plated articles are polished.)

What kind of articles worker will polish.
(Slightly different skill is required to polish costume jewelry, rings, chains, cases, and bracelets.)

What polishing operations worker will do.
(Some workers specialize on such operations as cut and gloss, oil, mat, satin, or gloss finish; while others are able to do all.)

VII. *DEFINITION OF TERMS*

Oiling: The act of cutting through the surface of metal using an oily compound which must be washed off.

Gloss: A high luster finish produced by polishing with a fine abrasive; also a term applied to the operation of producing such a finish.

Cut and Gloss: The procedure of smoothing metal surfaces with a fairly abrasive compound which requires little oil and the immediate polishing to high luster on another wheel with a fine abrasive. The operations are combined when the cutting can be done with a compound which need not be washed off before glossing.

Supplementary Sheet

Schedule Number _____

Date   *11/17/58*

Sheet 6 of 6 Sheets

Job Title   *POLISHER*

VII. *DEFINITION OF TERMS* (Continued)

> *Mat:* A dull finish produced by polishing with a coarse abrasive; also the act of producing such a finish.

> *Satin:* A soft finish produced with a wire brush wheel.

> *Clean Wheel:* A light polishing operation in which no compound is used on the polishing wheel.

VIII. *COMMENTS*

Job Title and Alternate Title: There is some justification for using the alternate title JEWELRY POLISHER in these items because there are POLISHERS in other industries who while using somewhat different techniques, are capable of being confused with this job.

Relation to Other Jobs: Experienced POLISHERS are usually hired, but occasionally WASH BOYS or male JIGGERS may be promoted to the job.

INSTRUCTIONS FOR
FILLING OUT THE
JOB ANALYSIS SCHEDULE

1. *Headings.* Items 1–14 on the Job Analysis Schedule are included in the term "headings." This part of the schedule provides for naming and locating the job industrially and for recording of certain identification data which are needed for every job.

2. *Item 1, Job Title.* Here should be entered the name by which the job being analyzed is commonly called in the establishment (plant title). All job titles (Item 1) or alternate titles (Item 8) should be written in capital letters in the singular and in the natural form as used in industry, such as BARTENDER, not TENDER, BAR. The only exception to this rule is that the words "assistant," "helper," and "apprentice" should not be used to begin a title. A descriptive word should precede these such as MACHINIST APPRENTICE, PRESSMAN HELPER.

3. *General Terms.* Such general terms as "manager," "foreman," and the like should always be editorially qualified by a descriptive phrase if these titles stand alone. For example, FOREMAN (BRICKLAYING); but BRICKLAYER FOREMAN would require no editorial qualifications.

4. *Agreement with Dictionary Form.* Extreme care should be exercised to make all titles other than plant titles in the Job Analysis Schedule and in the *Occupational Dictionary* agree in form; that is, if a title appears in inverted form in the *Occupational Dictionary,* it should be used in inverted form in the Job Analysis Schedule. A few titles are always used in inverted form, to avoid unreasonable alphabetic placement. The words "assistant," "helper," "apprentice," and "foreman" always follow the descriptive portion of the title showing the type of assistant, helper, apprentice, and foreman.

5. *Item 2, Schedule Number.* This item is used for identification and filing purposes primarily.

6. *Item 3, Number Employed.* Here is entered the number of workers engaged in jobs identical with the job being analyzed in this particular establishment.

7. *Item 4, Establishment Number.* This entry is used for identification and filing purposes.

8. *Item 5, Date.* Enter here the date on which the job analysis is completed.

9. *Item 6, Title of Verified Job.* This entry is left blank until the job under consideration is verified as to content.

10. *Item 8, Alternate Titles.* All names by which the job is known, other

536

than the one entered in Item 1 above, should be entered in the space opposite Item 8. These job names should not include slang terms unless such terms are widely used and recognized in the industry.

11. *Items 10 and 11, Dictionary Title and Code Number.* If the job which is described in this analysis is defined in the *Dictionary of Occupational Titles*, enter the specific dictionary title and code number here.

12. *Item 7, Industry.* Here enter the accepted name of the industry in which the analyzed job is observed.

13. *Item 9, Branch.* A branch represents a larger division of an industry, made according to type of activity carried on, as contrasted with a department, which represents a division made according to phases of a single activity or process.

14. *Item 12, Department.* Enter here the name of the department of the industry in which the analyzed job is found. The analyst is responsible for specifying either the division in which this job exists, or the fact that no division exists.

15. *Item 13, Analysis Prepared by.* Here is entered the name of the person who is responsible for preparing the job analysis.

16. *Item 14, Field Office.* Enter here the name and the code number of the field office which services the area in which the industry is located.

17. *Item 16, Job Summary.* The job summary presents in concise form the essential and distinguishing characteristics of the occupation. Since it is a summary of all of the information collected by the job analysis, it is not written until all of the job analysis has been completed. Hence the details for preparing the job summary will be discussed in paragraph 53 of these instructions.

18. *Minimum Qualifications.* The source of information included in Items 16 to 19 is the person responsible for hiring workers for the job under analysis. This person should define the minimum acceptable standards for employment. It should be recognized, however, that employers generally have a tendency to demand higher qualifications when discussing jobs than when they actually hire workers. It is the problem of the analyst to determine tactfully and accurately the actual minimum requirements and to record these rather than the ideal standards.

19. *Minimum qualifications for employment* always remain the minimum requirements for success on the job, even though an employer may at the moment prefer applicants of a certain nationality and of higher educational requirements than necessary. He may feel that these requirements are necessary to meet the needs of other jobs in the plant when promoting or transferring workers from one job to another. Minimum qualifications for employment at the time of analysis are not necessarily permanent hiring factors, since hiring requirements readily fluctuate with changes in the labor market. If other than actual minimum job requirements are noted, the entry should be qualified with an explanation.

20. *Item 16, Sex.* Enter here the answer to the question, "Does the employer hire men exclusively, women exclusively, or either men or women, for this job?" Enter "M" for male, "F" for female, and "O" if there is no preference.

21. *Item 16, Age.* Enter here the minimum and maximum age which the employer will require in hiring people for this job. If no special range is desig-

nated, enter a zero (0). Thus if the employer is willing to accept people between the ages of eighteen and twenty-five only, the entry in Item 16 appears as "18–25."

22. *Item 17, Necessary Physical Requirements.* Here are entered any special physical requirements that are necessary to adequate performance of the job. If average, ordinary, not unusual requirements are specified, the entry should be zero (0). The data should include all necessary characteristics, such as: "Small and agile to climb between girders"; "Not under 5'10" tall to reach high shelves"; or, "Strong and husky, weight 160 pounds or over, to carry heavy lumber."

23. *Item 18, Education.* Encircle "S," "R," or "W," or all three, to indicate that the ability to speak, read or write English, respectively, is the minimum literacy requirement for employment. If the minimum education required is more than ability to read and write, it should appear after "Other"; as "8 years elementary school"; "business-school secretarial training"; "college graduation with major in chemistry."

24. *Item 19, Experience.* Here indicate any prior work experience which may be required of the applicant. When questioning the employer, it is important to determine exactly what he considers as minimum experience requirements in the light of the normal labor market situation.

25. *Item 20, Relation to Other Jobs.* Item 20 is intended to provide information with reference to the job from which qualified workers come to the job under analysis, as well as the jobs to which qualified workers may be promoted. It points out ways in which workers are or can be interchanged between jobs within the establishment, as well as the manner in which interindustry transfers may readily be made.

26. *Item 21, Supervision Received.* Here enter a rating of the degree of supervision received by the worker, by marking an "X" in the space after the appropriate item: "general," "close," or "medium." It is essential that the analyst indicate the amount of responsibility placed on the worker for the quality and quantity of his product or performance. The term "general" indicates the usual type of overseeing which most workers receive. "Close," at the other extreme, denotes a constant overseeing of the worker by the supervisor, with almost no responsibility placed on the worker. "Medium," between these extremes, indicates that the worker is given specific detailed instructions, particularly at the beginning of a task and, hence, is assigned a certain amount of responsibility.

27. *Item 22, Supervision Given.* If no supervision is given to other workers by the worker under observation, an "X" should be entered in the space after the word "none." If the worker whose job is being analyzed has, as part of his duties, the supervision of others, the number of workers supervised should be entered following "No. Supervised." The titles of the jobs supervised should be entered following the word "title." Where the titles of the job supervised are numerous, an indication of the group supervised is sufficient, but it should be possible to ascertain the title from the statement made, supplemented by a note in Item VIII, Comments, if necessary.

28. *Item 23, Seasonality.* In certain industries, as in canning, the number of workers employed is closely related to the season of the year. In canning, the greatest number of workers are employed during the months of September and

October and the smallest number in February. If the job being analyzed, or the industry in which it exists, is affected by seasonal fluctuations, the weeks and months in which the hiring and the laying-off occurs should be recorded. The weeks or months during which employment is above normal are known as the "peak" of employment, and the period during which employment is below normal is known as the "trough."

Filling Out Supplementary Sheets

29. Certain kinds of information which are needed to describe a job fully, vary so much in form, extent, and content, that little more than a heading and a general explanation can be given. Of such a nature are the eight items of the supplementary material. These items are:

I. Work performed	V. Hazards
II. Equipment	VI. Special information
III. Material	VII. Definitions of terms
IV. Surroundings	VIII. Comments

30. Not all of these eight supplementary items will be of value on every job. On some jobs the detailed treatment of work performed may be unnecessary, especially if ample descriptive material is contained in the job summary. In jobs in which no hazards exist, or in jobs which involve few or no special terms, these items will not be required.

31. *Work Performed.* The primary purpose of this supplementary item is the description of the duties of the job concisely, precisely, and explicitly so that a reader may be able to visualize the tasks composing the job, preferably in the sequence of steps taken, and may be able to recognize the skills, knowledges, and judgments or responsibilities involved, with a minimum of reorganization of the data in his own mind after reading. The purpose of the information on work performed is to furnish the interviewer with enough detail about the job to enable him to do effective interviewing, selection, and placement work.

32. In *Supplementary Item I* should be entered a statement or description of what the worker does in a series of either chronological or logical steps, setting forth what he does, how he does it, and why he does it.

33. A statement of work performed will usually consist of a series of numbered statements, each comprising a description of a task or major step in the job. The statements should be brief, and the job title of the worker is implied as the subject of each sentence.

34. *Knowledges and Judgments.* It is not enough to record simply a description of the motions performed by the worker; it is generally of greater importance that the interviewer have a record of the knowledges, training, and experience necessary to perform these motions at the right time, in the right order, and in the right manner. Consequently, it is vitally necessary in every instance that the analyst determine whether execution of the motions depends on any skills, knowledges, exercise of judgments, or other intangible factors, and that he make specific statements emphasizing the significance of such factors. This comment applies to each separate task in the job, as well as to the job as a whole.

35. *Rating of Percent of Time.* After each numbered element of the work

performed, in the column headed "Percent of Time" should be indicated the percentage of the worker's time that the element occupies as compared with the job as a whole.

36. *Rating of Degree of Skill.* After each element in the second column headed "Degree of Skill," should be indicated a rating of the skill that is required of the worker to perform the element. Expressions of the degree or rate of skill are indicated by the figures "1," "2," and "3"; "1" being used to express the lowest amount of skill, and "3" the highest amount. When assigning the ratings to job elements, only the job being analyzed is to be considered. This practice must be followed strictly because it is not possible to compare the skills involved in different jobs, since what might be rated a "3" skill for the element of one job might deserve only the rating of "1" in another job.

37. The *"Work Performed"* item should include a statement of the duties that are performed infrequently, as well as in the normal work cycle. Such tasks as the occasional setting up of a machine, occasional repairs, infrequent reports, and the like, should here be included. In each case a notation should be made concerning the frequency of occurrence of the performance.

38. *"May" Tasks and Alternative Tasks.* If a task may be performed by one worker or by another, the description of it should be introduced with the word "may." All alternative methods of performing a task should be stated: "Either . . . (the one) . . . or . . . (the other) . . . ."

39. *Simultaneous Tasks.* In cases in which a worker may start several tasks at the same time, none of which is completed for several days, each task should be completely described before beginning the description of a second task.

40. *Miscellaneous Cautions.* In preparing the "Work Performed" item, care should be exercised to avoid the simple listing of the tasks performed by the worker without any explanation of how they are performed. The inclusion of too many duties in one work element should be avoided. Even closely related duties should be broken up into more than one element if the item has become too long and involved.

41. *Equipment.* Under this item enumerate, in the order mentioned under "Work Performed," all machines and all special or unusual equipment used by the worker on the job that is being analyzed.

42. Under *Description of a Machine* should appear the following: a statement of the function of the machine; a description of the physical appearance of the machine and its essential parts; and a description of the operation of the machine and its relation to the worker. Only essential features of the mechanical equipment should be included in the description. Structural details, such as gear ratios, types of power drive, and other technical features, need not be included unless some specific job duties are performed in relation to these features.

43. *Tools.* For simpler devices, particularly for hand tools, it will be necessary to include only a definition of the device rather than a complete description. In every case the purpose for which the device is used should be shown.

44. *Relating the Description to the Drawing.* If a drawing has been included in the Schedule, all descriptions of equipment should be related to the drawing by placing the letters appearing on the drawing in parentheses after the names of the component parts of the device to which they refer.

45. *Material.* Under this item should be listed and described the components used by the worker to make a finished product, if such activity is being

performed on the job. For example, a baker makes bread from flour. A core maker makes cores from sand, but a cab driver or elevator operator does not use material in this sense.

46. *Surroundings.* Under this item will be described the physical conditions under which the job is performed. The statement should show the nature of the conditions and the manner in which they affect the worker. The statement of the surroundings may begin with the word "inside" or the word "outside" if this fact is not obvious from the statement to follow. Three situations may arise in analyzing surroundings. These are: First, situations in which the analyst determines that no significant entries need to be made concerning surroundings, such as might be typified by a large group of clerical workers who perform their duties in "normal office surroundings." In preparing schedules for such jobs, a zero (0) should be placed after Item IV, Surrounding. Second, situations in which the surroundings are significant and inherent factors on the job. Third, situations in which the analyst is in doubt whether the significance of the surroundings or their inherent identification with the job adds to the job analysis. When in doubt, the analyst should include the data as reference information, leaving to others who use the information the decision as to its relevance.

47. If the job is of such a nature that its performance involves possible injury, death, or damage to health, these dangers should be described. Only those hazards that can be connected with the job itself should be included. For example, traffic hazards to which everyone is subjected are not considered occupational hazards for most jobs, but in the case of a traffic patrolman, the danger of being struck by a passing vehicle is a very real occupational hazard.

48. The material in this section should enumerate the factors in the job, the presence or absence of which may have a direct bearing on occupational classification or on placement. A substitute heading for this item might be "Registration and Placement Aids." This item should be used to emphasize characteristics in which the job under analysis differs in important respects from other jobs of its kind. It should assist in anticipating variations in the job which may occur in different establishments.

In this item two main headings are kept in mind, "Basic Requirements" and "Variable Requirements."

Basic requirements are the "performance" characteristics—those qualifications which are definitely required by the nature of the job itself. These may be beyond or aside from any qualifications of "evidential" nature which may be demanded by individual employers in keeping with their labor policies. Such factors as "the ability to do art work," or "the possession of engineering training," should be mentioned here. The analyst must be careful in all cases to state the minimum rather than the maximum qualifications for success on the job. Even when no experience is required for the job, some knowledge or ability may be specified as needed for its successful performance. For example, the employer may specify one of the following: "Eighth-grade education or its equivalent, to provide ability to solve problems involving multiplication and division of fractions"; "Sufficient physical strength to stand continuously and lift articles weighing approximately 50 pounds from the floor into the feed hopper at frequent intervals"; or "Worker must possess or obtain a food-handler certificate."

The description of variable requirements should bring out the differences that may be expected between workers, all of whom are employed in the same job, in either the same or different establishments. This information should guide interviewers in obtaining supplementary information that will indicate a worker's fitness for a specified position after it has been determined that he is qualified to perform the duties of the occupation. Here would be noted such factors as wide variation in procedure followed, equipment used, or the number of workers supervised.

49. *Information for the Applicant.* In Supplementary Item VI, information should be included such as the applicant might request concerning the job. Obviously, all factors listed below will not necessarily apply to any one job, nor does the list include all of the possible items that might apply. Among the more common types of information requested by applicants are: specialized knowledge of machine operation which is required, use of attachments, tolerances or accuracy required, rate of production required by employer, opportunities for training on the job and in the community, length of the learning period, base rate of pay, hours of work shifts, transportation to and from the job, housing and boarding facilities in the neighborhood of the plant, etc.

50. All unusual or technical terms that are used throughout the analysis should be underlined as they are used. In Item VII, these technical terms should be listed in the order in which they appear in "Work Performed." Each term should be defined. The definitions will vary with the terms to be explained. Each definition should include a clear statement or explanation of the word or thing by describing the attributes, properties, or relations which distinguish it from all other words or things. The term may be defined by stating its use.

51. The style to be used in preparing "Definitions of Terms" is illustrated in the following examples derived from an analysis of the job of polisher in an establishment where costume jewelry is produced:

Gloss: A high-luster finish produced by polishing with fine abrasives; also, a term applied to the operation of producing such a finish.

Satin: A soft finish produced with a wire-brush wheel.

Cut and Gloss: The process of smoothing metal surfaces with a medium fine abrasive compound which requires little oil, and the immediately polishing or high luster on another wheel with a fine abrasive.

52. This item contains miscellaneous material not elsewhere classified. It should be used for footnoting all other parts of the job analysis. If the space allotted in the printed form is insufficient at any point, the information to be entered may be continued in Item VIII.

53. *Job Summary.* Refer again to paragraph 17 of these instructions. The job summary presents in concise form the essential and distinguishing characteristics of the occupation. It should be so constructed that it characterizes the job accurately. The job summary must be an abstract of the entire analysis; hence, it is written after the Job Analysis Schedule proper has been completed. It should be so complete that it can be used independently as an adequate presentation of the essential facts about the job. It should be a concise over-all definition of the job, and not simply a summary of the work performed. Such items as the following should be taken into account in determining the content of the job summary:

What the worker does
How he does it

Why he does it (for what purpose) and his place in the process
Under what conditions he does the work
The degree of his responsibility
The kind of establishment in which the work is done (if the industry includes more than one)
Considerations controlling his trade judgments or decisions
The special qualifications which he must possess

Undesirable Differentiations

ADJUSTER.—Receives complaints from customers in person or by telephone concerning merchandise and bills; investigates complaints and makes adjustments.

ADJUSTMENT CLERK.—Notes complaints made by customers; as TRACER checks complaints and informs customer what adjustment will be made.

Desirable Differentiations

ADJUSTER.—Receives complaints from customers concerning qualities of merchandise, credits to be allowed for defective merchandise, and the like. Investigates complaints, decides what adjustment is to be made, and authorizes replacement of merchandise or the giving of credit.

ADJUSTMENT CLERK.—Receives complaints of customers concerning routine matters such as nondelivery of merchandise and erroneous charges. As TRACER ascertains reason for the complaint, what adjustment will be made, and informs customer.

Another example is cited of an unacceptable job summary and an acceptable revision:

Unacceptable Job Summary

CORE PASTER.—Mixes paste; removes baked core from rack; cuts vent holes through sections; applies paste, presses sections together; spreads flurry on seams, checks dimensions.

Acceptable Job Summary

CORE PASTER.—Assembles baked-sand core sections to form a core by brushing the adjoining surfaces with flour paste, to make them adhesive, and fitting the sections accurately together, smoothing the surfaces with a plastic mixture and inspecting the dimensions for accuracy.

Two acceptable job summaries are cited in conclusion:

PUNCH PRESS OPERATOR. Sets up and operates a punch press to punch or shape small aircraft pieces from sheet aluminum. Checks dies against blueprints and fits dies into press, bolting them securely in place. Sets gauges and makes trial run to test position of dies and gauges, making adjustments so that the completed work conforms to specifications recorded on blueprints. Places piece of aluminum stock in position against gauges on the punch press and operates the machine by stepping on a pedal, periodically checking completed pieces to be sure they are according to requirements. Supervises a PUNCH PRESS OPERATOR HELPER.

ROAD PAVER OPERATOR. Operates a one-yard capacity gasoline-powered road paver to mix wet concrete and spread it on a roadbed by manipulating hand levers and foot treadles to lift and dump the ingredients from the skip (loading hopper) into the rotating mixing drum of the machine. Empties the drum contents into a bucket, moves the bucket horizontally along the boom, and distributes the contents of the bucket onto the roadbed as the bucket is being emptied. Moves the road paver on its crawler treads during the paving process.

CASE PROBLEMS

The following case problems have been adapted from actual practice and are presented in relatively short form. (Of course, names used herein are fictitious.) It may be noted that a short statement does not contain all of the facts about any case, but the same can also be said about long cases. Hence the cases given here have been digested to a point where the students can visualize an actual situation, yet do so without complaining that the cases require so much reading time that little time is left for critical analysis. It may be noted, too, that in addition to descriptive situations, a number of cases have been included which provide an opportunity to exercise some simple statistical and mathematical skills. The latter are intended to illustrate some of the quantitative aspects of problem solving in the personnel area.

The order in which the cases are presented follows broadly the chapter outline of the text. A regular *plan* of problems, exclusive for each chapter, would be difficult to provide because the actual business world does not produce such neat arrangements. Hence the instructor should use his judgment in assigning problems and in interpreting the solutions in the light of his own standards of how much the students should be expected to cover and accomplish.

In regard to solutions to these problems, the author prefers to see what imagination and good sense each group of students can bring to bear upon the materials. However, it is recognized that the student will usually bring to the analysis of these cases what he has learned from his readings, classroom lectures, and discussions. In each instance, therefore, the instructor should be the best judge of the standards of comparison he will apply in reading the submitted reports. The questions at the end of each case are merely suggestive; the instructor and the students may well prepare and propound others.

Nor does the author have a rigid plan of assigning case problems. Sometimes few, and sometimes many, are assigned. This must always be a matter to be decided in the light of particular conditions. It is felt, however, that problems should not be assigned merely to keep students busy; a problem should be assigned only when it serves a definite objective in the instructor's plan of advancing his students' knowledge and critical powers.

CASE 1. EDUCATING AN EXECUTIVE

A supermarket grocery chain offered excellent opportunities to promising young men in its organization. In the summer of 1963 the manager of one of the stores was selected by the company to attend a midwestern university to study for a master's degree in merchandising. This store did not have a comanager, so it was necessary to transfer in a new manager.

The old manager left the store during the first week in September, but the new manager did not take up his duties until the third week. During the two-week period, both men took their vacations, but this left the store without a manager.

When the new manager arrived, he found the store in a deplorable condition. Merchandise had been overordered by some trainee managers who had been sent in during the two-week period. Yet, some shelves were unstocked, since the work force had been depleted because some clerks had returned to school, leaving only part-time help as the main, but inexperienced, working force.

The new manager exerted every effort to get the store back into shape. He used high-pressure methods, and kept every one hurried and on edge. He barked his orders, boomed his commands, and became irritated at the slightest delays in carrying out his orders. But between his dictatorial methods and the fact that fall business was extremely good, he straightened out the stock situation and had the merchandise flowing smoothly through the store.

But his rating with the employees was very low. The morale of the group fell lower when inventory taking revealed shortages for two consecutive four-week periods. In this company, three to four of these shortage periods was usually grounds for discharge. So the manager, fearing for himself and feeling that some of the shortages might be due to employee practices, became even more observant of his crew. The employees' resentment showed itself in discontentment with the manager.

After the next inventory period the condition was found to be satisfactory. The manager immediately became a changed individual. He was more friendly with the employees, and they began to relax. On one occasion, he asked the head cashier what the employees thought of him. She told him of their views on his practices and attitudes. Upon hearing this, he changed his tactics to an even more friendly manner. He no longer hounded everyone, stopped making cutting remarks, and started to give consideration to the individual problems of the employees.

The change was reflected in employee attitudes and productivity. A concrete example of this showed up in the reports on man-hours of work per $100 of sales which was computed weekly for each store. Whereas the ratio was one of the poorest for the entire chain for the first five months the new manager was on the job, the trend moved to the point where in the last month this store stood among the top in the chain.

Employees are satisfied with working conditions and their relationships with the manager. And the manager is a much more easygoing, yet more effective leader.

Questions

1. Was the new manager inherently a good manager of people? If he was, why didn't he show it in the first five months?
2. What do you think of the manager's method of finding out the attitude of employees toward him?

CASE 2.   A LETTER TO EMPLOYEES

To counter some of the claims a union had been making during a strike, the director of industrial relations of the struck company decided to send the following letter to the striking employees:

To All Our Employees:

You have now been out a week on your union's strike. We have heard it said that we "forced" you out on strike. Nothing is more ridiculous. We would be pleased to have you return. Some already have. We deny we forced you out.

We have heard it said that you must struggle against the company to secure justice. May we point out that our wage offer would place our rates at or above every company in this neighborhood. We deny that you must struggle with us to get a fair offer.

We have heard it said that your union has received congratulations for taking a militant stand against a repressive company. We question that militancy is a part of good collective bargaining. And we deny that we have ever been or intend to be repressive.

We have heard it said that a strike is necessary to get an honorable settlement. We have been honorable in our dealings with the employees from the day the factory opened, and with the union from the day it came into the lives of our employees. We deny that a strike creates honor.

To repeat, you have lost a week's wages already. Besides, it would take a year to make up the week's wage loss from the increase per hour which the company is ready to grant. Why add to your losses? We deny that these losses by strike are needed.

Question

1. What is your judgment of countering the union through this medium of a letter and through such arguments?

CASE 3.   INFORMAL EXECUTIVE RELATIONSHIP

The Home Bakery has five major plants and a number of branches located in four states. It has grown from one small plant to its present size because of a product of superior quality sold at a competitive price. Its personnel program was based for many years on the personal relationship between ownership top management and the employees. But as the company has grown, it has become impractical for top management to maintain the personal touch and also to select, train, and evaluate people effectively.

Recently, the company turned to a consulting psychologist for help. On his advice and through his active direction, a personnel department was established. The psychologist was instrumental in developing a program by which young men were taken directly from college to be trained as future personnel managers. Since the personnel program was based largely on such refined ideas as psychological tests, planned interviewing, and conference training methods, college men were preferred for personnel work. The supposition was that other factors related to the company and its practices could be learned on the job.

Among the men so hired for one of the major plants was Richard Roe. When he was hired, he stated that his education had been in liberal arts, but he was told that he could learn the practical side of things on the job. Roe was installed as assistant to the plant personnel director.

After six months, during which time Roe had been learning the ropes, the personnel director was made plant manager. Roe was promoted to personnel manager with the assurance of the newly promoted plant manager that "if you need any assistance, we will be glad to help out." Roe eagerly tackled the job, even though he realized that he had much to learn before he would feel confident. Apparently, this was the opinion of the employees, too, since most of them still go to the plant manager with their personnel problems.

After the situation continued along these lines for a number of months, under-the-surface friction developed between Roe and the plant manager. Roe's function as personnel manager regressed to the point that he was little more than a glorified employment clerk. Roe conferred with the plant manager about his plight. The plant manager stated that he was powerless to make employees come to the personnel office with their problems and that he appreciated Roe's feelings in the matter.

Questions

1. What should be done about Roe?
2. What advice would you give the plant manager?

CASE 4. CHANNELING YOUTHFUL ENTHUSIASM

The produce department of a chain grocery unit employs five people: the manager, two full-time employees, and two part-time employees. Of the latter, one works in the afternoon with the manager and full-time help, and the other works evenings, at which time he is the only member of the produce department in the store. In the evening, therefore, he is under the jurisdiction of the grocery manager. Each day before the produce manager leaves, he assigns specific jobs to be completed by the evening employee.

The produce department requires an area apart from the sales floor in which certain processing functions may take place. It shares this area with the dairy department, which handles milk, cheese, and eggs. This area has also become a hangout for helpers from other departments to gather during their spare time.

During the past few weeks, egg spots from broken eggs have been noted on the walls of this area. There were also indications of tomato spots. The situation reached a climax when eggs broken during the night were found in the morning by the produce manager. That afternoon the produce manager accused the part-time boy, in the presence of other employees, of throwing eggs. The boy denied this charge. His story was that in the evenings when the store got busy, the grocery manager would call on him, contrary to store policy, to carry out customers' groceries. And while he was outside, the grocery boys would come into the area and throw things around. When he told them to leave, they would refuse. When the grocery boys were questioned, they accused the produce boy of acting up and said he only got what he deserved if someone threw eggs at him.

Questions

1. What suggestions do you have to cure this situation?
2. What suggestions do you have to prevent the animal spirits of youthful helpers from getting out of hand?

CASE 5. EXTRACOMPANY BEHAVIOR OF EMPLOYEES

In a given company, two somewhat related incidents have brought on some soul-searching sessions on policy by the management of a given company. The first case arose when the company restaurant unexpectedly could not operate one day. Employees therefore had to go out into the neighborhood for their lunches. One of the employees, Bill Calm, a supervisor, happened to take a few alcoholic drinks with his lunch. In his happy condition, he made some bright (as he thought) but ungentlemanly remarks to one of the secretaries who was eating lunch at the same restaurant. When she returned to work, she indignantly reported Bill's conduct and remarks to the personnel manager.

The second case arose in connection with Art Swift, a valued engineer, who, after working hours, used to follow the primrose path to various taverns in the town. This part of his life did not affect his work. But stories started to drift back to management that Swift's actions reflected unfavorably on the company. Some of the comments implied that one couldn't put much confidence in the company's products if they were made by employees such as Swift.

Questions

1. What action, if any, should management take in each case?
2. What policy would you advocate, if any, governing the personal lives of one's employees?

CASE 6. WAGE INCREASES AND BREAK-EVEN POINTS

The Peghole Company is faced with wage and salary increase demands by its factory and office employees. The executive committee is desirous of knowing what the increases would do to its break-even point and profit position. With this information at hand, the committee will be in a position to determine what course of action it should take in regard to the request for increases, or how the request could be financed. You obtain the following information:

Sales price per unit of output.............................$1.70
Annual fixed costs currently.............................$1,750,000
Direct costs per unit.....................................$0.80
Current annual sales in units............................ 2,250,000
Current annual capacity of plant in units................. 3,000,000
Factory wage increase demand per unit.....................$0.10
Office salary increase demand annually.....................$150,000

Questions

1. As a result of this increase, what would the new break-even point be? How much is it above the old break-even point?
2. In view of your calculations, what alternative courses of action might the executive committee explore?

CASE 7. THE NEEDS OF EMPLOYEES

A wholesale and retail flour and feed business employs four truck drivers or deliverymen, two clerks to handle the retail trade at the store, a bookkeeper, and two outside salesmen. The proprietor himself actively manages the business.

A serious symptom in this company is the relatively high labor turnover. In the past year, six truck drivers and one retail clerk had to be hired to fill vacancies. The employees express dissatisfaction with the pay, hours of work, and oppressive management. Yet, in the community the owner is considered to be fair and is held in high respect—an apparent paradox in views.

One of the main difficulties as far as the employees are concerned is the lack of definite policies. For example, the truck drivers often work overtime when the roads are bad in winter. There is no payment for this overtime, the owner usually saying: "I'll give you some time off with pay during slack days in the summer." He intends to do this but sometimes does not, so the drivers feel that the pay situation does not even out. In addition, the store and plant do not always close promptly at the scheduled closing time, so that employees are neither certain when they will get home nor are they compensated for these little over-hour times.

The owner gave each employee an insurance policy for a Christmas present and is in the habit of making gifts regularly to employees throughout the year at various holiday periods. He does this to show the employees he is interested in them and to keep them in a good humor.

Yet, to his friends, he has expressed the opinion that despite his generosity and interest, "people won't work like they used to."

Questions

1. To what extent is the owner realistically and reasonably satisfying the needs of his employees?
2. How do you stand on the opinion of the owner as expressed in the last sentence of this case?

CASE 8.   ORGANIZATIONAL AUTHORITY RELATIONSHIPS

In the course of selecting a given employee, some differences of opinion arose between the personnel department, the sales manager, and the legal department. The trouble came to a head when the sales manager refused to accept a candidate sent to him by the personnel department. He argued that he alone was the best judge, in the final analysis, of who would or would not be successful in his department. Moreover, he argued that as a line executive, his authority could not be diluted.

The personnel manager insisted that his choice had to be accepted. He argued that because of the careful screening processes which were employed, he had every confidence that the particular candidate was capable and would be a productive salesman. In addition, it seemed to him that it would be futile for him to operate in the company if his expert advice and thorough examinations were to be contradicted by rather superficial judgments by the line.

The company lawyer had been brought in by the personnel manager because when he asked the lawyer about the case, the latter had expressed the opinion that the man should be taken because the company otherwise left itself open to a lawsuit by the man who was hired and then quickly "unhired."

Questions

1. In the case of each of these executives, what authority did each have—and think he had?
2. How should these executives be handled so that their authority relationships do not conflict?

CASE 9.   ESTIMATING MANPOWER REQUIREMENTS

In a given company an expected stepup in production would require additional workers to be hired. The requirements were not sent to the personnel department until shortly before the men were needed. Yet the personnel manager was expected to hire thirty-five men in such skills as welders, machinists, assemblers, and semiskilled helpers.

Unfortunately, the personnel department could not fill all the requisitions. As a consequence, the production line fell behind, and some shipping dates fell a week in arrears. The general manager asked for an explanation and was told that in a tight labor market, men could not be hired on short order.

The general manager told Joe Mallon, the personnel manager: "We will have to sacrifice some product quality and lower employee qualifications in order to meet production schedules. We cannot let down on our present orders. It means future orders." Mallon did not agree that future orders would be easy to come by if quality were sacrificed, but he went along with the policy. Fortunately, things returned to normal.

After the rush was over, the general manager complained that he was stumbling over all the help in the plant. So that very afternoon, he told personnel to lay off 25 men, effective immediately. Mallon argued against this action, stating that the men were trained and would be hard to replace in an ever-tighter labor market. But the general manager said that costs had to be cut, and they would have to take their chances. So Mallon checked out the 25 most reluctantly.

A week later, Mallon answered the phone to hear the general manager say: "Joe, I hope you've been keeping in touch with some of the men we just laid off; we're going to need all of them and more besides. There's a big job coming through that we've been bidding on. I'll send you a requisition."

Questions

1. What plan of action will Mallon have to take?
2. Was the general manager justified in his decisions?

CASE 10.   IMPLEMENTING AN OPERATION

To perform a certain office operation, which is expected to continue for ten years, a company has narrowed its choices to three methods.

Alternative No. 1 would require (a) two clerks, each of whom would be paid $300 monthly, with fringe benefits amounting to another 20 percent; (b) two machines, each costing $500, with a life of three years and a trade-in or scrap value of $50; and (c) supervisory and administrative overhead of $600 a month.

Alternative No. 2 would require (a) one technical assistant at a salary of $450 a month, with fringe benefits amounting to another 20 percent; (b) one machine costing $10,000, with a life of five years and a trade-in or scrap value of $1,000; and (c) supervisory and administrative overhead of $400 a month.

Alternative No. 3 would involve (a) contracting out the operation to an outside office service company at a monthly cost of 900 and (b) an administrative overhead cost of $200 a month.

Question

1. What would be your decision in this case?

CASE 11. RESPONSIBILITY FOR PERSONNEL SHORTCOMINGS

An optical company employs fifty people in its laboratory where lenses are ground and surfaced. About one half of these are immigrants and have been with the company for more than ten years. Twenty of the employees are women. Due to the low wage structure, reliable employees are not easy to hire. And except for those of immigrant background, the turnover rate is excessively high.

In the lab are two supervisors. One is in charge of grinding, and the other supervises the surfacing department. Both men were hired when the firm was founded and have progressed to their present positions. They report to Mr. Contact, who is in charge of the laboratory. Mr. Contact checks every lens that is produced, hires help for the lab, and keeps necessary records.

Recently, the lab has been plagued with a series of difficulties. For one thing, the turnover in the lab has reached the point where it is necessary on the average to hire two new employees each week. The quality and quantity of work has slipped to an all-time low. Absenteeism has increased; on the opening day of hunting, more than half of the new employees were out. Also, it is not unusual for a quarter of the new employees to take either Mondays or Fridays off. Recently, too, liquor bottles have been found in trash cans; employees have been caught sleeping on company time; personal calls have been made by telephone during working hours; and one woman, passing out religious materials, was conducting a revival meeting on company time.

Mr. Convex, executive vice-president, made an investigation of the situation. His interview with Mr. Contact brought out the point that work in the laboratory was exacting and placed a severe burden upon people. His interviews with Mr. Contact's supervisors brought out the cliquishness of the immigrants. They seemed to resent it when a new employee was brought in. They would ridicule the new employee and would not cooperate with him. But Mr. Convex also felt that the supervisors seemed to side with the immigrants.

In an interview with one employee who was quitting, Mr. Convex got the impression from him that no one seemed to care whether he succeeded or not. Moreover, the employee felt that there were too many "odd-balls" around the place.

Questions

1. Upon whom would you place responsibility for what is happening in this case?
2. What plans would you recommend for the improvement of the short-comings?

CASE 12. PROBABILITIES IN DECISION MAKING

The Widget Company is considering bidding on a contract the profit on which could amount to $250,000. Its chances of getting it are affected by (1) the possibility of a strike being called by the union and (2) competition.

If the company agrees to the demands of the union, there will be no strike, but labor costs will increase by $60,000 annually. If it refuses the demands, the company believes the employees will weary of the strike and eventually settle without a raise. It estimates that chances of settlement without a raise are 70 percent after one week, 80 percent after two weeks, 90 percent after three weeks, and 100 percent after four weeks of striking.

But the company calculates that for each week of the strike, it will lose $10,000 of profits.

It further estimates that its chances of getting the contract are 50 percent if there is no strike or if the strike lasts no longer than two weeks. If it lasts longer, the buyer will have less confidence in the company's ability to deliver on time, so the chances of getting the contract would go down to 40 percent in a three-week strike, and to 30 percent in a four-week strike.

Question

1. What should be the strategy of the company in this case?

CASE 13. EXCEPTIONS TO A POLICY

One Friday afternoon, as employees were leaving for the weekend, a supervisor noticed a large bulge in the pocket of one of his workers,

Fred Fast. He asked Fred what he had in his pocket. Fred appeared very nervous but replied, "Oh, nothing." He excused himself and hurried off to his car. The supervisor waited a moment and then followed Fred to the parking lot. Just as he got there, he saw Fred put something under the front seat. Feeling certain something was amiss, he walked up to the car and told Fred to get out. Then he reached under the seat and pulled out a torque wrench.

The wrench was a type used in the assembly department to tighten bolts. It could be adjusted so that all bolts were tightened equally. It was valued at $70.

The supervisor told Fred to go home and that the case would be taken up on Monday morning in the office of the plant manager. Fred said nothing but got into his car and drove off.

The supervisor returned to the assembly department and replaced the wrench in the tool cabinet. He then checked the tool inventory list. He found that all tools could be accounted for except for the wrench. Having finished the inventory, the supervisor left the plant. During the ride home, he thought about his relationship with Fred during the past five years. He recalled an incident when Fred had found another employee's gold ring on the washroom ledge. Fred turned it in to the supervisor. When the owner had tried to give Fred a reward of $5.00, he had refused it, saying he couldn't take money for something like that.

The following Monday, the supervisor came to work an hour earlier than usual. He went to the personnel office and reviewed Fred's file. The file gave him the following information:

1. Fred had worked for the company for the past seven years.
2. He had never been disciplined, and his tardiness and absenteeism record was far below the average.
3. All of his supervisors had made favorable comments about his attitude, personality, output, and quality of work.
4. Fred was next in line for promotion to supervisor of a section of the assembly division.
5. Fred had a wife and three children. He lived in a newly purchased house on the outskirts of the city.

The supervisor took this information to the plant manager's office. After he explained the situation to the plant manager, he went to get Fred.

The plant manager asked Fred if he was familiar with company rules concerning removal of company property. Fred said he was. The manager still felt he should quote the company manual so that there would be no doubt in anyone's mind. He then read the following passage:

RULE #34. Any employee found removing any property of the company, or of its employees, from the company area, is in violation of company policies and is subject to immediate discharge.

Having read the rule, he asked Fred if he had anything to say about the incident.

Fred said he did. He explained that he was working on the engine of his car. He had finished assembling the motor Thursday night except for tightening the two heads. To avoid warping the heads, he needed a torque wrench. He knew that no one would need the wrench in the plant after Friday because the plant shut down during the weekend. He didn't consider it stealing because he intended to return it Monday morning.

Questions

1. If you were the plant manager, what would your decision be, and why?
2. Would you rewrite Rule #34 in any way?

CASE 14. A WORK ASSIGNMENT GRIEVANCE

In a certain rayon mill, textile yarn is manufactured and knitted into underwear cloth, a continuous process which keeps the mill in operation twenty-four hours a day, seven days a week. Three shifts are employed.

A grievance was cited at a special meeting requested by the district representative of the union, concerning job assignments in the dyeing and finishing department. Present at the meeting were the personnel manager, the area supervisor, the head of the D & F department, the district representative of the union, the president of the local union, and two employees of the D & F department.

In the D & F department the knitted cloth is put through the final processes, preparing it for packing and shipping. Here the cloth passed through dye tubs, extractors (water whirled out), folders, dryers, first-pass machines (steamed and inspected), and second-pass machines (steamed, pressed, inspected, and rolled).

The jobs in the department include the following: second-pass operators, tub operators, first-pass operators, dry-end-of-dryer operators, and helpers. The grievance in the case is concerned with helpers.

The district representative of the union stated that the helpers were dissatisfied with the arrangement concerning their job assignments. They were currently being rotated on various helper assignments, but they preferred permanent assignments. Rotation involved learning too many different jobs. The representative suggested that the helper job be broken down as follows:

1. Dyehouse helpers:
   a) Dye-tub unloading
   b) Dye-tub loading
2. Finishing helpers:
   a) Folding machine
   b) Wet end of dryer

The head of the D & F department then described the current method of rotation. He pointed out that rotation among various jobs was primarily done weekly to give everyone a chance on all jobs. But as work loads required, or as breakdowns occurred, rotation had to be used to accommodate for these conditions.

The personnel manager asked if there were any preferred jobs. He was told by the employee representative that the loading job was preferred. The personnel manager asked if it would be satisfactory for the most senior employee to be given this task, with less desirable tasks going to junior employees during normal runs. The department head agreed that this could be worked out.

When it came to the finishing tasks, the discussion soon revealed that there was too much variation in the work to permit a permanent assignment without causing either too much work at some times and too little at others. Yet the union representative was adamant and insisted on some form of permanent assignment.

Questions

1. What solution would you propose to this situation?
2. Has the union usurped the prerogatives of management in this case?

CASE 15.   ADDITIONS TO THE STAFF

The chief of office services has been approached about the problem that technicians faced in getting materials from a central storage area. The technicians often must wait for materials because there is only one attendant at the disbursement window. The chief of office services contends that adding another attendant would increase costs unduly, but agrees to look into the matter.

A sample is taken of the arrival time of technicians at the storage area. It is found that arrivals during the sample period were as follows: The first technician arrived at 8:45 A.M., the second at 8:48 A.M., and so on as follows: 8:50, 8:51, 8:52, 8:56, 9:06, 9:16, 9:26, 9:34,

9:46, 9:59, 10:14, 10:22, 10:25, 10:26, 10:39, 10:43, 10:44, 10:45, and 10:51. The sample was concluded at 11:05 A.M. It was assumed to be representative of the problem.

The average service time was five minutes. The attendant's salary was $80 a week, or $2 an hour. The technicians' salaries average $120 a week, or $3 an hour.

Question

1. Should another attendant be hired for the central storage area?

CASE 16.   TURNOVER IMPLICATIONS

The Executive Insurance Company had grown to the point that it had reached the $100-million premium level. While it had taken 40 years to reach the first $50-million premium level, the next $50 million had been reached in a few years under 10. While business had grown to the satisfaction of the company directors, they were becoming aware of some storm signals.

The company discovered that it did not have adequate personnel to take care of the new business. It had been selling service, but it found that it could not give that service. Not only was it a problem of securing adequate personnel to run the company, but it was also a matter of retaining the employees who were then with the company. Its officers were shocked to find that the company had an annual turnover figure of 31.2 percent. Appalled by the figure, the company's management obtained a breakdown on the figure from information acquired from exit interviews. The results were disquieting to company officials, for the figures indicated that not only were a large number of employees being discharged, but many people were leaving for reasons which indicated that they did not like their jobs or the company.

This was an alarming set of facts for a company which was selling service to its customers through employee contacts with those customers.

BREAKDOWN OF ANNUAL TURNOVER, 1957

Reasons for Leaving	Percentage
Quit voluntary (unclassified)	0.7%
Unknown reason	2.8
Discharge	6.4
Health	2.1
Disliked job	8.5
Another job	6.4
Unavoidable (pregnancy, death, etc.)	3.6
Do not like job conditions	0.7
	31.2%

The company believed that this turnover figure was definitely excessive and decided that something must be done. Years before, the company's management had decided that there were certain undesirable conditions or results inherent in the company's personnel program. Like so many other companies, the executives adopted a practice of paternalism. Recreational, pension, and insurance programs were set up in an attempt to foster employee good will toward the company.

In 1940 the management decided to inaugurate a company-financed annual party and set aside $50,000 per year to finance the party. The idea was continued until 1945 and then abandoned when it was realized that the amount of money spent did not produce corresponding improvements in relations; and as an additional factor, certain disagreeable incidents which occurred at these parties had actually produced negative results. The money was diverted to increase employee retirement benefits.

At the time of the turnover study in 1957 the personnel department consisted of one man and one woman, both low-salaried. Into their hands had been placed the responsibility for administering some 2,200 employees. The personnel director was a low staff employee with no executive status. Screening of job applicants and hiring of many of the company's employees was done by this man, who attempted to compare employment candidates with what he thought were the requirements of a particular job. The candidate was usually given an initial screening by the personnel director and was then referred to a line supervisor, who made the selection on the basis of his own experience.

Questions

1. What steps would you take in order to reduce the rate of turnover in this company?
2. What additional information regarding turnover would you like to get in order to be on surer grounds regarding your course of action?
3. What is your opinion of this company's personnel setup and policies as factors in the high turnover?

CASE 17. LABOR ALLOCATIONS

The Outdoor Tent Company makes two standard products: tents and sleeping bags. Its machine installations are relatively simple. Hence, labor is the biggest element of cost of manufacturing operations, with more labor being utilized in the production of sleeping bags than in tents. This (apart from respective selling prices) explains why the contribution to marginal income by each unit of output is $6 for tents and $4 for sleeping bags.

The company is desirous of allocating labor to that product mix which would yield the greatest contribution to total marginal income. The technical limitations on output are as follows:

	Tents per Month	Sleeping Bags per Month
Cutting operation	300	600
Sewing operation	400	500
Finishing operation	600	500

Question

1. Assuming that the company can sell any amount within its technical limitations, what would be the best allocation of labor to possible product mixes?

CASE 18.   A SELECTION AND INDUCTION PROCEDURE

The superintendent of a factory did the hiring for all factory jobs. When he needed help, he would either hire casual labor or notify the office manager in the front office who, in turn, used his own methods to attract applicants. In the latter case the superintendent would screen the ones sent to him by the office manager. The superintendent selected employees on the basis of his personal judgment; there was very little interviewing; and only casual attempts were made to check on the applicant's references, past experience, or education.

After being accepted by the superintendent, the employee was referred to a factory clerk, who filled out a personal history data sheet and arranged for a physical examination in town. The clerk would assign the new man a number and show him how to punch his daily time card and job cards.

The employee would then be taken back to the superintendent, who would immediately assign him to a machine, give him a few minutes of instruction, and leave him to do as well as he could. Only when some job went wrong would there be any follow-up.

Labor turnover in this plant was relatively high. Each month a number of employees left the payroll. Some were discharged because they did not come up to the standards set by the superintendent. Others left of their own accord because they could not adjust to the impersonal attitude of management toward employees.

The superintendent was aware of the turnover, but his view was that production was satisfactory and the company was making money, so why worry about the turnover or the views of employees?

Questions

1. How do you counter the superintendent's views?
2. What suggestions do you have as far as the selection and induction procedures are concerned? Remember this company doesn't do a lot of hiring, so an elaborate program is not justified.

CASE 19. AN INEFFECTIVE EMPLOYEE

Ed Smith had been in four different departments in seven months. In none of them did he get a rating of better than "fair." Yet, according to his tests and interviews during hiring, the personnel director thought Ed should have done much better.

Now, Mr. O. L. Wade, Smith's present and fifth supervisor, reports that Smith is loafing on the job, stepping out for frequent smokes, and occasionally interfering with other operators by his gossiping.

Wade called Smith into his office for a talk, his intention being to find out why Smith didn't work more effectively. The conversation in its essential parts was as follows:

WADE: How do you like the job you're on?

SMITH: Oh, it's all right.

WADE: Well, I've noticed you seem to have a lot of spare time on your hands. Seems like you might put out a little more effort.

SMITH: I think I do as much as anyone else on this job.

WADE: But Ed, you don't keep yourself busy.

SMITH: There's nothing else to do; if you look at the charts, you'll see I do as much as the guy on the shift before me.

WADE: Well, let's see if we can't keep a little busier in the future.

SMITH: O.K. (*He leaves.*)

A review of Smith's personnel and work records revealed the following information:

Age:	20
Experience:	None previously in a factory
Education:	One year of college; studied art; quit, no funds
Military status:	Deferred, perforated eardrums
Days lost:	None
Late to work:	None
Accidents:	None
Productivity:	Average
Characteristics:	Quiet, slow-moving, defensive when talking with superiors, lacks initiative

A review of job reports showed the following:

First job: Carbon cutting; broke in with Old Harvey. Didn't exert
                himself on this job. Supervisor asked to transfer him
                out.
Second job: Carting saggers; temporary during vacation period for regu-
                lar man. Did the job passably.
Third job: Piecework in forcing department, traying carbons. Earned
                above-average per hour at regular rate. This was a
                vacation fill-in.
Fourth job: Helper in mixing room; worked slowly.
Fifth job: Transferred to new CWS plant as helper in calcining room,
                where he is presently employed.

Questions

1. What would your decision be now as to what to do with Smith?
2. Could anything have been done to prevent this situation from developing?

CASE 20.   THE SALES DEPARTMENT STORE

The Sales Department Store is located in a medium-sized city in an agricultural area and does a business of about $2 millions annually. It is owned and managed by A. B. Comer, who is elderly, resistant to change, and opinionated in most matters. His son, James Comer, manages one of the large departments, does some of the top administrative work, and also handles the personnel duties. A son-in-law, D. E. Jones, runs the accounting office, supervises maintenance, and handles some of the top executive functions. These are the top executives of the company, under whom are the department managers and buyers.

One function that Mr. A. B. Comer and Mr. James Comer will not delegate is that related to personnel. They receive requests for new employees, but they do all of the hiring. However, they give almost unlimited authority to department managers in buying and selling. Their success has been through other people's rather than their own personal merchandising skill. The difference in their ages and background sometimes gives rise to clashes in matters pertaining to employees. This was illustrated in the case of Mrs. Jane Doe, who was hired for the cosmetics department, which is one of the seven departments managed by Mr. John Swift.

A few months later, and after Mrs. Doe had been transferred to the book department, young Comer came to Swift about Mrs. Doe.

JAMES: Mr. Comer is really mad about that Mrs. Doe now. He says fire her today, give her a week's pay in advance, and get her out of the store. He said she's been absent two more times; and he has received a complaint from a customer about her; and every time he sees her, she is sitting around reading a book. This afternoon at 2:30 he saw her sitting in the kitchen drinking coffee and reading a book, and it was forty-five minutes before she came out.

SWIFT: Well, he might have bothered to find out why, before jumping to conclusions. One of the other girls is sick and didn't show up today, but phoned in. That made us shorthanded, with two others away on vacation. Jane volunteered to work in two departments so the girls could get away for lunch, then she was going without her own. About 2:30, I insisted that she take time off at least to get a sandwich and rest awhile. It would be unfair to fire her for being considerate of other people—and if he does, I quit, too, right now!

JAMES: Oh, that's different. He wouldn't be sore if he knew that. But what about this reading all the time?

SWIFT: I've asked her to read every chance she gets. That's the only way she can know these new books as they come out. She reads all the book reviews, and keeps the bulletin board posted with them for the benefit of the customers. Have you noticed the board she put up over there? The customers like that. When she isn't busy, she reads the fly leaves of different books. Then, at noon she reads and at night takes books home with her. I check them out to her, and she keeps them in perfect condition, brings them back, and we sell them at no loss. She has a remarkable memory for books and can really talk to customers about them. It used to be that nine out of ten people were just browsing around; now, nine out of ten are buying. Have you noticed those book sales?

JAMES: Yes, but Mary is selling a lot more than she used to. As much as Jane, according to the sales slips.

SWIFT: Mary isn't selling anything. She couldn't sell anything if her life depended on it—you know that. She is a sweet girl that most of the people like, and she just waits on them to get them what they ask for. But that works out swell with Jane. Mary handles the miscellaneous trade on stationery and stuff and writes up the sales tickets on Jane's sales while Jane is waiting on another book customer. That's why Mary has more sales slips now; she writes them out while Jane sells. [*No commission on sales had resulted in such working arrangements between the girls.*]

JAMES: Of course, it looks bad if she is reading on the job. But it's fine that she is finding out so much about the merchandise.

SWIFT: She isn't sitting down reading a book out in the department. She stands at a book rack, arranges the books, checks stock, and reads fly leaves, and is Johnny-on-the-spot when a customer approaches. That is exactly what she should be doing. Does Mr. Comer prefer Mary's just standing around doing nothing when a customer isn't there?

JAMES: Can't you keep Mary busy?

SWIFT: By giving her specific tasks, but I can't watch her every minute. She hasn't an ounce of initiative.

JAMES: Would you like to replace her?

SWIFT: Not necessarily. She works out well with Jane. But I'd much rather lose her than Jane.

JAMES: I have suggested to Mr. Comer that we let Mary go or transfer her to the office because she can't sell. She is the complete opposite of the sales type. But Mr. Comer insists on keeping her there. It seems you and I disagree with the boss on people, doesn't it?

SWIFT: Well, a couple of them, anyway. We seem to agree on all the others, though. What was the complaint about Jane?

JAMES: An older woman, an acquaintance of Mr. Comer's, said she didn't think that girl was the right kind to have working here, especially with a sweet girl like Mary. Thought it would contaminate Mary and give the store a bad name having such people for lady clerks.

SWIFT: Oh, I know who you mean now and what the complaint was about. It was the only real boner Jane has pulled on the sales floor; but oddly enough, it helped business, and I got the best laugh out of it that I've had all year. See that book rack built around that post? Jane was standing on this side of it, that old prude on the left side, and two fellows from the university on the right side of it. All were talking to her. The woman had wondered when Jane had had a chance to read so much, since she knew so many of the books, and Jane told her she read every night when she went to bed. The college fellows asked if she had any more books like *Forever Amber*. Jane pulled three books from the rack and started telling about them. The woman interposed in an insulting tone: "Young lady, do you read such trash as that? I'm surprised that you don't read something to improve your mind!" Jane was half indignant, and said: "Lady, after I work here all day, then go home and cook supper, wash dishes, clean house, and take care of the kids, and finally get to bed, I go to bed to be entertained, not educated!" The boys started roaring; then, it dawned on Jane how it sounded, and she put her hand up to her mouth and started laughing, too. The old lady left in sort of a huff. Mary and I had overheard the thing, and we were both laughing, too. The boys bought all three of the books, have come back twice since then and bought stuff, and brought friends with them both times. That bunch has bought almost $100 worth of stuff, including a good suitcase from the luggage department, and they are definitely Jane's customers. Of course, we haven't seen the old lady since.

JAMES: How about her absences lately?

SWIFT: She hasn't been absent. She worked on her scheduled day off last week so Mary could get away for a church function. So this week, Mary worked for her, and that's why she was gone an extra day. And she needed the rest; she's been working at two jobs and is looking rather tired.

JAMES: Where else is she working?

SWIFT: At night, as a waitress. She took on the extra job for a few weeks to make money to pay off the loan she took on the house. Now, she has decided to stay there permanently and quit here because she heard via the grapevine from the office that Mr. Comer wants to get rid of her. She told me just before you came down. She said she would stay here, though, to help me out until I could get someone to replace her. I thanked her for that. I would like her to stay here permanently, but I didn't press the point because she is earning over three times as much there as she is here, counting tips.

JAMES: Well, it's best, in a way. It will get Mr. Comer off our neck.

SWIFT: And lose a lot of business. I'll bet you ten to one you can't find anyone, at her salary, who will sell half as much merchandise in that department as she has. And she would have stayed in spite of the salary difference because she likes to work so well here, except for Mr. Comer. But this case has taught me something. There is no future in working for a place where prejudice overrides facts and business considerations, so I'm leaving. I'll stay till the first of next month. That will give you a chance to find a replacement, and me a chance to make an inventory and get everything shipshape.

JAMES: Do you feel that strongly about the girl?

SWIFT: Not personally, but as a matter of principle I do. That could happen to any of the individuals here if it happened to her, and it could happen to me. Under such conditions, there is no future in this place.

JAMES: I don't want you to leave, and I know Mr. Comer won't. You have done a grand job with these departments. Think it over, and talk to him before you do anything definite.

Mr. Swift did not leave then but did leave two months later, in good grace, when he accepted a much better job in a salary range the store could not meet. The store lost the top salesclerk in the seven departments and the manager who had the largest volume of business for the seven departments in the history of the store. The elder Mr. Comer was quite pleased to get rid of the girl who was "no good," and young Mr. Comer was relieved of a critical point of friction.

Questions

1. Criticize the handling of this case.
2. Was there any other logical outcome?

CASE 21.   A DISCIPLINARY INTERVIEW

A typist in the general office of a retail establishment had become a tardy case. Employed only a year, she had developed into an efficient, all-around worker. Her ability and productivity were praised by both her office manager and the executives for whom she did work.

During the last month or so, however, she had been late to work a number of times anywhere from 10 to 30 minutes. In the beginning, her tardiness was attributed to transportation delays. The office manager spoke to the girl and told her she must report on time. As time passed, her record did not improve, nor did she offer any excuses for her tardiness. Her work assignments were completed with an excellent rating. Nevertheless, the situation caused unrest among other office personnel. The office manager heard murmured complaints, morale was lower, and general efficiency was decreasing.

The office manager decided to have another interview with the girl. Following are significant selections from the interview:

"Do you like your work here?"

"Yes."

"Do you enjoy working with the other members of the office?"

"Yes."

"Are you satisfied with your salary?"

"Yes, for the present."

"Do you have transportation problems in getting to work?"

"No, sir."

"Do you meet someone who keeps you from getting to work on time?"

"No, sir."

"Are home problems causing delays?"

"No, sir."

"Then why are you late so often?"

"I don't know; I just can't make it sometimes."

Questions

1. What decision would you reach in this case if you were the office manager?
2. If the girl was discharged, what would this mean in taking disciplinary action?

CASE 22.   INDUCTION PROCEDURES

This is a report on the induction procedures used in a job-order foundry employing from 150 to 200 men.

Originally, new employees were inducted as follows: Upon completion of the hiring process the employee was escorted from the employment office to the foundry by an office messenger boy. Entering the foundry, the new worker was taken directly to the superintendent's office, whereupon the messenger presented the superintendent or his assistant with a slip of paper bearing the employee's name, age, home address, telephone number, and previous foundry experience, if any. There was no other introduction.

The superintendent or his assistant would then briefly explain that the policy was to have new men work their first week in the grinding and inspection department, where the products of the foundry were given the finishing touches and inspected. The new employee was then escorted to grinding and inspection; on the way the superintendent would make some such comment as this, "You will find your time card in that rack over there," and point in the general direction of the foundry time clock.

In the grinding room the new man was put to work with other men loading and unloading rough castings into large drums which rotated, in order to grind off sharp edges and to detect any flaws in the castings.

The second week he was returned to the superintendent's office and assigned to the foreman in charge of the type of work for which he was hired, or wherever he happened to be needed. The foreman usually assigned a new man as an assistant to one of the older men for the purpose of learning the job. This was particularly true in the case of molders and sandcutters.

The above is a complete and accurate account of the induction procedure used by this company for several years.

A new personnel director, fresh out of college and inexperienced, arrived on the scene. He took immediate steps to correct the method of inducting new employees. A brief resumé of the number of grievances, and the fact that 50 percent of all employees leaving did so during the first three months of their employment, indicated something was wrong with the original breaking-in process.

The personnel director installed the following induction procedure:

1. Each new employee is presented with a small handbook containing the rules and regulations of the company. Sufficient time is taken to elaborate on some of the more important rules, thus eliminating the possibility of some of the misunderstandings which frequently result in grievances.
2. A fifteen-minute film is shown on the production process as well as how the product is used and distributed. The counselor is careful to emphasize certain key points of the film and at the same time attempts to install a certain feeling of confidence in the company product. Generally speaking, most workers want to be a part of a good production team.
3. The pay scale and promotional possibilities are discussed in detail. New employees are assured that promotion is possible, providing of course, that they produce satisfactorily in accordance with established standards. This gives the new worker something to look forward to and constitutes somewhat of a challenge to him.
4. Sufficient time is taken to show and explain the following facilities:
   a) Location of time clocks and how to ring in and out properly
   b) Location of rest rooms, showers, and lockers
   c) Location of facilities for eating lunch (most of the employees carry their lunch)
   d) Location and use of the employee parking lot
   e) Location of the first-aid room
   f) Recreational activities, which include company-sponsored softball and basketball teams, and a picnic each year
5. At the conclusion of the orientation, each employee is invited to come back to the personnel office to discuss and talk over any problems pertaining to work or personal matters relative to housing, transportation, medical problems, and so on. The personnel director feels that this procedure is essential to good morale, since it instills a feeling of security in the new worker.
6. The personnel director or his assistant personally escorts each new man to the foundry superintendent's office and makes a proper introduction.

This is a prime prerequisite for getting the work relationship off on the right foot.

Questions

1. Under what conditions might the casual induction procedure as originally employed have been effective?
2. Why do you think the new procedure is more effective?
3. In what ways might the new procedure of induction be made more effective?

CASE 23. A SHIFT PROBLEM

The Makem Parts Company had to add a third shift because of increasing business. There are three major divisions in the company. In section A (see diagram), initial manufacture of parts takes place. Here is found the heaviest and dirtiest work. Hourly wages here do not always compensate for these conditions. However, some jobs here are liked better than others. Many good jobs are located in section B (a finishing and paint-spraying unit), but it is also the hottest section. As a consequence, many good jobs go unwanted in the summer but are desired in the winter. Section C is final assembly. Conditions here are generally the best, but the work is controlled by a mechanical conveyor and, as a result, is tiresome and monotonous.

Section A	Section B	Section C
1	2 2	3

1. Welding and assembling
2. Paint spraying and ovens
3. Mechanical conveyor

Each section has a supervisor and assistant supervisor for each shift, with a general foreman over all.

The company is adding a midnight shift to the day and afternoon shifts. This is being done by hiring more men from the outside and training them, by transferring men between sections, and by promoting employees.

The union contract, which applies to all employees except supervisory and above, states:

All vacancies shall be posted, at least a week before they become available, on the various company bulletin boards. Any man wishing to bid for a job should do so in the department office for which the vacancy occurs. Men bidding for jobs will be given preference in the following order:

1. Persons who are in the same section of the same department in which the vacancy occurs will have first choice. However, if two men from the same section apply, seniority will rule unless the company can prove the senior man to be incompetent.
2. All other men in the same department have next preference. Seniority rules here in case more than one man applies.
3. The rest of the employees have next preference with seniority ruling, of course, in case more than one man applies.
4. All outside hiring will be in order of application.

Questions

1. What difficulties do you foresee in the light of the union contract?
2. What changes, if any, in the union contract would you try to bring about?

CASE 24. SENIORITY

The collective bargaining contract in a given company specified that seniority was to be considered on a groupwide rather than a plantwide or departmental basis. This meant that by mutual agreement the company and the union had set up eight groups which had common characteristics and job interchangeability. Anywhere from five to ten departments made up a group.

Promotions and layoffs were to be governed by seniority within the groups. In the present instance a layoff raised a perplexing problem.

For purposes of the layoff, seniority lists were prepared for each group. It was found, however, that there were a few jobs that were common to all groups, such as porters, laborers, helpers, and truckers. To lay off by seniority meant laying off a porter in group A with five years' service, while a porter in group B with only a year's service was safe from a layoff. This was due to the fact that the porter in group A was in a group in which layoffs were necessary, but there were no layoffs scheduled in group B.

The company could not transfer the porter in group A to group B and thereby give him preference over the porter with less seniority because, according to another section in the contract, any employee transferred from one group to another must be in the new group for a year before he could transfer his hiring-date seniority with him.

Questions

1. What could be done now to arrive at a fair decision?
2. What could be done about writing a new seniority clause that would be fair under all conditions?

CASE 25. RATING SUPERVISORY EFFECTIVENESS

In order to fill a vacancy in a general manager's position, five executives reviewed the qualifications of a group of supervisors. Out of this group, five have been selected as seeming to have the ability to fill the vacancy. The committee of five is now going through the process of checking and rating the candidates on a number of factors. Among the factors is that of their effectiveness as supervisory leaders of their particular organizational units. In respect to this factor (as well as with the other factors), the members of the committee have asked to rank the candidates in order of their merit and to indicate the degree of excellence by marking after each ranking one of the following: good, very good, or superior.

The following table shows the results of the committee's appraisal of leadership effectiveness:

	RATER									
CANDIDATE	No. 1		No. 2		No. 3		No. 4		No. 5	
	R	E	R	E	R	E	R	E	R	E
RDA	4	G	5	VG	4	G	4	VG	3	VG
CRB	2	S	1	S	2	VG	1	VG	2	VG
JKC	5	G	4	G	3	G	5	VG	5	G
LSD	1	VG	3	G	1	VG	2	S	1	S
TWE	3	VG	2	VG	5	G	3	S	4	VG

NOTE: R = ranking order; E = excellence rating; G = good; VG = very good; S = superior.

Question

1. On the basis of the foregoing information, what would be your judgment of the candidates insofar as the factor of leadership effectiveness is concerned?

CASE 26. TRAINING TECHNICAL SUPERVISORS

The expansion needs of a company called for an increased staff in the accounting office. To this unit were to be added five supervisory personnel and fifty operative employees.

The requirements for supervisors were as follows: The applicant had to have a college degree in accounting; the minimum age was 23; the candidate had to be physically fit and had to pass a personal interview.

The requirements for operative employees were as follows: The minimum age was 21; the candidate had to have a high school education and a knowledge of bookkeeping; and he had to pass a mental test and a physical examination.

About 10 percent of the supervisors' time was spent on accounting matters, largely to do with weekly and monthly reports to be sent to the controller. The rest of their time was concerned with dealing with employees, organizing work assignments, handling grievances, interviewing prospective employees, and counseling and training present employees.

After the expanded department had been in operation for several months, results had failed to come up to expectations. The personnel department was asked to see if there were any personnel difficulties or problems. It reported that the main cause of trouble was the lack of supervisory competency. The supervisors were experts in accounting practices and systems but rather inept when it came to dealing with employees as people. It suggested the following:

1. Hire for supervisors people who had some courses in personnel and office management as well as in the specialty of accounting.
2. Set up a supervisory training program that stressed personnel and human relations aspects.

The personnel department also suggested that greater care be taken in screening prospective candidates, particularly for the supervisory positions. And it argued that after hiring, training emphasis should be on personnel matters, as justified by the percentage of time the supervisors now spent on this phase of their work.

Questions

1. What is your opinion of the conclusions of the personnel department?
2. What would be some of the specific subjects that should be included in the human relations training of the supervisors?

CASE 27. THE OPEN-DOOR POLICY

Whenever employees of the Proco Company do not get the action or answers they want from their immediate supervisors or from the personnel department, they may take the matter up to higher management or directly to the chief executive. That is what Mr. A. W. Topper, the president, wants them to do. He has found that because they know his door is always open to them, workers ask to see him only when it seems absolutely necessary. And he has not been swamped by employees bearing suggestions, requests, or "gripes."

The open-door policy is augmented by morale surveys that are conducted every few years. In these, individual responses are kept confidential. They are sealed by the employees and go to an outside firm of consultants for analysis and review. The company gets detailed reports of the survey results, but no names. The employees have developed faith in the surveys because over the years the items brought to the attention of management have in the main been acted upon.

A newly appointed supervisor has felt somewhat upset by this system of communications. He has found that a number of employees have gone around him to higher management to voice opinions and complaints. In a meeting with his superior, he has argued that company policy should require employees to come to the supervisor either before going to higher levels or before expressing their views on questionnaires. Otherwise, he argues, action cannot be taken at the lowest possible level, and that higher levels must be bothered by details that have to be handled by the lower levels in the final analysis.

Questions

1. What is your opinion of the supervisor's opinion?
2. What is the basis for the company's success in human relations, assuming that it has been successful?

CASE 28. EDUCATIONAL SUBSIDIES

The Scitechno Company has been in the vanguard of manufacturing highly technical machine controls. It has grown to a size of over five thousand employees. Concern of the executives with technical matters left little or no time for labor relations during its early history. As a consequence, the company, until the 1950's, had no formal personnel program. But in the past several years the company has interested itself, among other things, in education. It inaugurated an educational subsidy for talented young men and women. Under this plan the company employs "co-op" students, offers summer employment to college students, and makes grants to individuals in the form of unrestricted scholarships.

Most of the scholarship recipients were connected with the company in some way or other. They usually slanted their education toward fields in which the company was interested. Such slanting was not, however, stipulated in the grants.

After the scholarship program had been in effect for several years, the company made some casual surveys of those whom it had sent through school. It was found that while the scholarship holders held the company in the highest esteem, few of them sought jobs with the company upon graduation. It was further found that the company itself exerted no effort to recruit any of the graduates, even though it considered some of them to be top managerial material and technically competent. It seemed that the company was underwriting a program for training personnel for other companies, some of whom were competitors.

The president, although a believer in higher education, is wondering whether the scholarship program should be dropped.

Questions

1 What would be your advice to the president?
2. How might the program be retained with more benefit to the company?

CASE 29. SUPERVISORY-SUBORDINATE PERCEPTIONS

A given company has been concerned about the quality of leadership of its first-line supervisors. Among other matters, the personnel director was asked to examine the attitudes that supervisors and employees held in regard to each other. One approach the personnel director took was to survey how supervisors perceived their jobs in relation to subordinates and how subordinates in turn perceived the job the supervisor was doing in relation to them.

To take the examination out of the realm of qualitative conceptions, the personnel director developed a set of scales to measure perceptions. Reproduced below are two of the scales administered to the subordinates and two to the supervisors:

Subordinate Scale #1—Taken all in all, do you have enough knowledge about your leader's evaluation of your work to know where you stand in his opinion?

Know very well where I stand	Know fairly clearly	Don't know too clearly	Don't know at all clearly

Subordinate Scale #2—How would you rate your supervisor on his knowledge about the attitudes and feelings of the people in his department?

Perfect	Excellent	Good	Poor

Supervisor Scale #1—To what degree do you think your subordinates accept the evaluations you communicate to them about their work?

Very high	Above average	Below average	Quite low

Supervisor Scale #2—To what degree do you think that logic, as opposed to feelings, influences opinions of employees about departmental matters?

Very much	Often	Moderately	Very little

When he tabulated the ratings, the personnel director obtained the following results:

On Subordinate Scale #1:
5 rated between "Know very well where I stand" and "Know fairly clearly."
11 rated as "Know fairly clearly."
16 rated between "Know fairly clearly" and "Don't know too clearly."
42 rated as "Don't know too clearly."
22 rated between "Don't know too clearly" and "Don't know at all clearly."
4 rated as "Don't know at all clearly."
On Subordinate Scale #2:
2 rated between "Perfect" and "Excellent."
8 rated as "Excellent."
12 rated between "Excellent" and "Good."
18 rated as "Good."
55 rated between "Good" and "Poor."
5 rated as "Poor."

On Supervisor Scale #1:
3 rated between "Very high" and "Above average."
2 rated as "Above average."
On Supervisor Scale #2:
1 rated between "Very much" and "Often."
2 rated as "Often."
2 rated between "Often" and "Moderately."

Question

1. What conclusions would you draw from this sample of the study (recognizing, of course, that this is a very small sample)?

CASE 30. COMMUNICATION PRACTICES

The Furnace Control Manufacturing Company makes thermostatic heat controls for coal and gas furnaces. It employed twenty-five women and two men in its assembly department. The majority of the women were married and ranged in age from 17 to 35. Assembly work was not difficult but required considerable finger dexterity to perform the operations. The women were seated at three poorly lighted workbenches (which ran one half the length of the room), and rarely had to stand during the performance of their work.

Close social relationships had been formed among the employees, and personal problems concerning husbands, relatives, and children were discussed openly every day. In fact, the employees produced more work when these conversations were allowed to continue ungoverned.

A problem arose when management decided to have the plant studied by an outside consultant for the purpose of increasing efficiency and production. Rumors passed through the plant that management was going to compensate all employees on an incentive basis. Most of the employees feared production rates would be increased, with less take-home pay for more work being the ultimate result.

Management did nothing to relieve the fears of its employees. One morning, a new man (carrying a clipboard and a stopwatch) was shown around the assembly room by the department foreman. It was explained that management was making a time study for the purpose of simplifying the work and thus increasing production. Contrary to rumors, no change in the method of compensation was to be introduced. A feeling existed among the employees that management would eventually change its mind and soon base pay on output.

A general slowdown in production occurred during the time-study period. More rejected controls than usual began turning up, and absenteeism increased. The consulting agency then suggested several plant-wide improvements. Power tools were introduced, more comfortable chairs were purchased for the women, and a better lighting system was installed. The attitude of the employees changed soon after these improvements had been made. Production reached and surpassed the old level. The assembly room employees appeared to be satisfied with the present changes. One thing was different. The employees no longer trusted management.

The crowning blow came a few weeks later. Management, for the sake of economy, combined the assembly line department with the parts fabrication department located on another floor. The employees in parts fabrication were also women, but they were 10 to 15 years older than the women in the assembly section. Resentment grew up between the two groups of women. The younger women said and did things that shocked the older women.

The assembly department was split into two sections after the move was completed, and sometimes the older women were spaced between two younger ones. This division was made for the sake of efficiency and was not merely used to divide the two groups of women.

The production of the fabrication employees decreased because the older women spent much of their time watching what the younger women were doing. Management immediately put up production charts showing what each person was expected to produce each week. The fabrication women got together and decided to "show those younger girls how to produce." Their production increased 150 percent. This increase put added pressure on the assembly women. The foreman came around and complained that production in assembly work would have to increase. No incentive, other than the urgings of management, was given to motivate the greater effort, and many employees soon quit.

Questions

1. What has this company communicated to the employees, and by what means has it done so?
2. What should it have communicated, and how?
3. In what respects, if any, should the communication program have been different for the younger and older women?

CASE 31. CALL-OUT PAY

The Jones Company is faced with a grievance in reference to a clause in the union contract in which the company is to pay employees for a full day when they are asked to report for work but no work is available.

The present case arose out of the unexpected breaking of a water pipe during an unprecedented cold spell. The pipe broke, water got into some motors, and the boilers turned off automatically. The night watchman called the plant manager, who tried to get the motors dried out before work started. After the employees arrived, management asked the men to stay on and await repairs. The temperature in the plant was disagreeably cold with the boilers out; after a couple of hours, some employees rang out, but some stayed on. Heat came on by 11:00 o'clock; but since some of the key men, such as crane operators, had left, the rest of the crew was sent home.

The following day, the union asked if the men were to receive call-out pay and was informed that they would not. After the next payday the union filed a grievance. The case finally came to an impartial umpire for a decision. In the hearings, he received the foregoing information as well as the following contentions:

1. The union argued that the workers should receive call-out pay because they had reported for work and there was no work. They were not sure that repairs could be completed that day.
2. The company argued that the broken pipe was an act of God, that work was offered, and that pay would be granted only to those who had remained until officially sent home.

Questions

1. On the basis of the information, what would your decision be?
2. How, if at all, would you improve the call-out pay clause?

CASE 32. AN ANALYSIS OF A WAGE STRUCTURE

With a view to evaluating its wage structure for selected jobs, a company has gathered data both within the company and in the community on wages in the various job classes. The table below contains the data that have been gathered:

Company Wage Class	Points for Class	Company Average Rate of Class	Community Average Rate of Class
1	30	$58	$ 75
2	40	68	76
3	50	70	90
4	60	76	92
5	70	90	104
6	80	96	111

Question

1. In your opinion, (*a*) is the wage relation between classes fair? (*b*) Does the wage curve for the company compare favorably with that of the community? (*c*) What, if anything, would you propose about changes?

CASE 33. ARRANGING FOR LAYOFFS

Early one spring, a manufacturer of shoes was faced with a two-week shutdown due to an unexpected leather shortage. The amount of orders on hand was so large that lost production time would have to be made up before fall, or it would not be possible to meet all delivery dates.

Operative employees were paid on a piece-rate basis and got a week's paid vacation in August with the privilege of working that week and collecting double pay.

The lost production could be made up in one of two ways: (1) by working overtime, although this would run costs above the contracted selling price; or (2) by persuading the employees to take their vacations during the layoff and working during the regular vacation period.

The task of selling the latter option to the employees was assigned to the industrial relations director. He realized that early spring was not a good time to take vacations; but he thought that if he gave the employees the facts, they would be willing to go along with management.

He called a meeting of the employees and told them that there would be a two-week layoff in April, but that the lost time would have to be made up before October. He went on to say that the cost factor ruled out overtime to make up lost time, but that costs would not be out of line if the employees would take their vacations during the layoff period and work during the regular vacation period. He pointed out that if this solution was not acceptable, it could easily mean lost orders to the company and some lost jobs to the men. He also stressed the fact that by taking their vacations during the layoff, they would only lose one week's wages. At the close of the meeting, he told them that a vote would be taken the next day, in cooperation with the union, to determine what was to be done.

That evening the union leaders called a meeting of the members to discuss management's proposition. They found a flaw in management's case which made them doubt the sincerity of the proposal. They noted that the industrial relations director had overlooked, purposely or otherwise, the requirements in the state unemployment compensation law that an individual must be unemployed for more than a week before he was eligible for compensation.

The union leaders explained this provision of the law and went on to infer that the real reason management wanted the employees to take their vacations during the layoff was to make them ineligible for unemployment compensation. By not drawing compensation, the merit rating of the company with the state compensation board would remain favorable, and its premium payments would not be raised. The union leaders argued that it would be better for the employees not to take their vacations during the layoff; they could then draw one week's unemployment compensation, and in August they could work the week of their vacation and draw double pay. This suggestion for getting more money appealed to the members; so at the election the next day, they voted against the company's proposal.

Questions

1. What mistakes did the company make?
2. How should the plan have been presented?

CASE 34. THE FIVE-DAY WEEK

John Williams works for a large machinery manufacturer. He is a graduate engineer and has worked for the company for over three years. He is well liked and is happy with his work. He has received training in all divisions of the company. His present job is the beginning of an interesting career with excellent opportunities for advancement.

The company is very progressive, providing numerous fringe benefits such as medical care, a pension plan, performance bonuses, liberal vacations, educational support, and low-cost loans for home purchases. The low labor turnover is indicative of good employer-employee relations.

Notwithstanding all this, John walked into his supervisor's office and told him he was going to quit. This was quite a surprise to the supervisor, who regarded John as one of his best and most satisfied men. The following discussion ensued:

SUPERVISOR: Why are you thinking of leaving? Are you dissatisfied with your work, pay, or advancement?

JOHN: No, I'm satisfied on those items, but I don't like to work on Saturday mornings.

SUPERVISOR: What's wrong with working on Saturdays? We have to here.

JOHN: Well, there are a number of reasons. Most of my friends have Saturday off; and when they plan picnics, golf matches, and other things, me and my wife are left out. My wife and my friends can't understand why I have to work on Saturdays. Besides, I bought a new home, and I would like the time to work out a number of minor improvements. I'd be willing to work a nine-hour day to make up for Saturday mornings. I just want that Saturday for my purposes.

SUPERVISOR: Let me tell you why we're working five and a half days a week. This started in the shop. You know we're not mass production. Our men need a lot of training before they can do their work properly. With our work load, we just couldn't go out and hire enough shop men to handle the schedules on a five-day basis. And even if we could, when work fell off from the present schedules, we'd have to lay off some good people. This way, when a drop-off comes, we can go to a five-day week and still keep our present force. And when the shop works on Saturdays, we in engineering have to be around to help on technical matters when they arise.

JOHN: That is all well and good, but I still want a five-day week.

Questions

1. What should be done about John Williams?
2. If this feeling is very prevalent, what should the policy of the company be?

CASE 35. SALES COMMISSIONS

Mr. Smith established a small business selling garden supplies. At the time of the store's opening the demand for plants and garden supplies was at its peak (1950). Mr. Smith had underestimated the demand for his services, and the company grew faster than he had ever expected. Because of the highly seasonal business he was in, he resorted to hiring high school and college boys as part-time help. Many of these boys liked the work and continued to work with Mr. Smith during vacations and some evenings after school.

As the business grew, new lines of merchandise were added to the list of over two thousand items Mr. Smith handled for the gardener, among them power mowers. Most of these were small mowers that could be sold without demonstration. Mr. Smith felt that there should be some form of higher compensation given to the employee when he sold a mower—sort of an incentive plan—since the company would recognize a greater profit margin on these larger items. The employees were very favorable to this setup, since it was often possible to pick up $20 to $40 extra per week during the peak mower-selling season.

Mr. Gray, one of the salesmen, had been with the company for seven years and was one of their best mower salesmen. He was attending school and depended on the commission paid on mowers for a large part of his school expenses. During one week in early May, Mr. Gray turned in his time slip with a list of the mowers he had sold. When he received his check, he noticed that the commission was less than half of what he should have received. He went to Mr. Smith, who told him that Mr. Brown, another salesman, had put many of the same names on his list and had told him that if he had not demonstrated the mowers, they would not have been sold. Mr. Gray then told Mr. Smith that if he had not taken the customer's name and talked to him about the mower, Mr. Brown would have had no one to whom to demonstrate the machine. Mr. Smith said he would have to work out the situation.

One week later, Mr. Smith told the employees that they would have to get together with one another and decide who should get credit for the sales—that he had too much to do to fool with little "gripes" like these. He said the men knew well in their own minds who should get credit for the sales and should be men enough to admit it. After the meeting, everyone felt a little better about it.

This plan, however, did not work, and there was a great deal of hard feeling between the employees. It even got to the place that employees were sacrificing sales rather than giving another employee the chance to demonstrate the mower or talk to the prospective buyer.

Mr. Gray worked one week under the new plan and went to Mr. Smith and said he would have to quit since he was doing the business far more harm than good and he was not enjoying his work—nor did he think the commission plan was fair. Within two weeks, three of the other part-time employees who had been with the company for more than two years quit.

Questions

1. How would you set up the commission plan if you were in charge?
2. On what grounds, if any, could Mr. Smith conclude that this issue was too small for him to take up?
3. How would you put up safeguards so that other facets of salesmanship besides writing up orders and giving demonstrations received attention?

CASE 36.   SAFETY

The Motor Manufacturing Company makes auto parts, which are sold to various automotive companies in and around Detroit. The company employs approximately five hundred men. It was unionized in 1940 by the UAW.

The company uses punch press and drop hammer operations in the manufacture of some of its products. There are about fifty employees in this department who operate approximately twenty machines in two shifts. Operation of these machines is extremely hazardous unless all safety rules are strictly observed. It is the responsibility of the foreman to enforce these rules. He is aided in the enforcement by group leaders.

The accident rate in the operation of these machines has been very high. A check of the safety rules shows that the following procedure is to be used in the operation of the machines: The operator picks up the unformed part with his left hand, grips it with tweezers in his right hand, and places it in the machine. The machine is set in motion with his foot. After the machine completes its cycle, the operator removes the part with the tweezers and, at the same time, grasps an unformed part with his left hand. The cycle of operations is then repeated.

The operators are on incentive work and tend to disregard safety in an effort to boost their earnings. Consequently, they have developed the habit of grasping the unformed part with the left hand and placing it in the machine while they remove the formed part with the right hand.

In an effort to reduce the number of accidents, the safety engineer had the machines equipped with a sweep-motion mechanical guard. The guard brushed the operator's hand aside when the machine was set in motion.

This brought a complaint from the operators that the guard was removing their hands far enough to clear the descending die but that their hands were being hit with the guard. The complaints continued, and it was eventually agreed to discontinue the use of the guard, provided that the workers used the tweezers.

However, the rule of using the tweezers was disobeyed, and the accidents continued.

The safety engineer investigated other safety devices in an effort to reduce accidents. The investigation disclosed a device which was being used for similar machines in other plants, which automatically pulled the worker's hands away from the machine when it was set into operation.

At a safety committee meeting of the department the safety engineer explained the device and went into detail as to how it functioned. The foreman of the department opposed the device on the ground that he had seen it in operation at other plants and had found that employees cooperated reluctantly after such devices had been installed.

The committee, because of the foreman's objections, voted against the use of the safety device.

Later, in a further investigation of the same device, the safety engineer conferred with a representative of the firm that manufactured the device. At his suggestion, it was decided to experiment by installing the device on a machine. The foreman agreed to permit the installation on a machine that was used for odd jobs. At his suggestion, the device was installed without any notice to the workers or to the union.

Several men tried the device, which proved to work satisfactorily, but reserved their opinions on it. Others refused even to try the machine.

At this point, the union steward saw the device and requested that it be removed at once. He objected to it for two main reasons: (1) that the device was not actually foolproof and (2) that the device would restrict the worker's actions and make him less efficient.

All efforts by the safety engineer to disprove these beliefs were rejected by the steward. The machine remained in the shop for several days and finally, upon the insistence of the steward, was removed.

In the light of the facts given, the problem still remains of how to cut down an excessively high accident rate. The problem is accentuated by the fact that the attempts to install various devices have been rejected by the employees, the union, or the foreman.

Questions

1. Who is responsible for safety?
2. Why has management failed to take positive action?
3. Why do employees seem to have insufficient regard for their own safety? What is the moral?
4. What should management do in this case?

CASE 37. A SELECTION CHOICE

Two qualified and able men are being considered for promotion. The job in question is that of department head in a governmental agency responsible for the administration of the procurement and supply of coal.

The two candidates are Mr. Blow, who is currently the chief of a major unit in the coal department, and Mr. Doe, who is a technical consultant to the department chief. Their background and qualifications are as follows:

1. Mr. Blow has been employed by the government for twelve years and had been interested in getting promoted to a higher grade. He has purchased a new home and has a wife and five children to support. He is forty years of age and expects to work until retirement age.

    Mr. Blow belongs to a minority religious group. He worked his way through college and went on to earn a master's degree in business administration. He started his career in the present department as a clerk and has worked his way up to his present position.

    After several years' experience in this department, he became an expert in the supply of coal for the government and was of valuable help in establishing procedures and policies in this area. He spent long hours in his office without extra pay in order to accomplish his work.

    His superiors regard him as a very capable man. Oftentimes, he is consulted by other agencies on coal problems and is helpful in policy decisions that affect the government. His coworkers respect his ability, admire his efficiency, and enjoy working for him. His department chief has told him on occasion that he would be considered for promotion at the first available opportunity.

    Mr. Blow has one shortcoming: He uses flowery language and talks excessively over minor details. He has been cautioned about this, to no avail. In fact, he has been relieved of the duty of attending important conferences because the conferees complained that time was wasted by his pointless talk over details. But since his technical knowledge is respected, his opinions are sought, but they must be submitted in memorandum form.

2. Mr. Doe is approximately at the same grade level as Mr. Blow, but he is a consultant rather than a supervisory executive. He is about forty-five years of age and has no children. He enjoys his work and would like to stay on in government service in order to earn retirement benefits.

Mr. Doe is a graduate mining engineer and has had about twenty years' experience with private coal firms. He has held administrative jobs in industry, but his jobs with the government have been primarily technical.

As a technical consultant, he also attends many conferences and is noted for giving clear, concise, and dependable reports. He is well liked and respected by higher officials, and his immediate superior has rated him as a key man in the organization.

If Mr. Blow is turned down for the job, he may think that he was discriminated against because of his religion, that he is not being rewarded for the many hours he put in without pay, and that his long and loyal service is not appreciated.

If Mr. Doe is turned down, he will remain with the agency another year and then return to private industry. It will be difficult to replace him, but he has promised to stay long enough so that a replacement could perhaps be found and trained.

Questions

1. In terms of the available information, which man do you prefer?
2. Is there any other information that would be helpful to you in reaching a correct decision?

CASE 38. SAFETY PRACTICES

Jim, an experienced crane operator, was setting down a load of steel sheets for a working crew. Bill, a maintenance man, was working in the area while standing on a ladder. The descending load struck Bill a glancing blow, knocking him from the ladder. In the fall, Bill's wrist was broken, and he had to lay off work for a month.

The safety engineer reviewed the accident with Jim and Jim's supervisor. It was noted that this was the second lost-time accident in which Jim had been involved.

After further study, the safety engineer decided to send Jim to the personnel department for reassignment to a job on which the probability of his being the cause of injury to others would be minimal. He told the supervisor to inform Jim of the decision. Jim was called in and told in a kindly and considerate manner about the decision, and why it was necessary to protect the other men.

Jim said that he liked his work as a crane operator and that he would file a grievance if he was taken off this job.

Questions

1. What right had management to make the decision it did?
2. What practices of a personnel nature might have prevented this accident from happening, if they had been adopted?

CASE 39.   PREPARING FOR BARGAINING

The Auto Parts Company has a seasonal peak period from May through September, when the annual model change is taking place. This peak is usually met by adding temporarily 200 or 300 college students. At times, the peak period has been handled by increasing overtime hours and working Saturdays by the regular crew. The college students obviously like the summer jobs. It gives them 12 to 15 weeks of work with take-home earnings of over $100 a week.

But the regular crew has expressed open opposition to the summer-work plan. They resent the fact that temporary workers earn about as much as they do. They also claim that students undermined rates by going beyond production standards, which they argue can only be done for short periods of time, but not over a year's span. They noted, too, that the students had no interest in union affairs. And they complained that the college students had no desire to enter into the social life of the regular crew, either during or after working hours.

Although no formal grievance has been presented, the industrial relations director has a feeling that an issue is to be made of this situation at the next bargaining period.

Questions

1. What preparations should the industrial relations director make to meet this issue if it comes up?
2. What stand do you feel he should take on this issue?

CASE 40.   HANDLING OLDER EMPLOYEES

Mr. Brown, tiring of retirement—he had sold his small machine shop a few years ago at the age of 55—decided he would like to work again for a while. He applied at a company which had numerous defense orders and was very short of help in a tight labor market. Because of Brown's mechanical background, he was hired as a technical assistant in the engineering research department.

The work Brown did was varied and nonroutine. He was given particular jobs to do by various engineers, who either gave him oral instructions or drawings and sketches. Because of his previous experience and his ingenuity, Brown soon became one of the best assistants in the department. And because of his skill, agreeable personality, and willingness to help other assistants, he got along very well with and was influential among his fellow workers.

One of the engineers, Mr. Jones, was known as a "slave driver" in the department. Technically, he was competent and demanding, but he rated very low when it came to his personal relations and interactions with the assistants.

Brown, in particular, did not get along well with Jones, and the feeling was reciprocated. Brown disliked (as he put it) "Mr. Jones's surly attitude." The situation came to a head at a time when Brown had been assigned to Jones as an assistant on a particular project. In checking up on the progress Brown was making, Jones was so displeased that he yelled at him in a loud, contemptuous voice: "When the blankety-blank-blank are you going to get this job done?"

Brown just walked away from Jones. He went to the personnel manager, told him his story, and said he was going to quit.

Questions

1. Would you try to convince Brown to stay? How could you assure him he would not be subject to the same treatment again?
2. Do employees like Brown need special treatment?

INDEX

This book has been set in 12 and 10 point Garamond #3, leaded 1 point. Chapter numbers are in 10 and 18 point Spartan Heavy; chapter titles are 18 point Lydian Bold italics. The size of the type page is 27 by 46½ picas.